MORE BACK ROADS
of the
Central Coast

by Ron Stob

Bear Flag Books   1996   Arroyo Grande CA

ISBN 0-939919-26-5

Since the chapters in this book first appeared as newspaper features, it is necessary to update information and phone numbers at book presstime. Verify addresses, hours of operation and fees when planning visits to these areas. Lone hikers and travelers in particular should guard against accidents, sudden illness or assaults. The author and publisher assume no responsibility for your safety. Please exercise normal caution when traveling.

Published by Bear Flag Books/A Division of Padre Productions
        P.O. Box 840
        Arroyo Grande CA 93421-0840

Bear Flag Books   1996   Arroyo Grande CA

Contents

Foreword

Those of us who live on the California Central Coast know deep in our hearts that we are among the most-blessed people of the world. This is God's Country, a land of beauty, marvelous climate and intense feeling. It is a land that combines most of nature's wonders in a relatively small area. It is a land of hidden splendors and enormous possibilities.

This is what Ron Stob writes about— the possibilities for reflection, peace of mind and renewal that exist within our reach.

All of us who live here—from the native to the recent arrival— often leave the territory of our own backyard unexplored.

Ron Stob follows those little signposts as they beckon him on the back roads, and he takes us there with him on his adventures.

In his columns you will find inspiration to explore the wonders that lie so close to us in every direction. The good life is out there, within easy reach. This book is your guide to help you find it.

George DeBord, Editor
San Luis Obispo *Telegram-Tribune*

Introduction

Our Central Coast—it's a veritable treasure-trove of natural beauty.

What a wondrous feeling it is to discover its riches, in forms both barren and lush, rugged and smooth.

In his "Back Roads" columns, published monthly in the *Telegram-Tribune's Focus* magazine, Ron Stob is our guide.

By foot, bicycle, motorbike and horse, Ron leads us across the stark flatlands of the California Valley, into the tree-shrouded wilderness of the Big Sur Coast, over the pastel landscape of the Nipomo Dunes.

In his writings of wanderings down craggy trails and country lanes, he introduces us to the far-reaching beauty that lies off the beaten path.

This book celebrates Ron's second compilation of columns that have been published in *Focus*. Let us, too, celebrate by donning our walking shoes and joining him in further explorations of our paradise.

Shirley Howell, Features Editor
San Luis Obispo *Telegram-Tribune*

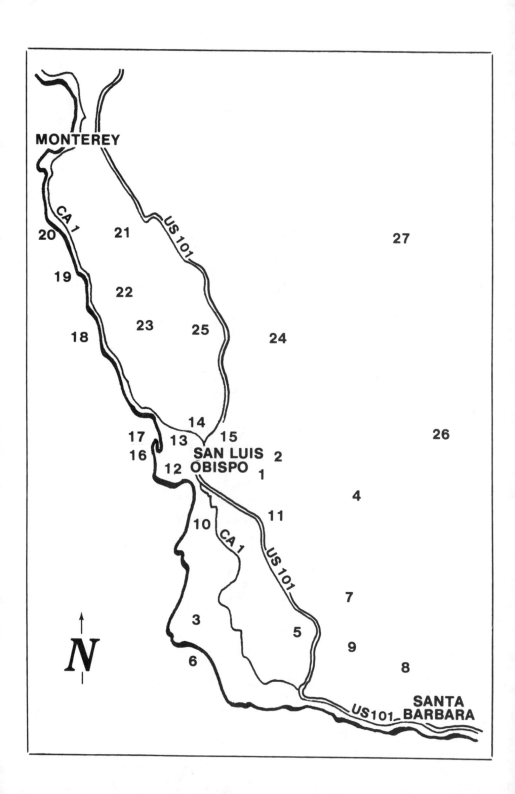

I Points South

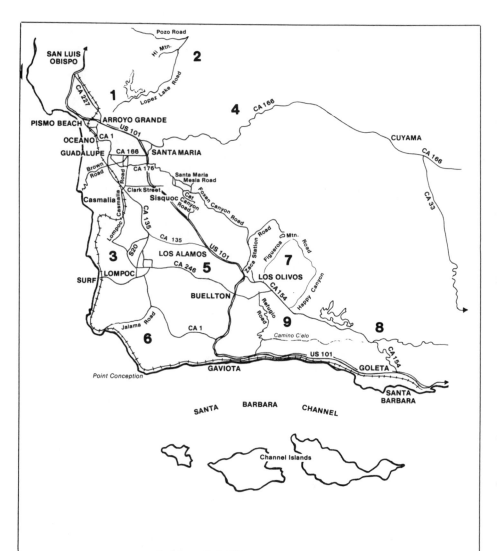

1 **Lopez Lake**
2 **Roads to Pozo**
3 **Lompoc Flowers Fields**
4 **Adobe Trail**
5 **Los Alamos**
6 **Jalama Road**
7 **Figueroa Mountain**
8 **Cold Spring Tavern**
9 **Camino Cielo**

1—LOPEZ LAKE: HISTORY LIES UNDER THE SURFACE

It was a year of torrential rains. The dam at Lopez Lake was just completed in January 1969 when the rain began to fall. For most of the month there was a steady succession of storms that produced all-day drizzles and drenching downpours.

February followed with days of endless rains, and by the end of the month 49 inches of rain had fallen on the Lopez Lake watershed. In one three day period the water rose 30 feet.

By April of 1969 the water came over the spillway and the lake was filled. What had been estimated to be a five-to-ten-year filling time was accomplished in just four months.

It had been more than a year since I had been out to Lopez Lake, and I had forgotten how beautiful it is. If I were a newcomer to these parts and saw the shimmering lake at the base of the mountains, I'd think I was in one of the most scenic spots in the country, and I would probably want to move here.

A group of us had arranged to take the nature boat across the Wittenberg Arm of the lake to the head of the Two Waters Trail. We drove out to Cottonwood Cove, north of the marina, and boarded the pontoon boat for the short trip.

As we approached Miller's Cove and the beginning of the trail, we observed several large drowned oaks standing in the water near shore. These trees are frequently used by great blue herons, but neither nests nor birds were in evidence.

When Lopez Lake was created, all the trees and buildings were removed from the valley floor to prevent barns, houses and privies from bobbing to the surface. Santa Manuela School was saved and now resides at the three corners junction of Highway 227, Huasna Road and Branch Street in Arroyo Grande.

We began the .7 mile hike to the top of the ridge, along grassy hillsides of wildflowers. The hummingbird sage was beginning to bloom and buttercups and lupine were everywhere.

The hike is an easy, pleasant walk, and most of us took long breaks along the way, looking at the boats on the lake and enjoying the scenery.

The Las Palitas fire came through here in 1985 and left the California live oaks blackened, with gnarled fingers of fired limbs; but new shoots have emerged from the charred trunks.

We rested on a bench at the top of the ridge and viewed the Lopez and Vasquez arms of the lake. Dorothy and I took time to look at the sweet smelling flowers of poison oak, their tiny flowers attracting a large number of bees and flies.

The trail up to the Duna Vista Lookout is through a wooded parkland that thins at the top. We waded through a field of bushy lupine as we approached the lookout point.

Ernie, 73, had beat us up there by half an hour. He was cool and dry, wondering where we had been. We all refreshed ourselves on the vistas that extend to the dunes on the coast and back into the Santa Lucia Mountains.

We returned to the junction with the descending trail to the Lopez arm of the lake where the ranger was to pick us up. Along a moist ravine were sword fern and maidenhair. Buttercups and popcorn flowers grew in the sunny spots.

The Encinal campground is at the water's edge, serving picnickers and overnight campers. The ranger arrived while we were having lunch and agreed to walk with us along the old county road that ran up this valley. For a quarter mile the old road emerges out of the lake on the south end, runs along the side of the hill and descends again into the lake.

For a moment I imagined the jangle of harnesses and a team pulling a buckboard up the dusty road, then the vision was lost as the wagon sank into the water on the north end.

"These rocks are full of fossils," the ranger said in a loud, startling voice. "Twenty-six million years ago a warm sea covered this part of California, and scallops and oysters lived in the waters. Their impressions can be seen in many of these sedimentary rocks."

Many of us began splitting the layered rocks and in a few minutes we had a dozen beautiful fossilized shells. Dorothy, who has never shown greed for anything, was clutching as many as she could hold, stacking them on her arm like a truckstop waitress.

"Oh, my kids at school will love these," she said excitedly. So we collected rocks and fossils for Dorothy and her kids, until her loaded pack bent her backwards into an obtuse angle.

We boarded the pontoon boat for the ride back, making sure Dorothy didn't get near the sides. Ranger Davis gave us an interpretive tour of the Lopez arm of the lake, steering the boat into the backwaters of the canyons where fishermen, as quiet as monks, were angling for dinner.

On the north rim of the lake is a large clump of cactus planted above the hillside of a youth camp. On the opposite shore were the first commercial strawberry fields, planted by John Rodriguez who harvested 20 acres of strawberries and shipped the fruit to market around 1901. The Vasquez Arm was the site of El Campo, a camp of primitive summer cabins shared by Ruth Paulding and a number of Arroyo Grande residents.

Underwater was the 280 acre ranch of Juan and Jesus Lopez. Juan Lopez was an outrider for Frances Branch in the 1800s and when the Tulare Indians came through Pozo to raid, Lopez would have time to get word to Branch about their activities.

Near the dam are three underwater Chumash sites 160 feet below the surface. There were two large villages here and an associated area of bedrock mortars. In this area also was the Jatta

home which lay in the broad valley between the Lopez and Arroyo Grande Creeks. The log-adobe cabin and second Jatta home became the location of the 40-acre Routzahn Park, a favorite picnic grounds for many years.

We cruised slowly near the intake flumes that carry the lake water down to a holding pond on Orcutt Road. The rocks along the roadway are a combination of Monterey shale and black-brown volcanic rock. The younger Santa Margarita sandstone is the rock that is full of fossils. It lies above the shale and is extremely faulted, undulating in gold layers like the folded pages of a giant geology book.

The droning of the engine was enough to put Alison and Jeanette into a hypnotic trance and they dozed off as we moved through the Arroyo Grande Channel into the Wittenberg Arm of the lake.

It was near here, far below us, that Newton Wittenberg stepped onto the porch of their ranch home and saw a grizzly bear scratching himself on the oak tree in the yard. Newt ran back into the house to get his rifle and killed the last grizzly in San Luis Obispo County. The beast was eight feet long.

The nature boat runs from the marina Friday evening, and all day Tuesday, Thursday, and Saturday on a two hour long interpretive ride that takes visitors into the Lopez Arm with stories from the past and observations of the wildlife of the region...and Dorothy collecting fossils. Sunday is reserved for special groups. Cost is $2 per person. For the current schedule call 489-1122.

Lopez Lake is 19 miles from San Luis Obispo.

2—ROADS TO POZO:
GETTING THERE IS HALF THE FUN

There are two roads to Pozo. One is 25 miles long, beginning from Arroyo Grande, and takes two hours. The other is 25 miles long from San Luis Obispo and takes a half hour. The long way is exciting, scenic and breathtaking. The short way is smooth, pleasant and pastoral. You ought to take both.

Pozo? you say. Why would anyone want to go to Pozo?

Well, for one—Pozo is a hundred years back in time and the ride across the furrowed fields and wooded slopes is a beautiful way to revisit this woebegone community; and the other is that you will want to eat at the Pozo Saloon, especially on weekends when they have their famous oakwood barbecue.

On Sunday Archie Johnson punishes the old barroom piano while he sings ballads of broken hearts, fallen angels and 18-wheelers, and on Saturday they feature the Pozo River Bottom Band and other country western groups. With nary a town in 16 miles the rockin' and rollin' is known to get a little wild.

The civilized way to Pozo is via Highway 101 from San Luis Obispo to Santa Margarita, then Highway 58 to Pozo Road which runs south 18 miles along the west side of Lake Santa Margarita to Pozo. The road has recently been paved and is an absolutely perfect back country road.

The long way (same 25 miles but it takes longer) to Pozo is out of Arroyo Grande at the south end of town on Branch Street, then on to Lopez Drive to Lopez Lake. Just before the entrance to Lopez Lake Recreation Area, I turned right on High Mountain Road and set the odometer to zero.

Pozo is 16 miles away on a partially paved, but mostly dirt road which crosses the 2076-foot summit. This road is paradise to four-wheel-drive vehicles in the wet season when the clay berms and gumbo ruts become taffy, but in the dry season most family sedans can make it, albeit they'll look like they've aged 10 years by the time they reach Pozo.

In one mile Upper Lopez Canyon Road goes left (to Little and Big Falls), but I continued straight ahead through the gateway of the Ranchita Cattle Company. It's a land of rolling grassy slopes and oak trees dripping with Spanish moss. The rush of springtime flowering is over in June and the senescent vegetation is mellow and ripe; the elderberry is still in bloom and the hemlock and thistles flower along the roadside.

Up the road a short distance is the Arroyo Grande station of the U.S. Forest Service. They have information on road conditions, campgrounds, motorcycle trail maps and a place to park bike trailers for those who use this area as their jumping-off point. Beyond the Arroyo Grande Station the pavement ends and the dirt road begins.

I came through a section of curving roadways, babbling creeks and woodlands (3.6 miles) that reminded me of the 19th century Hudson River artists who attempted to record "divine architecture." This idyllic landscape begs to be painted or photographed.

Nearby is an old oak tree with a latched gate across the road. I unlatched it and swung it wide open, then ran to my car to get through; but the gate is so hinged that as soon as you let go it closes itself. After three tries of mad dashes and spinning wheels I discovered a large boulder that kept it in place until I got through.

A mile beyond the gate the road ascends sharply and becomes rutted and bumpy. It dips and weaves out of the canyons, crossing creeks and getting narrower as it climbs.

The yucca are in bloom near the top and a turnout provides magnificent views of the hills and canyons. At 13.4 miles I crested the ridge and came to the junction of Hi Mountain Lookout Road. I turned left on this scenic nine mile (deadend) spur for a brief side trip. Lookout Mountain Road runs the ridge northward, separating the Salinas River drainage on the right (east) from the Lopez Canyon drainage on the left (west).

At 15.7 and 17.6 miles on Lookout Mountain Road are two vantage points overlooking Lopez Lake, the Arroyo Grande valley and all of the dunes to Mussel Point. The vertical canyon walls are a kaleidoscope of green sculpted fabric as sun rays streak through the clouds.

Even if you don't go all the way to Pozo, at least come this far. The terrace turnout at 17.6 miles is my favorite midnight picnic spot. Views of the mountains in the moonlight with the twinkling city lights 20 miles away are extraterrestrial.

The trail heads to Little and Big Falls are up here, at 20.5 and 22.4 miles respectively (end of road). As I made my way back to Hi Mountain Road, a brown snake came across the road and we talked for awhile; but he got bored and went back into the brush.

I have never seen Wooly Blue-Curls (bush) in the back country, but they're resplendent along Lookout Mountain Road, and so is the chamise with its soft forms of creamy colored flowers.

Pozo is four miles below the Lookout Mountain Road junction at the top of the grade. The descending road meanders across the creeks that drain the eastern slopes, so your family sedan will be slipping and sliding across the rounded stream boulders, but in the dry season the way is no threat to cars or people.

I had had enough of dirt and white talcum dust for awhile and the thought of wetting my whistle at the Pozo Saloon urged me on. At the blacktop (Pozo Road) I turned right and drove .2 miles to the Pozo Saloon, a wrinkled old place with sagging lines and a genuine hitching post out front under a 125-year-old cottonwood.

A lot of horse power was tied up there—street bikes, dirt bikes and an assortment of pickups. Most of the cowboys were lying around embracing a Pozo martini, a pint-sized Kerr jar of beer with an olive.

Inside, Archie was keeping things jumping for a crowd that included families and bikers. Rhonda and Brian Beanway were hustling out huge portions of barbecued chicken and beef amidst the din of smacking pool balls, clanking glasses, honkey tonk piano and 50 people singing and laughing. I think you call this a "happening."

Outside, people gathered around the oakwood barbecue or threw horseshoes in the pits. . . and out front the guys were still sprawled across their bikes or slouching on the porch benches discussing everything but religion and philosophy.

For current hours and entertainers call the Pozo Saloon—438-4225.

The ride back to Santa Margarita on Pozo Road was smooth, pleasant and peaceful—about the right antidote following an afternoon on Hi Mountain Road and the celebration of life at the Pozo Saloon.

3—BICYCLING THROUGH THE LOMPOC FLOWER FIELDS

Our kids gave us new bikes so we thought we would try them out touring the flower fields of Lompoc. Every year there is a celebration with a float parade, displays in the fields, and a show in town.

Lompoc has long been the nation's leading producer of flower seeds, with 50-75 per cent of all seeds coming from this valley. The discovery of the Lompoc Valley as a prime growing area began with the La Purisima Mission, 1787—1834, followed by bean farmers, one of whom, Robert D. Rennie, was approached in 1907 by an English company looking for a grower to provide them with sweet pea seeds. He succeeded admirably and sold his seeds also to the Burpee Seed Company of Philadelphia. In the 1920s Bodger and Denholm Seed Companies arrived and continue to operate in the valley today.

We loaded the bicycles on the pickup and headed up Highway 101 to Clark Avenue in Orcutt, then west on Highway 135, past the Highway 1 (formerly S20) turn-off to Vandenberg, and turned right on the Harris Grade Road, formerly called Highway 1, or Cabrillo Highway. Confused? So were we. They just finished renaming all these roads. At this junction the flower field show begins. Acres of Iceland Poppies and Schizanthus (poor man's orchid) fill the fields, along with cauliflower raised for seed. While the flowers are gorgeous I was amazed to see how pretty the cauliflower is. It's like the story of the frog and the prince. The warty, bulbous cauliflower head is simply the precursor of a magnificent bouquet of pink flowers.

On the right of the road the fields are like a flag of colored stripes.

We followed the Harris Grade Road into Lompoc, coming in on H Street... (the early city planners, in an uninspired moment labeled all the streets with letters and numbers)... and went to 113 North I Street to pick up a Flower Field Tour Map at the festival office.

Ocean Avenue (the city planners also had a pragmatic strain), which runs down to Surf Beach County Park on the ocean, cuts the town into north and south sections, and is the main route to the fields. At Ocean and O is Ryon Park, the center of the festivities set for June.

We turned left on V Street, then right on Olive Street (in a renaisance of vision and inspiration later, city planners began using names of flowers and trees, like Prune and Olive), alongside Bodger Seed Company, to the observation road that winds up the hill to a scenic lookout. It's a pretty view from up there, but not a ride that you can do easily on a bike. The grade is very steep and the surface of the road is bumpy and lumpy.

After we came down we parked the truck at nearby Miguelito School and rode our bikes down the dirt road adjacent to V Street.

The Bodger Seed Company fields are the most diverse and beautiful collection of field flowers in the valley. The impact of these large beds of flowers is greatest when you stand near the ends of the rows, with the plants at your feet stretching away to the horizon as far as you can see.

Along Ocean Avenue we came to Floradale Avenue (now there's a descriptive name) and admired a small Victorian frame home, dwarfed by a cluster of towering eucalyptus; all around fields of sweet peas nodded and waved in the persistent ocean breeze.

The seed industry estimates that an acre of sweet peas produces about 3,200,000 seeds. I raised an eyebrow in disbelief when workers told me this, and they sniggered, "Go ahead, count 'em."

4—THE ADOBE TRAIL — EXPLORING THE PERMASSE ADOBE AND BIG ROCK MOUNTAIN

Twenty-two miles east of Santa Maria there is an adobe home on the Permasse Ranch, east of one of the many bridges that spans Highway 166. The roof is caving in and daylight streams into the rooms, but it's still intact and each window looks out onto a view of the ranch like a scene from an Andrew Wyeth painting.

It's cool inside, even on hot afternoons, and the only sound is the breath of the wind in the pepper trees. An animal has moved into the adobe, burrowing beneath the plank floor, leaving signs of its comings and goings. It's good to see someone is still living there.

The last time a human lived there was in 1937 when cowboys John Skinner and Frank Reed used it while herding cattle for the Glines, McDonald and Gifford Cattle Company, who ran cattle on the Permasse Ranch.

Bernard Pemasse came from France in 1888 and homesteaded 200 acres with his partner, Pete Labord. Permasse built the adobe in 1890 and lived in it for a number of years, but when the partnership dissoved Labord took possession of the 100 acres that included the adobe and Permasse moved up the canyon (west) several miles, where he built the permanent Permasse home on the old highway.

Twenty years ago the road between Cuyama and Santa Maria rode high in the hills, parallel to the existing highway, but farther up the slope. It cut into and out of more than 60 canyons on its way from west to east, and travelers would stop halfway at a gas station where they would get fuel, water their radiators, and drink a bottle of Coca Cola.

The scuttlebutt is that during Prohibition they were enjoying more than Coca Cola up there, and the adobe might have been the place where the moonshine was made. The adobe at that time was far below the highway, along a dirt ranch road; now of course it's right along the highway. The gas station is gone but sections of the old highway still exist and can be driven, walked or bicycled.

Two miles east of the adobe, toward Maricopa, there is a section of old highway that you can drive for about three miles. It curves in and out of the canyons, then comes to a barricade. The old road is discontinuous, so you can't stay on it with a car, but there are stretches that you can walk or bicycle to see remants of the past.

The adobe is near the head of the adobe trail that a group of us hiked. The trailhead is 500 yards east of the adobe, and parking is behind an unlocked fence a few hundred yards to the west, near a bridge that spans the highway.

We decided to take a number of shuttle cars to an end point so we would be able to hike a one-way trail. The drivers of the cars re-entered Highway 166 and drove 3.9 miles east to Branch Creek Road which is also the entrance to Rock Front Ranch.

This gravel road, with patches of blacktop, runs through the bottom of the canyon. The languid stream makes its way back and across the road a myriad of times. Within a mile we came to Big Rock Mountain, an isolated group of hills that are made up of cemented conglomerates that are eroding into huge boulders. On the top are several 20,000-ton balls ready to roll down.

On the far (north) end of the mountain is a trail that goes up and between these unique formations. Climbing to the top you can see for miles. The surrounding mountains are rolling hills of chaparral and oak-studded grassy slopes, unlike the peanut brittle geology of Big Rock Mountain.

As we drove by Soto Springs the road became a series of puddles and running rivulets. The cars were in and out of the water, and we began to think that Ian Begg, our guide, hid from us the true condition of the (underwater) highway to Cable Corral Spring where we were going to leave our cars. At points we were hub deep in water and a few of us had the nagging feeling that we might spend the morning in the middle of a slow-moving stream with water wandering in one door and out the other.

Eventually we came to our shuttle point at 4.4 miles from the highway, then returned to the gang waiting for us near the adobe on Highway 166. Soon we were on the trail, looking at the wild flowers in bloom and finding everything new and interesting.

The trail leaves the parking lot to the east, traverses a meadow, then switches back and forth, eventually running above the adobe east of the trailhead. The hike was continuously uphill and we finally entered a wet canyon where we stopped to rest near a watering trough. Several people in the group were faltering from the rigors of this first stint, and they stayed behind as the rest of us left to climb the next mile in a continuous ascent.

At the top of the canyon we followed a jeep trail that runs along the ridges. The group became strung out and silent, walking alone or in groups of two or three. In a half mile we came to a trail junction and stayed right.

The blue oaks grow in a parkland atmosphere along the ridges, spaced in nearly equal increments among the waving grasses. It's an atmosphere of unusual idyllic quality. The views on the trail are quite unlike what we saw from the road, and justified our exertions on the strenuous uphill sections of the trail.

At 2.6 miles and an elevation of 2,470 feet, we came to the Big Rock trail junction and turned right. In another mile and a half we turned left near a farm pond, wending our way toward Logan Ridge and the descent to our shuttle cars.

This trail is poorly marked, and if it hadn't been for Ian and the Sierra Club Trail Guide we would still be wandering around in the woods; but heading in the direction of Branch Creek Road (east) is a sure way to find the road to the cars.

See also the Los Padres National Forest map for an alternative trail from the Permasse Ranch on Highway 166 to Branch Creek Road. This trail duplicates the first half of our 6.5 mile hike, but is shorter.

5—LOS ALAMOS AND DRUM CANYON — RECALLING WHAT THEY USED TO BE

There's nothing like a ride in the country to undue the tinsel and noise of the holidays.

I started down Halcyon Road of Arroyo Grande to Highway 1 and headed south through the produce fields of Oceano, climbing the grade onto the Nipomo Mesa, catching views of the Amtrak line and the dunes along the coast. Through the old eucalyptus groves of Nipomo I sailed past salvage yards and rural homes in idyllic country settings.

Highway 1 rolls off the mesa into the Santa Maria River basin, the newly tilled fields furrowed like corduroy. Beyond Guadalupe it continues through a patchwork of green—the deep color of broccoli, the vibrant shades of sprouting barley and the shimmering green of pastures awakening from a long summer drought.

West of Orcutt, Highway 1 joins Highway 135, and together they become four lanes until Highway 1 squirts off the right to Vandenberg Air Force Base. After San Antonio Road, Harris Grade Road (formerly Highway 1) heads west to Lompoc across the Harris Grade, but I stayed on Highway 135, south, along the old Pacific Coast Railway bed. I felt I had peeled away the final impediment to rural sanity. Now I was in the country with the aroma of manure, and sweeping flocks of blackbirds making kaleidoscopic images against neat rows of grape vines.

But fancy horse farms are taking over this land of natural farmers and free-roaming herefords. Indolent horses live in New England style barns, giving birth in climatically-controlled foaling

barns and being bred to hired studs in mating parlours. All this horse vogue seemed to bring a little of Grand Avenue and Broadway into the country and prevented my total escape.

In the town of Los Alamos, named for the cottonwoods that grew on the Bell Ranch, I stopped by the Union Hotel where I met Dick Langdon, a whimsical guy who has re-created the facade of the original 1880 hotel that burned in 1888. Another hotel was constructed (1906), and into this 80-year-old relic Dick has stuffed a warehouse of antiques and collectibles, making it a museum-restaurant-hotel. It's only open Friday—Sunday because Dick is convinced that any more than that would diminish the fun he's having.

A few doors down, Dick is turning a giant yellow turn-of-the-century Nipomo home into Victorian a la mode, adding fluff and frippery to satisfy his nostalgic fantasies.

I stopped at the end of Shaw Street to photograph an old windmill in the field. A group of kids came over to see what I was up to. "Hi, what are you doing?" the biggest kid asked.

"I'm just taking pictures of this old windmill," I replied. Then I thought about the park that was used in the railroad days when people from San Luis Obispo came on the train for picnics.

"Do you kids know where the park is?" I asked.

"Yeah, it's by the school," the small blonde kid said. They were all eager to show me where the school and park were and so they led me down the street, the two bigger kids on bicycles pulling the blonde kid on a skate board, the spotted dog with no tail sauntering along, my big red car following slowly behind and the little girl with fat cheeks and a bicycle with a pink basket taking up the rear. For two minutes and two short blocks we were a parade.

At Centennial Street, I turned right at the school and waved off my escort. A hundred yards beyond the school yard is the Los Alamos Park.

Before the coming of the railroads, the Los Alamos canyons were hideouts for thieves and cutthroats who held up stagecoaches and cattle drivers. The attacks were so numerous that this canyon was called Canon De Los Calaveras, "Canyon of the Skulls," a name that still appears on some maps. Zorro, the legendary Robin Hood of California, was no less than Pico Salomon, the "hood" from Los Alamos.

After 1882 the Pacific Coast Railway brought San Luis Obispo people out to the park on holidays and weekends. There were Maypole dances, picnics and quadrilles, a square dance routine on horseback where eight pair of riders performed movements sung out by a caller.

The park is still a favorite back roads getaway for picnicking. Over the small bridge beyond the caretaker's home I walked an old road that girdles the hill. It affords panoramic views up Drum Canyon (the present name for this canyon) to the old cemetery and down to the town.

According to Al Moneghetti, one of the longest living resident-historians, Drum Canyon was a former stagecoach route between Lompoc and Los Alamos. It's a good macadam road that winds to the top of the Purisima Hills along steep sides of exfoliating limestone. Sharp hairpin turns make it scenic and slow, and crossing the saddle there are magnificent views into the Lompoc Valley.

There are a couple of good wildflower shows going on here in the early spring, the south slopes providing a different display of wildflowers than the north (Los Alamos) side. Then, of course, there are the cultivated flower fields of the commercial growers along the 19 mile drive around Lompoc.

Drum Canyon approaches Highway 246, where I turned right and drove west through a broad valley until I came to Purisima Road (beyond Cebada Canyon Road). La Purisima Mission is up the road, the only completely-restored California Mission with outbuildings, water system and an active docent interpretive program.

From the mission I followed Purisima Road to Harris Grade Road, then turned east across the Purisima Hills.

Harris Grade Road is one of the most tortuous, but scenic, routes tying the Los Alamos Valley to the Lompoc Valley. It's a road to avoid at night and during heavy rains because of sharp drop-offs and deep canyons on the north side as it comes down the Harris Grade to join Highway 135.

Coming through the flower fields Harris Grade Road joins Highway 135, completing a circuit through a country peaceful, wild and full of fascinating tales from the past.

Total round trip from Arroyo Grande on this circuit is about 100 miles. One way to Los Alamos via Highways 1 and 135 is 39 miles.

6—JALAMA ROAD — A PERFECT PLACE TO ROAD TEST A CONVERTIBLE

Everett, when you buy that convertible you've been coveting, I've got just the road for you to travel. It's a road in the country where vintage ranch homes nestle against pastoral hills and the horses graze in pastures of grass as high as their bellies. Dorothy and you will love it.

This road approaches the ocean where the coreopsis blooms, and the breaking surf chills the air.

Take Highway 1 south from here, beyond Santa Maria and Orcutt. Continue on Highway 135 beyond the Highway 1 turnoff to Vandenberg AFB, and another 3.5 miles to Harris Grade road, old Highway 1 (beyond San Antonio Road).

From the piney hills atop the grade you'll catch magnificent views of the Lompoc Valley. The ceanothus (California lilac) and the prickly phlox are absolutely outstanding going down the grade toward Lompoc in April. You'll never see a more floribund chaparral than this.

Remember that old tune "June is bustin out all over..."? April is June in California when all nature seems on edge, feverish with the urge to reproduce.

Take Highway 1 into Lompoc along H Street and then to Ocean Avenue. Out of Lompoc Highway 1 dives into the hills and gets very scenic again. About five miles out of town Jalama Road comes up on the right side.

The scenes up the 15 mile long Jalama Road remind me of the Irish Hills beyond Prefumo and See Canyons in San Luis Obispo—. cows on green hills, giving perspective to the towering hills behind them.

Freshly-tilled fields in the valleys show the grooves of the disc and harrow. Oak forests canopy the road at places and the buttercups and wild hyacinth (blue dicks) bloom between the trees in a park-like setting.

Authentic ranch homes cuddle into the hills and you'll feel grateful that suburbia and split-level homes haven't yet discovered this section of rural California.

A covey of quail may run across the road in front of your convertible, and a few stragglers trying to catch up to their buddies will probably fly over your car, barely skimming your sport cap and making Dorothy cry out, "Did you see those birds, Everett? We nearly hit them." And she'll look back to see how they are, but they'll be lost in the bush.

And then Dorothy will quickly regain her thoughtful composure, and focus on the wild clematis scrambling on the roadside hedges; and the anise, with its ferny leaves growing up through a base of last year's dead stalks...and the hemlock—that deadly hemlock that will kill an adult with barely a mouthful—getting ready to bloom.

Over more ridges and into other valleys you'll ride. You'll probably slow down as you go because the smells get sweeter and the views of flowers and awakening valley oaks is something you'll want to see closely.

The trees thin out as you approach the ocean, and then there are none at all. The coreopsis begin to appear with their bright yellow daisy flowers on elephant trunk stems. How they love the cool damp air near the ocean.

Then you'll see the Amtrak Railroad lines coming along the coast. The 28,000 acre Bixby Ranch is at the end of the road before you cross the tracks and begin your descent into the park. The ranch extends all the way to Point Conception.

Jalama Beach Park is a 23.5 acre ocean-front park along the Jalama Creek. A portion of the park was a Chumash Indian settlement prior to the Spanish influence and La Purisima Mission. The padres "converted" the Indians from a life of surfing, fishing and perpetual picnicking to a life in the Lompoc Valley picking beans and squash.

The surfing, fishing and picnicking are still going on. In addition there are campers and people that just drive out to look around and eat one of the camp store's Jalama burgers. It feels good to just sit in the warm sand with a Jalama burger and watch all those young guys out there surfing and trying to score with the girls.

On the way home, Everett, go three miles back north on Highway 1 and pick up Santa Rosa Road east to Buellton. Santa Rosa is a favorite bicycling road that meanders across the gentle hills and even valleys, skirting tilled fields and groves of walnuts, until it reaches Buellton. There's a wonderful aroma in these valleys, something akin to a blend of wood fires and apple sauce.

At Santa Rosa Park, six and a half miles from Highway 1, there's a bit of bucolic peace under the trees where the noisiest thing is a wren in the laurel tree. It's a wonderful place to throw down the car blanket and snooze in the afternoon sun.

In another eight miles you'll arrive in Buellton with time to put the top up for a quick ride home. Have fun . . . and tell Dorothy to wear her babushka.

For information on weather and tides, call the Jalama Beach Park, (805) 736-6316.

7—ENJOYING A DAY TRIP TO FIGUEROA MOUNTAIN

We were on our way south to Figueroa Mountain but there were a couple of old historic homes in Nipomo that we wanted to see on the way. We got off at Tefft Avenue in Nipomo and turned left (east) to Oak Glen, the frontage road along Highway 101 on the east side.

South on Oak Glen one mile, on the left side, is the William Dana adobe, down a long driveway flanked by locust trees. William Dana and his wife, Maria Carillo, had 21 babies in this house, 13 of whom grew to adulthood. Their 30,000-acre ranch extended from the Nipomo foothills all the way to the ocean.

The San Luis Obispo County Historical Society owns the home now and has a caretaker in residence. Unfortunately it is stalled in its tracks toward rejuvenation and is not open to the public, but you can stand there and imagine what it was like when the stagecoach rumbled by on its way from Santa Barbara, or when the narrow gauge Pacific Coast Railway ran nearby—just east of the house, down the hill.

Frank Dana, one of the sons of William and Maria, built a frame home a few miles from his father on Mehlschau Road, a mile north of Tefft. A quarter mile east of Thompson Road is the blue and white 1882 Frank Dana home at 535 Mehlschau, on the left side of the road, across from a citrus orchard.

Frank's great grand daughter, Judith Dana Powers and her husband, Sehon Powers, live in the home pouring their heart and soul into the old place. They've made it house beautiful, maintaining some of the simplicity and charm of turn-of-the century life, while enriching the home for their personal use.

37

The home is private and opened only on special occasions, but the Powers are used to being ogled and even a glimpse of the house from the road is worth the trip.

Continuing our trip to Figueroa Mountain, we took Highway 101 to Highway 154, San Marcos Pass, south to Los Olivos, and stopped in front of Mattei's Tavern (1886), another old relic from the narrow gauge railroad-stagecoach days.

Off to the east, nearly opposite Mattei's Tavern, Figueroa Mountain Road wanders among the peaks until it makes contact with Happy Canyon Road, forming a 60 mile loop. We set our odometer at zero and headed up the road.

Figueroa Mountain Road begins in the valley of the Alamo Pintado Creek, where broad fields of golden grain lie against a background of dark hills. Baled hay lay in curvilinear rows like ingots of gold in a field of flaxen stalks.

The road parallels the creek, then climbs out of the valley, passing the Midland School and ascending into hills of pines. There's a turnout where the road makes a 180 degree right turn over a cattle grate at 6.2 miles. A foot trail to White Mountain takes off over the road guard on the left side of the bridge.

The road rises sharply with views of White Mountain, the sacred place of the Chumash shaman, the mystical men of the tribe. Green serpentine rock lined the roadside cuts as we drove along, and a pair of bluebirds flitted from a rail fence. Overhead two red-tailed hawks sailed above us so close we could see their red tails.

We entered Los Padres National Forest at ten miles and White Mountain fell behind us. The road zigzags upwards and in a few miles we came to Figueroa Mountain Lookout Road. This is the high point of the drive. The views from the top are eastward toward Cuyama and westward across the Santa Ynez Valley. There are picnic tables and ideal spots for spending an afternoon. The Pino Alto nature trail is an instructive way to become acquainted with the area.

This is good point to end the trip and return the way you came—round trip from San Luis Obispo is 166 miles—but we decided to camp overnight so we continued on.

At 17 miles we ran along a ridge with a steep dropoff on the left side. There are many mature firs here and the area had the look of the Sierra Nevada Range.

Cachuma Saddle Station, an information cabin usually open during the summer, came up in two miles and we turned left on Sunset Valley Road to Davy Brown Campground five miles away. It's all downhill to Davy Brown and I anticipated this would make true the claim that water always runs in the creek at Davy Brown. We weren't disappointed. Each of the sites is set against the hillside next to the babbling brook. We chose a 40 foot diameter clearing under a huge old sycamore. Alders lined the creek and the water gurgled over the terraced rock in a scene remiscent of the images of Tolkin's Hobbitt. Lemon-yellow Mariposa lilies grew along the creek, and the air was filled with the sounds of twittering birds. Up on the slopes digger pines waved in gentle breezes that whisper lazily in and out of the canyon. It was a scene of extraordinary peace and calm.

In the evening we built a fire and watched the inferno with child-like fascination. It was a satisfying experience living simply in the outdoors, dawdling, puttering, dabbling—making do with little and being thankful for much. The next morning there was time to read in the sun, prepare meals on a smoky fire and swat invisible gnats and other flying creatures that have a perverse curiosity for the inside of your nostrils and ears.

Late in the morning we left Davy Brown and turned left to look at NIRA Campground two miles at the end of the road. After the first creek crossing we passed Catway Road, a rough dirt road that takes off by the stock station for Figueroa Moutain. Our source said this is an okay two-wheel-drive road, but I doubt it. The boulders, ruts and heavy brush say "truck or four wheel drive."

The NIRA Campground is a favorite jump-off point for hikers going to the backcountry campsites of Potrero, Coldwater, Lost Valley and Fish Creek. The hills back here are gray-brown and languishing from drought the first weeks of August.

Driving back to Cachuma Saddle Station we turned left on Figueroa Mountain Road again over to Happy Canyon. At 32 miles from Mattei's Tavern we left Los Padres National Forest and Figueroa Mountain, and entered the private realm of manicured horse ranches, where pastures look like golf courses and indulged stallions chase mares in a heaven of limitless food and sex.

At another ranch of endless white fences in Happy Canyon a doe grazed with her twin fawns beside the corpulent herefords. The little ones were spooked when they spotted us and bounded off on springy legs, their mother running anxiously behind. No wonder they call this Happy Canyon. It has an indefinable, but unmistakable, aura of idealism, harmony and order.

At the Santa Barbara Thoroughbred Farm and Training Center we turned right on Armour Ranch Road to Highway 154, then right, past Mattei's Tavern to Highway 101.

Summer temperatures are high in the Santa Ynez Valley, but cooler at the upper elevations of Figueroa. Approximate round trip distance from San Luis Obispo is 200 miles.

8—A STAGECOACH RIDE TO COLD SPRING TAVERN AND AN IMAGINARY TRIP FOR KIDS

They built a stagecoach road over San Marcos Pass in 1868 using a gang of Chinese workmen who made the grade with picks, shovels and wheelbarrows. On the north side of the grade the coolies built a bunkhouse near a cold artesian spring, far back in a horseshoe-shaped canyon.

The stagecoach trail ran into the Santa Ynez Valley to Ballard (later to Los Olivos and Mattei's Tavern when the Pacific Coast Railway arrived in 1887). One route ran through Foxen Canyon with a stage at Foxen's adobe, then to Dana's adobe in Nipomo and beyond to the Ramona Hotel in San Luis Obispo. There were many stages in the Flint and Bixby Stagecoach run to Santa Barbara, places where the team of six horses could be changed and the "seasick" passengers given a chance to stabilize themselves. These stages, or stops, gave rise to the name stagecoach.

From Los Olivos to Santa Barbara there were three stages, one of them being near the top of 2,225 foot San Marcos Pass, by the cold spring where the Chinese had their bunkhouse. It was an idyllic spot under the bay trees where the horses could be watered and people could have lunch and dinner at the tavern and hotel built in the 1890s by J.D. Parish.

Parish made his residence at Cold Spring and built a house and a barn big enough for a livery stable. Since then the Doulton family, of the Miramar Hotel in Montecito, owned it and added tourist cottages.

Today Audrey Ovington leases it to a couple of guys who know how to keep the old tavern working as a mountain watering hole and gathering place for people along the trail.

41

We thought we would take a look so we drove up Highway 154 past Mattei's Tavern to the entrance of Lake Cachuma, where we set the odometer. Exactly six miles beyond is a Los Padres National Forest sign on the right and the original Stagecoach Road on the left. The road is big enough for a Concord (stagecoach built in Concord, New Hampshire) and six horses, but not for much more. The road winds around the hills while Highway 154 shoots straight ahead at a higher elevation.

At 7.4 miles (from the Lake Cachuma entrance) we crossed Paradise Road, a back country road to serene camping spots along the Santa Ynez River, above the river's impoundment. The utility lines had been on the left as we drove up Stagecoach Road but when we left this place the poles moved over the road from left to right, through a clearing of sandstone outcroppings.

We got out again (at 8.4) and looked for evidence of the original trail. The wagons had iron wheels that rutted soft sandsone, and I thought just maybe . . . and then I saw them—parallel cuts in the stone, sometimes six feet long, carved sharply by an iron wheel. And then farther up I saw more of the same. There's little doubt that at this point an older trail went up this grade; but heavy brush and fallen trees prevented my exploring the trail any farther than a hundred yards.

At 8.9 miles we came into full view of the 1500 foot Cold Spring Arch Bridge, built in 1963, where Highway 154 spans the long horseshoe-shaped canyon. Soon we began to encounter the vehicles of noonday visitors to Cold Spring Tavern. Crowds of people sat about in the warm sun, sipping drinks and listening to the music.

Tom Ball playing harmonica and Kenny Sultan pickin' guitar, were performing on a bench in front of the log cabin, tapping their feet, raising dust and wailing old-time traditional blues. On the back porch over the stream Ben was sending an intoxicating smokey aroma around as he grilled tri-tips and got lunch ready. The sun was warm, the crowd was at peace and everybody seemed as mellow as a cat on a sill.

Cold Spring Tavern is a collection of slip-shod buildings in various stages of arrested decay. I don't understand how anything so decrepit can be so charming; but charming it is. We came back in the evening for dinner and sat in the white room, actually a back shed used as a bunkhouse and storage place in years past.

Through the window we saw the original Chinese workmen's 1868 bunkhouse with a big sycamore tree growing through the roof; and up the trail the old Ojai Jail (1878), adopted by the owner, sitting friendly next to the outhouse that leans into the hill . . . and farther along the walkway old ivy-covered tourist cabins built by the Doultons.

All of the restaurant's rooms have fireplaces, and I imagine that on a cold winter night when the rain pelts the roof and the fire crackles in the hearth, a romantic soul could lose control savoring the atmosphere and the rabbit and venison dishes prepared so deliciously here.

In the log cabin next to the restaurant the music had turned louder with a crowd dancing to an amplified group on stage in front of the fireplace. Above the mantle a boar's head with sunglasses looked down on a mass of gyrating pelvises and flailing hands.

Earlier in the afternoon we continued on the Stagecoach Road beyond Cold Spring Tavern toward Santa Barbara, winding out of the Canyon, bypassing a spur that runs up to Highway 154 (at 10.2 miles), until the two roads were within 100 feet of each other close to the top.

Five hundred feet south is Kinevan Road, known as the trotting grade on the Flint and Bixby Stagecoach Line, the only level stretch over San Marcos Pass where the horses could run. It's a

very narrow, winding road of extraordinary charm and nostalgia, meandering under a canopy of laurels and sycamores alongside the ferny slopes of San Jose Creek.

In less than a mile, Kinevan joins West Camino Cielo; then turning left we came up to Highway 154 again. A mile and a half down the southern slope of Highway 154, toward Santa Barbara, the Old San Marcos Road goes to the right, just prior to Painted Cave Road on the left.

Much of this steep paved road of double U's going down to Goleta is part of the original Santa Ynez Turnpike Road of 1868. Squabbles with landowners over open gates and straying cattle forced the stagecoach lines and road builders to occasionally change the routes, and one of the most important relics of stagecoach days, the Slippery Rock section, where the wagon's iron wheels left deep gouges in the exposed sandstone, is nearby on private property.

Old San Marcos Road ambles down across Maria Ignacia Creek, by the "Laurel Of San Marcos," said to be the tallest bay tree in the world, where linesman, affectionaltely called Jehus (see 2 Kings 9 vs 20) would shade their horses before the strenuous climb ahead. Left on Cathedral Street, in Goleta, Turnpike Road continues to Hollister, concluding a path of California history that ran from 1868-1901.

If my grandson were here, and were about eight years older, I know what I'd do. I'd take Dillon for a ride along the Old Stagecoach Road; then we'd have lunch along Lake Cachuma and I'd tell him about times the stagecoach stopped by the chalk cliffs, a place now 60 feet under water. I'd show him the ruts in the trails and then we'd go to to Santa Ynez Carriage Museum at 3596 Sagunto Street, in Santa Ynez, and we'd feel the hard iron wheels and imagine we were linesmen high up on the wagon snapping a 16 foot bull whip over a team of horses, cussin 'em when they got out of hand . . . and we'd sweat a lot and feel mighty proud we had brought Miss Kitty and her aunt from Back East into town, safe and sound.

Then we'd go for an ice cream cone and drive on home—quiet and feeling good, and happy we were together—just Dillon and me.

Carriage Museum hours are 10 a.m.-4 p.m. Tuesday-Thursday and 1 p.m.-4 p.m. Friday-Sunday. Call 688-7889.

Cold Spring Tavern's phone is 967-0066.

9—CAMINO CIELO —
EXPLORING A ROAD IN THE SKY

Every time I traveled to Santa Barbara over San Marcos Pass I came across signs to East and West Camino Cielo and wondered where those roads went. Now I know.

The maps indicate that West Camino Cielo runs from Highway 154, west, all the way to Refugio Road across the ridge of the Santa Ynez Mountains; and East Camino Cielo runs eastward along the ridge, eventually winding down into Santa Barbara city limits.

I explored West Camino Cielo by riding up Refugio Road from Santa Ynez. In the 1860s Refugio Road was an old burro trail that connected the Ortega Ranch on the ocean side with the mission of Santa Ynez. The Flint and Bixby Stagecoach Company considered Refugio as one possible location for a stagecoach run over the mountains, but San Marcos Pass was an easier grade to negotiate and Refugio never came into extensive use.

A mile and a half east of Los Olivos, Roblar Road bisects Highway 154. It immediately branches to create Refugio, which runs straight as a lot line across the valley, past nifty horse ranches and country homes. Across the Santa Ynez River and Highway 246, it climbs into unpretentious ranch country of herefords and barbed wire fences.

The road winds deferentially through a maze of huge sycamores and gnarly oaks that have stood there for hundreds of years. I stopped where the road comes down to the spring and got out to stretch and take a few pictures. The air was still, and heavy with the scent of sage and composting earth. Moisture dropping from the overhanging branches splatted on the crunchy bed of fallen leaves. I began to understand why Ronald Reagan finds his peace

47

here. His ranch is only five miles up the road, across the ridge. It's a place of quiet charm where the music is the drone of bees visiting the flowers.

The pavement ends half way up, and a good gravel road continues the last three miles to the summit (elevation 2250). West Camino Cielo is to the left and a Forest Service facility to the right.

There's a gate across West Camino Cielo about a mile from Refugio, but half of the time it's open and you can travel the 19 miles along the ridge of the mountains to Highway 154.

It was open on the day I was there so I pulled my bicycle off the truck and started up. Three guys from Santa Barbara caught up with me and we rode together for awhile. They were completing a circuit ride that began in Santa Barbara and had been on the road for over two hours, peddling up Highway 154, over San Marcos Pass, then down the Santa Ynez Valley, west along Highway 246, and up Refugio Road.

Now they were going through on West Camino Cielo to Santa Ynez Peak (elevation 4,298 feet), a gain of 2,000 feet in five miles on paved road; then down the ten mile long dirt section of West Camino Cielo to San Marcos Pass (Highway 154) and back down to Santa Barbara.

I tried to keep up but these jocks were too much for me. Soon I was peddling—and walking—by myself. There were grades where I could ride, but too soon I was back on the pavement hoofing it to the top.

Frequently I was interrupted with the sounds of helicopters coming and going, and after a half hour on the road I caught views of the Reagan 688-acre ranch behind me, just west of where I was. If West Camino Cielo continued west of Refugio Road, beyond the Forest Service facility, it would go right through Rancho Dos Vistas.

The views along this road in the sky are breathtaking: dark green canyons run down to the ocean, far away groves of avocado dot the gentler slopes, and ghostly images of the Channel Islands appear through the sea mist.

When the gate near Refugio is open, you can drive your car on the paved road to Santa Ynez Peak, and continue beyond on the dirt road. It's a dusty, bumpy and rutted road for ten miles as it winds along the ridge, but there are excellent views of Lake Cachuma and the San Rafael Mountains to the north.

The shooting of firearms is a popular pastime along this desolate ten mile section of road, and I got a queazy feeling when I saw men with loaded arms looking at me like I was moving target. I make a special effort to wave and throw a toothy smile . . . haven't been hit yet.

Pavement begins again at the Winchester Gun Club's Trap and Skeet Range. Just beyond the second entrance to the gun club, on the right (ocean) side, is a system of well-worn trails that amble over the boulder fields to a prominent lookout called Lizard's Mouth.

Continuing down this four mile paved section eastward toward Highway 154 I discovered many trails that meander through gardens of huge boulders. Reportedly, numerous caves in this area bear the artwork of Indians who lived here.

Within a few miles of Highway 154 there are a variety of quirky homes among the boulders and then West Camino dips down to meet Kinevan Road. I turned left and followed Kinevan, the original stagecoach route, to a point where it comes up to Highway 154. Across the road is East Camino Cielo, a stretch of paved road that wanders further eastward, eventually descending into the city of Santa Barbara.

There's a short jaunt up East Camino Cielo that's worth your time. Within a couple hundred yards, east, along East Camino is a full service watering hole where you can get gassed, fed and entertained—The Cielo Cafe, Gas Station, Store and Starlight Dinner Playhouse—all in one.

More significant is Painted Cave State Park, a .7 mile ride up the road to Painted Cave Road then right a half mile, beyond the Painted Cave community of homes.

Up the hill, along a trail, is a gated cave with genuine Indian petroglyphs. The cave isn't very deep so you can view the paintings easily through the grate.

You can stay on Painted Cave Road and exit again onto Highway 154 a few miles below (south) of East Camino Cielo.

If you stay on Kinevan Road, northward, over San Marcos Pass, it becomes Old Stagecoach Road and runs by Cold Spring Tavern. Here the common man enjoys a bowl of chili and a cold glass of beer by the gurgling stream, and the yuppies sit in the restaurant sipping martinis and eating gourmet luncheons.

The next time you're going over San Marcos Pass and someone in the car says, "I wonder what's up that road," you'll be able to sally forth with a detailed account of Painted Cave, Lizard's Mouth, Broadcast Peak and the close-up views of the Reagan Ranch. They'll be impressed.

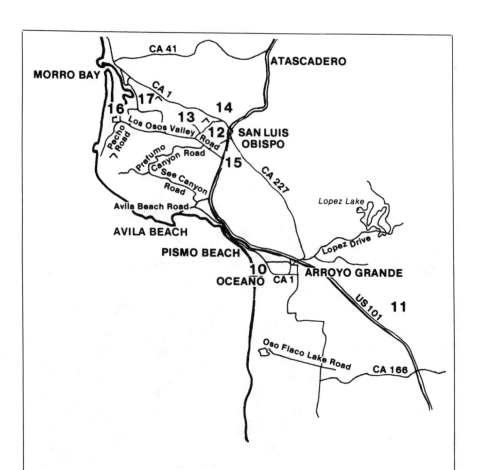

10 Oceano Dunes
11 Pacific Coast Railway
12 Laguna Lake
13 SLO Peak
14 Poly Canyon Hikes
15 Farmer's Market
16 Baywood Park
17 Morro Bay's Blue Herons

II In the Heart
of the Central Coast

10—A WORLD OF GREEN MOORS AND FLOWERING PLANTS — HIKING THE BACK DUNES OF OCEANO

"This sand dune area is unexcelled, both in scenic quality and in extent, by any similar area in California... and nowhere along the California coast do sand dunes of comparable scenic quality, extent and height occur."—from a recreation report made by the National Park Service in 1959 about the Nipomo Dunes, an 18-mile stretch of Pacific coastline from Pismo Beach to Vandenberg AFB.

But you don't get the best impression of the dunes from the beach side where the wind blows hard and the cold ocean wind forces sunbathers under blankets. You have to get beyond the first hummocks along the beach, to the secondary and back dunes.

There flowering plants have tamed the mounds, and green moors of mock heather and bush lupine provide food and shelter for coveys of quail and a host of bush tits, sparrows, towhees, and brown thrashers.

By seed, by rhizomes and by the strength of their roots they invade the sand and hold it, grain by grain, until a whole dune is in their grasp. Buffeted by wind, they climb the hills until the next storm tears the fabric and the sand runs rampant again. Then creation moves back to the first day and the building begins anew.

To see a little piece of this drama, drive down Grand Avenue in Grover City, beyond Highway One and the Southern Pacific Railroad tracks, to the beach and parking lot. Opposite the parking lot kiosk is the trailhead marker to the Grand Dune Trail, up a

4-foot bank of sand. The trail ambles .9 mile through the back dunes to the campground of the Pismo Beach State Park in Oceano.

Beyond the crest of the first hill is a world of pastel colors and flowering plants. Nearly 100 per cent of the sand is covered by vegetation, living comfortably in the lee of the foredunes that absorb the brunt of the beach's stormy blasts. It's a miracle anything can live on the totally inorganic sand (quartz), which is hotter than a tin roof at midday, reaching temperatures of 130 degrees.

But only six inches below the burning surface the sand is moist and less than 70 degrees, a difference of more than 60 degrees between the surface and the subsoil.

Eriastrum shows off its bundles of baby blue flowers and Indian pinks stand out of the brush and sage. Bush lupine is still in bloom in August with many of its pod-like ovaries pregnant with the seeds of the next generation, and running down the draws are spangles of sand verbena, each of their little flowers a wallpaper designer's dream. Scattered throughout the back dunes is mock heather, a large, almost evergreen shrub, growing to six or seven feet, looking like green spiked balls. We stopped to photograph an idyllic setting of croton sprawling across the sand, next to the blue flowers of bushy Eriastrum. Buckwheat, with its massive heads of frail white flowers formed the backdrop.

Mourning doves coo plaintively from the brush, and finches and sparrows flit nervously in their search for seeds. A pair of towhees appeared on a limb long enough for me to identify them, then they vanished in a thick bramble.

The ground is marked by a myriad of footsteps and scratches of field mice and lizards, and dung beetles who forage in the path for the trail horse's contribution to the local ecology.

The trail is up and down, with views of the marsh to the left (east) and the rising dunes to the right. It's a strange juxtaposition of wetland and semiarid habitats.

At times the ocean surf is barely audible, then it comes through clearly where the long sweeping valleys run to the foredunes.

Willows grow along the edge of the marsh, with pearly everlasting and dune grasses taking the higher places. Dudleya snuggles in the sand with its succulent basal leaves, sending up a stalk of winsom red and yellow flowers.

It was during a morning walk that I came to understand the importance of morning fog in the survival of the plants of the dunes. The fog lay across the tules like gauze. The air was quiet and atmospheric water hung suspended, clinging to everything it touched.

The plants were wet and drops of water fell to their thirsty roots in a trickle system so slow it is difficult to imagine that in a year's time as much as 12 inches of moisture falls to the ground.

The droplets become drink for insects and browsing animals, and the sustaining element in a world of severe hardship. It had been over three months since there had been a real rain but the plants were thriving as though it were the first week of spring.

I took a walk up one of the draws where pines grow in the moist hollows. They have been recently planted and are doing well despite the lack of moisture. The pines grow in a horizontal configuration, similar to conifers growing at high elevations, a posture called krumpholtz, or crooked wood. Sand driven by high winds shears off the terminal buds and only the horizontal buds survive to form the new growth.

The Grand Dune Trail came into a section of moving dunes where European beach grass has been introduced, a species the Southern Pacific Railroad found useful for controlling drifting sand at the turn of the century. They're a beautiful sight with their dark green tubular stems and buffy plumes, but they have been both savior and villain. Although they have been an excellent stabilizing force in the dunes, they out-compete the native plants. In time they may totally tramsform the dunes from a native landscape of many endemic species to a foreign landscape of only one or a few species. We stopped to look at a cut of an eight foot dune being stabilized by the European beach grass. The roots had extended at least four feet into the sand forming a network of fibrous strands similar to woven cloth.

The trail becomes undiscernible as you walk through the beach grass and into the open dunes. Stay to the right, away from the tules, crossing over a large dune, then down into a trough, aiming for the distant evergreens on the horizon of the Oceano campground.

In the campground turn right for the return walk along the open beach, or left to walk the campground road to Pier Avenue where you can catch a bite to eat.

The U.S. Fish and Wildlife Service published an inventory of California's important wildlife habitat and found the Nipomo Dunes . . . "possessing the highest aesthetic and ecological values remaining in California." No wonder there is an organization called People for a Nipomo Dunes National Seashore.

11—TRAVELS INTO YESTERYEAR ON THE PACIFIC COAST RAILWAY

It was the 1880s. Down at the train station on Higuera Street the warehouses were full of grain and feed. From the corrals and box-cars restless cattle and hogs bawled and squealed, and the odor of manure lay over the city like a blanket of fog.

There was a lot of activity: men moving cattle through chutes and ramps, crates of produce being loaded onto cars, and people hurrying with baggage to and from the station. The train took on the belongings of everyone like a serpentine beast of burden.

The Baldwin engine sat impatiently on the track, seeping steam and issuing a light white smoke from its stack.

Engineer Masterman watched the last of the passengers board, then, glancing at his big pocket watch, reached up and gave the whistle three short blasts, with the last one trailing into a thin, mournful sound.

The track cleared and the engine chugged, sending a gray cloud of smoke into the air. Drive wheels strained. In slow motion, the two passenger cars and a string of freight and cattle cars moved down Higuera Street to Port Harford and the steamer Queen Of The Pacific tied up at the wharf.

San Luis Obispo wasn't yet a college town in the 1880s . . . or a prison town. It was a railroad town, the heart of the Pacific Coast Railway, the link between the southern valley towns of Los Alamos, Los Olivos, Santa Maria, San Luis Obispo and the pier at Avila.

From Harford's wharf (Port San Luis Pier), ocean steamers hauled people and goods up and down the coast. Lumber from Redwood City and Oregon came in, and cattle, dairy products and crops went out.

At Higuera and Madonna Road, where a derelict railroad warehouse stands, there were railroad car paint shops, machine shops, a roundhouse and office.

The railroad began with John Harford's horse drawn railroad in 1873. Horses hauled cars onto a high point along the cliffs of Avila, which then rolled by gravity onto the pier to waiting ships.

In 1876, there was the San Luis Obispo-Santa Maria Railroad, which by 1887, included tracks to Los Alamos and Los Olivos, when the name changed to Pacific Coast Railway. The end for the PCR began in 1936 and by 1942, it was all over.

The PCR was not only there to haul cattle, pigs and oilwell equipment; before the advent of the automobile it was also a principal way for the people in the city to go for an excursion into the country. Trips in the spring and summer were very popular, and the Telegram Tribune of 1883 gives an account of over 1400 people jamming boxcars, flat cars and passenger car compartments for a 3.5 hour ride to Los Alamos and the picnic grounds at the end of Centennial Street.

You've missed your chance to ride those rails, but the second best alternative is to retrace the path of the PCR. There are a few places where your imagination can help you see the old train running through the hills.

SAN LUIS OBISPO TO AVILA

From San Luis Obispo, the train ran down South Higuera, toward Avila, with a spur going northwest to Bishop Peak where they quarried granite. The main line ran parallel to the old highway (Ontario Road) in the southbound lane of Highway 101 (before its construction), then in front of the old school house, crossing over Ontario Road at the bridge on the north side of San Luis Creek, where you can see and walk the grade.

The tracks crossed the creek by the Avila Water Department building on Avila Beach Drive, then crossed again over a trestle, adjacent to the present bridge. Look to the left (west) of the road bridge and you can see some of the remaining concrete anchors of the old trestle, and a deep cut in the bank on the far end. The present roadway is where the double sets of tracks ran.

John Harford built the Port San Luis pier in 1871 and it has endured every winter storm. The original old port buildings burned in 1915, and modifications have been made, but it's basically the same old railroad pier.

Five hundred yards from the Port San Luis parking lot, at the "$1,000 Fine For Littering" sign, you may be able to identify the tunnel in the rock for Harford's horse drawn train. Imagine a line running from the littering sign through the decorative anchors at the entrance to the trailer court. Up the slope by some pilings and a telephone pole is a conspicuous rock. Just below it and to the right is a closed-in tunnel through which the train ran. The horses pulled the cars to an 80-foot summit and then by gravity rolled to the pier, or to the flats along San Luis Creek.

SAN LUIS OBISPO TO LOS OLIVOS

The train left San Luis Obispo for Arroyo Grande along South Street, crossing Broad near the Mazda car dealership, running parallel to Broad Street and the Southern Pacific Railroad tracks. It crossed Orcutt Road 500 yards down the hill from Broad, then ran along the left side of Broad (Edna Road or Highway 227) into Edna Valley.

Across from the airport (east), the train crossed the De Piedra Creek over an existing trestle (behind the yellow farm house with twin gables). A mile south, at the bridge that spans the Southern Pacific Railroad tracks, look north for the PCR cut to the left of the existing tracks.

The PCR narrow gauge crossed the Southern Pacific tracks at the mouth of Price Canyon, then headed east crossing Highway 227 (Carpenter Canyon Road), 1.5 miles from Corbett Canyon Road, about 50 feet east of the east fork of Pismo Creek. The railbed is raised on either side of the road, curving slightly eastward, then crossing the creek over a trestle that can be seen left of the blue water tanks in the field.

The train moved northerly across the Patchett Ranch, crossing Corbett Canyon Road near the Downing Arabian Horse Farm. Here it made a big U turn before it climbed the grade and proceeded in a deep cut on the left side (north) of the road, through a eucalyptus grove. This is commonly referred to as the Verde Canyon cut.

The tracks ran right and left of Corbett Canyon Road, entering Arroyo Grande along the base of Crown Hill where E.C. Loomis operated for many years. A plaque on the sidewalk marks the spot.

It took 300 Chinese workmen to pick and grade the railbed to Arroyo Grande from San Luis Obispo, but it was completed on October 12, 1881.

The ranchers had watched the laying of the rails through Corbett Canyon and had stacked 25,000 sacks of grain at the station ready for shipment. As soon as the tracks were laid, the train began to run, making three trips a day to Port Harford.

The Chinese tracklayers inched their way out of town, circling behind the high school on Fair Oaks Avenue, then along Valley Road near the Pitkin residence (the Rose Victorian Inn) and up Los Berros Road on their way to Nipomo.

There isn't a lot you can see of the grade until you cross Highway 101; there on the east side, near the northbound exit sign, is the raised grade with a curving fence, and a hill with accompanying utility poles. From here to Los Olivos, utility poles, often unstrung, are guideposts to the Pacific Coast narrow gauge.

The PCR crossed Tefft Street in Nipomo, 60 feet south of the Adobe Plaza shopping center. A historical plaque, hidden by grass, marks the Nipomo station site.

The train continued in the gentle valleys between the present highway and Thompson Avenue, running just down the hill from the Dana Adobe at 671 Oak Glen Street in Nipomo.

At the Santa Maria Speedway the train came through a narrow cut (look for unstrung utility poles) on the east side, crossing the highway and traversing the speedway before going over the Santa Maria River.

On Main Street, one mile west of Broadway, across from the Toyota dealership, you can see another plaque and a remnant of narrow gauge rails at the site of the Santa Maria station. The PCR right-of-way runs south along Railroad Avenue toward Orcutt, and after a short distance becomes the standard gauge Santa Maria Valley Railroad, which is still in operation.

Along Blosser Road, south of Stowell, we sighted the trail to our left across the cabbage fields, old utility poles marking the way. During the way years, Blosser Road and the PCR gave way to the U.S. Air Force that bought 3,000 acres for a P-38 training base, but the road and track bed continue south of the Santa Maria Airport.

The PCR roadbed continues southerly past Clark Avenue, but Blosser dead-ends there, so we turned left to locate the Orcutt station, a block west of Broadway on Markum, by yet another historical plaque.

We drove down Clark Avenue to Highway 135, then south up the Graciosa Canyon on 135. This section of the line was called the

Divide, a 500-foot climb out of the Santa Maria Valley into the Los Alamos Valley.

To the left of the "10 miles to Vandenberg" sign is the vicinity of Graciosa, once a thriving little burg that was burned to the ground by Mr. Hartnell, its owner, who decided the only way to remove squatters from his land was to set fire to their homes and businesses. So much for Graciosa.

Across gently sloping land the PCR chugged though the Righetti Ranch, the small power lines with the V-shaped hanger on the left marking the way. At San Antonio Road, I picked a red Iceland poppy for Winston Wickenden, my 81-year-old companion and guide on this trip. There are 100 acres of crimson poppies, stretching to the base of the hills and the Harris Grade (Highway 1) beyond.

At the Highway 1—135 intersection, we were again surprised with the beauty of fields of purple alyssum, spread like sheets into the distance.

Near this intersect was the Harris station-warehouse, on the Harris Ranch, where crops and cattle were shipped out by rail to Port Harford.

Traveling south we came to Bell Street, just south of Los Alamos. We turned left on Bell, 200 yards east of Highway 135, to see the parallel tar strips in the road where the tracks were pulled up

years back. Winston recalled a tragic accident at this intersection when a gasoline truck rammed engine 101, destroying itself, the engine, two boxcars and a waiting automobile.

The train came into Los Alamos along Leslie Street where the station and warehouse are intact, still dealing in 19th century goods and articles, now called antiques.

Los Alamos is full of memories for Winston. He was born here in 1905 and remembers climbing the old sycamore tree on St. Joseph Street. He also recalls occasions when city people came out to the country on the train to picnic at the the park up Drum Canyon, near the cemetery where his ancestors are buried.

It was also around 1905 when Mrs. Lyons came from Los Olivos on the train to substitute teach for a week in Los Alamos. When she went to board the train on Friday for her return home she was provoked, learning there was no passenger car on the train.

The station master said, "No problem, Mrs. Lyons, we'll work something out," whereby he added a flat car to the train, bolted a rocking chair to it and placed Mrs. Lyons in it. One and a half hours later, a sooty Mrs. Lyons was back home in Los Olivos.

Along Highway 101 toward San Marcos Pass, the PCR ran to the right—along the utility poles, crossing the left side south of Alisos Canyon Road.

At Zaca Station Road there was another PCR station-warehouse. Just beyond the second fence line on the east side of northbound 101, you can see the grade. It crossed Zaca Station Road, climbed along the hill, then swung east along Highway 154. After ascending to the 960-foot summit, the roadbed rolled into Los Olivos at the Oak Tree Station under the big tree across from Mattie's Tavern.

The fashionable place to stay at the end of the line in early railroad days was in town at the Los Olivos Hotel, completed in 1888, but it burned to the ground two years later. In its place is the Los Olivos Grand Hotel and Restaurant on Grand Avenue.

A scenic alternative return trip is down Foxen Canyon Road into the Sisquoc River Valley, where the PCR sent a spur in 1911 to service the rapidly developing oil businesses up Palmer Canyon.

Total round trip distance from San Luis Obispo is about 150 miles. For more information check Gerald Thompson's "Memories of the PC," or Gerald M. Best's "Ships and Narrow Gauge Rails, The Story of the Pacific Coast Company."

12—LAGUNA LAKE: A RECREATION AREA IN SLO'S BACK YARD

I remember seeing pictures of peasant people stuffing a goose. They'd put the bird between their legs and force feed the poor beast until it could hardly walk.

I didn't think they did that around here, but one day I stopped at Laguna Lake and discovered there are a lot of people into that—and they don't even eat the goose.

Most anytime, but particularly on weekends, you'll see people trundle in unimaginable edibles to feed the birds at Laguna Lake; things like platters of kitchen leftovers, loaves of bread, mashed potatoes and bags of cracked corn and grain. I even saw a kid sharing his Pepsi with a mallard. The duck liked it.

I've been there when flocks of geese in the roadway forced traffic over to the shoulders. The bossy geese hardly raised their fat bottoms off the pavement as cars passed, except of course, when somebody stepped out with a loaf of Langendorf's swinging from their hand; then the geese were up honking and wiggling their tails like happy dogs.

What begins as a handout to a few happy ducks and geese invariably turns into a melee of hundreds of gluttonous birds vying for food. This is no Thanksgiving feast of sharing and loving; this is every bird for itself, where vengeance is heaped on the hapless bird who takes another's morsel. I saw a ringed-bill gull chase a coot above and below the water for over a minute, in what seemed to be unnecessarily mean, ugly and malevolent. I know that's anthropocentric, but that's how it looked.

Little kids standing in the middle of this harangue of snapping bills usually end up with their hands high over their heads, pressed by straining geese stretching for food hidden in their clenched little fists. Sooner than not the children are climbing their parents to escape.

Some of these ducks are comical, some bizarre in their strange feathering and colored masks, but all of them are loveable. In their innocence, dependency and insatiable need for our benevolence they beg until our hearts bleed and our hands reach for another loaf of day-old bread.

Morley and Douglas Weir and Lisa Trayser joined me one morning to see how many different kinds of waterfowl we could spot at the lake. We saw coots, ring-billed gulls, Western gulls, mallards, domestic Pekins and farmyard geese on the edge of the lake close to Madonna Road, where most the feeding occurs.

Away from the feeding area, westward, along paths through the smartweed and rushes, we saw cormorants, bitterns, egrets and high overhead, a red-tailed hawk.

Laguna Lake is more than a bird feeding ground. It's a 320-acre park of mountains, grasslands and sparkling water. It's a bit of wildness within the city limits, a back roads in our own back yard.

People come to fish the lake for trout, blue gill , crappie and big mouth bass. Windsurfers and small sailboats play in the gusting winds that whip across the lake from Los Osos Valley. At mid-morning, mothers watch their kids run in the grass or climb the beamed fortress. At lunch time, office workers break for a breath of fresh air and a fresh view; and in the evening after work, people run their dogs and themselves along trails and across the fields. At the end of the paved quarter mile road at Laguna Lake, an exercise trail continues west along a fence.

Primitive trails along the inlets of the lake run through a network of willows and tules to good fishing and birding spots. I parked the car at the end of the road and walked a path that arches around past a restroom. At the upper (west) end, I crossed the stile over the fence and headed uphill past the water tank where a group of turkey vultures drank.

Jagged rocks form an unceremonious cross on top. Hikers have built a human nest up there, and I imagine they sit against the rocks and look over the city, out to the airport and left up Chorro Valley and the Cal Poly campus. The city owns all the acreage up there, all the way to the next barbed wire fence, so you don't have to think you're trespassing if you climb the hills.

Behind is the broad Los Osos Valley. I was surprised to see that the valley rises out of San Luis Obispo and doesn't begin descending to the ocean until you're past the Monte Mills Ranch. Laguna Lake holds the runoff from this slope of Los Osos Valley and Prefumo Canyon. From the lake, water flows under Madonna Road toward Higuera Street, then parallels Highway 101, joining San Luis Creek, until it enters the ocean at Avila Beach.

As I walked back down the hill through a eucalyptus grove, I marveled at the diversity of this park. It's a place that offers rest from the city, a long view of a broad valley across a shimmering lake, water to fish and sailboats... and even a good place to stuff geese.

Laguna Lake Park is on Madonna Road, halfway between Los Osos Valley Road and Higuera Street; the entrance is near the Post Office building, on Dalidio Drive.

13—SLO PEAK
AFFORDS BREATHTAKING VIEWS
OF THE VALLEYS

My daughter Cynthia was in town for a few days so we went out for lunch at the Inn at Morro Bay, enjoying the best of man in the best of natural settings.

After lunch we drove up Black Hill Road, which is opposite the Inn, and motored through the golf course, past the club house to the end of the road. The views of the bay are exceptional from here with the sloping greens and piney hills of the golf course as foreground.

A foot trail ascends from the end of the parking lot, through chaparral and pine trees. After an easy 15 minute walk we approached the top of Black Hill, elevation 665 feet.

We looked eastward, into the Chorro Valley. Hollister Peak was nearby, looming above us at 1,404 feet. Beyond Hollister are the rest of the Seven Sisters, those magnificent granite peaks, or morros, that separate the Chorro and Los Osos valleys.

All these hills are ancient volcanic domes, or remnants of intrusive plugs, 23 million years old. The highest is Bishop's Peak at 1,559 feet, and across Foothill Boulevard in San Luis Obispo is Mount San Luis, elevation 1292 feet, more properly called Cerro San Luis Obispo, but commonly misnamed Madonna Peak.

It was still early in the day so we headed over to Foothill Boulevard to catch the trail to Mount San Luis at the end of Tassajara Street (a half mile west of Santa Rosa).

A staircase leads over the Madonna Ranch fence onto a well-worn path that ascends the grassy slopes. The meadow larks were on the fence posts announcing spring and the western sun was

glowing behind a veil of showers dripping from a fast-moving purple cloud. It was strikingly beautiful. From up the slope we glanced back at Bishop Peak, a monument of green swells with miniature cows upon her hills.

There is a system of trails running along the foothills, but the main trail runs straight ahead to the tree line and the jagged face of the mountain.

At the junction in the trail we went left, not sure where either one would lead us. The trail is an obvious road with the sides of the hill cut like a wall. Just beyond the trail junction is a fern grotto with water that trickles, or gushes during rains. The trail is well protected with the bluff on the right side and a canopy of oaks on the left.

The road becomes boulder strewn, and rolling between them came Rod Hiltbrand on his trail bike. Rod said that most bicyclists use the right hand trail, circling 'round the mountain on the Los Osos Valley side, then descending on this trail that faces Santa Rosa and Foothill.

Views of the Johnson Avenue area were around the next bend, then Highway 101 as it weaves through the city on its way up the Cuesta Grade.

George and Clemence Hinds hiked by us like we were dawdling; no heaving chests and parched lips on these people. They do
the whole hike with smiles on their faces, unlike some others I
know who look like they're dying. The Hinds are staying in shape
to do a Grand Canyon hike, so they churn up these hills daily.
They said they go from the base of the mountain to the top in 20
minutes.

A half hour after we began we came around a bend in the trail
and overlooked the entire city. The airport beacon on Islay Peak
(elevation 775 feet), last of the Seven Sisters, was in front of us,
preceded by a few button hills lying before it. The entire Poly
campus came into view, all in miniature, a post card view of life in
San Luis Obispo.

In another ten minutes we were at the summit, looking at the
cement-encased pole that supports the lights that the Madonna
family erect at Christmas time, the lights that some find a desecration and others find symbolic and inspirational.

From on top you can see forever. Highway 101 swirls away in
a neat concrete ribbon to the south, the Madonna Road shopping
plaza looks like a variety of flat-topped boxes, and up the Los Osos
Valley the Seven Sisters line up pretty as a picture. One night we
watched a sunset from up here, and the fog came rolling down the
valley from the ocean, gobbling up people, cars and buildings until
the entire city was devoured.

Following the bicyclist's directions for circling the mountain
on the Los Osos Valley side, Cynthia and I began our descent, but
it looked like we were going to end up on Madonna Road, while the
car was back on Tassajara near Foothill. I decided to send Cynthia
back with the keys to the car while I explored ahead, with the
agreement she would pick me up near the Madonna Inn or Laguna
Lake.

Ten minutes after she left me I discovered a trail that cuts
back the 180 degrees toward Foothill Boulevard, while the main
road led down to Madonna construction yard. I made the turn back
and began to wonder how Cynthia would ever find me if I returned
to Tassajara while she was looking for me with the car at Madonna
Road. I became convinced I had to beat her back to the car.

I guessed that Cynthia would run back, so I picked up my
pace, trotting at first, then running hard past cool, wet fern

canyons, through muddy puddles, under idyllic canopied woodlands; catching views of the foothills of Bishop Peak across the
ravines.

I tore past a wild blooming peony yearning to be stroked.
Monkey flowers, wild raspberries and Indian paint brush became a
blur in a jolting panorama.

Through the trees I could see that the car was still parked by
the staircase. I ran harder, stumbling breathlessly along a medita-
tive trail with trickling rocks covered with moss and ferns.

By the time I reached the junction of the trail I could see down
to the car. Approaching it was a loping blonde woman with a green
shirt, Cynthia. I whistled, but my parched lips wouldn't purse
properly, so I screamed a hideous call that got Cynthia to turn
around. She saw me.

Since then I've walked (slowly) this section of Mount San Luis,
in a more sane state of mind. It's the prettiest side of the mountain
and needs to be seen leisurely.

It's the kind of place where Edith Hall walks John Dog, her
daughter's big malamute, and sees the fuchsia-flowered
gooseberry and the feral goats; and Craig walks hand-in-hand
with Kelly, and Bob and Lisa take their guinea pig, Spunky, for
walks, picking fresh grass for him... and where Ron careens
through the trees like a lunatic, trying to catch up to his daughter
who is about to take off in his car and leave him behind.

14—POLY CANYON HIKES — BACK ROADS IN OUR BACK YARD

San Luis Obispo is often mentioned as one of the nation's most desirable places to live because it is charmingly tucked away in the mountains, and the rolling terrain is an integral part of the city landscape.

You don't have to drive out into the country to make contact with the natural world of canyons and streams; you can find them right in the city, and in a few moments be in a realm far removed from the hustle of town.

There are a variety of walks and bicycle rides in Poly Canyon, on the Cal Poly campus that take you into the country so fast you can't believe these places have stayed secret so long.

The Poly Canyon walks begin across from the Clyde P. Fisher Science Building on Perimeter Road. To get there take Grand Avenue in San Luis Obispo all the way to the end where it deadends with Perimeter Road, across from the University Union. Turn right and follow Perimeter Road as it circles around to Poly Canyon Road; park in lots H4 or H5 or drive up Poly Canyon Road one-half mile to the end. The gate is open all day on weekdays but closed from 5:30 p.m. to 7:30 a.m.

The Poly Canyon Road and trail goes through a eucalyptus grove along Brizziolari Creek. To the left is the Cal Poly maintenance yard with its clutter of equipment, but that soon changes to relaxing views of cattle in pastures and swooping waves of blackbirds.

The canyon is a shady lane of green serpentine rocks on the right and the gurgling stream on the left. In fall the poison oak along the stream is red and the elderberries look just right for pie filling or jam. In the spring the canyon is a moist, shady lane and a dramatic avenue to the fields of wildflowers beyond the university ranch house gate.

The trail is a favorite for Poly students, and a great resource for the whole San Luis Obispo community. On a quiet Sunday morning when I went out, student Bill McDonald came by on his horse, planning to ride the trails across Cal Poly ranches, possibly going all the way to the Cuesta Ridge. Mountain bicyclists with spatters up their backs were coming back from a morning of riding the trails, and a young professor jogged by with legs fit for an anatomy chart.

Poly Canyon is for everyone—from the spartan athlete to the happy wanderer looking for an escape from the city.

Beyond the old ranch house at the end of the canyon the landscape opens up to expanses of suede hills undulating upward to the ridge. The quiet of the country is overwhelming, and the transition from strident city noise to pastoral calm in just 30 minutes can bring sweet relief from the requirements of our daily lives, and a setting where our instincts make contact with the natural world of free creatures.

Here are five walks—all of varying lengths and qualities, some for the body, some for the soul. All the hikes begin at the gate to Poly Canyon, off Perimeter Road on the Cal Poly campus.

Hike No. 1: From the end of Poly Canyon to the ridge by the letter "P"

At the end of the Poly Canyon Road, about a half mile beyond the gate, take the foot path on the right over the creek. The trail goes through a grove of laurel, then over a foot bridge, ascending gradually through open fields past an old water storage tank. It gets rough as it climbs sharply through more laurel and coffee berry.

In a field of Fuller's teasel I observed two does and three fawns. The trail meanders diagonally across the hills, climbing until it comes along a fence of the neighboring private ranch. It goes straight up then and crests the ridge, with views of Highway 101 and Reservoir Canyon. Going left along the ridge the trail descends towards the big "P" on the mountain, a sloppy cement-pouring job one foot wide and six inches deep.

The trail ends at the parking lots behind the student residences along Perimeter Road.

The time for this hike is about 1.5 hours and a distance of 3 miles. The trail is moderately strenuous and uphill most of the way, except for the final descent which is precipitous and treacherous. Hiking shoes are advised.

Hike No. 2: To the Gravel Pit and Beyond.

At a distance halfway between the gate to Poly Canyon and the end is a road off to the right that climbs steeply to the gravel pit. A trail ascends the hill beyond the pit, circles left onto a higher level where the gravel is crushed, then continues at the far end, ascending steeply until the pit is far below.

The grades are extremely tough and most of the time I was on my toes, like climbing a ladder. The trail becomes narrow, leveling off some as it plies the side of the hill facing the canyon.

Thirty minutes after I began this hike I reached the end of the trail. A broad clearing (fire break) runs the length of the hill. To the west is the letter "P" above the Poly residences. A ten minute scramble puts you on top of the mountain, or a ten minute descent down the fire break brings you back to the Poly Canyon Road.

The time for this hike is 1 hour; distance is 2 miles, and is recommended for those wishing to build hard sinewy thighs.

Hike No. 3: To Future World and a Romantic Setting of Rocks and Trees.

At the end of Poly Canyon, walk through the archway to Poly's architectural experiments, where imagination and dreams become concrete and steel. A trail meanders along the stream with pathways to futuristic living units, park shelters and barbecue pits. At the upper end a trail goes up the hill and to the right, circling past an old exercise station.

Coming back toward Poly Canyon Road, on the other side of the draw, the road passes a beautiful clump of laurel in a rock garden setting, a perfect place for serious talk, no talk at all, or lunch on a hot summer day. Straight ahead is the university (Petersen) farm house and gate.

This easy walk is 1 hour and a distance of about 1.5 miles.

Hike No. 4: To the Southern Pacific Railroad Tracks and Beyond, or Back On a Steep Terrace Trail.

From the end of Poly Canyon (1.12 miles from the main gym) continue along the road, over the creek and toward the university farm house. It's okay to walk through the farm yard, staying left of the barn, through the "user friendly" gate and out into the country beyond.

Stay on the main road, passing an old milk truck box on the left. In .9 mile you'll go through another gate and the trail will take a decided turn to the left, with views of Cuesta Ridge and the railroad tracks.

It's a mile of continuous climb up a predictable but relentless grade to the 2.82 mile marker (from the main gym) where you'll be within 100 yards of the railroad tracks and a fourth gate. A marker at the gate indicates the elevation of 940 feet.

A hike to Cuesta Ridge is possible from here by crossing the tracks and continuing upward.

A yellow arrow points left along the fence, while the orange arrow points straight ahead. If you continue straight ahead you will wind down to the Poly sheep barn on Stenner Creek Road. A 4.13 mile marker (from the main gym) and an orange arrow will lead you through the sheep yard to Stenner Creek Road. From there walk the road out toward Highway 1, under the train trestle, turning left on the roads that run along the dairy barns and poultry sheds, until you come to Highland Drive which ties into Perimeter Road. This whole circuit is about 3 hours, and 8 miles in length.

If at the top of the hill by the railroad tracks you follow the yellow arrow up the hill (left) along the fence, instead of going straight to Stenner Creek Road, you'll end up on a trail that reverses the direction of the road coming up. It skirts deep canyon draws and meanders under a canopy of oaks, until it comes to another gate a quarter of a mile back.

The thin trail gradually becomes a ranch road beyond several gates. It intersects a road coming up from the old milk box. (See below for an optional return by turning right on this road) Stay to your left and amble down to the milk box and the ranch road that you came in on. Turn right on the main ranch road and the farm house will come up in a quarter mile.

This is a very scenic 4 mile walk of easy grades and idyllic lunching spots. Total time is about 2 hours.

If you opt to turn right at this intersection with the road coming up from the milk box, follow the road up the hill to the saddle a quarter mile away. Don't jump the locked gate to a private ranch at the top of the hill, instead follow the well-used trail down— across the slopes, moving in the direction of the (visible) Poly Canyon. At another junction, after you have climbed over a gate, it's a right turn to the architectural works or straight ahead to the university farm house past a clump of bay trees in a rock garden.

Hike No. 5: A Walk on the Treeless Hills Above the University Ranch House

From the end of Poly Canyon, follow the yellow and orange arrows through the university ranch house yard to the main back country road, letting yourself through two gates.

Turn left up the road by the milk truck box. In 200 yards you'll come to a junction with a road from the right, the exit for Hike No. 4. The road swings left and climbs a gentle slope up to a saddle a quarter mile away.

There is a locked gate to a private ranch at the saddle and a lot of NO TRESPASSING signs. Don't jump the fence; instead follow the trail to the left that heads in the direction of Poly Canyon. This well-used trail cuts across the slopes, goes through a gate and then branches.

The right branch goes to the architectural and environmental design park, or over the hill to the Cal Poly horse unit on the west side of the hill.

If you continue straight ahead you'll pass an exercise platform and a clump of bay trees in a rock garden setting as you walk downhill to the University ranch house.

This is an easy, pleasant trail of about 2.5 miles that will take 1.5 hours.

Optional Trail along Brizziolari Creek from the End of Poly Canyon to the Gate:

At the end of Poly Canyon, near the gate to the university ranch house, is a trail on the north side of the creek that takes off near the picnic spot under the huge oak tree, across the road from a foot bridge that begins hike No. 1.

It's a narrow ledge walk that hugs the creek and gives an intimate feeling of the canyon and the babbling brook. It follows the irregularly contoured slopes, eventually coming down to the creek and crossing it, about half way back to the gate.

If you missed the creek crossing, or the water is too high, continue on the north side of the creek until you enter the stockades and corrals of the Beef Unit where you can walk the university roads past the Horseshoeing Unit. Stay left and walk up to the Poly Canyon Road.

15—THE WORLD IS A STAGE AT THE SAN LUIS OBISPO FARMER'S MARKET

It's a practice carried on the world over. In Merida, Tangiers, Beijing and Bombay, villagers come to the market where farmers from outlying areas lay out a giant smorgasbord of food and supplies down the center of the street. Smoke from charcoal fires fogs the air while townsfolk queue up for food from the street vendors. They perch on the curbs like blackbirds on a telephone line, teetering flimsy paper plates loaded with messy-but-good sweetbreads, ribs and sausage.

Small children break away from parents, playing tag among the bodies and the overloaded tables creaking from a ton of melons and nuts.

Teenage kids group together grooming each other affectionately, rearranging hair and articles of clothing. The girls resemble the boys in dress, but their face colors are dramatic and eye catching, reminiscent of Mandrill baboons that probably inspire their mimicry. The upper body clothes are a chaotic arrangement of layered shirts and jackets while the too-short pants flash white, green or pastel blue socks. Their hair is shingled, often streaked, and cut in a long visor shape that droops off to one side, shading one eye, creating a veiled effect. They primp, they strut. The market is their stage.

And it all happens right here in San Luis Obispo on Thursday night. A fine old tradition has come to flourish down six blocks of Main Street (Higuera) where the entire town turns out for its weekly get-together.

As at a family reunion, the folks renew acquaintances. Fashionably decadent punkers preen, children scream, adults jabber and wave, and lovers stuck together like taffy move silently through the crowd. The shops are open, the lights are their brightest, everything seems to be on sale, stocks are at their fullest and the latest of everything is just being unpacked.

Farmers' trucks pregnant with fruits and vegetables line the street like Saturday night in Pella, Iowa. The nut farmers from Atascadero and Paso Robles offer great buys and generous samples. Cal Poly students urge passersby to try the new Feijoas, a tarty fruit sometimes called pineapple guava. A lady from D&L's Onion Patch hawks mandarin tangerines: "No spray, no seeds. C'mon, try one."

An Asian farmer with hands as big as pie plates holds out fresh broccoli, picked just hours before. A 12-year-old kid sells popcorn on the cob. Just stick it in the microwave and watch it explode. A clown makes long balloons into animals for kids. His sign reads, "Prices according to your attitude." Everybody smiles.

Some folks hurry through the market as if it were the last shipment of fresh produce they'd ever see. They buy until their arms ache, then trudge home with that satisfied, tired look. They know they're going to be healthy.

Others like Phil and Janice walk the whole length, looking, making notes and doing comparisons; then with a final sweep they go back and pick up the good deals.

There is a certain amount of aimless herding as people move with the flow, hooked on the conveyor of humanity that seems content to simply be there.

Occasionally they'll stop to stare at the street musician who plays guitar and harmonica. His high-top tennis shoes, quilted pants, plaid jacket and blond hair tied in a bun are a ridiculous curiosity. However, his little orange bucket is filled with contributions to the lively arts from an audience that is stunned but supportive.

The street gourmets are out in big numbers. Lots of guys take their ladies out to eat on Thursday night. They're on the curbs of Higuera eating barbecued ribs, skewers of beef and vegetables, and even fresh Morro Bay oysters on the half shell, a gourmet touch for 75 cents each or 3/$1.00. With the tremendous variety of foods available, there isn't an unfilled molar in the crowd.

Most of the portable barbecue pits are down by McLintocks, near Broad Street. By 5:30 p.m. the fires are going and Higuera is closed off from Osos Street on the north, near the Assembly Line Restaurant, to Nipomo Street on the south. Trucks loaded with produce wheel into position and set up shop. In five minutes Higuera is transformed from boulevard to country fair midway. At 6:30 a whistle signals the official start of selling, and the early bird shoppers who have been cruising the street and sizing up the good buys, move to make their purchases.

Around 9:00 p.m. the energy is spent and the crowds thin. The Thursday night circus winds down like a calliope that has run out of steam. The vendors pack up their things, the poets, thinkers and late-night music lovers move over to Linnaea's Cafe on Garden Street, and the street cleaners begin their pickup. By 10 p.m. the street has returned to normal.

The San Luis Obispo County Farmer's Market Association organizes and operates markets throughout the county. The markets are the shortest link between local growers' fields and the consuming public.

In 1978 the first market opened in San Luis Obispo at the southern edge of town on the William's Brothers Market parking lot. Five years later, when the San Luis Obispo business district faced a slump in downtown shopping and the problem of Thursday night cruising down Higuera and Marsh Streets, the idea of a market in the heart of the shopping district sounded like a solution. Instead of being simply a farmer's market Thursday night became a fair-type atmosphere with community oriented activities, barbecues, merchant's special promotions and street entertainers.

Thursday night is more than shopping and eating. It may be reviewing the lineup of new cars when the auto dealers have their share of the street, or observing bleating sheep or chickens that lay blue eggs, brought to town by 4-H kids from Creston and Templeton. Another night the Cal Poly band entertains near Garden Street or Cuesta College artists project slides on a stone wall.

In January there's a ski night featuring equipment and trips. February brings Valentine's Day sweetheart dances in the street. In March the street turns green for St. Patrick's Day and features Irish music and dancers. April ushers in the Poly Royal festivities. May is La Fiesta, another celebration that doesn't look for a reason for being.

In June classic cars are at the curbs, and the Renaissance dancers and singers appear. They're always splendid, the women buxomy and the guys debonair and flamboyant. July brings the annual rib cookoff. August is for kids and babies. September introduces the world to WOW week (Week of Welcome) at Poly, a party parade of incredibly corny, fun-loving, creative, hilarious and stupid goings on that may—or may not—be described as WOW.

October has witches and goblins running through the streets. November has dance groups and steel bands; and December is the Christmas parade, and snow brought in from the North Pole.

The Downtown Business Improvement Association is to blame for all this, but what they have created is commonly acknowledged as San Luis Obispo mental health night. A lot of hot air is released, spirits are buoyed, attitudes are adjusted and a lot of psychologists are amazed at what a little shopping and partying can do for a person on Higuera Street on Thursday night.

Hardly back roads you say? Just imagine it's Merida, or Tangiers, or Bombay.

No other community matches the carnival atmosphere of San Luis Obispo on Thursday night, but they all offer good food and the atmosphere of the town gathering together to shop and visit.

Here is what's happening around the county.

LOCATION	DAY/TIME	PHONE #
Arroyo Grande		
City Hall parking lot	Sat/noon- 3 p.m.	544-9570
Oak Park Plaza	W/9 a.m.-11:30 a.m.	544-9570
Atascadero		
City Hall Sunken Gardens	W/3 p.m.-7 p.m.	466-2044
Baywood Park		
2nd and Santa Maria Sts.	M/2 p.m.-5 p.m.	528-4884
Cambria		
Veterans Hall	F/2 p.m.-6 p.m.	927-4715
Lompoc		
Ocean and I Sts.	F/2 p.m.-dusk	736-4567
Morro Bay		
Young's Giant Food	Th/3 p.m.-5 p.m.	544-9570
North T-pier	F/4 p.m.-7 p.m.	772-4467
Nipomo		
Tefft and Mallogh Sts.	Tu/3 p.m.-7p.m.	343-2135
Paso Robles		
14th and Park Sts.	Tu/10 a.m.-1 p.m.	238-4103
12th and Park Sts.	F/4 p.m.-8 p.m.	238-4103
Pismo Beach		
Dolliver and Main Sts.	Tu/4 p.m.-dusk	773-4382
San Luis Obispo		
Higuera St.	Th/6 p.m.-9 p.m.	541-8000
So. Higuera, Market Place	Tu/3 p.m.-6 p.m.	543-3269
Central Coast Plaza	Sat/8 a.m.-10:30 a.m.	544-9470
Santa Maria		
Broadway and Main Sts.	W/2 p.m.-6 p.m.	343-2135
Templeton		
Templeton Park	Sat/9:30 a.m.-1 p.m.	

16—BAYWOOD PARK — GOOD FOOD, RUSTIC HOMES AND GORGEOUS VIEWS AT THE BACK EDGE OF THE BAY

Illiteracy in the area of geography is said to be one of the nation's educational shortcomings.

So dire is the condition there are people in our county who know little to nothing about nearby communities and points of interest.

Here is a simple test to help you discover your geography literacy.

1. What community has as much charm as San Luis Obispo, is a neighbor to Los Osos but has only one overnight motel?

2. What community has a glass house, a patisserie and a grocery store featuring Shorty's Meats?

3. What community has more wind chimes than barking dogs?

4. What community thinks that if you can't find it on Second Street you probably don't need it?

5. What community resembles Carmel of the '30s?

6. Where can you find a town with a pier that extends into a sea of mud? (at low tide)

7. Which town has these three memorable restaurants—Rodney's, the Salty Pelican and La Patisserie?

8. What town has a black and white dog asleep in the middle of its main street?

If you answered all those questions with Baywood Park you're not as dumb as you thought. Baywood Park is the answer.

We went there one afternoon to discover this town at the back edge of Morro Bay. We made plans to stay at the Back Bay Inn, an unpretentious place in an idyllic setting, situated on a notch overlooking the bay.

Our room was in a corner of the building with views of the piney woods and the shimmering water. Killdeer railed from the edge of the bay and myriad coots, pintails and American widgeon nibbled near the waning pools and streaming rivulets as the bay drained to the sea.

We took a walk around the point where the barnacled ribs of an old boat lie near the shore. The bay was draining fast and new land began to emerge, some gelatinous and shiny, some green with mounds of eel grass, which is the base of the food chain in the bay. The new muck was a clean slate for the signatures of the shore birds: some tiny scratches, some long and lobed, and the duck's prints as big as snowshoes.

Small mounds with oozing holes suggested apartments of geoduck clams and mud shrimp, below in the muck where there is neither day or night, storms or sunshine, just the constancy of mud and darkness . . . and birds running across the roof waiting to eat anything that moves.

We walked around the point to the public access beach at the end of Santa Ysabel. The town by the bay is quiet and rustic. The only sounds are the wind in the pines, an orchestra of tinkling chimes and the staccato voices of barking dogs.

Up Second Street we caught the downtown action. A big black and white dog lay in the middle of the street and a couple was walking the center line like it was a trail marker.

It was eventide at the pier on the end of Second Street and people gathered for the ritualistic setting of the sun. Judy and Bernardo and their little girl Kendahl were there from LA, clearing their heads of big city stuff and just sitting on the benches of the pier in a moment of reverie.

Many of the celebrants had tripods and cameras. Couples clung to each other as if they shared internal organs; funny what a setting sun does to people. It's celebrated like the first or the last epochal event of the universe.

But the dogs didn't fall into a trance. They chased each other and the birds; and one golden retriever totally disgraced himself by plowing through the slurpy, sucking mud of the draining bay until he was exhausted. He stood up to his belly in nature's black cement, a despicable family pet gone berserk.

The flock of geese moved around the last moments of daylight until there seemed to be a settling, somewhere safe, far from mad dogs.

We rested a bit and then went to dinner at Rodney's restaurant, a few doors down from the Back Bay Inn. The sky by the bay was a crimson red at the horizon, paling to orange and blue above the sand spit, and finally a deep purple with two big stars and the man in the moon winking from his cradled position straight overhead.

The mud flats and the draining streams became irridescent, a surrealistic mirage of violet and blue fingers.

Later that night the moon followed the path of the sun, falling into the sea and smearing yellow reflections across the bay and the mud flats. As the moon sank into the ocean, the image of the moon came up in the water. It was breathtaking. I don't know if they do this every night in Baywood Park, but it was stupendous.

While the Salty Pelican restaurant is always reliably good, and we hear Don Eduardos is a fine place for Mexican food, we think Rodney's At The Bay restaurant is the star of Baywood. This accomplished chef with extensive experience at the San Luis Bay Inn, Santa Maria Hilton and Embassy Suites Hotel brings elegance to Baywood Park.

And therein is the anomaly, but Baywood Park is that sort of place. It's a town that loathes curbed streets and city glamour, yet has charm and grace. It combines rustic with gorgeous, burping mud flats with symphonic sunsets, barking dogs with wind chimes tinkling in the sea breeze.

It is a reminder that back roads don't have to be hot dusty trails and cowboy saloons. They can be finding the secrets of the back bay, savoring a succulent frog leg at Rodney's or becoming sated on tempura fingers of mahi mahi with lime chile sauce—and staying a night at the Back Bay Inn, far from the world of otherwise.

MORE TO SEE AND DO

La Patisserie at 1218 Second Street is a dream for breakfast—great buttery croissants, fresh squeezed juices and lots of big city newspapers. The Sculptured Egg (1326 Second Street) is another good breakfast joint.

Tiger's Folly is a Morro Bay cruise ship that leaves from the pier in Morro Bay for cruises in the harbor and bay. There's a Sunday champagne brunch cruise, dinner cruises, special party cruises and no-food cruises. Call 772-2257.

Kayaking on the bay: 1/2 hour complimentary kayaking to guests of the Back Bay Inn. 1391 Second Street, Baywood Park. Phone 528-1233. Rates: $50–$110.

Montana de Oro's seven mile drive. Begin in Los Osos, drive Pecho Road to the end. Pack a lunch.

17—LOVE IS IN THE AIR FOR MORRO BAY'S GREAT BLUE HERONS

There were 6th graders from Bakersfield there, and docent Tom White's group from the museum, and passersby—all looking into the trees, smiling and talking in hushed tones, like people standing in front of a nursery window.

That's what they were doing, actually. In March the great blue herons begin their mating season and the nests are full of eggs and young ones. Like grandparents, uncles, aunts and cousins they stood viewing the babies. They couldn't really see the eggs or the babies, but the nests were certainly there: large tubs of sticks and branches swaying in the upper canopies of the eucalyptus, often dozens of them in one tree, staggered at various levels. The high rent housing is in the sun on top, with lower-ranking birds taking the cooler, more obstructed inferior positions. The males arrive in January, staking out territories and choosing nesting sites. Three weeks later females fly in and the pairing-off begins.

The males initially fend off all comers, male or female, attacking anyone who is a threat to their claim, but having won their real estate, they then turn their attentions to a mate. Flopping their wings excitedly the couple dance about, entwining their necks, grabbing each other by the beak, clucking and howling and lovingly carrying on for hours. Eventually the male offers a twig to the female. If she accepts it and works it into the nest, the bond is made. The real estate is now in joint tenancy and the two work as one in getting the nest ready for the eggs.

Each drawn-out amorous episode, described by Tom White as "clucking, fussing and stamping around," results in a ten-second moment of copulation. In several weeks, after a lot of necking and repeated unions, the female lays her fertilized eggs in the nest. The romance continues with frequent copulation through the egg laying period and up until incubation, a period of about a month.

Babies in the nest leave less time for the loving couple, and taking care of the babies becomes a consuming activity. As the chicks grow, innocence gives way to unmitigated greed and viciousness, and invariably the nest becomes the sole possession of only one chick who has monstrously kicked all his siblings out of the nest . . . and to their deaths on the forest floor.

Overlooking the sins of their youth, the hapless parents continue to shuttle endlessly back and forth, regurgitating goodies like fish, lizards, snails and gophers to the insatiable, undiscriminating mouth.

Despite the parent's heroic and selfless service to this one surviving offspring who has garnered the family's total larder of incredible edibles, only 30 per cent the fledglings survive the first year.

In nine weeks the robust youngsters—and the fatigued parents—celebrate graduation. It's time to fly off into the world of independence and uncertainty. This is a momentous occasion, and not a few adult great blue herons have been observed smiling at this time, a rare phenomenon in birds.

The adults resume their isolated lives along the shores and in the fields . . . until the next year, when the memory of the ordeal fades and they resume the tradition of building another nest—to be observed by another group of sixth graders from Bakersfield and a group of people led by a docent from the Morro Bay Natural History Museum.

The best way to see the rookery is to drive to Morro Bay and take South Bay Boulevard and Country Club Drive through Morro Bay State Park to the museum.

The museum has an observation deck overlooking the bay where you can see teeming birds on the estuarian mud flats at low tide, feeding on the tons of invertebrate animals that burrow in the mud and small fish caught in the shallows.

Through that frenzy of feeding birds you'll see the great blue heron rise off the surface, slowly beating its huge wings, until it is skimming the surface, long legs stretched straight behind, neck crooked in an S shape.

Rising higher the heron reaches the tops of the eucalyptus trees along the bay. The bird brakes midair, dangling those long legs toward the nest and teetering over it, a tense moment in the gusting sea breeze that will make its landing either ludicrous or beautiful.

For a closer look at the nests, walk the scenic path from the museum along the bay to the grove of eucalyptus.

There's a fine old log by the water's edge where you can sit and wonder how all those birds find enough food to eat . . . and how those wiggling morsels they pull from the mud taste.

The bay is a garden of Eden on a bright warm day and a veritable bread basket for 50 adult herons and 25,000 other birds who spend the winter here.

Up the hill, by the display sign, there is an excellent viewing area, across the uncluttered clearing of the Fairbanks Reserve. The nesting trees are clearly visible and the traffic of birds to and from the nests can be observed. For the handicapped there is a parking area just 50 feet away, off Country Club Drive.

The herons begin pairing off in January and February, and incubation of the eggs continues through March, April and May. There are numerous cycles of courtship, incubation, brooding and fledging, all the way through August, so there are many months of viewing the rookery in all stages of activity. Love is in the air and the evidence of new life that comes with spring on the bay gives us a vision of eternal creation.

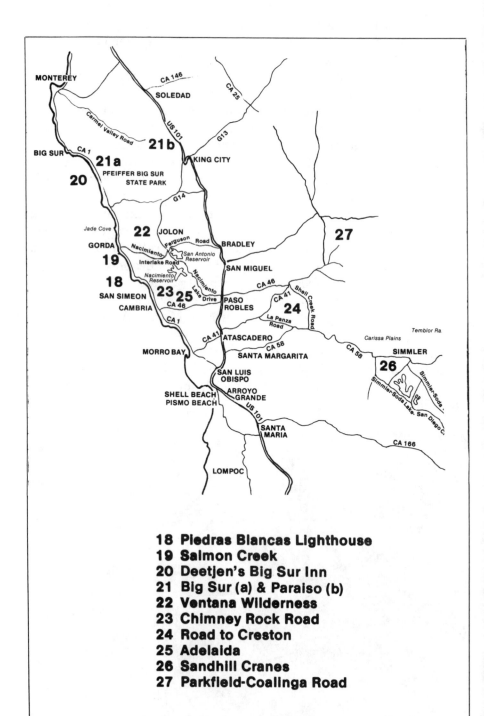

18 Piedras Blancas Lighthouse
19 Salmon Creek
20 Deetjen's Big Sur Inn
21 Big Sur (a) & Paraiso (b)
22 Ventana Wilderness
23 Chimney Rock Road
24 Road to Creston
25 Adelaida
26 Sandhill Cranes
27 Parkfield-Coalinga Road

III Points North

18—PIEDRAS BLANCAS LIGHTHOUSE ILLUMINATES NORTH COUNTY'S PAST

I think some of our fascination with lighthouses comes from what we imagine life was like on a windswept seacoast at the turn-of-the century, a time of sailing schooners and tragic shipwrecks.

Lighthouses have a lonely, forlorn feel about them, a reclusive place where I imagine keepers and their wives had a lot of quiet time—to read and spend unhurried days making bread, tending livestock and sewing their own clothes. Of course they had the light to watch and repair but that couldn't have taken up much of the day.

Captain Thorndyke, the first lighthouse keeper of Piedras Blancas, liked it. He stayed 30 years, raised two sons alone after his wife's death and saw the govenment ship only once a year when it brought kerosene, coal and food staples. A supply boat stopped by every two or three months to bring in other materials as they were needed. In those days, before Highway 1, the sea was the main access to coastal sites.

Pherbe Luchessa recalls a time around 1906 when her mother bundled her and her siblings for a boat trip up the coast to visit ailing Grandma Plaskett. The small launch was heavy with oats and a brewing storm threatened to capsize them. Fearing disaster the boat headed toward the beacon of Piedras Blancas.

Captain Thorndike, resembling Popeye with his corn cob pipe and black captain's coat and hat, met them at the dock. He took the mother and her three little ones up to the house where they spent the night. The storm howled, but they rested securely in a home built to weather storms, and in the morning the trip to Gorda continued.

Those old storm-proof houses aren't there any more. In 1962 some were razed and one was rolled down the road to Cambria where it sits on Chatham Lane, off Moonstone Drive, the gray-blue house on the right side, second from the end. This story-and-a-half house is built with nothing less than 2x6s (no 2x4s) and moving it was reputedly a losing business deal for the housemover, who didn't know what he was getting into.

The top of the lighthouse is in Cambria too. The Coast Guard discarded the top 40 feet of the lighthouse in 1949 following extensive storm damage. The Lion's Club of Cambria found it lying in the field near the lighthouse so they took it home and erected it on Main Street, next to the veteran's hall and Pinedorado, .5 miles south (east) of the blinking light on Windsor Boulevard and Highway 1.

Originally the lighthouse stood 150 feet above the water, 110 feet from the ground, producing light by five kerosene wicks that consumed five tons of fuel a year. Large lead crystal prisms magnified the candles and cast their light in horizontal striations 25 miles to sea.

Now the lighthouse is only 70 feet tall, and despite its more powerful light, its reach is shorter by 7 miles than the old French kerosene wick light and Fresnel prisms.

Our guide, Ron Jameson, advised us before we toured the interior of the lighthouse that Captain Thorndyke's ghost was still around, and sure enough we all sensed it. There was a sepulchral atmosphere in the damp rotunda as we stood silent and looked around. A metal staircase wound its way up in a tightening twist to the hatch at the roof that went out onto the deck.

With clanging sounds we climbed the cold iron staircase and stepped out onto the deck, looking squarely into an airport beacon (romance is dead). It has a concave reflector that concentrates the light waves of the 1,000 watt bulb into a narrow 800,000 candle power beam that pierces the mist for 18 miles. In place of the elaborate system of weights and chains that turned the kerosene-fired Fresnel lamp in the old days is a cluster of gray metal cabinets that house the electronic gear.

There isn't much light-tending for anyone to do anymore so all the lighthouses along the California coast are unmanned. Research biologists looking for a place to study the California Sea Otter have come to Piedras Blancas, so for a while humans inhabit the point again.

Two miles off shore the whistle buoy sighs with the regularity of the waves, sounding more like a person blowing across a Coke bottle than a real foghorn. The hollow tube inside the buoy fills with air as the buoy rises and is compressed as it falls.

The point had a real foghorn in earlier times, powered by a one-lung kerosene compressor. Captain Thorndyke complained about the noise of the foghorn when it was installed in 1906—said he couldn't sleep; so he retired that same year at the age of 75.

Piedras Blancas means "white rock." Actually the white rock is the outer island just off shore, and it's the cormorants and gulls that have "painted" the rock white. Ships used to come to harvest the stuff. Nobody has cleaned the rock for a hundred years, but this does not discourage the Pelagic and Brants cormorants, Western gulls, shearwaters and a variety of mammals who continue to use this address for indolent pleasure and voluminous deposits.

There is a loose assortment of trails along the coast to the south of Piedras Blancas for good viewing. Since our visit, additional restrictions are in effect. Although the lighthouse area is under the jurisdiction of the U.S. Coast Guard, Group Monterey (Operations Officer, 408/647-7312), at book reprint press time it was being used for research by the National Biological Survey, and is closed to tours. The lighthouse is 46 miles from San Luis Obispo via Highway 1.

19—SALMON CREEK HIKE OFFERS PERILS AND REWARDS

Before we started up the trail to Salmon Creek, Ben assembled our small group and advised us to stay close to each other and not wander off by ourselves. Good advice from an old (not very old) Boy Scout leader.

In a hundred yards the main trail to Spruce Creek and Estrella Campground went right, up the hill, but we continued straight ahead on a ferny trail towards the falls of Salmon Creek. Barbara Horner knelt for a nose full of wild iris along the way, humming in a little girl voice, "My Wild Irish Rose." This was not a good omen.

Like a bunch of kids just out of the car after a long ride, it was difficult for us to reign in our enthusiasm as we approached the falls. The nearly two-hour-long car ride from Arroyo Grande left us eager and energetic. The trail broke up as it entered a garden of boulders, and we all scrambled excitedly until we were down by the stream below the falls, the fine spray of the falling water misting our skin.

Laurel and alder trees overhang the rushing stream where a million gallons a minute rush to the sea. Everyone scrambled along the streamside boulders for a more perfect view. Some of the boulders are big enough to form small caves as they loosely couple together, and some are so big it's difficlult to get a hand or toe hold to cross them.

Eventually we came to a point where we could see Salmon Creek above the falls. We continued another 15 minutes along a weakening trail, the brush and poison oak crowding in on us. Allen, wearing shorts, pirouetted and sidestepped through the grappling tendrils, doing a perfect bourree, with hands arched gracefully overhead dangling a camera.

It became evident that this creek-side path was not going to get beyond the brush of the creek, so we made our way back to the main trail junction, and headed up toward Spruce Creek. The shooting stars and Indian paint brush were blooming in a wet meadow fed by the last of the spring rains.

Ted was setting a mean pace on the ascending trail, hauling in his pack everyone's water and lunches. We all followed like hounds on a trail, never losing sight or scent of Ted and our lunches.

The trail ascends to a ridge that looks disturbed, as if mining or clearing operations had stripped the land. A field of poppies and new silvery swords of yucca grew against the bleached rock.

Ben decided to call a lunch break at the top of the ridge, where a trail goes out to a jutting plateau. We sat cross legged on the warm earth and drank in the world of Salmon Creek. The highway was far below us, making the big sweep past the ranger station.

Brenda got a chance to carry the big pack after lunch and her ebulient spirit fell silent under the strain of the load, but as soon as Ted resumed the role of pack mule we had more lighthearted monologues and dialogues that covered everything but Christmas in Iran.

Ten minutes beyond our lunching spot we crossed a damp tributary that feeds Salmon Creek, but there wasn't a drop of water in it at this elevation. I wondered about the source of the millions of gallons at the waterfall. It wasn't coming from up here. Then I saw water running out of the rocks about 30 feet below, the first of many rivulets that join to make the roaring creek below.

Eva and Brenda carried on about how they would like to hike. They wished a helicopter would drop them off at the top so they could hike downhill... and that goats would clear the way for them, eating the shrubbery, especially the poison oak. "Why do all these hiking trails go uphill?" they wondered.

The trail makes a wide loop in and out of the canyons, with the hikers at the front straight across the chasm from the hikers in the rear.

"Courtney," Brenda called out from the rear of the string of hikers.

"Hi, Mom," Courtney called back from his lead position in the front.

"You're way over there," Brenda shouted insightfully.

"You are, too," Courtney said.

The rest of us trudged along through this brilliant dialogue until we saw a few young fir trees. New sounds of another creek greeted us, and a look at the Trail Guide to Los Padres Forest indicated we were approaching Spruce Creek, misnamed by the early miners who mistook the Douglas firs for spruce.

The air was cooling as we climbed and the ground in many places was saturated with water. Fructicose lichens ornamented the toyon and fir trees like beautiful lace. The firs got bigger until they towered above us, many of them with darkened trunks from recent fires that destroyed the younger trees.

We crossed through a paradise of poison oak growing in a seepy bowl. Allen again assumed his "Baryshnikov In The Woods" role, dancing and threading his way through the leafy pestilence, while the rest of us bowled through like Texas Longhorns, being so thoroughly polluted with this morbific plant we didn't think it necessary to use discretion or caution.

We came to the trail junction sign and discovered to our amazement and disbelief that we had marched only two miles uphill. Some in our party called the sign a lie. Others scoffed, "Well, maybe that's all the farther they've come. I know I've been hiking for at least six miles."

Ben comforted us with the assurance that the Spruce Creek campsite was close at hand, only .1 mile downhill to the creek. We all looked at him with suspicion. But he was right. It was a short walk in and it was the payoff for the trip.

Spruce Creek, at 1,325 feet, is paradise. A babbling creek has created a hundred quiet pools and rock garden waterfalls under a canopy of big toothed maples and alder trees. The group quickly broke up and the tempo slowed to the measured pendulum of a grandfather clock in a reading room. Brenda found a miniature sand bar, a perfect little beach, where she stretched out and was soon asleep with the creek lapping at her heels.

Eva discovered a "little box with a lid on it," situated up the slope from the campsite, behind a large boulder. It's as idyllic a situation as you could imagine. Everyone sat on it and agreed that the call of nature has never been heard in more glorious surroundings of stream and woods... and privacy without walls.

The walk back to the cars was without a memorable incident—except that Brenda finally got around to talking about Christmas in Iran. I thought she might do that.

To get there: take Highway 1 north, past San Simeon and Ragged Point to Salmon Creek, a few miles inside Monterey County. The highway makes a big sweep into and out of the gorge and passes a Forest Service building. Parking is alongside the road with the trails beginning on the right (south) side of the creek.

The distance from San Luis Obispo is about 60 miles.

20—DEETJEN'S BIG SUR INN: IT'S PERFECT FOR LOVERS

At Doris's barbershop we engaged in the usual light conversation.

"So what have you been up to, Ron?" Doris said as she draped me and turned the chair toward the mirror and began snipping away.

"Well, Doris, we just got back from a trip up north to Big Sur where we stayed at one of the funkiest, most charming Hansel-and-Gretel sort of inns I've ever been in."

"Really," she said, "Tell me more."

"It was black as ink along the coast when we finally arrived at Deetjen's Big Sur Inn at a curve in the road, seven miles north of Julia Pfeiffer Burns State Park.

"We stopped at the restaurant-reception desk—and got our room name, no number, just a name—and no key. 'No, we don't have any keys here,' they said, 'we don't need them. You can latch yourself in at night.'

"So we got our directions to Champagne, our room, and walked down a small road (the old coast road before Highway 1 was built) that brushes the fronts of the cabins, each one different, a fresh inspiration of the builder who used discarded barn sidings and waste lumber to build the cabins.

"Dim light glowed from the windows and wood smoke curled from their chimneys. The air had that delicious fragrance of an evergreen forest and burning wood. We got to our room and opened the door. It was cold and dark and we stumbled through the room searching for a light."

"How do you want me to cut your hair, Ron?"

"The usual, Doris, make it full and wavy, but don't make me look like I've just had a haircut."

"OK. Go on with your story. The room was cold and dark..."

"After we got the lights on we saw the small iron stove in the corner and a neat stack of firewood, kindling, paper and matches, so I stoked up a fire and went back to the car to bring more things in.

"There was a large uncovered window on the far side of the small room. The clean window panes were black, so deep was the darkness, and all I could see was a reflection of myself.

"In the bathroom was another uncovered window, right in front of the toilet. I had no idea if I was entertaining someone but I used it anyway."

"Did they pay you to stay there or did you pay them?" Doris quipped.

"Oh, Doris, you've got to see this place. It's wonderful.

"We went to dinner after we put some things away. The restaurant is the original home of Helmuth and Helen Deetjen. It's got the same feel as all the buildings, dark redwood paneling, low ceilings, dim lights and candles, fireplaces in every room and a cat on the mantle. They were playing Beethoven's Moonlight Sonata when we walked in and I melted in a maelstrom of gushy emotions. It was awful."

I could tell that Doris did not comprehend the depth of my experience.

"They've got a great young chef in the kitchen and the service was excellent. After dinner we slid between the cold sheets and snuggled under the down comforter, and when we awoke in the morning guess what we saw out that bedroom window that was black as coal the night before?"

"What?" Doris said, as she stopped snipping and looked at me in the mirror.

"From our bed we were looking into the middle of a forest of giant redwoods. I got up and stood at the window and discovered that our little cottage was perched on the edge of a 50 foot canyon. The ground dropped like a vertical wall. Huge redwoods stood down there... and above us for another hundred feet.

"The second night we stayed in Grandpa's room. The rain began to fall toward dusk, and big drops from the redwood limbs smacked the thin wood roof.

"Helmuth Deetjen was called Grandpa by everyone, though he was never a father or a grandfather. The room has all his personal possessions—his record collection, the old pump organ with missing ivories, neglected lamps with shades turned yellow and pictures of Grandpa in earlier times with his beret and pipe. He looked very debonair then.

"On the last morning we were there a light drizzle kept the woods dark. Drops of water hung from the bay trees and from the eaves. The fire had gone out and I tiptoed across the cold plank floor to the record player and put on Chopin's Nocturnes, while Eva stayed buried beneath the fluffy feather comforter. The old player gradually got up to speed and filled the room with music. What peace—to spend a cold, wet morning in a warm, down bed listening to Chopin's moody nocturnes. I secretly hoped they would close the road so we would be stranded there."

"What kind of name is Deetjen?" Doris asked, as she snipped away the curl and shortened up the sideburns.

"He was a folk art craftsman, Doris. He made everything from kitchen utensils and bowls to the buildings on the grounds. His decorating media was lemon and linseed oil, and that's the finish on everything.

"He had a love for the classics and insisted that only the masters be played in the restaurant. In his native Norway he is said to have lived next door to Edvard Grieg and heard him play the piano.

"Deetjen's Inn was the gathering spot for Bohemian poets, writers and thinkers. Staying there was almost on invitation, and he never advertised his inn. His was a place that waited to be discovered, a hiding place. It's still that way.

"The Inn is AAA in food, grace and charm, but FFF in some other things—like heating and air conditioning (none), locks on the door (none), knotholes and cracks in the doors (some), makeshift plumbing (most), shared bathrooms for some rooms and no telephone or television. They have one pay phone—outside.

"But no one minds these inadequacies; in fact it's part of the appeal of Deetjen's. There seems to be a purposeful disregard for modern contraptions and a cherish of the natural and simple.

"When Deetjen died in 1972 he had no heirs so he willed his estate to the State of California—who refused it. It was then offered to the county of Monterey—who also refusd it. It is presently in a not-for-profit estate operated for the benefit of the people. Are we ever lucky!"

"So, what do you do there, besides eat and sleep?" Doris inquired as she kept shortening my hair.

"Eating and sleeping are the favorites there, Doris. There are no tennis courts, hot tubs or recreation rooms.

"I observed a lot of hand holding, hugging, long tender looks into another's eyes, walking up the Seven Dwarfs trail in Castro Canyon and sitting among the sorrel . . . things like that.

"On our full day there we drove down the coast (south) a mile to Fuller's Beach where the surf is giant, and then went on to Partington Cove, 5.3 miles from Deetjen's.

"At Partington Creek, where the road comes into the canyon, we parked the car and walked through the iron gate onto the trail that meanders down towards the ocean. At the creek level there's a foot bridge that leads through the tunnel John Partington cut in the 1880s when he operated a loading dock at the cove. They shipped tanbark oak that was used for tanning hides, and in later years shipped hides and cattle. The cove was still used in the '20s when they brought in supplies for Highway 1 during its construction. The weathered timbers of the loading boom are still standing. It's a delightful walk, and the cove is pristine and quiet, a wonderful place to just sit for awhile.

"Down the road two miles is Julia Pfeiffer Burns State Park where a waterfall cascades into the sea. The falls are extraordinary. McWay Creek drops more than 50 feet into the sea from Saddle Rock. We watched the sun set there our first evening. It was perfect."

Doris was finishing my hair by this time, removing the drape and turning me toward the mirror.

"There you are, Ron, how does that look?"

"Great Scott, Doris! You made me look like Ollie North. This is the last time I'm going to tell you what I've been up to!"

Deetjen's Big Sur Inn
Highway 1
Big Sur, Ca 93920
408/667-2377
100 miles from San Luis Obispo

21—BIG SUR AND PARAISO ARE RICH IN HISTORY AND BEAUTY

Rain continued and the steep mountain walls began letting loose boulders that rumbled across Highway 1 north of San Simeon.

The waning afternoon sun over the ocean cast piercing rays through gray clouds. Waves crashed against the shore with an intensity that created the feeling that something was wrong. The sea was muddy, with white caps sheared off by the whistling wind.

We were on the last leg of our 100-mile drive up to the lodge at Big Sur, and we wished we were there.

Highway crews scurried along the road in the dimming light, working rapidly to scoop the crumbling gravel and stone that sometimes trickled from the hills, and sometimes came in torrents of flying rock.

By the time we arrived at Pfeiffer Big Sur State Park, only the faintest glow of daylight remained. We eagerly followed the incandescent path to the lodge desk, got the key to our room and then drove the winding wet road, blowing with wet leaves, to the cabin at the top of the hill.

We quickly built a fire to chase away the gloom and dampness, and laid out books and magazines sufficient for a Siberian exile. The rain splattered against the roof all night and kept up a continuous patter until the early morning light.

In the morning the sun broke through the clouds and we awoke with that delicious expectancy of discovering a place that we had blindly stumbled through the night before.

The stellar jays were outside our window screaming at a crow that sat composed as a judge on a nearby limb. They squawked denunciations, fulminations and vilifications until the crow finally took off, flapping its wings in ponderous beats like a mechanical flying machine.

113

The big leaf maples and chestnuts were electrified by sun shining through their yellow leaves, and light bounced off the ground where a mosaic of gold and brown leaves scattered light beams.

At breakfast in the lodge we looked through a wall of glass onto a slope of wet, glossy fern sprinkled by a canopy of redwoods that were shaking off the last of the evening rain. The Big Sur River ran full, and birds flitted through the brush in search of morning morsels. Everyone and everthing appeared washed in prosperity and happiness.

Late in the morning the sky darkened and a heavy mist fell, the kind that forms beads on an old felt hat. The fire within us kept us warm as we walked the trails and rock-hopped up the Big Sur Gorge.

We came to the end of the trail, where huge multi-colored boulders filled the river. The river was in its winter condition, muddy and yellowish, with white foaming caps, sluicing aggressively between the rocks. A large golden poplar stood in the distance, coloring an otherwise moody gray scene.

The prospect of returning home along Highway 1 through a mine field of rolling stones and possible landslides led us north to Carmel.

Seven miles out of Big Sur State Park we passed the Big Sur Lighthouse, sitting imposingly atop a monolithic fortress of rock, surrounded by water and a broad expanse of beach.

The canyons of redwoods were now behind us, and the road coursed through undulating treeless dunes of iceplant as red as strawberries.

Three miles beyond Point Lobos Reserve we turned right on G16 for a 50-mile ride through Carmel Valley, a nifty area of expensive country homes, golf courses, farm stands, quaint stores, hideaway music and fine art centers, and private ranches with elaborate iron gates.

In the town of Carmel Valley we stopped at the Iron Kettle for tea, a charming frame cottage with lace-curtained windows overlooking flower boxes of red geraniums.

The road beyond, going east, follows the Carmel River, skirting the Ventana Wilderness—winding, twisting, changing elevation frequently and running through forests of golden valley oaks dripping with moss. This road is a favorite of motorcyclists touring up to Laguna Seca Raceway.

Two hours and 75 miles from Big Sur we came into the Salinas River valley and G17 (Arroyo Seco Road, or Old River Road). We turned left (north) eight miles to Paraiso Springs Road, then left again five miles to an old relic hot spring resort that flourished in the 1880s when hot mineral baths were cure-alls for anything that ailed you.

Claus Spreckels, the sugar king, and others built Victorian cottages near the spring that issues 40,000 gallons of hot mineral water a minute. In those times the tallyho went over to the Soledad train station to pick up the elite clientele that patronized Paraiso Springs. Society ladies in long, white gowns and heavy socks with bathing shoes could be seen on the grounds, discreetly venturing to the baths. It was a 19th century institute for attitude adjustment that I suspect did as much good as today's health spas.

The Indians used Paraiso for hundreds of years; then came the Soledad Mission padres in the 1790s who used the hot springs for healing their sick and irrigating their adjacent vineyard, where 5,000 vines produced the sacramental wine. They called the springs "Eternidad Paraiso," eternal paradise.

I wouldn't call it paradise, but it's a fascinating place. The resort is committed to wholistic health and spiritual nourishment. A recent brochure promoting a women's retreat featured water therapy, herbal hikes, massage, dances of life and empowerment, yoga, meditation, passing the talking stick, singing and dream guests.

The old hotel burned down years ago, but the grounds on this 1400 foot plateau overlooking the Salinas River are still gracious with old palms and Victorian cottages. Thirty-five homes are for rent, from single room cabins to two story homes, but only the cabins are available for overnight stays. Rents start at $121.

Your stay includes use of the pools and, at extra expense, the use of the baths and the therapeutic massage technician.

For $20 per person you can use the picnic grounds and the outdoor pools; $25 per person will get you camping privileges. A snack bar serves soup, sandwiches, liquor and soft drinks. They recommend restaurants in nearby Greenfield, Soledad, and Gonzales.

Paradise is 100 miles from San Luis Obispo via US 101, off Arroyo Seco Road through the town of Greenfield. For more information call (408) 678-2882.

Big Sur Lodge, (408) 667-2171, is 100 miles north of San Luis Obispo on Highway 1.

22—WOMAN IN EAGLE'S NEST KEEPS WATCH OVER VENTANA WILDERNESS

There's an eagle's nest in the Ventana Wilderness, where a human lives. She sits a mile high in the mountains overlooking the ocean and Big Sur, scanning the hills with eyes as big as Coke bottles. She watches for signs of trouble, and when she sees smoke, she cries FIRE, and in an instant the roads turn dusty with trucks and men.

Her steel-legged perch is at the end of a dirt road, on the top of a ridge. We went to take a look.

We took Highway 1 north of San Simeon and squiggled up the coast past Gorda where the South Coast Ridge Road takes off to the right. It goes up to the ridge and then along it, north, until it bisects Nacimiento Road at the fire station.

An alternative way is to continue six miles on Highway 1 to Nacimiento-Ferguson Road, beyond Mill Creek. That road is paved all the way up and over, with a number of scenic turnouts to view the coastline.

At the top of Nacimiento-Ferguson Road we turned left (north) on the seven-mile-long dirt ridge road, going through dense stands of madrone, laurel and California maple. It got curvier and bumpier as we continued, but a grader had been along recently and there weren't any boulders big enough to hang us up.

Ninety miles from San Luis Obispo we passed the trailhead to Vincente Flat campgrounds and came around a bend with a grand view to the east. We surprised a deer that was standing in the road and she bounded up the vertical road cut wall, sending rocks flying.

In a couple of hundred yards we passed the San Antonio River Trail, and staying left on the main road noticed outcroppings of unusually white fractured rock that looked like marble. Garlands of poison oak hung insidiously over the roadway, an indication of the fertility and moist soil conditions along the ridge.

Six miles from Nacimiento Road we approached the trailhead to Cone Peak. In another mile the road ends, and in the last mile you can get a good look at Cone Peak (to the left) and the stilted fire lookout perched on top. The Gamboa trails to Goat Camp and Trail Spring Camp take off from the end of the road. These camps are primitive campsites lying at the base of Cone Peak on its westward slopes.

The trail to Cone Peak is only two miles long, but it's continually ascending, and the last mile really opens up the pores. The trail is used regularly by mule pack trains that bring provisions to the fire lookout. Within a hundred yards of the trailhead we went through a healthy grove of madrone trees, their caramel-colored trunks showing as smooth as skin from beneath scaling bark. There is some poison oak along the trail, but it thinned out as we climbed.

It was 10 a.m. when we left Morro Bay and now it was 1 p.m., not a good time to get on a trail in summer. I anticipated the weather would be cool at this elevation, but the temperature was already 86 degrees.

We came around a bend in the trail to an open grassy slope overlooking the coast. The rich purple flowers of Turkish rugging were all about, their heads of tiny dried flowers resembling more the nap of Turkish towels than Turkish rugs. On the dry slopes scarlet bugler flowers, looking just like their names, were sounding off.

"It's all uphill," my wife complained as we trudged along, with salty perspiration running into our eyes.

"Yup, usually happens when you climb peaks," I retorted unsympathetically.

We crossed a number of places on the trail where slides of exfoliating rock cascaded over the trail and down the steep slopes. Rolling stones flew crazily down the hills, smashing their way to the Limekiln Creek below.

To the right of the trail is a sheer face of strikingly white rock, similar to the rock we had seen on the road. I learned later that this is marble, Paleozoic limestone, 250 million years old that has been recrystallized and metamorphosed. The white stone, streaked with golden and silvery veins, is gorgeous. It's part of the Sur Series of marble that runs northwest along the ridge.

After an hour on the trial we came through a deeply shaded grove of mature oaks, where we rested and had lunch. Fifty feet beyond is a wonderful viewing point over the coast to the south. We felt we were viewing a table model of the coastline. Below was the bridge at Limekiln but there were no sounds of surging waves or the drone of traffic. Everything was still. The surf was lined up in sequence but wasn't breaking. The tiny cars were on the road-way but weren't moving; and out in the ocean an aircraft carrier and escort were still figures, though their visible wakes proved they were moving.

The mule clinkers on the trail got me to thinking about the advantages of being a mule with four feet on the ground, and of the perils of walking upright. It seems preposterous to balance a six-foot vertical column of muscle and bone over a trail of uneven rocks on a mile-high peak.

We were close to the top now, and in one more switch-back we caught a view of the fire tower and a woman leaning on the bal-cony railing, watching the hills and our progress up the trail.

"Is this the Eagle's Nest Bar and Grill?" I called out to her when we were within earshot. "We could sure use a couple of cool drinks."

"Welcome to Cone Peak," she called back. "How was the hike up? My name's Soaring. What's yours?"

I knew it. A fire lookout sitting atop Tinker Toy legs in a 20-square-foot glass cage swaying in the wind would have a name like Soaring.

We climbed the steps to the balcony and she welcomed us into her 5,155 foot high nest. It was a setting of immense charm. A Haydn concerto for cello and orchestra was coming from the radio, and around the edge of the all-glass room was a bed with a hand quilted cover, a mandolin, some books and magazines, a table and lamp, clothes, food and a small stove. In the center of the room was a large table with a map and sextant for pinpointing fires on the surrounding ridges.

To the west we could see the ocean and coastline; to the south smouldering fires near Hunter Liggett; to the east the massive Junipero Serra Peak at 5,862 feet; and to the north the land of Big Sur.

"I love this land so much," she said. "I'm the eyes of the Forest Service. The faster I get firefighters to the fires, the faster they can stop them. I'm just so happy being alone in this beautiful place."

Two mules had brought Soaring and her meager possessions up to the peak the first week in June and she'll stay until November. When she needs more water, propane or other supplies, a helicopter drops in on the pad adjacent to the lookout.

They have had a rash of fires lately, and Soaring described the night fires: "It's incredible. It's like a big crater, all glowing red. The night was dark except for this huge fire ring that just grew."

By 4:15 we left Soaring and headed back down the ridge where I spotted a group of endemic Lucia firs—a rare find. They have a limited range in the rocky upland sites of the Santa Lucia Mountains and it's not an everyday experience to come across them.

It took us 2 1/2 hours to hike up to the peak, with a lunch break and a fair amount of gawking. The way down was fast and took about an hour.

The best time to take this hike is early morning, or when the fog enshrouds the coast. The trail will be cool then, and coming out of the clouds to the sunlit peak could be like arriving in heaven.

Round trip from San Luis Obispo to Cone Peak is almost 200 miles, whether you take Highway 1 to Nacimiento Road, or Highway 101 to Jolon Road to Nacimiento.

23—CHIMNEY ROCK ROAD — A LAND OF IMMENSE CHARM AND FASCINATING HISTORY

"Here herbs of every leaf abound, here dwells a healing grace. The burdened boughs their golden fruit afford; here arbors spread their vaulted restful shade, and lofty hills are crowned with kingly groves." (Franz Joseph Haydn, The Creation)

When I got on my old motorcycle and rode down Chimney Rock Road I felt I was entering a realm that could inspire great music and heartful prose. The hills and meadows rise and fall in broad movements and oak trees nestle into the swales like a vision of Eden.

Chimney Rock Road begins off G14, Nacimiento Lake Road, north out of Paso Robles, and ambles toward the ridge that separates San Simeon and Cambria on the coast from the eastern side of the Santa Lucia coastal mountains.

Chimney Rock got its name from a rock prominence on that corner, to the left, across the creek. It doesn't resemble Mount Rushmore or anything like that, simply a big rock that looked like a chimney to somebody.

Down the road .2 mile is the San Marcos Mennonite cemetery, 1898-1911. I got off the bike and walked among the nine simple grave markers.

In fall Chimney Rock Road has the feel of summer but the nostalgia of the changing seasons. The air is warm and sweet but the trees have begun their descent into winter, and their leaves are turning lime green to yellow, falling to the ground in frumpled heaps. Then intermittent showers put spring right behind fall and meadows are greening with new life.

It's a grand mix of seasons. The emotions run from hot to cool. At times I was laying old thumper into the curves and going over the hills like I was in a hurry to see eternity; then as quickly I mellowed, and slowed to a pace where I could see the acorns fall from the trees. I'd stop and listen to them hit the ground and watch the woodpeckers beat their brains out for a meal.

Another motorcyclist came along with his sweetie, easy riders going nowhere but to smell the air and be baptised with the extravagance of country charm. When you know the road will dead end in the next 14 miles, you make the best of what's there. No sense getting to the end in a hurry.

I stopped by the Chimney Rock Ranch Lake up the road and watched the geese on the water. This lake is a watering hole for bobcats, mountain lions and all the wild and free creatures.

Farther west on Chimney Rock Road is an old roadbed on the left, across San Marcos Creek. This is believed to be the wagon road from the 1880s and probably the mission cart trail of the 1780s referred to in early descriptions of the area.

Wesley Burnett, an early land holder who amassed 19,000 acres at one time, named his ranch headquaters Corral of The Mules, possibly referring to the place where the mission mules were quartered. The trail went from the San Miguel Mission to Cambria over the Santa Lucia Mountains.

Fraser MacGillivray, local gentry and area historian, thinks it's likely the trail went over parts of Chimney Rock Road and Cypress Mountain Road. The beams of the San Miguel Arcangel Mission came from the Santa Lucia Mountains in 1797 and could have been carried over this trail.

In 2.5 miles the 1917 Adelaida school house came up on the left. It's an unadorned country classic, square as a crate but with edifying pillars on the corners. The local ranchers still use the school for their monthly farm meetings. This is not the original Adelaida school that nurtured the immigrant kids of 1880. That one, along with three other schools, declined into the dust years before.

Around the next bend is the Pierce walnut processing plant and the Gertz ranch. Ted Rehberg was running the machines and took a few minutes to show me how the green skinned walnuts are hulled and dried.

A quarter mile beyond the Pierce place is Klau Mine Road and behind the cyclone fence is the Adelaida cemetery. Mary Burnett was buried there in 1878. She was kicked by a horse and spent a number of years in pain and suffering. Her husband, Wesley Burnett, donated six acres for a cemetery so Mary could have a resting

place on the ridge overlooking the beautiful valleys of their ranch. Around her are a lot of old friends in plots with lichen-covered headstones and rusting iron fences—Maudie Alwilda, the Ramages, Browns, MacGillivrays, Irvings and Dubosts. These are the names of fourth and fifth generation families that still live in these parts and work the land.

The Episcopal Methodist church was established at the base of the ridge, near where you park your motorcycle, but it was only a tent-camp church then. It wasn't long before a permanent church was built, but in the 1890s it was abandoned as people left their homesteads.

The Mennonites obtained the abandoned building around 1910, sawed it in half and hauled it to Paso Robles where they reconstructed it on 24th Street. It's still there. At the junction of Cypress Mountain Road, Chimney Rock Road continues as Lake View Drive for another 5 miles alongside Las Tablas Creek, coming to a dead end at a locked gate. Lime Mountain is 2.5 miles beyond. Lime is hauled out for use in glass making, sugar refining and as an amendment in chicken feed. A truckload a day goes down to Egg City in Moorpark where the chickens turn it into egg shells.

On my return trip I took Cypress Mountain Road back to Klau Mine Road. It's a beautiful gravel road along Las Tablas Creek where the scrubby dogwood is turning the color of wine and the poplar trees are yellow as gold.

A bobcat ran up the brushy hillside and disappeared over the crest as I came around a curve.

At Klau Mine Road I turned left onto pavement toward Adelaida Road. Near the Dodd Ranch I came across a flock of wild hen turkeys scratching the ground for acorns and berries. Pick a little, talk a little, pick, pick, talk a little.

They crossed the road and scurried under a fence, getting nervous as I closed in for a photograph. With an instant crank of the throttle they burst into the air, then glided into a running landing. These are the same strain of gobblers the Pilgrims feasted on. They ranged from the mountains around San Francisco all the way to New England.

The way home can be along Adelaida Road to Chimney Rock Road, past the 1881 red and white Ramage Victorian home, or back along Adelaida Road past the beautiful stone fences of the MacGillivray 1885 home.

Either way you'll regret leaving this valley of charm and serenity.

24—TO CRESTON
VIA THE LAS PILITAS FIRE AREA

When you ride through the Las Pilitas fire area in April it's hard to imagine the inferno of 1985 that blackened the hills. It's not that you can't see the ghostly shapes of carbonized manzanita and scarred trunks of pines, but nature has created new life out of the chaos, and fields of flowers flourish where death by fire seemed final.

The mustard swayed in the wind on the slopes up Cuesta Grade as I made my way up to Santa Margarita. I set my odometer in town and began a 67-mile tour along Highway 58 to Pozo Road and around Santa Margarita Lake via Las Pilitas, Parkhill and River Roads.

In a field along Pozo Road, a mile beyond Highway 58, black cows stood in a surrealistic landscape of blue lupine. On rounded mounds oceans of tiny goldfields covered the ground in golden waves.

I turned left onto Las Pilitas Road, five miles out of Santa Margarita. The valley oaks are sprouting new leaves and Spanish moss hangs gracefully from the trees. No fire damage here. Along the seeping roadbanks blue dicks, violas and forget-me-nots are in full bloom.

At 6.5 miles I crossed the Salinas River, downstream from the dam that forms Santa Margarita Lake. The fire ran through here in July 1985, and I got out to take a look at the charred landscape. Clusters of scrub oak are budding out, while clumps of blackened manzanita show no sign of life. The willows along the stream are sending out new shoots from their roots, and some of the larger pines have growth at their branch tips; but young pines are burned beyond survival.

The ground is totally covered with a luxuriant growth of miner's lettuce, chickweed, grasses and little yellow pansies (violas). In the creeks, the water runs clear, suggesting seepage from the soil rather than water running across the surface.

Several miles beyond the Salinas River, on Las Pilitas Road, are fields of purple owl's clover interspersed with blue larkspur and a million beaming daisy faces of goldfields lying close to the ground.

The hills on the left are barren and burned, while the right side shows broad green pastures and hills of unharmed valley oak and live oak. Shooting stars bloom along the road and down a shallow slope to a stream.

The Forest Service did not sow any flower seeds in the fire areas, so what you see is the natural survival of species resistant to fire, or enhanced by fire through the elimination of competing plants.

Las Pilitas Road twists around, finally joining Parkhill and Huerhuero roads. It was noon, and Creston looked like the only spot for lunch, so I headed north on Huerhuero Road, dipping through Huerhuero Creek which meanders across the road a half

dozen times. At Highway 58 I turned right (east) to O'Donovan Road, then north again across flat ranch land to Creston, a 100-year-old town of country vernacular homes landscaped with rabbit hutches and immobiles (stationary cars).

There are two places to eat in Creston, the Long Branch Saloon and the Loading Chute. The Long Branch is the kind of place where city folks stand out like golf balls on a green. The last time I was there a dozen ranch hands were hitched up to the bar, swigging beer from a bottle and smoking short cigarettes. The women were big and strong with tools in their back pockets and the men were raw boned and leathery, looking more authentic than the cowboys on the Coor's posters on the walls. The Long Branch serves a terrific ortega burger, too big to bite, and has a well-appointed interior of pool tables, arcade games and colloquial wisdom tacked to the walls.

I had heard about the Loading Chute's Sunday brunch, so I drove a block east on the main drag to check it out. As I walked in, Archie Johnson was playing his inimitable style of honky-tonk piano, wailing, with his head thrown back like a dog howling at the moon. A number of people were at the bar, and in the middle of

the room a lanky woman in jeans leaned over a pool table and smacked the eight ball into the side pocket. Shouts of laughter came from the onlookers. A wistful young boy in a corner watched the woman as she sauntered around the table and slapped a Marlboro man on the back with a hearty laugh.

In the rustic back dining room, with tables and chairs and blood red carpeting, I got the house special, a Hangover Omelette, a concoction resembling the ortega burger down at the Long Branch, but with eggs.

I headed back to Highway 58 via O'Donovan Road.

An alternative is La Panza Road to Highway 58, then to Shell Creek Road and the Avenales wildlife area. Four and a half miles north, along Shell Creek Road toward Shandon from Highway 58, is an extraordinary array of baby blue eyes, goldfields, owl's clover and tidy tips. It's an unfenced area of the privately-owned Sinton Ranch, whose owners allow the courteous public to walk through and view the flowers.

Retracing my steps, I picked up the trail again on Parkhill Road, going left, or east, to complete a circuit around Santa Margarita Lake, an area consumed by the July 1985 fire.

Parkhill Road is a scenic, curving Macadam road with flowering peonies along the roadside and scattered fields of goldfields and fiesta flowers.

Turning back west (right) on River Road along Toro Creek I caught sounds of outboard motors on the lake, just over the ridge to the north. The hills come in close to the road making this drive exceptionally pretty, and the slopes of lupine are the finest I've seen anywhere.

Back on Pozo Road I crossed the bridge over the Salinas River and cruised back into the town of Santa Margarita, a total distance of 67 miles, including the trip to Creston for the brunch.

If you are interested in identifying the wildflowers, take a look at Belzer's "Roadside Plants of Southern California," Hoover's "Color Supplement to the Vascular Plants of San Luis Obispo County," Coffeen's "Central Coast Wildflowers," and Muntz's "California Spring Wildflowers."

25—ADELAIDA, ADELAIDA — BACK ROADS NOSTALGIA

There are times during the summer when fog covers us like a wet blanket and we get to complaining, thinking whoever is in charge has the seasons turned around. Summer is supposed to be hot so you can have picnics and play baseball, and sweat a lot and drink like a fish.

For just a little while I would like it as it was back in Illinois, when a sweltering, humid day was followed by an evening of the same—just darker. People would sit outside with neighbors drinking "black cows" and the kids would run around like they never had to go to bed, chasing lightning bugs until their jars were full of flourescent blips. Lying in bed the evening would be quiet—and hot—and the crickets, who love hot nights, would sing until morning.

We heard they were having summer up in Paso Robles so we groped our way through the fog to the car and drove up Highway 101 over Cuesta Grade. Sure enough, the sun was shining, the temperature was 80 degrees, and it wasn't yet 10 o'clock in the morning.

At the County Fair exit (24th Street) we picked up Lake Nacimiento Drive and headed northwest into the country through hills of orchards loaded with ripening almonds. We turned left on Adelaida Road, past Resthaven Park, a former swim resort and watering hole patronized by the hot and dusty horse-and-buggy travelers coming out of Adelaida and the quicksilver mines generations ago.

Adelaida Road dips and weaves over wooded slopes and brushlands, past manicured walnut groves interspersed with fields of golden grain. Ten miles from Paso Robles we came to the Brown's

131

rustic 1912 frame house, where Marie was standing near the house, looking as prim as a lady going to a Republican Tea Party. We stopped to chat, her animated face lighting up as she told stories of deer, coons, badgers and mountain lions. "We have a favorite lion here that comes by in the morning and goes down to the creek," she said.

The road beyond Marie Brown's is ruggedly wooded with cultivated fields breaking the sameness. Around the bend in the road an imposing two-story white frame house with ornamented doorways and latticed balcony railings came into view. It was a civilized oasis in the middle of unbridled nature.

Fraser MacGillivray is the sovereign of this old English-style estate of 1885, and the guardian of Adelaida's mysterious past. We sat one night and talked abut mining and farming, the early pioneers who homesteaded in the 1870s, and the great exodus of the late 1880s as settlers, struck by epidemics, a scarcity of food and endless winter rains fled the wilderness for more predictable opportunities.

And we talked about Adelaida. Was she the 15-year-old daughter of Jose (the blacksmith) and Susana Corelle who lived next door to the post office in 1877 where Milton Sunderland was postmaster? Did Milton abandon his wife Adra for the affections of this young woman and rename the post office after her? Or was the town named after Adelaida Carlon, a member of an influential family? Or could it be Adelaida Price (daughter of Captain John M. Price of Pismo Beach), the wife of Bartolo Brizzolari who had financial interests in nearby mines?

What we do know is that in 1877 Las Tablas, renamed Adelaida, was on the mail route to Cayucos and Cambria. There were no road connections to Paso Robles, and Las Tablas (Adelaida) was considered the frontier outpost of Cambria. All of the district's cattle and produce had to go over the mountains to the coast, following the same dirt roads that wander across the hills now.

Beyond the MacGillivray house we began to catch glimpses of stone fences—some crumbling, but others masterfully constructed in intricate finger joints. Then came Vineyard Road (formerly Los Tablas Road) that runs southeast to Templeton.

We continued on Adelaida Road and came by the red-gabled house of the Ramage's who were having a yard sale. We had a chance to talk to Arian Ramage, who spoke about early days. "Adelaida was just a store and little service station and a post office and a dance hall. But that all disappeared in 1936. That was the last of Adelaida, when they closed the post office down. The little store and everything couldn't survive without that."

Just up the road we turned left on Klau Mine Road, but if you continue around toward Chimney Rock Road, you'll come to a few houses 200 yards from the intersection, at 2825 Adelaida Road, the heart of Adelaida in 1877. Of the original buildings, only some of the outbuildings of the 1880s Dubost sawmill remain. The original Dubost Victorian home, store, post office and dance hall have vanished.

On up Adelaida Road a quarter mile on the right is the Adelaida cemetery, where Mary Burnett was buried in 1878. Mary was kicked by a horse and after years of suffering died. Her husband, Wesley Burnett, who bought many of the homesteads from the starving settlers, donated six acres for a cemetery so Mary could have a resting place overlooking the beautiful valleys of their ranch.

Backtrack now to Klau Mine Road, a wonderfully tortuous, good gravel road that changes elevation continuously, running into Cypress Mountain Road where much of the mining took place. Mining began here in 1871 when cinnabar (red mercuric sulfide) was discovered. When price supports for strategic metals ended in the 1960s, mining stopped. Today the corrugated sheet metal buildings creak and pop in the noonday sun and the underground ovens that heated the ore are cold. The Buena Vista Mine is on the left side of Cypress Mountain Road as you climb the hill, and the Klau Mine further along on the right.

Three miles beyond Klau Mine we crossed a clear running stream and took time to eat lunch in the middle of it. It was a perfectly hot day and we sat with our feet in the water, dragon flies darting around, and the resident cows watching us intently.

The road got rougher and narrower as we moved westward toward Santa Rosa Creek Road, some 24 miles from Paso Robles. The views at the top of the mountain are exceptional, a picture point of unusual breadth and scope. To the right is Cambria along Santa Rosa Creek Road and to the left is Highway 46 and the way back to Templeton and Paso Robles, a round trip of about 36 miles.

We returned to Paso Robles that night to enjoy an open air concert at the gazebo in the park. The temperature was still deliciously warm and we spread out the blanket on the lawn to listen to Jack Artusio play Schumann and Chopin.

It was good to have summer again.

26—STALKING SANDHILL CRANES IN THE CARISSA PLAINS

The woods get thicker as you go toward Pozo. Tilled fields border the road, and beyond the hedgerows more fields, barren now, their corrugated surfaces awaiting the seed and the rain and the sun of spring.

Then it's over the chaparral mountains to Pozo summit (El. 2675) before you reach Highway 58 again. In a short distance you enter the valley, broad and plain and whistling with wind.

Every time you go, there is less of man and more of nature. The restaurant in California Valley of the Carissa Plains is closed now and the gas station has "No Gas" signs pasted on the face of the pumps. The motel is still open but no one was staying there when I went by.

The streets of this phantom village are grassy mounds and the street signs are bleached so you can hardly make out street names like Gypsum and Calcium.

The Carissa Plains is becoming a wildlife sanctuary again. With recent legislation, federal funding and Nature Conservancy acquisitions, the valley floor and BLM land in the Temblor Range and Caliente Mountains will become a 180,000 acre, 10-mile wide, 40-mile long preserve for the sandhill crane, kit fox, tule elk, and pronghorn antelope.

I came to find the sandhill cranes who arrived on the plains from their northern (as far away as the Arctic Circle) breeding grounds in November. They stay until March, feeding in the hills during the day and finding refuge at Soda Lake and its safe wetlands at night.

Thirteen miles from the Highway 58 turnoff I caught sight of the lake and the crystalline salt beds. There wasn't anything moving.

I got out of the truck and scanned the horizon like a hunter. Nothing.

Then I heard them. It's a call I haven't forgotten. I've heard it in the skies along Lake Michigan and in the Okefenokee Swamp of Georgia—that raucous call, a wooden machine gun sound, a cadenza of clucks.

My field glasses scanned the hills, and just above the horizon I caught a glimpse of them jumping and flapping around.

I ran back to the truck and drove north on Soda Lake Road. A ranch road took off into the Caliente Hills and I rumbled over the dirt road until I saw the whole flock in a draw. There were probably 300 of them. I crept as furtively as a fox, slowing my pickup's speed to an idle.

A few of the birds were leaping and spreading their wings in exhibitive courtship rituals while others appeared to be nibbling the new shoots of winter wheat and catching whatever small varmints might be available.

Cranes are mostly gray with visible red crowns. The younger birds are more brown than gray, and lack the red crown. They're incredibly big when you see them up close. They have wing spans of seven feet and long spindly legs, so they stand three feet off the ground.

I checked the cameras to be sure they were ready—one with a 150mm lens, the other with the softball-sized 500mm mounted on a tripod. I sat and waited for the right moment, but without provocation the right side of the flock sprang into the air, sounding their cacophonous alarm until the whole flock was squawking and beating their way skyward.

I scrambled out of the truck with both cameras, blasting away with the 150, then turning the big 500 on them as they crested the hill. In 30 seconds I had only gotten off nine rounds.

I watched them cross the sky in the direction of the lake—long sinuous strands of birds in formation, heads stretched out long and straight, the spindly legs pointed backwards, a flying arrow beating great ponderous wings. My senses were as alive as a hunting animal. My heart raced, my skin was flush with intensity. I was spellbound.

In another moment they were within the protective realm of the lake and its salty wetlands.

Regaining my senses I reminded myself that stories need pictures, so I threw my cameras back into the truck and turned to follow them.

The birds had already reached the lake and were circling for a landing on the dry soda bed. I retraced my route and drove onto Simmler-Soda Lake Road, a levee that cuts the southern edge of the lake from the northern.

The birds had settled down, and I positioned myself at a point a quarter mile along this roadway, waiting for the next opportunity to observe and photograph them. The sun was setting and I realized that if they didn't move again, I had seen the last of them for one day.

Picking up my tripod and the cumbersome camera with the 500mm lens, I walked down to the edge of Soda Lake and headed out across the surface toward the cranes.

The ground was saturated with water and mineral. Each footprint was deep, and water quickly filled the indentation. I walked flat-footed to prevent digging in. The color of the surface changed and became whiter. Drier I thought.

Wrong. My feet sank deeper, the alkaline slurry now coming over my shoes and grabbing my ankles. I quickened the flat-footed pace, now nearly running to prevent from being sucked into the quicksand. To stop and turn meant a moment when I could sink up to my knees.

The thought of being trapped in sinking sand at sunset a million miles from help, with only a company of cranes nearby, was horrifying. In a large circle I arched back toward shore and finally found sure footing. I looked out across the white lake bed to the cranes—who hadn't moved. They knew.

If birds talk, I'm sure there are 300 cranes on Soda Lake retelling the folly of a guy who sought to invade them by walking on water.

HOW AND WHERE:

You can come to the Carissa Plains by following Pozo Road from Santa Margarita. This scenic country road is beautifully paved to the megalopolis of Pozo (16 miles), but beyond the saloon the road becomes a narrow, winding dirt road as it winds into the La Panza Range, cresting a high ridge (El. 2635).

In 15 miles from Pozo it rejoins Highway 58 on the eastern side of the mountains. Simmler and the Carissa Plains are another 15 miles east along Highway 58.

The quicker return trip is on Highway 58 to Santa Margarita, a distance of 50 miles. The road is well-paved and marked, but slow-going in places as it winds through rugged country of deep canyons and steep hillsides.

27—EXPLORING THE HILLS NORTH OF CHOLAME TO PARKFIELD AND COALINGA

The road from Cholame to Parkfield over the grade to Coalinga is one of the area's most diverse and scenic roads. It begins in the high plains off Highway 41 and wanders over a 4,000-foot summit before it ambles down the eastern side to Coalinga, Priest Valley and points of obscure intrigue.

We drove up to Paso Robles, setting the odometer at zero, and headed east on Highway 41 toward Cholame. At the Shandon exit we turned left onto McMillan Canyon Road, a ranch road that cuts diagonally over to Cholame Valley Road through the treeless hills turning gold with ripening grain.

Aged fence posts stand dark against the platinum grain, and blackbirds swoop and sway on the summer wind, disappearing into the grain, then exploding in a great flurry from their hiding as you ride along.

The air is sweet and it sings through the stiffening stalks of oats and wheat like the hissing of an overheated radiator. Beyond the paved section we stood in the middle of the gravel road and drank a full measure of country. It was summertime and the temperature was climbing; grasshoppers were jumping and the mourning doves sang their doleful song. The cattle and horses rested in the noontide heat under the big oak trees, barely moving except for the swishing of their tails.

A huge turkey vulture left its post as we resumed our trip, flapping its wings just a few feet above the windshield. We could see its naked head, and its eyes made contact with ours. It soared over the descending valley catching the breeze, higher and higher, until it was just a silhouette in the sky.

At each fork we turned right until the road ran nearly straight east and descended a 500-foot grade into the Cholame Valley. The landscape changed to savanna woodland, and jimson weed grew scattered across the fields, its dark green foliage and trumphet-shaped white flowers prominent in a panorama of anemic pastels.

Squirrels were everywhere, racing across fields, running up the trees or standing in the road in a reckless game of "chicken."

At 24.2 miles we came to Cholame Valley Road and turned left, down a broad valley with oak-studded slopes. From across the valley we saw through the shimmering heat waves the etheral image of a mowing machine cutting swaths in an alfalfa field.

Digger and Coulter Pine began to appear along the hills as we left the valley and entered Monterey County, ascending a grade alongside the gurgling waters of Cholame Creek.

In ten miles we came to Parkfield-Coalinga Road and turned right, rolling into Parkfield in a half mile. Parkfield, elevation 1530 feet, population 34, is a sleepy little burg of rustic cottages, a forestry fire station, and the epicenter of seismic study.

Never has there been a town of such obscurity and simplicity that has been visited by so many academicians, geologists and news-people, for it's here that the experts believe the next big earthquake will begin.

Down Park Street, lined with Tree of Heaven, we were greeted by a tiny black poodle and a big black lab who ambled out of the shade, curious about our interest in their library. We got out and talked to them about library hours and books, but they just squirmed around and wagged their tails and smelled our pant cuffs.

The library is one of the more interesting buildings in town, being about 12 foot square, with red siding and a white shuttered window. It's refreshing to see a back roads town with no saloon, gas station, card parlor, or drive-in liquor store . . . but with a library. It tells you something about the people here.

Beyond town, the Parkfield-Coalinga Road ascends Parkfield grade, a gravel section that climbs nearly 2,000 feet to the summit. The gravel road climbs relentlessly into the chaparral and then into the pines. Along the way a road runner raced us for 50 yards, doing more than 10 miles per hour before he darted back into the chaparral.

There are magnificent views of the surrounding hills and a number of scenic pull-out points. This road is a popular enduro motor-

cycle course, but the grade is not too rough for family sedans and should be considered one of the area's choicest back roads for a summer afternoon ride in the country.

At the summit (elevation 3,498 feet) we crossed into Fresno County and caught a glimpse of the San Joaquin Valley with its checkerboard plots of produce.

The road descends toward Coalinga across smooth undulating slopes accentuated by massive outcroppings. It's a photographers' paradise, each turn in the road providing another view of unusual form and composition.

The gravel road became blacktop near the bottom of the grade, past Robertson Bros. Ranch, and climbed one more set of hills before it finally settled into a fertile valley.

The stream crosses the road at several places here, leaving a bed of gravel across the road. We met the first vehicle since we left Highway 41 near Shandon.

Highway 198, also called Warthan Canyon Drive, to Coalinga (east) and San Lucas (west) came up shortly at 54.6 miles. It was already after 4 p.m. so we gave up the sights of earthquake damage in Coalinga, and the only source of food and gas in these parts, for a look at Coalinga Mineral Springs County Park, up Highway 198 toward Priest Valley.

We turned up the five-mile-long road leading to the park, past free roaming sheep and horses. The park, site of a former mineral spring resort, today is simply an obscure picnic and campground oasis; all that remains of the resort is a delapidated bath house.

A hiking trail leaves the far end of the grove, crosses a dry stream bed and threads its way up Kreyenhagen Peak, a scenic lookout at 3,558 feet. It's a good two hour hike to the top, with magnificent views into the surrounding BLM land and the San Joaquin Valley.

We chose to return home via Highway 198 to Priest Valley and San Lucas, a beautiful two-lane road winding through hills and scenic valleys.

The odometer read 101.8 back at Highway 101, and 142 miles by the time we returned to Paso Robles.

A shorter way home may be via Highway 33 out of Coalinga to Highway 41, then westward home. No matter which way you go, you will find extraordinary beauty and peace in the hills north of Cholame.

Index

Padre Productions   ORDER FORM
P.O. Box 840   Phone/FAX (805) 473-1947
Arroyo Grande CA 93421-0840

Yes, I am interested in California history, travel and nature studies. Please send me the following titles:

☐**California The Curious** by Ray Reynolds $12.95
(0-939919-25-7) Illustrated. Indexes of famous and infamous persons and places. "A book of facts, a book of lists, a catalog of curiosities—a Zen garden of California history that is eminently useful and sheer reading pleasure."— Kevin Starr
☐**Columbia: A History of "The Gem of the Southern Mines"** by Bonita M. Cassel. $9.95
(0-939919-08-7) Illustrated with many historic photos, tables, index. From Gold Rush days to establishment as Columbia State Historic Park, the most fully restored boom town of the Mother Lode.
☐**Pioneer California—Tales of Explorers, Indians and Settlers** $12.95
by Margaret Roberts. (0-939919-33-8) 296 pages, index, references. Seven suspensful tales of exploration from Indian days through the Gold Rush. Portraits, Indian glossary, mission dates, historical landmarks.
"Well written and worth reading."— *The Pacific Historian*
☐**Teacher's Guide to Pioneer California** by Margaret Roberts. $5.95
(0-939919-30-3) Lesson plans, activities, word exercises. Comb binding.
☐**Where the Highway Ends—Cambria, San Simeon and the Ranchos**
by Geneva Hamilton $9.95
(0-939919-04-4) Many historic photos. Index. Fourth Printing.
"Bursts with local history data...a solid portrait."— *Westways*
☐**The Story of Lytle Creek Canyon** by Virginia R. Harshman
(0-9633727-0-X) Hardcover, $15.95. (0-9633727-1-8) Paper, $9.95.
Chronicles a fascinating San Bernadino County wilderness by-way. Index, maps, references. "An artfully written history that will inform, entertain and challenge readers."— Larry Burgess, Library Director, A. K. Smiley Public Library, Redlands
☐**Nature Walks on the San Luis Coast** by Harold Wieman $6.95
(0-939919-19-2) Fourth Printing. Illustrated. Becoming a classic.
"Would every coastal county had a guide this good!"— *Sunset*
☐**Morro Bay Meanderings** by Harold Wieman $5.95
(0-914598-22-8) Second Edition. Illustrated. Entertaining columns.
"Indispensable guide and companion."— *Fresno Bee*
☐**Back Roads of the Central Coast** by Ron Stob $9.95
(0-939919-28-1) Second Edition. Maps, illustrations, index. Twenty`-seven byways adventures from Santa Barbara to Big Sur.
"An adventure to read."— San Luis Obispo *Telegram-Tribune*

⊔**More Back Roads of the Central Coast** by Ron Stob $9.95
(0-939919-26-5) Maps, illustrations, index. Twenty-seven additional explorations in California's countryside and coast.

☐**Course 095 to Eternity** by Elwyn E. Overshiner $9.95
(0-936940-07-7) Destroyer squadron wrecked on the California central coast in USN's greatest peacetime disaster.

☐**Flower Tumbles: Story of an Esselen Indian Boy** by Robert M. Walton (0-939919-39-7) Illustrated by Art Salvagno. Recommended by teachers for the new social studies curriculum. $5.95
"An accurate portrayal of Esselen life. — Tom "Little Bear" Nason, Esselen Spiritual Leader

☐**The Painted Rock of California** by Myron Angel $5.95
(0-914598-14-7) Photos and drawings of the archaeological landmark, including reissue of the 1910 legend, with foreword by rock art expert Georgia Lee, Ph.D. and archaeologist Robert L. Hoover, Ph.D.

☐**Nature Walks in Orange County** by Alan McPherson $9.95
(0-939919-09-5) Maps, illustrations, index. Guide to beaches, parks, and back-country mountain trails of Orange County, California.

Books by Angus MacLean

Angus MacLean retired from ranching to devote his time to recreating the speech and customs of Early California. Five volumes are filled with vivid, entertaining, humorous and true-to-life tales.

☐**Legends of the California Bandidos** Includes Murieta, Vasquez, etc. (0-939919-21-4) Hardcover, $12.50; (0-939919-20-6) Paper, $8.95

☐**Cuentos: Authentic Folk Tales** Stories of the rancho era. (0-914330-27-6) Hardcover, $12.95

☐**From the Beginning of Time and Other Stories** (0-914598-67-8) Hardcover, $14.95; (0-914598-68-6) Paper, $8.95

☐**Curse of the Feathered Snake** History and tales of Painted Rock. (0-914330-42-X) Hardcover, $9.95; (0-914330-43-8) Paper, $5.95

☐**The Ghosts of Frank and Jesse James and Other Stories** (0-914598-72-4) Hardcover, $10.95; (0-914598-73-2) Paper, $7.95

To order, indicate quantity desired of each title; where appropriate indicate hardcover or paper binding. California residents add 7.25% sales tax to the total; include $2 shipping for the first copy and 75¢ for each additional copy ordered. Make check or money order payable to:

Padre Productions, P.O. Box 840, Arroyo Grande CA 93421-0840

WHAT READERS ARE SAYING

"This book is exciting, warm and captivating. It presents Sai Baba and His teachings in such a loving, humorous and welcoming way. It is wonderful! It will be a great teaching book that will help to awaken many to the truth of their divinity." Dr. Gloria Ryder, Psychotherapist and Author of *Destiny in the Wind*.

"Connie's book brought tears to my eyes as her compelling stories opened my heart. Having personally visited Sai Baba's ashram, I know the power He bestows on His devotees and Connie is powerfully blessed with His grace. This book is a testimony of her devotion and dedication in her service to uplift the consciousness of mankind into love and peace."
Patrisha Richardson, TV Talk Show Host and Executive Producer, *Mystic Insights;* author of *Transforming Darkness Into Light.*

"It is an adventure story – suspenseful and full of action; it is a love story – bringing tears to the eyes. The descriptions are superb and the themes of Sai Baba's teachings serve as pegs for telling the story. This book is a spiritual treasure." Dr. Betty Broadhurst, Professor Emeritus, School of Social Work, Colorado State University.

"108 thumbs up for *Wake Up Laughing – My Miraculous Life With Sai Baba.* Indeed, 'God is alive, magic is afoot.' Throughout this book, Sai Baba's omniscience, omnipotence and omnipresence come vividly to the fore. One could sit at Connie Shaw's knee eternally – wowing and laughing, listening to her compelling adventures." Sandy Karng, Author, Poet, Talk Show Host, *Wednesday Morning Alternative*, KGNU Radio, Boulder, Colorado.

"How remarkable to find that one woman's worldwide journey through the maze of historical and mainstream spiritual modalities is ultimately rewarded when she locates, in India, the divine planetary Avatar, Sri Sathya Sai Baba. Each spell-binding story reveals Sai's "footprints in the sand" throughout Connie's life. I laughed in joyous wonder at Connie's journey and wept in heart-felt recognition of the divinity, love and truth He embodies in the Oneness of life in which we all live and have our Being." Jean Peterson, Author of *Oneness Remembered.*

"This book shows how to draw on the power and wisdom of one's higher Self. I strongly recommend the reading of this book." Rev. Robert Pipes, Baptist Minister and Author of *What Every Woman Needs to Know About Her Black Man*.

"Totally captivating. It touches the deep heart and nurtures the soul. Like the morning sun, she, too, enlightens and enlivens our journey together to God." Barry Berns, M.D., Author of the forthcoming book, *Path of Remembrance*.

"Connie demonstrates fearless courage and strength throughout her book. We observe her metamorphosis as she pursues her Teacher and path...Connie, thank you for reminding us that we are all on this path together. Your having written *Wake Up Laughing* is a truly wonderful way to 'love all and serve all.'" Pat Fregia, Co-author of *Know Your Dreams, Know Yourself*.

WAKE UP LAUGHING

My Miraculous Life
With Sai Baba

Connie Shaw

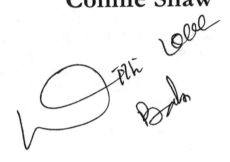

Om Productions, Inc.

Cover design by Connie Shaw
Cover photo by Jim Wright

Wake Up Laughing
My Miraculous Life With Sai Baba

Copyright 2000
by Connie Shaw

First Edition, August, 2000
Second Printing February, 2001

ISBN 0-9649202-3-9

Printed in U.S.A.

For additional copies, for permissions or serialization,
condensations, adaptations, or for our catalog of other
publications, write the publisher or visit
www.connieshaw.com.

Published by Om Productions, Inc.
P.O. Box 548
Johnstown, CO 80534 USA

www.connieshaw.com

Table of Contents

PART 3 - WHO PRACTICES?

DEDICATION

This book is lovingly dedicated to my Beloved Lord Sri Sathya Sai Baba that I might dwell in the Heart of Being more continually and know myself to be You and to see You ever more consistently in all that I encounter. There are no words, Dearest Swami, for all that you have graced me with in terms of awareness, darshans, lessons, laughter, challenges and opportunities, not to mention countless blessings, healings, boundless grace, family companionship and worldly comforts. Since I know this personality does not in reality exist except as an aspect of You in the dream called "life on earth," I know that all gratitude and appreciation for any outworkings in this so-called embodiment belong to You, the only Doer. This play of consciousness is an exquisite, eternal drama. Forgive us if it sometimes seems like a Sai Soap Opera!

ACKNOWLEDGMENTS

My special appreciation and unbounded love are ever extended to my eternal friends, helpers and colleagues Beloved Mother Mary, Jesus, Beloved Kuan Yin, Archangel Michael, Saint Germain, Beloved Portia, El Morya and Kuthumi. Deepest gratitude is sent to the Ascended Master MAP Team which has helped me so continually. To the saints and Realized ones who have so richly blessed me with their time, interest, mentoring, shakti-pat, benediction, darshan, and satsangs, I thank you: Gia-fu Feng, Mukthananda, Guru Mayi, Mother Teresa, Anandi Ma, Gangaji, Ammachi, Robert Adams, His Holiness the Dalai Lama, Shiv Yogi, Karunamayi and Ramesh Balsekar.

To my darling husband Jim I have no adequate words of praise and appreciation for your endless support, kindness, wise listening ear, sweet surprises, long late hours on the computer, great good humor and steadfast companionship in this dream adventure and on this book project. What Swami says is true – "Your husband is a very good man! He is always helping you." How fortunate I am.

To my dear, devoted friends who have spent so many hours editing and proofing the many drafts of this manuscript, I am indebted to you for your patient, meticulous seva. How blessed I am to share the pathless path with you: Mary Spahn, Irene Hibbs, Gloria Ryder, Marvin Boone, Betty Broadhurst, Marilyn Wilkinson, Donna Bamrick, Rob Hardcastle and all my other friends who had a hand in the final outcome. Many blessings to each of you and may you see the joke in every situation faster and faster and laugh out loud with head thrown back, saying, "Oh, thank You, Lord, that was a really GOOD one!"

How can I ever, ever thank my treasured friends who, when I was recovering from surgery due to a broken leg and ankle, helped to heal and nurture me? While I hobbled to the computer on crutches to finish this book, you acted as hands and feet, you fed me, encouraged me, gave freely of your time and energy. To you I am eternally grateful: Jim Wright, Jannie Williams, Dona Bosse, Betty Broadhurst, Marvin Boone, Donna Bamrick, Gloria Ryder, Rose Higel, Irene Hibbs, Vukja Andrich, Jason and Heidi Strehlow.

AUTHOR'S PREFACE

Wake Up Laughing - My Life With Sai Baba is an intimate spiritual autobiography beginning with my early 1980's adventurous travels throughout Asia and the wonderful and exciting experiences I had as I first searched for, then found God Incarnate. Underlying everything in the chapters that follow, is the extraordinary transformation that I've experienced over these nearly 20 years with the greatest Being Who has ever appeared on earth.

The story commences when, as an American business woman, I move to Singapore for a year with my husband, Jim. I do not know the Holy One's name as I search eight Asian countries for Him, then finally learn that His name is Sri Sathya Sai Baba, Creator of the cosmos. The day I learn His name, I am diagnosed with a brain tumor and on that evening, my birthday in early 1982, He appears beside my bed and invites me to come to South India - to be immediately healed by Him! A few weeks later, there I was in India and was indeed, healed by Sai Baba in India, immediately and permanently changing my entire life.

The first chapters, under 'Contemplating Divinity,' detail the fun-filled hide-and-seek search for Him, as well as the trials and adventures which are an inevitable part of such an arduous investigation and discovery. The second phase, called 'Deeper Practice,' highlights my encounters with my ego, as projected upon India, people and circumstances, during the first twenty or so journeys there. Having been a long-time student of *A Course in Miracles*, I used the daily lessons to assist in my healing. Finally, in part three, 'Who Practices?' I become more stabilized in witness-consciousness and begin to comprehend the jokes of this incarnation.

Aside from the joy, grace and blessings extended to me, there is a much deeper message within the book. Beyond Sai Baba's having saved my life many times, through rescue and healing, the book reveals His unique spiritual training for each of us and His apparitions, miracles, resurrections and manifestations. Sai Baba, Planetary Avatar, is God in human form, the One Who hears and uniquely answers the prayers of all people, no matter to which aspect of God they plead and petition. Further, Sai Baba, through His devotees worldwide, is now providing healings, teaching and many of the spiritual gifts for which He, Himself, has become well-known.

Sathya Sai Baba has urged me to write in such a way as to uplift and educate others, as well as to inspire courage, devotion and a resolve to implement His ageless teachings. The vast number and types of intimate grace, blessings, instruction and miracles which are mentioned in

Sai literature far surpass anything chronicled about a given individual in any of the holy texts of the world's great religions. There are three reasons for that. First, this Avatar is living among us. Secondly, He will live to ninety-five years. Finally, He demonstrates, as the Poorna Avatar, or fullest Embodiment of God yet to come on earth, more of the aspects and qualities of the Creator than any of His previous Incarnations. In short, the sheer quantity of works and wonders of this Avatar is, frankly, off the charts. There never has been nor will ever be Anyone like Him in power or capability, not to mention demonstrable love for all beings.

The ancient holy books of all religions, being prophetic storehouses and treasures of human heritage, each contain ample descriptions of Sathya Sai Baba. Further, He will never be surpassed in His fame or glory by His future Incarnations, since mankind's future evolutionary attainment will, by then deem it unnecessary.

Sai's healings, teachings and miracles are taking place today in staggering numbers and variety, with devotees who represent both clergy and laity of every spiritual path on earth. Sai Baba also teaches that all men are brothers, with the twin tasks of awakening to their Inner Divinity and serving God through serving the Light in one's fellow man.

In this book, I have kept the diary form to maintain the immediate impact of Sai's teachings and interactions. As many spiritual aspirants know, the methods for the gradual annihilation of the personality can and do take place according to the decision of the Teacher. He heavily reinforces each lesson in order to teach love, courage, humility, surrender, detachment, selflessness and compassion.

In order to protect the privacy of the many characters from several countries who appear in *Wake Up Laughing*, I have given them pseudonyms. There are, however, a few exceptions: when characters are already well-known in the community of Sai Baba devotees or when they figured in a public situation which was witnessed by a number of people.

Finding Sai Baba became the goal of my life for nearly a year. In the hide-and-seek game which He played with me, I undertook arduous investigative travel throughout China, Thailand, Singapore, Malaysia, Indonesia, Hong Kong, Nepal and India. Since finding Him in South India, the focus of my days has been the implementation of His teachings while living a life in the world as a house-holder, author, speaker and publisher. A nineteen-year period of testing and cleansing has just ended, thanks to Baba's love and grace.

When I arrived in India and received an unsolicited audience, or "interview," with Sai Baba, I felt that I had known Him forever, which I had, and immediately recognized His Divinity. That deep recognition caused an unforeseen, inexplicable weeping jag, known as the uncontrollable release of bhakti tears, at the spiritual heart's awakening memory of past times with the Lord. He healed me of a brain tumor on the spot, with no fanfare or swagger, but with the tender love of the most wise, noble, humble, compassionate Mother imaginable. He is the Divine Father-Mother which all humans unconsciously and unsuccessfully seek in most human relationships.

It was immediately apparent to me that His Presence on earth is a profound benediction for all beings, with His rescuing-healing-protection and with His work of world uplift and restoration of dharma (balance and integrity) to the planet. In fact, It is the biggest news, the happiest and holiest news of our times. Yet, since the entire planetary population is in need of help, advice, solace and guidance, Sai Baba has chosen, strategically, to allow Himself to be known by only a few hundred million people until His imminent Revelation of His Presence on earth. There are two primary reasons for His low profile. First, each person who earns the chance to know of Him and to see Him, has won that opportunity through countless Godward choices in thousands of lifetimes. Secondly, Puttaparthi village, the birthplace of the Avatar and the new Holy Land, can only accommodate, feed and shelter a limited number of anxious pilgrims per day. Nevertheless, Sai has quietly cycled millions in and out of His precincts during the past sixty years.

They have, like this author, seen Him teach, heal, manifest food for thousands, and perform awe-inspiring miracles. He has performed ten public resurrections. Sai Baba has built hundreds of free schools, many colleges, clinics, hospitals, community halls, temples and mosques. Millions of rural Indians in nearly a thousand villages now enjoy clean plentiful piped-in water for the first time, due to the love, grace and ingenuity of Sai Baba. He has also provided paved roads, free education and health care to countless villages and towns. One of His promises to India was that He would not allow news of His availability to spread to the media in wealthier nations until He had fulfilled His responsibility to clean up and to uplift India. Bharat, or India, is the historic home of Avatars which has safeguarded for all seekers the world treasure that is Vedantic wisdom. You might be surprised to learn that Sai Baba has also come to earth to prevent all-out nuclear war, to shift human consciousness to higher and deeper levels and to inaugurate a Thousand Years of Peace and Plenty.

When I first met Sai Baba in person, I expected wonderful teachings. Such teachings have been provided in abundance, both through His individual instruction and through the vast body of literature available, in over forty languages. But what Sai does, which is of greatest value to each "individual," is to force one to face seeming inner darkness and error. Through meeting my erroneous patterns of thought, belief and culture, which have kept me bound, I have found vast Light and love within, as the Self. As the veils of ignorance have been lifted, I have found new compassion and forgiveness for myself and renewed love and acceptance for others.

While it is not necessary to make a pilgrimage to see Baba's physical form, such a trip is unimaginably salutary. Every journey to Sai, and there have been, for me, nearly thirty, burns away karma, lifts veils that shroud perceptions, and inflames the heart with greater love for all beings. The spiritual heart, as a result, develops a longing for freedom from separation which comes to rest in the deep, abiding knowledge "I AM That." In other words, That for Which I have sought in strange and myriad ways throughout time, is the Self within, the Atma resident within all, Which animates every form.

In writing this book, which has been a fifteen-year process, I had several challenges and several objectives. The challenges centered around the fact that the book is an abridged version of stacks of diaries. As a consequence, there are occasional repetitions as one finds in other intimate journals and diaries. My objectives in writing this book were:

⋄ To share my search for God without and within.

⋄ To familiarize the reader with some of the rich history and culture of China and India.

⋄ To acquaint readers with the Asian cultural overlay and value system as it relates to women and the family.

⋄ To inform people about the most important news of our time – that God is on earth and that He loves each of us more than we would have ever imagined.

⋄ To share my observations and experiences of Sai Baba's teachings, healings, miracles and audiences or interviews.

Ultimately, I have come to see, through Beloved Sai's perpetual grace and benediction, that the entire cosmos is enfolded within the Self. I am whole and complete. I am, and so are you, an embodiment of peace, love and truth. I refer not to personality but to the Self.

This book testifies to the pain, struggle, delusion and eventual awakening of the spiritual aspirant – all in God's Divine timing. As Ms. Byron Katie Rolle, the beloved American Self-realized Teacher says, "The Truth works. Everything else is like Prozac – it stops working after awhile."

My tests and challenges have included several surgeries; two kidnappings and a hi-jacking; fires and floods; bouts with pneumonia, malaria, ptomaine poisoning, Epstein-Barr Syndrome, and heart failure, all of which were eventually healed by Baba. There have been attempts on my life during public talks, slander and inevitable disappointments while learning detachment and surrender. For the past twelve years, while practicing witness-consciousness, I have been asking, "To whom is this happening?" Insight and laughter immediately follow.

Conversely, and more importantly, the Avatar has blessed me beyond measure with countless gifts, with nearly sixty apparitional visits to our home, as well as many interviews. He has materialized vibhuti ash, amrit and gold leaf flecks on our photos. Hundreds of people in several countries have been unobtrusively but definitely healed by Him during dozens of talks and workshops which He has directed me to offer. He has, at times, manifested vibhuti ash and amrit during the talks and has blessed audience members with visions of Him and of saints. There have been healings of audiences of radio and TV interviews which He has arranged. He is the only Doer. We, in fact, do not exist, except as aspects of That Love Which pervades the cosmos.

Finally, He has, in His vision and graciousness, sent me (to my initial perplexity) to eleven Realized people for brief darshan, observation and instruction. To them my debt is unspeakable. They are: Mukthananda, Guru Mayi, Anandi Ma, Gangaji, Ammachi, Robert Adams, Karunamayi, Shiv Yogi, Byron Katie Rolle, the Dalai Lama and Ramesh Balsekar. When, face-to-face in interview with Baba, I thanked Him for such magnanimity, He laughed and, patting my hand, said, "It is My duty to give you all these good things. I am your Mother."

The cosmic joke which we each play on ourselves upon taking up yet another embodiment-cum-veil-of-ignorance, is the mistaken notion that we are limited and imprisoned by time, place, body, relationship, livelihood or circumstance, when that is patently untrue. It is our view of or belief about our circumstances which seem to imprison us. We are free but remain unaware that the jailhouse door of the mind is open.

We are addicted, throughout most embodiments, to unnecessary suffering. We believe we do not deserve happiness. We wallow in the warm mud of delusion, attached to people, places, things and concepts in the vain hope that they will relieve our misery. Periodically we may slip into one or another of the prevailing brands of Jacuzzi Spirituality and briefly experience a warm, bubbly sensation.

But afterwards, nothing much seems to remain. That is exactly as it should be. To accept (relative) reality is the first step in surrender. Each person's "programming" for awakening is unique. As we begin to awaken to Reality, the joke is revealed. The bubble of illusion is popped. We learn that our own unconscious soap operas are the funniest. To grasp the joke and to enjoy it, is the essence of freedom. May you live skillfully in joy, drinking deeply of the bountiful wellsprings within, until you awaken to the Truth of Being. Then, as you snap out of the cultural trance, may you wake up laughing.

PART ONE

CONTEMPLATING DIVINITY

CHAPTER 1
MOTHER INDIA

"India's culture is unexcelled…. India gave the message of peace to the world in ancient times because of its spiritual leadership. Then, as well as now, the Bharatiya message has been: 'Let all the people everywhere be happy.' " Sathya Sai Baba, SS June 1995 P 151

Bombay, India
October 6, 1979

We have arrived in Bombay, India! Jim Wright, my fiancé and best friend, and I have booked the "Highlights of India Tour" and have just arrived at midnight in the recently-burned-down Bombay Airport. We step into the remains of the airport with Brian Flemming, our zany, ethereal British tour guide from Brendan Tours. Brian assures Jim and me, the youngest of the group, and our twelve other tour companions that we are in very competent hands. He has been to India twenty times in the past twenty years and his father spent most of his army career in India. Thus, "I know India and Indians," Brian asserts confidently. He also knows theater and regales us with stories of his acting avocation on the San Francisco stage. The fact that the airport would lie in smoky ruins on our arrival was a surprise he hadn't anticipated.

As Brian tosses off one joke after another to put us at ease, his beautifully shaped white hands flutter to his temples to smooth his impeccably barbered sideburns, then fly down to adjust the poufed paisley ascot which smartly accents the throat of his khaki bush jacket. His animated blue eyes wink and twinkle in a handsome pinkish English face. Jim and I smile at each other in the pleasurable anticipation that this is bound to be a very entertaining trip with such a witty tour director. I am constantly taking notes, as always.

As we look around it is shockingly obvious that the disastrous fire has gutted the building interior, leaving only a few walls remaining. A makeshift arrival hall has been thrown together from olive green tarps hanging from wires. The tarps are serving as walls for a lobby and baggage arrival area against the stifling humidity and 95 degree temperature. The airport fire has destroyed the air conditioning system.

Our compatriots huddle together clutching their beige Brendan Tours complimentary tote bags which serve to identify us. They gaze nostalgically back across the airport rubble to the sleek white Air India plane on the runway which we have just left. We gaze at the huge crowd of noisy Indians in colorful turbans and saris, shouting and pushing each other in a frantic search to find their luggage and relatives; hopefully the uniformed customs officials will quickly usher the arriving passengers out into the night. Though the other tour members stand sullen and impatient, fanning themselves industriously with their passports, I brim with energy and excitement, smiling broadly at the delicious joyous awareness that we are actually in India. Ah, India - land of the *Mahabharata*, birthplace of mystery, home of Moghul emperors, of mosques and temples, manse of sacred motherhood.

For the next few hours, while we await the porters and the arriving baggage, our eyes lap up the various interesting scenes in the tented arrival hall. Pretty women comfort crying babies; functionaries stamp entry cards and passports; soldiers in khaki knee socks and shorts patrol the airport; dazed tourists push heaped luggage carts over the gray granite floor. Overhead in the tent a few desultory fans whir next to the dim yellow bulbs that dangle from black cords. The air is oppressively humid and smoky-sweet. All of us are soaked through with perspiration and fervently hope that the hotel is air conditioned. The glossy brochure for "Highlights of India Tour" promises to introduce us to the Taj Mahal, ancient caves, exotic temples, and tours by elephant back.

Only one of the people with us, a red-haired, fiftyish widow, has been to India before. The others are primarily people in their fifties and sixties, most of whom are old enough to be our parents, except for a fortyish black couple from Brooklyn and Heather Bayliss, a young Canadian from Montreal. On the whole the group is extremely well traveled, even more so than I am, with only forty countries in my experience. Most of them tell us that they take two or three trips a year and that they have had "the gypsy wanderlust" all of their adult lives.

Suddenly, Brian claps his hands for attention and abruptly ushers our cluster over to the airport window which looks onto the street in front of the airport. He cautions us to protect our purses by turning the flap and zipper sides against our bodies. Brian briskly makes "go-away" gestures out the window to the hundreds of people pressing their faces against the airport terminal glass, who are shouting "bakshish, bakshish!" They all want money.

"Those people," Brian informs us, "are beggars and thieves who will immediately try to clutch you, pick your pockets and steal your purses and wallets the minute we file out that door. Now your first objective is to get through that throng on your own power, single file, head down, running as fast as you can to that bus which is parked across the street. The driver has the door open for you and he and I will supervise the porters bringing your baggage. Everybody ready? Now then, make a run for it!"

One by one we push through the pressing, crying, chaotic crowd. Outstretched hands are thrust into our faces and there is a tugging and pulling at our clothes. All around us the cry goes up, "Change!" "Cigarettes!" "Some money, please!" The cries vary from the shrill and insistent to the pitiful and/or hopeless.

Suddenly, a twelve-year-old leper boy, without forearms or legs, whizzes from out of nowhere on a creaky homemade wooden roller pallet in front of me. Vigorously pushing his pallet on the stumps of this elbows, he aggressively clamps his teeth on my shirtwaist dress. The result is that as I walk I'm pulling him along. I'm acutely embarrassed, never having encountered an even remotely similar situation. His eyes plead. I stop. He stops. Then I resume walking and he automatically whirs along beside me, his teeth biting my dress. What am I to do?! Finally I stuff a few dollars in his dirty khaki shirt pocket. He smiles, releases me and says, "Thank you, Ma'am." Although I smile back at him, I'm trembling slightly with unfamiliar emotions of deep pity, guilt, revulsion and fear.

Behind me one of our group hisses under her breath "God! I hope it's not going to be like this the whole trip with beggars trying to tear our clothes off!" Cars and taxis drive pell-mell right through the crowd without slowing down and several of us are nearly knocked down in the traffic. We finally realize that Indians drive on the left, like the English, and that we have been glancing in the wrong direction as one after the other leaps into the oncoming traffic lane, mistakenly thinking it to be on the safe side of the road.

Just before stepping into the welcome haven of the parked tour bus I glance up and notice that the black sky overhead is dusted with stars and that the bus driver's clock says that it is three o'clock in the morning. It has taken us three hours to clear customs, gather the baggage and get to the bus. Inside the bus tiny fans above each seat pit-pit the air conditioning against the ceiling in miniscule gusts.

Ten little boys from the crowd across the street have converged upon our luggage and make a major production of hauling it on top of the bus; some look to be only seven or eight years old. Another hour elapses before all forty suitcases have been tied down with rope and the boys paid. We finally leave the airport four hours after our arrival in India.

As the driver negotiates traffic, Brian stands at the front of the bus beside him and clears his throat for an announcement. Enthusiastically he announces our itinerary: Bombay, Aurangabad, the Caves of Ellora and Ajanta, Udaipur and Jaipur, Agra, New Delhi, Srinagar. He informs us that Srinagar is in the magnificent mountains of Kashmir. The bus bounces along as we listen to his lively monologue and I notice from my window seat that the buildings, bridges and fences outside have peeling paint or stucco and seem dilapidated and neglected.

Jet lag begins to weigh upon us and our London stopover fades from memory. But I struggle to stay awake so as not to miss a single moment of this unfolding adventure. The packed Bombay streets at 4:00 A.M. seem more crowded than our own daytime thoroughfares. However, I must remember that India is roughly one third the land size of the U.S. and contains three times the number of people. The overall impression is of nine times as many souls crammed together in a concomitant space in the States.

Someone sitting in a seat in front of me muses "What are all those lumps and bumps on the sidewalks and walls - piles of dirty laundry? Good God - it's people! Look! It's sleeping people. They're everywhere -

the gutters, on the awnings, in culverts, on windowsills, in doorways, on gratings, in sewer pipes, under bridges, on doorsteps, on street corners…. And look! Rats as big as puppies scuttling right among them." It's true. On every dock, trellis, outcropping and cantilever of any kind lie thousands of sleeping Indians in the muggy morning darkness of Bombay. The bus narrowly misses the scores of drivers that brazenly speed toward us in suicidal oblivion of our lane of oncoming traffic. I peer into the blackness to get a better look at the condition of the dozing people.

Most of them haven't even a towel or a hanky between their faces and the filthy sidewalk, not to mention the luxury of a pillow or a blanket. It's dizzying to realize, in person, that all I have read of India in this respect is true. Mothers and babies here on the streets haven't even a bed sheet for rest and privacy. Worn-out beggars, curled up in a fetal position in ghastly charcoal gray rags lie next to scruffy- looking goats, bony cows, rusty bikes, thread-bare pallets, and piles of excrement. Numbed by the enormity of such grinding daily deprivation I wonder what on earth these people do in the monsoon season with its unpredictable floods, destructive winds and relentless rains.

As I glance around, I think of Mother Teresa, whom I heard speak recently in Denver. She has always been one of my heroines and there's a photo of her in my office with one of her sayings beneath it. "The life not lived in the service of others is a life wasted." But how on earth could a simple middle-class American like me, a householder and career woman, possibly serve the masses of India and make any sort of dent at all in the poverty?

Upon our arrival at the hotel, I am further shocked by the contrast with the scenes of sleeping Bombay homeless people. Brian had said our hotel would be "quite good" but he hadn't said it would be palatial. What a shock! After our final lap through endless rows of cardboard and tin shacks we have arrived at the sumptuous Hotel Oberoi Towers. Through mile after mile in Bombay, I have been telling myself that even if our hotel is substandard, according to American convention, that it will still be dry, secure and devoid of animals and insects.

The bus purrs to a stop at the top of a steep hill and rolls to let us out in front of immense gleaming glass doors and windows reflecting a small army of elegant doormen in sparkling white tunics and trousers, scarlet turbans and red cummerbunds, not to mention lavish black handlebar mustaches. We had finally adjusted to the starkness of numberless poor without roofs or homes. Now there's a new adjustment to opulence. I wonder if India is going to be a continual experience of lightning-quick reality reversals. Hinduism has a saying that "Happiness is a point between two periods of sorrow and sorrow is but a stage between two periods of happiness." Accommodating the contrasts of life, I see, is part of the learning of acceptance.

The world of the Oberoi Towers holds glistening ten-foot crystal chandeliers, shiny marble floors, elegant sofas, attractive urns, fine mirrors, gold leaf and brass appointments. It's the kind of five star hotel which Erma Bombeck would have described as one where practically every registered guest would have old money and new underwear!

An air of calm assurance and subdued poise radiates from the desk captain and porters who display fine continental manners with our jet-lagged, soggy, bedraggled little crew. Brian indicates that we are to "circle up the wagons" and settle comfortably into the velvet lobby chairs so that he can give instructions and agendas before we collapse into exhausted slumber upstairs in our beds.

When someone remarks on the shocking contrasts between the thousands of homeless and the palatial grandeur of the Oberoi, Brian, missing the point, says that he's pleased that we like the hotel and that this sort of setting will be typical of our accommodations in most cities. He says that most hotels in India are either abominable or extraordinary; he prefers the latter. I can see that our daily excursions between poverty and lavishness are going to be a challenge to my ingrained democratic American sensibilities. Since I pride myself on an ability to thrive on change, this is a perfect test to find out where I experience anxieties as my comfort zone of tolerance on both ends widens. Further, I have learned through countless experiences with both polarities of extreme pleasure and extreme sorrow, that there is no lasting happiness in the world. That is, nothing in form can give infinite peace or satisfaction. The mind is fickle. My purpose in visiting India is spiritual – to find a Teacher who can help me to subdue the mind and find lasting inner peace.

Since my fiancé Jim, Heather Bayliss of Montreal and I are the only ones in our thirties in the group, the others immediately start referring to us as "kids"(!) and tell of their own children and grandchildren back home in New York, California and Florida. Our traveling companions seem very amiable and I am relieved at the prospect that there will be harmony and cooperation as we encounter the inevitable challenges of India.

Heather, in jeans and tee shirt, announces that she will wear jeans and caftans the entire trip and hopes we won't have to get dressed up very often. Marie and Charlie Wilson of Florida wear matching shirts and slacks in contrast with the five older single women who wear printed sundresses. Jim looks and feels comfortable in his sport shirt and slacks and I conclude that the skirts, slacks and sandals that I've brought will be perfectly suitable though I'm hardly as well turned out as Dr. and Mrs. Ligeti, the wealthy Hungarian refugees sitting next to us. In fact, it has always been my custom, in contrast to most American travelers, to wear my oldest sturdiest clothes while traveling so that I don't attract attention to myself. Further, this is helpful in order to emerge from the uneven climates, conveyances and laundry facilities without any regrets, such as shredded, spotted, dyed or accidentally bleached clothing. Teddy and Olga Frett, a genial African American couple from Manhattan, draw numerous comments as local people have assumed they were from Africa rather than the U.S.

Brian reminds us to take our malaria tablets faithfully and to keep a check on the healing progress of our vaccinations. Several of the group members have also experienced severe typhoid inoculation reactions yet we and our traveling companions are all in excellent health and are eager to retire to our rooms. Two of our group comment that they never take malaria or cholera since they are only forty percent effective and they don't want to pollute their bodies with vaccinations. Their voices trail off as we enter the elevator.

Upstairs Jim and I remark on the room's two most outstanding features: a refrigerator set into the wall paneling and an impressive view of the bay. In the soft gray pre-dawn light we notice that the waters are dotted with tiny wooden fishing boats bobbing gently in the breeze.

Bombay, India
October 7, 1979

This promises to be not only a colorful but a jarring day from the standpoint of cultural differences between the U.S. and India. In fact, I find India to be one of the most disconcerting experiences of my life. India's overall sensory input of unusual colors, odors, noises, pressing crowds and tumultuous begging for money.

There are more armless boys on unpainted pallets, fitted with baby stroller wheels, pushing themselves along the street with their elbows. Toothless children beg for candy, money and clothes. Next come some men with no legs and boys with deformed legs who hop about and shout for money, food and chocolate. Vendors selling postcards and jewelry insistently ask us to buy their wares. Brian has told us not to give them money because they'll bring their friends and ask for enough for the whole neighborhood. He says the smaller children will just get beat up by the older ones who'll then forcibly take any money from them. It's a heartbreaking dilemma and my head swims with the faces and cries.

At the boat dock we notice a pretty young woman wearing a yellow silk punjabi outfit of tunic and slacks. She will be our tour guide for the day and chats with two men who squat in the front of the open wooden boat cooking some food on a stove. "Welcome to Mother India," she shouts to us above the roar of the boat motor.

The bay, ruffled in a light wind, is gunmetal gray from the wastes of Bombay, the huge vessels at anchor, and from the waste of the immense power plant across from Elephanta. Rats and garbage float on the water's surface and it is clear to me that unless the air is sweeter elsewhere in India, I'll have to breathe through my mouth so as to survive the putrefaction and pervasive stench. As we cross the bay, the various tour members snap photos and write in journals.

As excited as a child to be seeing Elephanta, I learn to fend off the awaiting beggars at the motor launch area near the stone steps to the Elephanta Caves. Overhead in the trees, large gray monkeys nurse their young and chitter to us on our climb up the many stone steps. We are passed by local women in silk saris of lime green, wisteria purple, and turquoise who carry babies on their hips and heavy brass jugs on their heads. Even the old women wear their thick hair in a fat ample braid that falls straight down the spine to the back of the knees.

What a marvel I find in the skillful execution of the four enormous rock-cut temple rooms of the Elephanta Caves. The magnificent bas-relief sculptures are dedicated to Lord Shiva and have survived 1200 years. Originally called Ghapapuri or "Fortress City," the island was renamed by the Portuguese who unfortunately desecrated the sculptures by chopping off the private parts of many of them. Nevertheless, the power, majesty and sheer size of the statues create awe in even the most uninformed visitor. Shiva statues in various forms smile serenely from their twenty-foot-high niches in the damp dark recesses that perpetually challenge photographers and light meters.

On the motor launch back to town the stench, heat, and noise of Bombay assail me. Back at the hotel I flop down on the bed and cry for two hours over the plight of India's poor. Jim and I talk about the lesson behind my reaction. We also discuss *A Course In Miracles,* namely that my thoughts are giving meaning to a neutral landscape. These are my projections of fear of poverty and sickness. It's clear that I must find a way to encounter beggars and handicapped Indians without collapsing into tears. I remember something Mother Teresa says. "When you walk among beggars, see the Light of Christ in them. Ask their names and tell them your name. Begging is their job; it is what they do for a living. Just be light and friendly and you'll have no problems."

Aurangabad, India
October 8th

Although we were scheduled to leave for Aurangabad this morning, our Indian Airline flight was ten hours late. Since we had no idea how long it was going to be until it arrived, the entire planeload sat reading book after book under a canopy in 98 degree heat beside the fire-damaged airport. It rained heavily last night, leaving deep puddles over the wavy tarmac. In the hammering heat an optical illusion was created which was rather amusing: while reading our books on the airport runway, we looked as if we were soaking our feet as the puddles lapped at our ankles. Since the water, juice and milk aren't safe to drink, our little group of fourteen consumed a few crates of the Italian soft drink Limca (pronounced Leemca) during the ten hours of waiting in the sun. Naturally by the time we arrived in Aurangabad, forty minutes after departure from Bombay, we had missed the scheduled tour to the Ellora Caves. We rescheduled our flight for the next day.

Aurangabad looks delectable and verdant after the putty-gray aspect of Bombay. In this countryside setting the people and animals look generally much healthier - fatter cows, fatter goats and chubbier children are everywhere. Here in Aurangabad, trucks, or 'lorries' as they are called, barrel madly down the center of the road, the way they do in Bombay. Part of the local color is created by bewitching almond-eyed white oxen bullocks pulling gaily painted wooden carts of periwinkle blue or Kelly green.

As the bullocks clip-clop along on bony legs they rock from side to side and swing the scarlet silk tassels which hang from their painted horns of crimson or royal blue. Every cart displays scenes of flowers, birds or sunsets painted on its sides, and is driven by a skinny boy or man wearing a white dhoti hitched up between his legs and tucked into his waist. Beside the carts, lending an ancient charm to the landscape, sari-clad women glide along the road balancing gleaming brass water pots on their shawl-covered heads. Unaccountably I feel a familiar kinship with the land and its people. "Could I have lived here in a past life?" I ask myself.

As I appreciate the area's rural sounds and scenes, I find myself thinking that this is the type of scenery which I had hoped to encounter in India. Maybe the rest of India won't be like Bombay after all. But my real hope is that, charming landscapes aside, I will find a spiritual mentor to assist me in the next step of the spiritual path. Will there be such a One in India? Is it too much to hope that a Being like Jesus, Buddha or Krishna could be among us today? The search for God, or at least an accessible Realized Master in human form is, for me, the objective of our trip to India.

It would be such a relief to be able to ask such a person why it is that recently I have been having so many unusual spiritual experiences. For example, there are about five inexplicable things which have recently happened to me. They are:

1. Seeing a large blue orb, rather like an eye, while meditating.

2. Feeling as if the top of my head has either opened up or turned to transparent glass so that I can see in all directions at once.

3. Feeling as if I'm about to suddenly levitate upward, defying gravity. Sometimes I hold onto furniture so that it won't happen.

4. Experiencing myself in meditation, everywhere in the universe simultaneously.

5. Finding myself suddenly outside my body, standing about three feet behind it, looking at the back of Connie's head! How did I get there? Which one is the "real me?" Does this happen to other meditators? I've been meditating for four years now and most of these experiences began nearly right away. Am I doing it incorrectly? If only I had someone who knew about such things to guide me.

Even though we had to come on a tour, instead of by ourselves, which we would have preferred, at least we are in India and it feels very familiar in many ways.

It seems to me that I am ready for the next step in spiritual growth but I can't seem to take it alone, without a teacher. *Lord, help me die daily to this personality.*

Hotel Rama International in Aurangabad is a celery green fairy tale castle bedecked with pools, fountains, and a gazebo that is smothered with giant saucer-sized Persian blue morning glories. Even the dining room is graced with marble pools and fountains set off by dining tables draped in pink linen. As we came into the lobby this evening we were garlanded by smartly uniformed doormen who salaamed before placing the hotel's welcome garlands around our shoulders. These fluffy floral necklaces of white honey-suckle entwined with red-orange bougainvillea have a heavenly fragrance. Imagine – there's even a framed photograph sitting on the hotel reception desk of a big-haired guru in an orange robe. Only in India....

Upon awakening from a restful sleep to birdcalls in nearby tree branches, and an elegant buffet breakfast, optimism has returned to our group. Now we'll see the "real India," starting with a day tour from the hotel. Today's vivacious Sikh guide, Mr. Singh, is obviously eager to see us and begins our bus tour commentary by educating us concerning his white costume set off by a maroon turban and sash, a silver bracelet, a dagger.

He tells us that Sikhism is the youngest religion of the major world religions. Guru Nanak, who was born in 1496, was its founder. He explains that Sikhs may never cut their hair or beards, hence wear a turban "to look presentable." They pay homage to five "k's" which carry sacred significance. They must not cut their hair (kesh). They wear a special steel bracelet (kada) and carry a steel comb (kanga). Further, Sikhs carry a short, sharp ceremonial dagger, called a kirpan. Finally, they wear special underwear (kachcha). Sikhs say prayers to divine embodiments of God. Mr. Singh further adds that they are a warrior caste and are non-vegetarian.

"Our Preceptor, Guru Nanak, is deceased but lives in our hearts. He teaches duty to God, family and country and that God is within each person. We meditate on the divine light within. Our holy book is called the Granth Saheb. There are no statues in our temples and no elaborate worship there. We study the sayings of Guru Nanak and a collection of hymns."

As the bus moves along rural roads, I notice from the window that there are more varieties of birds and flowers than I can count and many which I've never seen in my travels to dozens of countries. Since I enjoy talking to the guides and driver, I sit in the front aisle seat whenever possible and take notes while Jim photographs people and landscapes from the window.

Beside the bus driver there is a little wobbling stack of white cardboard box lunches. We'll eat our hotel-prepared meals near the caves at midday. Mr. Singh announces that the Ajanta Caves are about 112 kilometers from Aurangabad, a city which was named for Aurangzeb. Cotton and peanut fields abound along the bumpy road; wide brick ground-level cisterns, or tanks, proliferate throughout the farmland amid lush rows of cultivated crops. More white oxen move among the nearby women who wear silver bells jangling on their ankles and silver rings on their toes.

The nostrils of the women are fetchingly pierced with silver, gold or rhinestones which glint in the sunshine. On their braided heads ride jugs of shiny tangerine copper or yellow brass. Little puffs of dust swirl up around their bare feet and skoosh out from the wooden wheels of the white canvas-covered ox carts. Pastoral scenes in this landscape seem like those one would imagine from the Bible. The architectural features of ancient brick arch ruins and pungent colors of the silk-garbed women are the foremost clues that we are indeed in India.

As we alight from the bus in the early morning we are besieged by throngs of vendors clamoring vehemently for us to buy agates, geodes, semi-precious necklaces and textiles. So far this is the most persistent flock of merchants, perhaps because they are cloistered in the hills away from the continual stream of tourists afforded vendors in the city. India abounds with hundreds of varieties of colorful birds, masses of fragrant blossoms and vines and a dazzling array of butterflies. Such natural wonders, combined with the ethnic costumes, geography and architectural offerings, make it a visual treasure trove. But its spiritual heritage outshines everything else and is, of course, the wellspring of artistic innovation.

On our way up the wide concrete stairway to the Ajanta Caves, our attention is caught by blue-winged parakeets with red beaks clustered in treetops overhead. The secluded aspect of the remote caverns set high on ledges strikes me as being reminiscent of the cave ruins of Mesa Verde Colorado. One of the caves reminds me very much of Balcony House of the Anasazi Indians. It has taken about half an hour's climb to reach the richly ornamented gray caves of Ajanta.

To escape the merciless heat, we hurry toward the cool blue shadows of the mountain ledges. Although it is early morning here in this remote country setting, the caves are already thronged with tourists and school children who lean panting and giggling against the door sills, walls and cave entries.

A gaggle of men bearing four plump elderly white-haired European women on sedan chairs trots by us to deposit their red-faced load on the top steps. A little ripple of discreetly suppressed amusement passes through the crowd as we note the expressions of their pop-eyed, terrified passengers, eager to stand again on terra firma. Boys educated in the

School of Barking and Hustling thread their way about the crowd yelling, "Chair, Sahib? Chair, Madame? I give you cheap price on good chair!"

Twenty-four monasteries and five temples housed monks in these perfectly fashioned ancient caverns. Inside we are met with cool temperatures, marvelous acoustics for chanting and a peculiar odor of urine and incense. Two Western women read from a book containing passages from *The Dhammapada*. One reads aloud, "As rain seeps through an ill-thatched hut, passion will seep through an untrained mind. As rain cannot seep through a well-thatched hut, passion cannot seep through a well-trained mind." TD P 79

We are told by the guide that as Buddhism waned about the seventh century, A.D., in favor of less rigorous religious practices, the occupancy of the caves diminished until they were abandoned. The caves were not rediscovered until 1819 by a hunting party of British officers.

Tinkling laughter of children floats up to us from below. The half-moon-shaped cliff housing the caves overlooks the clear greenish Waghore River. Wind whistles onto my neck and chills the rivulets of perspiration which stream into my cotton blouse. The grotto where I stand provides a view with a foreground of a rock ledge beyond which one can see silver fish flashing in the Waghore far below and the swooping arcs of green parakeets amid mahogany trees on the river bank. Brown hawks wheel and cry in the crystal blue sky as if protecting ancient Ajanta.

As we stroll through the caves, Jim and I softly discuss the best time to "pop the question" to Brian about the fact that we'd like to be married in India in a day or two. We expressly came to India to be married and don't want to delay our vows any longer. We want to be married as we tour India.

Inside the latest series of caves we notice that the frescoes are remarkably fresh-looking. Old men hold naked electric light bulbs on long extension cords inside the pitch-black caves to illuminate the paintings. Astonishingly well-executed paintings of the story of the Buddha's life are depicted in fresco-like tempera, mellow in tone and color yet sharp in detail. Subtle shades of pink, gold, rust and creamy white seem to glow with a vivid yet discreet life of their own. Buddha sits surrounded by opulently jeweled women who unsuccessfully tempt him with attractions of the senses. In this, but one of dozens of magnificent paintings, the scene's detail work showing rich canopies, luxurious floor cushions and comely serving girls is exquisitely clear. As I admire the cave paintings, I again wonder if someone like Gautama Buddha lives on the earth today. Surely we would have heard about it if he does.

In the twenty-nine caves at Ajanta, one finds a variety of everyday scenes portraying teaching, merchants in bazaars, and people dining in elegance. The effect of the paintings is one of serenity, quiet opulence and dignity. Ceilings and columns are adorned with birds and elephants and elsewhere fine sculpture enhances the paintings. Wooden scaffolding at the cave entrance holds two art restorers applying fresh pigment to the entry ceiling. Brian announces that we'll now proceed to our picnic lunch in the gazebo on the lower hillside.

Instead of hiking down the cement stairs we take a shady gravel path through over-hanging bushes and lavender shadows to a white gazebo set in a clearing of tropical birds and red hibiscus. "This would make a great setting for a movie," someone shouts. Purple bougainvillea cascades down the hill banks near the sun-splashed glade where we rest for our picnic box lunch prepared by the hotel. Small, bird-like boys emerge from the shadows to serve our lunches and soft drinks. Under the trees several yards away a small family patiently waits for us to finish lunch so that they can eat our leftovers.

I'm never more keenly aware than at this moment that Americans throw away more food in a day than many Indians get in a week. Our raven-haired serving boys reverently wrap our food scraps in paper napkins and tenderly take the bread, apples, boiled eggs and cola to a distribution spot beside the gazebo. They will parcel out the booty after we leave. Beggars whimper for money as we dust crumbs off our faces and straighten our clothing and tote bags in preparation for leave-taking. Brian has warned us again not to give them any money so we all sit mutely staring at our fingertips feeling overfed and guilty. At least I have the consolation that I purposely left most of my lunch in the box so that the family in the shadows could have it.

Once again I'm reminded that I've never had more than four months of success as a vegetarian. "As the food, so the mind." It would seem that it is difficult, so far, to get healthful food on this trip. But how self-righteous I am to be thinking of food preferences when these local people aren't even minimally well-fed!

On the way up the hill I slip some ball-point pens (the pen being a much coveted item in India) into the hands of a few beggars and stealthily hold an index finger of caution to my lips in indication that they are not to tell anyone. In appreciation they light up in smiles, bow their heads, peek out from under their thick bangs in a final grin, and pad off down the hill to the river below.

Even the air-conditioning of the bus doesn't diminish our heavy breathing in response to the ever-present heat. It is about 105 degrees F. Everyone simultaneously glances out the window at the herd of blue-black water buffalo contentedly floating chin-deep in rainbow colored valley pools. Their wide mouths seem to curl up in broad smiles causing us to laugh out loud at the happy picture they present.

"Now those guys have the right idea: a carefree life and a float in the tub!" one of the men remarks.

It is four o'clock by the time we reach the Cave Temples of Ellora and the shadows beside the old trees in the dirt parking lot are growing long. Jim and I finally decide to tell Brian of our wedding plans on the return bus trip. The wide bare plains and flat-topped mesas in the arid countryside remind me of Colorado. It was throughout many different historical periods that Jains, Hindus and Buddhists created the temples and courtyards in these thirty-four caverns that emerge from the mysterious hillside.

The rock-cut sculptures feature a pantheon of gods and goddesses, spectacular architecture, and enormous, perfectly chiseled columns. Interiors of the caves and grottos feature worshipping chambers, grave mounds and passageways. There are dark monk cells with stone beds, pillared verandas, chapels and shrines. Perhaps some of the finest bas-relief sculpture features the River Goddess Yamuna, Lord Siva - King of Dancers, and Parvati Winning A Dice Game. Outside in the courtyard the once-creamy-colored building exterior still displays red, blue and green designs of flowers, birds and elephants. Gray basalt is elaborately carved with voluptuous women and courageous warriors.

All at once the photographers among us virtually leap up the many angled staircases to pillared balconies and recessed lookout points to shoot carved roof supports and ornamented temple enclosures.

On the bus ride back from Ajanta, we tell Brian that we plan to be married in India and would like his help in arranging the details. After quizzing us as to the seriousness of our intent, he announces that he is delighted. Imagine being married in sacred Mother India, home of Hinduism, Buddhism, Jainism and countless other religions and paths! We will dedicate our marriage, the relationship and our lives to service and to world uplift. But how can we possibly organize a wedding in forty-eight hours? We'd like to be married as we tour India.

CHAPTER 2
A WEDDING IN RAJASTHAN

"Marriage is a training ground for fostering trans-sensual love."
Sathya Sai Baba

Rajasthan, India
October 9, 1979

After initially congratulating us about our wedding plans, Brian shifted into a role of responsible patriarch and began cross-examining us to ensure that we were serious. "Now kids - you're sure this isn't a whim, aren't you? I can't be responsible for any hasty, starry-eyed wedding ideas inspired by all this romantic scenery, you know."

"Thanks for your concern," Jim says, "but we're older than we look. We're in our mid-thirties and have three sons between us. They're in school in the States now. We've both been single for several years and have been friends for quite a while. In fact, one of the reasons we specifically came to India is to marry here since this country is the birthplace of so many of the world's major world religions and is a vast treasure-trove of spiritual tradition."

"Yes," I chime in. "Spiritual life is very important to us. Believe me, we know what we're doing."

"Okay kids," Brian laughs. "I see that you're determined, with or without me. Why don't I plan the wedding since I know India and have planned quite a few weddings? But I warn you - it will probably have to be a Hindu wedding with a Hindu priest and a fire ceremony outside. All the missionaries have left, you know... heh-heh! Now let me see... how about if we have the ceremony near the Lake Palace at Sunset, if we can arrange it? You can design the ceremony and I'll get the local costumes. You, Connie, must be married in the red and gold sari of the region and you, Jim, must wear the traditional gold lame jacket and crimson turban of the rajas. And of course there will be palm fronds and garlands and banquet servers in matching turbans and sashes. We'll ride to the ceremony in an elegant white boat with a blue awning.... By the way, when did you want to get married?" Brian's mounting enthusiasm is momentarily interrupted by the practical matter of time.

"In two days, if possible," Jim announces, eyes twinkling.

"Two days! My God! You don't want much do you? Only a miracle! Never mind - miracles are my specialty. They have to be with all the lovebirds I get on these trips. Why once a few years ago I had a couple approach me with the same look in your eyes that you two have today. At least I'm getting to recognize signs of an impending wedding in advance! But we were spending two days with the Masai tribe in the middle of Africa. In that situation I had far less to work with, so this one should be easy by comparison. Just imagine it: the bride and groom wore the local raiment with these huge shadows being cast on all of us by the roaring bonfire. The tour group started passing booze around and the Masai warriors all started getting high and whooping it up. I was afraid things were going to get out of hand but the only result was that the whole tribe got whipped into a frenzy of ecstasy for forty-eight hours. When it was time for us to leave we were all like one big family. That was about the most spectacular wedding I ever planned. Of course my background in theater helps give me a feel for the dramatic. But don't worry, kids, I won't get too carried away this time. Of course, it won't be boring either!"

Who knows what will develop under Brian's flamboyant hand. I am getting anxious. We want to have a spiritual wedding, not a brawl. After having lived a fulfilling life of intentional singleness for nearly eight years, I now find myself with greatly mixed feelings about marrying, even though we have been discussing the subject for months. My independence is priceless and has been hard-won. Yet, I deeply love Jim and feel that he is the most easy-going, self-actualizing man I know. He is calm and centered, spiritually-oriented and largely free of most of the limiting and conventional ideas about women and their roles that would suffocate me.

Of the several men who have indicated an interest in marrying me these past several years, Jim is the one with whom I could live most happily, without threat of possessiveness or stagnation, not to mention role-bound behavior. Since my lifetime goal is high spiritual attainment, or awakening, it is essential that my life partner be spiritually like-minded. Anything less than that is unthinkable. Spiritual agreement (in essence, not form) is the foundation of all successful relationships.

October 10th

We've arrived by plane at Udaipur, the lovely whitewashed city of fairytale palaces and lakes as well as the residence of Maharana Bagwasin Mewar, last of the rajas of Rajasthan. Since "pur" means village, Udaipur is the Village of Udai, founded in 1559 by Maharana Udai Singhji. It remained the capital until 1947 when India gained Independence and the old states were merged to form Rajasthan of which Jaipur is the capital.

Two outstanding threads run throughout Udaipur's history. The first is the long continuity of the ruling family which traces its ancestry to at least the beginning of the Christian era. The second is the area's devotion to Hinduism in the face of wars, the sacking of towns and persecution. "Listen to this," I hear someone behind me in the plane reading to a seat companion. "Someone named Sage Shuka once said, 'Fools who cannot grasp the Truth, who cannot recognize Divinity and measure the power of God, live in the delusion that their petty plans will save them and that they can triumph through their own efforts. The fact is that not even the smallest success can be won without God's grace.' " Hastily I scribbled the quotation on my airplane paper napkin for further reflection.

To look at Udaipur now in its pristine wedding cake architecture, one wouldn't think it had harbored anything but tranquility for centuries. It is known as the city of gardens, lakes, fountains, temples and eighteen colleges. There's also a museum and a market although the entire labyrinthine city is a vast market of gray-cobbled streets, white-washed walls and blue-green wooden doors. Involuntary comparisons to Tangiers spring to mind as we amble the narrow curving streets to our boat that will take us to the fabled Lake Palace Hotel, a filigreed white castle which is one of the finest hotels in the world. The Lake Palace, home of the last Mewar king, is but one example of a palace considered too expensive to maintain by its owner, hence converted to a lavish hotel by the government.

From our crisp, canopied blue and white motor launch we see scores of jewel-like birds. The lake is said to be the home of 250 species which dart and swirl over its black-olive waters. The ones we can easily identify are bluebirds, herons, parakeets, sandpipers, parrots, pigeons, wrens and hawks. The bougainvillea here comes in more colors than I've ever seen. There are blossoms of lavender, fuchsia pink, scarlet red, tangerine orange and milky white.

From the middle of Lake Pichola we can see Jagmandir Island in the distance with its deserted white palace and turrets; along the streets on the shore of Udaipur the fabled women of Rajasthan glide in gold and red saris beside ox-cart traffic jams. Three-wheeled auto-rickshaws, bikes and busses weave among the painted horse tongas which are reminiscent of Sicilian horse carts. Green wooden cart wheels are painted with flowers. The carts themselves are further accented with red, green and white flags and the horses wear red plumes and tinkling brass bells.

Throughout the morning I have been folding and unfolding the colorful tour brochure to familiarize myself with the spectacular sights we are about to enjoy. An obscure sentence that I haven't noticed before suddenly jumps out at me. Tucked neatly in a paragraph that casually mentions that India is suited for more "adventuresome" travelers is this piece of advice: "Your victory will lie in your surrender to India."

After the baggage handlers help us off the boat and lead us to the lobby of the Lake Palace Hotel, we await the distribution of the room keys and I spot a foot-long white lizard slithering along the lobby ceiling of the hotel. Our group stands in the spacious lobby searching purses and pockets for pens and reading glasses in order to jot down room numbers. Suddenly, another white lizard of the same size falls off the ceiling onto the head of Florence, a plumpish tour companion, which causes her to whoop and scream in fright. She shrieks sharply three times, spins around in a circle four times scratching at her head and shouting.

"Help! Help! Get it off me! Do something! It's on me. Get it off!"

Both Florence and the lizard are terrified. Her cries bring all the porters and desk employees running to the lobby to see what is happening. Florence knocks the trembling lizard off her head and shoulders and onto the marble floor where it skitters under a satin chair. The lizard tussle, combined with being the unwanted center of attention immediately upon arrival in a strange hotel, causes Florence to burst into tears. None of us knows each other very well so far. It's obvious that we all feel a bit awkward for her and are mutually uncertain as to whether she would prefer a consoling pat on the shoulder or to be left alone. Porters dash about searching for the offending lizard and summarily excommunicate him from our presence, explaining that lizards, like cobras, spiders and poverty, are unfortunately a fact of life in India.

This explanation does little to ease the fears of the single women in the group who are now afraid to enter their rooms until the porters open the closets and drawers to ensure that there are no further creatures lurking there.

"Yes," murmurs one of our group as she crosses her doorsill across the hall from our room. "F-E-A-R. Fear is just False Evidence Appearing Real." She squares her shoulders, takes a deep breath and says, "India is not going to get me down. I'm here to take new risks and to have a good time – not to be the timid little 'fraidy cat' I've always been! If my grown kids in New Jersey could see me now...."

This morning, after we have been charmingly received and settled in by the staff of the Taj Mahal Hotel Chain, which the Lake Palace now represents, we visit a batik cottage industry in the home of a large local family. More as a gesture of support rather than in appreciation of the batik samples, we buy a few small hangings. We are captivated, however, by the Rajasthan region with its Persian, Moorish and Chinese influences in architecture. Brian quizzes us again about wedding plan preferences and we re-confirm that tomorrow is the big day.

In the fields around Udaipur there are tall piles of ochre-colored twining which we at first mistook for coils of rope about four feet high and three feet wide. It seems that what we were actually seeing is row upon row of beautifully shaped dung patty piles. We later saw some people meticulously shaping them into precisely-indented "pies" about ten inches across and overlapping about a dozen pies in a circle until a stack was completed. The dung is sold and used for fuel. In fact, trains of little gray donkeys carry huge sacks of these dung patties along the road. Esthetics are such a basic and natural part of life here that even the dung stacks have artistry in their arrangement.

This evening Brian announces at dinner that our wedding will take place tomorrow afternoon at sunset on the hillside opposite the Lake Palace. Our group will travel by motor launch from the Lake Palace to the Hilltop Hotel garden where a Hindu priest will be awaiting our wedding party. He says that the local tour office is so excited that they'll spend tonight and the entire day tomorrow in preparation. They'll be making flower garlands and buffet dishes as well as lending us their own local traditional wedding clothing and even a richly caparisoned horse for the groom's arrival to the hilltop setting. Let's hope the clothing fits since, at five feet five inches and six feet one inch we are considerably larger than most Indians who would normally be about five feet and five and a half feet respectively.

Rajasthan, India
October 11th

Today we are to be married in native costume in Rajasthan. Brian called the entire tour group together in the Palace lobby this morning to distribute our hand-written invitations, which he had carefully prepared himself. Everyone was delighted and surprised to be included in the actual plans themselves. It's been a rushed day with rings to buy in the palace gift shop, naps, baths, the ceremony to write and our wedding contract to design. One of the reasons we have felt so strongly about involving the entire group in the ceremony itself is that, as a group, we have not yet coalesced. Therefore mutual involvement in the processes leading up to the wedding event itself can be utilized to bring out all of the personalities and to help everyone to feel involved through making a verbal contribution.

Before boarding the motor launch I outlined the parts that Jim and I will both read during the ceremony, having mutually worked them out with much discussion and refinement. After all sixteen of us have seated ourselves in the boat, I hand out pieces of paper and explain that we would like for this to be a three-part ceremony and that we would appreciate their individual involvement. First, we'll have a recital of our commitment. Next, we'll invite group presentations of "Five Essentials For A Quality Life and Union."

Finally, we'll move from the Hilltop Hotel reception room to the garden on the hillside for the final portion that features a Hindu priest and the Hindu traditional rites and fire ceremony. Jim and I will be seated on the ground beside an outdoor fire pit that overlooks the lake and Lake Palace. Red henna powder will be applied to our hands and we will pledge our love, support and faithfulness to each other as we walk around the fire and the priest chants ancient Vedic scriptures for matrimony.

The royal blue boat canopy flaps overhead as we roar over the lake. I give instructions for the group to divide themselves into five groups of three people each. Each person will join a group by selecting one of five topics he'd like to comment on during the wedding ceremony. Each triad of people then creates two or three statements from his own experience on the value of work, study, prayer, service or laughter for a balanced life.

When the tour members look a bit puzzled, Jim explains that I'm in the personal growth field and lead workshops and seminars for a living. With his usual good nature, Jim remarks that I'm so accustomed to leading and organizing that I "even feel compelled to turn our wedding into a personal growth workshop!"

"Is nothing sacred to a workshop leader?!" I exclaim in chagrin.

Everyone laughs, relaxes and starts to get into a cooperative spirit. Each trio completes its task and selects a spokesperson from each group to read their contribution. After our hasty rehearsal the boat arrives at the jetty and we enter the awaiting cabs to meet Brian at the Hilltop.

Dressed in a flowing snow-white caftan with a batik scarf at the throat, Brian flutters his manicured hands in greeting. He ceremoniously welcomes us into the lobby reception area and whips around the room announcing that today he's alternately standing in as the father and father-in-law of the wedded couple. "Sometimes in life we have to play two roles at once," he winks.

Two Indian women arrive and take me into another room to dress while a cluster of men tell Jim that his costume and steed await. By now I'm paralyzed with apprehension at the thought of sharing myself and my values so openly with so many strangers.

"Am I out of my mind to be marrying in a Hindu fire ceremony on a hilltop in Udaipur, India?" I ask myself.

Instead of a spontaneous celebration of life, perhaps this is but one more flamboyant flashing of my ego. Maybe a justice of the peace would have been more sensible. No, that would be too drab. Brian has told us we'll have to be married again in the States since every country has its own individual laws. We will indeed do this but as far as I'm concerned, this is our spiritual wedding, our real one with heartful commitment. When we get back to Colorado, Jim would like to either be married by a Justice of the Peace, or have our friend Maryann Downs, a Methodist minister, marry us in the living room of our new house.

Frankly, I favor being married in a hot air balloon. There's something about the freedom and upward direction of it that appeals to me. Since most things can be done with verve and flair with just a tiny bit of extra effort, why would one want to have a drab wedding? In any event, the second ceremony will be the legal one but this will be our real wedding.

Suddenly I realize that I'm keeping the guests waiting. As I see myself in the mirror, it's a hilarious picture. The gold-bordered red bridal sari is too short by eight inches and too small by two sizes. My bosom is smashed into a tiny doll-sized blouse and overblouse then covered with a flowing red veil. No doubt Brian's local friends have found the largest wedding sari available, but the owner must be about five feet tall, or nearly six inches shorter than I am. On me, it looks as if the crimson Rajasthani wedding outfit has shrunk! Oh well, it will just have to do.

Clutching their readings, the tour members have assembled in a circle of arm chairs to hear us pledge our love and loyalty. They are visibly surprised, however, at the wording of our commitment and its implications. It is as follows:

Part One
Five Essentials of a Satisfactory Life and Union:
Prayer, Work, Laughter, Study and Service

* Prayer: and meditation for constant awareness of the Divine in all
  things
* Work: for contribution and perspective
* Laughter: as a celebration of awareness and joy
* Study: for exercise of the intellect and imagination
* Service: We are not placed on earth merely to gratify ourselves

We would like to begin our wedding ceremony by reading our contractual
commitment.

We choose to embrace, in our marriage, larger concepts than the conventional roles of men and women in relationship. Therefore, we take this
opportunity to affirm some of the more important premises on which we
agree.

A. We consider the Care and Maintenance of our Minds and Bodies to be
   our ongoing duty throughout our lives. Our daily habits which will
   contribute to healthy minds and bodies entail nutritional diet and exercise; meditation and reflection; attention to cleanliness in grooming;
   thoughtfulness of gesture, speech and attire, and ongoing study and
   lively interest in life outside the relationship.
B. Names. We both strongly believe in the necessity for maintaining
   individual identities and therefore will maintain our separate current
   names for public, private and legal purposes. We'll continue to be
   referred to as Constance B. Shaw and James D. Wright.
C. Careers. Both of our careers have equal value, therefore neither of us
   is to be considered the primary wage earner. As individual
   opportunities arise we will continue to give cooperative consideration
   to such things as change of job location, travel demands, overtime and
   company benefits.
D. Finances. We will establish and maintain joint financial goals and
   plans for savings, investments and day-to-day needs, using joint
   accounts as appropriate. We will also maintain individual investments
   and need not be accountable to each other for expenditures outside of
   our mutual plans. We will be individually responsible for the financial
   needs and educational expense of our children.
E. Children. Inasmuch as Jim has already contributed two children to the
   planet by a former marriage and Connie has one child by a former
   marriage, we do not intend to procreate. Further, we will be jointly
   responsible to ensure that such eventuality will not occur.
F. Changing and Risking. We cannot maximize our union and celebration
   of work, prayer, laughter, study and service without changing and
   risking on a day-to-day basis. We will therefore review our contractual
   commitment at least semi-annually in a formalized manner. We will

continue our weekly family meetings as a format for ongoing dialogue
and problem solving and will continue to have quality interactions.

Connie: Jim, I am a very different person from the one you met six years
ago and so are you. Six years hence we will probably be yet quite changed
in various ways. This marriage commitment to each other is based on
who we are today, both individually and in this union. It will not be given
up lightly. In the face of major conflict we commit to bring all of our
internal and external resources to bear on resolution.

Jim: Love and Fear. Two major feelings are love and fear. In recognition
of these emotions we understand our individual responsibility to husband
the thoughts which create our own reality. Implicit within this idea is
continual forgiveness of ourselves, each other and all we encounter. This
absolves us of the need to feel guilt or to take pleasure in causing each
other or anyone else to feel guilty.

Miracles and Healing. We believe in miracles. We can choose whether life
is difficult or easy. We choose a path of healed vision and attitudes to
facilitate the Five Essentials of work, prayer, laughter, study and service.

Part Two
Five Essentials of a Satisfactory Life and Union

At this time we invite the thoughtful verbal contributions of our
friends and travelling companions regarding five of the necessary
elements for our life and marriage together.

A spokesperson for each group reads the three contributions of that
group:

Work: may it always be stimulating, meaningful and rewarding.

Prayer: may you keep your connection with God strong, be ever thankful
and express the Divine within you.

Study: select areas far larger than your ability to overreach them, such as
nature, travel or gardening; apply your studies and share your knowledge
with others; support scholarship in others.

Service: live to help others and be a haven and a blessing to all whom you
meet.

Connie: In recognition of the divine office invested in this Hindu priest
we hereby participate solemnly and joyfully in exchanging our wedding
vows. We hereby dedicate our lives, our union, our resources and talent
to God and to the service of humanity. It is our especial privilege to be
married in India on this hillside at sunset since India has been a fount of
spiritual inspiration throughout the ages.

After our groups have made their own verbal contributions to the
ceremony, we form a procession and move down the steps, across the
drive and through a green archway of vines and palm fronds onto the

expansive lawn. Dressed in a white dhoti and pink turban, the elderly Hindu priest awaits at the ceremonial spot.

Upon stepping through the archway I am given a red "tika" dot at the center of the "third eye" chakra. Everyone else is daubed on the head with red paint and we're all garlanded with white flowers. A chair has been set for me near the stone wall that overlooks the city. We are told that the palm-frond archway represents the bride's home and family which will shortly receive the groom.

If I think I look slightly comical in my petite sari, Jim is acutely aware of the fact that his "horse" is the largest pony that could be found and that his lavish costume is more than a bit too small. However, he's undaunted by such trifles and carries himself with his usual dignity. His costume and that of the costumed white horse create a stunning effect. A red plume waves from the horse's forehead as the thousand mirrors of his gold blanket twinkle in the sun. Jim, dressed in a gold jacket and matching turban with a red plume, cuts a fine figure. Like an ancient warrior, he dismounts from the horse and enters the archway with the sword in his gold cummerbund glinting in the setting sunlight. Even though our costumes are too small, no one seems to notice. They are enthralled with the pageantry.

Although I've feared I'd not know how to proceed at my own wedding, there are abundant "helpers" giving me cues throughout.

"Let the groom garland you now," exults Brian.

"Sit over here, please," intones the priest.

"Offer your hand, please," prompts another.

Brian instructs me to welcome the groom to my home and for us to join the priest on the platform where he builds a fire of cinnamon-colored roots and twigs. The wrinkled, wizened man must have done this a thousand times; he chants a rote nasal prayer then directs Jim in the sprinkling of water and marigold petals into the flames. Next he mixes red henna powder and applies bright crimson henna paste to our hands. Our wrists are bound with yarn strands. Yarn strands are tied to the wrists of the wedding guests. Still chanting, the priest ties our arms together with the large red sash from his waist and requests us to walk around the fire with bound, henna-painted hands seven times, as women in the dark blue saris behind us beat drums and chant. *Occupy my mind night and day, Oh Lord. Let me be your worthy servant and a good wife and companion to this dear man whom I now marry, with Your blessings.*

We vow to put God first, ahead of each other, in all things. We pledge that we will honor and trust God and one another and that we will be loyal partners and friends throughout all the ups and downs of life. We will support each other in living a spiritual life for the upliftment of others and the betterment of society. After all the rice, herbs, leaves, water and marigold petals have been fed to the fire, the priest bows to us, smiles and wishes us happiness.

We're led to our two chairs near the fire where local women in saris approach us with their babies since it is considered good luck for babies to sit on the lap of the bride to ensure a fertile union.

Since I've specifically mentioned our intention to bear no more children between us, the irony of the custom causes everyone to laugh. Someone jokingly shouts, "Watch out, Connie - you don't want any babies sitting on your lap!" More laughter. Photos are taken, drinks and snacks are served by stunning white-suited men in red turbans and cummerbunds.

As stars emerge overhead and the lake sparkles and glistens in the moonlight I'm reluctant to relinquish this magical moment. However the mini-cabs have arrived to take us to the wedding feast at the Lake Palace.

It's a quiet, rapid motor launch ride across the lake to the Palace Hotel where the hotel staff meets our wedding party at the landing. We're greeted with a pair of lovely brass vases, a basket of flowers and the announcement that the bride and groom's belongings have been moved to the spacious air conditioned honeymoon suite, free of charge. Upon arrival there we're presented with more flowers, a note and fruit basket from the hotel. The corner suite is decorated with a chartreuse velvet sofa, coffee table, twin beds, as always, a modern bath and an exquisite view of the lake. Plush indeed. Our air conditioning is the talk of the group who joke loudly that they're so wilted that if they'd only known you could get an air conditioned room by getting married, they'd have planned to get married too!

After re-arranging our tiny uncomfortable wedding outfits we join the group in the dining room for the lavish, surprise wedding dinner they've arranged. Applause breaks out as we enter and see the pink-draped tables which hold fuchsia bougainvillea blossoms spelling out "Best Wishes." Brian toasts any number of circumstances in the candlelight amid lovely décor, a sumptuous meal and superb wedding cake. He presents us with an autographed book from the group entitled, *The History of the Mewar Kingdom of Udaipur.*

We fall exhausted into bed with dazed amazement at all that's transpired and the stark realization that we have several more cities ahead of us in our final week here.

October 12th

Jaipur, the Pink City of India is extremely cosmopolitan, in a romantic sort of way, compared to other Indian cities we've seen. Have I been here before in another lifetime? It seems hauntingly familiar. The buildings are indeed varying shades of pink, ranging from salmon, to flamingo, to cinnamon, coral and bubble-gum pink. They are trimmed in pristine white and look like Walt Disney fantasy creations. Also of note is the Observatory built by Jai Singh, the famous astronomer, which seems more like an outdoor playground for giants with its immense sundials, towers, pits, mounds and staircases. The Palace of the Winds is a marvelous construction of waterways, fountains, gardens and in-laid semi-precious stones in the building itself.

After Jaipur we explored the wonders of Agra (the fabulous Taj!) and New Delhi. It was thrilling to tour the Red Fort and palaces and to fly to Srinagar in the Himalayas. We stayed on a romantic Victorian houseboat on Lake Dal in Srinagar for our honeymoon. There are tombs for Jesus and Mary in Srinagar, though we didn't personally see them. Now that little fact, if true, would certainly turn Christian theologians and historians on their ears!

India has captivated me. My eyes have been opened by the gentleness of Indian people, the brilliance of Indian culture and spirituality and the visual splendor of the sub-continent. However, there is so much squalor, noise, disease and just plain ugliness that I doubt that I'll ever return to India. This trip will last me for a lifetime.

Littleton, Colorado
October 29th

The trip to India was the best trip of this lifetime. We will have Maryann marry us in our new house so that the American wedding will be legal. Nothing could top our spiritual wedding in India, though. Sadly, I have not found a spiritual mentor or teacher, as I thought I might in India. It is all very well to say that God is within. But I just don't have very clear, steady, consistent guidance yet and can't help but feel that someone somewhere could help me. And while it is enjoyable to meditate with Jim each morning and evening and to practice *A Course In Miracles* together, I don't know how much longer I can sustain myself without a *human* Teacher. I have investigated the Denver Zen Center, the Jung Center, where I'm a board member, several meditation groups and many other leads. I went as far as I could with Gia-Fu Feng, who was a lovely and mirthful mentor to me. Surely there is someone who is far superior to me in matters of Spirit who will "take me on" as a student.

CHAPTER 3
TRIALS IN SINGAPORE

"I do not know what anything is for." ACIM, WB P 38

Oakland, California
Spring, 1981

Jim and I have been offered a once-in-a-lifetime opportunity. It entails living in Southeast Asia, on the tropical island which is the Republic of Singapore. 'Clean and green Singapore' lies across the water from Malaysia and just north of the countless islands of Indonesia. Our equatorial sojourn will last for about a year and will give me the chance to do some consulting in Asia and to travel to at least ten countries while I'm based in Singapore. Jim will be working for a subsidiary of his company and will travel to Borneo and to other exotic tropical places within easy travel distance of Singapore.

Tonight we are visiting the Siddha Yoga Dharma Ashram of Oakland, California, because Jim is eager to meet Mukthananda, the famous Indian Guru. Although I have been looking for a Teacher since we were married in India, a year and a half ago, I still haven't discovered such a Being. Maybe Swami Mukthananda will be The One.

We are sitting on the floor of the large hall with several hundred other people. A very slow version of 'Om Nama Shivaya' is being sung by the crowd. It is so slow that it sounds funereal to my uninitiated ears but the devotees seem totally enthralled by the rhythm, the incense, the twang of the veena and the hum of the harmonium. Many of the attendees are dressed in shades of orange such as coral, pumpkin, salmon, peach, ochre or tangerine. I'm told that orange is the color of renunciation, much as black or gray would be for priests or nuns of Christianity.

After quite some time, Mukthananda comes and the crowd is instructed to form long single-file lines in order to receive his blessing. From where I am standing, I can't see what is happening near the Swami, but I see that he is standing under a canopy, that he wears a small round red brimless hat and that he is waving something in the air. There are people standing near him as the line moves slowly forward. Meanwhile, the hypnotically slow chanting continues and nearby devotees look entranced, swaying slightly as they inch forward to gaze at Mukthananda, eye-to-eye.

Eventually the line in front of us shortens and it is nearly my turn to be blessed. The woman in front of me is a well-groomed, long-haired brunette who said she is a secretary for a local corporation. She wears an elegant silk punjabi suit from India and large gold hoop earrings. As Swami Mukthananda comes into view, I see that he is smiling as he taps each devotee lightly on the head with a long peacock feather. He is wearing a long orange robe and an orange shawl. His black hair, worn short, is slightly graying and his face looks to me like an ordinary brown Indian face, neither astonishingly handsome nor unpleasant. I know that when the woman in front of me is finished with her turn, I will be certain whether or not Swami Mukthananda is my Teacher. All I have to do is to look deeply into his eyes and I will be sure, one way or the other.

At last I am standing alone in front of Mukthananda. He swings the peacock feather back over his head and, before it comes forward, toward me, I look deeply into Mukthananda's brown eyes. What a shock! I feel nothing. His eyes are lackluster and he seems to me to be either slightly ill or about to become ill. I try to hide my disappointment as the peacock feather, symbol of Enlightenment, hits me on the brow chakra, between the eyebrows. Without being able to explain how I know, I simply know deep in my bone marrow that he is not my Teacher. Now what? If Gia-fu Feng and Swami Mukthananda are not my Sat-guru, then who is, pray tell?

Singapore
April 20, 1981

Our flight to Singapore was uneventful, which is always desirable. But the moment I walked down the flight of stairs from the plane to the tarmac, the most stupendous thing happened. My heart chakra started vibrating and I received a vision that the One for Whom I'm looking is in Asia, in one of the largest, most populous countries. I saw, in the vision, lots of brown-skinned people and some Westerners surrounding the Person, Whom I couldn't see, as there were so many gathered around.

The devotees wore long clothing, looked blissful and were receiving something in their cupped hands, which seemed very precious to them. They brought it to their faces as they pulled back from the crowd and sat back down on the ground in a large orange-colored sandy area in front of an odd-looking building, which seemed to be a temple or shrine. I never caught sight of the Being, because of the crowd in the vision, so I don't know if It is a He or a She, but I do know that the Person is the most holy Person on the planet, and even more powerful than Jesus, Buddha or Krishna. That certain knowledge came with the vision. Accompanying the vision, I heard a locution, or inner voice, say, "The One for Whom you have searched is here in Asia. God is on earth!" I must find this Being. My immediate thought is that He or She must live in either China or India as they are the most populous countries and are probably the least tainted by Western values, media and products.

As soon as the vision came, with deplaning passengers surging all around us, I told Jim. He knows perfectly well that I have lengthy experience with the fact that God is within each one of us. However, he also knows that I believe that there is Someone on earth Who can help me to access deeper states of consciousness and to attain Realization. As we hurried to the luggage carousel, I asked Jim if he would mind if I scoured Asia, looking for God, while he worked on the various nearby islands of

Indonesia. He indicated his complete support and I decided that as soon as we get settled into a house I'm going to China to find God.

Singapore
April 25th

Little eruptions of excitement arise in my throat as I contemplate that we have actually moved to the Republic of Singapore - for a whole year. The past year and a half has flown by since we were married in India, then again in Colorado by Maryann Downs. When we were offered the chance to move to Singapore from Colorado, we conferred, discussed and negotiated. We decided to seize the chance for Jim to expand his career experience in engineering and management and for me to do a little consulting, writing and touring of Asia. But the real reason I decided to uproot my career was to continue my search for a spiritual Teacher and I have proof that He or She is hiding somewhere in Asia.

Obviously I had had no luck whatsoever in finding a Great Teacher in India on our wedding trip. I must find this Being.

New friends have told us some amazing stories about living in Singapore. Carol, from Australia, said that she had a nine-foot boa constrictor in her back yard. She called the fire department to come and get it but they took three hours to arrive and actually called before coming to ensure it had already wriggled back into the jungle before they came. She asked them why they had bothered to come. They replied, "To make sure you were still alive. Besides, we're all married Muslims and our families are important to us. If we're going to support our families we need to be prudent and not put ourselves in any danger."

"That's a novel way of looking at things," Carol had laughed. "Yes, what about the rest of the population they're supposed to be protecting?" a friend of Carol's had said, rather archly.

Susan, another new friend, had read an article to us from the Singapore Straits Times about a python which had entwined itself around the pole at the bus stop and frightened all the commuters away. But still, we wanted to live in a house away from the center of town instead of a high-rise apartment. We are from the wide-open spaces of Colorado and like fresh air and nature.

"You'll be sorry," I'd been told by numerous Americans when I announced that we'd be moving soon to a suburban house from our temporary base in the posh Marco Polo Hotel.

"I tried it once but didn't last four months," Carol had said in her charming Australian accent. "There were hoards of insects, fruit bats flying in the windows, noises from the neighbors, floods from rainstorms. And the heat! It's impossible for us Anglo-Saxon types to live without air-con in the tropics. I admitted defeat. Moved into a cool luxury apartment in town. Now you couldn't pry me loose with a crowbar."

These well meant words of warning come to mind now as I contemplate the house on Greenleaf View - all the work yet to be done to make cozy our new home away from home. After looking at dozens of places all over the island, I finally located a suitable house off Old Holland Road and Ulu Pandan. It's a semi-detached duplex with four bedrooms, a two-story layout with small balconies off the bedrooms facing the tiny front yard. It should be adequate for our year's stay here but it's a far cry from the modern house and large yard we left back in Colorado. Nevertheless, having brought only a few things - mostly books and clothing - it will be a lark to add my personal decorative touches to this sparsely and mundanely furnished place.

I intend to meet as many Singaporeans as I can, and to jump into our new life here with gusto. I plan to explore every aspect of this tiny island republic and its people and culture. Wahid (wah heed), our Malay driver who comes with Jim's job, offers the first opportunity in this department. I can hardly believe my good fortune in having him with us. It's obvious from his quiet, sensitive manner and frequent references to Islam that he's a devout Muslim as well as a devoted husband and the father of two young children. Upon meeting him, I immediately felt as though I had known him forever. We seemed to be resuming an old conversational pattern rather than beginning one. There were, of course, the usual initial questions on both sides and light exchange of information. Since I've always wanted to learn more about Islam, this will be an easy way to do so.

Wahid-the-Handsome is a good listener. When he smiles, a diamond shower dances over his black eyes, wide nose and dark cheeks. His stocky body, gleaming black hair and square hands make him appear more like a stereotypical wrestler than the artistic, considerate person he reveals himself to be through our delicious conversations. Somerset Maugham aptly described Malays as lovely, starry-eyed people. Malays, who look Polynesian, perfectly grace and animate this lush green Singapore-Eden in a quiet grounded way that contrasts sharply with its restless commercial hustle-bustle.

With a young father's irrepressible pride in his child, Wahid tells of his daughter's many recent elementary-school singing prizes, winning awards though she's only six years old. Pretty, precocious and extremely talented, Wanisa is very charismatic for one so young. Two-year old son Mohammed Hosni (pronounced Ohs' nee) is already showing early signs of having the medicine-man-priest potential of a Bohmo like Wahid's father. Wahid, like most Malay fathers, insisted that his son's black hair be left uncut until well into his second year, "like Samson" so that he would gather and retain strength for a wise, sturdy start in life.

As the sixth child of sixteen children, Wahid learned early in his life to share with others, to be respectful and polite to his parents, elders and employers and eventually to keep to the requirements of an extended family - or he would risk reaping the family's rejection and criticism of his errant ways.

"When I was a younger single man I was a very naughty fellow," he confides. "I would drink and I played the drums in a rock band. And I knew many women. My father even beat me because I was so bad. Muslims don't drink or stray from their families so my family was very ashamed of me and I was very confused. Finally I got fed up with such a life and I found Sanih (Sahn' ya), my wife, who is a good woman. But she told me I had to start praying every day again and go to the mosque and keep my beliefs or she would leave me. We got married and decided to have two children only, which is the modern Singapore way. Two only, boy or girl, never mind. We have a small flat with a hall (living room), kitchen, bath and one bedroom so it is very crowded with the four of us. But I remember my life growing up with sixteen children in the family when we had only two bedrooms and a hall, which was much more crowded. When I remember those days I don't mind."

Wahid is quick to tell me that there are two things I must know about him. One, he smokes but is trying to kick the habit and won't smoke in the car, for which I am eternally grateful. Two, he carries a green and white prayer mat in the trunk of the car so that in between driving me to appointments throughout the day he can find a quiet corner and pray the required five times. I nod in understanding and show him my ratty, well-used copy of *A Course In Miracles* – my holy book, like his *Koran*. He is surprised by my enthusiastic response to his mention of Islam. He's further intrigued when I mention that I too, "tune in" or meditate a few times a day and announce that I'd like to visit as many mosques as possible while in Singapore and I'd like for him to take me. His sparkling black eyes register alarm.

"But you have to leave your shoes at the door. And women must stay in the upper gallery and not mix downstairs with the men. And you must wash yourself before entering. And... you're a Western woman." As he delivers each sentence he scrutinizes my reactions in the rear-view mirror. It is obvious that Wahid has more on his hands than he had bargained for. How is he going to explain this to his family and friends? "Your Mem wants to do what? Why doesn't she pray to her own God in her own church?"

By now he is nervous and firmly but gently tells me that he believes that Allah the Almighty is the one and only omnipotent God. Monotheism is the truth as far as he is concerned. He announces these beliefs in hope that I'll be put off. But I agree with him. He's further confused. Next he launches into a patient explanation that Muslims do not go in for the prolific images of Hinduism or for the magical demons and spirits of Singapore's currently corrupt and populist form of Taoism. Neither do I. Why on earth, he wonders, do I want to visit mosques? I explain that I believe that God is in everyone and that I respect the major world religions and find that I can turn within and connect with my Higher Self, God within me, anyplace - in a temple, church, forest, or mosque.

In fact, my Course lesson today is "God is with me. I cannot be deceived." (i.e., that He is not.) ACIM, M P 40, 42 I tell Wahid that I've bought a copy of the *Glorious Koran* but that it seems very confusing to me and is difficult to understand, whereas I have enjoyed reading the *Bible,* the *Bhagavad Gita* and the *Tao Te Ching* as well as Buddhist writings.

He asks if I am interested in conversion to Islam, to which I reply that I'm not. My interest in Islam involves a need to expand my spiritual understanding to include more people, to appreciate Asia more, and to observe how an over-riding Spirit moves within and between people through various languages and cultures. Wahid consents to take me to visit as many mosques as I like as long as we don't go on Friday, the day of worship when the mosques are crowded and when political speeches are sometimes delivered from the pulpits. He is willing to take me inside them as long as he's not seen by anyone he knows. Since none of the Mems of the other drivers have shown any interest in visiting mosques or conversing at great length about religion and local culture, Wahid has a unique challenge with me.

But the next challenge entails my belief, and a typically American one, that all men are created equal and that he need not treat me with such elaborate deference nor insist that I ride in the back seat "like all the other Mems." I want Wahid to learn about democracy and about metaphysics and positive thoughts and the women's movement. Daily I have taken great pains to explain that:

⋄ Our beliefs create our reality and that we can do and be anything we wish.

⋄ Wahid can just as easily get out of his financial difficulties by deciding on a clear objective and aiming for it - such as a better job.

⋄ His wife (who's pressing to get a job) is equal to him in ability and can help him out by working and thereby assuage her frustrations and develop her abilities.

⋄ I don't like riding in the back seat and would rather sit next to him so that we can see each other better during our marathon conversations.

⋄ Although I appreciate Jim's company's having provided a car and driver for us in Singapore, I don't like being chauffeured around and have driven since I was fifteen years old. But I realize Wahid needs the money from driving as many hours a day as possible and am therefore willing to let him drive me everywhere.

Just as patiently and eminently more diplomatically, Wahid persists in explaining to me that:

⋄ Malays know their place in Singaporean society and their place is not to upset the status quo. They cannot do and be whatever they like. What a foolish notion!

- ⋄ Being a driver is considered a very good job here and he is glad he has it. Poor finances are a way of life. One has to expect that.
- ⋄ His wife will not work. He will not allow it. She will care for their little son no matter how tight the budget. That is that.
- ⋄ It's not proper for a Mem to ride in the front seat like a laborer. Mems ride in the back seat. It would make Wahid look very bad if I were to ride in the front. His colleagues would think he had lost his training, his manners and his mind. They would think I was common and had no training or that I was being rebellious in throwing off all the niceties that make for the smooth functioning of a society. It would look cheap and suggestive and Wahid and I would both be disgraced.

To ensure that this latest crazy idea of mine - brazenly sitting in the front seat - does not take hold, Wahid carefully piles the front passenger seat with newspapers and cassette tapes so that I can't sit beside him. He becomes more and more speedy at opening the rear door for me as I approach the car each day so as to divert me from my intention of sitting beside him and causing an irreversible scandal.

Several weeks of Wahid's resistance and tactfulness have worn me down, as he knows. We're so telepathically attuned that each of us can usually tell when the other is preoccupied. The time has finally come to bring up the touchy matter, in his mind, of what to call me. I have invited him to address me as Connie, which he has refused to do, finding it too familiar for an employee to use with a boss. Next, I suggest that he call me Ms. Shaw, since he seems to be vacillating between the term "Mem" which we both detest and not using any name at all. He decides to address me as "Mrs. Connie."

He probably thinks that this, like the Chinese reversal of surname and given name, is correct but I cannot dissuade him from "Mrs. Connie" which to me, has unfortunate overtones of southern American plantation days when Luke was employed by Miss Martha. It occurs to me, however, that Wahid is fully aware of American surname usage since he always calls Jim "Mr. Wright" rather than "Mr. Jim." In any event, I am now Mrs. Connie to Wahid and his family, whether I like it or not and am forced to quell any raised eyebrows of my own friends who overhear him address me this way by shooting daggers toward them which mean "don't-you-dare-laugh-at-him-because-that's-what-he-wants-to-call-me."

However, as soon as my friends and associates observe the respectful way in which Wahid and I treat each other they realize that this is no ordinary driver-Mem relationship but that something is taking place on another level entirely which is neither sexual, employer-employee, or distant and unconscious. Rather, it is extra-conscious and aware and has elements of a brother-sister interaction at times and at other times it has the hallmarks of teacher-student, with each of us changing roles, depending upon what is transpiring in our lives. It simply doesn't fit into any category and we are both paying close attention to what this situation has to teach us. One of my favorite expressions from the Course is, "Teach only love for that is what you are." ACIM, T P 87, 94

Mr. Lee, our slender young entrepreneurial landlord is meeting me at the empty rental house today to negotiate furnishings and appliances. Because of the acute housing shortage in Singapore this drab, old fashioned four bedroom house commands a rent of more than three times its stateside value. It's considered an enormous find, since most Singaporeans are apartment dwellers. We stroll about the house discussing the need for armoires, since the houses have no closets. He tells me that he has engaged a kaboon, or gardener, named Kim Sing, but that I will have to hire an amah myself to do the housework.

There is, mercifully, a huge lush jungle area behind the house which will absorb ubiquitous pile driver noises and construction crane din for which Singapore is infamous. Banana trees, a stream and a kampong cluster of ramshackle houses lie in the shallow ravine below our stilted home in a tangle of greenery. One of the odd things about homes in the Maryland Estates is that the back yard is made entirely of concrete over stilts and the front tiled patio gives onto a token entry yard about the size of a beach blanket. A six foot brick wall and black wrought iron gate enclose the front yard and driveway. Like all houses here there are no window or balcony screens whatever and heavy iron grillwork confines every door and window to discourage what Mr. Lee calls "petty thieves who are tempted by seeming great wealth."

Mr. Lee announces that he has shopped in the local furniture stores, as we have, and has also found that indeed the local beds are built for shorter Chinese bodies and that he realizes Jim's tall six-foot-one-inch frame would hang over the edge. He has therefore engaged someone to build an American size bed for us and has ordered a clothes washer and dryer. Mr. Lee confides that since he is thirty-two years old and single, living with his mother, he has seldom looked into these furniture matters and has learned a great deal. "My Mum takes good care of me," he chuckles then nervously concludes our business and wafts his elegantly attired body into his new gray Mercedes.

In an afterthought he rolls down the window and calls out "By the way, I'm also in steel construction equipment and in electronic acupuncture equipment in case you have any needs in those areas. It's very good steel from Korea. Very cheap too. Anyhow, just call me straightaway to make an order." With that he waves and zooms off to another appointment.

The sign at 21 Scott's Road says American Club, Private Drive, Members Only. It strikes me that this sort of sign is rather ironic since Americans have historically prized the sort of open society that gives everyone a fair chance and access to goods and services. Jim's company has graciously provided us a membership to the club which is valued by both Americans and Singaporeans alike for its restaurants and swimming pool, bowling alley, gym, slot machines, ballroom, bingo games, library and numerous outstanding classes and tours. The outings and trips are organized by the American Women's Auxiliary, a worldwide organization that assists families with quick, intelligent adjustments to overseas living. Outside the sprawling building there are scores of Mercedes autos parked along the sloping drive - a testimony to the membership which is largely one of highly placed corporate executives and their sophisticated spouses and families.

Drivers gather in clusters on the grass to gossip or to nap in the heat while awaiting the return of their Mems. After showing my membership card to the guard at the entrance I'm struck by surprise and delight that the air-con coolness inside is like a soothing mentholated liquid salve on a wound. As I pass through the dining room, on my way to the library, I notice efficient uniformed waiters in burgundy and navy livery, smile in welcome to their regular customers. Walking in the hallway outside the bowling alley, I encounter two "oil wives" (married to men working on rigs in the oil fields) pumping coins into the slot machines. They alternately swear and drag on the cigarettes which dangle from their glossy red lips. In the turquoise swimming pool below the dining room windows, babies and their mothers splash delightedly in the cold clear water, as the equatorial heat steams and shimmers the pool pavement. A few feet from the oil wives, on a hallway sofa, a missionary and his wife spread maps out, discussing a recent trip to Borneo.

Through the open door of the downstairs library I can see Kala, the pretty young Indian librarian sitting at her entry desk reading a novel. As I show my temporary ID card, introduce myself, and inquire about library hours and rules, Kala smiles and rearranges her fuchsia-colored sari. As she moves her head in animation, the rhinestone in her nostril glitters appealingly and her thick dark braid ropes down across her shoulder and dangles back and forth over her stamp pad.

"The rules are very lax here," she laughs. "Just don't play your radio or eat your lunch here. You can take as many books as you like. If you have any requests I'll order books and magazines for you but it takes between two and four months to get packages from the States as you probably know. You'll probably do a lot of reading during your stay in Singapore. Most Americans carry books with them everywhere they go because of the long queues at banks, taxi stands and the post office."

We chat a bit more before I hungrily peruse the shelves of this main source of free reading material for the next year. Kala tells me how fortunate she feels regarding her work in that she is paid to read novels all day. "The only problem is that the books make me a bit dissatisfied with my life, if you see what I mean." She remembers to tell me that there is an exceptionally good book store chain called MPH which has an extensive collection of travel books as well as the latest titles in psychology, religion, philosophy and metaphysics, as well as photography, art and literature. I make a mental note to investigate a few of the nearby bookstores this week.

My roving inspection of the American Club library leads me to conclude that there are about ten thousand volumes which include some very obscure titles about Asia, an overwhelming percentage of romantic and adventure novels, a detective/spy thriller section, a few atlases, some classics, children's books in dilapidated condition, numerous newspapers and magazines and a few art books and art magazines. The reading diet of many Americans here, if this small room is any indication, seems to be heavily weighted in the carbohydrate and dessert categories of reading tastes. The section on religion and spirituality is sparse to non-existent.

Readily acknowledging to myself that reading has always been an addiction, I wonder if the hundred books that I've brought over will last even five months. I've always managed to devour five books a week since I was in elementary school, regardless of a full-time work load, family duties, journal-keeping, community board work, travel, a large correspondence and occasional appearances on radio and TV shows.

Singapore
May 1st

Today is May first which is Labor Day in Singapore and May Day in Russia. It is also Jim's thirty-sixth birthday. We have celebrated his birthday, equipped the kitchen and started unpacking the wok, dishes and household items that will get us started in the new house. We are elated at the smooth transition we're making and wonder why more Americans and Europeans don't have the foresight that we've displayed in renting a nice large breezy house instead of a stuffy high-rise apartment. The overhead fan putt-putts the moist warm air around the open room while Jim reads on the sofa and I kneel on the cool marble floor experimenting with new oil paints on a seascape of the harbor.

From time to time our reveries are interrupted by the hawking and spitting of the Chinese grandfather next door who sounds as if he's in the room with us due to the acoustics of marble, tile and concrete in both houses. Next door the children of the Indian Member of Parliament play badminton and soccer with hoots and shrieks of jubilation. The concrete back yards reverberate every sound in the neighborhood.

Later in the evening while Jim and I cook dinner, two eight-inch chartreuse "chik-chak" lizards skitter in the window and scramble along the ceiling. Having a dozen in the house is not unusual so at least I'm past the screaming stage on seeing them and realize that absolutely everyone here has them, despite meticulous daily house cleaning. There are no screens in Singapore and it's too hot to keep the windows closed in the tropics.

Deciding to turn in early, I say good night to Jim and proceed up the terrazzo stairway to our bedroom. As I turn on the light, I'm greeted by a three-inch brown shiny cock-roach which waves its antennae at me from the nightstand next to my pillow. After four sharp shrieks, I emit a string of angry explosive words. Jim dashes upstairs to the rescue. Drat! Is it really necessary to have a zoo right in our own house? More to the point, is it possible to not have one in this sultry tropical clime with water and jungle all around?

Jim hugs me and laughs gently, saying, "You'll get used to all the bugs. We can spray." But he knows that I don't believe in killing insects. Of course it's been easy to live by my "non-violence principles" in Colorado where we have very few insects due to the dry climate. We turn off the light and snuggle into our sleeping positions.

In the darkness I feel something rustle under my nightgown. It moves across my chest toward my throat. I yowl and levitate four feet off the bed, stiffly horizontal, while yanking the lamp string. My howling hopping voodoo dance routs the culprit. An outraged cockroach jumps out the scooped neck of my nightgown and leaps onto the headboard before disappearing. Fuming, I march into the bathroom to get a drink of water, switch on the light to find a two-inch cockroach cheerily sitting on my toothbrush. Oh-yuck. Yecchh. By now I've become temporarily insane and jump up and down on the tile floor like a mad woman to Jim's utter consternation. It doesn't help my pique that he reminds me that today's lesson in *A Course In Miracles* is "I am not the victim of the world I see." ACIM, WB P 38

"This is impossible! We've got to do something. I can't live like this," I state emphatically. A tap-tap sound whaps outside the bedroom window. Upon investigation it turns out to be a fruit bat and I notice that the moonlit sky outside the window is silhouetted with a score of wheeling, darting bats. We decide to solve the invader problem of the moment by closing the windows and using the bedroom's tiny air-conditioner while we sleep. Safeguarding the rest of the house from beast invasions remains a challenge, however. I simply have to find an amah, or housekeeper, to help with the daily invasion of tropical reptiles and insects.

Singapore
May 3rd

This first week of May brings surprise to our gate in the form of a smiling Malay amah named Mariam, which she pronounces Mahd ee AHM. Mariam is a bony, petite forty-three year old whose life struggle causes her to look ten years older than her actual age. A shiny gold front tooth twinkles in her wrinkled dark face, with its cloudy brown eyes. Her heavy black hair hangs to the waist of her baju kurung traditional dress that covers all but her face, hands and feet. Her long-sleeved over blouse and sarong is a cheerful orange printed silk that matches the orange umbrella she carries in case of sudden downpours which are frequent now. Her voice is high and thin and she speaks a passable broken English. She holds a sheaf of "introduction papers" and references from past employers and says she has heard that I need an amah for my housework and that I have no children living at home now. She states that she would like to have the job. She often lapses into Singlish, or Singapore English with the suffix "lah" for emphasis. "This is very good job, Mem. Not too much work-lah. Mariam do good for you, Mem." Mariam tells me that she was married at thirteen, bore her first child at fourteen and that her daughter is now twenty-nine and has five babies, despite Singapore's policy of two children per family. There is no doubt that Mariam, as she artfully tells her story, has made a calculated point about her hard life, designed to gain my sympathy. She perpetually smiles coquettishly. However, I have an odd hesitant feeling about her that I cannot place. A fleeting thought that she is untrustworthy and dishonest flashes across my mind and is immediately dismissed. I am desperate and hire her.

We agree that Mariam will begin tomorrow and I plan my schedule accordingly. But on the appointed day Mariam fails to arrive, due, she says later, to heavy rains. She comes the next two days and works hard, scrubbing the floors and walls, as is customary, because of the constant arrival of ants, lizards, birds and roaches that fly in through the open, screen-less windows. The next day Mariam fails to arrive because her mother is sick and thus, my business appointments must all be re-arranged. The next time Mariam comes she cleans and prepares a curry. The following day she fails to appear due to a headache. The day after that she fails to show up because her daughter is having another baby. My patience has worn thin and when she finally arrives I tell her that I feel that I have been more than fair and that if she is to continue in my employ, I expect punctuality and dependability henceforth. As we speak I head for the door with briefcase in hand to go to the American Embassy to do some work which has been postponed several days since she has continually stood me up. She looks alarmed and tugs at my dress gently, looking as if she's about to cry.

"Oh Mem! Don't leave Mariam. Mariam will do very good for you. How many days you be gone, Mem?"

"What? I'm not going on a trip, Mariam. Where did you get that idea? I'm just going to the American Embassy for a few hours to do some work.

"No, Mem. Mariam sees suitcase. Mem has clothes in suitcase so Mem is going away," she announces proudly, like a detective who has produced an incriminating bit of evidence.

Suddenly it dawns on me that Mariam has never seen a large-size Samsonite briefcase, especially carried by a woman, and that she indeed feels guilty and thinks I'm leaving.

"This isn't a suitcase Mariam. It's a briefcase. See? Look inside - only papers inside."

"Why Madame has suitcase just for papers?" she asks, amazed that any papers could be so important as to warrant their own large and expensive suitcase.

"This is a special suitcase for papers so the papers will stay clean and not get dusty or bent or ruined in the rain. It rains every day here in Singapore and it's very important that these papers stay dry."

"Very funny, Mem. Very, very funny. Suitcase for papers! Only to keep papers dry. Very funny. Oh Mariam so happy Madame is not leaving Mariam!" She slaps her thigh and throws her head back and forth so that the light catches her gold front tooth and the sheen of her parted black hair.

In the car I tell Wahid my concern that charming Mariam is taking advantage of my patience and generosity and that I've been a sucker for her pathetic sob stories. He says that there are many amahs like Mariam who fail to show up for work and go from employer to employer, working when they feel like it with little sense of responsibility. Some of the employers write glowing references just to rid themselves of incompetent parasitic amahs. He mentions something that I've heard elsewhere, which is that Chinese amahs often steal from their employers whereas Malays tend to have a very casual attitude toward work. Wahid tells me that his thirty-eight year old sister, Fatima, is a good worker and might be able to assist me temporarily though she speaks no English. Since English is the official language of Singapore and I don't yet know Malay or Chinese I feel unwilling to drop the language requirement for a future Amah. He says that her outstanding cooking should make up for lack of English. "Mrs. Connie, Fatima makes very good horse meat," he says proudly, to impress me.

Startled, I reply, "Horse meat?!"

"Yes, it's very good. Mem should try it if you have not."

The next day Mariam fails to arrive and I interview throughout the weeks a number of amahs who display the same pattern. Meanwhile the equatorial heat wrings buckets of perspiration out of me and I find that Singapore is a three-baths-a-day place for those without air-conditioning and the laundry is mounting up alarmingly with a hamper full of three sets of soggy underwear and dresses for each day of the week. Furthermore, the heat and humidity, combined with the relentless armies of insects and my schedule of writing, travel and work, mean that dependable household help is essential. So far in this brain-numbing heat, I've found only two air-conditioned places to write - the American Embassy and the library at the American Club.

Another frustration adds itself to the dilemma. A thick gray mold, like a luxurious squirrel fur, is growing on my typing paper and books, leather belts and camera straps, the chopsticks and even the crystal glassware. Black mildew is beginning to pool on the ceilings and I am suspicious that this newly painted house is situated in a humidity pocket next to the jungle which exacerbates a problem shared by people who have no air-conditioning. The Straits Times ran a story today about the cholera epidemic which has killed sixty Singaporeans this month. This is a final top-off to a frustrating pile-up of aggravations. My daily lessons in *A Course In Miracles* have improved my attitude to the extent that I'm coping with these circumstances better than I would have in years past but I'm chagrined and bemused that they still bother me. And, despite my affirmations about the insects and critters, they still persist.

Determined not to give up living in the house so easily but perplexed as to how to resolve its many unsatisfactory aspects, I ponder various solutions while strolling about the National Museum of Art. Its two floors house a modest collection of Straits Chinese costumes, furniture, porcelain and jade and an aboriginal Malay display in addition to a modern painting gallery. Three types of aboriginal Malays are featured in an upper room containing artifacts such as blow-guns (still used in nearby Malaysia), pouches, wood combs, bark cloth, mats, drums, axes, fishing spears, bamboo-incised water holders and poison dart quivers.

Photographs of nude aboriginals, Senoi and Negritos line the walls next to the glass cases. Intrigued by some silk embroidered Chines robes downstairs that contrast so highly with the Malay blowpipes, I continue wandering about the old building admiring Indonesian shadow puppets and masks, antique brass and a kriss collection of wavy daggers. China has haunted me since I was a child and the Chinese artifacts here only fan the flame of the old desire to wander throughout that beguiling country. Actually, China is only about three hours by jet from Singapore. There's nothing that should prevent my going to China now. Finally I can begin my search for the Teacher which my Guidance told me is in Asia.

In an air-conditioned wing of the National Museum of Art, I discover the most ancient and priceless pieces of the museum. These include gray stone-carved Buddhas, Chinese porcelain, and red, Asian textiles. There are no Asian visitors in the museum at this time, but the other Americans who stroll about talk among themselves in animated appreciation of the unique assemblage of pots. The pottery collection ranges from the delicate luminous green Sawankoloke Wares of the Middle Ages through Vietnamese blue-on-white stoneware and dark Kmer wares.

Upon reaching the last hall, the Jade Room, my senses are sated but I'm surprised and delighted to see ten shades of jade represented in superb format. The informative signs tell me that the Chinese loosely classified quartz and other semi-precious stones as jade and used them with stunning effect in their fanciful carvings of birds, dragons, deer, scholars and fish. Inside the glass cases there are vases of crystal and urns of rusty cinnabar red, aquamarine blue, chocolate brown, celery green, olive green, pink, gray, white, yellow and inky black.

As I search my memory for the three ways to discern a genuine piece of jade I wonder absent-mindedly if it might be possible to book a trip to China soon, although I've only been in Asia about a month. Then I encounter a showcase sign which confirms that jade is real if:

1. It has a clear, ringing tone when struck.
2. It has a hardness when scratched.
3. It lacks spots or blemishes when held up to the light.

Art, like meditation and nature, has always returned me to a sense of balance and inner peace. The museum has satisfied my need for a sense of order and beauty in my life during this transition to a foreign culture where I am a minority and everything is strange. With the same sigh of satisfaction one feels after a superb meal, I skip down the marble steps and wave farewell to the museum guard.

Back in the car, I enthusiastically describe the museum to Wahid, who has never been inside, and who declined my invitation to come with me. He feels it is not his place to be visiting museums while he's supposed to be working, even though I have explained that the museums are air-conditioned and he'd be more comfortable inside than sitting out under a tree in the merciless heat simply waiting for me. His response is that he's used to the heat and never notices it but realizes that Westerners have quite a time adjusting to the climate. He has concluded, that he probably would react adversely to the fierce cold which he has heard exists in the U.S.

He asks me to describe snow, which he can hardly imagine. He wonders if it is like moth flakes or even feathers, only cold. The moth flake analogy strikes me as quite imaginative and I add that sometimes snow when it is falling seems like tiny thin, flat, frozen flowers or chips or mosaics. Sometimes it's heavy and wet and other times dry and powdery. In Colorado, I explain, we have some of the best snow for skiing in the whole United States. But the very idea of zooming down mountains covered with big icy piles of cold moth crystals is quite beyond Wahid.

The marker in my ever-present book in the back seat lies on page 389 of *An Autobiography* by Frank Lloyd Wright, which I resume reading, while Wahid contemplates snow and mountains. I'm reading the section called "Honorable Interval" and chuckle at his discussion of consistency. I've been wrestling with the idea of chucking consistency and heading for the cooler temperatures of China rather than frustrating myself further with insect hoards, mold, mildew, floods and rainstorms, amahs and the cholera epidemic.

Wright says, in the passage, "That word consistency! It is seldom the word for the imaginative man of action, is it? I sincerely believe I have not been very "consistent." Off on holiday too often. But direction has never changed nor development hindered. I've always returned refreshed for the work in hand - having learned much more from every "aside" than from the "line" itself." AA P 389

Something about Wright's writing clicks for me. That settles it. I'm going to China. Jim is happily absorbed in his work and has a pleasant air-conditioned office with an efficient staff to assist him. He encourages me to travel and has always been very self-sufficient regarding his own meals and laundry.

Then, in my imagination, I review the worst alternative scenarios that might occur if I were to set off to China:

1. Nothing unusual or wildly different would happen. It would be a pleasant trip.

2. The trip might be slightly inconvenient or uncomfortable but that, after all, is part of the adventure of travel. Besides, I've spent nine years of my life living overseas and have so far traveled in 40 countries so what could possibly happen? Not to worry.

3. There might be some genuine excitement which I would weather, as I always have.

4. The worst that could possibly happen, in my mind, is that I couldn't go alone because of political restrictions, and would have to book a tour wherein none of my companions would speak English. But that seems highly unlikely. In any event, it could be an interesting challenge.

On the positive side, I could search for the Holy Being who is supposed to be on earth. Surely He's in China or India. I'd get a much needed rest of several weeks after having spent the past few months involved in packing, moving and unpacking as well as in negotiating the bureaucratic labyrinth of Singapore for residency papers, driver's license, visa, university course registration, medical record filing and piles of other documents.

Yes, I will definitely go to China. As we drive along the immaculate, shaded boulevards of Singapore, I mention to Wahid that I'd like to stop by a few travel agencies to pick up literature for China. He is immediately attentive.

"You mean China for yourself? Just you?!" He's incredulous that I'd go so far alone in Asia, especially without my husband or a friend or relative. He tells me that he's never even been outside Singapore except for a few short trips to Malacca, Malaysia, to visit his wife's aunt since travel authorization is very difficult for most Singaporeans. Strict government regulations prevent pleasure travel for all but those who are over thirty years old who have government connections and permission to go abroad backed by assurances they will return.

He does his best to convince me that it might be dangerous to travel around Asia as a Western woman alone. I reassure him that I've traveled the world my entire life and have very few fears. Furthermore, I tell myself, I'll hopefully return to Singapore in a better frame of mind, with a more appreciative heart after experiencing China. China it will be.

As we drive to the travel agency, a thrashing rainstorm vents its fury overhead without warning, banging outdoor restaurant furniture against balcony rails and deluging building interiors with torrents of water. Rain in the tropics doesn't sizzle the sidewalk as it does in the West, but roars and smashes everything in its wake. It clatters mercilessly on rooftops sending sluices over gutters, sidewalks and roads. Rivers and lakes appear from nowhere to drown dry land and to overwhelm the gigantic canals and storm drains lining main streets. Thunder crashes and erupts from roiling black clouds which rumble menacingly low on the landscape. Tree limbs are flung out over the ground like missiles and sidewalks quickly become littered with a wet mat of refuse from shredded shrubs and palms.

A tenacious wind snatches laundry from clotheslines and rips the garments before tossing them like wet rags against the wall. Pedestrians in crosswalks gasp as their skirts are whipped overhead, blinding and confusing them. They wheel round and round in panic and embarrassment, as their white cotton slips are drenched in seconds. They stagger, calf-deep in flood-waters, clutching their purses, coiffures and dress hemlines alternately.

Surprised at the fury of the storm, I realize that I know little about the climate of China. I wish I had done more reading about China before now, but it's too late. Hopefully the weather will be less dramatic there than in Singapore. At last I will be able to pursue my spiritual quest. Where is God-in-human-form Who was in my vision as I stepped on the soil of Singapore?

CHAPTER 4
CHASTISEMENT IN HONG KONG

"The greatness of an individual depends on the cultural perfection he has attained. Culture does not connote mere diligence. It means the removal of evil thoughts and propensities, and the promotion of good thoughts and qualities." SBIB, P 2

Singapore
June 1, 1981

Crowds of Chinese are jammed shoulder to shoulder at the Singapore airport as I press my way toward the departure area in search of my Ik Chin tour group to China. So far I haven't spotted anyone else wearing the round blue and yellow Ik Chin badge which I received three days ago. I spontaneously decided to take a three week tour of nine Chinese cities with an imminently departing group of about sixteen Singaporeans. I had called ten travel agencies, all of which had full tours except Ik Chin, which could take me if I made an immediate deposit and could be ready to leave in sixty-two hours. Perhaps I'm being rash to head impulsively for China having only arrived from the States six weeks ago.

"By the way, you'll be the only Westerner on the tour," the pretty travel agent had mentioned tentatively, to gauge my reaction.

"That's fine," I replied. "In fact, I'd rather travel with Singaporeans so that I can see China through their eyes and get the true flavor of the country. Believe me, I'd much prefer to see Asia with Asians if at all possible and I certainly don't expect to see America transplanted wherever I go."

She had smiled and seemed relieved. "Would it be a problem if they didn't speak English?"

"I don't imagine that it would, as long as I have an English-speaking guide. Part of the fee does pay for an English-speaking guide, doesn't it?"

"Yes, of course. No problem. I am sure that our Singaporeans will take good care of you, too, so not to worry Madame."

Now it was my turn to smile, unaccustomed to being addressed as "Madame" (pronounced Mohd um with the gravity and respect once accorded to English women when Singapore was a British colony.). The term, although meant to confer politeness and dignity, had a feeling of ladylike anachronism to it and felt prissy and stifling. Hopefully living in Singapore would not be stifling or confining in any way. In my imagination I recollected images of myself engaging in my customary adventuresome activities. For example, climbing the Colorado Rockies outfitted with tents and backpacks. On one trip throughout Europe, a friend and I huddled in sleeping bags on the spray-soaked deck of an Adriatic ferry amid hoards of Yugoslavian peasants. My life had taken me to remote caves, to pyramids and great monuments, to primitive tribes and secluded beaches. There had been trips to dozens of countries as well as the challenges of my daily life as a management consultant wherein I had provided CEO's and U.S. Army officers with consulting assistance on personnel policy.

As I browsed through glossy tour brochures while talking with the travel agent, more images of my travels and work sprang to mind, such as exploring Mayan ruins in the Yucatan jungles. In the field of women's rights, I had addressed a convention crowd of three thousand people on social issues in our rapidly changing world. Just before moving to Singapore, I had taken flying lessons and had obtained a ham radio license. No, I mused, I'm definitely not the Madame type, but there's no point in taking issue with the term or its implications.

"Here you are, then," the Ik Chin travel agent had said crisply. "You'll have to start packing immediately if you're to leave for China with the Singaporean Chinese group in only sixty-two hours. 'Bye now and have a wonderful trip. I'm sure you'll be well taken care of with our countrymen to fill you in on Chinese culture." She waved after handing me the travel packet and vouchers and I backed out the door with a happy, jumpy feeling of anticipation in my heart. *Will I find You in China, Lord? How long will it take me to discover You?*

Still searching the airport crowd for anyone wearing the same circular Ik Chin tour badge, I sigh and once again remove the trip itinerary from my purse along with the Ik Chin brochures. Suddenly, there's a stir and a cluster of excited people emerge from the larger airport crowd. The Singaporean China-bound group is composed of two distinct sub-groups. The first group is "Old Style" Chinese couples wearing traditional Cheong Sam apparel, or loose silk pajama overblouses worn with silk trousers of black or brown and black felt slippers. The second group is comprised of their very chic adult children, who are "New Style" Chinese, dressed in the latest Western fashion. The older couples wear the tour badge and nervously check and double check their tote bags, boarding passes and carry-on luggage. They shout to those standing next to them in what sounds to my uninitiated ears like harsh, barking Cantonese dialects. Upon spotting my yellow tour pin they noisily nudge each other and stare. The older women tell their thirtyish daughters to inquire.

In well-modulated British English, several pretty daughters inquire for their mild, shy parents if I am by any chance going to Hong Kong and China with the Ik Chin tour which leaves momentarily. I nod and smile. A young woman, one of the daughters who'll stay behind, comes forth to act as the spontaneous interpreter for the group. Without preamble or introduction, she looks me over, peers at my badge, hears my affirmative answer, notes my brochures and nods to the others, who look horrified.

Young woman: "Yes, yes, she is! She is part of the Ik Chin China Tour group."

All of them are excited now and loudly talk at once, saying that there must be some mistake since there is no husband or father within sight to accompany the foreign lady (me).

Everyone knows that women simply can't and don't travel alone. What kind of a father or husband would let his wife travel all by herself?. It's unheard of. Surely her husband is somewhere in the airport and they will travel as a couple.

Young woman "But alone? All alone?! No one accompanies you?!" They are obviously incredulous at the situation. Here we go again. Asian women never travel alone. Never.

Connie: "Yes, I'm alone. My husband had hoped to come but he has to work and I'm on vacation so I came by myself."

They nod, then translate rapidly to the curious group.

Young woman:" You are the only Westerner on the whole tour. Do you know that?" She asks with a twinkle and a smile, expecting a shocked reaction.

Connie: "Yes, I know. I prefer it that way, actually. That way I can get to know some Chinese people by traveling with them."

Young woman: "You do? Really? Our parents are taking the trip, but we are not. They don't speak English, but they understand a tiny bit."

It seems that I'll be the youngest person on the trip to China. Closest in age to me are an attractive Chinese couple who are also in their thirties, named Danny and Yu Lan Loh, and a plumpish Chinese man who is about forty named Jimmy Ng. The three of them are friendly and speak the best English in the group.

More excited talk follows. The cluster moves forward now, inspecting me minutely, from hair roots to shoe soles. Suddenly I am acutely aware of the unadorned American simplicity of my appearance compared to their fashionable opulence. Both older and younger women wear an abundance of genuine jade bracelets and pendants and gold rings, chains and earrings. The daughters sport the finest Parisian dress and shoe brands, or Hong Kong knock-off look-alikes and fresh manicures and elegant coiffures. In my plain floral blue print sundress I seem at last to pass muster. They expertly take in, with a visual sweep, my simple shoulder purse, unpretentious shoes, freshly-coifed shoulder length curly hair, manicured fingers and toes and light makeup. They themselves are impeccably groomed and seem relieved that I am, also.

After their glance rakes me down to the floor, they rake me up to the scalp again, this time smiling and nodding their approval. Since I happen to be a head taller than anyone in the entire group of sixteen, excepting three men and a woman, they must lift their chins to look into my eyes and beam at me. At five feet five inches, my height appears considerable in this crowd. It is an odd feeling, after having been considered small to medium most of my life, to suddenly seem a giant here in Asia. This must be how American men feel, gazing over the heads of a crowd.

These sudden reversals of relative reality brought about by travel are not only amusing, but helpful to one's perspective and mental health, I feel. What a glorious sensation - being taller than all these men! I could crow except that Jim, the true giant is a constant reminder of my "real Western size." Then the realization hits me that we are not our bodies and that size is of no consequence, therefore why should I be feeling elated at suddenly being taller than other people? After all, we aren't our bodies, minds or emotions - we only have them. The ego asserts itself again, when given half a chance.

At this point I'm reminded of Ram Dass, the well-known American author, lecturer and spiritual teacher. In his radio interviews he often said that we're all trained by our society to be Somebody. This is a no-win game because there will always be a Somebody who is more of a Somebody than you. If you keep striving in that direction of being Somebody you'll eventually drive yourself crazy.

There are fifteen people on this tour besides myself and we're told that a Mr. Lo from Beijing will join us in Guangzhou, China. Mr. and Mrs. Sun are the tallest couple, fiftyish and wear Christian medals on chains. A strikingly beautiful, elegant and dignified white-haired woman of seventy-seven dressed in black slacks and slippers and gray jacket is accompanied by her tall slender son of about forty-five. She is Mrs. Lim and he is a handsome farmer-musician, Neo Lam Heng (Neo rhymes with Cleo). Next are Jimmy Ng and his parents, then Danny and Yu Lan Loh, Mrs. Muey Low, Miss Tan, Miss Wu, Mrs. Fu and extremely tall, gangling Mr. Wee with his short, demure wife, Mrs. Wee.

The gates and doors swing open and the passengers surge forward, the chirping timid group of Ik Chin travelers weaving along behind me. As soon as we are seated aboard the plane we are served a pink perfumed face cloth, chilled, to refresh our hands and faces. Next, orange juice. From the overhead storage loft I take a blanket and pillow, placing the pillow behind my back.

From the corner of my eye I notice that from two rows of seats across the aisle there follows a flurry of blankets and pillows being taken from overhead by my Ik Chin companions who scrutinize my every action. The menu card peeks out of the elasticized seat pocket in front of me so I pluck it out to read. Everyone else takes theirs out, but I notice that some of the women are holding theirs upside down. In a flash of realization it occurs to me that my companions have not flown before and are copying my every move. Perhaps they are also illiterate since they stare with furrowed brows at the menu card and chatter excitedly among themselves.

The awareness of my new role creates more alertness to my own actions lest I mislead them inadvertently. As lunch is served with Western cutlery rather than with chopsticks, I begin to eat, as always, with my left hand. I have always been left-handed, though left-handedness in Asians is extremely rare. In fact, left-handedness is considered rude, unfortunate and usually tragic since the left hand is reserved for "toilet functions." Hence, one never shakes hands or offers a business card or other article with the left hand without risk of extreme insult to the other party. However, all six gray-haired Chinese women within view of me begin to eat with their left hands as they copy my actions. They despair of knife and fork and mutter to themselves in vexation until they hit upon a solution. They put their fork in their left hand and their spoon in their right hand, simultaneously.

They save the butter and pudding dessert until last and by mutual consent, proceed to skewer and eat the butter with their knives. This proves such an efficient process that they lean across the row of triple seats to confer, and again decide to devour the pudding with knife as well. They innocently lick their knives with great pleasure, smacking their lips and burping with unconscious abandon in satisfaction. Then they dust crumbs off of their bosoms and rearrange their gold and jade bracelets, watches and earrings and remove their shoes for the long flight ahead. The women have intrigued me, considering that they are obviously not poor, yet seem to have led somewhat sheltered lives, judging by their unfamiliarity with airplanes and Western cutlery. Surely they will have similar thoughts about me and my unconscious gaffs owing to my unfamiliarity with Asia.

A vague sense of uneasiness floods me at the realization that we are quickly leaving Westernized Singapore and its holdovers of British colonialism. Soon it will be my turn to be the foreigner amid chopsticks, Cantonese and Mandarin street signs and table manners as strange to me as mine are to them. Perhaps I should have curbed my enthusiastic desire to see China so soon after arrival in Singapore so that I might first do an in-depth study of Chinese culture and prepare intelligently for the trip, as I normally do before embarking on a journey abroad. But it's too late. I'm eager to find God in human embodiment.

A pert stewardess moves down the aisle distributing disembarkation cards to be filled in by all passengers. After finishing my card I glance up to see six pair of eyes beseeching me.

"No can write," smiles a woman named Mrs. Muey Low. "You write." Unbelievably, they are all illiterate in both Chinese and English.

She hands me the cards and tells me the name of each woman, then gestures that they will each place an "X" in their own hand on their cards as the final authoritative embellishment to my English printing. They giggle and take great pride in making very large, distinguished X's next to their printed names. They all nod in triumph, smile and exhale in great relief to be past this latest hurdle. My heart goes out to them in sympathy and I pat the nearest woman on the shoulder and tell her "never mind," an expression that is constantly used in Singapore by the Chinese.

Mrs. Muey Low leans over and says, laboriously, "You berry clebber," meaning very clever. "Tank you," she giggles and her friends applaud her English.

Our tiny guide, a Chinese Singaporean named Karen, bounces along the aisle in black slacks and yellow jersey to inquire about our comfort. She announces her name and position and then tells me she is nineteen and that this is her first job. She lives with her mother in Singapore.

"You are having fun? You are happy?" she asks, concerned that I am enjoying myself, especially since I'm the only Westerner on the tour and have no friend or seat-mate to talk with.

"Yes, I am having fun. I am happy." Jubilant, in fact, to be flying to China, and in such a down-home and Old-Style Chinese way, with kind, simple, unpretentious people. A lifelong dream is materializing in a surprising way. Hopefully this long-awaited trip will be valuable in every sense.

In the seat behind me, an American teenager shows a tattoo of a dragon on his forearm to his seat companion, a Chinese businessman. "My Mom was furious when I got the tattoo," he says. "She said that 'a tattoo is permanent proof of temporary insanity!' But I like it and have no regrets."

Hong Kong
June 1, 1981

Eventually after about three hours, the glistening skyscrapers of Hong Kong, or Fragrant Harbor, swing into view beneath the silver wing. The Singaporean women across the aisle clap their ears and make alarmed little yelps at the sudden changes in cabin pressure during our rapid descent. Perhaps this is indeed their first plane trip. The green hills of the Fragrant Harbor are a glorious sight after the flatness of Singapore, but the overall architectural effect is no match for our own Orchid City, as Singapore is called. The fact that there's more space between Singapore's skyscrapers also helps. These buildings, to my eye, lack the architectural variety of Singapore's and seem rather like the upended shoe box skyscrapers of New York, Denver or Los Angeles in conception. Some of the Hong Kong buildings have turned black with mildew and air pollution. They stand packed together claustrophobically next to cranes, pile drivers and other bits of construction flotsam and jetsam. The dirt and unrelieved ugliness of parts of Hong Kong cause me to fervently hope that majestic Singapore will never deteriorate to this state. Since Singapore is a benevolent dictatorship, however, there are strict laws to prevent visual deterioration of architecture and infrastructure.

A bus arrives to take our group to the Ambassador Hotel and chubby, gray-haired Mrs. Muey Low, my roommate, accompanies me to our double room. We hastily unpack before dinner and as I hang clothes in the wardrobe, the unlocked door to our room opens without knock or ceremony and in troop three of Mrs. Low's rotund, middle-aged companions: Miss Tan, Miss Wu and Mrs. Fu.

They immediately inspect our bedspreads, curtains, rugs and furniture. Next they walk over to the closet and peer inside it to see what I've hung on hangers. They walk into the bathroom, make comments, come back into the bedroom, nod and then abruptly leave. A glance at my watch reveals that we need to grab the room key from the bed and immediately join the group for the short walk to the restaurant where we'll have dinner.

We are ushered into the Capital Restaurant and Night Club down the street from the hotel by weary, frozen-faced waiters who appear to have long ago lost any natural enthusiasm for tourists. Two round tables for ten await our group of sixteen and delicious food is brought instantly. We dine Chinese style, without napkins or Western cutlery. I am a novice at using chopsticks. Conversations are shouted simultaneously in Teo Chew, Hokkien, Hainanese and Cantonese. Finally there is a call to order by Danny Loh, unrelated to Mrs. Muey Low, to decide what to do about the American.

"Most Chinese are named Low or Lee or Tan," Danny laughs. "In Singapore we have 80,000 Tans (pronounced Tahn) in the Tan Clan Society for example." Danny Loh speaks the best English in the group, followed by Jimmy Ng. Danny is a slender tailor who owns his own shop and is traveling with his wife, Yu Lan, a pretty, elegantly dressed woman in her late-thirties. Her full lips periodically push into an exquisite pout, like a gorgeous spoiled child. She is lively, animated and amusing. Stout Jimmy Ng is a driver for an American family who live at the Ardmore Park high rise apartment complex; he is accompanying his parents to China.

Danny, Jimmy and Yu Lan decide that whoever sits next to me at each meal will tell me the names of each dish and take some food from each serving plate and put it on my dish or in my bowl. Eager to learn, I thank them in immense relief and explain that I'm brand new in Asia and haven't yet mastered using chopsticks to move masses of food from serving dish to plate. Across the table, lanky, silver-haired Mr. Wee - tall and distinguished in his crew cut and well-tailored clothes - is fuming. He is apparently greatly offended that a white woman is on the tour and he has tried several times to leave the table and to sit elsewhere but his wife restrains him. He hisses his indignation at having to sit with "Shaw."

The others at the table glance at each other surreptitiously, embarrassed that Mr. Wee is making such a scene at our first gathering.

"Neber mind. We take care of you," Jimmy Ng says, holding his hand across his laughing belly. He smiles shyly and fills my plate at the outset of each of the ten courses before taking any food for himself. He tells me he will do this at each meal throughout the entire trip. It is humbling to be so sweetly and considerately treated by such a good-hearted stranger.

Obviously I will have a lot to learn from these people about family, service, community, and mutual accountability.

"You will probably eat lots of new things on this trip," Jimmy says. "You see, we Chinese have a well-known saying that 'The people of China eat everything on four legs but tables and everything that flies but airplanes!'" Everyone laughs.

"Yes," says Yu Lan, "those mainland Chinese people even eat dog and cat – but we don't. We are much more civilized than that. Besides, Singapore has the best food in the entire world, so we are very lucky not to have to eat bad things."

Toward the end of the meal I notice my table companions ducking down below the table, one by one. Curious, I bend down to see what's down there the next time someone near me swoops down. They are wiping their mouths on the white linen tablecloth and Jimmy and I nearly knock each other unconscious as we clunk heads at table level. Next there is a flurry of bones and gristle being spat upon the table itself. Bowls are upturned and the contents dumped in piles, creating rings of dark grease on the white cloth. There ensues much smacking of lips, loud extravagant burps, slurps and more spitting. The final chewing of food is done with open-mouthed abandon and immense enjoyment.

Waves of nausea sweep over me and I avert my eyes from everything but the empty plate in front of me. Their table manners are so foreign to me! I've heard of cultural differences – but this is too much. I am bending over backwards to be as polite and well-mannered, according to my own cultural upbringing as I possibly can. Next the toothpicks are passed around the table, yet I decline to take one, having been instructed since childhood never to pick my teeth in public. There is horrified silence at this.

"You must clean your teeth at the table so they won't fall out," Danny Loh admonishes me.

"Thank you, but Americans usually use a tooth brush in the bathroom. Alone. I'll brush my teeth after we get to the hotel," I explain.

"This is better," he says, as he and the others make elaborate smacking noises and insert their toothpicks into elusive crevices behind cupped hands. Still I decline, with vivid images of my mother's earliest training in my mind's eye and ear. "Never pick your teeth at the table. Don't smack your lips. Never burp outside the bathroom. Chew with your mouth closed. Make sure that everyone has been served before you start to eat. Don't slurp your soup. Chew silently. Don't spot the tablecloth. Always use a napkin. Do not make any noise whatsoever when eating or drinking. What goes into your mouth with a fork comes out of it with a fork if it can't be swallowed. Never touch food with your hands unless it's expressly 'finger-food.' "

She never mentioned that we shouldn't throw gristle and bones into piles on the table or that we were not to wipe our mouths on the table-cloth. That's what napkins were for. But it was obvious that my new companions had never met my mother and I doubted that she would have sat as calmly as I had through the ten course meal. If this is the way things are starting out, how are they going to develop? Will I have several sets of parents telling me what to do the entire trip, like a huge extended family? The days ahead will surely tell. *Let me be kind and considerate, Lord. Let me not offend anyone.*

After dinner I'm invited by our guides Karen and Florence to "go loitering" in Hong Kong after dark. I enthusiastically agree, not knowing what "going loitering" means, but gauging that Karen and Florence seem innocent enough, both being highly protected Singapore teenagers who live at home, like most well-brought-up Asians do before marrying. Besides, nothing dangerous can happen to three of us together.

As we ride the red double-decker buses through narrow, crowded streets, Karen tells me of her life as a tour guide and the unbearable loneliness that she feels each month as she spends a few days in Hong Kong away from her family in Singapore, especially her mother.

"You will find we are true Singaporeans," she says, nodding brightly to include Florence. "All we like is shopping and eating." The two favorite Singaporean pastimes are well-known in Southeast Asia and help account for the two thousand restaurants and innumerable shopping centers on the tiny island. Hong Kong, too, boasts of food stalls of every description, as well as hawker stands displaying sandals, tee shirts, underwear, cassette tapes, toys and fabrics. I see a humorous cardboard sign at a hawker stand: Look both ways before crossing the street. Death is nature's way of telling you to slow down!

Karen and Florence hold my hand as we wend our way through crowds and they insist on paying for the subway and bus tickets, treating me as a royal guest and exulting in introducing me to the shopping treasures of city alleys. They confide again, with faces contorted, that they miss their mothers terribly when they come to Hong Kong for a few days. Tired and satisfied with our loitering adventure together, we return to the hotel in time to get a good night's rest.

At breakfast the next morning we are served Dim Sum - more than ten sumptuous courses again, which arrive in brown wicker steam baskets. I'm wondering how to politely decline the meat dishes since I've never been fond of meat. In addition to translucent, thousand-year-old eggs, there is green tea, porridge, spring rolls, pork rolls, prawns, cake, white dumplings filled with meat, ha tow, sui mai, chee cheong fan, choi chew poa and a white dumpling which has a little wafer baked to the bottom. After chewing and swallowing the thin white communion-type wafer attached to a vegetable-filled dumpling, I notice the others spitting their wafers out.

Alarmed, I stiffen, sit up, and ask Danny Loh, "Why are you taking out your wafer?"

"That's not a wafer. It's a piece of paper. For decoration. Where's yours?"

"Gone."

"Gone?! You mean you swallowed it?" he asks in disbelief, attracting the attention of the entire table and several tables around.

"Yes. I thought it was food, so I ate it. You know, like the little paper-thin communion wafer you get in church to eat."

"What? You eat paper in church?" He blinks.

"No, no. It's similar to paper. It's flat bread that looks like paper. It represents the body of Christ.... Some Western churches...." By now he's really excited and I'm getting choking visions of his mistaking the Christian communion ritual for some type of secret Western cannibalism so I stop in mid-sentence, tensely waiting.

He starts to tell the others that I thought the dumpling paper was like the paper that Americans eat in church. I wave my hands, trying to stop him but it's too late. Everyone stares at this news. They eat paper, these Americans. How odd. Then they all start to shout at once. The noise is deafening.

Finally they bring the discussion level down to a medium roar and Danny raises his hand to indicate silence. They have given him several instructions and I see concern registered in every face at the table.

"This is a good time for us to talk to you," Danny begins. "We all wonder why you are not happy. You are not having a good time. Why are you not enjoying the food and our company?"

"But I am, truly, Danny. Why would you even think such a thing? Just because I ate the dumpling paper by mistake? I've never even seen these foods before, so I don't know how to eat them, but they're delicious."

"We know you aren't happy and don't like the food," he says with stern emphasis, refusing to believe me. "Would you like Western food at each meal?" "Of course not," I answer, reddening at being the center of attention, my heart hammering audibly through my rib cage.

"Why on earth did you even think I haven't been happy?"

"Since you ask, I will say," Danny began. "First of all, you show no manners at the table and we use very nice manners so we think you are unhappy and we are offended.

"What do you mean, exactly?" In my own recollection I've been scrupulous. My parents, husband and former teachers would have been proud of me in my representation of the U.S.

"You just eat without any sound. Very bad manners. We show our appreciation of such good food by making noise. You make no noise with your lips and tongue, so we think you are angry with us. Also, you never wipe your mouth on the table cloth. You don't burp. You don't put your bones on the table. You eat so silently as to be invisible. We can't hear you, so we know you are unhappy with us and don't like Chinese food."

At this detailed pronouncement of my appallingly ignorant manners I start to laugh and then quickly stop, not wanting to cause further confusion.

"Danny, you must understand that when I was growing up, my mother gave me very different instructions in table manners than your mother gave you. Just the opposite, in fact."

His eyes grow huge as I tell him the ways in which our two cultures differ in the matter of conventional table refinements. He shakes his head and mentions that it's difficult to believe.

"Never mind. You are with Chinese now. You act in the Chinese way. When you eat soup you make noise like this," he says, slurping loudly. "And do this many times," he says, burping outrageously several times in succession, like a pained sea lion. I wince, then make a placid face.

"Be sure to let your noodles hang out of your mouth into the bowl like a beard," he instructs during the noodle course. "And always clean your teeth at the table." Everyone nods with satisfaction and pursed lips at the conclusion of Danny's mild upbraiding.

They have done their job in educating the ignorant American. Somebody had to do it. We can't have a barbarian travelling with us and causing embarrassment.

My face feels purple with conflicting feelings, long ingrained, as I slurp my soup, inhale parallel rows of noodles with noisy snorfeling and smack my lips in between loud "Ah's" of faked pleasure. Summoning every shred of thespian ability available, I exaggerate my enjoyment while keeping a wary eye on the restaurant door lest anyone that I know should suddenly walk in and see me bent over the bowl of mee with a wide row of the yellow noodles trailing in their greasy liquid. By the end of the tenth course, my popping eyes and genuine groans of bloated pain are mistaken for true satisfaction of the highest sort. It's liable to be a long trip.

"Don't worry. I like you. I will help you." These sympathetic words are spoken by Yu Lan Loh, Danny's wife. She explains that her name means Magnolia and that she will come to my rescue. She is aptly named and seems flower-like, with her unusually pale, clear complexion, brown eyes and glossy, pert coiffure. Yu Lan is elegance itself, in the latest European fashion. She, Danny and I are the youngest members of the tour. Neo Lam Heng, a tall thin music teacher strolls over to offer his assistance, should I need it in the future. He speaks a passable broken English and again mentions that he and Jimmy Ng are taking their mothers to China since both mothers wanted to see China once more before they die.

"I talked to everyone on the tour and said we must help the American. They all said they will help. We are your friends now." Neo Lam Heng exchanges business cards with me, then Danny Loh and Jimmy Ng follow.

"You will like China very much and you will be safe with us." They all smile warmly to me then shoot each other glances of satisfaction as we leave the restaurant and board the tour bus.

With notebook perpetually in hand I ask the guides to illuminate me as to some basic Mandarin words I'll need for navigating through China in case the English-speaking guide which I've paid for doesn't materialize for some reason. I present a list of two dozen English words to Karen, which we practice, accompanied by giggles and guffaws from my companions who nod and nudge me approvingly. Over and over I attempt the melodious words while the group tolerates my repetitions and encourages me to practice. I write out the Mandarin phonetically as no one seems to know the characters or Anglicized versions. We sound like a gaggle of parrots in anarchy as the Singaporeans bark out the Chinese-accented English words and I attempt to croon the mellifluous Mandarin ones as Karen does.

"Okay, start again," Karen commands patiently, as she reviews my list. "'Nee how ma', which means 'how are you?' "

"Mai-Mai is the Cantonese term for 'I don't want it.' " (as in declining a purchase or bargain)

"Sieh Sieh or sheh sheh, 'thank you'. Always tap your cupped fingers on the table and tap them a few times when you thank a waiter."

After reviewing the numbers one to five, a few greetings and farewells and about ten handy adjectives, Karen tells me the lesson is over and we'll do more later. But Danny, with a mischievous glint in his eye tells me that "oolong" is a very useful word and that I should use it often while bargaining in stores in China. An argument breaks out among the Cantonese-speaking tour members and some of them start laughing. Finally Jimmy Ng tells me not to believe Danny because oolong means "rubbish" and that he knows I'm a polite person and wouldn't want to offend the Chinese. At every opportunity they tease me but I haven't yet found a way to joke with them in return without offending them.

Our introduction to Hong Kong begins in a foggy drizzle which dimples the gunmetal gray waters of the harbor which are soon lashed into choppy waves. The tour bus has sped past endless rows of grim cement skyscrapers in Kowloon, into the clean, well-lit harbor tunnel and out into another Hong Kong world of Kelly green trolley cars, lush emerald hills amid clamoring rows of white balconied flats. We have beheld the stunning vistas of Repulse Bay and admired the glistening ferns beside the pink and blue bubble cable cars gliding up the hill at Ocean Park.

Everyone seems at ease with me now and I am learning a great deal from the group. Our day tour is relaxed yet stimulating. The masterfully conceived aquarium and the sea lion show have provided our first real opportunity to become acquainted with our traveling companions of the next three weeks. I feel completely at ease about asking any kind of questions now. As my first employer used to say, "Don't be afraid to ask dumb questions. They're a lot easier to rectify than dumb mistakes."

Yu Lan and Danny Loh, tailors, comment on the apparel of all those who pass by and one by one the other tour members begin to ask me how much I paid for my rain jacket, watch, shoes, dress, purse, umbrella and notebook. Invariably they nod and indicate that I have gotten a good price. The morning has fled in a blur of well-known tourist attractions, ticket lines, tour-guide patter and China departure preparations.

At last we stand in the Kowloon Train Station and amuse ourselves for an hour by watching and commenting upon the travelers who have exited the train from China. They shove their way through the swarming hundreds of waiting passengers in the vast, unadorned terminal.

No matter how spiritually advanced a person imagines himself to be, it seems that total immersion in another culture puts those ideas to the test. Although it is said that humility is the first step for a spiritual aspirant and I had thought I had been feeding on humble pie most of my life, I was wrong. I was merely having delusions of humility!

CHAPTER 5
TRAIN TO THE PEOPLE'S REPUBLIC

"I am never upset for the reason I think." ACIM, WB, P 8

Hong Kong
June 3, 1981

China, at last! The knowledge that we'll be there in a few hours causes my heart to leap up and down in a little jig. A whirlpool of images from films, museums and art history books swirl through my head in anticipation of the fulfillment of a long-awaited dream. I am wondering what my cousin Joe, a Hong Kong banker, had meant last night when he kept stressing that the China of actuality is nothing like the glossy, aesthetic China as captivated by the censoring cameras of the *National Geographic*. But upon being pressed for details he demurred, saying that China should be a surprise. He never mentioned the word "shock." He just said I would be sure to be surprised, no matter what.

After some wheedling and pleading on my part he had dropped hints that the Cultural Revolution had erased most of the cultural artifacts that spiritual seekers and art pilgrims to China would expect to find there. What could he have meant?

"Just don't start handing out sugar packets and American flags," he had said wryly. When my face registered a blank he explained.

"You wouldn't believe what some Americans would do over here in Asia. A few weeks ago when I toured China I found myself on a tour with some Europeans and some Texans. The Texans, believe it or not, had brought suitcases full of sugar packets - the kind you get in restaurants back home - and little American flags the size of postage stamps. Every time we visited a school or a commune they would start rushing around giving out sugar packets and American flags, telling the Chinese how good democracy was. I was so embarrassed for our country that each time it happened I just wanted to hide and deny my citizenship or to stand up and explain that all Americans aren't like that."

"Don't worry, Joe, I won't let down the U.S. or you, either, for that matter," I had laughed. "Besides, I've traveled in scores of countries and am always treated kindly wherever I go and I don't expect to run into any difficulty whatsoever. Furthermore, although I maybe look delicate and lady-like, back in Colorado I'm very independent and outdoorsy. I fly small planes, climb mountains and camp out in the woods, so I'm very hardy and self-sufficient in every imaginable situation."

"Okay, okay. I've done my duty and now I won't worry about you," he'd said as he drove me back to the hotel after a long dinner of reminiscing about our mutual childhoods and the intervening twenty years since we had seen each other. We had last met at a family reunion at his parent's home in another state when both of us were on the brink of puberty with its accompanying afflictions of acne, shyness, coltish gangling physiques, and general adolescent bewilderment.

In the subsequent decades, Joe had experimented with college fraternity parties and numerous sports cars. As a bachelor he had been in the army in Viet Nam, had subsequently met many beautiful women, and had enjoyed a distinguished banking career in Europe and Asia. During the same period I had had a happy and successful college life in the Shenandoah Valley of Virginia, a brief teaching career, marriage to a navy pilot who had become an attorney, the birth of my son, and exciting travel throughout Europe, North Africa and the Middle East. Additionally, I had also worked in radio and TV, had a career as a management consultant, and had done lots of writing and lecturing. The most difficult aspect of the last decade had been a divorce from my first husband which had, however, been balanced by a happy second marriage.

We were as dissimilar as our families were. Joe was inclined toward pessimism and was jaded on life's pleasures, by his own admission. I, on the other hand, was an optimist, and still found much that awed me in the small things of life as well as the grand ones. Perhaps it was this quality which prompted him to consider me naïve and to say, as we parted, "I just hope you're ready for China."

While I've been daydreaming the Kowloon train station has filled to capacity and the throng has expanded to a line six abreast and a block long. Still more passengers were pressing against the large floor-to-ceiling windows outside, screaming and gesturing to be let in. Meanwhile, more tourists from arriving China trains smash their way into our crushing mob of outbound travelers. Our curious eyes devour the file of people spilling from the platform door on our right, fresh from their journey. Rather, not-so-fresh. They all look haggard and weary, in need of sleep, a bath, and a shampoo. The Westerners among them pant under hilarious loads of boxes, tote bags, walking sticks and backpacks. But it is the hats they wear that catch our attention and send a ripple of laughter through the crowd. Several Americans each wear comical columns of six to ten assorted hats. There are olive green soldier caps on top of the high stacks. Next come straw topees, then conical coolie hats, straw farmer's wide-brims, construction-worker bonnets, shellacked rattan cones, and finally, an immense white cotton hat resembling a giant pizza pan.

As the hatted tourists thread their way through the crowd under their precariously wobbly piles, titters escape from my companions, who nudge each other in disbelief. They roll their eyes at me and jerk their heads in the direction of the Americans to check whether I find the parade as amusing as they do. In response I toss back a look which I hope conveys several things simultaneously.

Grinning and rolling my eyes in return I intend for my facial expressions to imply, all at once: "Aren't they resourceful? Isn't this exciting? Yes, they do indeed look screamingly funny and they are obviously Americans."

They smile, nod, sigh, and relax. A forward surge of the crowd lifts us up and everyone shuffles forward a foot or two, then comes to another long standstill as everyone struggles to maintain balance and to re-examine their possessions once more. (Passport. Carry-on luggage. Snacks. Purse or wallet.) The men in our group start fumbling inside their undershirts and stroking their chests, provoking my curiosity. Next they unbutton the top buttons of their short-sleeved business shirts and pull the necks of their undershirts out in front of them and look down inside to ensure that passports and money are still safely inside their neck bags and chest pouches.

"Pick-pock!" they hiss quietly to me in warning of possible train terminal thieves who might be immediately next to us in the tightly packed crush of damp bodies. I nod in appreciative acknowledgement and throw back my shoulders to indicate a competent readiness to meet whatever foolish fellow should be so misguided as to interfere with me in any way. Good grief... I had no idea we'd be bruising our way through this impossible human tangle merely to board the train. Even India wasn't this crowded. If this is the trip's overture, what will the journey be like?

The crowd twitches, lurches, then moves into a roll that becomes a shuffle and finally breaks into a wild scramble as the noisy excited passengers mash their way into the aluminum passenger cars. With the feverishness of homesteaders staking a claim on the prized dream of a lifetime, our group dives for the padded seats on both sides of the aisles. As quickly as the melee began it ends and miraculously everyone finds a seat in one of the numerous quartet groupings up and down the car.

The train picks up speed and zigzags through the New Territories' shanty-towns which are homes to thousands - hovels made from cardboard packing boxes, plywood scraps and sheets of discarded tin. Mud-caked, naked children stare at us from hillside shacks where emaciated dogs scavenge in weeds for sustenance. Steep hillside gardens climb vertically from the tracks, perilously close to the train. Gradually the landscape becomes filled with pastoral scenes of green paddy fields, mud puddles reflecting cumulus clouds, and imposing blue mountains in the distance.

"Tea, Miss?" The canteen hostess holds a lidded china cup out to me while she indicates with a glance the cookies and other snacks in her wagon.

"Thank you, yes." Jimmy Ng sits in the seat next to me, his mother and father opposite us. His parents speak no English but ask him several times in Cantonese to make sure that I have been eating all my meals, sleeping well and taking care of myself on the trip so far. He reddens as he carries out their request, explaining that he himself is over forty, married, and has grown children. Yet still, his parents treat him like a child when he's with them, even though he is essentially their chaperon and guide through China. I reply that I understand, have a child of my own also, and that my own parents are similarly solicitous when I visit them back in the U.S. Since Jimmy's parents don't understand English we can freely discuss older parents in general. I am, however, touched and appreciative that Jimmy's parents have decided to look after me in their fashion on this trip. So far the members of our group have been kind and friendly to me and for that I am greatly relieved.

Pale blue linoleum covers the interior walls of the passenger car. White lace curtains accent the blue velvet seat cushions of our car. Fluorescent lights and a small color TV set at the ceiling in the front and rear of the car complete the decor. The TV comes on automatically and a young uniformed Chinese communist woman begins to speak to us in English and Mandarin about the train rules. She wears a black beret with a red star in the center and begins her two minute presentation by explaining the location of the restaurant car and mentioning the imminent arrival of the rice trolley as well as the location of ashtrays in the arms of the seats.

The TV clicks off automatically and the rice trolley hostess arrives with box lunches for sale. Squeaky, jerky Chinese music comes over the air as we leave Kowloon far behind. Our Chinese group, having settled our parcels and baggage, nod to two Nigerians and a foursome of obese, red-faced Germans in the car. In high spirits due partly to their minimal travel experience, all my companions talk loudly and excitedly. They gesture to the scenes outside the window of the strangely juxtaposed picture of kampongs, skyscrapers, garbage dumps, and orchards, all jumbled together without much apparent zoning or modern urban planning. Hillside Bonsai nurseries display twisted specimens on row after row of gray wooden benches. Next we notice, outside the opposite window, rusty derricks, red and yellow double-decker buses, and finally, a picturesque lone red temple perched on a verdant hill as the smooth, quiet train winds its way into mountainous country. I am reminded that, resident within everyone, is the same impulse to love and to worship.

For some reason a verse from *The Dhammapada* comes to mind with the appearance of the red-column Chinese temple.
"Cross the river bravely,
  Conquer all your passions,
  Go beyond your likes and dislikes
  And all fetters will fall away." TD P 195

All staff servers on the train wear the same uniform comprised of a midnight blue beret with red star, black slacks, white socks and black slippers, wrinkled white cotton shirt with front buttons and rolled up sleeves at the elbow. At the front of the car the tea hostess boils tea in an antique kettle on an ancient stove.

The window reveals hilly country villages with flat-roofed, square concrete houses. The scene has a dismal aspect of people just barely hanging on to the slender thread of life with last wisps of energy. Further on a landscape of snowy white ibis perched upon black water buffalo is embellished with peaked rooftops and a jumble of lush vegetation, pierced by winding brown paths leading down to low paddy fields with standing pools of water reflecting a lavender gray sky. Rectangular billboards advertising White Cat Detergent, in English and Mandarin, jar us back into the moment as we round a curve onto a view of low, oblong buildings roofed with woven beige straw.

We examine the mud-wall irrigation system while a traditional Chinese opera, beautifully costumed, comes on TV. Though it is June, the train is damp and chilly like the weather outside, and it is still three hours to Guangzhou, pronounced Gwong Joe.

Guangzhou, China
June 3, 1981

At Guangzhou, or Canton, as Westerners call it, the pandemonium of train station exits and entrances is repeated as the mob presses out of the train and rushes headlong into the numerous immigration lines. We are officially in China and I want to get a good, full look at the station which resembles a huge bare warehouse with a dirty concrete floor. It is devoid of furnishing, color, or warmth. Passport examination booths are located opposite the train cars and are staffed by exceedingly youthful green-uniformed male guards. The station has an other-worldly feel to me, like a setting out of the American Civil War era, devoid of modern-world touches that we in the West have come to take for granted.

When I step up to the passport booth, opposite the railway car, the two young guards stare at me, nudge each other, smile, bow, and gesture that I need not show my passport like my tour colleagues. They make a sweeping gesture of welcome and wave me through to the opposite side, into a large outside corridor, lined with cheering mobs smashing against the chain link fence. The crowd begins to applaud and wave so I turn back to the station to see who is arriving. I stand there alone, expecting to see some famous celebrity, accompanied by press and an entourage of companions. The crowd still cheers and points in my direction. I turn all around in a circle, looking left and right, which causes the throngs behind the fence to laugh and to applaud even more. Suddenly it hits me. I'm the only Westerner in the crowd of arrivals and they are actually applauding me! A crimson blush creeps up my neck, past my ears and temples as I sheepishly wave back, nod, and bow stiffly at the shoulders. Whereas I was feeling at one with my surroundings until now, this unusual treatment causes me to feel like a Martian who has just landed. *Hold me fast to you, Lord. Show me where to go and what to do.*

Someone appears at my side just in time. "Ms. Shaw? Connie Shaw, American?" asks a tall, thin guide. "The bus which will take us to the hotel is parked over here," says six-foot Mr. Wong, who introduces me to his five-foot compatriot, Mr. Lee. Both guides smile and tell me they listen to *Voice of America* to improve their English. They are the day guides and would like nothing better than to study in the U.S. someday. They look about twenty years old and sandwich me between them, earnestly grasping my elbows and guiding me to the bus as if I'm fragile cargo. My tour companions look on from the bus windows smiling in amusement at their conscientiousness in firmly clutching my arms.

Mr. Wong begins the tour in Mandarin patter as we move toward the API or "Welcome" Hotel. Mr. Wong tells me not to worry about crowds which might gather about me wherever we go since they are not accustomed to seeing many white women, especially "such a very tall person as you." I chuckle, explaining that, for a Western woman, five feet five inches is not considered at all tall. My own brothers and husband are well over six feet tall," I add.

"Then they are like our Mr. Wong, here," giggles tiny Mr. Lee. "He is our giant. But you Americans have a whole country full of giants."

As we file out of the bus we are cautioned to never keep the hotel room key, to arrive at all meals and functions on time, and are told that attendance at every function is mandatory. We are then told that since it is of the utmost importance that we enjoy our vacation that we must all go everywhere in a group and never venture out alone or try to stay alone in our room for a nap because then we wouldn't enjoy our vacation. We must always think of the group, not ourselves. Apparently free will, free choice and spontaneous action are discouraged, at least on this trip.

The lobby is the first disconcerting scene which greets us. The terrazzo floor is filthy and the grubby, once-white furniture dust covers which hide the chairs and sofas are stained with acrid-smelling urine. As we stare at the furniture, declining to be seated until the luggage arrives, we are informed that this is one of the finest hotels in China and that in three weeks' time we will be returning here.

A hotel clerk shows us to the twentieth floor where our group will be staying. Room 2004 will be for Mrs. Muey Low and me. The ancient floral carpet on the hallway floor is urine-stained and the floor baseboards are thick with black soot. My companions chatter in angry undertones at the condition of the hotel and we all pause in simultaneous dread and expectation before the doors to our rooms. Mrs. Low crosses the threshold and surveys the room's terrazzo floors, small wood desk, plain twin beds, tiny wardrobe covered with black soot, tiny table fan, lamp, and thermos. We peer into the bathroom, surprised to find - hooray!- a Western toilet, sink, and bathtub. The bathroom is a relief since the train's unisex Asian restroom was a slab with a hole through which the railroad track could be seen.

While Mrs. Low and I stand looking at the broad brown muddy water stains which run down the wall from ceiling to floor we hear whoops across the hall. Yu Lan rushes into the room and cries in outrage, "Our room is no good-lah!"

"It stinks. Very bad stinking. Pee-pee and mildew. Bah! No good-lah! Come see." She pulls my shirt and hauls me across the hall, with Mrs.

Low on my heels. The stench is overwhelming. We all run back into the hall to gulp fresh air while Yu Lan roars down the hall to the desk in the elevator lobby to demand a new room. Her shouts bring the rest of our tour members out of their rooms with question marks across their faces.

A crowd has gathered at the desk where the desk clerk informs Yu Lan that nothing can be done about the situation as she is merely a government employee who has no authority.

"What is wrong with the smell?" she asks in genuine innocence. This is one of China's finest hotels. These smells never bother us so why should they bother you? I do not understand why you request another room."

Danny Loh strolls up behind the crowd and says to me, "Oh dear, there's no air-con. There's no TV. Whatever will we do in China at night?"

"It's a good thing I brought ten books to read," I laugh, trying to lighten the mood. "I guess we'll retire early and sleep a lot," I remark, but the group is glum. They return to their rooms, shoulders drooping, after Danny and Yu Lan finally convince the desk clerk to give them another room.

Back in our room Mrs. Low mops her brow with a hanky as we're perspiring in the afternoon heat and this is the twentieth floor. She walks over to the strip of wood paneling under the window and, mistaking it for an air-con control-panel door, grasps it firmly in both hands and inadvertently rips it off the wall. We both stand there bewildered. It wasn't an air-con panel. It was just a square piece of wood nailed to the wall to cover a football-sized hole in the plaster. It seems that makeshift patchwork is typical in China these days from what we've seen so far.

Next we lift back the bedspreads to find grubby gray sheets which look as if they have been used for several months without laundering. The towels and washcloths in the bath are charcoal gray, limp, and putrid. Mrs. Low wrinkles her nose and stamps her foot in disgust, saying "No good-lah! with vehemence, as she starts out the door, down the hall to the desk to ask for clean sheets. At the desk, the clerk is amazed that we would like clean sheets. She says that everyone in China uses linens a long time. "The people who used them the night before didn't complain, so why should you?"

I patiently explain that our group cannot sleep in filthy bed linens, nor can we use filthy wash cloths and towels. She asks why. I mention germs. She wants to know what germs have to do with the conversation. In exasperation I explain that the Singaporean Chinese and Americans launder their sheets at least once a week and only use their bath towels once or twice so that they will be fresh and sanitary and prevent the spread of disease.

The young woman tells me that she thinks these are wasteful luxurious habits that would never be practiced in China. The commotion has brought Beijing Mr. Lo, the official government guide who will accompany us throughout China. The desk clerk is explaining that soap and detergent are so expensive that most Chinese people can't even afford them so they often wash their clothes in cold water with no soap. "And we have seen some Americans even wash their hair every day while we only wash our hair once in two weeks, without shampoo," she explains, her temper rising at the thought of such extravagant wastefulness.

Beijing Mr. Lo has remained silent during the discussion, his scholarly face impassive behind his wire-frame glasses. He stands greatly interested at the edge of the crowd in his gray Mao jacket and pants. His pencil and notebook are poised in his slender hands. He steps forward and respectfully asks my name, occupation and complete educational background. Upon hearing that I have pursued, though not completed doctoral studies, am a management consultant on sabbatical in Asia, and that I am a writer and lecturer, he bows, formally faces the group, and earnestly addresses me in a loud voice so that all might hear. I'm as curious as anyone about what he has in mind.

"Connie Shaw, would you please tell us, in your opinion, and with your vast experience, the most important reason that you think the hotel should provide clean sheets and towels each day to a completely new group of tourists who only use the bed for one night when we in China don't even supply our own people with such luxury?"

"Yes, Mr. Lo," I begin carefully, not wanting to appear rude or ungrateful. "I understand from our guides Mr. Wong and Mr. Lee that since the Cultural Revolution you are most eager to build a new China. And that most of your tourism comes from the U.S. and from Japan, with a certain percentage from overseas Chinese like my colleagues, here."

Mr. Lo, hanging on my every word, has pencil ready and smiles in encouragement for me to continue, apparently approving of my low-key tone.

"Well, then, Mr. Lo, if I were an important official like yourself I would want to make sure that my superiors back in Beijing, as well as in Canton, knew what tourists expect so that the tourists who are paying for the rebuilding of China would be happy and would tell their friends that they had a good time in China and that the very expensive price of the trip was worth it. The very least that the many tourists will expect for the many thousands of dollars they are paying is to have very clean white sheets and towels every single night after a long hard day of travel. If they do not get good service they will be very unhappy, will cry and complain and want to go home. But worst of all, they will tell their families and friends that the People's Republic of China charges high prices but gives little in return and their friends will not want to visit China. Then tourism will dwindle and there will be little money for a new China. It could be very sad. But of course that is only my opinion," I finish, gravely looking at the floor.

Beijing Mr. Lo still takes rapid notes, nodding his head all the while. The crowd begins to talk at once, in four dialects, agreeing with what I've said.

Mr. Lo thanks me and says the idea of clean sheets is excellent and makes good sense. In fact, anything that would help build a new China made good sense. He will see that new linens and towels are placed in our rooms while we are out touring the area in the afternoon. Obviously he is pleased that he has hit upon a revolutionary new way to ensure the happiness of future foreign guests. Beijing Mr. Lo next announces with a triumphant flush that we will be honored this evening in a most unusual way. We will be treated to the rare opportunity of viewing Chinese television. The excitement with which he makes the announcement makes it apparent that we've indeed earned a rare distinction. However, television is available in each of our homes and apartments so the group is less than jubilant at the news since watching TV is the last thing any of us had hoped to do in China. But we do not show our disappointment out of consideration to Beijing who obviously wants very much to please and to impress us.

Beijing Mr. Lo claps his hands together in enthusiasm. "Now please be ready for lunch and our tour of Guangzhou directly afterward," he calls out. "I will see you downstairs in ten minutes. And, oh yes, welcome again to China. It's people like you who are helping people like us to build a New China of great glory and honor to her people. Remember, ten minutes. Think of the group, not yourselves. Remember, you are in China now, and must think of your comrades every moment." We are a bit taken aback at his brisk officiousness. But even more than that, we Singapore residents are totally unprepared for the strict rules being immediately imposed on us at the outset of our vacation trip

Beijing Mr. Lo then steps briskly into the elevator and departs from view as our group for once stands silent and dumfounded.

Upstairs, after we have hung a few items in the filthy, sooty armoire, Muey Low, my roommate and I comb our hair and freshen our lipstick. As we putter around the room, I wonder how I will feel when I finally meet God in human form. Suddenly, I recall my fondness for my first spiritual mentor, the famous author, calligraphist, T'ai Chi instructor and translator of the *Tao Te Ching* and other ancient Chinese spiritual texts.

Gia-fu and his talented photographer-physicist wife, Jane English, had provided me and my fellow spiritual seeker, Will, meals and instruction at their retreat home, Stillpoint, in Manitou Springs, Colorado during the early seventies when I was just learning to meditate and to discover Eastern traditions. We would drive from Denver to Manitou Springs for the day, eager for any insights or teachings which Gia-fu might confer upon us.

Two of my most vivid recollections of Gia-fu, aside from his wisdom, his great sense of humor and twinkling eyes, concerned two idiosyncrasies. First, he did not observe the usual Western modesties and would often come downstairs to greet day guests dressed only in an old red belted corduroy bathrobe. After a terse but sincere greeting of welcome, he would gesture for us to be seated and he would immediately begin a brief meditation. Now I realize that by meditating with us he was helping to ground us after our long car trip and was also assessing our depth, capacity and state of being at the moment. He could ascertain by the quality of our silence and by any display of restlessness the degree of discipline and resolve which we had attained.

The second habit from which Gia-fu never veered was his daily hike, nearly at running speed, up the vertical mountain beside Stillpoint. In the ashram kitchen, before the hike, he would make a few giant peanut butter sandwiches on whole wheat bread,. talking animatedly about how wonderful it was to be regular in spiritual practice and about how much he would welcome our company on the "walk." Then he would bolt out the door with backpack bobbling, gesturing for us to run along beside him. Few people could sustain his pace for more than fifty yards and would finally beg off, panting hard as Gia-fu, who, from our surmisal, was at least in his sixties, jogged up the steep incline and disappeared in the distance with a friendly wave.

Gia-fu was the first spiritual teacher who pointed out to me that stilling the mind was essential for freedom and that the Tao (pronounced Dow), or flow of life, is virtually palpable to those who live in the heart. When one is gentle, one will be treated gently by life. Whereas Westerners often think of Eastern paths as passive modes, they are but openings to a dynamic receptivity to the strength, power and light within each of us.

But for those on the spiritual path, humility is lesson one and it recycles throughout one's life, touching every facet. Discernment inextricably follows from discipline and is joined by detachment and increased joy. I remember the old Buddhist adage, "It is good to be a mother. It is good to be a father. It is good to follow one's dharma (right conduct of life). But best of all, it is good to be an enlightened sage."

While I muse, in our hotel room, Muey Low clears her throat and points to her watch, signifying that it is time to go downstairs to meet our group and Beijing Mr. Lo for lunch. Muey is a quiet, thoughtful roommate. It seems that I am the first Westerner that she has ever known to any extent. What lessons will the trip hold for the two of us and for the group at large?

CHAPTER 6
THE GLORY OF NEW CHINA

"Life is a march from 'I' to 'We.'" Sathya Sai Baba

Guangzhou, China
June 3, 1981

Directly after lunch the Singaporeans and I stroll along the faded red carpet runner beside the murky green fish pond in the fly-infested hotel lobby. As instructed, we assemble to await our local guide, Miss Feng. The dining room door swings open and three Japanese Buddhist nuns file past us, clucking and obviously horrified at the insects on the luncheon table, the soiled table linens, chipped tea cups and tumblers, and swarming flies in the reception area. We sympathize with them, having just experienced similar feelings. With admiration, we note their impeccable appearance, from shiny bald heads to carefully pressed dove gray nun's habits and hose, and simple black felt shoes. Yu Lan and Muey Low catch the eyes of the nuns and nod vigorously in agreement with them.

We laugh about the fact that the highly-touted Chinese television program never materialized, either because of the unavailability of a TV set or some other snafu.

Miss Feng then arrives. She is a smiling twenty-year-old, bristling with an obvious love and excitement for her work. We later learn that such sentiments of job satisfaction in New China are exceedingly uncommon. Miss Feng explains in American-accented English that she will translate everything that Mr. Wong and Mr. Lee say in Chinese. Privately on the bus she explains to me that she will also tell me about her life and various aspects of the Cultural Revolution. She would like to hear about my career and life as well. She tells me she listens to *Voice of America* and keeps up on the latest trends in the West by radio. Radio is a vital lifeline of culture and a source of correctly-spoken standard American English for Chinese government guides, officials, scientists and business people.

Guangzhou, situated on the banks of the Pearl River, has long been one of the most important industrial port cities of China. This southern gateway to China, with its sixteen parks and wide boulevards, gives no hint that the city has a long history as a center of insurrection, rebellion and civil war. But the sprawling city population of over three million people leaves Westerners with a claustrophobic feeling which is unrelieved even on the waters of the Pearl River, our destination and much-touted tour highlight.

Our bus drives past a television tower offering Miss Feng a chance to announce that China has both black and white and color television but that most of the programming involves children's shows. Education is a priority among the fifty million people of Guangdong Province. We pass the Flower Drifting Hotel in the district of the same name, then pass the Canton Trade Fair Building where the fair is held twice annually. The Orient Hotel which houses the American Consulate is pointed out to us. We are told that in 1957 the government mobilized the populace to voluntary labor and cleaned up Guangzhou. Until that time, it had been a city of vice, corruption, disease, crime and prostitution. Now however, we're told, most robbery, murder and social diseases have been eradicated from China.

Ironically, as she speaks we drive past apartment balconies which are surrounded by iron or bamboo cages to deter break-ins. When I ask about this Miss Feng replies that there is quite a lot of "petty thievery" still in Canton but that one's physical person is not in danger as in the old days.

"At least we don't have to face seeing people shoot each other with guns on the streets like you do in the U.S." she ventures.

I laugh and assure her that although the U.S. does have a bad reputation abroad for violence and crime, I have never even witnessed a crime from a distance, much less at close range, nor have any of my friends.

"I don't know whether that's because I always feel safe wherever I am or whether I'm just lucky. Anyway, I do know that most people in the world prefer safety to upset. They prefer harmony to fighting and prefer to eat and sleep well in the security of their homes than to engage in the excitement of upheavals, as thrilling as they may be for a short time. People are people everywhere. Each one counts and is needed. We all bleed, laugh, cry and rejoice the same, wouldn't you agree in part?"

So far, this is the first philosophical conversation that I've had on this trip. Suddenly I miss the stimulating daily conversations with Jim and Wahid that I've taken for granted. During the past week, no one has even mentioned religion, meditation or anything to do with spirituality. I feel a thirst to interact with anyone on such topics.

"Oh am I going to enjoy this day with you," Miss Feng responds and launches into a long story about how she and her family had to hide often during the Cultural Revolution when millions of people were killed merely for knowing how to read and write or for knowing another language. Most of the gifted doctors, professors, artists and scientists ranging in age from thirty to sixty were killed. It was a class war fueled by frustration, greed and envy by the have-not illiterate peasants. Some of her family members were sent hundreds of miles away as punishment because they were artists or musicians.

They had had to work long hours in wheat or rice fields in the brutal sun for months or years on end before being reunited with the family. Miss Feng's appreciation for her job as a guide and translator is due in part to the fact that such positions are coveted and considered to be among the finest jobs available in the country. The additional bonus of daily contact with foreigners who often give her magazines, candy, books in English and other gifts make the entire situation one that is almost unbearably sweet after all the torment and anguish which she had undergone during the eleven uncertain years of the Revolution.

From the bus window we can see the cream-colored No. 1 People's Hospital and are told that newer buildings are often designated with numbers rather than names. Next, a Moslem restaurant comes into view and we're informed that over 4,000 people comprise the city's Moslem population but that the majority of the people in the ancient province are Han in culture.

Banyan trees mark the oldest parts of town and the majority of the buildings, which seem to have been constructed in the 1920's and 30's, are made of brick or concrete. An unpretentious square building is apparently a local movie house where films cost the equivalent of fifteen to thirty cents, U.S. currency.

"The most recent and most popular American film we see here is "Modern Times" with Charlie Chaplin. Not very modern, is it?" she twinkles. Miss Feng is sensitive, interesting and amusing. She continues with her tour guide patter. "There are, however, British and American TV shows translated into Chinese and censored. At the age of ten children learn either English, German, Japanese or French as a second language, with Mandarin serving as the national language. English is the main foreign language at the moment."

Suddenly there is a crash and a scream as the bus screeches to a halt. The bus has hit a teenage bicyclist and knocked him onto the pavement. The driver, furious, gets out and yells at the boy, shaking his fist. From my window seat, I can clearly see the interactions below and describe them to Miss Feng and the others. The boy, scraped but impassive in the face of the driver's invective, calmly and with great dignity gets up, dusts himself off, once more mounts his bicycle and rides away at a right angle to the bus. No one has taken much notice of the incident on the street.

Hundreds of cyclists throng the streets and hundreds of bikes are parked along the sidewalk, without bike locks. The bikes are usually black without even modest accessories such as reflectors, lights, or baskets. Later, across the street I notice an outdoor restaurant with a few rusty metal tables plunked on the hard-packed dirt. The scene is so reminiscent of India that I inadvertently make a comparison of scenes in India and those I have seen in the past day.

So far, if Guangzhou is in any way representative of China and the current state of its people, then China at least feeds and clothes her people. Just barely. I am told by the guides that each person in China has one suit of clothes and two meals a day. In India not everyone has a presentable outfit or even one full meal a day. However, India is delightfully clamorous with colorful birds and flowers, music, architectural and spiritual wonders. It has a stimulating culture both ancient and modern and a liveliness that is juxtaposed with the undeniable grinding poverty of far too many people in the space available. Both China and India have their mysteries, their contributions to humanity, their challenges, their enduring people.

Eager to discuss our mutual love of good writing, Miss Feng, in a burst of emotion tells me of her regard for Thomas Hardy and of seventeenth and eighteenth century British and American literature. She further states that twentieth century Western literature is far too lustful and decadent for innocent Chinese people to embrace. Moreover, it would only corrupt the morals which the government has worked so hard to purify. She continues to say that young people are discouraged from marriage until they are twenty-five and that, of course, all are virgins when they marry.

Miss Feng prefers living in a dormitory to her own family's house since she can listen to *Voice of America* at 8:00 and 10:00 P.M. and can study without interruption. This is impossible in the family commune which is constantly crowded and noisy with three younger children and two parents occupying an area sixteen feet square. She asks me if it's really true that most Americans actually have houses or apartments which have separate rooms for cooking (a kitchen), for eating (dining room), for reading (living room or study) and for sleeping. She finds it hard to believe that even the poorest people in our country have such lavish amounts of space and privacy as to manage to rent a three bedroom apartment with a family of only four or five people. She has heard that many American people even have a special room for their private automobiles and garden tools (a garage), an excess that is beyond her most vivid imagination. One car is unthinkable, but two or more seems like an impossible attainment, if not an outright waste.

Miss Feng asks whether I have to haul water and whether I own a television and a radio. As I tell her that I've always had running water, two or three TV's and many radios, but that I seldom watch TV. I am acutely aware of my profound good fortune. She is astounded that I speak so casually about such seeming excesses, although I have been reluctant to answer her questions in detail, lest she feel an even greater sense of deprivation. We look at photos of Jim, my son Scott, and my parents and talk about our work, dreams and challenges as women.

She mentions that women are still not treated fairly under the current government but that things are much better than in the past. Miss Feng frankly admits that reading the authors Dickens, Bronte, Shaw, Hardy and Austen makes even the most difficult moments bearable for her. She and her friends have an elaborate book-borrowing system since each owns only one or two books in English, given to them by American tourists. Foreigners also send her the *New Yorker*, *Time*, and *National Geographic*, which she reads faithfully, along with the *Peking Review* and *China Reconstructs*.

"I like American foreign friends the best," she said. "They are always making jokes and laughing and they are very kind people. They also sing the most. Have you ever heard the song 'Daisy, Daisy' or 'You Are My

Sunshine?'" She then laughs aloud and tells me a saying she heard from an American from Georgia, which is that "Happiness is like a perfume that you can't spray on others without getting a little on yourself."

"I think that if I were not Chinese I would like to be American," she sighs. "And when we get off the bus the next time I want to ask you a question." The gravity with which she says this piques my curiosity. What question could be so important that it would have to wait?

We pass day-care nurseries and are told that children stay overnight during the week and go home on the weekend to see their parents. We're assured that children are well looked after and that they are healthy and happy. By now I am wondering if the subject of religion or spirituality is taboo here.

Miss Feng explains that the name Canton was given by foreigners and that no one really calls it that except tourists who can't pronounce Guangzhou. She again mentions that the many American influences, such as speaking English with an American accent and driving on the right stem in part from *Voice of America* and from trade influences. As she talks about Americans she has met I realize with a pang that I miss my countrymen. I have not spoken with a Westerner in three days and have nearly three weeks to go until we return to Singapore.

As we alight from the bus to visit a paper lantern factory in Foshan City she indicates that the group should enter the factory. She then leads me to the back of the bus and pops the question she has been harboring all day.

"Connie Shaw, do you believe in God?" she whispers, waiting expectantly for my answer, which is obviously important to her.

"Of course," I say, gauging her reaction. "I think God is in everyone, even people who don't know it or who don't believe in a deity." I am instantly reminded of the passage in the *Bhagavad Gita, or Song of God,* where Krishna says "having pervaded this whole universe with a fragment of myself, I remain."

Her eyes fasten on mine before she speaks again. "You may not believe this, but we, too, believe in God, even though we are officially supposed to be atheists!" she announces with the weighty drama of an informant, caving in at last to reveal treasured national secrets to a foreign investigator.

"We have many underground churches and fellowships. We have every kind of Christian denomination. We also have Buddhists, Taoists, Moslems. Just imagine – we have Protestants, Catholics, charismatics. Everything. I just wanted you to know." She quickly glances around, obviously relieved to have unburdened herself of her secret, and sighing again, links her arm in mine. She proudly moves to the head of our assembled tour group which has gathered inside the paper lantern factory's lobby-cum-shop to await a tour of the lantern production facilities.

Round, red paper lanterns, adorned with long gold tassels, hang over-head. The glass cases of the shop display red paper cut-outs of dancers, acrobats, temples, trees and children. There are ornamental fans, greeting cards, and silk-painted scrolls. It seems that the word factory is used loosely to indicate a shop employing from ten to fifty workers. Factory working conditions are difficult at best and the work areas usually consist of ancient wooden tables on unpainted concrete floors in bare, badly-lighted rooms. Such stark cells are bereft of heat, air conditioning, electric fans or even ventilated windows.

Our tour takes a brief five minutes and we are once again aboard the bus, passing schools, temples, cotton and silk factories, and Friendship Stores, the national chain that sells souvenirs only to foreign tourists. The more we see of Guangzhou and nearby Foshan City, the more crowded, dirty and depressing it all seems. There is a brutish sameness about the buildings, streets, difficult laboring conditions, and the lot of the citizens. The disorderly, rubbish-strewn streets are filled with workers carrying heavy loads on shoulder poles, while three-wheeled trucks, wooden carts and wagons jam into each other in a traffic pattern without lane separation or any discernible sense of order.

From all that I have heard and seen of post-Revolutionary China, a dawning awareness of the severity of Chinese governmental repression settles heavily upon me. I am seriously concerned that perhaps I won't find my Master, the Great Teacher – God – in China after all. Is this trip a wild goose chase? Have I drawn the experiences of the trip to myself merely for spiritual growth and deeper understanding of cultural differ-ences and of human nature? *"Where are you hiding, Lord?"* I ask silently. *"Besides being inside of me, where is Your Form?"* I know He or She is on earth, but where?

At the next stop on the city itinerary we visit an old temple known for its artifacts and porcelain figurines. In the courtyard of the Sung Dynasty Taoist temple we are informed that the building has become a museum, like so many other temples in China. Before the colorful images fade, I'm seated on a museum bench, writing journal notes from memory of the tour as about twenty-five people gather around me. They press in so closely that I can hardly breathe or see to write.

"Are you a newspaper journalist?" an open-faced school boy asks.

"Why do you write with your left hand? Didn't your mother scold you and forbid you to do so?" asks another.

"What is your occupation?"

"Are you an American?"

"Do you listen to *Voice of America*?"

I chuckle at the barrage of questions and ask them to give them one at a time so that I can give each person a specific, clear answer. As I put my pen away they all crowd closer and push each other aside, trying to get a look inside my purse. I notice that I haven't yet seen anyone carrying a purse or a bag of any sort except Miss Feng. Such is the poverty. After I have satisfied the questioners Miss Feng appears and asks the crowd to give me room to breathe and not to stare at me as if I am a zoo creature. They giggle with embarrassment, and we all wave and nod on our way into the temple antechamber. A gnome-like priest inside gives us tea and historic information about the artifacts in the courtyard and the antique carved rosewood chairs and tables where we sit.

"Our people won't hurt you," she says gently. "They are fascinated with your Western way of writing from left to right and with your colorful American clothes. And they seldom get to see a woman with curled light hair, or makeup and nail varnish. If you feel like an exhibit on display, it's because to them you are. But they are kind people and they would never hurt you."

I assure Miss Feng that I'm not worried and that I have become accustomed to being stared at in most countries of the world. The tiny temple priest raises his hands and folds them in front of him to indicate that he is about to divulge some historical information. He tells us that the nine hundred-year-old temple had previously been burned and restored. There were formerly over a hundred temples and churches here in the Foshan City area but this and a few pagodas are all that remain of a rich religious and cultural past. The Revolution decimated culture, business, education, religious practice and agriculture as they were practiced up to the 1960's. It has begun to rain gently. The rain reminds Yu Lan and the other women that we need to find a bathroom

Yu Lan asks directions to the restroom and we are told there is a toilet at the rear of the temple. We are ushered around to the outside rear of the temple, for a brief break before continuing the tour of the temple grounds. The facility turns out to be a rectangular slab on the ground surrounded by a primitive enclosure with no roof. Raindrops fall on our heads as we use the filthy reeking facility. Inside the cubicle there is a red plastic bucket filled with dirty water; a foul oily rag hangs on a nail outside the wooden enclosure for hand- washing.

As we stroll back to the temple courtyard we notice that it is charmingly shaded with acacia trees, which contrast strikingly with the red lacquer columns of the buildings and the blue-gray paving stones of the inner court. The interior of one of the temples displays immense metal kettles, giant wooden gilt warrior statues, and an assortment of fighting axes, picks, hatchets and lances on long red poles. I wonder if these weapons are actually part of the temple furnishings or have they merely been assembled and installed here since the destruction of the original building? Buddhists and Taoists are notoriously peace-loving.

The temple roof trim is what really catches my eye and admiration. Thousands of twelve- inch high colored porcelain figures grace the upper outside eaves. There are merchants, warriors, sages, artisans. The effect is stunning and takes my breath. It is rather like a European frieze, except that this is three-dimensional and each figure is unique in gesture and costume. The main, middle, and front halls, and a stage and pool are situated in a square around the courtyard. Two stone singhas or lions guard the entrance. In the charming temple pool, there is a concrete sculpture of a serpent riding a tortoise. A water god statue oversees the pool and scores of twittering swallows dart amid the tree branches.

By the time we arrive at the museum's treasure room of Ching porcelain, silk, pots, and stone-age flint, we are overwhelmed by accounts of a past filled with wars, revolution, intrigue and revenge. An indescribable darkness seems to hang over the temple building and grounds, like a gossamer black shroud. What is it? Is it the vibrational residue of the murderers of the priests that yet persist? One of Frank Lloyd Wright's comments on war, in his autobiography, come to mind: "War itself is denial of civilization, its very nature a failure." AA, P 540

Miss Feng herds us aboard the bus which once again carries us toward the long-awaited boat trip on the Pearl River. As we travel through city streets, we notice scenes which are peculiar to the People's Republic of China. Along the sidewalks swallows chirp and chatter in the shade trees as cyclists in straw pith helmets weave between trucks and buses. Unpaved side streets ooze with a thick red mud about a foot deep. Strange conveyances sploosh their way along: vans, lorries, motorcycles with side cars, bikes pulling carts, wooden carts built from bike wheels. Suddenly a green 1954 Dodge, nearly thirty years old, emerges from the tangle of vehicles and I realize with a start that it's the first automobile that I've seen in China.

Miss Feng explains that cars, being symbols of the landlord class, were destroyed during the Revolution. Peasant revolutionaries believed uniformly that the "landlords" oppressed the people and that all landlords were evil. She adds that the peasant class, in their rampage, methodically destroyed everything that belonged to or represented the landlords. Among the devastated items were prized houses, cars, furniture, appliances, books, records, gardens, art objects, musical instruments, fountains, plumbing, sinks and toilets, sidewalks, stone walls, bridges, museums, churches, schools, hospitals with their supplies and equipment, surgical instruments, major landmarks such as tombs and bridges and irreplaceable architecture, such as churches, temples, mosques, stone gateways and towers.

She continues to explain about Mao Tsetung's last years and about the Gang of Four who terrorized the people before their final downfall. As she speaks, a deep, powerful feeling of revulsion keeps trying to sweep its way through my consciousness and body. With a supreme force of will I suppress it, during my stay in China, only to have it rise again and again each time I behold the immense destruction that resulted from a long period of chaos and civil war. Obviously I would have been one of the first to have been killed, considering that I am well-educated, have studied a number of different languages and have been blessed, through karma, no doubt, to enjoy a comfortable, productive life.

As we drive along city streets toward the river, she points to bombed-out buildings and to cratered temples choked with weeds. With the burgeoning awareness of the extent of the violent destruction of the ancient Chinese culture, nausea floods me and I fight the urge to vomit.

As we near the ferry dock Miss Feng begins to tell me that this is Dragon Boat Festival Day and that we will be seeing the slender festooned boats from our ferry. She is unaware of the shock waves which registered six points on my Internal Earthquake Scale as she specifically detailed the horrors of the Cultural Revolution. All at once it becomes clear to me that my emotional turmoil has to do with several issues all at once. First, the trip itself is forcing me to overcome an attachment to the familiar. Secondly, I am unable to be in control of information due to the language barrier and I have to rely upon my observations, interactions, and on what meager facts and details that I'm told. Third, and most important, the encounter with China and the Chinese is dredging up a host of compelling, yet abhorrent emotions and reactions of which I have been totally unaware in my consciousness.

The third issue actually concerns modern physics and spirituality and I can't escape the ramifications. Specifically, and simply put, Heisenberg's Uncertainty Principle completely destroys the myth of the impersonal, objective scientific observer. Every observer brings unconscious biases to the quality and act of his observations. The very act of observation even affects, on a sub-nuclear level, that which is being observed. In short, we all see through the filters of our cultural heritage, racial point of view, gender biases, and values and beliefs. Our own perception of reality changes what we see on some level and we in turn are changed by what we observe. Our perceptions are selectively censored and, furthermore, reality is co-created continually with others.

As Jane Roberts, the popular American author would say, "Our beliefs create our reality." *A Course In Miracles* would put it another way. We make continual choices which act as a screen for our perceptions. Further, the universe resides in consciousness, therefore, if we are harboring fear, for example, we will perceive a fearful world. We project the dominant theme or emotion of our minds onto our immediate world. In other words, the *Course,* Jane Roberts and modern psychotherapy would all agree that most perception is merely projection.

So why am I experiencing such revulsion at the thought of past revolution, death, destruction? Is it because I, as an educated, middle-class person would have been killed by revolutionary peasants if I had lived in China in recent years? Or am I much more attached to materiality than I have allowed myself to believe? Am I addicted to comfort? Or is it a dawning recognition that Communism, like all human ideologies has yet to deal effectively with the lower, more self-centered aspects of people, and that classism and racism exist the world over, in all cultures?

As the bus pulls up to the ferry dock I can see through the gray haze across the khaki-colored Pearl River that every acre on the opposite bank is either under cultivation or construction. Wharves and warehouses are jammed together next to a rusty assortment of ancient, dilapidated vessels. There is an anticipation in the air. What is it? Why this expectancy? The flat yawning river is choked with ships and boats of every size and description, the most immediately interesting of which is our No. 1 People's Ferry.

The light green boat bobs at anchor as we step aboard and are offered refreshments of soda pop and hard candies. The guides apologize for the quality of the drinks and candy, explaining that they are a new experiment in the country and that they have not yet found quite the right combination of ingredients. My companions' faces wrinkle with grimaces at the truly awful tastes and leave the drinks and candies unfinished on the metal tables under the ferry roof.

Taking advantage of a moment alone, I stand at the boat rail writing in my notebook, peering through the misted air at the last dirty rags of horizontal fog clinging to warehouse roofs across the wide-mouthed river. An occasional sampan disappears into the silent embraces of the fog while I become mesmerized by the slick, shiny river surface. With a churning engine hum, the ferry rocks and we pull away from the dock, roiling the waters into a sudsy beige dishwater color.

Under my arm I carry Strunk and White's *Elements of Style*, to which I refer periodically to pass the time.

"Are you writing a poem?" asks petite, cheerful Mr. Lee, craning his neck over my shoulder to see my notebook writing.

"No, not this time, although I do enjoy writing Japanese Haiku poetry because of its classic simplicity. I'm just writing in my journal. I've kept journals most of my life and find that it's a comfort to me, especially when I'm in a foreign country without close friends or companions to talk with."

"Yes, I suppose it would be," he said. "This is a poetic sort of day, is it not? There's the fog, the crowded masts bobbing on the water." I am surprised at his poetic nature and his grasp of English. He spots Strunk and White's *Elements of Style*. "What is that book you have there? A style book. Is it about fashions in your country? Does it have pictures?" he asks hopefully.

"No," I laugh. "Not that kind of style. It means style in writing. It's a very famous book about clear writing that is used by college English professors and writers. See? It's just a small reference book that I'm re-reading."

He examines the book and a faraway look comes into his eyes. He talks of his family, his aspirations to study in America, his love of poetry and theater, and finally, his desire to marry someday.

"Would you like to hear a short poem by Li Po, one of China's great ancient poets?" he asks tentatively.

"Absolutely – that would be lovely."

"It's called 'The White Heron'. It goes like this:

The White Heron by Li Po

That great flake of snow which has just floated
Over the lake was a white heron.
Motionless, at the end of a sand bank,
The white heron watches the winter." POTO P 218

"Do you have any of your poems with you?" he asks.

"I can remember a few haiku. You know, the haiku is an ancient Japanese form that can be written in one long line or in three short lines, but it must have exactly seventeen syllables. Haiku poetry is fun to write and most fourth graders in the U.S. and Japan like to write haiku. I've always liked to make up Haiku while traveling or while waiting in lines. So here are two that I've written:

The wind howls. It is late.
I must fasten my hood
and walk home through the snow.

*   *   *   *   *   *

Thunder rumbles in
a yellow sky. Look! a
gray mouse darts for cover."

"Oh, I like these haiku very much," Mr. Lee chortles, clapping his hands. I hope that the girl I marry will also like poetry so we can share it. My ideal girl will be strong and a good citizen and she will have a sweet nature, a fine character and will look up to me and will defer to my ideas and judgment," he announces. I ask if it would be difficult to find a girl with strength of character in combination with deferential behavior. He replies that, in fact, this is exactly the problem, since he has not so far found anyone who is sufficiently competent but equally pliable - but he's sure such a perfect creature exists. In any event he isn't worried since he is only twenty-one years old and doesn't need to consider marrying until four more years when the government deems it a proper time for men to settle down to family life.

"Look! Dragon Boats!" Mr. Lee is thrilled.

Far down the river we see rows of tiny slender boats heading our way through the fog and drizzle. As they draw nearer we can see that the boats carry five gongs, a drum, red flags, and several paddlers. A tug boat which is loaded to the water line with men in blue jackets and trousers pulls three dragon boats behind it. All nearby piers and bridges are packed with observers who shout and clap in anticipation. Black bumboats and decrepit junks jockey for a better view of the imminent proceedings, threading in and out past wharves of gravel piles, factories, cranes and barges. The dragon boats furnish an unexpected flash of joy, color and excitement amid the otherwise unrelieved impression of a drab and difficult existence.

The humm-chug of the ferry engine is joined by the moaning fog horns. Then there's a sudden blaring of the cheerful, staccato rhythms of "Yellow Bird," a well- known Chinese song through the boat's loudspeakers. As the ferry music starts, four hostesses in ironed, white blouses and pressed skirts begin to circulate about the boat, distributing newly invented "powder ice cream," stale peanuts, and soggy vanilla wafers. Once again, the tour group finds all the food either rotten, unpalatable, or otherwise inedible. Everyone is starving. Finally fresh-tasting watermelon arrives, reviving the group's sagging energy and spirits. The tour group is served cold wet towels with tongs and they remark on the earnestness of our hosts and their willingness to serve well.

"They try very hard but they have been so poor for a long time and very isolated so they don't know what to serve or how to do it most of the time," remarks one of my companions. Suddenly a scratchy, raucously loud Elvis Presley tape roars over the public address system, causing all aboard to cup their ears and to ask that the music be turned off. We are told that this is a newly acquired tape and that it is customary to play it at least ten times during the ferry trip! One of our tour members tells the hostess that he and his wife have headaches and that we would all, in fact, appreciate some silence. He elaborates, explaining that there is also a great deal of other noise with the gongs and cymbals from the dragon boats, the tug boat whistles and the roaring crowds lining the shores. The young hostesses look hurt but comply and turn off the music.

There's a loud "Whonnng" of a gong and the Dragon Boat Festival begins. Miss Feng comes over to tell me how much more she enjoys the city than the country and that she, herself, during the Revolution was sent to the country for five years of hard labor "to learn how to be a strong worker."

"All in all, it was a good exercise but I much prefer city life and all its benefits," she says. She displays a mounting enthusiasm for the boat race and has an obvious love of the noise and crowds both on and off the water.

After the boat ride we board the bus and our bus is swallowed up in heavy bike traffic. On the way back to the hotel a bike cuts in front of the bus, narrowly avoiding a collision, but knocking a toddler to the pavement who was crossing the street with her mother. In the next instant a speeding taxi hits a cyclist, knocking him down and not even stopping to offer apology or assistance. On all sides people on black bikes mash their way forward as horns blare, bike bells jangle, and police whistles chirp above the traffic roar.

From the bus window I notice two gigantic pink and black pigs lounging atop a pile of garbage, which obstructs the sidewalk. Their mouths are upcurved, as if smiling, and their front paws are crossed, as they watch a street fight. In the pouring rain, two teenage boys punch each other in a furious fist-fight as a crowd gathers under dripping laundry that flaps from bamboo poles jutting over the street. Already the crowd of about fifteen starts to shout and take sides in the fight as traffic is snarled by the onlookers spilling into the street.

The overwhelming combination of pigs and refuse, black oily mud, mildew and green moss covering the buildings, the ever present crowds and earsplitting, unabating noise, conspire to depress me. Vainly, I stare out the window searching for an interesting or colorful scene to dispel the oncoming gloom. Hungrily my eyes search the winding side streets for the sight of a flower pot, an attractive doorway or a vivid vendor stall to relieve the brutish, miserable scene before us. Every canal, river and fountain is brimful with debris. I have put my camera away since the scenes are not those that I wish to record and I cannot bring myself to believe that all of China will be as joyless and lackluster. Back at the hotel, the bus pulls up to the entrance and our eyes come to rest on the welcome, beaming face of Beijing Mr. Lo, eagerly awaiting our arrival. As we step down from the bus he rushes over to me with notebook in hand and draws me aside from the group, his face alive with anticipation.

"I have been thinking quite a lot about your special skills as a consultant," he begins. "Also there's the fact that you will be with us for three weeks in China so I would like to ask you to consider a very important request." He delivers his lines with gravity and a certain excitement.

"I think that we would be wasting a great opportunity for the building of a glorious New China if we did not ask for your assistance. You can render a noble service to our recovering country if you'll act as a consultant to the China International Travel Service and the People's Republic of China - at no charge to us, of course, since we are a very poor country. You can help us by pointing out specific ways in which we can improve our service to foreign guests.

"We need their travel funds to rebuild, you understand. We have only been open to foreign guests for a few years and we ourselves cannot travel abroad very much so we don't know how to run our hotels and airlines and other services. Since you travel quite a lot you know how things are supposed to be in exchange for the money you spend. So you see, it makes perfect sense that you should be the one to help us since you travel frequently and know the most about how it should be here for our visitors. If you will be so kind as to think it over and let me know by tomorrow I will inform my cadre in Beijing of your decision."

After smiling and bowing, Mr. Lo efficiently moves to the end of the row of stragglers leaving the bus and welcomes the group back for dinner. He would make a wonderful capitalist sales manager. He has actually used the words glorious and noble. His request has the tenor of an urgent appeal which could only be refused by the most heartless individual, totally unmoved by the tragedy which the Chinese have brought upon themselves. It's comical, really, to consider the situation. I am supposedly in China on vacation, on a rest from a hectic year, as well as on a search for my spiritual Master, and yet the trip has been anything but restful. And now, to top it off, I'm being asked to use my vacation time to do free consulting. If I politely refuse I'll perhaps get some peace and quiet. If I agree I'll have to ask myself the perennial question: am I being soft-hearted and soft-headed? The request will indeed bear overnight reflection.

As we approach the elevator in the corridor, we notice a hand-lettered sign taped to the door of the lift. A hammer and screwdriver lie on the floor under the sign, which causes me to chortle softly. The sign announces: "This lift is having repair. We are regrettable but today you will be unbearable. Please take the correct steps. Thank you for giving us your corporation."

There is a smaller sign taped to the smudged wall a few feet to the right of the elevator. It says:

"Laundry announcement. When the comrade knocks you at 6:00 A.M. you must surrender your clothes. This is our laundry policy. Clothes come back when they are finished."

CHAPTER 7
MUTINY IN HANGCHOW

"Buddha taught that truth, right conduct and non-violence constituted the most sacred qualities. You consider ahimsa (non-violence) as merely not hurting others. This is not the whole truth. Speaking too much, working too much, harping on the mistakes of others are all acts of violence (himsa) and should be avoided." SS July 1995 P 190

Hangchow, China
June 15, 1981

Hangchow, usually pronounced Hong Joe by Westerners, is reputed to be one of the most scenic cities of China. Although it experienced brutal devastation during the Cultural Revolution, to our senses it has a spell-bound feeling, as if the city is about to spring to new life and prominence. No prison escapee ever hailed the ground outside his jail with more relief than I've greeted Hangchow. The vibration of Hangchow is much higher than in the other cities we have visited and there is slightly more visual charm and order in the buildings and gardens than we have seen so far. Although I have been trying to interest my fellow travelers in their own splendid heritage and culture, I understand the depression they have been feeling due to the almost unrelieved ugliness throughout China caused by the destruction of the Revolution. The trip has been arduous but compelling. Beijing Mr. Lo, constantly bristling with enthusiasm, finally wore me down; I've consented to spend part of each day of this precious vacation to China doing free consulting "for the Glory of New China." I'm considering it service to future tourists to China as well as to the government of the People's Republic.

Immediately upon checking in at the Number One Hotel we are launched through the time-stopped landscape to visit silk factories featuring sumptuous brocades, and to pass by tenantless temples in the afternoon's smoky blue haze. On our way to well-known West Lake of ancient Chinese poetry we notice that the dozen or so Nigerian male high school students who are also staying at our hotel are being chauffeured about Hangchow in long black shiny limousines, complete with red flags rat-a-tatting in the stiff breeze from the lake. They must be related to dignitaries to merit such VIP Status and treatment.

At West Lake's shore we are ushered by pretty Mrs. Shen, our local guide, onto a blue and white motor launch, for a sedate ride across the lake for refreshments at the island tea house in the distance. It saddens us to see that the lake which is known around the world through painting and poetry is now polluted with rubbish. Flower Pond Park must have been breathtaking at one time with its pagodas, arched bridges and carp ponds. There are white moongates in the stone walls on the island and a green-painted tea house with large, sunny windows. We are offered the Dragon Well Tea for which Hangchow is famous, along with a paste of powdered lotus roots which tastes and looks like glue. The guide mentions that the powdered lotus roots cure virtually anything. Whether or not that is true, we all summon resolve and swallow it, not wishing to appear rude. Floating in the lotus pond beside the tea house are round, platter-shaped leaves bearing pointed pink and white blossoms. We are told that the lotus is an ancient symbol of spirituality because it is still beautiful though it grows in the mud. After tea we admire triple rows of blue and gray misted mountains in the background behind the lake. Remnants of the Cultural Revolution abound here. Sidewalks are broken, fountains smashed and ruined.

"The Red Guards even pulled up flowers here because the landlords enjoyed planting flowers. Therefore they considered flowers bourgeois. Such madness!" laments Mrs. Shen. "Let us hope that our Great Proletariat Cultural Revolution is finished forever," she adds softly.

A trip to the Xiling Seal Shop and the local Friendship Store ends the day but the mood aboard the bus is gloomy. My own mood is light in contrast, and I realize that I have at last adjusted to China and really appreciate the opportunity to be here. My companions are on the verge of either individual hysteria or a gigantic group temper tantrum since their images of the fabled city don't match the reality.

"You said Hangchow would be nice," Danny grumbles to Beijing Mr. Lo like a petulant child. "It's not nice. It has war wreckage everywhere, the streams are polluted, the lake is full of garbage."

All the while we had been hoping that the journey would improve in scenic beauty and comfort. China obviously isn't going to materialize itself into the sleek architectural grandeur of Singapore as my friends hope.

The elevator whirs and stops at floor "san" or three. Without a doubt, this is the finest hotel room so far on the trip. There are clean linens and blankets, a clean bath, and even carpeting. A sign on the main floor announces that there is a barber shop and a hairdresser - the first we have seen in a hotel in China. It is such a novelty that I decide to go downstairs and have a shampoo.

The "hairdresser" shop contains two antiquated red leather barber chairs from the nineteen thirties era as well as a small sink and a mirror. The only sink, designed for a gnome, is about two and a half feet off the ground and the barber chair seats are five feet high in the air creating a mystery as to how one goes about getting a shampoo.

"Ni hau," I say, practicing my newly acquired Mandarin.

"Yes, what do you wish?" asks the twentyish young man in the shop.

"Hello. I'd like to have a shampoo. But I don't see any hair dryers or blow dryers. Do you do shampoos?" I ask.

"Of course. This is a barber and beauty shop, as you can see by the sign."

"Fine. Shall I sit in this chair?"

"Yes. What do you want me to do?" he inquires.

"Oh, just a regular shampoo and a cream rinse."

"How should I do it?" he asks, with a perfectly serious expression.

"What do you mean, how should you do it? Just the usual way. Nothing special."

"But you must show me. I'm new in this job. I am a Communist and I work for the government. I don't know what to do."

"Didn't they train you before you got the job?" I ask, beginning to be alarmed that he's not joking and that he hasn't a clue as to how to begin.

"No. I was told to 'let foreign things serve China' and that the foreigners would train me. You must show me what to do."

"Well it's actually very simple, just like shampooing your own hair," I say, eager to be rid of my itching scalp.

"We Chinese are very poor and I wash my hair twice a month with soap. Soap is expensive."

For the first time I notice his greasy hair and realize that, once again, I am training a service person in China who has no idea how to do his job and that he'll probably charge me as well.

"All right. Just open your palm and pour about a spoonful of shampoo into it and then lather it up."

"What is lather?"

"Oh never mind, just hand me the shampoo, please and watch me very carefully… then you'll know how to shampoo your customers." I pour the liquid into my palm and lather it onto my scalp. He explains it will be necessary for me to kneel on the concrete floor before the tiny sink. I turn on the water and swirl the shampoo into a suds, then rinse it off. There is no cream rinse. Next I stand up, dry off my hair and ask where the dryers are to be found. There are no dryers. One is expected to utilize Mother Nature's method: the air. It's too late: my hair is sopping wet so I'll have to stay here several hours since my hair is thick, curly and shoulder length and takes two or three hours to dry naturally.

He takes a box of ancient, grimy rollers out of a cupboard and asks me to show him how to use them. I agree, and slowly take a section of hair, tuck it under each roller, and fasten it with a bobby pin, explaining how certain directional rolls create certain effects when the hair is brushed out later. I explain that since my hair is extremely naturally curly I must roll it after each shampoo to make it straighter. He doesn't understand and wonders why I want straight hair when other people want curly hair.

In two and a half hours the hair is dry. There are no magazines or other amusements in the shop so I occupy myself by scribbling notes into my journal and writing postcards until brush-out time.

"You must do the next step," he insists, meaning the comb-out.

"It's very simple. Nothing to fear. You just take out all the pins and rollers and brush or comb the hair out. See? Like this? It's all finished."

"Yes, very nice. I knew I would not like this job. In China we cannot choose our occupation as you can in the West. Now that will be two yuan, please."

Upon leaving the shop I wonder whether I have been the recipient of a "Tom Sawyer" episode or whether the man is actually as inept as he seems. An amusing fantasy scenario occurs to me wherein the U.S. has become a socialist state and a visiting tourist enters a state-run beauty shop operated by federal employees. The hairdresser in charge is new at his post and says "How do you expect me to know how to attend to your hair? I've worked for the Bureau of Reclamation and have never been taught about hair. After all, I'm a government employee; they told us that the tourists would teach us all we would need to know." Unthinkable. Preposterous. But such encounters have happened to us so far at least once a day in China.

As I walk toward the dining room I remember something that one of my first spiritual teachers, author-philosopher Gia-fu Feng, used to say. "Even if you strive for perfection in your work and you do it without heart, then your work will have no soul."

The ballroom-size dining hall around the corner from the registration desk on the main floor, is filled with French, German, and American groups who have just arrived. After being seated at our assigned table I overhear some handicapped Anglo-Americans from San Francisco at the next table tell their companions about Chinese reactions to them. Attractive people in their thirties, they are in wheelchairs and begin to speak Mandarin with good accents. It seems their entire tour is composed of handicapped people who have been preparing for years to make this visit.

A spectacled New Yorker in his early thirties walks past my table and vainly asks the puzzled waiter where he can find a piece of apple pie. The waiter's bewildered look, the man's request, and his nearly desperate, whining tone of voice prompt me to tell him that he probably won't find any apple pie in China. After all, it's an American dish and we are in China.

"That's exactly what I was afraid of," he laments pathetically. "It must be the fact that I know I can't get it here that causes me to have apple pie cravings all day and all night. I never have apple pie cravings in the States. I guess I'll have to wait two weeks when I get back to New York to have some."

"I've found it's helpful to constantly focus my attention on something else when I have thoughts like that," I say, patting his arm in sympathy. "You may also find that visiting China is really more of a revelation about yourself and your attachments and perceptions than it is a revelation about the country and the people. I myself have experienced any number of ups and downs and surprises which are just continual chances to let go of my old expectations and to see things differently. Travel is a challenge to our mettle and flexibility, don't you think?"

"This is my first trip overseas and after this I don't know if I want to see any other countries," the New Yorker replies. He wanders aimlessly about the dining room and finally strikes up an animated conversation with some other Americans who have apparently just recently come from, of all places, New York. It's amusing to me that I haven't seen any Westerners in over two weeks until now. He, however, immediately discovers some other countrymen in the dining room who are from his own state. We each get what we need at the moment of our need. I must not be needing to encounter Americans on this trip since none have appeared until now.

The rest of our party join me at the lunch table and stare down at their plates with mounting glumness. To me the cuisine seems attractive and delicious, though a bit repetitious, whereas my companions barely conceal their frustration at what they consider inferior fare. They mention that Beijing Mr. Lo has not told the truth about Hangchow or about any of the other cities. They say they understand fully why their parents left China during the Liberation and that circumstances here do not seem to have improved since. They are bitterly disappointed in their experience so far, having lost hope in China and faith in Beijing Mr. Lo's integrity.

"Just look at this meal," barks Danny. "We have had the same meal seven times already. Singapore is a tiny island but we are known around the world for over 5,000 specialty food items. We have over two thousand restaurants for our tourists. China is supposed to be famous for food but if you ask me it is all propaganda. I have seen enough of China to last a very long lifetime!"

Later, upstairs, as I lie on the hotel room bed jotting notes in my journal, I am again struck by the fact that most people waste lifetime after lifetime in the trivial concerns of the world. The necessity for discipline and for a continual focus on God are essential to avoid suffering. The mutinous caprices of the ego conspire to keep us separated and unhappy, when Spirit is ever-present within.

When old age weakens the mind and body and the will has given way to comfort, what hope is there for a sudden enlightenment in the last years of life, except through God's grace? Personal exertion is indispensable on the path, moment to moment. In other words, every use must be made of each day, of our spiritual practices and of our every encounter, so that we might awaken in this lifetime and not be bound to the wheel of birth and death like a planet of sleepwalkers, somnambulating throughout time, making but negligible progress.

Abruptly, the door bursts open unceremoniously and four of my tour companions enter, obviously upset and on the verge of tears. Without announcement or preamble they stride to the center of the floor, radiating the red auras of fiery anger. In a chorus, obviously rehearsed, they simultaneously chant "Oh my Gott! Oh my Gott!" Then they all commence to cry real tears and to stand helplessly before me like contrite school children, about to unburden themselves on their teacher with a confession. Ironically, they are older than I am, yet they somehow seem to think that I am the person in charge of our party. It's also hilarious to me that this is the first time they have mentioned the word God, yet in relation to comfort. Clearly, this is also my projection. I've been complaining in my mind and in my journal about comfort throughout the trip, just as they have. They're just more vocal, whereas I've been trying to set a good example about being a happy camper and a cheerful traveler. Isn't that funny?

"We heard these words in a movie in Singapore and we know how to say them when something bad happens," Yu Lan begins, referring to "Oh my Gott." "Now something bad happens and we come to you to help us. We don't like China. We very, very much don't like China. Too dirty. Very rude to us. Not much pretty things in China. Food, no good-lah. People not pretty-lah. We not happy-lah. Want to go home to Singapore. We ask you to tell Beijing Mr. Lo to stop tour now-lah. We finished with China now. We miss our children. Connie Shaw miss husband, yes? Okay, so you tell Beijing Mr. Lo all is finished."

Miss Tan, Miss Woo, and Mrs. Fu all nod vigorously in support of Yu Lan.

Stupefied, I realize in a flash that these women, like myself on occasion, are reacting to the continual discomfort and shock of China's devastation with an intolerable sense of loss. Most of them have never left Singapore. At home they have cooks, amahs and gardeners, live in attractive homes and ride in expensive cars. They have never camped out or suffered hardships except during the Japanese occupation of Singapore during World War II. By and large, they are unaccustomed to such difficulties as those posed by the trip. They are disillusioned in the "old country" with the constant insects in our food, mice and roaches in the rooms, outdoor privies, the hauling of heavy luggage without assistance, and the endless waiting in airports, restaurants, train stations and tour lines. They are no different from the New Yorker with apple pie cravings, or from me or from most Japanese we have met who have all grown accustomed to a tidy, convenient, comfortable urban lifestyle. To be plunged backward in time, vicariously exposed to the atrocities of the Cultural Revolution, and to be deprived of the daily interactions of their extended families back home is becoming too much to bear.

How ironic that they turn to me for assistance when China is even more foreign to me than it is to them. But we can't stop the tour. We've been told that repeatedly all along. We are only halfway through the trip and the China International Travel Service would never reimburse the money, though we all feel we have paid five-star prices for flop-house service at best. It's obvious that the situation calls for diplomacy, logic, and motivational inspiration. We must go on and we must find a way to enjoy it. Summoning a cheery smile and in my most convincing pep-talk mode I stand up and speak with vigor.

"Just think of the adventure we are having. Your families back home will ask you to tell about it many times," I proclaim, waving my arms for emphasis.

"Besides, in five years, this China we are seeing will be very different. We are very lucky to be seeing living history in the aftermath of the Cultural Revolution. Pretty soon there will be Coca Cola machines on every block and boutiques and movie theaters," I announce, hoping my meaning is obvious.

"Then we should come back in five years, not now," Yu Lan sulks.

"Anyway, it's too late. You know they won't let us stop. They never stop tours in China. We just have to put up with it. Besides, I just talked with some Americans downstairs this afternoon who were in Beijing yesterday and they said it is very exciting to see such a clean, modern city as well as the famous art and gardens in the Forbidden City. They also went to the Great Wall and later had Beijing Duck, which they said was the best duck they had ever eaten."

At the mention of the Forbidden City, the Great Wall and Beijing Duck their eyes light up. Of course! They have forgotten Beijing Duck. In the future I must remember how effectively the mention of food gets the attention of a Singaporean.

"Maybe we can wait. Yes, we can see if the real Beijing Duck is as good as Singapore Beijing Duck. We will go tell everyone." Yu Lan and the others race out of the room as swiftly as they have entered, hope renewed once again. Morning begins with boggling, contrasting sights and sounds, causing me to wonder if, after all, I myself have adjusted to China. "The universe is in consciousness," I tell myself, meaning that the interpretive part of my reality is self-created. The perceptions certainly spring from beliefs and attitudes so deeply held they are virtually imperceptible to the conscious mind.

We assemble in the hotel lobby and board the bus for a day-tour. Mrs. Shen will be our guide today through the silk and brocade factory and the Chinese medicine factory later in the day. Eventually she leads us into a charming red and yellow two story house. Across the front veranda of the house clusters of fat grapes hang amid curly vines. It is inside that we will experience the traditional welcoming tea while sitting in the ubiquitous stuffed sofas with white crocheted antimacassars, and receive a "briefing" about New China and the role of its manufactured goods.

The vision of New China begins to shimmer before my eyes as our dumpling-round, enthusiastic host, Mr. Wu, weaves his tale. Half of the workers in the factory of one thousand employees are women, which is very unusual, we are told. He looks at me as he announces with pride that women play a crucial role in the leadership of New China. He thinks China will be a leader in assisting women to realize their larger roles and gifts for organization, communication and influence.

He entertains us with anecdotes about the charming, much-admired Chou En-Lai, former co-leader of China and champion of the emancipation of women. He relates a well-known story from Chou's biography. "When the head of an Italian news agency came to Beijing, Chou asked him when he was going to send a man to cover the Chinese People's Republic." "We're not," was the reply. "We're sending a woman." The Chinese Premier clapped his hands in delight. "Ah," he beamed, "in that case our pleasure will be double!"

Mr. Wu warms to his task. "There was another occasion when Chou was visiting with his old friend Andre Malraux, General Charles de Gaulle's Minister of Culture. As they discussed the difference between Western and Eastern concepts of freedom with Malraux, Chou declared that the Chinese Revolution had freed wives from the tyranny of husbands, sons from fathers, farmers from landlords, workers from bosses, and all from corrupt and brutal warlords. China had found freedom, but it wasn't France's type of freedom or America's freedom. It was uniquely China's freedom."

His stories cause all of us to reflect on the various sorts of freedoms and tyrannies which abound in the world and to appreciate the great distance that China has apparently come in drawing nearer to her latest ideals. It causes me to reflect also, on the tyranny which humans in general have historically thrust upon each other, with the victory temporarily going to the larger, stronger, more wily, more educated, more sophisticated. Thus, parents have oppressed children, older siblings have abused younger ones, colleagues have outsmarted each other, neighbors have betrayed each other and lovers have broken each others hearts. However, karma is the great leveler, as a comeuppance, or karmuppance.

Suddenly, the tone becomes lighter as we hear about how brocade themes and patterns are taken from old Chinese folk stories and from famous art works. Technicians copy the patterns and paintings, often using as many as sixteen colors in a brocade design. There are four main workshops: designing, spinning, weaving, and quality control. We are told that we will now proceed outside to the spinning workshop to see fabric earmarked for export. Ninety-five percent of all industrial goods are sent abroad. Only five percent are sold inside China.

A narrow lane leads from the briefing cottage to the plant, which is a large concrete floored room with high ceilings, rather inadequate lighting and wooden tables. Designs are copied from original works, pictures and books, then punched onto oblong cards like computer cards. In the machine room there are three-foot skeins of pastel yarn hanging from the ceiling. The bright, fresh colors include strawberry pink, pistachio green, vanilla and almond beige.

Spoons on electric spinners combine rayon and silk threads for later weaving. As we stroll among the workers I ask a few of them if they like their work and they reply that they don't but that in China no one has a choice of career. Although the goods produced in Chinese factories are colorful, the people themselves wear drab clothing, no make-up, have neglected hair and nails and seem tired, plain and homely. There is little variety in appearance or in the workers principal possession, the bicycle.

Since the average bike hasn't even a reflector or any adornment, I was wondering how people manage to identify their bike from the thousands on the streets. Or does it matter? Someone could do well to create a bike-reflector business in China.

The secret of bicycle identification in Hangchow is revealed to me as we pass between buildings along the grass-bordered sidewalk to the weaving halls. Row upon row of identical black bikes are differentiated by colored bows of yarn or ribbon tied to the handle in the owner's own unique fashion. It's lovely and humorous all at once, those hundreds of bikes in neat lines, set off by perky knots and loops in every color imaginable.

As we step into the weaving halls I am unpleasantly astonished. The weaving halls offer the most unbelievable scene I've yet encountered in all of the thirty factories we've so far visited. From the dim room's interior, we are assaulted by the ear-splitting din of hundreds of China-made (wretchedly-constructed) machines, all banging and clattering at once, the horrendous racket reverberating off the concrete floors, tin roof, walls. There are no hard hats or helmets, nor even ear-plugs, or noise shields of any sort. This is like the perpetual nightmare of a mad-man trapped in a railroad yard with all the locomotives racing by simultaneously without cessation.

How can the workers endure this for one hour, not to mention day-in, day-out for months and years on end - if they survive that long? Recollections of printed articles outlining the scores of physical and psychological disorders and malfunctions caused by unabated noise and vibrations pass through my head. These workers must all be addled and deaf by now. Maybe they are in shock and don't even know it. Horrific conditions! I'm shocked into numbness and run out of the building, unable to bear the vibrations which rattle my body through the floor; even my teeth are chattering from this damnable, demon-like din. Dashing to a wooden bench across the sidewalk, I notice that my nose, teeth, ears and forehead feel numb and tingly, as if my head has been shot in several spots with Novocaine. My arms and legs feel as if they no longer belong to the rest of me, without feeling, unconnected.

Is it useful or necessary that any human being should endure such a nightmarish existence, merely for the sake of selling fabric to foreigners to bring in money to New China? These people are martyrs for China and don't even realize it.

When Beijing Mr. Lo joins me on the bench he is puzzled that I am so upset about the working conditions since this is considered a model factory. In any event, I add some more suggestions for improvements to the list he asked me to make throughout the trip.

By now the sidewalk is lined on both sides with watercolors hanging from clotheslines strung between trees. It is an art contest by the workers. The designs and paintings have been copied from books and several of the pictures have been created as a group effort. "Hello, do you like my horse?" asks one of the artists wearing a smock and pigtails. "My friend did the head, another friend did the body, and I painted the mane and tail." In most of the factories we have visited it has been rare that only one artist has worked on any object, whether it be ceramics, a jade carving, a wall hanging or a snuff bottle. The "hand-made" articles are mass-produced in design and passed from person to person to finish as many as possible in the shortest possible time. Perhaps that's a clue as to why even the artisans fail to enjoy their work and develop little feel for creation in the traditional sense.

Clouds of thick, black air pollution choke the streets on the drive to the Pagoda of Six Harmonies, the six harmonies being harmony of body, mind, speech, opinion, wealth, abstinence from temptation. It is strangely mollifying, after the silk factory experience, to take in the visual effects of curly roofs and weathered burgundy wood as Jimmy Ng and I climb to the top of the old building. As usual, I am the only one of our group interested in seeing the well-known sights of the area; Jimmy is accompanying me at the request of his parents, who sit in the bus with the others. They can't understand why I enjoy seeing these old temples and pagodas when "everyone knows that you visit China to buy silk, jade, and Chinese medicine."

It is cool and dark on the winding wooden staircase as we ascend the Pagoda of Six Harmonies. The thin board steps are so narrow under my Western-size feet that I have to walk up sideways, much to Jimmy's amusement. Puffing as we emerge out to the lookout spot on top, we are overjoyed that we made the effort to haul ourselves up here. The view of the wide river is spectacular with its double-decker steel bridge for cars and trains. Below us the wide crowns of thick trees embrace an orchestra of warbling, chattering, twittering birds. Even up here, the rustling breeze is a reminder of time's passing and that we mustn't keep the others waiting too long in the bus. *Thank You, Lord, for this blessed life and the countless, graced opportunities You afford me to see Your spectacular marvels on this jewel of a planet. I am endlessly grateful.*

Mrs. Shen next takes our group to the Hill of Hills Restaurant for a memorable meal of fish, shrimp, soup, beans, chicken, duck, pork, tea, beer and Chinese cream puffs. The event of the evening is a visit to the "concert." Yet the entire group, except Mrs. Shen and me, are so tired they beg to return to the hotel and to lie down, even though we have been asked to participate in everything. Mrs. Shen takes pity on them. After dropping the others off, she and I sit in the front seat of our reserved, otherwise empty bus, and swap life histories on the way to the auditorium. Most of her family were killed for political reasons over the past several years. She was formerly a music teacher and is thankful to be a guide due to the educational nature of the job. When she is not conducting tours, she explains somewhat sadly, she is usually very quiet and reserved. After all that she has seen and survived during the Revolution, her once joyful spirit has become considerably subdued and reflective.

There are several aspects of the evening that catch my attention as significant of the spirit of New China. The first is the condition of the restrooms we visit in the auditorium before the program begins. The floor, like every restroom floor that we have seen in China, is shoe-sole deep in urine. But the aspect that I notice most of all is the fact that the toilets are Western ones, accompanied by signs saying "Please don't stand on the toilets." There is a circle with a pair of bare feet drawn in the middle, crossed out by a red x, like a road sign. Despite the sign, there are numerous black shoe-prints on the toilet porcelain, the toes all pointing toward the wall, instead of away from it.

Throughout the evening the mood of the music is gay and international, with occasional punctuations of poignancy. There is a definite attempt to attract and satisfy tourists here. Burgundy velvet stage curtains contrast sharply with the concrete floor and metal folding chairs of the auditorium. Even the walls are gray concrete and create a slight echo effect from the three Hawaiian guitars, the organ, tambourine and drums.

The young woman who announces the program wears the same color and style dress as the announcers in Canton and in Shanghai did at the musical programs we attended there. Even her white high heels with the arch strap are the same. Throughout the evening the other entertainers also wear costumes which we have encountered elsewhere in China. Such uniformity in entertainment garb between cities is somehow novel to me. There must be some sort of national cultural committee which designates a dress code for entertainers.

It is startling, as always, to see makeup on Chinese women. Mrs. Shen tells me that most Chinese women consider it too much trouble and that, furthermore, the party frowns upon people trying to distinguish themselves too much through makeup, hairstyle or clothing. It is considered needless vanity.

In consulting the printed flyer which serves as the evening's program, we notice the international flavor apparent in the song titles:

Pigeons
Oh Susannah
Red River Valley
Ching Tao
I Wish To Become A Small Swallow
The Laughing Song
Jingle Bells
Moving Into A New House
Meow The Cat's Song
Beautiful City
Flight Of Wild Ducks
Beautiful Land - A Pakistani Song

Matador Dance
Sousa March
The Farmer And The Snake
Lark - A Rumanian Tune
Mama - An Italian Song
A Husband's Declaration To His Wife - A Japanese
Song
Beer Barrel Polka
Happiness Is Not Drizzle - A Chinese Song

The audience here is very different from the Guangzhou audience which didn't applaud the musicians. Here, the audience roars out approval of any American or Japanese song. They are quite familiar with all the music and are attuned to the musicians who are dressed in matching navy blue creased slacks, white business shirts and red ties. Several of the songs are accompanied by interpretive dances of exquisite execution and costuming. Mrs. Shen tells me that Hangchow has always enjoyed the arts, has been noted for the arts, and that it is starting to come into its own again. The political struggles of the country have subsided so that a more normal life can be resumed.

"Tomorrow your friends will truly enjoy themselves," she promises. "We're going to a Chinese medicine factory which is quite large and very unusual. It's too bad they missed such an excellent performance."

At the end of the evening, back at the hotel lobby, a glance at my pocket calendar reminds me that the day after tomorrow we'll fly to Beijing for a few days before visiting Xian and, at last, returning home to Singapore. I wonder if Jim and Wahid are receiving my postcards and letters. It's beginning to look as if God-as-a-human-Teacher may not be in China. This is an awful thought, but I won't give up until we have seen Beijing and Xian. Surely someone knows how to find Him or Her.

CHAPTER 8
ACCIDENT IN BEIJING

"Nothing ever happens without proper reason, however accidental or mysterious it may appear." Sathya Sai Baba, MBAI P 22

Beijing, China
June 17, 1981

Peking, or Beijing as it is now called, is one pleasant surprise after another to our changed sensibilities. Now that we have adjusted to China, Beijing, compared to other cities, is delightful. It is perfect that we are seeing Beijing and Xian last, before ending the journey with a return to Guangzhou. The reason that it is perfect is that, after our seeming privations in other cities, Beijing's people and offerings will stand out in a shining contrast of progress and modernization. Beijing Mr. Lo, the zestful cosmopolitan, is home at last and is eager for us to see what he considers to be the ultimate in Chinese cities.

Our trip to ten Chinese cities has been completely different from what I had expected, but has been a priceless experience nevertheless. I'll never forget the kindness and hospitality that I have been shown continually, nor the hilarious mix-ups and misunderstandings due to cultural differences and language impairment on my part. As the bus moves through the wide, tidy streets of Beijing, I recall the recent highlights of our trip to Kweilin.

For many years I had wanted to visit Kweilin and Shanghai. Now that we have seen them, my feelings about both are mixed. Kweilin is definitely worth a visit with its famous karst (limestone) mountains. Kweilin has an otherworldliness that is, in part, created by magical circular moongates set in enchanting, high-walled garden enclosures. The cavernous, gumdrop-shaped hills further the visual fairy-tale effect of Kweilin. Life must have had an extremely romantic flavor there in times past with the many secluded tea houses perched on tiny islands in still, lotus-accented lakes, reached by painted boats or by charming red-lacquered curved bridges.

It's easy to understand why artists have journeyed there to paint and to write poetry. The local names of points of interest are enough in themselves to inspire creativity. For example, we visited Hidden-Dragon Rock, Pagoda Hill, Elephant Trunk Hill and Seven Star Cave.

There were, in Kweilin, two events that stand out in my memory. The first is that I got lost from the tour group while we were exploring a captivating botanical garden. I was so entranced with investigating the small goldfish ponds, with running over lots of little hump-backed bridges, and strolling the shaded curving pathways, that after awhile I realized that my companions were nowhere to be found. In fact, there were no friendly human voices nearby – only the calls of Asian birds. I kept going around in circles in the maze-like park, past clumps of golden bamboo, under the dark cool shade of huge ancient cassia trees and over the same bridges. Round and round, up and down. Where could the entire group have gone? Finally I had to admit I was lost.

"Okay, Lord, I admit it, I'm very lost and don't know how to get out of here," I prayed. *"How about a little help?"*

"Just sit down on this bench and wait a few minutes," a small inner voice said.

"Should I shout 'Here I am!'?" I asked the voice.

"No. Help is coming. Just relax."

Sure enough, in about two minutes Mr. Neo Lam Heng came rushing red-faced around the corner. When he saw me his face broke out into a relieved grin.

"Oh, Shaw! We were all so worried-lah! We thought something bad happened to you. What happened? Oh, never mind. You are found. Let's go back to the others now. Come, all is okay now."

When we got to the bus I sheepishly apologized to the group and our local guide, Miss Cheng, and told them that the paths are like a complicated maze and that somehow I just got lost while examining the fish ponds and scampering over the little curved bridges. They laughed, all except Mr. Wee, who was furious that I had become a big inconvenience to the group, just as he had expected. I've always been friendly to him and his wife (poor wife – what a grump he is!) and have otherwise stayed out of his way.

The next incident caused me to think for a moment that I might be about to find some clues to finding my Elusive Master. It involved the first overtly spiritually-inclined man that I had yet met on the trip.

Kweilin, romantic city of art and gardens, was such a fabulous contrast to some of the other cities in China that our whole group was buoyed up with lots of chatter and laughter. We all felt the energy and fresh enthusiasm of imminent exploration. The first day we were there we drove through curving shaded streets onto a dirt lane that climbed up a thickly wooded hillside. The bus driver and Miss Cheng indicated that a surprise awaited and that we should exit the bus for a pleasant walk. As we clamored up the steep hillside our clamor was accompanied by jokes among our group about who had chicken feet and which of us were climbing on pig's feet.

Suddenly we came to an intimidating set of four hundred steps that lead to one of Kweilin's premier look-out points. Surely this was a heavenly spot in earlier times with the fragrance of apricot blossoms and vivid fuchsia hues of bougainvillea flowers that grace the stone stairway entrance. After we toiled up the last flight of steep curving steps we lunged, gasping, onto the gray stone deck at the summit. We were richly rewarded for our tenacious efforts with a magnificent view of the Li Jiang River which snakes its way through emerald fields and open meadows. All the while the river reflects the aquamarine sky, pearl gray hills and lavender mountains in its flat, placid waters. By this time my burning lungs were feeling like naked, skinless flesh-sponges dowsed with iodine.

Then, in perfectly-cadenced English, at my elbow, the most charming man spoke to me with an American accent, though he was Chinese. He was white-haired, about sixty years old, dressed in royal blue shirt and pants and rubber sandals, and sat on a ledge overlooking the city. He welcomed me to Kweilin and explained that he (Mr. Mak) was the son of an American Baptist missionary. For several years he had lived in San Francisco and in Singapore. He explained that he is a retired language teacher and that he belongs to an amalgamated Christian religious group. The fellowship consists of seventy people of diverse Christian denominations who have joined together to worship and to do service in the aftermath of the Revolution. Sensing a mutual spiritual bond, we carried on an animated conversation about all that is most immediate and meaningful in our lives (God, family, spiritual practice and service, work) for fifteen minutes.

He asked me if I were enjoying China. I replied that I was indeed overcome and was humbled every day at the tales of the Revolution and at seeing aspects of the old and new cultures of China.

"China has been humbled over and over," he said. "But G.K. Chesterton said that "Humility is the mother of giants. One sees great things from the valley; only small things are seen from the peak." TQC P 152

"But how have you been able to keep your faith so strong in the face of such a long period of violence?" I asked him gently.

"Chesterton also says that 'True faith is able to withstand the onslaught of any mood, event or condition, no matter how severe.' " As we admired the valley from the viewing platform I realized how much I enjoyed speaking to someone who understood my English but even more my life-orientation and values.

"Besides, they say a writer has become a classic when he's only quoted instead of being read. People are fond of quoting Mao at the moment. Things are changing."

"Mr. Mak, do you think that it is possible that there is someone in China like Lord Buddha or Lord Jesus now, who has come to inspire, to heal and to uplift people," I asked, in a whisper.

Before he could answer, time-conscious Miss Cheng began her group round-up. We reluctantly said our farewells, two strangers – philosophers both, and instant friends – on the windy hilltop. While shaking Mr. Mak's soft, bony hand, I was startled. I noticed that behind the scene of reflected sky in his wire-rimmed glasses, a solitary tear was sliding down from his left eye. It traced its way down the side of his nose and into the well-worn channel between his cheek and lips, to rest at the corner of his mouth.

What had caused the sudden sorrow? Was it memories of his youth in the States? Was he touched by the intimacy of my openly-extended friendship, naïve and unafraid, in contrast to the terror and suspicion which has permeated the country during and since the Revolution? Did he feel a comradeship with someone who loves God as much as he does?

I squeezed his hand, patted his arm, smiled, waved, and reluctantly began the steep descent down the 400 steps. Our whole group was galvanized with curiosity about my conversation with Mr. Mak. Who was he? Had I known him before? Why was he crying? What were we talking about with such animation?

Finally I explained that I had no idea why he was weeping. Perhaps he was suddenly struck, upon seeing all of us, with a great nostalgia for the freedoms he had lost. Maybe he wept for his lost youth or for his departed loved ones.

Danny Loh had asked these questions on behalf of the group.

"You know, Danny, I told him, someone named Joseph Addison once said, 'The great essentials to happiness in this life are something to do, something to love, and something to hope for.' Maybe Mr. Mak has nothing to do, nothing to love or to work for and nothing to hope for, in his own estimation of things."

Danny walked beside me down the stone steps. "We think you are a different kind of person, Shaw. We have discussed it. You are always talking to everyone and soon people are either laughing or crying. Why is this? The waiters in the restaurants serve you very carefully and people always want to speak with you."

"It must be that people are eager to practice their English with me. Besides, I believe that everyone is my brother so I simply assume that if I am kind and friendly to them they will be willing to talk with me. Talking with people in other countries is one of the ways I learn about culture and current events."

Miss Cheng, who spoke the least advanced English so far, had overheard part of our conversation. At the foot of the steps she drew me aside and told me that she believed in God and that she "liked very much Burner Saw, was crazy for Burner Saw." After five minutes of questioning her it turned out that Burner Saw referred to the author Bernard Shaw. She was so frustrated that I couldn't understand her *"Voice of America* English" that she told me it was just too much trouble to talk with me. She sat at the other end of the bus sulking for awhile on the trip back to the hotel.

After sleeping on varnished boards for three nights in Kweilin, we were all astonished to find real mattresses on our beds in Shanghai. There was even a mirror and the towels were fairly clean and didn't feel oily. Wonder of wonders, the toilet even had a lid, there were no urine stains on the carpet or the walls and there were no obnoxious smells in the hotel. Things were definitely looking up, if this were any indication. As soon as I got off the bus to visit People's Park near Nanjing Road, however, a crowd of about sixty people swarmed me. Our new guide, Miss Ho, in her early thirties, was a crisp, no-nonsense gray-uniformed cadre member. The crowd separated the two of us from our group and then the usual questions began.

"Are you a spy?"
"Are all American women as tall as you?"
"Are you as tall as your husband or father?"
"Are you a Capitalist?"
"Do your parents live with you?"
"What is that on your finger nails and why do you wear it?"

Miss Ho, like a salmon swimming upstream, finally was able to plunge through the morass to retrieve her charge and upbraided the people for peering into my purse while I searched for a Kleenex. She told them it looked ignorant to stare at foreign guests and that they shouldn't ask so many questions.

Shanghai, we were told, ranked with Beijing and Tianjin as a thriving industrial and commercial center, except for massive unemployment. We noticed from the bus that rows of ten men walked abreast on each side of the broad boulevard. There were miles of twenty abreast who were out walking in order to avoid thinking about their unemployment. It was a government program to keep order and structure, like the morning T'ai Chi exercises in the local parks for the elderly. Upon confronting the vast sea of humanity, all the men dressed exactly alike in royal blue pants and shirts, and rubber thongs, I found new meaning in the hackneyed phrase 'the masses of China.'

Next, we were told that Shanghai was opened to the West after the Opium Wars and that since it was a treaty port it was ultimately dominated by the merchants of England, the U.S., France and Japan. Miss Ho is militantly loyal to "Beloved Chairman Mao." While we choked in Shanghai's sooty air, Miss Ho told us of the dangerous bourgeois ideas brought to China by capitalists. She told of the millions sent to labor camps and that suicide and murder had been common during the Revolution.

Finally she mentioned two words that sent my colleagues into raptures: Chinese medicine. Most of the group had come to China expressly to buy jade, silk and Chinese medicine. A stir of anticipation whipped through the little group. The excitement was almost too much for them. They dug into their purses for long shopping lists of items from friends and relatives. Upon entering the glass-fronted store, they handed over their lists to the man and woman behind the counter. The wall behind the clerks was filled, floor to ceiling, with brown cubbyholes containing nature's mysterious healing agents. There were pots, bottles, bags and packets of powders, seeds, liquids, salves, ointments, unguents, balms, creams, potions, nectars and liqueurs.

Muey Low and her friends were nearly swooning with ecstasy. They discussed the specialty of such shops – remedies for piles – as well as rejuvenators; virility-restorers; items for energy; recipes for improved circulation; relief from gallstones or hernias; corrections for poor eyesight; a cure for warts and relief for the common cold. As people were handed their orders and stepped away from the glass case that served as a counter, I could see the objects which had caused virtual swooning. China is a notorious violator of international game poaching laws and is responsible for the vanishing of countless species used in Chinese aphrodisiacs. Now I could see where the poaching booty had led.

There was, under glass, an astonishing assortment of rare, if not disgusting animal parts. There were rhino horns, snake skins, pearls, goat's hooves, ginseng root, lotus roots, dried bear testicles, brittle leaves, dried flowers, and a motley assortment of unrecognizable objects. While my companions deliberated inside the medicine shop for two hours, I caught up on my journal notes and contemplated what we might find in our last city, Beijing.

We attended a first rate, lavishly costumed acrobatic show on our last night in Shanghai. My heart was very happy to have, at last, seen China, as disturbing as it is in many respects.

Our flight has been uneventful and at last we have arrived in the city that has been touted as the best in China by Beijing Mr. Lo. The bus slows down and Beijing Mr. Lo's voice takes on a rare timbre and excitement as we near the hotel, which is one of the finest in the country, usually reserved for foreign diplomats. By now we have become accustomed to the rigors of travel in China and no longer have high expectations for accommodations. We're keenly aware of China's poverty and have relinquished our previous disappointments concerning the disparity between the expensive trip outlay and the resultant inadequate service.

At the hotel a chubby, jovial guide about forty-five named Mrs. Teng, bolts out the front door and leaps into the bus. Bristling with energy, health and enthusiasm, she introduces herself and welcomes us. She laughingly tells us that she keeps fit through lots of walking and especially through early morning calisthenics in the park with her comrades. I wonder what Mrs. Teng's survival story will entail concerning outliving the Revolution. The survival stories continually inspire me.

Two porters follow her out of the hotel entrance and move swiftly to the rear of the bus to carry our bags. Porters! They are the first baggage carriers we have seen in the entire country. We set up a chatter about sinking back to decadence now that we have carried our own luggage in and out of buses and trains, up stairs, and through the rain and mud of every city and hamlet. Porters indeed. Our outlook has changed. Maybe it's because we're in our last week and will be back home in Singapore within seven days. The group has become more capable in the face of hardship and is far more appreciative of every bit of grace we encounter. We are thankful for our customary blessings at home in a way that would have been impossible without the difficulties of the trip. The privations, as with any trip, are an invaluable part of the experience of growth and gratitude.

The lobby is large and relatively elegant compared to our previous hotels, in a dark 1930's kind of way. There are four modern elevators. But it is the guest room itself that draws a gasp from Muey Low's usually silent lips. "Ah... good luck. Air con!"

The room is a vision of lavish comfort. It has air conditioning, wall draperies, carpeting, modern furniture, reading lamps, bedspreads, sparkling sheets (two, in fact, and a clean pillow case), and, amazingly, the towels are fluffy and pristine. The huge sliding glass door opens onto a balcony, which overlooks a park. It is our first encounter with a balcony in China. There is the usual sign beside the bed which warns that guests must pay extra for all electricity they use.

Another sign is tacked onto the door to the room. It apologetically warns: "It is forbidden to take hotel towels. If you are such a person who would never do such a thing, don't read this notis."

Downstairs there is even a huge, modern dining room and a coffee shop. There is order and cleanliness here in Beijing. The hotel appears to be indicative of the local values for cleanliness, efficiency, grandeur and beauty, unlike the values of other parts of China.

Later, we report to the lobby for the announcement of the day's itinerary, which includes a visit to a model commune, a city tour, a look at a school and exploration of the Forbidden City. Despite the hundred and five degree heat our spirits soar upon learning that tomorrow we visit the Great Wall and the famous tombs of Ding Ling.

Although I have interrogated temple priests, guides, scholars, Mr. Mak and old men about the whereabouts of a Great Master, no one has been the slightest bit responsive. I truly fear He's not in China. But I've taken every day tour just in case I should bump into him in a temple. I have a hunch that he lives in a temple compound in a rather remote area in a very populous country.

Aboard the bus Mrs. Teng stands to give a twenty-minute history of modern China on our way to Tienanmen Square, translated as Peace and Harmony Gate Square. We learn about the Monument to the Heroes of the People, Mao's Tomb, which we'll visit while here, and about key events in Chinese history from 1911 until the present. The other Chinese cities we have seen have been, to our eyes, colorful in their way and visually disorganized.

The main thoroughfares of Beijing stand in stark contrast, with miles and miles of immense sterile, beige Stalinist structures. The avenues and main squares are surprisingly gargantuan having the resultant effect of dwarfing human beings in their vicinity. At first glance there is a surprising lack of architectural warmth or originality of building facades. Yet there is nevertheless a bustling urban atmosphere of charged hope and shared vision in Beijing that is almost tangible. We sense it in Mrs. Teng and Mr. Lo and it emanates from people on the streets and in nearby towns. It's as if China has seen the error, tragedy and futility of Civil War and is rolling up its sleeves to modernize and to stabilize.

Peking, or Beijing, as it is called by the Chinese, is a sprawling capital city where the first skull fragments of that anthropological wonder, Peking Man, were unearthed in 1929. Only an off-and-on capital, and one of many previous ones in China, the city has had a rich and exotic past, not to mention a current era that has been both tumultuous and controversial. It was once even the capital of Mongolia.

My heart begins to thump in anticipation as we drive through the Tienanmen Gate, an immense red stone structure in a red wall, toward the Forbidden City. Why am I so strangely affected by the familiar-seeming golden-tiled roofs, dark red columns, green beams, and alabaster white bridges of imperial architecture? Did I live here in some distant past life?

Gardens, moats and watchtowers embellish the Imperial Palace, which is the largest and most complete congregation of ancient buildings still in existence in China. My mind staggers to comprehend it. Nine thousand rooms of wood and brick sprawl over the grounds as a remaining vestige of the ceremony and exclusivity that prevailed until 1911. Here it was that one could be put to death for failing to keep downcast eyes in the presence of the emperor. Brutality and beauty, juxtaposed.

Lovers of art and history give thanks that, due to a government decree, this architectural fairyland with its cobbled roadway, thrones, art and artifacts, has been officially designated as one of China's most precious historical sites. However, we see the paradox all too clearly. The objects of art also symbolize, to the citizens of the People's Republic, previous tyranny, exclusivity, and unshared fruits of feudalism. Where Westerners see breathtaking human achievements in the fine arts, the Chinese see the results of power and vanity. That awareness puts art history in a new light altogether and creates in us the mixed emotions of awe and bewilderment.

Energetic Mrs. Teng links her arm in mine as we mount the steps of the Hall of Supreme Harmony. We pass large bronze incense burners, bronze storks, and tortoises flanking the staircases. On cue, everyone looks up to admire the "Florentine" ceiling, which originated in China, and begin an intense conversation which continues through the Hall of Complete Harmony, to the Hall of Preserving Harmony. Dragon-emblazoned gold columns and black marble bridges and floors serve as an incongruous back-drop for Mrs. Teng's story of survival. During the Cultural Revolution she lived with her husband, a laborer, and her twenty-year-old daughter, a medical student.

Against magnificent ceilings and walls stand four turquoise cloisonné jars on gilt stands.

"They were used for the burning of ceremonial sandalwood incense during the reign of the emperor," Mrs. Teng explains. Then, as the group members move to inspect the huge jars, she looks around conspiratorially.

"Tell me, Shaw, do you believe in God?" Mrs. Teng asks suddenly, on our way to the Palace of Heavenly Purity, a strange irony of location and subject matter.

"Yes, indeed I do. And the longer I am in China the more sure I am that the Chinese people must have a tremendously strong faith to have endured all that they've undergone so far. I weep for China - for her poverty, courage, and disorder now. I mourn for the killing, destruction, and lost arts but cheer her recovery from hardship. She is striding fearlessly into the future with amazing eagerness and hope. Such enthusiasm! But she will be great in a brand new way that will surprise everyone, I think. What about you, do you believe in God?" I ask.

"Oh yes, I know there is a God. You see, we have lots of underground religious practice here. Atheism is an official party line but we do not really believe in atheism. It is only our religion that has kept us alive all these years when we all went crazy and started killing each other. Even now, things are not as calm as we would like but we now have a great faith. That faith will never be taken from us. That is the only thing they can't take away and it is the most important thing... so we win after all, you see?"

"How have you managed to stay so humorous about life and so full of pep after all you have endured," I ask, curious about her overall philosophy.

"It's easy. Just stay in each moment - not full of worries about the future or drowning in sorrows of the past. If more people knew how to do that we would have a very different world and everyone could enjoy happiness right now."

Beijing Mr. Lo, at the head of our procession, leads us with obvious pride to the Echo Wall and the Circular Mound Altar where previous emperors made sacrifices to their gods on the winter solstice. The arrangement of the walls surrounding the Imperial Vault of Heaven and the center ground stones of the vault provide an unusual acoustical effect resembling an echo. We take turns standing against the wall and, cupping our hands over our mouths, send "phone calls" to our friends standing many yards away up on the higher courtyard mound stones. Although we speak softly into the Echo Wall they can hear us very loudly from the Triple Sound Stones under their feet on the high terrace.

While we joke and experiment with the sounds, a mildly startling image comes to my inner eye. Wave after wave of civilizations have evolved toward a crescendo of artistic and scientific achievement only to be followed by decline and the destruction of strife, war, invasion or natural cataclysm. It seems that a lengthy, uninterrupted period of peace, prosperity and technical expression has so far not been possible due, perhaps to man's less advanced behavior at the mental, emotional and physical levels. Our technology is far more developed than our ability to love each other. Is the continual rise and fall of civilizations merely part of God's play, without much meaning, throughout eternity?

On the bus trip to the model commune, Mrs. Teng again sits beside me in the front seat. As she tells of her hopes and dreams, which mainly consist of better housing and a better job for her husband, she suddenly squeezes my hand with the strength of a wrestler and turns to stare at me.

"I like you very much, Shaw," she exclaims with her usual ebullience.

"Now tell me, how did you get your hair like that, with those bumps in it?"

I explain that it's naturally curly and just grows that way.

"All Westerners have big noses that stick out from their faces, I have noticed," she further muses. "We Chinese have nice little noses like knobs. I like Chinese noses better." I don't bother to tell her that my nose is perfectly proportioned for my face, is not large and that I've done both ramp and TV modeling in Europe and the States for charity fundraisers. Chinese people think that all Westerners have big noses and depict Westerners grotesquely in cartoons.

"I've been thinking about the color of your hair. It's like the shadows in the wheat mounds over there, across the fields," she gestures out the window. "During the Revolution I was sent to chop wheat, to build my character. I would rather be doing this tour work, but when you know how to live in this moment you can endure anything because eventually all moments change into other moments and other places, filled with other people. You must never get soft, Shaw, because when you are strong you can take anything and even laugh about it."

Each time Mrs. Teng makes a point, she sharply pounds my right thigh with her iron fist which sends a little knife of pain up my leg. This time she socks my leg with extra emphasis and, to my consternation, rests her hand on my thigh for the duration of the bus ride. This act exemplifies the child-like social innocence of so many people we have met here and is at once endearing and unnerving, due to our own more reserved training and mores. I ask Mrs. Teng The Question – if she thinks there is someone like Buddha alive now in China.

"No, not now," she says.

Our first treat at the countryside commune is visitation at a "peasant-home-which-is-typical." A dusty lane leads through shady fruit orchards and past mud pools of dozing water buffalo to a small flat-roofed brick house. Inside, a black garbed woman about fifty, wipes her hands on her apron and greets us, beckoning the group into her sitting room. When she smiles we see that she has no teeth, nevertheless she answers our questions patiently and explains that she is on cooking duty today and is preparing the main meal for her housemates who are out in the fields.

Two European calendars hang on the plaster walls as decoration above a simple wooden table with a small fish tank. Goldfish and black mollies swim lazily about. In the cool room we arrange ourselves on the red vinyl sofa and various unmatched wooden chairs placed upon the tiled floor. Our hostess has five children and explains that there is no stringency on birth control on this commune, something we have heard elsewhere on other communes from people who have three and four children. Mrs. Teng explains that the national policy of one child per family is very unevenly enforced from province to province, hence the wide variation in family size.

We are told that there is no electricity here and that water for cooking and bathing is hauled from a nearby well. The men take turns cooking with the women and the children attend a nursery school which we will see next.

Outside, the sun beats mercilessly upon our hatless heads as we march single file along the narrow dirt track behind Mrs. Teng to the nursery school. Rude cinderblock structures, chinked with mud and cement, are scattered about the huge compound, bordered with open ditches of swirling, muddy water. Mr. Wee's six-foot frame obscures the view in front of me. Suddenly he shouts in alarm and leaps across the ditch beside us, then dives to the ground on the opposite bank. He scoops his hand up out of the water's edge and holds aloft a drenched, terrified yellow chick. The quivering chick fell down the embankment and would have drowned, but for Mr. Wee's sharp eye and timely rescue. He scolds the chick for all to hear, then tenderly sets him down in the grass to endure the scolding of his approaching mother. As she roars up to her trembling offspring, it suddenly becomes obvious to me how we got the American expression "mad as a wet hen."

Mr. Wee shakes his finger at the chick in a final warning. "Make China proud of you and don't be so foolish again. Next time I won't be here to save you," he remonstrates in Cantonese. We are all touched with his kindness, but even more with his humor since he has been silent and glum most of the trip. For weeks he has been hissing and grumbling to his wife each time I walk near them. But now I have seen his soft side and wonder if he is grumpy because he is ill or perhaps ill at ease at being out of his element.

We glance up from the mother hen and her brood, feeling other eyes upon our group. While we have crowded around the chicks, the rescue scenario has been keenly observed by the compound barber and his customer. The outdoor barber shop lies thirty feet away across the flat, dusty yard between the tightly packed buildings. He lifts his straight razor to us in greeting and nods with a broad smile, obviously approving of the rescue. Then with a touch of flamboyance, he drapes the man on the stool with a dark blue cotton cloak and shaves him meticulously in the outdoor barber shop in the purple shade of the light plaster building.

We can hear the singing of the children from beyond the cement wall surrounding their school building opposite the barber. Upon our entry into their classroom they all stand up and sing with extra vigor, forming a choo-choo line and weaving about the room, praising Chairman Mao and

and the soapless Guangzhou hotel laundry, in washing some brand new white slacks turned them putty gray. There's also a used paperback book, a slightly torn shower cap, a melted lipstick and melted swimming cap. Out of the corner of my eye I gauge her reactions, not wanting to offend her. Her eyes are large with anticipation, fixed on the waste can as if on a newly-discovered treasure chest.

"Would you mind emptying my trash can?" I ask, happy to have been able to provide a few things for her.

"Yes, yes. I do now." She's thrilled and flashes out the door.

The Merthiolate-colored dawn streaks a dove gray sky when Muey and I awaken the next morning. We flip the room light switch and the table lamp but nothing happens. Either there's an electrical failure or the hotel turns the electricity off at night. Groping like the blind, we dress and comb our hair in the dark room, hoping our lipstick is being correctly applied and is hitting the right spots; we skip all other makeup.

We carry a flashlight to the elevator and whip the weak light-stream around the lobby and reception desk area. Han sleeps at the desk but awakens and explains that the elevators and electricity are turned off all night as a thrift measure. He disappears in the darkness to turn on the elevator then returns smiling and ushers us into the lift with a dramatic wave of his arm.

Our two reserved breakfast tables near the window have nearly filled with group members as Muey and I stagger over, thick with sleepiness and sit down next to Jimmy Ng and Danny Low. The dining room is beginning to be illuminated by the faint light of dawn. We all look up to say good morning and simultaneously burst out laughing. Danny wears a big blob of shaving cream beside his ear. Muey and I have missed our lips considerably with lip color, and Jimmy is completely oblivious to the fact that his shirt is on inside-out.

The next day, the highlight of the afternoon is the visit to the Ming Tombs at Ding Ling and an exploration of the Great Wall of China. The tombs and the extraordinary avenue were off-limits until recent times. Again, as with other architectural marvels, only royalty were allowed to venture there. The Sacred Way, as the approach to the tombs is called, is punctuated along its four mile path with the White Marble Gate from the middle ages, with a Great Red Gate, the Stele Pavilion, the Avenue of Animals and finally, the Dragon and Phoenix Gate. We stroll along the Avenue of the Animals, admiring the twelve facing pairs of marble lions, elephants, camels and horses.

The animals, all in either kneeling or standing positions, are life-size or larger sculptures which guard both sides of the road. In olden times, we are told, the penalty for entering the grounds was death, since this very road was used only to bear the body of the emperor to his final repose in the tomb at the end of the avenue. Even the living emperors used another route to visit the tombs. Museum buildings in the courtyard contain over three thousand artifacts which were found in the underground tomb. The three flights of stairs to the tomb itself lead to three vast, empty rooms where the Emperor Wan Li was buried. The immense scale and elegance of design are startling in this tomb and in the nearby gates, walls, courtyards and terraces. What a contrast the graceful, inspired ancient Chinese architecture is to modern, uninspired architecture throughout the world!

Outside again, we notice that the air here has an unusually soft yet vivifying quality which we've not encountered in China so far. Ding Ling itself is magical and must have been so when it was selected as a tomb site. Mrs. Teng walks briskly up to the head of our group, takes my hand in hers, and explains that the location of the tombs was selected with utmost care through divination. Two of the criteria for the chosen spot were that there must be protection from the north (the origin of evil spirits) and a plentiful, natural water supply nearby.

While herding us back into the tour bus, Mrs. Teng announces that the two best treats of Beijing have been saved for last. The first of our farewell treats will be a visit to the Great Wall, followed by a grand finale dinner this evening at the famous and incomparable Beijing Roast Duck Restaurant. There is a cheer from my usually composed companions who have been awaiting this meal for three weeks, their tastebuds virtually standing at attention at the announcement. My own tastebuds begin to align in sympathetic resonance with those of the group. I'm not complaining, mind you, but one can only survive for so long on Dragon Well Tea, lotus blossom roots, and rice without a few pangs of nostalgia for a change.

The bus speeds along the smooth highway over arid foothills, through the finest air in China toward the Great Wall, which was first built between 770 and 476 B.C. Mrs. Teng elaborates upon its three main uses. First, it was a fortress against the slave-holding northern invaders. It has also served as a communication link for the many provinces of China. Finally it has been a military road where columns of ten men abreast could march upon its lofty, undulating heights.

At the base of the Great Wall a cluster of eight workmen squat on their haunches eating lunch in the shade of a spreading tree. As we approach the wall entrance they all stare as if they have never in their life seen a Westerner. Come to think of it, maybe they haven't. They poke each other and remark about my height and comment upon my figure and clothing, then point to the Chinese women serving orangeade at the make-shift cafe who wear sleeveless undershirts and slacks, like most of the women I've seen in China. Not once have I seen a bra on any of the bamboo laundry poles, or on any of the women I have met. Obviously in post-Revolutionary China it is either a rare luxury or deemed by the government to be unnecessary and decadent.

Dirt-caked toddlers and older children come running as I approach then abruptly scamper away again to bring other gawkers. The children scrutinize me with open mouths to which I smile and wave in response.

From the top of the wall the view is a rugged one of steep hills, cactus plants, and purple distant mountains. Odd cries rend the air. Below us, in a courtyard there is a lavishly decorated, red-tasseled camel unwillingly tethered to an olive tree. He is furious. The camel which seems out of place here as I do to the Chinese laborers, releases a series of outraged wheezes, snorts and brays to be freed at once - all of which are ignored. He serves as a "photo op."

For Danny and Yu Lan it is a life's dream fulfilled to be standing on this wall and they heartily approve of its workmanship and the once-great China that it represents. They lament that, in their opinion, except for continual social reforms, nothing worth mentioning has happened in the arts or sciences in China in nearly a hundred years. I have too little knowledge to respond with any depth or certitude to the statement. But there is a persistent feeling within me that a great and important social experiment is taking place in China now. Since one in four persons on the planet is Chinese, it will surely affect all of us profoundly sooner or later. Is the experiment essentially the subjugation of the self in order for something brand new to take place in the world? Was it completely necessary that millions be killed and tortured to bring it about? Or was the killing a karmic result of mass murder in some ancient era? Is it subsiding now - this apparent madness - or merely dormant before another outbreak?

The enormity of China and of its potential significance to our world sweeps over me, combined with a resolve to return in the near future. A fascination for this country has gripped me which I am reluctant to shake off or to ignore. Despite my shock and revulsion at the chaos and filth I've seen here, I'm captivated by China. This evening, at long last, we are to experience Beijing roast duck. The Beijing Roast Duck Restaurant has reserved a small room for our party of eighteen. Like so many other restaurants in China it is unadorned except for two round tables covered with white table cloths and a brown wood lattice screen standing next to the tables.

We are to leave Peking tomorrow, enroute to Xian before returning briefly to Canton and Hong Kong. In my mind I review some of the more exotic gourmet fare that has passed my lips these past weeks: fish eyes, grass, flowers, seaweed, lotus roots, lotus root powder paste, Dragon Well Tea (which looked like seaweed), jellied duck wings, thousand-year-old eggs, pig's intestines, bamboo roots and shoots, gallons of mineral water and cases of the ubiquitous orange-ade. There were two rare and memorable cups of coffee and two counterfeit Cokes, complete with fake logo, but made in Hong Kong and shipped to China. They have perfected the can but not the taste.

Eventually the chef arrives bearing, with tremendous import and fanfare, the large platters of steaming Beijing Roast Duck. He and his assistant chef waft it under our noses and wait expectantly for our approval, which is instantly forthcoming. We are ravenous beyond belief and imbibe mineral water until the roast duck is returned to the kitchen to be deftly, ceremoniously carved and accompanied by brown sauces and a tortilla-like bread. Yu Lan entertains us with a folk tale about an ancient emperor and his beautiful lover until new serving platters arrive.

There are three roast ducks per table, served complete with head, wings, and even feet. Nothing is wasted among the Chinese and the ducks are no exception. First we are served "Soup of the Bones of the Duck" followed by bamboo shoots in sauce, meat dumplings, green beans, rice, mushrooms, duck meat and sauce. There is more duck meat and sauce. After the fifth helping is pressed on me, when I begin to suffer acutely from an engorged sensation, I protest loudly at receiving any more and, covering my plate with my entire upper body, tap the table and say "Sieh-sieh" meaning "thank-you."

But we are not finished, though the room is a blur and I have released my belt to the last possible notch.

"Now, Shaw, we give the best part to you. You must sample our very famous webbed duck feet, which is a delicacy that we eat last," announces Mrs. Teng mercilessly. She plops a pair of bouncy, wart-covered webbed duck feet onto my plate and stands over me holding her breath expectantly for my praise.

Webbed duck feet! How will I swallow them? What if they don't stay down? This is the ultimate challenge so far in China. I stare at them for a long moment. Then, using my old stand-by trick of pretending that certain food is something else that I enjoy, I smile weakly and proceed to chew the tough, prickly, rubbery webbed feet which have been dipped in sauce. They qualify as being the most ghastly things I've ever eaten and I myself qualify, in my own mind, as having passed the supreme test of tactfulness and decorum by giving the impression of relishing them and neither fainting nor heading for the washroom. Another triumph. The others smile in approval.

The dinner has been worth our anticipation and already, as we stagger down the stairs, bloated, our companions tell Mrs. Teng they will return next year to Beijing if only for the roast duck. Tomorrow we leave Beijing and a note of nostalgia lingers in the air.

Since I have seen no sign whatsoever of my Master in China, I think He/She must be in India. But where?

Our final day in Beijing has arrived, regrettably. It is ten minutes before flight time in the Beijing airport so we busy ourselves with planning to have a last soft drink before boarding the long flight. A soft drink machine is enshrined on a four-foot-high platform in the center of the departure hall as an indication of its importance. There is no ledge around the machine, just the steps up to it and about a four-inch tile trim around it to set it off magnificently. Fascinated with its unusual prominence and location I stroll over, place some change in the slot and get a soft drink. Immediately a long line forms behind me. As I turn from the machine to let others approach it I step to the ledgeless side of the machine. Into thin air. I had forgotten for a moment, in my zeal to be polite, that there was no place for me to stand when the crowd quickly formed behind me, pressing to get a soft drink.

Then I realized I was falling and suddenly became horizontal, like the cartoon character, Wiley Coyote, falling off a cliff. I clawed the air until the hard, cold marble floor of the airport slammed the entire horizontal length of my body. Whap! I have fallen four feet on hard ground. Stars wheel about in my head as the cold marble floor of the airport slams against my cheek while a searing pain rips through my right ankle. I have hit my head really hard and have broken my ankle. The realization of these facts combined with overwhelming pain sinks into my mind, along with a feeling of helplessness and the knowledge that I could go into shock at any moment.

I have broken my ankle and have perhaps given myself a concussion five minutes before boarding the plane for Xian. I am in a foreign country and don't speak Chinese and there may not be a doctor in the airport or on the plane. Immediately a crowd surrounds me and Muey Low and Danny help me to my feet, or, rather, my good left foot, as I sag in their arms and fight off waves of nausea. A Japanese woman sitting in the closest chair drops her book and yanks a large roll of white gauze out of her purse, explaining that she is a nurse, and wraps my rapidly swelling and darkening ankle. As she does, our flight to Xian is announced. My temple throbs and the goose egg over my eye swells to the size of a tennis ball. In a blur of pain and confusion, I thank her and, flanked by my two companions, hobble to the plane. Mr. & Mrs. Sun, who are the tallest in our group, help me up the steps and into a seat where we learn that there is no aspirin, nor a doctor aboard the plane, and that the flight will take several hours. The ankle definitely seems broken and it is too late to get off the plane and go to the emergency room of the nearest hospital.

Now what am I going to do... with a broken ankle, a probable concussion, and several hours to wait before we can find a doctor?! This venture to look for God is taking every scrap of courage I can muster. My helplessness and the necessity for total reliance on God have seldom been more apparent in my entire life.

"*Help me, Lord! Please, please help me,*" I pray silently, hitting my first true low point in Asia. "*Please don't let me go into shock or into a coma. Please, please help me find a competent orthopedic surgeon to set the bone, Lord!*"

CHAPTER 9
ACUPUNCTURE PARTY IN XIAN

"Service to man is service to God." Sathya Sai Baba

Xian, China
June, 1981

Throughout the flight to Xian (See AHN) I try to meditate so as to separate my consciousness from the increasingly sharp stabs in the leg. The ankle swells further and continues to change color. By the end of the flight the leg has a dark purple, misshapen appearance and is stiffly swollen to twice its normal size, and the foot is much too large for its shoe. In fact, it looks like a giant black sausage. After we land in Xian, the two petite stewardesses ask me to remain in the plane until all the other passengers have disembarked. Next, they ask me to hop down the aisle to the exit door where they will assist me in getting down the metal staircase. It is a comical spectacle of a wounded Gulliver vainly assisted by two Lilliputians, each under five feet and less than eighty-five pounds. Both of the flight attendants sag under the weight of someone who is half a foot taller and weighs one hundred and twenty-three pounds.

It's obvious this solution won't work so I wave them off and use the last remaining strength to hop laboriously down the staircase a step at a time. Finally, as I reach the last step, perspiring and breathing heavily, I flop over the railing as limply as a rag doll and hang there, in full view of my astonished Ik Chin companions standing beside the Xian guide and her awaiting tour bus far across the wide runway.

It would be untoward, in virtually all circumstances, for an old-style Chinese Singaporean man to touch a Western woman, even to assist her. As the five men and thirteen women of the group stare at my plight I am reminded of the tragic story of a beautiful and beloved Queen of Thailand where there were taboos against touching the Queen. During a water festival her royal boat sprang a leak and sank.

The Queen drowned in full view of her adoring subjects who, because of tradition, felt themselves helpless to save her life. The law was changed after that, but it was too late for the Queen.

The frustrating absurdity of the situation, in combination with the unremitting pain of the ankle chokes me to tears and the ferocious heat slams down on my head like a plank. This is a good test. Can I truly "give thanks for all things? Even now?" The stewardesses are immobilized and speak no English. The crowd across the asphalt stand frozenly expectant. Time is ticking by. The air-conditioned bus is waiting. Such an occurrence has obviously never happened before. It is more than awkward and no one knows what to do. My strength is spent, after hour upon hour of unrelieved excruciating pain. For a moment patience fails me. *"Good God,"* I think vehemently. *"Will no one have the decency to help me?!"*

Finally, with a mixed expression of exasperation and personal triumph, tall Mr. Wee bolts from the tour group and lopes across the runway in a lanky, self-conscious stride. He is the last person from whom I would have expected aid. It can't be Mr. Wee - who has been so incensed all along at being forced to travel with a Western woman in the group. But it is indeed crew-cut, silver-haired Mr. Wee, the retired factory worker who has never ventured outside of Singapore. He, who has never shown any leadership throughout the trip, except to insist that the American be educated in table manners, is now lifting me up, as a father would a child, and shouting Cantonese encouragements all the way, he trots toward an empty jeep parked about thirty feet from the plane. Smiling broadly now, he looks positively youthful for the first time of the entire trip.

"Nevah mind, Shaw, nevah mind. All is okay-lah." I am stunned that he knows English and that he uses my name. He starts to laugh a joyful laugh of relief and, as he gently sets me down into the passenger seat of the Army jeep he gives a command, "Shaw: stay-lah" and nods, bounding away, alive with a plan. The canopy of the jeep is a temporary respite from the intense sun and a welcome change of scene from the tense anticipation across the tarmac. Suddenly I am reminded of the line from *A Course In Miracles* which states that a miracle is really a shift in perception which allows something new to take place. Somehow Mr. Wee must have seen that he and I are not the enemies he had thought we were - or else the entire group would have been left standing out in the sun all day until someone got the American off the stairway from the plane and into the bus.

A uniformed Army man trots over to the jeep, jumps in, revs up, and peels away from the plane, with a screech of tires leaving rubber on the runway. At the door of the airport lobby he gestures for me to get out and go into the lobby. He makes a point of looking in the other direction while I climb off the jeep and hop the four yards into the lobby where an assemblage of perhaps fifty men inside turn and stare. As I lunge for a chair and fall into it they edge closer. Tears slide down my cheeks, the ankle throbs and the entire assemblage of men starts to laugh - nervously at first, then in unison. Despite my knowledge that Chinese emotions often do not mean what they seem to Westerners, I find myself feeling helpless and enraged. They are actually just nervous at an injured Western woman in their midst and feel embarrassed that I am showing tears in public. It's bad form on my part, as far as they are concerned. The more they laugh the more I cry silently. *"What am I doing in a situation like this?!"* my mind silently screams.

Abruptly the far door opens and in walks a pretty, composed woman in her late twenties who announces herself to be Miss Wong, the Xian guide. She stands above me for a moment, radiant in an embroidered lemon yellow blouse and a royal blue pleated skirt, a black purse on her arm. Even through the pain and embarrassment I realize she's the first non-uniformed woman I've yet encountered. Maybe I'm starting to hallucinate. Her hair is curled and she looks more like a Singaporean than a citizen of the People's Republic of China.

"You are Connie Shaw. Don't worry, the bus is parked close to the door over there and I have sent for a wheel chair. We have never had an injured passenger before so you are giving us a chance to practice how to act in an emergency. I'm sorry it is taking so long. These men are laughing at you because they are nervous. You should not be crying. You must be strong. All Chinese people are strong and never cry in front of others. Be brave, Connie Shaw, be brave. You don't want to disgrace your country and your companions, do you?"

"Of course not, but this ankle may be broken and I have been in pain for over five hours now. May I please have an aspirin and go to the hospital right away?"

"We don't use aspirin here. That is something from Western medicine. We will take you to the hospital later but first we have planned a nice tour of the area on the way to your hotel, which is a very nice old guest house." Immediately I start an inner chant designed to thwart an oncoming mutiny of emotions. *"This is another opportunity to learn patience."* Then, *"I am not my body. I feel no pain."* The wheelchair arrives and takes us to the bus where the driver helps me aboard and into the front seat. Miss Wong immediately begins her tour spiel, some in Mandarin and also in English, as we weave in and out of thick traffic consisting of trucks, buses, and cyclists. Factories, communes, schools, and offices are pointed out and statistics are given about local production and about how this city is different from others of its relative size in China.

Two hours later we arrive at our guest house where three young men stand on the steps to greet us. Seven hours of pain so far. It has taken all my concentration to transcend the throbbing. Miss Wong leaps down the bus steps and directs the largest man, who looks about twenty and is about five feet nine inches tall, to bend over as I jump down the steps on one leg. Thinking that his deep bow at the waist is a special Xian sort of welcome, I too bow down low, while standing on one foot. This brings whoops from Miss Wong and the other men who wave their arms and shout "No, no."

"You have misunderstood. He is stooping over so you can ride upon his back," Miss Wong explains. "You are injured and he is the strongest man here so please get on. This is called 'piggy-back' in English."

"Get on? Piggy-back on a complete stranger?" I ask, afraid that I'll crush the man, as I nearly crushed the two stewardesses at the plane. A few hours before, I had been a pariah and now, the piggy-back extreme. Everyone is waiting so I inhale and, hitching up my dress, hop clumsily up on the back of the hotel employee praying that we don't collapse into a helpless tangle on the sidewalk. But he has the strength of a Burmese bullock and easily mounts the stairs and heads down the dark old hallway to deposit me in the first double room on the left. I thank him heartily and gratefully fall into the twin bed against the far wall, wondering when I'll have the opportunity to see a doctor and be relieved of the dull ache.

Two hours pass. It has been nine hours since the fall and the ankle is black, resembling a hideous dark shiny bratwurst with puffy toes. The leg refuses to move below the knee, and has lost all feeling, except intermittent shooting pains. Muey rests on her bed until we are told that dinner will be served in an hour but I have lost all appetite and fall into a deep sleep, awakening three hours later. It has been twelve hours now and the room is empty except for the gnawing and rustling of a mouse beside my bed.

Suddenly there is a knock at the door. In walks Miss Wong and a woman doctor who is visiting Xian. She looks at the leg, shakes her head, and tells Miss Wong to have me taken to the hospital by wheelchair at midnight when there will be a competent team of people who can help me. That is three more hours away and she has no pain relievers but asks the hotel staff to bring me some tea and sweets. The man puts the tray on the bed but two cockroaches pounce on the cookies before I can reach them.

In and out of wakefulness I repeat, for the five hundredth time since the fall, a string of silent affirmations to hypnotize myself into enduring the situation. *"There is no pain in this body. I am not my body, or my mind, or my emotions. I am beyond anxiety. There is no fear. This body heals itself."* It has been fifteen hours since I fell in the Beijing Airport. How long can I keep this up?

At midnight there is another knock on the door and Miss Wong and Mr. Neo arrive with a rusty ancient wheelchair to take me two blocks away to the nearby hospital. The stars are out and we travel slowly over bumpy dirt paths through a park toward the light of the hospital in the distance.

As we hobble across the threshold of the doorway - the wheelchair being too wide to go through - I am vividly reminded of my intermittent, persistent desire to see the inside of a hospital in China. I wonder how many times the thought has crossed my mind, *"I would really like the chance to see acupuncture being used in China. Preferably in a hospital and at close range."*

This isn't what I'd had in mind, though. Not with myself as the patient. I should have qualified the statement. The Xian saying comes to mind: "There are only two misfortunes in life - not getting what you want, and getting exactly what you want."

The emergency room is the first door on the right, mercifully close, and illuminated with fluorescent tubes. The walls are white, the tile floor is white, and the sheets upon the two iron-framed cots are nearly white. There is a straight-back chair and a tiny wooden table with a small drawer, otherwise the room is bare except for the cots. It looks as if it could be a room from the eighteen hundreds and I expect to see an ancient doctor arriving at any moment. The ancient-looking doctor does indeed arrive, yet it is three hours later, after I am plied with more tea from a kindly nurse who appears each half hour and tells me that the tea will be very good for the pain. It's regular tea, however, and has no effect. The eighteen hours that have now elapsed without any pain relief since the fall have caused the world to recede behind a giant, intermittent screen of bizarre fantasy, interwoven with scarlet ropes of slashing, searing knife-thrusts across the consciousness. Numb throbs advance into a front-row position and maintain a dominance followed by sensations of separation from the body and a halting of time.

Mr. Neo, however, is acutely aware of our waiting three hours before an orderly arrives to announce that we must proceed down the hall for an x-ray. He is incensed at the interminable delays and unavailability of representatives or of explanations. There is silence in the hospital, since it is nearly three o'clock in the morning, and the patients are presumably sleeping.

At the x-ray room the orderly gingerly mentions that he is unfamiliar with the procedure for using the X-ray machine and inquires whether Mr. Neo or I know how to make it work. Having had annual x-rays throughout my life I give him simple instructions on how to operate it, whereupon he leaves the room, peers through the window and starts the machine. We are all elated. Then he re-enters and tells us that he will take the plate down to the lab but is unsure whether anyone there will know what to do. Meanwhile we are instructed to go back to the emergency room and wait for a doctor.

At the nineteenth hour when I have relinquished all hope or expectation of either obtaining any pain relief or of ever seeing a doctor, in walks an elderly, smiling gentleman wearing a straw hat, a sleeveless undershirt, a pair of olive cotton shorts and brown rubber sandals. His hair is gray and he seems to be about seventy, although he is lithe and suntanned and could be much older than his appearance. He is a living example of the famous barefoot doctors of China, except that now they are all equipped with sandals, straw hats, and acupuncture kits, complete with herbs and moxibustion.

Dr. Yuan radiates peace and competence as well as shyness. He explains to the nurse, the orderly, and to Mr. Neo that he speaks no English and that he will explain his procedure, then asks the orderly and the nurse to translate to Mr. Neo, who will translate the planned procedure to me. If I agree, he'll needle my ankle and shin in three or four places to bring down the swelling and to get the skin color back to normal as quickly as possible. He is unsure whether it is a broken ankle or merely a severe sprain.

Eagerly I agree, explaining that I have been in pain for nineteen hours without relief and that I have complete confidence in his abilities. He smiles broadly at this, bows, and shows me his oblong case of acupuncture needles. There are short, squatty ones like miniature swords, medium thin needles and long thin ones about four inches in length. He has over a hundred needles and asks if I'd mind if he stabbed a few needles in my head. Yes, I would mind very much. No needles in the head, please. (Why can't we just get on with it?) An involuntary moan slips out whereupon Dr. Yuan concludes that perhaps it would be best to needle now and to educate later.

He asks the orderly to hold the unaffected leg and for the nurse to hold one of my arms in case I react to the stabbing of the needles with too much vigor, being unaccustomed to Chinese medicine. I have only seen acupuncture performed a few times in the States. He smiles sweetly, tells me to be brave, and slaps my shin immediately before inserting a needle in several places between the ankle and knee. A stinging pain plunges deep into the leg and stops, as swiftly as it began. Numbness, like spreading ice-water, follows the stinging. Dr. Yuan twirls the needles and removes them after twenty minutes.

For the first time in nineteen hours there is no pain and we are all elated at Dr. Yuan's rapid results. He then announces that he has seen two other very bad ankles like this but that the color and swelling in this one are the worst he's encountered, so he was unsure, at first, how successful he would be. The ankle is broken. He will come to the hotel at nine o'clock in the morning for another treatment and will administer three treatments in all. Now I must go back and get some sleep so I will be ready when he comes over in a few hours.

By nine in the morning I have washed my face and combed my hair and lie in bed under the covers, in my nightgown, awaiting Dr. Yuan. The door bursts open, unceremoniously and in march Muey Low, Mr. and Mrs. Sun, Jimmy Ng's parents, Miss Tan, Mr. Neo, Danny and Yu Lan. Danny explains that word traveled fast via Mr. Neo that Dr. Yuan was coming at nine o'clock so everyone decided to take advantage of his visit and ask him to needle them as well. They are all, both men and women, dressed in identical pajamas: tailored polyester pastels with dark piping around the shirt pocket, pointed collar, and long sleeves. No robes, just pj's. Without invitation or request, they each take a seat on the opposite twin bed, on the desk, the desk chair, the window sill, or my bed. If I had known there would be company and an audience I would have dressed but it is too late. Dr. Yuan will have to do his best with a partially exposed leg sticking out from the covers because I'm not exposing myself in front of all these people.

There is a knock and we all chorus a welcome in our various languages. Dr. Yuan arrives with acupuncture kit and straw hat, still wearing his same undershirt and shorts. He is surprised to see the crowd and asks what is happening. All the patients start talking at once in a variety of Chinese dialects.

"My lower back is killing me," Muey Low announces and promptly dives onto her bed and yanks down her pajama bottoms without embarrassment, offering the top half of her chubby derriere to be treated - obviously an old hand at acupuncture.

"My arthritis has been terrible here in China," Mrs. Sun cries, flinging herself across the desk, yanking up the back of her pajama top in readiness.

"I just came to watch but now I want you to stop the pain in my knees and wrist," Mr. Sun meekly requests.

"Well I just hurt all over," Miss Tan says quietly, rolling up the sleeves and pants cuffs of her pj's.

Mr. Neo, who has been translating for me, reminds the group that Dr. Yuan is actually here to give me another treatment and that he can treat them after he discharges his first duty. They say they will happily watch me and will await their respective turns. There is never any question of my own wishes or privacy in the matter of being on display. In fact, the concept of privacy seems to be a very different matter for Westerners than for the Chinese, whether they are Overseas Chinese or citizens of the People's Republic.

My leg is really broken. Dr. Yuan again repeats the procedure of several hours before and slaps or socks each acupuncture point before slamming the needle into it at an angle from his closed fist. Again comes the deep, searing sting, followed by icy numbness, then cessation of all feeling, followed by a pulling sensation and relief after twenty minutes. A yelp from me causes all the others to frown in disapproval of my chicken-hearted display. They stoically endure four needles each in various parts of their anatomy without so much as a grimace.

The spectacle of my compatriots in their pajamas bristling with acupuncture needles, like a convention of porcupines, suddenly strikes me as hilarious. As Mr. Neo translates, I ask the group if they would have thought that we'd be decked out flat, draped over the furniture, filled with an assortment of needles in all parts of our bodies, in an old-fashioned guest house in China. Muey Low replies that Dr. Yuan is the best acupuncturist she has ever encountered and that she is coming back to Xian in the future just to see him. The others echo her sentiments and we all thank him profusely, to which he responds with a few nonchalant waves of his tanned, bony hand. He refuses to be paid, saying that his work is a gift of the People's Republic and that he only wishes that he had learned English. He considers it a failing that he hasn't because it is the emerging technical language of the world. He asks me the word for acupuncture in English so he can tell his colleagues.

"Ahh cue punc ture" I say slowly four times. " Aht choo poon sue" is the closest he can get to the strange sounds the American utters. He shakes his head and says that he has no ear for language and will just stick to needles. He picks up his straw hat, leans over to shake my hand, and after giving his address to the others, waves to all of us and backs humbly out of the room, saying, "We only want to serve the people. Thank you for letting me serve you." To me, Dr. Yuan exemplifies the saying that "The life that is lived in the spirit of service is always new."

The sharpest disappointment concerning the broken ankle is the inability to see Xian itself, the ancient beginning point of the old Silk Road which served as an interchange for culture and products between Han China and Asia Minor and Europe. Today the promising attractions of Xian, which I'll miss, include the Xian bell tower, the small Wild Goose Pagoda, the Banpo Museum, a hot spring, and the very famous Qin Shi Huang Mausoleum, where a giant pit filled with life-size pottery warriors and their horses was discovered in 1974. Two particular acts of kindness befall me the day of our departure from Xian, both of them especially meaningful since all I have seen so far is the hospital and my dark mouse-and-roach-infested hotel room.

The first thoughtful gesture involves the hotel man who piggy-backed me to the room on arrival day and who has since brought me all meals and frequent pots of tea. He comes to the room with a pair of large blue and white men's rubber thongs as a gift from the hotel since my swollen foot is still too large for a shoe. He says the staff regrets my having missed the sightseeing and that they hope that I can return in the future to Xian. An official of the local cadre, Mrs. Wan, in white shirt and gray skirt, visits to ask if I have any requests before we leave, to which I reply that I'd love to somehow get a ride to the museum to see the few samples of the famous pottery soldiers on display. She agrees to accompany me herself and promptly calls a gray cadre limousine to come for us immediately and take us to the museum. For the first time in China it dawns on me what it must be like to be a cadre official as we whiz along the streets in the quiet car with flags flying from the front fenders. The interior of the car is gray velvet and every window except the front one is adorned with pull-down shades for privacy. People on the street stop and stare at the car as we drive by and when we alight a crowd gathers at a respectful distance in anticipation that something is about to happen. We walk as swiftly as possible considering my limp and the fact that one foot wears a high heel sandal and the other a new men's rubber thong.

The lift in the dark museum lobby takes us up to the second floor where we are shown the biscuit-colored terra-cotta soldiers, rows of ancient bronze kettles and drums, exquisite scrolls, and the Forest of Steles - one of the oldest, richest collections of stone tablets in all of China. It's a moving experience to stand among such rare and superb artifacts and to be personally accompanied by Mrs. Wan and the museum guide, who tell me that Westerners appreciate Chinese art and antiquities far more than the Chinese themselves who are usually ignorant of their own culture and heritage. I remember that the finest Chinese art collections are said to be in the Toronto Museum and in Taiwan, and that countless priceless objects were destroyed during the Cultural Revolution. Mrs. Wan pats my arm, amused at my continual ecstatic sighs on our walk along the museum halls. "Now you can be happy. You have seen your art. When you return to Xian in the future, you will stay longer and run about on strong legs," she adds. Tears of gratitude well up in my eyes and I thank her profusely. She is moved that I am touched since she feels she is merely carrying out her duties to New China.

It is astounding to me that I am able to walk quite easily without a cane or crutches, from having had only a few acupuncture treatments. No surgery, no cast, no pain-killers, no antibiotics.

At the Xian Airport there is a strange assemblage for so seemingly mundane an event or circumstance as my departure. The occasion, for it is too unimportant to be termed an event, is the implementation of a new procedure for the escorting of a wounded party aboard an aircraft. The Xian guide, Miss Wong, heads a convocation at the airport terminal building which consists of Beijing Mr. Lo, Mrs. Wan, two stewardesses, a dozen uniformed Army men who are passengers, and our tour group. There is a new wheelchair at the head of a processional line of two abreast. The idea is that the "injured patient" in the wheelchair will be rolled out to the aircraft at a glacial pace at the head of the line of passengers. The new procedure is a part of professionializing the boarding process for the future and will become routine after today.

It seems like a fine idea but it isn't actually necessary in this case, except as a practice measure, and it has come a bit too late. I am the "injured patient" and am merely cooperating so that the measure can be implemented with someone playing the part of the patient. Miss Wong glances back at the crowd of restless passengers sweating in the June heat, who are eager to board the plane and to depart for Canton. With an authoritative nod she steps forward and the two stewardesses push the wheelchair at a turtle's crawl toward the plane. The double line of passengers shuffles along, talking and checking watches, fanning themselves restlessly at the agonizingly slow movement.

"We can pick up speed, Miss Wong, since my ankle is much better now," I suggest, embarrassed to be the cause of all the delay again, especially after having been the cause of delay upon our arrival a few days ago.

"No, we must do it right. Chairman Mao said to let foreign things serve New China and this is our chance to serve China so we must pretend you are a sick person so when we get another sick or injured person we will know what to do. It caused us to lose much face and to bring shame on China when we didn't know what to do with you when you arrived with a broken ankle. We must use every moment of opportunity to its fullest and you are our opportunity at this moment."

Eventually we reach the plane and the two stewardesses make a great display of thrusting me by the elbows out of the wheelchair and onto the bottom step of the metal staircase. Miss Wong, Mrs. Wan, and Beijing Mr. Lo all shake my hand and thank me for having given them so much opportunity to practice new procedures. After shaking hands and waving, I silently thank all of them - wryly - for the many opportunities to learn patience. Just how much patience, though, does one person really need?

Our day-and-a-half stay in Canton on the way back home proves to be one of the most gratifying experiences of the China trip for me personally. Beijing Mr. Lo had left orders that all recommended improvements on my consulting list were to be carried out in our three-week absence. As impossible as it seems, they have been, to the very letter and spirit of my suggestions. The hotel lobby, without flies or soiled slip-covers, sparkles. Much to our amazement, new linen and dishes rest on the dining tables. Even the elevators and fish pond have been cleaned. Now the guest rooms have clean sheets and towels, clean carpets and fresh air.

With twinkling eyes, Mr. Lo confides that since I had been willing to donate my know-how to New China, he had been determined to surprise me by the implementation of my suggestions before I left China - a gift to me. I'll miss our constant companion and tell him so. He bows one last time and invites me to bring my husband on the next visit. "Next visit...." Will there even be a next visit? If I can possibly arrange it, there will be indeed - within five years – God willing.

But since I have had no luck whatsoever in finding my Master in China, I wonder if I should seek Him next in India. For some unknown reason, a verse from *The Dhammapada* comes to mind: "Long is the night to those who are awake; long is the road to those who are weary. Long is the cycle of birth and death to those who know not the dharma." TD P 94

CHAPTER 10
THE RATTLING ROCKET OF SRINAGAR

"… danger and solitude are the two factors that go to form a man's character, that do the most for him." Anne Morrow Lindbergh, WWAW P 20

Singapore
September 28, 1981

When Jim and Wahid met me at the Changi Airport in Singapore upon my arrival from China, they had mixed feelings. Both Jim and Wahid were aghast when I walked off the plane with a bandaged ankle, from having broken it in Beijing, as they had not received any news of the accident. They were happy and relieved to see me but they mistakenly believed that I hadn't bothered to write them! Only a few of my postcards and none of my letters to Jim reached him from China. The phones in China seldom worked so it was nearly impossible to get a long distance call through to Singapore.

Now, ninety days later, after trips to Thailand and Malaysia, we are once again in the airport in Singapore and I'm about to leave on another trip, bound for North India and Nepal. I assure both Jim and Wahid, who are protective of me but resigned to my travels, that I will be safe and that nothing dangerous could possibly befall me.

It's been two years since we were married in India and I'm ready to have a real adventure – traveling in the Himalayas by bus with a group of American and European women. The American Club tour includes camping and sleeping in a tent in the coldest part of Asia. We'll be camping in mountain lion country which sounds exciting in itself. Hopefully I'll get some leads on whether or not God is in India, as I suspect. Surely the monks in one or two of the eleven lamaseries we will visit will know something about Him.

All of my searches for God in Singapore, China, Thailand, Malaysia and Indonesia the past few months have proven futile. One consolation, however, is my discovery of the Theosophical Lodge of Singapore, through its very kind president, Len Rodrigo, an attorney. He also informed me about the Annual Book Fair at the World Trade Centre, which I recently attended, looking for spiritual books and hoping to find clues to my Master.

Most of the books at Len's booth (the only booth with spiritual books) were either old Theosophical works or books about a big-haired Indian guru named Baba something. I haven't mentioned to Len, or to anyone, that I am looking for a Holy Being. Since I haven't found the One I seek, I'm returning to India, with the American Club tour that features a trip to Little Tibet, short treks to eleven Buddhist lamaseries in the Himalayas, an overnight stay on the houseboats at Dal Lake, Srinagar and a trip to the temples and monuments of Nepal.

This morning, the day of my departure for India, Jim and I told each other our dreams, as we always do upon awakening. Last night, for the third night in a row, Jim, who seldom recalls his dreams, had a dream with an airplane hostage-taking theme. This seems quite unusual, since neither us ever has fearful or negative dreams. Coincidentally enough, I also had a hostage dream last night without knowing of his hostage dreams. In discussing my own dream with him, I mention that I vaguely feel the dream is somehow connected with our trip. It seems to me that it may in fact have something to do with the departure phase of the tour or with the first half of the trip. From my feelings upon awakening and the emotional state in the dream however, it seems clear to me that there is no need to worry.

Jim and Wahid urge me to be careful and, after we have said our farewells, Wahid says "Goodbye and God bless you, Mrs. Connie. I will pray for you." That's not the sort of thing he normally says, though it isn't out of character for him.

Although I didn't find my elusive hide-and-seek spiritual Master in China, I feel that the trip deepened me and taught me a great deal about cultural differences. Underneath cultural, racial and gender differences, we are essentially the same. In fact, in truth, who we really are is exactly the same – the Mighty I AM Presence is in all humans. It is our task to see and to honor That in everyone. Also, it is clear to me that kindness and compassion are at the heart of all religions and spiritual paths. It's also crucial, I feel, for each person to heal his issues, or grievances, with God, church, clergy and the injustices which have been done in the name of religion, in order to move forward on the path.

Only four or five months remain for me to find my Master. It is autumn now and we return home to the States in early spring, at the latest. I feel fairly certain now that the God-Being for Whom I search is actually in India since the vision that I had of Him surrounded by vast crowds seemed to be located in China or India. If He's in China, He's doing a very good job of concealing Himself. It feels intuitively to me that He may be living in an obscure region of India. Hopefully I will find Him/Her or at least obtain some definite clues as to the whereabouts of this One. By the time we finally meet, I wonder if I'll be acknowledged in any way for this relentless tracking? Will I be ignored, summoned, contacted or greeted? I feel so very certain that this will be a turning point in my life.

We're off to Delhi - sixteen Westerners, of whom fifteen are women. One is the husband of a woman in our group. From Delhi we'll proceed to Srinagar, then to Little Tibet by bus to visit nine or ten ancient Buddhist lamaseries. It's an extremely sophisticated group as appearances go. Lilo and Thornton Milton, both attractive, smartly dressed and fiftyish, stand out even a bit from the rest of the group with their stylish blond good looks and expensive luggage. Though all of the other tour members save two (Gracia Lewis and Thornton) are spouses of corporate executives, each individual is interesting. From Balikpapan Borneo has come Elizabeth George, a tall Texas nurse who practices acupuncture. Agnes Holmes, a gray-haired, grandmotherly nurse also shares an interest in acupuncture with Elizabeth and me. Recently I've been taking an acupuncture course at the University of Singapore.

Norma Jean Ferguson, our tour leader, is a white-haired, sixtyish, vibrant individual who has lived extensively overseas and who has traveled to remote places most of her life. She continually makes the rounds to dispense tickets, information and cheerfulness to our remarkably tall, attractive group members. Since half of the women stand over five feet nine inches tall, being thus taller than the majority of Asian men, we draw lots of stares, smiles and comments about "all those tall Western women." Those who fall in the tall category are Bev Chapman, a pretty young American; Gunilla Rouxel, a stunning blond Swede; Gunilla Friis, who is a striking German blond; regal Regina Landry from Germany; Nancy Gjerlow, a fashionable blond American; and fair-haired Texan Elizabeth George.

Our shorter members, aside from petite Norma Jean, our tour leader and me, are Antoinette Krankowski from the U.S.; Gracia Lewis, a stylish brunette seventy-year-old from Singapore; Renate Schuller, a German American; and my red-haired French roommate, Regine Burgoin.

The same questions are probably on everyone's mind: how will we all get along together? Will we stay healthy in India, Little Tibet and Nepal? Are the high spirits and optimistic conversation really sincere and durable or merely a veneer? Anne Morrow Lindbergh once said, "The most exhausting thing in life, I've discovered, is insincerity."

New Delhi, India
September 28th

At night in Delhi we are greeted by hoards of begging men at the airport. They push and shove against the building doors while their compatriots sleep in rags on the airport sidewalk. I remember the moist hot nights of India. India looks and feels and smells the way it did two years ago. There seems to be a desperation among the street people. This time I don't experience the horror which I did on my honeymoon trip, having then come directly from the sanitized, orderly, prosperous U.S. It's a different experience for me now to travel throughout Asia while having a home in an Asian country.

My eyes are sharper these days and I observe the pluckiness of the beggars and notice them nudge each other as a "likely prospect" approaches. Does my attuned vision indicate lack of compassion? I think not. It is a more realistic acceptance of the situation whereas the primary shock of my first trip to India entailed my coming to terms with the extent of the ever-present poverty. I reacted to the depth and enormity of the poverty on the Indian sub-continent by incapacitating myself in a crying jag for an entire day. The next step in my growth, however, seems to be to discern when to offer a meal, clothing or money to the poor as inner guidance directs.

A bus takes us to the Ashok Hotel in Delhi for a short rest of a few hours. After pushing through throngs of restless people we find the royal blue and cream Italian Provincial decor of the hotel room a restful and welcome oasis. It is to serve as a napping spot, which is much needed, after the long journey and the retrieval of luggage amid the hot crowd.

New Delhi
September 29th

The morning departure for Srinagar entails the usual body and luggage searches performed by khaki-uniformed airport officials. We are bound for Kashmir in northern India, a state which has a long history of political struggle. My attention is captivated by the fact that there are a great many Sikhs aboard the plane. This, in itself, is not extraordinary, but the fact that there are so many of them, all wearing the traditional bright gauze turban, silver bracelet and dagger, is somehow noteworthy. They seem nervous. We are a noisy and exuberant group upon boarding, unaware of our accidental jostling of others with bulky shoulder bags, camera equipment and backpacks. The Sikhs scrutinize us and look at each other in seeming alarm as one after another of our group steps aboard. "Are we acting more outrageous than we realize?" I wonder. "Why are these Sikhs appearing so surprised and resistant to our arrival? Is it that we are foreign women travelling without husbands and therefore seem too free and a bad example to Asian women?" The Sikhs nudge each other and talk behind cupped hands about our group.

Indian stewardesses in jewel-like saris glide along the aisles serving refreshments. In heavy Urdu accents they ask each of the women in our group the same polite rote question. "Would you care for some tea or drinks, Sir?" The surprise at being addressed as "Sir" catches each woman off guard and the responses vary. Margit smiles and giggles softly while I suppress a chortle, attempting to make the strangled noise sound like a cough. Others grin broadly or plunge their faces into their napkins briefly.

Srinagar, India
September 29th

After a smooth landing we arrive without incident at the new Srinagar Airport. Two years ago, when I was here on my honeymoon, it was a small, dark cinderblock building cramped with a souvenir counter, ancient vinyl and chrome chairs and dirty floors. Tiny local children padded barefoot through the crowds hawking tea.

It is vastly different today with the high ceiling letting in soft shafts of Kashmir light and with plenty of attractive seating, a refreshment stall and even a small luggage carrousel. Through the huge glass windows we admire the curving, flower-encircled driveway in front of the building. As we lift our eyes heavenward, we gasp at the magnificence of the rocky lavender-hued Himalayas standing sharply against the cornflower blue sky. Wide fields of blond grass remind me that it is autumn here although every month in tropical Singapore looks the same. It feels to me that snow will be approaching in a matter of weeks – three or four at most.

It is easy to forget time and season while living in Singapore at the Equator. Perhaps that's the idea behind the tee-shirts one occasionally sees in Singapore that say 'Just another lousy day in paradise.' I can't recall ever having had a lousy or boring day in my life since each moment is so very precious. The fact that I've had numerous surgeries, have been kidnapped in Egypt, and have come close to death so often might account for this fact.

The local tour guide urges us toward five tiny yellow and black taxis, on top of which the drivers lash our bags. In a lurching procession we head for town, taxi radios blaring. The drivers try to out-race each other along the narrow winding roads until we restrain them with the firm assurance that there is no need to rush at breakneck speed. We'd rather survive the taxi trip.

"Please, Abraham," I tell the driver, "It's better to be five minutes late on earth than fifty years too early in heaven!" We all laugh and he slows down a bit.

Where there was farmland and cows a few years ago at the outskirts of Srinagar, there is now blue air pollution amid crowded rows of blatant billboards advertising the Kashmir carpets for which the area is well known. Lots of large, new brick houses have sprung up along the main road.

The essential character of Srinagar remains, yet the Tudor-style shops and houses of local orange clay brick speak clearly of recent prosperity from tourism and carpet sales. Taxi horns blare at the herds of shaggy goats glutting the narrow roads. As we bounce along city streets to our awaiting bus the houseboats of Dal Lake come into view. We wonder which of the commodious brown lodgings will be ours in a few days, after our return from Ladakh.

Across the immense Himalayan peaks from Kashmir sits Ladakh on the high Tibetan plateau. Its nickname of Little Tibet derives from Tibet's unmistakable influence on its religious customs, culture and dress - an influence which accelerated after the Chinese takeover of Tibet itself. We take cabs from the airport to meet the bus which will take us to Leh.

At last we arrive at the bus which will take us over one of the world's newest and most treacherous roads, the Srinagar-Leh Road. To refer to it as a road is a complimentary exaggeration, we understand, for the narrow, rocky, precipitous track is known for its mud and rock slides, cave-ins and general dangerous condition. Yet it's the only way to reach Leh except by air. Norma tells us that the trip took six months to plan because the letters to hoteliers and other contacts had to be sent in waterproof pouches by donkey over perilous mountain passes. We are one of the first Western tour groups to make this trip by ground transport and have packed for rigorous high-altitude camping.

We intend to camp out in the Himalayas and to see remote hamlets and colorful Tibetans along the route, hence the bus trip, instead of a plane journey. Although Srinagar has some modern buses, ours is not one. We alight from the taxis and stand staring for a few moments at the odd old conveyance waiting at the appointed meeting place. It is an ancient derelict vehicle adorned with a small, beat-up wooden shingle flopping below a side window. The shingle proclaims "Class A." Atop the bus is an overloaded luggage rack straining with tents, tarpaulins, food, cooking pots, sherpa equipment and a large wicker basket of squawking, cackling white chickens.

"There's an old Chinese saying that It's better to have a chicken tomorrow than an egg today'," someone quips.

As we continue to stare in a dumbfounded manner, the seven sherpas throw our luggage next to the protesting chickens and distribute individual box lunches in orange plastic containers to each of us. Each box lunch contains a hard boiled duck egg, two apples, a banana and a piece of mutton. The sherpas sell beer and mineral water since we'll not be drinking any natural water for the next two weeks. At last it is time to scramble into the bus. Our Tibetan guide, Faiz (rhymes with nice) explains that the uniformed, sockless boy in the seat next to him is the "assistant bus driver." We are introduced to the bus driver and his assistant who are both tall, dark Kashmiris, who smile and nod in greeting. The cook and the other three sherpas are introduced as a group. Since they are snowed in during the eight-month winter and can only work three or four months a year as trekking sherpas, the men are clearly jubilant to be in charge of our group. They usually cook and carry for male clients but assure us that they are very glad to have a women's group - excepting Thornton, who is our only man, and an extremely quiet one so far.

Faiz tells us the bearers say we "look like very nice gorels (girls) and they will give good service and take very good care of us." We smile broadly as he says this since most of us have traveled widely alone and don't need "taking care of." Further, the average age is probably about forty-five, which puts us, as a group, over a quarter of a century past the "girl" stage. I'm the next to youngest at thirty-eight. Such tender care and solicitude, however quaint it seems to us (all being the independent type), may be needed if we get into any challenging situations. A huge burley man named Rasool who is the cook, tells us of his pretty young wife and three young daughters who live on a small houseboat in Srinagar.

The back seat of the bus is packed to the ceiling with eggs in cartons, tea kettles, sherpas, sleeping bags and extra luggage which wouldn't fit on top of the luggage rack. Faiz and his colleagues immediately slouch deep down in the seats for naps on the long journey ahead. We, however, are too interested in the sights on the road to relax. Periodically Agnes and

Margit squat in the aisle to photograph a herd of motley sheep, a cliff-hanging village, or snowy mountain ranges. Chickens overhead cluck-cluck while we appraise our situation, each other and our circumstances inside the "Rattling Rocket" as I've dubbed it.

The lumpy gray road stretches beyond Srinagar's golden leaves and autumn haystack fields to wind up the mountain past sweet-smelling apple orchards and paisley-shaped rice paddy terraces. As we climb higher the tree crowns become red, orange and yellow from autumn frosts. Beside the road runs the teal blue Indus River - a vital glistening body which will be our continual companion for the next few days. Its waters look indescribably clear and majestic, changing its surface from Saran Wrap smoothness to roiling milky waves and back to a flat serenity again. Whether we admire the mighty Indus from high roads or low terrain, I never tire of seeing its unraveling aquamarine satin surface lacing its way through the blue-gray Himalayas. Its hypnotic, binding effect on me is puzzling yet welcome and soothing. The Indus River reminds me of an ancient verse from *The Upanishads*. "The flowing river is lost in the sea; the illumined sage is lost in the Self. The flowing river has become the sea; the illumined sage has become the Self." TU P 117

Herd upon herd of shaggy brown and white sheep waddle in huge flocks at the center of the road as we bolt forward along the ever narrowing track in the mountains. Woolen-cloaked shepherds in turbans decorate the landscape in soft patinas of beige, pearl white, mulberry or brown. They drape baby lambs about their necks, like shawls, firmly clasping the spindly legs in brown leathery hands and rubbing the fuzzy wool against their cheeks. This is Muslim territory and the local costumes have a Biblical appearance to our Western eyes.

In the fading light of afternoon our hungry glances lap up views of ocher-colored sod huts and khaki mud houses built in narrow valleys. Bright burgundy and orange herbs are stacked in brittle bunches on the roofs of the huts to dry in the waning light. Dilapidated brown wooden mangers lie about the hillside under a stormy iron-gray sky. From two eight-inch, saucer-sized holes in the floorboards near the driver dust from the gravel road puffs up into the bus. In minutes it becomes twilight and chilly. Women in long black Muslim chadri peer out from lace "lookout windows" of their veils and hurry home to their village. In the gathering darkness we can barely see the rickety log bridges spanning the Indus or the almond-eyed white buffalo heading homeward over rocky ground. White fog-curls nestle on the mountain crests and darkness enfolds the countryside now; we clatter along in silence except for a periodic wheeze of the engine.

Upon noticing that the assistant bus driver has not put on socks in the chilly twilight, I realize that he probably doesn't own any. I am swept with compassion for his icy feet and present him with the gift of a new pair of expensive wool socks which I had been looking forward to wearing this evening. His face lights up with a dazzling smile. He, the driver and Faiz all thank me profusely and all the men smile and nod their approval.

Our reverie is abruptly shattered, however, by the violent side-to-side jolting of the "Rocket" over large, sharp boulders. The macadam highway became a gravel road and now evolves to a weaving rock track. Big square gray rocks litter the grass-tufted field ahead; the tires of the bus are shiny and bald. In recollection of the fact that there are no gas stations or pull-off places for emergencies the next two days, I catch myself gritting my teeth and crossing my fingers and toes for a moment, like a child in hopes that we'll arrive without mishap. As the road snakes along the bottom of a canyon, I once again mentally affirm our safety throughout the journey, visualizing all of our needs being met speedily and completely.

The outlines of the cedars, willows and birches are dimly visible now in the gloom ahead. It begins to rain but the front windshield wiper is broken. There are no lights anywhere. What shall we do for lodging now that it's dark and raining? Snow on high peaks all around us shines starkly in the moonlight as a reminder that in two days our tents will be pitched in the coldest spot in Asia, according to meteorologists. We pull up hoods, button jackets, dive into mittens and shiver inside the unheated bus. From time to time the pale yellow headlights shine on a ravine's frail hanging bridge swinging in the wind over raging waterfalls and steep cliffs. On the golden tundra a few miles back, a sign welcomed us to Sonemarg. As we glance about, we see no town, shelter or life-signs of any sort.

Just as the interminable suspense of finding lodging seems unbearable, we come to a dozen ramshackle gray buildings clumped in a narrow valley.

"This is Sonemarg," announces Faiz. "We'll unload the bus and sleep on the floor of that abandoned green and white lodge across the road. Soon we'll have a fire in the fireplaces and tea and biscuits for all of you before dinner."

The sherpas unload the food, luggage and provisions while we dash through the rain into the lodge and unfold sleeping bags on the floors of the three bedrooms. Soon fires are providing a cheery crackling background to our jokes and laughter while we sip spiced Kashmiri tea prepared by tall, dark Rasool. An hour later we enjoy dinner, which consists of rice, curry, cabbage, mutton stew and vegetables. Candles and firelight illuminate the simple lodge rooms with an orange glow which links us together in an unspoken intimacy by the fact of our having safely survived the first hard day of Himalayan mountain travel.

After dinner the silhouette of short, slender Faiz frames the doorway. A brief log-blaze lights up his handsome, tanned Tibetan face characterized by unusually rosy cheeks, dazzling teeth and hazel eyes. He looks rugged and hearty in his yellow and navy plaid wool jacket and faded denims. His short blue-black hair shines in the firelight and his eyes dance with the dramatic devilment of an impending announcement. He definitely has a presence about him that gets our attention. As we all look up inquisitively he begins.

"You people are extremely lucky. So lucky, in fact, that you've just narrowly missed being hijacked and taken to Pakistan!" Everyone begins to talk and to question him at once.

"What?!" "How?" "What do you mean?" "Our plane this afternoon?"

"Just a moment, please," he says, raising his hand for silence and order.

"It seems that directly after you left your plane at Srinagar the Sikhs who were on board used their ceremonial daggers to hijack the plane to Lahore, Pakistan. We heard it on the portable radio just now and will see to it that your families are informed that you are safe and are enjoying yourselves in Sonemarg in case they fear you are among the hostages."

Suddenly it occurs to me why the Sikhs appeared startled at our noisy group. Perhaps they'd not planned on the possible unforeseen complications of having Western women aboard during the plane takeover. Next I recall Jim's hostage dreams and my own, which nevertheless carried the persistent feeling of ultimate safety. Jim will be surprised when I tell him that there was indeed a highjacking, but that we were spared a complicated, dangerous detour to Pakistan. *Thank You, God, for saving this life yet again.*

Three of us crawl into sleeping bags on the floor of the smallest room after liberally spraying the insect-infested floors and walls with bug repellent. Two others toss their sleeping bags onto rusty-spring cots beside us. In the room next to ours, the rest of our party make retirement preparations, their merry laughter mingling with the sound of Himalayan wind and rain. Our bones ache from being thrashed around inside the bus for several hours, like laundry in a washing machine. But neither the high mountain chill, nor fatigue can interfere with immediate, sound sleep. We make a few last remarks about the fact that our "motor coach tour" arranged by Cox and King's is turning out to be more of the type of adventure that we were hoping for anyway.

At dawn Faiz taps on the door and announces it is time to arise for breakfast which will be served on the wooden veranda overlooking the snowy peaks. After packing sleeping bags and luggage we put on sweaters and hats and sit down to eggs, biscuits and coffee made by Rasool and his helpers. Our bodies feel the effects of having flown straight to North India from sea level at the equator. Everyone is still too drunk with the altitude and time changes to talk very much. Gauzy shreds of white fog cling to the stubby little wooden shops across the road which sell prayer shawls, jewelry and Himalayan artifacts.

It is chilly inside the unheated bus and I notice for the first time that the rusty holes in the floor are sufficiently large so that I can see the rocks of the road through them. Wind whistles in through the chinks in the windows and little puffs of dust whoof up through the openings in the floor. Just a few hundred yards down the road from last night's lodging we come upon a large sign welcoming us to Ladakh. The road becomes a narrow one-way macadam at this point which makes passing other vehicles an event requiring the utmost dexterity since there are thousand-foot cliffs immediately beside the road. Bearing down on us is a wooden lorry carrying a green metal shield painted with a goddess on top of its cab. There is a checkpoint ahead, one of many on this impossibly narrow road, where we must wait until the lorry, a pony caravan and an army convoy pass, single file. All around us we see clear lakes, immense pinnacles and magnificent arid rock cliffs. It is so much like the U.S.'s Colorado Rocky Mountains I love, that my heart turns over in the realization that I've missed them, without consciously realizing it, while living happily in the equatorial steam of Singapore.

A tiny hamlet clings to a muddy hillside above us. From the open porch of one of the mud houses five black-clad Muslim women sit in a row observing the foreigners with great interest. Once it is obvious that the army convoy crawling along the one-lane road ahead will take quite a while to pass the check-point at the foot of the hill, we dash out of the bus and trudge uphill in the cold rain to visit the village.

Dozens of children run toward us yelling "Shoes!" and "Baksheesh!" (money). We are unprepared for the children, who are covered with mud, shoeless and dressed in rags. As a gift, Liz takes a Polaroid photo of a boy who has slid down the muddy hill with his friend to meet us. The boy's friend carries a baby boy on his back and, in his eager demand to have a photo taken of himself, drops the baby abruptly on the ground. The baby is unhurt but Liz, alarmed at the result of her generosity, scolds the boy. We are soon swamped with children of all ages who descend on us from gullies, cliffs, huts and streamlets. They all have hands out, demanding shoes and presents. Since I've left my wallet in the bus, I offer a box of raisins from my jacket pocket to a small boy tugging at my sleeve.

The boy, who speaks a bit of English, asks what the box is and what one does with it. I reply that it is raisins, dried grapes, to be eaten. Little fruits. He says he'll sell it to the soldiers who come through the valley. We empty our pockets of hard candy and ball point pens, then dash down the hill to the bus with two dozen children in hot pursuit, still screaming for more. Aboard the bus we debate our role in encouraging begging, knowing that we haven't enough supplies or coins to give to the people of every village we will encounter along the way. Some of the women on the bus have lived in Asia for years, unlike myself, and have brought dozens of ball point pens, boxes of balloons and lots of candy and change. But their supplies are also meant for barter later on, like the few things I have brought, and are packed deep in the luggage, inaccessible for now. Everyone has a theory about begging: all the theories conflict, yet they all make good sense.

The bus is ready to clear the check-point and as we round the corner it is obvious that the challenging part of the trip begins here. Yesterday's trip was easy compared to the scenery before us. The narrow road is only the width of the bus and leads around sharp blind curves with no shoulder, railing, or protection from the steep cliffs. It will be sickeningly dangerous the entire remainder of the trip. There are two choices. We can try to sleep in the chilly seats or can avert our eyes from the windows and either talk or stare at the floor. It is too bumpy to read and we lurch from side to side every few minutes as if we were on some thrilling, never-ending amusement park ride.

With glazed eyes we grip the arm-rests, corneas popping and knuckles white. We meet two trucks and a bus which necessitates Faiz and the assistant bus driver getting out to direct the treacherous passing. The process takes about ten minutes of moving our bus back and forth at the edge of the drop-off while the other vehicles crush past us, their wheels slanted at an angle three feet up against the mountain. The side of their bus nicks ours once or twice. Several of our passengers murmur that they are about to vomit. Others say "Don't you dare - it smells bad enough in here already!" We all stare at the floor, at our watches, at the floor. Again time drags.

We finally pass safely and exult in a vivid display of wildflower out-croppings clinging to the umber mountainside next to us. One doesn't have to be a botanist to marvel at the pristine perfection of purple showy fleabane with its bright yellow center and bright chiming bluebells nodding their demure heads like chaste maidens in bonnets. The road ahead is covered by a landslide from last night's rainstorm. It has brought down an avalanche of mud and broken rock which our vehicle clatters over without a pause. Mile after mile we weave along the rutted, rocky track, searching the cliffs and mountainsides for any evidence of human life. A cave appears beside the road and we startle at the unexpected sight of its inhabitants, an arm's length away from our bus. Five long-robed men drink tea, protected from the slanting rain by the cavernous overhang. As they sip from antique cups, I smile and politely place my hands in prayer position, Namaste-fashion.

Two more army trucks pass on a hilly curve. We inhale and stare at the floor, thinking that this latest passage seems a miracle since the road has dwindled to little more than a cliff-hung, stony goat path barely wide enough for a narrow truck. All around us there are globby channels of gray mud oozing their way down the mountain. It starts to snow, now that we have climbed above timberline and fog prevents our seeing more than a few feet ahead at a time. The road hairpins at alarming angles every few meters. If the driver misses a cue or if the brakes fail we'll sail off into oblivion within seconds. My stomach turns over and someone makes a crack about wishing she had made out a will before leaving home. "How can you even think of possessions at a time like this," someone else challenges. "All I want to do is to see flat land again. Then

I promise I'll be a good person the rest of my life after this - if we just live through it."

The driver stops the bus and we all jump up to look out the front window. The road has washed away in the storm and someone has placed a few weathered old boards across the yawning ravine. Undaunted, the driver jounces over the boards and I stare at the floor, forgetting the large holes, which are in my line of sight, through which I see the old boards and the thousand-foot drop. Fear flares my nostrils. Fear is stupid, I realize, yet the situation seems to arouse deep fears in all of us. No one speaks or moves. Several passengers have their eyes clamped tightly shut. Others fumble in their purses for sunglasses so as not to see any more.

Snow has churned the rutted road to sluices of slippery gooshy mud and I occupy my mind with endless affirmations since there is little else to do. The tundra wall beside the bus window is a rusty shade, enhanced occasionally by cinnabar lichens dappling bluish boulders. The sun comes out abruptly and shines on an immense blue and white glacier, tunneled with long bundles of pale green icicle spears. In a gray scree valley near the road we see a winding donkey train carrying piles of spindly firewood sticks lashed to their backs. Small clusters of ponies haul woolen blankets and wares to be traded. Caravans rest in mountain meadows at the top of the world, the leaders gazing at herds of thick-coated black yaks grazing hundreds of yards below.

Higher and higher we climb, beyond the fragile tundra now to a gray and beige moonscape devoid of all vegetation. Barren peaks heave upward everywhere we look, relieved only by the glinting satin ribbon of the aquamarine Indus down in the unreachable valley below. It seems like the only thread of continuity in this vast wasteland - like a familiar friend accompanying us to another planet. Just when we have adjusted to the idea that we will not be encountering any people in these heady elevations the bus rumbles down a hilly curve and we come out into a green valley filled with square, dun-colored mud pueblos, their flat roofs piled high with ocher-colored hay. Teen-age children play an unfamiliar sport with sticks and a ball in an open field beside the road. We wave enthusiastically at the children, relieved to encounter other humans in the mountain vastness.

After several more barren miles a town appears and my spine extends with an alert expectancy that it will be Drass, which is well known for its record-setting cold winter temperatures and heavy snowfalls. It is indeed Drass and we see that this charming hamlet near our designated campsite boasts an immigration office, a few vine-covered cottages, lots of green plantings, irrigation projects and the unpretentious simple Rahi Tea Stall. On the road directly outside of Drass our attention is caught by some khaki-colored seventh century Buddhist steles - upright carvings - in fair condition. It is chilly outside the bus and the feel of an early winter slices through the September afternoon air. Faiz announces a short tea stop before we proceed to the larger town of Kargil to repair the broken cooking stove. On the tiny porch of the minuscule tea stall two men sit talking and sipping tea. One is a very dark Indian who sharply contrasts with his companion, a white-haired, pink-skinned albino Indian wearing dark prescription glasses and an olive-drab shirt or uniform of some sort. He is startling in his unusual appearance and absolute composure. Although I'd like to talk with the two about life in Drass, I'm reluctant to impose on their intense conversation and realize we haven't time for more than a few quick pleasantries since night will soon fall. We have yet to fix the stove and set up camp.

It is sunset when we arrive at Kargil, a mere village at the meeting point of the Suru and Drass rivers. This hilly town of unpaved streets is noted for the Purik dialect, Shi'ite Moslem religious practice and obvious absence of women in public. Its population of about three thousand makes it the second largest town in Ladakh. The only main street is choked with squat, one-story tea shops and "hotels," which is the term for restaurant. It is quite evident that Westerners are seldom seen here, especially women Westerners, and so many tall blond ones at that, judging from the stares we attract and the gathering crowds beginning to mill around us in curiosity. There are numerous anti-American political posters glued to lumpy mud walls and nailed to large old tree trunks. They depict sinister-looking American eagles and a fierce, demonic Uncle Sam. We are told that Shi'ite Moslems have put them there but that they have not met any Americans and simply obey their mosque leaders who give political harangues during weekly worship.

After dark we move on to our campsite in a stubbled farmer's field beside a stream, high in the Himalayas. The temperature has fallen to freezing in the past few hours of driving. We all get out to help unload equipment and identify luggage while the encampment is set up. The large cooking and dining tent, with its red cloth floor, is surrounded by ten yellow nylon two-person tents. Overhead in the inky sky the Milky Way looks like a wide band of crushed glass. With magical swiftness Rasool prepares Kashmiri tea and chicken curry in the dining tent. We squeeze into the small dining tent and sit packed together cross-legged on the red ground-cover, savoring the hot food while wildcats scream in the mountains outside. "Will we encounter any leopards?" we ask each other nervously.

The weak yellow beams of our flashlights lead us to our tents after dinner to unroll sleeping bags, extra clothing for the frigid night and notepads for candle-light journal recording. Regine, a French sophisticate will be my roommate for the remainder of the trip. She is brisk and efficient as a packer and traveler. She reminds me of the well-known writer, Anais Nin, since she has a cosmopolitan ease with people of all backgrounds and a very good sense of humor. We joke a few minutes, blow out the candle and fall asleep exhausted, unconcerned by continual roars and screams of nearby animals of unknown description.

After breakfast, our morning departure is delayed two hours due to the challenge of securing our increasingly heavy load to the top of the bus so that it won't fall off. I decide to stroll up the dirt road to explore the area and am greeted by a scene comprised of dry roads, autumn roadside shrubs and an arid landscape of beige and burgundy striped mountains. The banded pinnacles resemble the colors of an Arab's robe and thrust up toward the porcelain blue sky in awesome beauty. Dogs and children can be heard making a commotion higher up the hill which borders the country road. Who lives here? An exploration seems in order.

Further along the hilly road, a cluster of buildings appears through the thick shrubs and a sign signifies that the tiny settlement is the Government High School. The low buildings are made of simple, gray stone construction. Since it is still very early in the morning, the school buildings are empty but I can see old slate blackboards through the large glass windows and rows of wooden benches. The laughter I heard down the hill is that of five children who bathe in cold water from a bucket beside the school building. They push and jostle each other as I walk by, then run out to get a better look after they think I've looked the other way. I wheel around suddenly and laugh and wave, causing all of us to laugh together.

At last the bus cargo is secured and the Rattling Rocket leaves the campsite to find its way back to the road between Kargil and Leh, our destination. We pass more mud-brick pueblo-style hamlets with six to twelve houses. Throughout the area we notice black-clad women carrying dung-collecting baskets. The wicker baskets are attached to a tump-line around the heads of the stooping women. Dung is used for fuel in this treeless region. In their search, the women climb and labor with difficulty up the nearly vertical mountainsides. *How easy, tidy and safe is my life, Lord. Thank You for this incarnation.*

A new landscape of black and white goats, gray-green willows, Russian olive trees and caves emerges. Oasis-like pueblos nestle in sunny, green valleys, bundles of twigs and herbs drying on their flat roofs. This road is wide, solid, pretty and leads to picturesque farm compounds and immaculate fields. We have entered the countryside of Tibetan people where tattered yellow and white prayer flags flutter from house roofs. Pueblos here are whitewashed and decorated with gray wooden window trim. An odd feeling of having lived here before washes over me.

The valley scenery becomes reminiscent of the Mesa Verde region of Colorado, which is visually rich with caves, crenellated rock forms, book cliffs, chimney rocks and striated mesas. As the bus rounds a sharp curve in the road, we abruptly encounter the chilling sight of an oil truck that has fallen off the mountain down into a ravine. Faiz tells us the truck is empty and that it was not there two days ago when he passed this way. Farther on we notice the crushed carcass of an army jeep and later a smashed tourist bus, both of which have plunged off the ledge in the past forty-eight hours. Our driver twirls the steering wheel round and round, unperturbed, mile after mile, as if entranced. My heart is in my mouth as I silently murmur more affirmations for safety, like mantras. Our teeth tingle and bones shake in the endlessly vibrating bus.

As we near Lamayuru monastery, the first of eleven lamaseries we are to visit, we are flagged down by two little Ladakhi boys bundled up in wool caps and jackets who hail the bus for a ride to school. We shower them with pens, nuts and raisins before dropping them off at our stop high above the valley in which the cream and burgundy-colored lamasery sits. Purple mountains loom high in the background, beyond the gray rock pinnacle in the cleft below the Kargil-Leh road. It has an aspect of a fairy castle, this Tibetan Buddhist lamasery, far below us in the deep ravine in the distance, thrusting up through the dry, clear air. We zip our coats and pull on wool caps as we file off the bus for our first Himalayan trek. A keening wind tears at our heavy jackets and slacks as we trot down the long, steep, scree-filled trail into the rocky valley toward the impressive structure.

Will I find God here? Will God appear in a male or a female body? Will the stature of my Master be tall or medium in height? Will He greet me in recognition and congratulate me for relentlessly tracking Him down? Or will He acknowledge me only subtly, or not at all? Will I even find this One Whom I can feel in my heart chakra, Whom I feel playing hide-and-seek with me, drawing me ever onward toward Him...?

Since the sky looks threatening, I have stuck a blue umbrella into my backpack and appreciate the fact that I had the foresight to pull on long thermal underwear before getting into my jeans this morning. My blue nose stings as the wind claws at our eyes, whipping dust and gravel against our cheeks. The trail drops into the shadows of the hills as we near the courtyard of the lamasery, panting, half an hour later. Young monks dressed in saffron yellow and maroon wool cloaks sit on the stone walls of the biscuit-colored clay courtyard. They arise and summon others as we approach. A brass gong is struck inside and chanting emanates from the ancient building.

Weathered wooden prayer wheels spin in the breeze at the courtyard entrance where a toothless, hunched old woman leads a cluster of children past the monks. A monk sitting on a low wall beckons to me; I approach him in curiosity to find that he has displayed on a blanket about twenty temple ornaments which he wants to trade. Am I perceiving this correctly? Trade? As in barter? Yes, he wants me to open my backpack and offers candles, bright prayer flags, Buddhas, finger cymbals, pounded copper squares which are "house blessings." He points to my watch but I indicate that I need to keep it. Next he indicates that his feet and mine are about the same size and that he'd very much like to have my tennis shoes.

The thought of a genuine Buddhist monk greeting future visitors in my scruffy American tennis shoes is both horrifying and comical. I feel as if I should be filing some sort of governmental environmental impact statement for ruining the visual environment. I shake my head about the shoes and open my pack. He is adamant and points to his open sandals and sockless feet after seeing that I have a spare pair of tennis shoes in my pack. His eyes light up at the sight of my blue collapsible umbrella, which I show him how to operate. The hot water bottle and extra pair of longjohns, which I had forgotten were in the pack, drive him into a contained sort of excitement. With a flourishing gesture he offers me, in exchange for the umbrella, tennis shoes, hot water bottle and thermal underwear: a yak butter lamp, a six-inch square copper shield, finger cymbals, a prayer wheel, a bronze bell and a dorje, or prayer scepter, for meditation.

His things are interesting, though I have no idea of what use they would be to me, except as decorative artifacts. He holds his breath in anticipation of my answer. How can I deny this poor man these things if they would keep him warm and dry and if they would bring him pleasure? We arrange an amicable trade and he appears very happy with the outcome. For my part, I find myself hoping that the tennis shoes keep his feet warm but that he doesn't wear them in public and destroy the aesthetics of the monastery. Halt. What on earth am I thinking? Where is my compassion? Where are my values? Have I become totally jaded and insane? These aesthetics are all part of the maya of illusion, anyway. The comfort of his feet should come before my preferences for an authentic scene peopled with properly outfitted monks. Always the past has been sacrificed to the present throughout history. Who is to say which aspects of culture should go and which should remain?

Since we are not allowed to enter the monastery we must content ourselves with a stroll in the empty courtyard, with admiration of the old wooden prayer wheels there, and a brief introduction to Buddhist religion, culture and artifacts by Faiz. Although several hundred monks lived here in the past there are only about twenty or thirty here today, many of whom serve as teachers throughout Ladakh. The lamas here belong to the yellow sect - as opposed to the red sect - and are dependent upon the villagers for food and donations as their own slanted hillside fields are inadequate in crop production to sustain their entire order. These same villagers still carry on a lifestyle from the middle ages at the base of the mountain lamasery. Our visual appetite has been whetted now by the architecture of Lamayuru and by the appearance of the monks, both in their costuming and more importantly in their quietude.

We will be visiting about eight or ten monasteries in the next few days and I am eager to spend time inside them, hopefully to observe prayers and chanting. I chuckle as I notice the curiosity with which my mind has riveted toward the more hidden or obscure aspects of these monasteries. That old curiosity, like a friendly stray neighborhood puppy, wanders away and returns, continually. Will it ever leave me for good? We tend to laud curiosity in the West whereas Asians of any spiritual attainment view it as one of the many amusing nuisance aspects of the limited, temporal mind, which is not the true Knower.

The afternoon journey's endless round of sharp curves and vertical cliffs merges into twilight driving, then an inky black road dissolves under a star-speckled velvet sky. Finally clusters of ground lights appear in the darkness to herald the outskirts of Leh, which has a population of about 8,500 and an elevation of 3505 meters. Leh was, at one time, a primary stopover on the famed Silk Route as well as having been a center of commerce. Tourism is its main attraction today with highlights being the town's back streets, the old Leh Palace, Leh Gompa (monastery), Sankar Gompa, Spitok Gompa, Beacon Highway, Shey Gompa, Tikse and Hemis Gompas and the nearby Tibetan Refugee Camp.

My heart beats louder as we pull into the courtyard of the two-story hotel where we are greeted by the bearded owner, Mr. Singh, who is a Sikh, wearing turban and vest. He is a robust-looking man with an unusual falsetto voice and rather vivacious effeminate gestures. As we stiffly stagger single-file out of the bus into the blue-white moonlight of the courtyard and up the three front steps of the entrance, each of us is garlanded with a white gauze prayer shawl by Mr. Singh or a hotel staff member. The tiny lobby of the hotel is illuminated by candles carried by the three young Ladakhi desk clerks.

"I'm so sorry that you have to arrive after your long trip in the dark but the electricity has failed us again as it often does here in Leh," Mr. Singh announces in his most sincere manner. We hasten to assure him that we are so pleased to be standing on solid ground that the absence of electric lights is not a matter for concern. We are marrow-chilled and ravenously hungry. Every bone aches. Our spirits are high, however, and we are thrilled to be here, full of anticipation for the events and sights of the next few days. It is an appreciative, uncomplaining troupe of visitors which Mr. Singh and his young men show to their rooms with much pomp and flourish. As we cross the doorsill to our room I receive an intuitive flash that here in Leh I will find a clue to the Great Being for whom I have been searching.

Regine and I investigate the Westernized toilet and shower fixture in our room, then tip the baggage boy and collapse on our twin beds with heavy sighs of ecstasy. Immediately there is a knock at the door. Faiz announces that dinner has been kept warm for our arrival and that we are to report right away to the dining room.

CHAPTER 11
A CLUE IN AN ANCIENT LAMASERY

"Your life is ultimately your greatest work of art." Anais Nin

Leh Ladakh
October 2, 1981

We cross the open courtyard at the center of the hotel to the lower floor dining room opposite our own room. After three days of cold, jouncing bus travel over treacherous passes, the dining room seems like a scene from Shangri-La with lavishly appointed buffet table set with fine linen and exquisite silver and candlesticks. Exotic Indian curries and sauces vie for our attention with creamed vegetables and garnishes. Samovars of tea rest next to frosted bottles of mineral water and sparkling tumblers.

Liveried waiters glide between the dozen tables of Americans, Australians and Europeans who murmur to their dinner companions in cultivated tones periodically punctuated with refined laughter. Our senses are overwhelmed with the food aromas, the comfort, the ambience of this secure haven which contrasts starkly with our harrowing, uncomfortable journey. We had finally let go of all comfort needs and settled into an endurance of discomfort and monotony this last day of the trip and the fact that we have truly arrived finally weighs in on me with a light-headed gratitude. Now that it's over it seems easy, like most ordeals.

Still in our jeans and sweaters we look and feel grubby in the setting but notice that everyone is casually dressed. Dinner is unceremoniously inhaled amid excessive compliments of our group. The altitude and fatigue conspire to cause sleep to overtake us in our chairs but we are able to resist, to ambulate to the room and to open our sleeping bags onto the beds of the chilly room before unpacking a few essentials.

We have unbuttoned our clothes when a knock sounds at the door. It is Lea, a young, beautiful local girl. Despite our exhaustion we invite her in for a talk. She wants to barter. She tells us about her family, who live in a hut near town which has no heat nor floor except the frozen earth. She and her brothers and parents do a little farming and a little bartering and selling of goods produced at the nearby lamaseries in order to survive. I'm especially taken by her outer beauty which is typical of the people of this region. Her cheeks are a bright, natural pink and her raven black eyes and hair shine with healthy vitality. She has a radiant spiritual attractiveness and a gentle manner which are immensely appealing as well.

As we speak she appraises our sleeping bags, which we'll be using on top of the beds throughout most of the trip and offers to buy them for three times what they cost. Regine curtly refuses and I explain that mine is borrowed from a friend of Jim's back in Singapore and isn't mine to sell or trade. Sadly, I explain that I haven't anything left to trade since this is my first time in the area and I wasn't prepared for trading. An hour later we escort Lea to the door and fall asleep in our clothes, too tired and too chilled to change.

In the morning Faiz announces that we'll be visiting Leh Palace, local gompahs and the home of a Ladakhi family for chang and yak butter tea. From behind him in the courtyard, however, we hear loud angry shouts from Rasool who yells at the dilapidated bus, as if it is a recalcitrant ox, and kicks the tires in fury. It seems the bus won't start and that we'll have an extra hour to wander the town this morning before boarding the bus to visit Leh Palace. With a whoop like the gleeful shouts of school children released early from class, we streak off in all directions to explore Leh in the golden autumn morn. Outside the hotel courtyard gate two little boys float sticks down a winding stream and I hunker down in a squatting position, like theirs, to observe the bobbling twigs being swept off in the icy mountain torrent. A klankle of goat bells, interspersed with bleating, diverts my attention toward the town market where most of my compatriots have gone.

The lanes between the whitewashed buildings are narrow avenues streaming with long-robed Tibetans twirling prayer wheels, women carrying produce to sell in the town square and young mothers with babies tied to their backs in colored shawls. Most of the women wear ankle length black robes with sashes of bright pink or green, topped with a Ladakhi black hat, turned up at the corners and resembling a Dutch girl's hat in shape. The population here contains an unusually large number of extremely old people, it seems. Many of the lined, hunched citizens seem as if they are over eighty or even ninety and quite a few are toothless. In the market square there are old men chanting prayers, women in twos and threes talking softly near their vegetable wares and young people unlocking sparsely outfitted tourist shops.

One of the men calls to me from an antique shop and says he has good bargains on rare religious items and that he will give me a good price with his calculator, which I notice he is holding upside down, while pretending to push the buttons.

An hour later Faiz gathers up his flock for the trip to Leh Palace which is grandly placed atop Tsenmo Hill overlooking the town. This sixteenth century, eight-storied structure was built by King Singe Namgyal. In order to reach the palace we have to climb a steep hill between the houses of the townspeople who are already busily at work on their flat roofs and in the winding streets. In the bright sunshine on one rooftop a determined mother purses her lips, wielding flashing scissors to trim her little wriggling daughter's glossy raven-black hair. Next door to them an ancient grandmother convalesces in her rooftop bed out in the fresh fall air. Spotted goats clatter through the narrow streets, chased by little boys in burgundy wool sweaters and brown baggy pants.

Inside the dark Leh Palace there are wooden stairs and ladders to the flat roof where the view of the surrounding territory is superb and breath-stopping. In the stiff winds colored cheesecloth prayer flags rat-a-tat over the Zanskar Range, looming huge and deceptively near. We stand mesmerized by the yellowing autumn-tinged trees in the distance and an expansive view below us of mud-brick houses, emerald valleys, fields in harvest and the intriguingly carved gray stone mani walls.

In anticipation of our imminent visit to Sankar Gompa, near town, we are acutely aware of our rather rude appearance in jeans, tennis shoes and wool caps. We look like a group of lumberjacks rather than a bevy of European and American professional women and corporate executive's wives. Hopefully the monks will not be offended by our attire nor feel that it in any way indicates even the slightest disrespect for their holy places. Breathtaking vistas render us speechless as we leave the palace. Prayer flags ripple and flutter in the slight breeze. In the valley below us, yellowing aspen quake and oscillate in the clear, dry mountain air beside a cold rushing stream.

We are struck by the stillness which pervades the landscape. Here in the Himalayas the Thunder of Silence, the Eternal Om, suffuses the hills and vales. It is both compact and diffuse – deep, eternal, endless, far and yet very near. It is charged with energy, like a roar - or a mighty hum. Yogis call it the Breath of Brahma.

In a few minutes we proceed from the palace to the gompa (monastery) and alight into a charming courtyard shaded by old trees which cast blue shadows onto yellow chrysanthemums in clay pots on the steps outside the huge double doors to the gompa. Faiz instructs us to carry extra wool socks with us, from now on, to put over our regular socks and stockings, since footgear must be left outside the door; the lamasery floors are often smeared with rancid butterfat. The heavy old door creaks open and our group, as one body, eagerly leans forward. A wizened monk greets us with obvious joy and takes us on a tour of the two floors in the dark interior. Faiz translates the monk's comments on the usage of the gongs, tankas, mandalas, yak butter lamps, murals and various artifacts. Like most gompas, the building is sparsely appointed and is without running water or electricity.

We pad along in sock-clad feet touring the prayer and chanting rooms, admiring more gongs and drums before finishing the tour back in the main entrance. The monk bows deeply and tells Faiz with a twinkle, in obvious admiration for us, that it has been an especial honor to host us since we are by far the cleanest people he has ever taken through the gompa! He further remarks that the most interesting and valuable aspect of our visit for him was to see all of us Western women in our native costumes! This is another reality check. While we've been entranced with the "native costumes" of the region the local people have regarded our rough clothing as "native costumes." To all of us, we're simply wearing our prosaic everyday garb. To others, it's exotic.

But clothing and cultural phenomena, as interesting as they are, are of the world of form, rather than the world of enduring spiritual substance, hence they cannot provide ultimate satisfaction as a field of study or enlightenment. The more we travel the more keenly aware I become that I have really been hoping at some level to find some common thread running through the major world religions that could give new purpose and meaning to people. It becomes clearer to me, by degrees, that such knowledge cannot be extracted from the environment, no matter how exotic, but rather is only gleaned from one's living, from giving and from service. Can it be as simple as this, that the common thread is love? Love of Spirit within us and love of Spirit in each other.

Perhaps Manly P. Hall describes best the various degrees of spiritual understanding as manifested in actions rather than as mere intellectual conceptions.

"Realization as conduct is the performing of Truth.

Realization as observation is the perceiving of Truth.

Realization as appreciation is the enjoyment of Truth.

Realization as speech is the utterance of Truth.

Realization as veneration is the acceptance of Truth in a spriritual mystery.

Discipline as Truth is obedience to the Law.

And sight as Truth is the discovery of Reality in form, line, color and composition." SUBDOR P 182

Faiz interrupts my reverie to announce that our long-anticipated visit to the home of a Ladakhi family will take place shortly in their second floor house above a second-hand book stall in Leh. As we clip-clop along the cobblestones of the dark, narrow alley to the destination, little boys peek out of doorways and smile at us. The unlighted stairway and cold cement steps leading to the upper apartment give an indication of the simple living conditions of even the most affluent people here at the top of the world. Faiz has told us that this family is one of the most prosperous for miles around and that they have recently been featured in an issue of *National Geographic* wearing their best Tibetan wedding dresses which they'll put on for us.

We are greeted by the mother and her daughter who have prepared chang and butter tea for us. We are ushered into a large room which has beige plaster walls and low turquoise green wooden benches along every wall. An open cupboard holds a treasure of silver and dishes and serves as a room divider for the kitchen sink where the two women prepare our beverages. High on one wall a poster of a Scandinavian rock group smiles down at us.

We've been told that it is impolite to refuse food or beverage in Asia so everyone smiles and accepts the steaming cups of yak butter tea. While we sip the tea we admire the daughter, who could be anywhere between thirty and forty-five in age, modeling her stunning dress that is black with red and turquoise embroidery and topped with a peraq headpiece made of silver and turquoise stones. Her matching jewelry is turquoise, coral and silver. Next we are served chang which contains alcohol, and which tastes like grapefruit juice to me and has the same color and consistency. Several seasoned Asia travelers of our group warn the others of the unwisdom of drinking alcoholic beverages at high altitude, especially since we have yet today to visit the Tibetan Refugee Camp, Sonam Ling and Shey Palace featuring the golden Buddha.

Reluctantly we leave the cozy, sparsely decorated home and thank our hostesses who bring in two rosy-cheeked grandchildren to invite us to return again.

At the Tibetan refugee camp outside of town, we are beset by scores of tots who speak a bit of very practical English and who yank our jackets and thrust pieces of paper into our hands with their names, ages, camp addresses and clothing size. Their mothers sit on the floor of a long barn-like building making wool rugs or spinning on miniature spinning wheels. The building is cold, unlighted and dusty, yet the women seem peaceful and chant, pray or talk quietly as we inspect their work. Two thousand refugees have lived here since the early sixties, surviving by way of church relief and world-wide assistance organizations. Faiz herds us quickly past the antique shop and rug shop, eager to round up the group and keep our appointment at famous Shey Palace. As I step up to board the bus a little girl and boy, about six years old, grab my hand and chant "I am size six. Please send me your children's old clothes. I am size six...." They stick their papers with vital statistics for each into my jacket pocket and wave merrily until the bus rounds the corner of the compound.

Their faces swim lucidly in my mind's eye the next few miles of our jouncing journey to Shey. I recall all of the children we've met along the way and the balloons, candies, coins and ball point pens we've dispersed, such trivialities compared to their more urgent needs. It's always an odd sensation for me to suddenly step into another world and to see myself as the poor local people of remote regions must perceive the exterior me - which is, of course, only a tiny portion of one's being and an often misleading one at that. If we were to magically change places and I were to become a Tibetan and one of them were to take my place on the tour, then what? Would I make more spiritual use of my life if I had far fewer resources available? More to the point, am I really making "good use" of my life, skills, abilities and understandings right now? I have so much more in the way of resources and possessions but am I doing anything significant for others with the advantages?

Shey Palace presents itself to us without pomp and yet each time we come upon a lamasery we are thrilled at the architectural feat, the hillside setting and the ambience and silence of the surrounds. This former summer palace of Ladakhi kings was built over 555 years ago and houses an incomparable huge golden Buddha, twelve meters high and adorned with blue hair.

Of all the gompas, however, it is at Tikse Gompa that I become most excited. It isn't the restored and painted library with its gilded, nine-inch square cubicles that intrigues me, although I admit that the forty cubbyholes contain priceless old manuscripts that would make Western scholars do gleeful cartwheels. Several of our group have wandered to other corners of the huge dark room and only a few of us stand before the monk. Realizing that this young monk may know the answer to my perennial question, I boldly but politely ask him. "Sir, do you think there is a possibility that there is, on the earth at this time, someone like Lord Buddha or Lord Jesus or Krishna who has come to help humanity. Do you think that God Himself might be here now on the planet?" My heart is pounding and I've stopped breathing in anticipation of his reply.

The slender smiling monk says, "No one has asked this question before. Kindly wait here a moment. I have something that will interest you very much. I'll be back shortly." After about five minutes the smiling young monk returns, accompanied by an older graying monk who is carrying an old brown wooden box wrapped in a red silk fabric. With great care and a dollop of ceremony they remove the red silk and take pains to let us know that we are being specially graced by God to receive a peek at this old manuscript and its accompanying history. They explain that it has been secreted back and forth from Hemis Gompa to Tikse over the centuries to protect it from invaders, adventurers and artifact collectors.

Ancient Tibetan Prophecies

"Because you have asked about God on earth at this time in history, we will give you the rare privilege of seeing the most prized manuscript in this monastery. In fact, it has been safeguarded for two thousand years, through fire, foreign occupation, plague and war. We have moved it from lamasery to lamasery over and over and will do so again after you leave. The answer to your question is that at this exact time in history, according to our prophecies, there is indeed a great Full Buddha on earth. He is probably somewhere in India, most probably the South and is in middle age now. He will live a long time and will eventually bring about world peace. He is gentle, kind, all-powerful, all-knowing, all-present. He will perform many healings and miracles and will be the wonder of the whole world. But, sadly, we do not know His name or whereabouts.

"It is said that His appearance will coincide with a great building boom throughout the world and that there will be many regional wars when he comes. There will be much hatred, prejudice and untruth. Hindus call this the Kali Yuga, the Age of Chaos and Darkness. It is also called the Age of Lies. But soon, by the end of the century, the Great One will make Himself known and will call his age-old teachers to

Himself to instruct them to begin to educate humanity about their purpose on earth. We feel very happy that you feel His presence on earth but we cannot tell you where He can be found." *Don't hide Yourself from me, Lord. Where are You?!*

The older monk bows and then, with a flourish, lifts the silk completely off of the box containing the ancient manuscript. He tells us very softly that Western eyes have not beheld the ancient manuscripts. The story the monk pays out to us in gradual, subdued sentences, translated by Faiz, holds me transfixed. Here, in these manuscripts, these two thousand year-old tomes, is the story of the life, studies and travels of Esa, or Issa (rhymes with Lisa), whom the West knows as Jesus.

These hand-written books are not bound pages, of course, but are loose sheets, most often wooden strips or vegetable-shellacked leaves, wrapped up in cloth, held between two boards. The sheets and boards are tied with straps and kept in the library cubby holes. According to our monk, Jesus traveled and studied with masters in the Himalayas during His "lost years" or the period of His youth and adulthood in order to master His ego and to prepare for His future work of teaching, preaching and healing. This manuscript is the very proof which theologians the world over would covet, as it outlines in great detail the life, spiritual education and itinerary of Jesus Christ, as well as His development as He studied with various Self-realized teachers and holy ones throughout Tibet, India, Egypt and elsewhere.

We profusely thank the monks for the great honor they have shown us.

"I have no idea why you have given us this special gift," I said, deeply touched, "But we are supremely thrilled and appreciative. You have answered a question that has been with me night and day for seven months. I have traveled to many countries searching for the Great One Who is here on earth now. From the highest mountains and from the solitary seashore I have called to Him, asking, 'Where are You?' Now I know I am on the right track in my search. My deepest thanks to you."

I bowed. They bowed. Then we all bowed again.

"If you find the Holy One," said the older monk, "we would like to know where He is, but it is said that each one will be drawn to Him at the exact correct time for that soul." They waved wistfully as we retrieved our shoes and left the courtyard.

Outside the gompa, when I mention the theological and philosophical ramifications of such information to the others I am met with blank stares. They've read little in philosophy or theology and think it's amusing that I'm interested in them. Desperate to talk with someone who is aware of such things, I seek out Faiz on the return bus trip and engage him in a two-hour discussion of Buddhism and his thoughts about the Dalai Lama.

He feels we are living in extraordinary times that will indeed presage a new era and mentions several of the local prophecies concerning the new golden age. He says that the local people also believe that in a time of moral degradation, war and much building construction all over the planet, a Master will come to comfort the people, to create peace amid the threat of annihilation and that wars will subside and people will emerge harmonious and spiritually strong. "It does seem that the prophecy could match these times, don't you think?" Faiz asks with a twinkle. "We could use someone soon; that I know," he murmurs.

"Maybe this really is that period of great change and we are all the Master in potential. Perhaps the Messiah is all of us, needing to come into a new awareness and commitment of love and responsibility together," I venture.

Faiz laughs and tells me that it is a sweet idea but that he has seen too many "rough characters" to have faith that everyone could have such high ideals unless pushed to the breaking point to give up selfishness and ego-bound habits. "It's very hard to keep your mind constantly on God in our busy, noisy world today. And it seems that when people need to work to earn a living for their families they sometimes forget God completely and start to think only of things they can buy and pleasures they can find to enliven their dull lives or to make them feel that their toil is worth the emptiness they feel."

"You'd make a good priest or teacher," I remark.

"No, all my people know these things but they are gradually losing their old ways and their knowledge both through contact with travelers and from having to live in refugee camps or to leave the camps and find work in the cities. Then many of them become lost, cut off from the nurturing influence of their culture, spiritual beliefs and practices." As Faiz talks, the twilight sky erases the last remaining light and we ride back to the hotel in silence. One of Emerson's famous lines comes to mind, "The reward of a thing well done is to have done it." It is thrilling for me to search for my Master, but for me, finding Him will be the reward – just to know He is here on earth, helping all of mankind, is enough for me. If He is the One to Whom I have prayed all my life – God Himself – that would indeed be too wonderful for words.

Today's clue in the lamasery and hearing the local prophecies from Faiz have been the most encouraging aspects of the seven-month saga so far. *"Thank You, Lord, for these clues. I feel jubilant."*

With each trip I make throughout the more remote spots of Asia, I am becoming a more hearty traveler and a more compassionate person toward those I meet. This, I feel, will be my last tour group. Although I am enjoying it hugely, I feel ready to travel alone, or with a friend, as I have, previously, in Africa, Europe, Canada, Mexico, Central America and elsewhere. However, I know that it is futile to seek enjoyment in the world and, as *The Upanishads* say, "The immature run after sense pleasures." TU P 90

Ladakh
October 4th

Our class A bus, cajoled into action by Rasool, jounces over the Upshi Road past Shey and Tikse, along the Manoli Road that winds beside the silvery blue Indus River. Only a dozen or so monks now live at world-famous Hemis Lamasery which was built in the early sixteen hundreds. Hemis is well-known for its masked dances in June, its harvest festivals and archery contests and its huge tanka which is only displayed in public every eleven years. We learn that, as in the other gompas, the monks subsist on a simple diet of vegetables, tsampa meal, butter tea and a little bit of sugar or butter.

Inside the dark chapel of Hemis there is an altar at the far end of the room. In the center a long silk patchwork fabric tube hangs from the high ceiling. Our host explains that this colorful cloth column measuring about three feet across and several meters high, is an ancient and efficient device to catch smoke from the lamps and to freshen the air. The wall paintings of various gods depict the lower nature of man in monstrous fashion. Creatures with bulging eyes stare ferociously out at us amid stark symbols of white skulls. The murals appear freshly painted yet use the traditional beast and monster motifs in colors of black, white, red, green and yellow.

A sense of the coming winter is in the cold clear October air as Rasool drives the Rocket to the airport for our departure by plane back to Srinagar in Kashmir India. At the airport the uniformed military luggage checkers exhibit rude, aggressive behavior and seem intimidated by so many confident Western women boarding the plane all at once. They demand bribes but we have exhausted our supplies and protest that we have nothing. They make us unwrap the Tibetan antiques purchased at the antique shops and exclaim that the antiques are required to have certificates allowing them to be taken from the country. We protest that no papers were sold with the goods and that we were not informed of the regulation before spending our money. They attempt to confiscate the goods. More protesting from the people who have bought tankas and temple ornaments. Tempers quickly flare to the flashpoint. Swiftly Norma Jean strides to the rescue and diplomatically calms down both sides. Next an officer appears and gives his permission for our group to board. Leading us onto the tarmac out of their hearing he apologizes for his men explaining that they are poor and inexperienced and had felt the need to display their manhood by flexing their bureaucratic muscles. They have seldom encountered a group of Western women traveling without husbands or fathers. (Presumably this show of authority on their part was meant to remind us that they still believe it is a man's world and that we had better watch our step!)

The steep ascent from the short runway into the crystal blue sky of the Himalayas is as thrilling as the needle pinnacles surrounding the little town. Leh's shops and houses quickly shrink to miniature size and the view out the plane windows is filled with snowy peaks as far as we can see. In a brief hour the plane has traveled the same distance that we laboriously climbed in the tattered bus over two nights and two and a half days. Soon impassable snowdrifts will close the passes to all travel during the entire extended winter.

Even as the plane approaches the Srinagar Airport we can see streams of merchants, hitchhikers, shepherds and students coming down the mountain roads to the more comfortable climate in the Vale of Kashmir until the snowbound roads can be reopened in June. Srinagar's altitude is 1,768 meters with a population of about half a million. The people here in north India are noticeably taller than those in the south and Islam predominates, whereas Hinduism is the most widely practiced religion in the south.

Kashmir and Ladakh are regions of the Indian state of Jammu and Kashmir, often spoken of as "J and K." Jammu, the southern part of the state, geographically comprises a connecting area between the Indian plains and the Himalayas. Authors and film makers have long used the large picturesque Himalayan valley in the northern state called the "Vale of Kashmir" in their lore and regional romances. The Kashmir region continues to be disputed territory by China, Pakistan and India.

Throughout Kashmir, the mogul emperors of old established elaborate, terraced, perfumed gardens whose formal designs are often hundreds of years old. Like the forts and palaces of the moguls, the gardens are an artistic and scientific wonder, constituting an historic treasure belonging to the whole world. The colors and designs resemble gigantic, living botanical Persian carpets. The floral fragrances calm the nerves and entice one to forget his cares and to tarry awhile in the splendors of nature.

The fabled houseboats of Kashmir, which will serve as our lodging, were introduced by the British in colonial times and attract as many visitors as the gardens, the carpet factories and the cool mountain climate of Dal Lake.

Strange feelings well up in me as we drive along the shaded avenues of Srinagar and I once again see the older brown and white Tudor-style houses with their bluish tin roofs and towers. This canal city where I spent my honeymoon is changing so rapidly that I fear it will be ruined in the hasty plunge toward profit and modernization. If only India had an active Historical Society and competent Chambers of Commerce or City Planning Commissions which could cooperate in preserving the best of the culture while attracting tourism without devastation. Brown wooden houseboats are lined up along the Ghelum River. Children romp about the decks as mothers wash laundry in the river and prepare family meals for the day ahead. These boats which pack the canals are far smaller and much less luxurious than the vacation houseboats on Dal Lake.

Having been refused land for housing by the reigning Maharaja, the British built the first houseboats in 1888 as living quarters for officials and their families. Today, for the most part, the houseboats retain their Victorian flavor, color and decor. The Dal Lake houseboats are generally sixty to one hundred and twenty feet long and about nine to 18 feet wide. They're rather reminiscent of old fashioned floating house trailers of the "double-wide" variety. A front porch leads into a living room area, behind which is a formal dining room, then a corridor leading to two or three bedrooms, each with its own private bathroom in most cases. The decor is charming, in a quaint English country cottage sort of way, though the floral chintz curtains and upholstery which set off the mahogany and cherry furniture are rather uninspired. The sundeck of the flat roof overhead can be reached by stairs near the small kitchen. The package price for the accommodation usually pays for three main meals and two tea-times as well as shikara transportation to land and back as many times as necessary in a day.

Dal Lake, which is really three lakes in one, swings into view as a confusing jumble. Sign-sporting houseboats are packed next to one another with their veranda ends facing the road. Colorful wooden shikaras (canopied boats) with gaily printed awnings ply the channels and waterways, their blue, red or yellow trim matching the boatmen's paddles. Causeways and bridges connect the islands for pedestrians and bicyclists; the lakes are choked with yellow-green lotus, cucumbers, snarled weeds, melons and tomatoes, all growing in a matted mass.

No sooner has Abraham, our host, paddled our boat out to the awaiting houseboat and installed us in our rooms, than persistent salesmen have paddled up to our boats and begun much shouted bargaining of their wares. Without invitation they board the boats and offer fruit, leather, fur vests and gloves, silver jewelry, embroidery, soft drinks, soap and Kleenex.

There are shikara police on the lake and shikara produce-sellers which farm and sell the vegetables that grow in the fetid waters. Middle-aged men dressed in round skull caps and woolen cloaks equip themselves for a day's trading of vegetables with hookahs, or hubble-bubble pipes and kangris. A kangri is an earthenware bowl brazier fitted inside a wicker container and carried under the voluminous Kashmiri pheran (cape) as an individual portable heater for the paddlers of the long wooden boats on chilly autumn mornings. Burn scars from kangri contact while squatting with burning embers are not uncommon here.

Regine and I decide to go into town and to stroll beside the British residency buildings along the Bund. The pedicab which transports us there rides beside signs for papier mache boxes, shawls, imitation saffron, honey, both real and imitation, carved wooden ornaments and filigree jewelry in the style of the moguls.

We walk from the cab along shaded streets to the well-known handi-craft store, "Suffering Moses." Regine tells me of the numerous wind-surfing championships she has won in Singapore. She is a tanned, well-muscled woman who looks thirty, rather than forty-seven. Her time is absorbed in the duties of being a corporate wife with a heavy entertaining schedule, bridge parties, interior design, reading and travel. She is the daughter of a French banker, who was one of the most powerful men in Saigon before it fell. She and her husband and son escaped Saigon by helicopter with their lives and a single suitcase. They left behind their luxurious home, furnishings, art objects and the fate of their servants to the Communists. As she describes the horror of the takeover and the family's various, subsequent ways of dealing with the trauma, a movement in the bushes ahead catches my eye. I notice further along the sidewalk, springing behind a skimpy hedge, five lively, healthy children between the ages of seven and ten, jumping up and down in the excited hatching of their imminent plot.

They have spotted us as their prey and demonstrate for each other which of them will fake each sort of handicap or affliction as they pretend to be crippled beggars. I nudge Regine and she catches them scrambling behind the bushes to lie in wait for us. When we come alongside the shrubs all five start up a cacophony of moans and appeals that are not only convincing but truly dreadful. One boy rolls his eyes pitifully, simulating a blind person while his friend crawls along the sidewalk dragging an inturned foot and drooling and whining. A little girl fastens onto my slacks with bulldog tenacity, requesting rupees and bon-bons. If I hadn't seen the planning of the ambush by these clever thespians, I would indeed be alarmed by their afflictions, enacted with such gusto and believability. Regine sharply tells them that we know they're only acting, that they should be ashamed of themselves and to stop harassing us. They are so shocked that we know it's a trick that simultaneously the chorus halts and their mouths fall open, their eyes pop in wonder and they stand there in mid-gesture. Slowly they all come to their feet and silently stare after us, their boldness demolished by our having somehow seen through the ruse which has obviously never failed before.

Back on the houseboat Yosef has prepared a lunch of chicken stew, the flat bread known as naan, cooked vegetables and spiced Kashmiri tea. Rasool stops by to leave his address and the clothing sizes of his children.

On the way to bed, I pass Gracia Lewis' room which is next to ours. A funny familiar feeling, like a shiver of precognitive goosebumps electrifies my body. Gracia would refer to it as "goose-flesh" and Regine would call it "horripilation." The mere thought of being in Nepal tomorrow is, in itself thrilling enough without any additional highlights. It's the sort of clue accompanied by a sense of expectancy which experience has trained me to notice. What will we encounter in Nepal?

CHAPTER 12
RHINO CHARGE IN NEPAL

"The closest distance between two people is a good laugh."
Victor Borgia

Meghauli, Nepal
October 6, 1981

After breakfast today we flew from Srinagar to Delhi to Kathmandu to Tiger Tops Camp at Meghauli. Royal Nepal Airlines has transported us to Meghauli's emerald green grassy airstrip where we are greeted by a collection of enormous lumbering charcoal gray elephants and a little clump of native mahouts (elephant drivers) waiting expectantly in the shade of a grass hut, which is the only dwelling in sight. As we alight to the ground it is announced that half of us will travel by Land Rover and the other half by pachyderm to the Tiger Tops Jungle Lodge where we will unload, have a snack and set out on foot to the tent camp nearby where we'll sleep tonight.

There is much hooting, wobbling and jockeying about in ascending the rickety wooden ladders to the howdah platforms on the elephant backs. There aren't enough elephants for the entire group to ride today, unfortunately. My reluctance to push my way aboard the few available elephants leaves me among the group who squeeze into the Land Rovers. It is sunny and hot as we lurch along rutted dirt roads and through shallow streams to the lodge. From all visual evidence we seem to be in Africa rather than in Nepal. The round lodge with its pointed, grassy roof further bears out this impression.

At twilight, after a brief lecture, we trot on foot behind our young American female guide through the jungle to the tiger blind to await game. But our patient silent vigil goes unrewarded. She senses our disappointment and announces that our tent camp will welcome us with dinner and a campfire, as well as a trek to a hilltop tiger blind. It's a short walk of a few miles through four-foot blond grasses and along a flat wide river to the tent camp where we are met by another guide and the camp chef.

This is a posh camp, indeed, with large attractive double tents, immaculate upper and lower sheets on comfortable cots, pillows, nightstands, buffet food and a large hut for convening and socializing. The atmosphere is so clean, safe and cozy, that a few of our group comment that they had hoped for more adventure than this and would like some sort of "episode" to match the continual feelings of danger that we experienced while traversing the road to Leh. Though we've already had a near-hijacking and several bad scares on the Rattling Rocket, I myself wouldn't mind a little excitement, either. We're probably becoming hooked on our own adrenaline.

G.K. Chesterton apparently used to say that "Dull people always want excitement." TQC P 98 Am I really as dull as all that to want a little adventure now and then?

After dinner a half-dozen of our group join some others who have arrived from the U.S. to swap stories and admire the glittering stars. From the indigo sky a silver moon brings to mind the famous words of Shakespeare in Romeo and Juliet.:

> "It seems she hangs upon the cheek of night
> like a rich jewel in an Ethiope's ear –
> Beauty too rich for youth
> For earth, too dear." IV 49 Act One

My head begins to pound again, as it has throughout the trip and I wonder if I have altitude sickness, having come from sea level, or if something else is wrong with me. Periodically I've experienced double vision lately and I notice that the moon seems alternately blurry then clear, then blurry again. The others assure me that the moon is quite sharply outlined, has been all the while we've been watching and that the sensation must be caused by my eyes. If this continues I'll have to have my eyes checked when I return to Singapore. Or are my eyes giving me a metaphor that I'm not perceiving the world correctly? This bears close watching.

One by one, the moon-watchers trail off to bed and an idea of George Leonard's comes to mind as I review my stay in Asia thus far. Leonard postulates that to experience a major breakthrough as individuals we must dispense with the most indispensable aspect of our own vision. What is the most indispensable aspect of my own vision now? It is that there is somewhere on this planet, a Teacher who is spiritually advanced far beyond me or anyone I have ever met. He or she is Self-realized in the sense that Jesus, Buddha, Krishna and Zoroaster were and can provide me with direct or indirect assistance on my spiritual path.

Further, perhaps this person can assuage this keen and nearly painful longing in my being to know how to know the "I AM" within myself and to discover whatever it is that I am supposed to be doing on the earth in this lifetime. To put it simply, I need a spiritual breakthrough. Suppose there is no such person and I'm forced to abandon my search? What then? Then I will continue as I always have, doing the best I can to make meaning and purpose of my own existence, serving the best way that I can. To tell the truth though, I am about to give up the search for a Messiah, Teacher, guru, or spiritual mentor. Or perhaps I'll let it go awhile, detestable though that thought is to me. Maybe I've been trying too hard.

When the monk in Leh told us about the Fullest Buddha (Highest Avatar) being alive now on earth, I initially felt quite elated and very close to finding Him. If they haven't found Him, though, how could I find Him, since there are billions of people in Asia and I haven't done anything meritorious to have earned the right to discover Him. So far, except for that lamasery clue, I've not seen any other sign so far of such an entity, though for some reason I was fairly sure He or She would be in China or India. Is it so terrible to want to know if an Exalted One is alive in my lifetime and to make contact if that is the case? I know we each need to do our own spiritual work, but a little guidance would be appreciated at this point in my life. We'll only be in Asia another three or four months if Jim's company projects are finished on time, and then I'll be forced to relinquish the search for the time being. I feel slightly discouraged about this.

The only thing that sustains me in this phantom pursuit is the continual work with *A Course In Miracles* wherein I genuinely feel that my true purpose is to know and express my divinity and to help others to know and express their divinity. As I let myself be made whole, I am better able to assist others to do so. Another idea comes to mind. It is that everything which appears in our reality is there to foster our awareness.

Meghauli, Nepal
October 8th

This morning we tour the area by Land Rover, dug-out canoes and on foot. Our guide explains that the Royal Chitwan National Park is a favorite haunt of naturalists from throughout the world because of the hundreds of varieties of birds and butterflies to be found here. The park, sizable and magnificent, is comprised of 360 square miles of jungle and grasslands.

We board long slender dug-out canoes for an excursion along the flat river in the fog. After the intense crowding of Singapore, it is indescribably exquisite to me to be enveloped in the hush and mist with only the splat of boat paddles to be heard. I have always felt at home in the forest, grove or jungle. Nature always restores me more quickly than art, music, or meditation. The headiness of the jungle explorations thrill me as I admire slanting sun rays filtering through leafy vines and dark branches to the forest floor. Large colorful birds flit, squawk and scream as we snap photos, take notes and write Haiku poetry.

A few hours later, at nightfall, we climb single file with flashlights for a few miles along hilly jungle terrain to crouch silently in the stockade-like tiger blind on a rise of land not far from our tents. Through peepholes we can see the hilly terrain far below us. Across a steep ravine, a deer is lashed to a stake to attract tigers. Apparently we are sufficiently far away to avoid having our scent detected by the tiger. At last, a tiger arrives and a bright spotlight shines directly on him. He warily attacks the prey, all the same. Confused feelings of revulsion well up in me.

Why have I unwittingly paid to see this? I feel like a peeping Tom and feel sorry for the deer as well as for the tigers and their ever-diminishing range area. There are apparently only about six hundred tigers left in this part of the earth and poaching still persists world-wide, despite restrictions and fines. What in heaven's name are we doing to this planet's fragile eco-system? We've spoiled the garden, or as the author Rene Dubos would say, "We've turned the garden of Earth into a garbage dump."

There is something rather faked about this encounter which I can't quite put my finger on. The scenery is marvelous, the air is clean and the accommodations are superb. Is there too much of a Disneyland feeling about it, I wonder? Too safe, too artificial? There is a dawning, persistent question that haunts me these days. How can we create sustainable tourism that maintains habitats and cultures?" It seems we need sustainable agriculture, fishing, architecture, business and now, tourism.

At last, the black cloak of sleep drops over me and I dream that I am in South India in some sort of ashram.

Meghauli, Nepal
October 9th

Thirteen years ago today, my precious son Scott was born. As I rush to dress for the elephant safari, a pang shoots through me. I wonder what Scott is doing at home and school now and what activities are occupying Jim and Wahid.

This morning, after a sound sleep in our jungle tents, the group has moved from Tiger Tops Camp down to the three-story barracks near the lodge and will fly to Kathmandu tomorrow. From our new twin bed double room in the Lodge, Regine and I can hear laughter and scuffling outside our window. Several members of our group hang off the second floor balcony preparing to leap onto the flimsy wooden-railed howdah riding cage that is strapped to the top of the towering elephants. As we run out to the porch to watch, we see in the distance the disappearing rear view of several massive elephants that have already started through the bush.

Eventually, after several groups of three passengers each have climbed aboard and trotted away on their towering, cast-iron beasts, it is our turn. Gracia Lewis, Regine and I leap onto the elephant platform, clinging to the creaky, wobbling side rails of the dilapidated howdah as our overwhelmingly tall elephant sways, lumbers and crashes through the underbrush. It's hard for me to realize that slender elegant brunette Gracia, dressed in boots and jeans, is actually nearly seventy years old. Her Yoga practice and frequent travel make her seem twenty years younger.

As we sway and creak in our wooden cage about fifteen feet above the ground, Regine whirs away with her movie camera, then talks in rapid French into her tape recorder before she resumes filming. Gracia speaks Hindi to Mahabudur the elephant, and cracks jokes about the huge leeches which are said to infest the area. We are just passing under a tall tree filled with cavorting gray monkeys when two big fat black leeches land on Gracia's hand and foot, presumably flicked off of the fifteen-foot elephant grass that surrounds us. She is non-plussed and says she'll remove the leeches back at the Lodge with a match-flame. Periodically, I steal glances at the two increasingly plump cling-ons that are nonchalantly gorging themselves on her blood

"You mustn't disturb the heads of ticks or leeches," she solemnly intones in her low voice, in case I should suffer the same fate.

We startle at a jackal's howls nearby before our attention is caught by red dragonflies that zit-zit through the marshes along the river ahead. Shadows of jungle birds fly across our faces. On the river bank a green-brown crocodile slides into the water, his slight splash alarms blue herons nearby which further frightens some black and white storks into an agitated lift-off. Further ahead the other elephants crash across the river. Yet, with the quirky "animal radar" that I've had for the past ten years, I sense a large beast of some sort up ahead of us in the underbrush to our right. Mahabudur, our trusty elephant, senses it too. He is acting skittish and snorts a threatening warning. Raj, the elephant directly in front of us, starts to trumpet and to rear up on its hind legs, in spite of the rickety howdah and startled female passengers.

Mahabudur starts an answering trumpet, lifting his formidable trunk and rears up, with our wobbly howdah creaking and shaking precariously. More bugle-snorts and prancing and rearing. The elephants are really frightened now. Do elephants stampede when badly upset? Our howdah slants dangerously as we crane our necks to see what it is that has caused all the excitement. Cool-headed Regine aims her camera toward the grass where the sound of crashing underbrush is coming from. Gracia and I cling alternately to each other and to the rails. Stamping, thrashing, stomping ensues. Dust flies and elephant grass crashes. Mahabudur rears again and backs up. The sky, from our crazily-slanted angle, seems to wheel around in circles. We hear screams, snorts, elephant bugeling.

Suddenly a great one-horned rhino mother and her baby charge us with all the fury within them. They have been surprised in our path and have panicked. The armored gray mother is ablaze with terror and desperation. She snorts and charges us again. Again Mahabudur backs up, rears, trumpets and paws the air with his front legs, jiggling us all the while in a dizzying, perilous swaying that threatens to pitch us all off into the path of the furious rhino mother and her young. The guides are frantically shouting and waving sticks amid more animal screams, monkey shrieks, clattering hoofs, swishing of dry grasses and our own hysterical, inappropriate, hooting howling laughter. We're so thrilled at all the commotion that we are nearly exultant. At last - an adventure!

"Isn't this wonderful?!" I shout above the din to Gracia and Regine. "Just think, we could get killed any minute – but what a great way to go, instead of dying alone in your bed, never having gone anywhere, nor having done anything really breath-taking!" Then I remember that Jim, Scott, Jonathan, Ben, Mom and Dad and my siblings would be grief-stricken if I were to die in an elephant stampede and I decide to be quiet and not to add to the mayhem.

Finally the guides and trackers manage to head the rhinos in another direction, regain their own composure, count heads and praise the elephants. But the guides were as badly frightened as the rhinos, which trot away on squat stumpy legs, their wedge-shaped heads held indignantly high at this unexpected encounter. Our guide profusely apologizes, then explains that rhinos seldom attack unless they believe they are being attacked. The mother and baby, like most species under threat, were at first frightened, then confused and finally, outraged.

Regine hopes her movie film has caught the action; Gracia and I nudge each other in celebration of this fine turn of events. She feels that suffering leach bites was definitely worth the outcome, though the engorged slug-like leeches have filled to the bursting point with blood. She'll remove them with matches back at the lodge, she assures us, unperturbed.

In recounting the entire episode in the evening, it occurs to us again, that we could have easily fallen off Mahabudur and either been trampled underfoot or gored by the charging rhinos. In fact, several times on this trip we could have kissed this sweet life goodbye. However, as we've concluded, if we allowed ourselves to think about that sort of thing, we'd never go anywhere.

As for Gracia and the two fat walnut-sized leeches, she extracted them by holding a porter's cigarette to them. They backed out, heads intact, thankfully, and Gracia laughed ruefully. She never gets flapped, it seems.

Kathmandu, Nepal
October 10th

Yesterday afternoon we flew from Meghauli to Kathmandu where we are staying in the Everest Sheraton, of all places. (From one extreme to another, we adjust and readjust again.) After a stroll around town on foot, which has proven shocking, due to the extreme filth and poverty, we end up in front of the house of the Princess of Nepal. It delighted me since for a year and a half I've had a *National Geographic* picture on my bulletin board as a reminder that I'm determined to visit Kathmandu - a photo of the princess leaning out of her window... and lo, here I am, in front of her house!

The reason that Kathmandu is most shocking to me is that amid the wooden-filigreed architecture of the Middle Ages there is the most unspeakable filth - excrement and blood from calf sacrifices throughout many of the streets. However, the temples - hundreds of abandoned ones - are quite interesting. There are courtyards with marigold blossom garlands hanging in graceful loops. This appears to be a festival day of some sort.

The people here look to be very poor, vacant-eyed and possibly hungry. I wonder if many are on drugs. They even use the street to relieve themselves, in plain view. How I grieve for them and for their privations — insufficient jobs, food, heat, toilets, running water. It will take every citizen of every town to end this wretchedness of worldwide poverty.

When they believe that a temple has "run out of magic" the local people shut it up and build another. Hence, the hundreds of vacant temples which answer no more prayers and sit silently amid the narrow, dark cobblestone alleys.

This morning we've taken a tour of the ancient city of Patan, a Tibetan Refugee Camp, some temples and Durbar Square. Most of the group are buying temple ornaments and hangings which are the finest we've yet seen anywhere. There are row after row of second-hand clothing stores featuring expensive jeans, gauzy shirts, filmy dresses and the patchwork vests of the American counter-culture. The second-hand fashions formerly belonged to very wealthy tourists, judging by the designer labels. Opium dens abound here as well, which probably accounts for the many new Western clothes and for the English books and other belongings that have been hocked.

In general, the vibrations of Nepal seem to be among the lowest I've yet encountered in Asia. Tomorrow we leave for Singapore. There is meditation, re-packing and journal-writing to do before bed.

Regine takes her sleeping pills and reaches for her eye-shade as I mention with a touch of concern in my voice that perhaps her having taken sleeping pills nightly for twenty years is dangerous to her brain and nervous system. She replies that she wouldn't be a Singapore wind-surfing champion if that were true. Besides, she adds, the pills are necessary to blot out nightmares. After the light is switched off, I reflect on my travel companions in the dark. In some ways I feel that I've known some of these people for years - Gunilla, Regine, Norma, Gracia Lewis. I wonder if I'll be seeing them again after we return to Singapore.

CHAPTER 13
GRACIA

"Love, not as an expression of separateness based on emotion, but as *compassion*, is that which holds the world together in Unicity. In Unicity we do not love others, we ARE them." Ramesh Balsekar
ANOJ, June 26

Singapore
October 15, 1981

At last, I'm back home in Singapore. Recently I've been spending a lot of time at the Theosophical Lodge of Singapore. Len Rodrigo, the president, who is an attorney, has taken me under his wing and has invited me to various lectures and events at the Lodge. There is another man there by the name of B.P. Yap who is also very kind. Most of the members are Chinese or Malay. So far I haven't met any Westerners who have an interest in spirituality, comparative religion or philosophy. Len says that most of the Westerners who come to Singapore are primarily interested in shopping, drinking, parties and the high life. So it would seem, from our casual observations.

Len and I talk of the early Theosophists, of Alice Bailey, Madame Blavatsky, Annie Besant and of the concepts of free will, reincarnation, the purpose of life and the Ascended Masters who help humanity from the "Other Side." He is a compassionate man whose wife, Peggy, is a nurse. They have four children. He has also mentioned a few times that he was a former member of parliament in Singapore, though he certainly seems unpretentious.

During the day I write and do research at the Theosophical Lodge or the American Club Library. My notebooks and journals are filling up and I'm keenly aware that in a few months I'll be back in the States, with my precious year in Asia but a memory. There is a lovely quotation from *Markings*, by the well-known Dag Hammarskjold, that captures my attention and I write it down. "Openness to life grants a lightning-swift insight into the life situation of others. What is necessary? - to wrestle with your problem until its emotional discomfort is clearly conceived in an intellectual form - and then act accordingly." M P 13

Since our stay in Singapore draws to a close in three or four months, Jim and I are taking sailing lessons at the yacht club. We've also been enjoying many dinners and Hobie Cat sailboat rides with our new friends, David Hock, an American from Kentucky, and his pretty, sweet Muslim girlfriend, Tati Shariff. Tati recently fell off the Hobie Cat during rough waters and hit her head on a rock in shallow water. I've been concerned about her but now she seems fine and refuses to see a doctor. She has, however, admitted to occasional headaches. We will miss David and Tati when we return to the States.

When I look back to my attitudes of just a few months ago regarding Asian people, and Wahid in particular, I have to laugh. I was so certain that if he would simply set high goals and think positively he could "better himself" and create a more prosperous life for his family. As a so-called liberated American woman, I have been more influenced than I had realized by my culture, by metaphysics (one can be and do anything) and by the grace and good fortune of my own dharma. Wahid is happy being a driver and everyone is doing exactly what he is supposed to be doing. It's none of my affair to try to "improve things" in the lives of others according to my Western female values.

Tomorrow I'm going to tour Chinatown with Gracia Lewis. The more I know about her the more I like her. Since the North India-Nepal trip, I've learned that I don't seem to have much in common with any of the others we traveled with except Gracia. She likes public service, history, philosophy, adventure, art, culture, travel, languages, architecture, literature, music – all the things I enjoy. Neither of us is at all drawn to drinking, gambling, parties or shopping.

Meanwhile, my headaches still persist. However, my work with individual and corporate consulting and counseling clients is going well. They are bright professionals who are CEO's of banks and oil companies in Asia.

Since I've now been to eight countries searching for the Fullest Buddha, I've decided that I'm going to give up the pursuit unless I get some sort of final, definite clue in Singapore. Surely the Great Being can't be here or Len would have said something. So much of my time has been spent touring other countries in Asia that I've rather neglected getting acquainted with Singapore. We found a city tour, Gracia and I, that is headed by Geraldine Lowe Ismail, a very well-known and respected long-time resident here.

October 21st

Chinatown at night in the company of Gracia Lewis! She is a cultural treasure of Singapore. She has information and insights which virtually no one else here has and since she is elderly the information may become lost. I feel compelled to take notes every time I am with her. Singapore is changing so quickly that much of the precious culture and heritage of the Chinese Singaporeans is fast disappearing before our very eyes in the pell-mell rush toward modernization. I can hardly believe my good fortune as I arrive at her apartment. She has promised to tell me about Singapore in the old days, when tigers and crocodiles were part of the landscape.

Gracia Lewis is well-known in Singapore for a number of distinctions all her own. Her late husband was connected with the Frazer and Neave Brewery and her father, a British colonialist, played a large part in the building of Hong Kong with elephant labor. Gracia's striking slender appearance and vivid personality probably had a great deal to do with her being the namesake for the tall red "Gracia Lewis orchid." She herself raised orchids for years and was a consistent prize winner before giving it up for travel, leisure pursuits in music and theater and volunteer counseling on the telephone hot line of a local social service center.

Visiting Gracia is always an event in itself since she is a kind, witty friend and hostess and is generous with her recollections of Singapore in the early days, during the colonial period. The ambience her bi-level flat in Leonie Towers on Leonie Hill parallels the same compelling combination of modern simplicity and classic old-world graciousness which Gracia herself brings to any relationship.

The gardens and pool on one side of the building form a screen of protection against the noise of Orchard Road only a few blocks away. The opposite side of the apartment overlooks a jungle view of an overgrown, notorious Malay cemetery reputed to belong to the Sultan of Jahore Bahru and is said to be haunted. It is notorious because Prime Minister Lee Kuan Yew has emphasized that available land for building in Singapore is extremely scarce and this plot is centrally located, therefor especially valuable. On three separate occasions three separate work crews have been sent into the old vine-tangled cemetery to begin uprooting trees for construction. According to Gracia none have returned or been heard from since. Trees and cemeteries have always been sacred in Singapore until now.

Many priceless Chinese antiques catch my eye while she pours tea from an old teal blue porcelain pot into delicate blue and white china cups. Gracia speaks with great warmth and knowledge of the history of this area. It is like reliving the recent history of the Orient to hear of her father overseeing the felling of giant old trees in "Fragrant Harbor," the English translation of Hong Kong.

"But how did your family get from Hong Kong, which is three hours by plane from here, to Singapore?" I ask, eager to hear the story.

Gracia smiles in merriment and shakes the sleek, shiny sheet of brunette hair that is her pageboy coiffure. When chic, good-looking Gracia was only twelve years old, her father died. "You see, Connie, I was an only child, born quite late to my parents, hence the name Gracia. It was a rather miraculous event by the grace of God that I even arrived on the planet since they were so advanced in age at my birth. They had in fact been married for twenty years when I came into the picture."

When her father died, he left Gracia and her mother with considerable wealth and a houseful of servants. Gracia began a life of travel, touring from India to England by ship. In fact it was in India, only ten months after Gracia's marriage that she and her mother were stranded for three years after the outbreak of the Second World War. Her mother fell ill and had to be nursed by Gracia who had recently joined the staff of the Red Cross as an income survival measure for the two of them. She and her mother were without any funds or any knowledge of the whereabouts and safety of Gracia's new groom, Max Lewis.

Eventually they were reunited after the war and settled again in Singapore where Max built up the Frazer and Neave Brewery by working his way up the ladder. "Our annual holiday trips were to the breweries of

Europe," she laments in her low cultivated voice as we sip tea in the cool, marble-floored living room. She chuckles over old memories and comments on the various carved antique stools, chairs and temple ornaments placed tastefully about.

From her living room window we can see the new C.K. Tang building which is a tall white tower crowned with green tiles and a curly Chinese roof. When I remark that C.K Tang must be quite a financial force in Singapore she laughs and says, "Why I knew him when he used to pedal a bicycle along our street selling rags! Later, as he became wealthier, he lived on our street, in one of the bungalows. Now he's a millionaire and is responsible for the Dynasty Hotel."

The subject of Sarawak comes up and Gracia tells me of having visited Sarawak a dozen years ago by ship and of swimming in a picturesque lagoon. She was later informed that the "lovely lagoon" was crocodile-infested and that she was lucky to still be in one piece.

"By the way, Connie, speaking of crocodiles, they were everywhere when I was growing up here. Once my Nanny was sitting on the sea wall doing her crochet, when along came a great huge one toward her. She nearly had a fit but was able to call for help. She finally caught the attention of some fishermen in a nearby boat and they chased it away. And furthermore, speaking of wild creatures, there actually was a tiger under the billiard table at the Raffles Hotel, exactly as the legend claims. Poor thing, it must have wandered in lost and laid down there to rest from the heat. Actually, I preferred Singapore in those days, before all the tidy plastic atmosphere came."

"Tonight when we see Chinatown at night you'll catch the flavor of the old Singapore with its smells, food stalls, characters and superstitions," Gracia intones.

Wahid arrives to take us to the appointed meeting place under the People's Park Bridge at Pagoda Street where we will join Geraldine Lowe Ismail - a hilarious and well-known guide. A block before we arrive at our destination Gracia requests that Wahid stop the car so that she can check the street sign and make certain that we are indeed in the right neighborhood. After she has stepped out of the car Wahid turns to me, bristling with curiosity.

"Is Mrs. Lewis really nearly seventy?" he asks, big-eyed at the thought.

"Yes, Wahid. And she's taking over the instruction of forty-six students at her yoga class next week when her instructor goes on a vacation. She went to China last year to study ceramics with the museum group and she works as a counselor."

"Western women are quite amazing," he muses. "Asian women sit quietly in their houses and seldom go out at her age. Here in Singapore people retire completely worn out at age fifty-five from working six and seven days a week all their lives. Mrs. Lewis is nice and thin, too. She looks twenty years younger, doesn't she?"

We both agree that Gracia is fully ensconced in life and has probably always been full of fire and verve. She returns and announces that the group of fifteen English people have arrived and that the tour guide, Geraldine Lowe Ismail is awaiting us.

Geraldine, a large imposing red-head of Dutch and Russian descent, is married to a Singaporean Muslim. Her Malay costume, tall portly frame and breathtakingly fast gait seem incongruous at first. She abounds with good humor and sparkling laughter and is bursting with amusing anecdotes. Chinatown at night is indeed different from daytime Chinatown, primarily due to the characters who haunt the streets and the services and entertainments they offer. Overhead in an ebony sky a silver sickle moon and bright Venus shine down upon the overwhelming conglomeration of Pagoda Street stalls and hawkers. Impenetrable crowds jostle and shove through street traffic of cars, trishaws and motorcycles. Enterprising "restaurateurs" of the seamy variety have plopped metal tables and chairs directly onto the asphalt street for instant open-air dining amid the traffic, with nary a sidewalk for the protection or separation of the "diners."

Makeshift stalls transform the night-time streets, displaying the latest in tee shirts, sandals, underwear, umbrellas and cassette tapes. Each time any of our group assumes the facial expression of a tempted customer, Geraldine generously intersperses her tour-guide patter with shopping tips.

"You've heard of Lord Buddha's Noble Eightfold Path? The Ninth Path is shopping!" someone in the group quips. We all laugh.

"You probably don't want to purchase those inexpensive umbrellas, even though they are pretty," Geraldine warns. "When it rains the cheap umbrella dyes tend to run all over the owner and there's nothing like having a river of royal blue runlets streaking your nice dress to spoil your outing," she laughs. She cautions us to be on the constant lookout for neck-high wires strung across the street in the dark and to take care not to fall into the immense rain puddles or disappear down the many three-foot-deep concrete sewer drains which booby-trap the sidewalks. "Mind your heads and feet, Dears, you don't want to break a leg or get decapitated now, do you?"

There are no street lights in most of the alleyways and side streets we navigate. An occasional cat flits in front of us and trishaw bells ting-a-ling in the darkness. Around the corner the unmistakably assaulting skunk-stench of durian fruit wafts like a heavy ocean roller, into our nostrils.

"Durian! How I adore durians," Gracia exclaims. "It's the season, you know. And it's rambutan season again, too. We have two durian and rambutan (fruit) seasons this year. That's very lucky, mainly because the durian is so expensive. Why, people pay as much for a durian as for a tailored suit or for a fine dinner for ten people."

"Yes," someone in our group chimes in. "Durian is also called the heaven and hell fruit because it tastes like heaven and stinks like hell!"

"Well it does necessitate acquiring a taste for it," Gracia concedes. "It's like a gorgeous custard in taste and consistency. But the aroma clings to you so long that you may want to plan to eat one when you're not going anywhere for about three days. Otherwise you'll smell like a skunk for that long, no matter how many times you brush your teeth or use mouthwash." The chartreuse green spiky fruit that lies in piles in the stalls is reminiscent of a mound of green prickly-skinned footballs. No matter how luscious they taste I can't imagine myself inflicting a putrid, rotting stench on all who would encounter me after a brief durian indulgence.

Further on there are numerous rows of flat-beds filled with the hairy red rambutan as well as stands selling brown mangosteens, orange persimmons, yellow creamy white frangipani blossoms, fifteen types of dried fruits and snowy white rice cakes. In the darkness of neighboring streets vendors bark out their seafood wares. Our stroll takes us past their stalls of salted fish, eel, prawns, squid, fried bread, hand-made noodles, a murky local drink called chandal, green sugar cane juice and mussels.

Laughing and talking all the while we walk, Geraldine soon brings us to the Hindu temple called Sri Mariaman, known for its colorfully detailed paintings of gods and goddesses overhead on the ceiling. While we stand in the outer room of the temple, Geraldine tells us that the Indians who came to Malaysia brought with them their systems of sultans and rajas. Throughout her talk I glance around at the several assembled Indian worshipers present and notice that the women wear saris and the men wear dhotis, as do virtually all of their Indian countrymen in Singapore. Further inside the temple I observe male worshipers with bare chests wearing red dots and white stripes on their faces and upper arms. Are they priests? Incense burns from a tall pot in the outer chamber and barefoot people walk near the statues in front and sit in prayer or prostrate themselves on the concrete floor.

Geraldine, with her green eyes sparkling in her pale face, describes the annual fire-walking ceremony which takes place in October in the courtyard beside us. Next she mentions the Thaipusam Festival coming up in a few weeks wherein devotees fast for several weeks. They achieve a heightened consciousness designed to entrance them into a painless state while swords, knives, hooks and skewers pierce their faces, tongues and bodies, to be worn several hours during a walking procession of annual penance. They chant and walk throughout the city while entranced, accompanied by faithful assistants should they falter or even faint. In addition to singing and chanting, fasting, penitential acts and sacrifice, the Hindu scriptures figure prominently in their worship as well. Geraldine speaks of the *Ramayana* stories and of the *Mahabharata* in her crisp, lilting English as we file through the enormous greenery-festooned doorway, into the inky tropical night.

Some of the signs on shops in the area catch my attention because of their amusing misspellings or vague meanings. One sign reads "Wine

Treader" instead of Wine Trader. Gracia chortles and tells of a sign that used to hang outside a tailor's shop on swanky Orchard Road. "Just imagine casually ambling past all the elegant clothing and furniture shops and coming upon a sign for a tailor announcing cheerily, in huge letters: 'Come In And Have Fits Upstairs'! I was always tempted to go upstairs and ask what sort of fits they had in mind," Gracia wisecracks. Most of the signs we see are in Chinese with an occasional English translation, such as one saying "Flats to Let" meaning apartments for rent. From time to time there appears a sign over a low doorway "Mind Your Head" in English, but primarily the signs are composed of Chinese characters painted in red, yellow, black, blue or white. Translations of commercial enterprises announce the wares inside: chemist, carpets, departmental store, cycle and carriage, dress-making, cameras and optics, antiques, flowers, electronics and beauty saloon. Movie billboards appear in hand-painted phantasmagorical colors, rather than the photographs which we are accustomed to seeing for the advertisement of films. The lurid expressions and protruding eyeballs of the film characters indicate that we are seeing ads for horror films, a perennial favorite of Singaporeans.

As we enter famous Sago Lane, the "death street," we see a funeral feast taking place out on the asphalt road. Two large round dining tables are filled with relatives of the deceased, eating and gambling over mahjong. Death isn't considered a sad occasion, we are told, and the lively chatter and bustling activity of this funeral dinner confirms the fact. Large white frangipani wreaths rest on tripods beside the dining tables and nearby an altar bears a black and white photo of the deceased, a middle-aged woman, as well as red candles, oranges, pink cakes, paper money - all provided to "keep the gods happy and far away from the departed one."

Across the street yawns the doorway to the casket maker. Banner makers, funeral wreath makers, a funeral band and paper model shops prosper in Sago Lane. Formerly there were fourteen funeral parlors here but with the development of the nine new satellite towns around Singapore most of them have moved elsewhere.

"White is the color of death among the Chinese," Geraldine explains. "Some Chinese refuse to wear white and they don't even willingly paint their houses white. In the same vein of superstition fall the Ghost Weddings of the Chinese. Very often, it is said, a deceased girl will contact her parents through a spirit medium to say that she would like to marry a certain deceased boy who is also on the other side with her. She requests that her parents arrange a "wedding" for them and that they buy the usual paper replicas which signify luck and prosperity. For example, there is an elaborate, balconied house with servants, a trishaw, plentiful food, red paper trunks filled with paper money, a Mercedes and even a canopied wedding bed with embroidered pillows. Inside the paper model production shop we do indeed see stacks of paper money, yachts and scores of colorful creations for the delight of the deceased.

On our return walk to Pagoda Street we pass an alley shop displaying from its covered porch some hanging papier-mâché lion heads for the Lion Dance parade. Bobbing from strings overhead, the white lion beards wave and separate in the breeze and the giant pop-eyed lion heads wobble and nod as if greeting us in friendly fashion.

During the final block of our stroll we happen upon the most interesting people and scenes thus far - fortune tellers and prognosticators. Numerous men sit hunkered beside kerosene lamps on the sidewalk telling fortunes in a variety of ways. Clients sit on tiny brown stools on the dark sidewalk and have their palms read or throw yarrow sticks for readings from the *I Ching*. Others watch parakeets use their beaks to select a lucky card for each customer from the stacks of cards on the ground. A woman sits next to a statue of Kuan Yin, the Goddess of Mercy. Her specialty is numerological card reading while a Thai astrologer next to her selects fortuitous dates for customer's business ventures.

On the corner, a crowd has congregated around a Chinese man who sells pills made from ground silk worms. A pile of wriggling white silkworms undulates in a basket at his feet. He dances agilely around in a circle doing T'ai Chi movements to demonstrate how unusually fit he is from using his pills. Business is brisk for him but his competitor across the sidewalk scowls. The competitor's specialty is, unbelievably, snake oil. Snake oil "squeezed before your very eyes." At his feet there are snake heads, snake skeletons and living and dead serpents. He mashes his oil glumly in silence, pouting at the paucity of customers in his vicinity while the dancing silkworm pill vendor piles up dollar bills and nearly cartwheels in glee with his own mounting success. Showmanship and the pizzazzy sales patter make the difference in the success of two peddlers. Attitude seems to make the rest of the difference. To love what we do and do what we love has a powerful effect on our own outlook and creates a magnetism that is irresistible to others.

Asia is one delightful surprise after another. Although its has taken several months for me to adjust to the tropics, I can finally say I'm exultant to be living here. In fact, there is a persistent feeling these days, like a distant drum roll, that in the next few months my entire life will change. In spite of the enrapturing beauties of Asia, I am fully aware that happiness and fulfillment are not to be found in the world and that this existence is a school for attaining awareness and, ultimately, Realization. One can only work so much, travel so much and study so much. Then one becomes surfeited, as with too much dessert. It's clear to me that to become lost in pursuing passions can set one back for lifetimes. Having said all this, with great conviction, where-oh-where is my elusive Master?

CHAPTER 14
LEN, MERRY MATAJI AND THE TRIPLE VISION

"It is not we who seek the Way, but the Way which seeks us. That is why you are faithful to it, even while you stand waiting, so long as you are prepared and act the moment you are confronted by its demands." Dag Hammarskjold M P 120

Singapore
February 24, 1982

Jim and I have packed and shipped our belongings to Colorado. We have moved into the Marco Polo Hotel since we'll be going home to the States in three weeks. It is my birthday today and I have had two shocks. The first was an hour ago when Dr. Mohan, a local neurologist, told me that he thinks that my long-term headaches, since living in Asia, are due to a brain tumor. The second shock causes mixed emotions within me; Len Rodrigo, in whose law office I now sit, has just announced that the large photo on his wall depicts Sathya Sai Baba and that Sai Baba is God. Len has seen Him with his own eyes at Sai Baba's ashram in Puttaparthi, South India. I am frankly stunned. After getting the extraordinary medical pronouncement from Dr. Mohan, on my birthday no less, I thought I'd walk across the street to Len's office and tell him that we'll be going back to the States in about three weeks As Len tells me about Sai Baba, I take notes. My heart is beating fast.

"Would you and your husband like to come to our house and see the videotape called *Aura of Divinity* about Sai Baba?" Len asks in response to my amazement at his incredible story. Could Sai Baba be THE ONE?!

"Yes, of course, if it wouldn't be too much trouble," I reply, hardly knowing what to think of the recent series of events. Len says that we can seek God all we want but that our finding the Avatar is the result of hundreds or even thousands of years of correct and dharmic choices, day in and day out on the endless spiritual path. He says that we have earned the right to learn about the Avatar through service to others in prior lifetimes as well as current service and spiritual living. He says that we are called by Sai Baba when He decides to "reel us in" rather than when we think we need Him.

Billions of people are praying (begging) constantly to be relieved and released from self-created pain and suffering. But if they don't learn compassion and other lessons from their suffering, they will go right back to the same errors, addictions and mistaken ways of living. There is a blessing in every form of suffering. When we really understand the lesson we will give thanks for the suffering and may even laugh at our prior stubbornness and blindness. Those are the main points that he mentioned in his opening remarks about Sai Baba.

Len, as I've mentioned, is a capable and respected attorney, a former Member of Parliament of Singapore and current president of the

Theosophical Society. He is a person of constant surprise. It seems that Sai Baba, as Len relates his story, has healed thousands of people, has produced numerous books of profound wisdom, established scores of schools, universities, clinics and orphanages and has even brought three people back from the dead. He is even said to know the past, present and future of all who come to Him. The list of His accomplishments is apparently endless and his followers number in the tens of millions throughout the world!

There are several things which puzzle me about these narrations. First of all, if Sai Baba has millions of followers and is so well known in Asia, why haven't I ever heard of him until recently, especially since I have always been very currently informed on any personalities who even remotely approach his unusual abilities? Is it really due to one's spiritual merit? Secondly, how could he appeal equally to Hindus, Buddhists, Christians, Moslems and Jews? Third, how could he materialize things out of thin air for his followers, day after day, with the greatest of ease? Fourth, is he genuinely an Avatar - or a fraud, like so many "holy men" of India?

Len is the second person today to mention Sai Baba. Can it possibly be that Sai Baba is the one I've been seeking for many months? When I explained to kindly Dr. Mohan for the fifth time in five weeks that I had suffered from unrelenting headaches shortly after arriving in Singapore, he inquired about any head injuries the prior year. There were only two things which, to my mind, could have caused double vision and the sensation of a hatchet lodging in my skull. The first is that back in Colorado, just before moving to Singapore, I had been shooting touch-and-goes, or take-offs and landings in a small rented plane that I was using to get my flying license. After I had parked the plane for the night and chained it to the tarmac, I tripped over the chain in the dark and fell flat on my face. There was no one around to assist me so I merely got up, brushed myself off and drove the forty-five minute distance to my home. There was a gigantic goose-egg over my cheek for a few days but I eventually forgot all about it and never went to the doctor. Perhaps I had given myself a concussion that only started to hurt in the change of humidity and altitude of Singapore. Denver's altitude is one mile high and Singapore is at sea level. The difference is over 5,200 feet and the change of altitude might exacerbate a head injury.

The other possibility was that I had somehow fractured my skull when I fell off the ill-constructed Coca Cola machine shrine at the Beijing Airport when I simultaneously broke my ankle. (Authorities, I'm told, later placed the vending machine on the floor where it belonged.) In giving my medical history to the doctor, I also happened to mention that both of my parents had had brain tumors and that many people who had lived in the state of Washington, however briefly, in the forties or fifties had, decades later, developed brain tumors, Grave's Disease (affecting the thyroid) or other maladies. A nuclear power plant was thought by many to be the culprit.

Tall, slender Dr. Mohan, after glancing at the stacks of x-rays, charts and reports about my case, at this point delivered the news that he thought I probably had a brain tumor and should proceed immediately to the States for brain surgery. He then got up from his chair, closed the door to his office and told me that he was going to "give me some magic medicine from his spiritual teacher whose name was Sai Baba and that millions of people had been healed by it."

"This is called vibhuti. It is fragrant-smelling, fine-textured ash that will stop your headaches until you have brain surgery. But, I just ask one thing. Please don't mention this to anyone here at the clinic. They simply wouldn't understand."

As he swirled the contents of a little folded paper into a glass of water, I glanced around at his framed degrees and certificates on the wall. They were impressive. He had been trained at the best European universities and had graduated from many other courses in neurology. But, really! This was outrageous – such a well-trained neurologist asking me to drink a glass of water mixed with ash, for heaven's sake. Nevertheless, I drank it and my headache stopped.

After thanking the neurologist and paying the bill, I walked across the street to drop in at Len's legal office. My emotional reaction is that if my time to leave the body has come, I am ready, as always. But it would be deeply disappointing if I had to leave without finding my hide-and-seek Master who has eluded me for nearly a year. When we return to the States, assuming I survive brain surgery, I won't be able to afford the luxury of traveling around Asia as I have the past ten months. The noise of Len closing his desk drawer yanked me out of my reverie about Dr. Mohan's news and Sai Baba's ash.

"Happy Birthday," Len said, smiling. "Speaking of birthdays, Sai Baba says that everyone has four birthdays:

◊   The first is at birth.

◊   The second is when you consciously commit to the spiritual path.

◊   The third is when you have attained the wisdom of the sages.

◊   The fourth is when you attain Self-realization."

In that case, I'm probably on my second birthday. Maybe Len is on his third.

As the news about Sai Baba supposedly being God began to sink in, Len noticed me glancing at his unusual diamond ring. It was entirely out of character with everything about him, since he usually dressed quite simply. The gigantic diamond in the gold setting just doesn't seem congruent with Len's down-played attire of simple pale blue short sleeved shirt and gray slacks. He is modest and reserved and continually seeks ways to serve others, although he himself was quite well known throughout the country. What on earth is he doing wearing that immense glittering ring when he wears no other jewelry and has no need to impress anyone about anything?

I must have been staring at it when he chuckled and started speaking very directly about its origin.

"I see you're noticing the ring which Sai Baba gave to me in India. Sai Baba is an Avatar. There are quite a few Sai Baba groups here in Singapore. I've even met people who have been healed by Him and I've observed some of His miracles. Believe me, these things I tell you are true."

"You see, Sai Baba shows all of the sixteen qualities of a true Avatar. They include control of the five functions, control of the five senses, control of the five elements of nature and infinite consciousness. His teachings are the most important aspect of His work, of course, but very often Westerners emphasize His miracles because they are unaccustomed to seeing such things. In fact, when I went to India to see Him for myself He selected me from a crowd in the courtyard and asked me to go to the porch of the temple, or Mandir, and sit there every day for six days in front of the large wooden doors. Naturally I did as He requested and on the sixth day He called me inside for an interview.

"During the interview He materialized some vibhuti, or light gray ash, out of thin air and asked me to eat it. Next He manifested this diamond ring for me from nothing, right before my eyes, and told me to wear it as a reminder to be as bright and spiritually clear as a diamond. He said the material value of the diamond is not important but that the symbol of clarity is significant. 'Diamond means (to) die, mind,' He said. He told me that the vibhuti was for purification of my system. You know, it's a funny thing, since He gave me the vibhuti to swallow and told me about my life and my work, I've found that I no longer drink a cold beer when I get home from work each day. I hadn't even thought much about it until now but I always used to enjoy that and now it has just passed out of my life and I don't even miss it." He smiled and sat quietly with his hands folded in his lap as he finished the story.

"I'd definitely like to accept your invitation to come over to your house and see the videotape tomorrow at 5:00," I muse. "My husband Jim will never believe this. He's in Borneo on business today, but he comes home tonight. Wait 'til I tell him that I might have found God after all these months of searching throughout Asia!"

February 24th (Evening)

The Night My Life Changed Forever

Jim has returned from Borneo and I have told him all about the doctor visit, the suspected brain tumor, my having drunk ash in water and Len's exciting news of Sai Baba.

"This will probably be the most unforgettable and important birthday of my life," I murmur after kissing Jim goodnight.

"I'd say so," Jim laughs. "But knowing the way your life seems to go, I'm sure you'll have plenty of excitement and adventures after this. And we'll get a second opinion about that brain tumor diagnosis as soon as we get back to the States in a few weeks."

After having fallen asleep, I am suddenly awakened and sit up in bed. At the foot of the bed I see two smiling Beings, both men, who radiate an enormous glowing light. They are Jesus and Gautama Buddha. After blinking a few times I observe that they are still there, still smiling and that they indicate they have something to tell me. Jesus begins to speak first.

"We have come to tell you that We have been with you throughout this entire embodiment," He says. "You are going to eventually have a world-wide work of teaching and healing, but first, you will have many years of purification."

"Now look, We will show you a vision," Gautama Buddha says serenely. They both point to the wall of the hotel room and, presto! – a movie-like scene appears. It is the scene of a beach at sunset. The sky is streaked with coral pinks and golden yellows as a lavender twilight falls upon the scene. The three of us, Jesus, Buddha and I, observe the beach at sunset from about forty feet above it. Foamy wavelets lap at the wet sands and I notice that there is a giant thirty-foot-long human footprint in the sand. There is a small figure about five and a half feet tall who is standing in the huge footprint.

"What's that big footprint and who's that little person standing inside it?" I ask Jesus and the Buddha.

"That's the footprint of a spiritual giant. It's a Self-realized person's print, symbolizing the great effect that Realization has on the landscape of life," replied Lord Buddha. "The small figure standing in the giant impression in the sand is you, as you now conceive yourself to be. Your Presence is already perfect but your experience of yourself is not currently as a Realized One. Eventually you will grow into this identity of Truth and will thus be a spiritual giant."

Smiling weakly, I sit staring at them and at the vision on the wall. They send warm emanations of love from their heart chakras and disappear.

After lying down and rolling over on my side, I am again awakened by another Presence in the room. I sit up again, curious, and see, this time, standing at the foot of the bed, Sathya Sai Baba, smiling and resplendent. He is wearing an orange robe and looks exactly like His pictures. He surrounds me with the most extraordinary vibrations of love I have ever experienced. He holds up one hand and speaks in a high clear voice that is saturated with compassion and a touch of humor.

"I AM Sathya Sai Baba, Mother-Father of Truth. Come right away to India. Bring your husband. I will heal you."

Then He smiles and fades from the room. I know in my heart that this event signifies a turning point in my life.

"Jim, wake up! You're not going to believe this. Jesus and Gautama Buddha just came and talked to me! They gave me a vision right on the wall of the hotel room. Then, when I thought I was just imagining it and started to go to sleep, Sai Baba just now appeared and said to come to India right away and to bring you. He's going to heal me! Wow! This is the most amazing day of my entire life. Just wait 'til we tell Len tomorrow. He'll never believe it."

After having spent a quiet Sunday together, Jim and I discussed last night's apparitional visits from Jesus, Sai Baba and Lord Buddha as well as his business trip to Borneo. Our year in Asia has been more blessed and full than we could have anticipated and it is just too good to be true that I might find my Teacher/Mentor/God before leaving Asia.

As we drive out into the country to Sembawang to visit Len and his family, Jim and I discuss the unusual and seemingly sudden series of events which revolve around Sai Baba. We have both had an odd sensation that the videotape is somehow very important and that it might have a significance greater than we can yet realize.

The affluent neighborhood and many cars parked in the driveways give evidence that Len and his neighbors are financially secure. Tropical plants line the wall enclosing the front yard and the hill setting provides a view of the houses on the sloping street below as well as of wild vegetation beyond the development. Len and Peggy come to greet us and to introduce us to their four children, live-in amah, and cat. Large color pictures of Sai Baba can be seen amid books in the bookcase as we sit in the cool living room on the floral velour sofa awaiting the videotape's emergence onto the TV screen.

As soon as I see Sai Baba on the videotape walking through the crowd manifesting vibhuti, I begin to weep without stopping for the next two hours. My head fills with mucous and I use the entire box of Kleenex that Peggy rushes to me. My body is trembling, I'm crying uncontrollably and my nose is running like a faucet. What is this unaccountable reaction to a video? Maybe the purification that Jesus and Buddha spoke about is beginning right now. It feels as if I've known Sai Baba forever and that I've sorely missed being in His physical Presence without consciously realizing it until now.

Throughout the hour-long color videotape we sit riveted to the unfolding story of this compelling and phenomenal individual. The narrator tells of Sai Baba's having been born on November 23, 1926 in the south Indian village of Puttaparthi, a three hour drive north of Bangalore. In His youth Sai Baba materialized objects for His friends such as candies and trinkets while sitting in the branches of a village Tamarind tree. He announced himself as an Avatar at the age of fourteen and has been healing countless hundreds of thousands ever since. In addition, He has been materializing thousands of objects for His devotees, such as statues for Buddhists, rings for Hindus, rosaries and medals for Catholics and necklaces for Protestants and Jews. In fact, His followers come from all the major world religions and He urges them to follow their hearts and conscience in the practice of their own religion in order to exemplify the best that it represents.

Len points out that the emblem of the Sathya Sai organization contains the symbols of the major world religions: Hinduism, Buddhism, Christianity, Islam and Zoroastrianism. He often says, "There is only one religion, the religion of Love. There is only one language and that is the language of the Heart. There is only one caste and that is the caste of Humanity. There is only one God and He is omnipresent." He further states that the only difference between Himself and others is that He knows He is God and others do not yet know that they, too, are divine. His teachings are extensive and fill over a hundred books.

"Sai Baba says, 'The one object of this human existence is to visualize the reality of the soul. I have come to light the lamp of love in your hearts, to see that it shines day by day with added luster. Love is the basic nature that sustains the resolve to march ahead. Without love this world would be a dark and fearsome jungle. Foster oneness between all people of all creeds, all countries, and all continents. All religions teach the removal from the mind of the blemish of egoism. They train their followers in detachment and discrimination so that they may know peace.' "

In the videotape Sai Baba walked serenely through throngs of ardent followers barefoot, in his red-orange silk robe, materializing vibhuti and rubbing it on the eyes of sick infants or offering it to various people seated quietly on the ground in the crowd. He creates vibhuti since His great theme is that all returns to ash, thus we must not become attached to the things of the world and let them blind us to our true divine state. Len tells us that Sai Baba never sleeps and that His task is to unite the religions of the world in harmony and to relieve human misery. I find myself overwhelmed with the feeling that this is indeed my hide-and-seek Master Whom I have pursued throughout the shores and mountains of Asia. His love for humanity is incomparable. I am still trembling and still blowing my nose and weeping.

Jim and I turn to each other at the same time and excitedly make plans to visit Sai Baba's ashram at Puttaparthi in three weeks on our way home to the States. We had planned to visit Tahiti for a much-needed vacation.

"Who needs Tahiti." Jim says, acknowledging my unusually strong reaction to the video.

"If the scenes on the videotape are genuine and if such a remarkable personage as Sai Baba actually exists we must see Him in person. It's our obligation to ourselves. His very existence could well be the most extraordinary circumstance of the century - in fact, of the past several centuries. If you want to go to India, Connie, we'll go as soon as we can finish our business here. Besides, Sai Baba personally invited you to come last night in the apparition. We should be there at Sai Baba's ashram in about three weeks from now."

We hear that Sai Baba doesn't "perform" miracles, but that they flow from Him as an expression of love. When He sees someone who is dear to Him and who is a beautiful soul, a ring comes out of the air and He presents it to that person. For another person who is ill some healing vibhuti comes forth as a blessing. When there is no loving response in that person there is no cure. "When there is a meeting between the negative and the positive and a conjunction results then my love and His love flow into each other and there is a cure," He says.

During the past six weeks that I've been having medical tests and x-rays which have resulted in the tentative diagnosis of a brain tumor located at the base of my skull. At the back of my mind I wonder if Sai Baba really will heal my excruciating headaches and make my suspected brain tumor vanish. I hardly dare hope such a thing and yet I know that I must get to Puttaparthi.

"Say Len, did I ever mention to you that Mother Mary has appeared to me several times? The only reason that I mention this is that I have a question. Do Ascended Masters immediately start to appear to people directly after you tell the people about Sai Baba? I mean, have you ever heard of anyone being visited by Jesus, Gautama Buddha and Sai Baba all on the same night, because it just happened to me last night and I'm wondering if it was a series of hallucinations because of the brain tumor or if it's really an actual triple apparition."

Len just stares at me for a few seconds without answering. Then a slight smile plays about his mouth. As he rubs his hands together preparing a response, I notice how much he looks like the picture in the video of Shirdi Sai Baba, Sathya Sai's previous Incarnation. The large brown compassionate eyes, the full lips and the sensitive hands are remarkably similar.

"Yesterday when you came to my office and I was telling you about Sai Baba, I myself had my first vision. You know we solicitors (lawyers) are not given to visions. We are very feet-on-the-ground sorts," Len laughs.

"Well I'm a feet-on-the-ground sort too," I cut in. "You know, I was accepted at law school several years ago but decided at the last minute that practicing law would kill my soul and that the only reason that I wanted to be a lawyer was to prove to my father that I could do it. I decided that was a spurious reason for dedicating my whole life to a profession that would cramp my spiritual expression. Anyway, pardon my interrupting you, I just wanted you to know that I'm not an air-head. Do go on, please."

Len chuckles. "While you were looking at that large photo of Baba on my office wall and telling me you didn't think God would look the way He looks, I was seeing a panoramic type of a movie in front of you, super-imposed across the front of you. It was transparent but I could see it just fine. It was a condensed version of your life from now on. If you hadn't told me about the apparitions of Jesus, Lord Buddha and Baba last night I wouldn't have told you. I guess this is a confirmation to both of us that our mutual visions are to be trusted."

Jim and I look at each other with gaping mouths. So Len had a vision too?

"Jim, this really, really is the most amazing birthday of my life!"

"I know, you keep saying that," he laughs. "Let's hear what Len's vision entailed. Calm down, relax." We're all laughing at my bounding exuberance on the sofa, and the impatience as well as the nose-blowing, weeping reactions to the video and now to Len's pronouncement. The waste basket in front of me is overflowing with soggy tissues. This is the most overwhelming physical and emotional reaction that I can ever recall having to anything in my life.

"So here was the vision," Len announces, warming to the revelation. "You get healed by Baba in India. Then you were receiving lots of visits from Mother Mary, Jesus, Sai Baba, angels and saints after you get back to the States. Then you start writing books and you eventually begin to speak about Baba. You travel to other countries telling people about Him and you write more books and eventually you are well-known around the world doing spiritual teaching and healing. So you see, that corresponds with what Lord Jesus and Lord Buddha told you."

Len's report is too much for me, so I toss it off. "But all that will probably happen twenty or thirty years from now, Len, so I don't even have to think about it. Either it will happen or it won't. My immediate priorities are to pack and organize a trip to India and then to find a Sai Baba group back in the States. Len, how can we ever thank you and Peggy for your many kindnesses and for telling us all about Sai Baba?"

"Thank Baba, don't thank us. Our wish for you is a wonderful stay at the ashram and an interview with the Lord."

"Thank you both so much," I say with a grin, "and I'm still going to look up Sai Baba's sleeves if I get a chance, just to make sure He doesn't have any little hidden pockets or strings up there!"

"Look at it this way," Len says, "even a magician takes back his scarves, rabbits and props. Sai Baba never asks people to return His gifts or talismans. He's made hundreds of thousands of them and says that these are just 'tinsel and trash' that are coveted by His devotees. You'll see that He's genuine."

Len gives us a color photo of Sai Baba wearing a white flower garland around His neck, His hands upraised, and a smile on His lips. We thank him profusely and leave, planning to be in India in only three weeks.

Back at our new temporary home in the Marco Polo Hotel, I finish reading the final chapters of a book which has recently come into my hands. It is by Indra Devi, the world famous yoga teacher. She sounds like a hilarious person and I chuckle as I finish the book and tell Jim about her. The phone rings. Len's voice on the other end says, after the usual opening formalities, "Would you like to attend a free yoga class given by Indra Devi which is open to the public tomorrow evening?" I can't believe my ears.

"Len, you're not going to believe this but I just this minute finished reading a book about Indra Devi and wished I could meet her some day. It's hard to believe she's coming to Singapore tomorrow. Of course I'd like to go."

"She'll be at the Sri Mariaman Temple for the evening. You'll need to wear comfortable clothes, leave your shoes outside the temple, and sit on the women's side. I'd suggest that you get there early since close to a thousand people will be there and it's best to get a seat near the front. You know, we have fourteen Sai Baba centers here and the thousands of devotees revere Indra Devi very much, not only because she has received many blessings from Sai Baba, but because she herself is like a saint and has helped countless numbers of people. Just get there early and bring something to read if you get impatient waiting."

Tomorrow I intend to take Len's gift picture of Sai Baba to the frame shop. The equatorial sun has set and the hotel house-keeping staff are making their rounds.

The hotel night maids have turned back the sheets on the bed and have, as usual, placed a lavender orchid and a miniature chocolate bar on each pillow. I glance around the room at the sleek blond furniture, opulent chartreuse draperies, carpet and bedspreads, the refrigerator, bookcase, dresser, chair and table, and try to imagine the dry heat of the simple village of Puttaparthi after the dampness and sophistication of Singapore. An ashram in the desert of India will be a quiet, welcome change after the busy year amid the noise and crowds of Southeast Asia.

As I climb into bed I recall what Dr. Mohan had said as he gave me the vibhuti ash in water. His words have taken on new meaning since hearing Len talk of Sai Baba.

"You know, the body is a miraculous instrument," he said. "Some-times we doctors can heal it and sometimes we can't. But faith is an altogether different thing. I believe that if you have faith you can be healed of anything. Would you agree?"

"Of course," I replied.

"Recently when I was in India, I happened to meet a very special man," Dr. Mohan had tentatively continued. "He is a holy man. He can heal others either directly or indirectly. He has the ability to bring the dead back to life and has done so three times. He also can appear in more than one place at a time and frequently does so in order to assist people in emergencies. He gave me several packets of vibhuti, which is a light gray healing ash, that I have used with great success with my patients. Regardless of what you may think of all this I am now going to give you some vibhuti in a glass of water and I believe it will relieve your headache much better than aspirin," he said, his eyes crinkling with humor.

"If I were you," he continued, "I would put all of my efforts into going to see Him and trying to get an interview to see if he would heal you. Who knows - you might not even need to have brain surgery upon reaching the States if he heals you first. Consider it. I really believe that's your best approach. Now just drink this ash in the water and you'll feel better."

Again I remembered his efficient staff and his impressive credentials and diplomas that covered his office walls. Surely such intelligent, prominent people as Dr. Mohan and Len Rodrigo couldn't have been fooled by Sai Baba, could they?

My headaches have stopped, I notice, as I fall into a deep slumber.

*　*　*　*　*

This morning my crushing headache has still not returned, for which I am supremely grateful. Further, I feel more energetic than I have in several months. My overall mood is very optimistic and I feel eager to meet Sai Baba in person.

A few hours later, as I step into the frame shop with Len's photo of Sathya Sai, the picture framer immediately recognizes Sai Baba. When he sees the photograph of Sai Baba wearing a white garland, he asks if I'm a follower or Sai Baba devotee.

"Not exactly. I've only recently heard of Him and intend to visit Him myself in a few weeks to see if all these stories are true."

"His devotees are very fine people. Very honest. We have framed many pictures of Him and He even cured my cousin of cancer. They say He can cure anything, even blindness and lameness. Many thousands of people in Singapore follow Him and in all of Asia He is very well-known. You can pick up the picture in two days," he says, smiling.

I thank the framer and ride back to the hotel with Wahid to pick up the day's phone messages at the desk. There's a message from our friend Tati Shariff, whom I had told about Sai Baba. Tati says she has a friend named Nancy Tan whom she wants me to meet. I call Tati and give her the results of the doctor visit as well as our impressions of the Sai Baba video.

"Amazing," she responds. "Nancy Tan actually spent several months in India at Sai Baba's ashram. Why don't we all have dinner together so that you can ask her any questions you'd like to have answered about Him and about the ashram."

We agree to meet in about a week and I sit in my room wondering why it is that the entire year I've lived in Singapore I haven't heard of Sai Baba until my birthday a few weeks before leaving Asia. This is the second year in a row I've received a spiritual birthday present. Last year on my birthday, I dreamed that Jim and I were going to move to a tropical island and saw many of the actual streets and buildings of

Singapore in the dream. A few hours later Jim received the phone call and invitation to work for a year in Singapore.

What does this mean? Why are there so many coincidences now which seem to point inescapably to the appropriateness of our going to India? "Before long, hopefully, we should know the answers to all of our questions," I reflect, perusing the day's To Do List and examining the mail from the States.

At seven o'clock I ask Wahid to drive me to the open-air temple on Serangoon Road for the Indra Devi lecture and yoga class.

"You're welcome to come in or to just wait in the courtyard or the parking lot, Wahid."

"Thank you, Mem, but I think I will just wait in the yard of the temple and watch what I can from there, since I am a Muslim and am forbidden to go into the mosques of other religions."

"Yes, I understand, Wahid. It should be over in about two hours."

As I approach the temple I see a book table being set up and decide to examine the books being unpacked from cardboard boxes on three low steps surrounding the large open-air, pillared structure. A thin Indian man with an Afro haircut walks quickly toward me, his palms touching and fingers pointing to the sky, as if he is praying.

"Sai Ram, and welcome," he says, smiling and nodding. "Are you here for the yoga class? For Mataji?"

Confused by the words "Sai Ram" and "Mataji" I began to fear I'm in the wrong place.

"Well I am looking for a yoga class but it's to be taught by Indra Devi."

"Of course," he says, chuckling. "Mataji and Indra Devi are the same person. We call her Mataji which is a term of endearment since she is like a saint with all of her kindness and good works. You aren't a follower of Sai Baba, then? I don't recall seeing you here before. In fact, we have no Westerners following Sai Baba in Singapore yet and we can't understand it since so many Asians know of him - several million, you know. Perhaps you'd like to look at the books until the class begins. He leads me to the books, bows slightly and continues with his other preparations. After perusing the book table at the rear of the temple, I buy seven books about Sai Baba - a week's worth. I glance at their titles on my way up the aisle to the front rows: *The Holy Man And The Psychiatrist; Bhagavan Sri Sathya Sai Baba; Sai Baba Avatar; The Heart of Sai; Sathya Sai Speaks, Volumes 1 and 2; and Sai Baba and His Message.*

Walking to the front of the hall I feel keenly conscious of being the only Westerner in the temple and the only woman wearing slacks. The first few rows have already filled, on both the men's and women's sides of the center aisle. Orange prayer mats have been laid on the concrete floor for the audience to sit on cross-legged. Mothers sit facing the altar with babies in their laps. A pretty, roundish woman with the uniform long black braid of Indian women beckons for me to sit next to her.

"My name is Jaya and we are happy to have you here tonight."

"Thank you, Jaya. My name is Connie and this is obviously my first time. I only heard about Sai Baba very recently and just finished reading a book about Indra Devi and amazingly enough she's here in Singapore for a few days."

"Yes, we are lucky to have Mataji with us. Now, do you promise not to tell anyone a very great secret?"

"A secret? Yes, besides, who would I tell since I don't know any of these people?" What could the secret be and why would she confide in a complete stranger?

"Mataji is staying in my home while she is here in Singapore!" She waits for my reaction but since I have never met Indra Devi I am stuck for an appropriate answer.

"That's a great honor, isn't it?" I offer, hoping that it is an all-purpose response suited to her obvious sense of responsibility about the situation.

"Yes it is. You are so right. In fact, all my friends are jealous. They beg me to get them in to see her, for a private audience but what can I do? She is 84 years old and even though she has a kind heart and a lot of energy, she cannot see everyone who wants to see her. It's like Baba - millions want to see him but only a few are so fortunate and I, myself have been such a one. He healed me, you know, and now I am totally devoted to Him as my teacher."

The temple continues to fill until about eight hundred men, women and children are packed tightly together in anticipation of Indra Devi's appearance. At the front of the temple there is an immense color photograph of Sai Baba which is draped with an opulent garland of orange marigolds. Joss sticks burn in a brass container at the base of the picture. An orange throne chair sits empty next to the picture and various brass pots and ornaments lie on the altar.

Across the aisle, past the colorful silk saris on the women's side, I notice a soulful-looking dark Indian boy about to play a harmonium. He leans his head back and closes his eyes ecstatically, while singing a phrase alone which is enthusiastically repeated by the crowd in response. Immediately I sit bolt upright, caught by the haunting, joyful beauty of the song.

"These are bhajans," whispers Jaya, pronouncing it 'budge'uns.' They are sacred Sanskrit songs to the Lord. Very joyful. Here's a song sheet so you can sing too. To remember how to pronounce the word, just remember to budget time each day to sing 'budge' uns' to the Lord. See? budget and bhajans sound a bit alike." She laughs at her little teaching device.

I thank her and attempt to sing along but each word seems to have fifteen letters and seven syllables. To my unaccustomed ear the bhajans have an unearthly beauty and I notice the women in front of me becoming entranced and swooning slightly in rhythm to the music. More songs ensue and then a rustle sweeps the crowd as Indra Devi approaches the front of the temple.

A rickety card table and microphone have been set up on the concrete floor before the crowd in order that Indra Devi might have an elevated platform on which to stand. Like everyone else in the temple, I catch my breath as the short, plump grandmotherly woman, clad in a peach-colored sari is assisted up on the wobbly table. Laughing heartily at the crowd's apprehension, Mrs. Devi immediately chides us and lives up to her reputation as a lively, outspoken woman with a mind of her own. The table rocks precariously back and forth and a young man rushes forward to catch her, presumably.

"Now stop that!" she exclaims in American-accented English. "I've been standing on walls and tables since before you were born - and before your mother was born too. I know what I'm doing. Just because I'm 84 doesn't mean I'm going to fall off this table. After all, I'm here to teach a yoga class, for heaven's sake!" The audience hoots and her spicy introduction heralds a galloping pace. She immediately assures the crowd that there will be time at the end of the evening to come forward in a line to touch the mala or necklace-like prayer beads that were given to her when she was in her forties.

"As you know, this mala, or rosary or strand of prayer beads is olive wood and has healing powers, just as it did when it was first given to me. Now when I say I want you to form a line later on, I mean a line. Not a stampede. Another thing, this is a holy japamala, not a washcloth. Some people have acted as if they were seized with the inspiration to take a bath in public and have scrubbed themselves all over - and far too vigorously at that - with this delicate item. One man even broke it in his ardor, so… not too much ardor, please!" Again the crowd laughs at her friendly bossiness and humorous way of expressing herself.

"Now let's talk about Baba and self-abnegation. That's why we're all here anyway - to know that the divine is in us, as it is in Baba. Self-abnegation can be achieved in two ways: love and service to others, and non-attachment to the fruit of your action. Erase your ego. Ask "What can I do to deserve Baba's grace? What can I give to others?""

The audience sits spellbound, even the babies are transfixed by the easy engaging delivery of this white-haired woman who is a marvelous mixture of witty sage, imperious school teacher and independent American. She tells about her Sai Yoga School in Tecate, a small Mexican border town next to California. The school is at Rancho Cuchuma, a ranch site where more than one miraculous event has taken place. For example, once a grass and forest fire swept across the land and nearly encircled the house, but left it standing. Family and friends had prayed fervently to Sai Baba to save the house.

Indra Devi's husband is in a wheel chair, paralyzed, yet Sai Baba always asks about him. This is an indication of Sai Baba's attention to small details, though millions of people constantly seek His help and intercession.

"Now I will tell you some of Baba's thousands of leelas of which I have personal knowledge. As you know, a leela is a divine play or sport - sort of a funny little joke or gift or miracle. Baba is famous for His sense of humor and for His generous love and grace. He even takes on the pains of others at times to relieve them of their suffering. Why once He took on some pain of a devotee by having a large, deep splinter in His foot which kept Him inside for ten days. Imagine - ten days away from His beloved people. When asked about it He merely said "We must have thorns as well as roses or life would be too dull." Chuckling and rocking the table, Mataji gazes lovingly at the crowd.

For the next hour, after the Sai stories, Mataji is swamped with questions on yoga asanas best suited for various ailments. She leads us in asana work interspersed with directions for their application to physical problems. Audience members want to know about relief of sinus problems, back pain, arthritis, headaches, and poor eyesight. I am intrigued since many of her responses echo the advice of my own current yoga teacher, Sally Hillis, whom I join with eight other women twice a week for instruction in Sally's Singapore apartment.

"Now I have a surprise for you. We will turn off the lights and see a short film which I made of Swami in his earlier days. He looks very sweet and you can see Him healing numerous people as He walks through the crowd. After that we will do a candle-light meditation together as a closing."

She hops off the card table and directs the placement of a film projector on the table where she had been standing. The room becomes hushed as the film projector whirs. Without voice or preamble, the film shows Sai Baba strolling calmly through a vast throng of people at a holiday celebration. People stand in the glaring sun under ornamented parasols along a city avenue. There are hundreds of orange costumes on the people and marigold garlands and palm frond decorations gracing the buildings, pillars and archways. Sai Baba's pet elephant, Sai Gita, is festooned with garlands and obviously adores her master. Sick babies, old people, young mothers are touched lightly on the head or given materialized vibhuti to eat for healing. It is a lovely silent film and whets my interest in seeing Sai Baba in person all the more.

A calm tranquility and surge of appreciation have moved through the audience by the end of the film. Indra Devi announces the concluding process and energetically directs us into circles of ten people each where we place a candle in the center of our group. We're instructed to gaze at the candle until we can close our eyes and see its details continually in our mind's eye. "Ask yourself now, how shall I live and what love can I give?" At this thought I open my eyes to glance around the temple. About eighty groups encircle their white candles, flickering yellow lights illuminating their rapt faces. The feelings of love that emanate from the circles are nearly palpable and I marvel that I have not sensed anything like this before - not even in worship services of Western churches or at any rallies or conventions I've attended. This is different: heart-centered, selfless, pure and spontaneous.

Jaya leans toward me and whispers "I have a feeling that you will be visiting Sai Baba soon. Is it not so?"

Eyes wide, I answer, "Why yes, Jaya. In three weeks, on our way home to the States my husband and I will go to India to see Sai Baba. That's a good guess on your part."

"I also have a feeling that you are a writer and that you will one day write a book about Sai Baba," she chuckles. As I nod, bemused at the possibility, she asks me to jot down my address and phone number at the Marco Polo Hotel, saying that tomorrow she and her husband will call on us at two o'clock in the afternoon with addresses of friends in India where we can stay, if necessary. She will also bring a packet of vibhuti which Sai Baba has personally given to her. Overcome at such generosity from a virtual stranger, my eyes quickly fill with tears. The events of the evening and of the past few days are getting to me.

"Now don't be tearful," Jaya smiles, patting me on the knee. "When the heart is full the eyes overflow... anyway, I'm sure you would do the same for me if I were in your country."

"Yes, I would indeed. In fact, it's exactly the sort of thing I usually do," I reply, recovering from the short burst of emotion I'm feeling. "There, you see," she continues, "you are under Baba's grace for your kindness to others. That's the way it works, you know. Someone helps us then we help another and he helps another. It's like a golden chain of love around the world, Baba tells us."

We close our eyes for the final aspect of the guided meditation which draws the evening to a close.

Later, as I skip down the temple steps the same curly-haired Indian man who had said "Sai Ram" to me when I arrived walks toward me. "Sai Ram" he begins. "Did you enjoy the evening?"

"Oh, yes, I can't wait to tell my husband all about it. He had to work in Indonesia today so he couldn't come. It's really fantastic. All this is so new to me. And Indra Devi is such a funny, vivacious person that I feel really lucky to have seen her here in Singapore."

He laughs at my enthusiasm and says, "We have many thousands of followers of Sai Baba here in Singapore. There are fourteen centers here now. Since you are the only Westerner who has ever attended our gatherings, I would like to invite you and your husband to my restaurant for lunch and for a surprise on Monday. It's called the Tipsy Topsy Bombay Restaurant and I'd be very honored if you would come. Here is my card and a picture of Sai Baba for you. Please say you'll come on Monday about one o'clock."

A bit taken aback, I say that we will of course be pleased to come to lunch at his restaurant. Wondering what the surprise will be, I jog across

the parking lot to tell Wahid all about the program. After I have summarized the events Wahid says smiling, "Yes, yes, Mrs. Connie. I put the car
in a good spot so I could see everything. I saw the old lady talking on top
of the table, I heard the nice singing, saw the film and the yoga that all of
you did together. Tell me, how old is this woman?"

"She's eighty-four, can you believe it? She lives part of the time on
her ranch in California, which has a yoga school, and part of the year in
India. Wahid, she told us some stories about Sai Baba that you just
wouldn't believe. This man is incredible, from all the things I've heard
about Him. How am I ever going to explain all of this to Jim?"

"Yes, I too, have heard many stories. Have you ever followed a spiritual teacher?" Wahid asks, trying to sound very casual and detached.

"No, Wahid. I'm not the following type. I've seen mystics and
masters all over the world and so far I haven't been too impressed -
except that they're mostly fine people doing what they think is right. For
me to follow someone he'd have to be really something. A man who had
fully attained his God-self like Jesus or the Buddha - a Self-realized
being. Even then, I might not sign up as a devotee. It would depend on
what He's like. Most of all, it would be a comfort to be able to ask Him
questions and to know that He is helping mankind in these troublous
times."

"I am happy to hear that, Mrs. Connie because in Asia there are many
tricky people who pretend to be powerful and I don't want to worry
about you and your husband."

"Thank you, Wahid, but my main problem so far has been how to
stop other people from wanting to follow me when I don't even know
where I'm going. In fact, I think that what each person is looking for is
actually within himself and simply has to be let out. No, I'm definitely
not the guru-following type. I'm thrilled to know that the Avatar Sai
Baba is on the planet and I'd like to see Him, but I'm not the type of
person who would just turn off her brain and blindly become a devotee. I
believe in personal responsibility and in each person making their
contribution to society through inner guidance. You don't have to worry
about me, Wahid." As I said these words to Wahid, it almost seemed as if
I could hear faint locutional laughter, as if these would be my 'famous
last words.' *You wouldn't be laughing at me, now, would You, Sai Baba?*

CHAPTER 15
A SURPRISE AT LUNCH

"The spiritual discipline must be of the highest character if one is to realize the Supreme Consciousness and be under the Grace of God, always." Sathya Sai Baba, TOSSSB P 8

Singapore
February 28, 1982

At two o'clock Saturday Jaya Rajamanikam and her husband arrive at the hotel lobby seating area, true to their word. She is dressed in a pink and rose sari and she sits next to her husband, who is a successful businessman, when Jim and I enter the mirrored lobby to greet them. Jaya presents me with a packet of vibhuti which Sai Baba personally gave her during her last visit. Her husband shyly hands me a folded piece of paper listing all the items we will need to purchase before setting out to Southern India. It mentions loose-fitting cotton shirts and trousers for both of us, preferably in white, due to the intense heat.

Also included on the list is a canteen, two padlocks and keys for our room, dark-colored twin bed sheets to be folded over and sewn up as emergency bedding, pillow cases, vitamins, snack foods, silverware, a drinking cup, bath tissue, soap and shampoo, detergent, inexpensive rubber thongs, cheesecloth or mosquito netting for window screening, a mirror, towels and washcloths, suntan lotion, travel iron, tissues, shawl, pen knife, rope for a clothesline, clothes hangers, alarm clock, malaria tablets, immunization records, inoculation update, passport and other I.D., sunglasses, hat, water purification tablets, luggage keys, fifty one-dollar bills, traveler's checks, nails and hammer, hard candy or lifesavers (6-8 packs for a week due to the heat and unpotable water), wet naps, bug spray, tacks, good air mattresses, sewing kit, masking tape, lomotil, brown paper and string, flashlight and batteries, a dozen small plastic trash bags.

"You see," begins Mr. Rajamanikam, "India is unbelievably poor and Puttaparthi is deep in the interior desert where there are no proper stores for many hours of travel in all directions. It is better to be prepared than to have your visit spoiled by the lack of some trivial item which could have made such a big difference. Of course you never know how crowded it will be when you arrive or what sort of accommodations will be available. They try to give Westerners suitable lodging but "suitable" can mean anything to Indians who are used to doing without even the most basic items which all of us in Singapore and the States consider vital necessities. Even though I am Indian I am always shocked each time I return to India and see once again how impoverished and dirty everything really is. Have you ever been to India?"

"Yes, we were married in India a few years ago and I was in Northern India a few months ago," I answer. "But on both occasions that I was there, I was on a tour and the circumstances were quite a bit more comfortable by comparison. However, we can adjust to anything and this list will be helpful. It was very kind of you to take the time to inform us this way."

"We also have some addresses which you may find helpful," Jaya says. "There is a list of hotels where we know the owners and you can feel quite safe. Also, you can buy your clothes in Serangoon Road and I can help you to tie sari if you like."

At this offer, all four of us glance at my tailored slacks, simultaneously realizing that I'd probably opt not to wear a sari in the hundred and ten degree heat of India, or at any other time or place for that matter.

"Thank you, Jaya, but I really would feel strange in the yards and yards of sari cloth and feel that such a lovely costume looks better on Indian women than upon Westerners. They will allow me to wear a long overblouse and loose slacks, won't they?"

"Yes, but sari is better," she pouts. "Sari is cool and pretty. It is easy to tie. You will like it once you tie it."

"I don't want to cause an argument over a sari, Jaya, but can you imagine my sari falling apart in a crowd, like it did when I was married in a sari? After I had to go to the wedding dinner with half of it wadded in a roll under my arm and all the banquet waiters laughing until they cried, I decided that traditional charm and costuming had its limits where I was concerned and I have sworn off saris ever since. Once you've become unraveled in public you never forget it."

We all laugh, conclude our visit with good wishes all around, shake hands and wave as the Rajamanikams exit through the immense glass hotel doors into the sweltering afternoon heat.

A telephone message at the desk from William Wong informs us that he would like to bring some Sai Baba books to the hotel. William, an English professor at the University of Singapore, was the second person to mention Sai Baba and to suggest that I go to India. He also has some new Sai contacts for us.

When William arrives we talk about recent meetings at the Theosophical Society and about how his English classes at the University are progressing. Although William looks much younger than his age, he spent some years in California before teaching at the University of Singapore. He chuckles as he recalls how Americans called him "Bill" and how they always hugged him in greeting.

"I was frightfully embarrassed at first," he says, reddening. "We Asians just don't touch each other so indiscriminately, as you know. But after awhile I realized that Americans are very friendly people who are bursting with good will and who show their feelings very easily. They are a bit naive, too, in a sweet way. After I finally adjusted to the shock of people rushing up to me and throwing their arms around me, I relaxed and hugged them back. At first I wanted to run away, though, from all that exuberance and affection. Things are so different in the States. Easier all around. I'd like to return there some day if I could arrange it."

William regales me with more stories he has heard about Sai Baba and lets me borrow some of his books about Him. He has read most of the books written about Him and has many friends who are devotees but is personally reserving a commitment until he sees Him in person. He still hasn't seen the *Aura of Divinity* videotape of Len's, though he's the one who first mentioned it to me. It's almost as if he's urging me to "scout out Sai Baba" for him in order for him to ascertain the wisdom of his making the journey to India himself. Who knows - this Sai Baba might turn out to be a materialist, a fake, or just another guru undifferentiated from all the rest. We part with plans to meet again soon to scour some of the old book shops downtown for more books on Sai Baba.

In the morning I awake with the vivid recollection of a dream about Sai Baba talking to me in a very specific manner. Before it fades I start scribbling in my dream journal that lies open on the nightstand. He was speaking to me in person and said that I would soon have three spiritual tests to go through. One would involve going to see Him in India. The following two tests wouldn't be revealed until they happened, then they would be obvious. I mention the dream to Jim, which has become a daily habit with us, then review the list of Stateside re-location preparations to be accomplished today.

As Wahid drives me to various appointments I ask him to stop at the framer's to see if the picture from Len is ready to be claimed. While I pay for the finished frame, the store owner sizes me up for a moment before speaking.

"Perhaps you have heard, Madame, of the many unusual events and circumstances which have taken place upon framed pictures of Sai Baba. There have been cases of vibhuti just clumping on top of the picture from out of nowhere. Some say it is a reminder of Sai Baba's love for His followers and an encouragement to remain steadfast on the spiritual path. Now I myself am a rational thinker and don't know what to make of all this but many of my friends believe that miracles take place all the time in the lives of His followers."

"Yes… it's beyond my comprehension, too. I've heard many such stories recently," I reply with sudden remnants of the previous night's dream of Sai Baba flooding my consciousness. After thanking him for the fine work on the frame, I join Wahid and again consult my "To Do List."

Throughout the day Wahid glances anxiously at me in the rear-view mirror and once ventures a direct personal question, which, for him, is unusual as it borders on insolence and invasion of my privacy in his own code of ethics.

"Don't be angry, Mrs. Connie, if I ask you this," he begins, in a soft quavering voice.

"Oh come on, now, Wahid. Have you ever once known me to be angry with you in the entire year that you've known me, in driving me all over Singapore for several hours a day, every day?"

"No, you are right. You are a patient woman. But before I haven't seriously asked you about your intentions concerning your religion."

"You meditate and read spiritual books a lot but you don't go to any mosque or temple or church on Christian worship day, although you are a very kind, compassionate person. So now you see many people who always tell you about Sai Baba and you even frame the picture your friend gave to you. Now I understand you liked the yoga class of Indra Devi and that you are even going to India to see Sai Baba. So I am very surprised. I don't know what to think. Are you really going to follow Sai Baba?!" He turns and looks beseechingly at me with a strange mixture of fear, horror and amazement rippling across his face.

"In the first place, I haven't seen Him yet. In the second place, I think that the things I have been hearing about Him are so unusual that I feel I owe it to myself to investigate them. So far I have been true to every single spiritual instinct that I have had and have not felt satisfied until I have made the next step on my path. Who knows what we will find in India? Maybe Sai Baba will turn out to be some sort of modern day Messiah to help us know God within us. Wouldn't it be a shame if that were true and I were right here in Asia and never even bothered to obey my own internal prodding to see for myself? Now don't you worry about me, Wahid. I won't do anything foolish. Besides, as I have told you many times, even if He does turn out to be some fantastic bomoh or great holy man, what does it matter? The divine is in all of us and it's our purpose to live the clearest life we can, in each moment. Sometimes I forget to be extra aware in every conversation but I realize when I have slipped and come back to remembrance of the commitment. I can't expect someone to take that responsibility from me, ever... even someone like Sai Baba."

Wahid seems to relax, since he has done his duty in warning his Mem. We finish the day's errands and part for lunch, agreeing to meet in the afternoon for another round of the same. The late afternoon holds appointments to pick up health records, to visit with the moving company, to purchase items for the thirty-three hour trip back to Colorado from India. There are farewells to friends and library books to return to the American Club. The interminable "To Do List" still has forty unfinished priority items as I finish the day and run up the steps of the Marco Polo. The large ornate vases of yellow, rust, and lavender orchids reflecting in the huge mirrored lobby walls speak to me silently as I realize I'll traverse the lobby only a few more times before leaving Singapore. Even the floor mat of the elevator makes me smile with its cheery message: "Good afternoon. It's Saturday at the Marco Polo Hotel in Singapore." The elevator lifts silently and opens on the first floor to admit two Australian men carrying the cameras and suitcases of new arrivals. They notice the floor mat and start laughing.

"Damn good idea, that. Many's the time I've been so tired in these foreign hotels that I've forgotten what day it is and even where I am," says the blond one.

"They have a great pool here. We were just looking it over. Would you like to go swimming with us this afternoon?" the other asks, winking at his companion and laughing nervously.

"No thanks. I'm married," I laugh good-naturedly, as the elevator stops at the chartreuse carpeting of the tenth floor.

The afternoon chambermaids are emptying waste baskets and turning down the bed linens as I enter the long mirrored hallway. I stop to chat with Fatima, Grace and Eng as they carry fresh towels, juice and ashtrays to the nearest room. We speak of their children, their anticipated vacations and the construction noise across the street.

"We will miss you," they say, reminding me once again that my days in Asia are numbered. Thomas Wong, a porter, nods as he passes me on the way to my room overlooking the pool, gardens and thatch-roofed patios. The room is cooler than the hallway and the open bath door reveals the fresh soaps, shampoos, sewing kit, shoe shine cloth and towels that have just been arranged on the white tile counter next to the large mirror. Everything glistens and smells of polishes and cleaners.

On Monday at one o'clock, Jim and I ride with Wahid to the Tipsy Topsy Bombay Restaurant, wondering what surprise awaits. In the tiny lift to the restaurant we are enmeshed with a jolly, chattering family of Indians shepherding toddlers in ruffled dresses and babies in arms. They, too, are going to the restaurant at the top of the building. As the lift opens they dash past us and we step out into a large dining room with about ten round tables and several green leather booths curved against the wall. Windows line the far wall and the tables are laid with white linen, candles and attractive place settings.

We see no signs of our host and take seats in a booth to wait. Half an hour passes. We inquire of the waiter if the owner is available and are told that he has gone to meet a large party of distinguished guests who will be arriving any moment. Ten minutes more pass and we contemplate whether or not to leave or to order lunch since we are ravenous and have left our work to accept the invitation to come to this restaurant.

While we are discussing our next step the lift door opens and out steps the restaurant owner with about ten Indians and Indra Devi in their midst.

"This is the surprise I promised you - luncheon with Mataji," he beams.

"You haven't been waiting long, I hope."

Upon seeing Indra Devi, two dozen people in the restaurant jump up from their tables and run to prostrate themselves before her. One after another they fall to the floor and touch her feet. We sit staring with shocked expressions then recover our composure and wait until the prostrations have finished, wondering what the protocol of the situation requires.

"Well I for one am not going to get down there and touch her feet," I whisper to Jim.

"I've never touched anybody's feet in my life and I'm not going to start now. I don't care if everybody in this entire room does it. I'm not."

"Relax," Jim whispers, convulsing at my emphatic reaction. "They can tell by looking at us that we're Americans and don't do that sort of thing. At least I hope they know that," he says nervously as the prostrations and embraces continue.

"Come and sit down at the head table with Mataji," our host calls over the excitement. The long table seats about a dozen people, including babies on the laps of two young Indian mothers. An assortment of eager, worshipful men in their twenties and thirties presses around the table for the lavish traditional Indian dinner.

At the end of the meal, while the others are having dessert, Indra Devi arises and comes to the end of the table to sit beside Jim and me. She finds that we have only recently heard of Sai Baba and begins to tell us about India in the old days when she lived there. Upon hearing that Jim's last name is Wright she chuckles in recollection of her old friend Frank Lloyd Wright, the architect. How odd it is that I've recently read his autobiography.

"Frank was such a dear fellow. He used to come and visit when he came to the Midwest. He was very talented, of course, and funny too. We had a good time." She tells us of her ashram at Tecate and of how she began following Sai Baba in 1966. I recalled being told that she had fled from the Russian Revolution as a young girl with her parents before studying with yoga masters in India. As I glance at her hand, I notice a large diamond ring exactly like the one Sai Baba gave to Len. He had materialized this one for her and she says that it's the only jewelry she wears even though she owns an egg-sized diamond and other family jewels that were smuggled out of Russia in her youth. She has held yoga seminars throughout the world as well as at her California ashram. She explains that her nickname "Mataji" means Holy Mother or Dear Mother and that it is used as a form of endearment and respect by her colleagues and friends throughout the world who also follow Sathya Sai Baba. "Sathya means Truth, you know," she says. "But if you are going to visit Sai Baba at Puttaparthi, I think you will be disappointed. I was just in India and He said He was going to Brindavan as He usually does at this time of the year, now that the heat is starting."

"We'll find Him somehow," I assert. "I really would like to go to Puttaparthi, even if He's not there, just to see the place. Besides, maybe we'll be lucky and find Him there. I can't imagine why we're having so many unusual coincidences regarding Him if we're not meant to see Him, sooner or later. We'll take the chance."

"Good for you. You never know what He's going to do. It's good to follow your heart and make your plans, then see what happens. You know, Baba says, 'I direct you to implant three ideas in your hearts: Do not forget God; Do not put faith in the world you see around you. It is changing every second and does not last; Do not be afraid. You are the imperishable Atman that knows no fear. I want you also to banish two ideas from your hearts: Forget the harm that anyone has done to you, and forget the good that you have done to others.' "

"It's wonderful to be in the presence of Baba, you know. He is kindness itself. He's healed thousands of people but never accepts any money or gifts in return. He's like Christ the way He loves all people and constantly comforts humanity. He's always saying that 'we all need to serve others with our five resources: food, money, time, energy and knowledge. The end of knowledge is love.' He's getting so well-known around the world now, though, that pretty soon we won't be able to get near Him for the crowds. That's why it's good you're going at this time of year, when it's hot, because most of the crowds go home then. You'll only have a few thousand people to contend with instead of more than a hundred thousand. And be sure to dress modestly out of respect for Baba and for the other people there. Now I must be going but I hope you get to see Him and God bless both of you."

Mataji arises, smiling and with her merry eyes sparkling and is once again besieged by fond acquaintances in the restaurant who prostrate themselves before her. Jim and I shake her hand, heartily thank her and our host, and leave the Tipsy Topsy Bombay Restaurant well satisfied with the luncheon surprise.

PART TWO

DEEPER PRACTICE

CHAPTER 16
FINDING MY MASTER

"The One you truly are is neither perceptible nor perishable."
Ramesh Balsekar

Bangalore, India
March 18, 1982

Although it's still morning the March heat is beginning to penetrate the dark cool interior of the Bangalore Airport. Most of the mob of deplaning passengers from Madras has just dispersed. Jim, B.P. Yap, and I huddle in the center of the airport discussing our plans to hire a cab to the Prashanti Nilayam ashram in the tiny village of Puttaparthi. "Puttaparthi is three or four hours north of Bangalore by cab," B.P. says, "and the ride will be hot. We'll need to fill our canteens now before we start out." While he speaks a dark, slight man with a mustache walks up to me and says "My name is Babu. I am a cab driver. My specialty is taking Sai Baba's devotees to Puttaparthi. You are going to Puttaparthi, are you not?" Babu looks a bit suspicious with his greased black hair, narrow black trousers and glittering eyes. His voice is soft and low yet he is insistent. He sighs at our reluctance to commit ourselves and brings out a tattered sheaf of "recommendation letters" from his bag.

Knowing that such letters can easily be faked, we step a few yards away for a discussion. We hadn't booked a cab in advance and have heard stories about bandits in India. It seems risky to go on a three hour journey into the Indian countryside with a stranger who approaches us so eagerly, but after half an hour of stalling around we have no excuses. Babu patiently tells us his unusually low fee for the fourth time. "Shall we go now?" he asks.

Alone with him in the airport, we look at each other and nod our assent. We have delayed too long as it is and must set out for Puttaparthi before the heat becomes too intense. "Let's hope he's what he says he is." I mutter under my breath.

Babu once more takes out his collection of photos, letters and testimonials from people around the world. As I examine them I see that they all extol his virtues as a guide, friend and cab driver. There is a letter on Esalen stationery and another from a Mama Theresa, his benefactor in Germany. She apparently sent him the money to buy three cabs for the sole purpose of ferrying Sai Baba's devotees back and forth between Bangalore and Puttaparthi.

"Six years ago I was a poor man but Baba helped me to have my own business through my German friend and now I am successful. I owe everything to Baba." Babu smiles as he ushers us into his small black cab and fastens the luggage to the overhead baggage rack.

It is immediately apparent that Babu is a skillful, aggressive driver. He deftly steers us around soot-belching lorries, past lumbering cattle, through narrow alleys and finally to the outskirts of Bangalore where the fields are green with a variety of healthy crops. After about an hour the villages and hamlets along our route thin out. There are fewer fields planted with crops. New colors are introduced to the landscape. The flat fields of reddish-brown and putty are handsomely balanced with the cornflower blue of the sky. To the west, a bank of lavender-tinged mountains entertains the eye with occasional gray boulder clusters and flat mesas barren of vegetation.

During the remaining two hours of the trip, B.P. assumes the responsibility of teaching Jim and me some bhajans. "You see, Connie, we will be singing bhajans every day for an hour before dawn, and hour at mid-morning, and an hour in the late afternoon, so it would be a good idea if you know some of the songs before we arrive." With infinite patience, B.P. and Babu lead us in several of the easiest songs until we can sing them alone. One line at a time B.P. sings the strange Indian melodies and foreign words, clapping his hands to keep up a rhythm.

The humor of our situation dawns on me as I glance over at Jim, who sings quietly with eyes closed against the dust clouds which swirl in on us. A month ago I had expected to be sunning on a white sand beach in Tahiti by now, relaxing after an adventuresome year of living in Asia. Instead, here I am bellowing strange songs at the top of my lungs while we rumble down the bumpy road toward Puttaparthi in Babu's funny little black cab, hoping we won't be waylaid and abandoned in some remote dusty field. How vastly different our lives are - B.P.'s world of finance and the Singapore Stock Market and Jim's worlds of jungle and city as an engineering project manager. Then there's my own life of consulting, travel and adventure, plus writing, speaking and counseling, and dozens of board meetings and service projects. I think of Babu's arduous life and the hundreds of times he has driven this road with foreigners like us - the curious as well as the devoted.

My own life of writing, consulting and public speaking has taken numerous surprising turns thus far. It's as if my arms have become elastic, embracing hundreds of new friends and colleagues, dozens of new countries, scores of unaccustomed ideas and attitudes. Now this. Sai Baba. Will He prove disappointing? Will He be a clever fake? Or merely an over-rated mediocre man of messiah pretensions? How can we know unless we see for ourselves, and even then....

Local farmers turn to stare as we sing Sai Baba's bhajans under B.P.'s direction. "These are wonderful songs. Sing with joy! Louder! Have confidence!" B.P. tells us. Dust clouds furl up in ocher plumes behind the car while strains of *Ganesha Sharanam* escape the cab windows. All lushness has vanished from the landscape now. The fields are dry and the ground is a harsh red clay, relieved occasionally by low tufa brick buildings, grape arbors, and dun-colored plains. A ridge of purple mountains appears faintly in the distance and a pang of homesickness for Colorado sweeps over me.

By now it's over a hundred degrees Fahrenheit and the dry air shimmers over the plains. Even in the heat, this clear dry air seems such a relief after the heavy wet cloud of tropical humidity ever-present in Singapore. I smile at my pleasure in seeing the immense sky overhead - so like the American West. "Yes," I think, "I have missed this kind of spare beauty... spacious, pared down landscapes of horizontals, earth colors, subtle simplicity of desert, mesa and plateau. Singapore's green abundance and floral excesses are balm in their own way yet even paradise can pall without variety or contrast. And Singapore is a vertical place with its tall palms, skyscraper-filled center city, ubiquitous deafening pile-drivers and angular cranes raising the steel skeletons of still more new buildings. This land of south India is stripped to the bare essentials of existence."

The closer we get to Puttaparthi the more Biblical the people and terrain seem. Waves of heat shimmer from the road and create images of lakes ahead. They are mirages. Packs of gray monkeys cavort beside the road, leaping down from the red-trunked trees bordering the narrow highway. Although this is my third trip to India, my whole body fills with tension as the opposing traffic charges toward us right down the center of the road. Both vehicles seem to accelerate as if suicide is the agenda on both sides of the mad convergence. At the last instant the oncoming vehicles swerve aside and we are once more miraculously spared an early death by head-on collision.

Scraggy clumps of corn and vegetables sag in the hammering sun. On the road ahead a patch of brilliant fabric color catches our interest. Women in saris and men in dingy white dhotis labor away with hammers, chipping gray boulders into gravel for the road bed. They must be of a caste which builds roads by hand. They painstakingly move the earth and stones from hillside to roadbed in woven baskets carried on their heads.

A bus roars by spraying gravel and dust, and blaring its horn. It bears a suffocatingly crowded-in load of humanity, heads pressed against the windows, standees crammed into the aisles, onto the dashboard, into the stairwell. Each seat appears to hold six people and they even seem to hang from the ceiling. We remind ourselves to resist the temptation to take the bus from Bangalore should we come this way again - no matter how romantic it might seem to our heat-addled brains at the time.

Long before we arrive at the ashram we drink the last of the warm water remaining in the canteens. We are covered with khaki dust like a quartet of hard-rock miners who have just emerged from a tunnel cave-in. The ground becomes hilly and a few simple huts come into view. Ancient gnarled trees make blue shadows in the biscuit-colored dust. Mongrel dogs bark half-heartedly in the heat. More small, simple, white-washed houses are clumped together near groves of trees. We are passing through a miserably poor village as our anticipation mounts.

Puttaparthi, South India
March 18th

The hamlets seem cleaner, more orderly and more prosperous as we near Puttaparthi. Approaching the ashram property, the town gates come into view and our hearts race with excitement. After having experienced the serendipitous plane trip where we met B.P. Yap, and this dusty taxi ride, we wonder if Sai Baba will even be here at the ashram. Visitors have frequently been disappointed after much longer journeys than ours.

After passing several white-washed huts with dirt floors and thatched roofs we arrive at the edge of Puttaparthi. A large pink multi-storied school comes into the frame of the front window of the cab, then small whitewashed houses with flat roofs. As we approach the pink, cream and blue gates of Prashanti Nilayam itself, it occurs to me that the ethereal-looking buildings appear like giant birthday cakes adorned with pastel angels. The Abode of Great Peace is indeed a heavenly spot, like nothing I have ever experienced. There is an unearthly quiet throughout the grounds. Green parakeets with red bills flit through the trees and gray monkeys scamper amid the shrubbery. There are no cars in the ashram. The only audible sound is birdsong and notice signs nailed to large shade trees petition: SILENCE IN THE ASHRAM, PLEASE.

Babu smiles triumphantly and says softly, "You see, I have brought you safely to Baba. He is here at the ashram now. My friends told me so two days ago. Enjoy your stay. When shall I return for you?" Immediately we agree on leaving a week hence, ashamed that we had mistrusted Babu at the outset. Smiling still, he unpacks the cab, and directs us to the Public Relations Office where we check in and receive instructions.

At the desk inside the small bare office, we are met by a handsome elderly man in white. "Please leave your shoes at the door and remember that in India we don't wear our dusty shoes inside" he chides us gently. "And you, Madame, will need to remove your Western clothes and cover your arms and shoulders with a large shawl. Everyone is very modest here in the ashram to keep our attention on our prayers and meditations, rather than on the distractions of the comings and goings of Baba's many foreign devotees. You have seen our signs requesting for silence? We also observe silence in the canteens. Men and women eat separately. The food is Indian of course. It is simple but you will find it nourishing and very filling. You may eat as much as you like and we hope you will have a comfortable stay."

We thank our host and set out to find our room in order to change into the white cotton clothes we have bought in the Indian district of Singapore. Although in Western society I would be considered modestly dressed, I am keenly aware that in my short-sleeved sport shirt and tailored slacks I seem flagrantly immodest here. It will feel wonderful to be dressed in the cooler cotton Indian kurta and slacks and to lie down on a bed before the afternoon darshan begins in an hour.

A group of shabbily dressed men and boys sit in the shade of a tree near the office. As we approach, they quickly surround us, each wanting to earn a tip by carrying a piece of luggage to our room. We have become accustomed to being pressed by people on the streets of India crying, "Baksheesh! Money! Denaro!" We are glad that Baba does not permit begging in the ashram, choosing instead to provide food for people in Puttaparthi and work for many of the villagers. Having selected some porters we say goodbye to B.P. for the moment, since his accommodation is in another building "for those who have stayed at Prashanti Nilayam before."

Leaving the other porters sullenly behind, we troop up several flights of stairs outside one of the dorm buildings and down a long veranda to our room. Upon entering, we are astounded to find that instead of a dresser, bed and closet, the room is completely empty. Absolutely. There must be some mistake. There isn't a stick of furniture in the room. The floor is unpainted concrete without even a small rug. Not even a closet. Nor even a clothes hook. The iron barred window is without glass, screen or mosquito netting. There is a small bathroom with a Western toilet, broken toilet seat, no mirror, sink or shower. Instead of a sink there is a naked pipe with a spigot over a red plastic bucket. A sign tells of a severe water shortage and instructs us to bathe from the bucket before eight in the morning or between eight and nine at night. "Water will be turned off between 8 A.M. and 4 P.M." Walking back to the green wooden door we notice that the padlock is broken. We have brought our own lock, as our friends in Singapore recommended, but don't intend to stay in this room, which is obviously just a storeroom of some kind.

Feeling certain that there must be some mix-up in our room arrangements, I rush outside the empty concrete cell and peer into the room next door to us. Large shade trees cast dappled shadows on the sandy courtyard below. The room next door, occupied by a Catholic priest from Brooklyn, is exactly like ours. Maybe we're on the wrong corridor. This wing must be for special people practicing asceticism. It's probably for extra-devout clergy. At a quick but apprehensive trot, I investigate all of the rooms along our veranda as well as all the cubicles on the other outside halls in the building and am dismayed that they are all the same, with the exception of a few sparse decorative touches, such as photos of Sai Baba, placed there by the Westerners.

Our neighbors seem to be an assortment of Americans, Canadians and Europeans of every imaginable type: students, business people, couples, families, nuns, rabbis, ministers and teachers. Many have placed candles in the single alcove of their rooms along with incense and pictures of Sai Baba. On the floors are straw mats and simple thin mattresses with piles of luggage beside them.

"This must be the place, Jim. They all look like ours. This is going to be pretty spartan. We'll have to hurry outside the ashram gates and buy mattresses and mats before the darshan starts."

In half an hour we have bought our mattresses, plastic buckets and grass mats. When people said this is like camping out with God, they weren't kidding.

With a sense of flailing resistance, I realize that the "Abode of Great Peace" is far more stark than I had ever imagined. My attachment to minimal comforts becomes painfully vivid as an old familiar pouting mood of years ago begins to creep into my consciousness. I laugh at this situation and at the contrast with our final thirty days in the Marco Polo Hotel in Singapore. It's a ludicrous comparison. A few days ago we were eating sumptuous meals, chauffeured everywhere, lulled by air-conditioned splendor; and enjoyed the fresh orchid and small Cadbury chocolate bar placed by chambermaids on the hotel room pillows each night. We've become slightly decadent in a very short time whereas at home in Colorado we live a simple life. However, an empty third floor walk-up cell in the strangling heat is not what I'd expectantly pictured in my mind during the past few days. How self-centered I've become.

No time to sulk. Darshan starts in a few minutes and there are several thousand waiting for the blessing of seeing Sai Baba. Does that mean that He is actually here or do they hold darshan even if He is at the Brindavan ashram near Bangalore? We change clothes and quickly run down the stairs two steps at a time in our white baggy pajama pants and loose kurta shirts and thongs. We pass more "Silence" signs on the walls and hurry across the courtyard, under trees from which immense flocks of black crows raucously ignore the signs' order. "Splat!" A white blob lands on my shoulder. A crow has just welcomed me to Puttaparthi.

On arrival at the Mandir courtyard my heart threatens to burst through its ribcage. Will He be here? In typical Indian fashion, the women are separated from the men in their own courtyard on the opposite side of the Mandir. After leaving my thongs at the gate I file into the sunny courtyard with the thousand women and place my new square mat on the hot sand. I sit silent and cross-legged, observing the crowd while waiting for Sai Baba to appear. Smelling a floral perfume, I glance around and notice that several of the women are wearing cream-colored jasmine garlands, caught in the middle with a bobby pin, and fastened to the top of their braid at the back of the head.

We sit in dozens of straight rows, packed together and overlapping. In front of me is a sea of shiny blue-black heads, each with a single fat braid down the back. Most of the women are Indian, in an assortment of saris, simple to opulent, yet there are still dozens of Westerners. By counting the rows of devotees and the number in each row, I count approximately eight hundred men present at darshan and about a thousand women, for a total of eighteen hundred people. About two percent are Westerners. The Indians carefully scrutinize the Western women who wear caftans, beach gowns, a few carefully wrapped saris, slacks with knee-length overblouses and long skirts in a variety of colors. Every woman wears the required shawl so as not to distract another human with even a hint of bosomy curve or spreading hip. On the other side of the Mandir, a crowd of men, equal in size to ours, sits patiently waiting in the oppressive heat for the Avatar. On both sides there are people in wheelchairs, several lying on stretchers and people who have come on crutches. There are babies in the arms of weary mothers and perspiring toddlers whimpering from the unrelieved solar rays of Andhra Pradesh State. Our attention is suddenly drawn to a stunning group of late arrivals - a tribe of bald Indian women on pilgrimage, wearing faded ragged gauze-like costumes. Though they are obviously desperately poor, they radiate a magnetic inner beauty and carry themselves like royalty.

The crowd emits a mood of silent expectancy as individuals jostle carefully, seeking a more comfortable cross-legged position. We peer toward the dark, open doorway of the Mandir for any clue that Baba is inside. A group of visiting white-uniformed junior high school boys sits in the cool shade of the Mandir veranda. In their cross-legged positions they suddenly become rigidly upright and lean forward as a body as Sai Baba emerges from the Mandir.

There He is at last, looking exactly like His pictures, in red-orange silk robe, barefoot, with a wide black Afro hairstyle. My heart melts. Immediately I feel that He is God and that I have known Him forever and have been with Him in other lifetimes. Like most of the people of South India, He is dark with wide nose and lips, small, exquisitely-shaped hands and feet, and an overall frame of about five feet. The small size of His actual physical body is a shock, yet He has a huge presence and seems much taller than He actually is. His expression is serene and composed as he accepts some of the nuts on a tray offered to Him by one of the schoolboys. He blesses objects which the boys hold up for Him and looks at them with obvious tenderness. He rolls up his sleeves and makes a gesture of rotation with His hand and immediately materializes some candy for the boys in the front row. From where I sit, I can see that the candy is even wrapped in shiny paper!

Baba then takes letters of petition from the boys and signs an autograph for one. He seems very kindly and affectionate with the visiting students, without any overt display of sentiment. They, like the entire audience of devotees, nearly swoon in His presence. Since the birds in overhead trees have stopped chirping, I notice that the silence is almost palpable. The ardent reaction of toddlers and children to Sai Baba is deeply touching to me. Every eye follows His slightest movement. He is simultaneously humble and majestic. How I wish that Scott and my sister and brothers could see Him now.

It has been several weeks since I have had any of the mysterious migraine-like headaches which began so suddenly several months ago. Now all pain and tension of past months fall away from me like a heavy blanket. Every muscle of my face eases into a broad smile. My heart leaps.

Sai Baba leaves the porch and walks directly toward us. Though we've just arrived, I've somehow drawn the great good fortune of sitting in the second row and notice that as He comes directly in front of me I'm holding my breath, still smiling. What's going to happen? He looks straight at me for a long, welcoming moment, causing heads to turn toward me, then He walks along the rows of adoring women. As He passes by them several of the women dive for His feet and miss, despite the strict prohibitions against grabbing Sai Baba or reaching out for Him. They scoop up the fine sand on which He has walked. He gently shakes His head and says "Tsk, tsk." They strain to control themselves and some weep to be so near to Him. Someone next to me tells me that because so many people are taking handfuls of souvenir sand upon which the Lord has walked, it is costing the ashram a fortune to replace it every few weeks.

It is about 105 degrees F. now and the heat is so merciless that I feel as if I might faint face forward on the sand, like a statue falling on its nose. Sai Baba stops and turns His head, looking back in our direction. He raises his hand, swirls it and smiles as a great liquid breeze arises, bending the trees and shrubs in its force. Palms sway and a nearby red hibiscus bush swoops toward the earth. The temperature drops about 35 degrees. He glances at the crowd and smiles again at having provided some relief from the heat. To myself I think "That's a miracle, making a breeze on command like that. Did everybody see that? Don't you people realize what's happening here?! Sai Baba just materialized candy and now He's making vibhuti and rubbing the ash on the eyelids of a sick infant. These are *significant phenomena*. His sleeves are rolled up, so He can't be tricking us by hiding objects in them."

I feel a great gratitude for being here. No - just for being, for existing. We take the same spirit with us everywhere so there's no need to come to Puttaparthi in order to sense and appreciate our being. In glancing around I see that no one else seems especially excited, except me, at what is transpiring. By the end of the hour's darshan I have seen Him create several piles of holy ash, the breeze, wrapped candy and answers to questions before the questioners had even finished formulating their thoughts - and in several languages. My own questions are how a spiritual aspirant can know if he is progressing. Further, is it necessary or even advisable to know our own stage or level of development? Does God automatically take care of our development? That would be the case if there's no free will.

Reluctantly we watch Him disappear into the Mandir for His interviews with about fifteen people whom He has selected, who have come from all over the world to seek His help and advice. The crowd sighs happily and joyfully begins singing bhajans in response to the leading voice inside the Mandir. The swell of sweet, light voices from inside the prayer hall is transporting in a different way than the darshan has been. It touches me so to share this experience with devoted people from so many different countries that I fight back tears of thankfulness and wonder why it is that I am even here and what it all means.

After eating in separate canteens, as is the custom, Jim and I meet to discuss our joy at all we have experienced. We are weary from heat and travel, but the trip has been worth it. In fact, it would have been worth coming to Puttaparthi just to participate in one darshan. We still marvel that there are tens of millions of Sai Baba followers around the world and most Americans, like ourselves until quite recently, have never heard of Baba.

Back in our cell, the unpainted, hard bare concrete floor is a practical matter that reminds us clearly that this is not, after all, heaven. At least as far as our Western bodies are concerned. Silently I recite to myself that "I am not my body. I am not my thoughts. I am not my emotions." Mosquitoes dive-bomb our bodies all night and a mouse rattles and scrapes a paper sack of fruit on the floor next to my head. By morning we are stiff, hot, tired and annoyed by our rodent roommate. This hamlet could really use a shop that rents cots, chairs and tables.

I try to talk Jim out of staying for the rest of the week as planned, confident that I'll succeed in persuading him since he's the one who is usually the most attached to creature comforts. "Let's just stay two more days," I suggest. "My bod can't take this concrete floor after a day of sitting cross-legged on that blistering sand and pressed into that crowd." Surprisingly, his response is negative. "Let's see how it goes. Oddly enough, I like it here. This austerity will be good for you."

"Good for me?! This is the first austerity you've been exposed to in a year! I've had plenty of it on a constant basis. What about those hundreds of ants, lizards, cockroaches and birds invading our Singapore house? What about having to take three baths a day after perspiration has puddled every pair of shoes I own? What about sleeping on boards in China and sleeping in freezing tents in the Himalayas? What about having to eat fish eyes, rubbery duck feet, weeds and roots? How about living through a typhoid epidemic and a cholera epidemic? Have you forgotten how our hotel in Singapore caught on fire on New Year's Eve and how we had to run down seventeen double flights of stairs in our nightclothes and trench coats? And don't forget my having been attacked by armless, legless leper beggars in Bombay, who hung onto my skirt with their teeth."

"That's easy for you to say. You're the one who's soft. You sat in an air-conditioned office with a team of secretaries and expediters all year while I battled the equatorial heat, the bureaucracy, the Mandarin, Cantonese and Malay languages and endured the long lines in the markets for us, while I was working, too," I remind Jim.

I realize, ruefully, that I'm shouting, in response to Jim's baiting and that all the suppressed tensions and challenges we've successfully met over the past year have flooded over me in my fatigue. I'm acting like a soldier-returnee who has suddenly slipped into post-traumatic stress syndrome. Of course Asia is far, far more than these things about which I have just ranted. It is rich, endearing, exhilarating. But now I'm exhausted, have been raving at my beloved husband like a maniac and only want a simple clean bed and uninterrupted sleep for about three days. Jim and I never fight or argue, so I am mortified and humiliated at how I must have hurt him. Brain-numbing jet-lag overtakes me. It looks as if my desire for a long, long recuperative sleep may not be fulfilled for several days.

CHAPTER 17
FACE TO FACE WITH GOD

"Above all, develop Prema (Love). Love all religions and all nations. Recognize and accept all religions as paths leading men to the same destination. All of them teach love and compassion, humility and forbearance. I bless all of you and ask you to promote love, sympathy, and compassion toward all beings; God is present in every one of them; and it is your duty to revere God in each of them."
Sathya Sai Baba

Puttaparthi, South India
March 19, 1982

Upon awakening this morning, I remorsefully apologize for my ugly outburst last night and tell Jim of the dream I had a few days ago in the Marco Polo Hotel in Singapore.

"Jim, you know I love you and I'm mortified that I snapped at you last night and said such mean things. I was just exhausted and it wasn't so much about you at all. I find that my emotional issues are coming up and I feel overwhelmed. In a recent dream Sai Baba came to me and was talking to me. He said I'd face three tests. Spiritual tests. The first one was to come to Puttaparthi." Ruefully I continue, "I think the reason I got so angry last night is that the second test is to endure all these discomforts and stay the full week. Let's just hang in here together at the ashram and make the best of things. It should be fairly simple to find some tacks or nails in the ashram store to create window-screens with the cheesecloth we've brought for this purpose. Our outlook will probably improve after breakfast."

"By the way, you're not going to decide to stay here in India and become one of these Sai Baba devotees, are you? I mean, you don't think you'll be wanting to stay here forever, without me, do you?" Jim asks.

"Are you kidding?! Not a chance! Don't worry – I won't do anything strange or make any major decisions without checking with you first. As for India, I can't stand the dirt, poverty and bureaucracy. I can't imagine ever, ever living here. Let's go have breakfast," I suggest cheerily.

Breakfast in the canteen is an idly pancake with spicy sauce on it, rose milk, and a brown vegetarian gravy of some sort. Again today I sit on the side of the room with the Indian women and eat Indian style, rather than congregate with the Westerners across the room who are afraid to drink the water and eat the food. Since I'm here I might as well be here fully and overcome these stubborn resistances of the body. There are attractive flower bordered signs on the canteen wall that relay maxims by Sai Baba on the virtues of love, compassion, humility and forbearance. The line-up for darshan outside the clean white walls surrounding the Mandir is the same as yesterday. The person at the head of each line of waiting people is given a number, and a number is selected for the "lucky first line" to enter the courtyard and take a front row seat on the ground.

In the morning darshan we women sit in rows in the shadow of the Mandir, across from where we had sat yesterday afternoon in the sun. This is one of the most representative crowds of humanity I've ever seen. There are young to old, rich and poor, clergy and laity of most world religions. People are variously reading, writing in journals, or meditating while awaiting Sai Baba's arrival. In the ashram handbook I notice the five key principles that He says should govern all relations and activities: Truth (Sathya), Right Action (Dharma), Peace (Shanthi), Selfless Love (Prema) and Non-violence. Finally He comes around to our side of the building, from which we can't see the men. I am fortunate to sit in the first row. As He approaches I stiffen, ready for anything, for any acknowledgment of us. He serenely passes by, however, not even glancing in the direction of our section. He takes letters, blesses articles held up to Him, places vibhuti on the heads of babies, hears requests. *Illumine my intellect, oh Lord. Remove my ignorance.*

A few Westerners hold up hand-made cardboard signs saying "Interview, please" but He ignores them and their signs. Today He ignores the ill and crippled and surprises people who have asked nothing by stopping to give them an encouraging word or a bit of counsel. "You never know what He will do" whispers an Indian woman beside me. When He speaks it is with a high, raspy voice that is not at all unpleasant. Every face is riveted on His form. The expectancy is nearly visible, like a giant, outstretched, petitioning hand. He looks at several poor souls with a bit of a scowl. In a few moments He's gone. "If only He will grant me an interview, I'll be very happy," someone says. "Yes," says another, "I've come thousands of miles just to talk to Him."

A Central American woman beside me says "You know, we're not supposed to be so selfish as to desire an interview, but of course we all do! Only a saint wouldn't. I'm Maria de Castillo and this is my mother, Maria de Servent. We're here with my younger brother for about three weeks from El Salvador. Since our country is falling apart, we decided to come here. Our father and the rest of the family think we're crazy but we don't care. They don't believe in Baba but that's okay with us." The younger Maria is about 35, heavy, with a very short haircut that has recently come into vogue. Her ears are pierced with gold earrings and she wears jeans (forbidden at the ashram), a cotton shirt, and a shawl. Her mother is a chic red-head who seems to be about sixty. Her seventeen-year-old son Rick soon joins us and tells me he was a high school student in Lakewood, Colorado, last year. Maria the younger had lived in Houston for 9 years and is divorced with an infant daughter.

We make plans to meet for dinner at a house where more varied meals are served - warned that it is a small crowded room and that we will sit on the floor. I search for Jim at our appointed meeting place which is in the shade of a huge old tree in the outer courtyard beside the ashram bookstore. Strolling along the main street of the ashram we are joined by a tall, stunning redhead who resembles a grown-up Orphan Annie. Her hair is a curly globe, like Sai Baba's. Her eyes are blue in a pale face that is lightly freckled. She wears a tee shirt, sandals, and a cream cotton skirt with matching shawl. Jillian is a French fabric designer from Paris who has been here three weeks and "knows everybody." We accept her offer to take us up to the hilltop rock to Sai Baba's childhood wishing tree where as a boy He manifested candies, various fruits, and pencils for His friends.

As we amble along the dusty red road past the souvenir stalls and small huts of the village, Jillian tells us of her travels through India. "This is the best ashram," she confides. "The others cannot compare. I have been to all the main ones in India." She feels this encounter with Sai Baba has changed her life. She is, however, "angry," she confesses, as Sai Baba has ignored her cardboard signs requesting an interview. "He won't even glance at me. I am mad with Him," she pouts, in her heavy French accent, like a pretty child who is accustomed to getting everything she wants.

In the blazing heat of late morning we toil up the steps of the hill to rest and meditate at the base of the tree where a local man has made a shrine and asks us for money. "Do you see how these local people try to profit from Sai Baba?" Jillian asks. Below us the riverbed is a wide, sandy stretch bereft of any water. Three women have dug a hole in the dry river bed and are washing clothes in the water that has seeped into the depression. Green fields and whitewashed huts give the rural scene a peaceful quality in spite of the punishing temperature on the scorching rock. Once again I feel the sacred quality of the village touch me. How can this remote spot be on the same planet as jet planes and computers?

At the bhajan class held for Westerners after lunch, there is an announcement that foreigners are requested to refrain from "scampering about in the midday heat" as the doctor fears he may find their limp bodies strewn about the village like fallen trees, collapsed from heat stroke. "Please control your enthusiasm" we are told. "India's heat is severe and you won't realize the repercussions until it's too late."

Another ashram official says, jokingly, "Baba says that 'God madness is the least harmful of madnesses' but we still don't want any of you going mad from exercising imprudence in the heat of the ashram sun!"

We are also told by the official that we must be patient while waiting in the various lines each day for darshan, food, the bank and the post office. He says that the very experience of sitting for long hours is part of our learning experience here and that it is good for our spiritual development. It builds character and is called 'tapas' or penance, sacrifice, or spiritual endurance for a higher cause.

The afternoon's darshan confirms to me that I haven't been imagining the materializations. By now we have seen scores of such creations, flowing effortlessly from Him, in silence with no fanfare and no bid for applause or approval from the crowd. He is complete nonchalance. In fact, there is absolutely no pomp or swagger about this man. On the other hand, I cannot help but consider the ramifications of His essence and of His acts. Suppose He can be equated with Christ, Buddha, or Krishna. What does this mean for my life, my habits, my lifestyle? Is it necessary to change greatly? For sixteen years I have been searching, reading, meditating, serving, traveling, looking for Truth. Surely we have to make our own Truth, to exemplify Truth instead of looking to anyone to rescue us. Isn't Sai Baba's role to help us each to discover the inner Truth, love and peace for ourselves and to help us, by example, to lead a meaningful life of contribution to our times? There seems to be another important issue here too. The trick, in following the teachings of a compelling master is to not get yanked out of one's own orbit and made a satellite. Rather, it is to release the steady radiance of the God-star that resides in oneself - which resides in everyone - if he would know it. *Possess my awareness, Lord. Make me inseparable from You, abiding in God consciousness.*

Once again I meet Jim under the shady old tree of the outer courtyard and we compare our darshan experiences. He wears an expression I've never seen on him before, tranquil to the point of seeming a bit vacant. We both feel wonderful, even "floaty." We agree to stay a few more days. Someone later points out to us an American by the name of Don MacDowell, a retired Air Force officer, who was recently healed of a brain tumor by Baba. The man arrived in a wheel chair and, having been healed, is now pushing it about the ashram to use as a comfortable darshan seat. The stories of healings and miracles we have been hearing about are truly astounding. I feel as if I have known Sai Baba before, maybe even many times. Although the ashram austerities are very challenging, still I feel very at home with Sathya Sai. The devotees say that He is hilariously funny and that He loves to tease, to joke and to play, showing us that life is meant to be joyful.

Mother Mary, who started appearing to me two years ago, keeps saying, "Be joyful, Beloved Heart, be joyful! It is not necessary to be so serious and it profits you nothing." Someone told me today that Baba often says, "A smile costs less than electricity and gives more light." Sathya Sai has truly thousands of pithy sayings which have been written down by devotees the world over. There are dozens of books about Him and His mission as well as many books about the stories of how devotees have been drawn to Him. I wonder if I really will write a book about Him some day as Len Rodrigo and Jaya Rajamanikam seem to think.

March 20th

Last night I dreamed that far in the future Jim and I will somehow be in India long-term. Jim was wearing black business trousers and a white ashram kurta, or long shirt, and he had been given the job by Baba to walk behind Him in darshan collecting letters from the crowd. I was very surprised since usually only long-time devotees or VIPs are given such a grace as helping to collect letters in darshan. Was this symbolic of a future bit of grace or will we live in Asia again in the future and come to India periodically? Truly, I think this is my last trip to India. Sai Baba says you needn't travel to India to benefit from His love and grace. He can even heal long-distance. I have relinquished all need to have Him heal me. I'm merely thankful beyond measure that He is alive on the earth now. Knowing that gives me immeasurable consolation. Now that I have seen Him in darshan I can return to Colorado and see what else He has in store for me. I'm no longer opposed to being a devotee of a Guru. I see now that to be the devotee of a satguru is one of life's great privileges and that Baba works at long distance with everyone in the world, just as we have always thought God does. I understand that it is not irresponsible to bask in the glory of an Avatar and, that one's veils melt away in the radiant power of a true Master.

We line up for darshan in the chit lines and sit in straight rows in the sand. Some people read while others meditate and young mothers chase toddlers who run about the crowds. The seva dals, or ushers, try to make the children sit down before Sai Baba comes out. Finally He appears and glides along the pale orange sand on His exquisite bare feet with His graceful hands held up to bless the crowd. A slight breeze ruffles His bouffant hair for a moment.

My legs feel permanently paralyzed by the cross-legged position we've assumed for three hours a day. Sai Baba again blesses the crowd with an abundance of ash, smiles, advice, medallions, candy, lockets and other materialized gifts. However, I observe it all from a glaze of discomforts - sleepless nights on the concrete floor, itching mosquito bites on tortured limbs and salty perspiration running into my eyes as the sun beats down on our heads. In the back of my mind there is a numb dread of the thirty hour plane trip home yet ahead of us.

All of my hopes of the past three weeks have been focused on the objective of seeing Sai Baba. After this, what awaits us? We cannot return to old friends and the same harried lifestyle after this experience. The darshan is over and the crowd of women arise in a frenzied stampede, carrying me along to the back porch of the Mandir for bhajan singing. I sit near a low window of the Mandir porch but cannot see inside. As we sing I become more and more animated, clapping to the rhythm. Without warning I start to shake and begin sobbing uncontrollably in a strange happy release. I feel extremely embarrassed, not being one to display my emotions in public and can't seem to stop. A woman nearby senses my acute chagrin and pats me, saying "Those are tears of devotion. Bhakti tears. Don't worry, it's normal." An orange-clad nun, who is bald, and obviously a Westerner, jumps up and generously trades places with me so that I can sit directly in front of the window and see Sai Baba perfectly several yards away, sitting in His chair inside the dark interior of the Mandir. At that moment He turns His head and stares at me for a long time. Once again I start crying. Now everyone around me starts to giggle. We all smile and clap and sing and sigh. I can't believe I'm having such reactions.

After bhajans the nun, "Sathya," walks beside me and tells me of her former life in Walnut Creek, California, and in New York, where she started a yoga school before coming here two years ago. I promise to bring her some vitamins as she has lost several teeth and has been sick. I look into her sparkling green eyes and embrace her, feeling a deep love for her. Still I cry and shake my head at such bizarre feelings and behavior regarding Puttaparthi and Sai Baba. She tells me that I must have some particular work in store for me since so many coincidences have occurred in only three weeks. "You are very blessed, you know" she says, but I'm uncertain of her meaning.

March 21st

There's an old Indian saying that "Discipline follows a devotee like a shadow." Obviously Jim and I need more discipline than we had ever imagined to sit here in the heat on the ground for many hours and to stand in long lines for food and services. I understand the tapas involved and see how it makes strong character. Although only a few days ago I was complaining about the discomforts of the ashram, my point of view has changed. I not only don't mind the lack of comforts but I feel it is almost essential in order to adequately experience the simple, immediate, spiritual environs properly. I don't want to leave but think that if we don't leave soon we just might stay here forever. Lots of Westerners here came for a week, as we're doing and have stayed months or even years. Since being here I've thought of the statement by Thomas Jefferson, one of my heroes, which was that "He who knows best knows how little he knows." Even though I've been on the spiritual path for fourteen years, I'm keenly aware that there's an entirely new world of spiritual experience with which Sai can assist me. At last I've found the One Who can help me to overcome the vagaries of the mind.

It feels indescribably serene to be insulated from all traffic, pollution, noise, TV, radio, papers, newscasts, work, junk mail and telephones. It is indeed a compelling, spiritually charged atmosphere here - even holy. Of course we want to return to Puttaparthi within the year if not before. Jim keeps saying "Now don't get any funny ideas about wanting to live here. If you do, I'll come visit you once a year, but don't expect me to give up the world and stay here too!" We laugh together nervously at the thought that either of us might be seized with a desire to stay.

A highlight of the day, in the evening after darshans and the lecture, is that on Wednesdays and Sundays (today) there is vegetarian pizza at the bakery. We are overjoyed at this change of diet from the tasty gruels - but gruels none the less - served in the canteen. Many of the Westerners have a difficult time with the South Indian vegetarian fare, but to us it is exactly like the meals we had at the Komala Vilas Restaurant in

Singapore. The delicious pizza is made by an Italian devotee who moved here seven months ago.

March 22nd

It's Monday and tomorrow we must leave for Bangalore and Bombay. Our time at the ashram has passed too quickly. The darshans have been indescribably exquisite. I feel absolutely blissful and dread entering "the world" again. We pack amid heavy sighs and humming bhajans that we've learned today from Liz, the perky gray-haired American singing instructor. We have bathed all week with cold water from the little plastic bucket in our room and haven't minded. It has been like camping out, in fact. We've hung our clothes on a plastic line across the room, have used tablets to purify our water and taken anti-malaria pills, all without resistance. The simplicity of our cell feels purifying yet I long to get back to our simple independent ways in Colorado after the continual extremes and reversals of Asia. We plan to leave our cushions and mattresses behind for the poor. A little boy comes to the door and says his father needs a new shirt. I give him my orange kurta, which is brand new and has never been worn. From my tote bag I remove about eight jars of vitamins, all that remain, and put them aside for Sathya and her friend Om, the other nun in a tangerine robe.

Last night I had two dreams about Sai Baba. In the first one He is giving me some nectar and saying "Here, drink." In the second dream Sathya, the Buddhist nun, is crying happily for me. These dreams stay with me as we walk down the three flights of stairs to breakfast. It's our last day and the stay has been richly laden with surprises, new friends and an overwhelming feeling of well-being. I had always thought that the "bliss" supposedly experienced by various individuals after a stay at an ashram was purely imaginary, airy-fairy stuff. But it's an actual elixir of inner poise and peacefulness.

March 23rd

After breakfast in the canteen we join the darshan line for the last time, just as the lines are moving into the inner courtyard surrounding the Mandir. I sit with eyes closed, remembering all the bountiful aspects of the week and finally even relinquish my earlier desire to have an interview with Sai Baba. In an hour we will leave in Babu's cab. A persistent feeling causes me to open my eyes and I see Jim standing on the porch of the Mandir, searching the thousand faces on the women's side for me. He spots me in the crowd at the same time I see him and waves for me to come. "Come on, quick!" he calls in a stage whisper. "We have an interview now." A wave of excitement flutters through the group around me as it does anytime someone is called for an interview. Hastily I climb over the pressed rows of women and jog-trot to the porch, with my cushion and notepad.

There is a collection of about fifteen people on the porch, all strangers to me except for B.P. Yap, waiting patiently for Sai Baba to summon them inside. My heart beats madly. Standing next to Jim I can feel his excitement too. Our little group is smiling and expectant as Sai Baba threads His way through the crowd. He calls a Japanese man to find his wife. The man searches the crowd in vain, then Sai Baba chides him gently and says "You will not find her. She is still asleep in her room." The poor man loses his chance for an interview and the whole crowd groans for him. I blush with embarrassment at the recollection that I had considered staying in my room today also and would have missed this precious opportunity. (Baba does, however, see spouses alone at times.)

Sai Baba glides back up to the veranda and says "Come, come. I will see you now." The room is small, with pastel green walls and a cool bare concrete floor. Sai Baba moves to His orange, high-back chair and foot-stool and gestures for us to take a seat on the floor. I sit next to Jim and Sai Baba says, "No, no! Now you sir, must sit over here, and you, Madame, must sit with the ladies." He chuckles. "You in the West are always trying to mix everything up, even the seating." We all laugh, then make a "men's side" and a "women's side" in the cramped little room. From the courtyard we can hear the sweet strains of the harmonium punctuated with the jingle of finger cymbals and cherubic Indian singing. Glancing around to see who is with us, I notice a family of about eight Indians, a young couple with their children and their aging parents. Uncle Kumarasamy, a key founder of the Sai movement in Singapore and much beloved devotee, is with the Indians. Sai Baba looks at the young Indian woman and at me and says to both of us, "Take this vibhuti and eat it." He then rolls His sleeves up to His biceps and swirls His hand. He shows us there's nothing up His sleeve but His arm. Out of thin air the ash appears and He swiftly turns His palm over to catch it and drops some into each of our upturned palms. The woman and I eat the ash in front of the others; it is pale and fine, like talcum and smells light and sweet. I suddenly realize He must have heard me say I'd like to look up His sleeves sometime, when I was back in Singapore three weeks ago. That means He not only reads minds long distance, He has a great memory, too!

I lick the remaining ash from my hands, hoping it's not caked all over my face. The older Indians begin to cry now, as a woman among them is ill and Sai Baba ushers them through a curtain into a small back room. We hear Him soothing them and then speaking very sternly, then softly.

There are six of us remaining in the outer room: Jim, B.P. Yap, my-self, an Australian man who tells us he is the head of a telecommunications section for a city in Australia, a male Dutch student, and an American fellow who is a physics professor. Jim seizes this opportunity to quickly tell me how we were called for the interview. "B.P. and I concluded that Baba was only taking groups for interviews, instead of individuals, so we formed "an international group" when we were in line outside," he explains. "We were sitting in the back row, but Sai Baba walked up in front of us and said 'Someone is leaving today.

Who is it?' " Jim chuckles and says, "I waved, and Sai Baba asked how many were in our group. I said 'This is our group, and I'll get my wife.' That's how we got the interview," he says, delighted with the serendipitous turn of events.

The Indian family comes through the curtain, all smiles now, thanking Sai Baba.

Sai turns to me and says that when people first come to Sai, especially Westerners, they are only interested in getting things.

"This Avatar moves a devotee from a position of 'getting and forgetting' (selfishness) to 'giving and forgiving' (service)."

He seemed to be sending me telepathic messages about the role of women and I began to remember all of the talks and workshops which I had presented on women's rights, minority rights and children's rights. I recalled my championing of justice for blacks and Hispanics and the book I had written with Marilyn Auer, *The Colorado Women's Resource Book*, a compilation of services for women and minorities. As I recalled the years of service to uplift women He suddenly startled me by saying, "You have been angry because of mistreatment by men in your life. I will heal that. Also, you have misunderstood the proper role of women in society." *Oh no, Sai Baba, now that I've found you and believe You're God, You're not a chauvinist, are You?!*

As I prayed this silent prayer-question I held my breath, hoping that He wasn't going to advocate that women revert back to subservient roles as mere chattel when we had worked so hard during this entire century to give women dignity, self-respect and confidence.

"You see, woman's role is a sacred one. She is here to uphold the lamp of spirituality in the home, the workplace and the community. She is the sacred flame of Love. All people are Atma but woman has this sacred function."

He says He will now give a few things to some of our group and turns to B.P. Yap and asks, "Are you a Christian or a Buddhist?" B.P. stammers a moment. "Oh! I was born a Buddhist, now my family are Christians, but I follow you, Baba." Sai Baba is teasing B.P. but B.P. doesn't yet realize it and is quite serious.

Do you pray to Jesus or to Me?" He asks. Without waiting for an answer He says "Never mind. I will make you a picture of Jesus." He swirls His hand in the air, sleeve rolled up, and materializes a ring which resembles scrimshaw in a silver setting. A picture of Christ is etched into the bone-colored background. Sai Baba starts to hand it to B.P. and stops. "Oh you," He jests. "I have just made this nice ring for you and now you are thinking, 'What if the ring Baba has made for me doesn't fit!' " Immediately B.P. colors and laughs that it's true. He had been thinking just that. We all smile and watch as Sai Baba puts the ring on B.P.'s finger. "Of course it fits perfectly. Everything Sai Baba makes fits."

Next He turns to the Australian and says "I'll make you a medal but not the chain because you are already wearing a chain." Astonished, the man opens his shirt and reveals a silver chain. Sai Baba repeats His materialization gesture, produces a medal with a picture of Himself on it, and hands it to the man. "Don't worry, it will fit the chain" He laughs. It does.

He gets up from His chair and asks our group to follow Him into the inner room, behind the curtain. It is a simple bare room like the first except for Sai Baba's chair. We sit on the floor in front of Him. He looks at me and begins His teaching. "You in the West need to remember to start the day with love, fill the day with love, and to end the day with love. Also, do not be dazzled with these gifts I have created for my devotees. They are not important; I only create them to forge a link between My followers and Me. The gifts are mere tinsel and trash. The only significance of a diamond is its symbol of spiritual light. (How does He know about my interest in the origin of Len and Indra Devi's diamond rings?) Remember this: SEE the light and BE the light."

Including Jim, He says, "You both must learn to do even more giving and forgiving and less getting and forgetting. This is the lesson of the Western world. People are so misguided in the West. Everyone on earth has the divine aspect; the only difference between Me and others is that I know that I am God and others may not yet know that they too are God."

He admonishes Jim to keep up regular meditation and spiritual practice and next He turns to the Dutch and Australian men, both of whom inquire about bringing their girl friends to India. He tells both of them that the women they have selected are not correct for them and that they must stay at the ashram awhile and develop more discipline. There are other women who are more spiritually mature whom they'll be meeting. Then they will see that He is right. They are disappointed. He tells the American professor to think for himself and to make up his own mind about his career. "It doesn't matter whether you stay here or leave," Sai Baba says. "I am leaving soon to go to Brindavan."

"May I go with you? I'd like to stay by your side" the professor says ardently. Sai Baba sees he is in earnest and says that He will arrange for the American to follow Him to Brindavan. Jim asks Sai Baba how my impending brain surgery will turn out. Sai Baba pats him on the shoulder and says "There will be no brain surgery." Then He announces that the interview is over and shows us out into the sunshine, where His followers still sit, singing bhajans.

Briefly, I recalled the many things I had wanted to ask Him, before I found Him:

1. Does free will exist?
2. Is there a uniform experience of Self-realization?
3. Are there different levels and gradations of samadhi?

4. Do we select our life lessons between lives or does the I AM Presence do it, or both?

But my questions have fallen away in the Presence of God and I feel deep peace and gratitude in their place.

The cab is loaded and ready. We have a new fellow passenger, Paolo, an Italian airline pilot for Alitalia. We discover that Babu is fluent in self-taught Italian as he converses with Paolo. (Of the six languages I have studied, Italian and French were my best. They have now evaporated, though, from lack of use.) Paolo tells us that when he first heard about Sai Baba in Rome a few weeks ago, he rearranged his whole schedule to make Puttaparthi his first priority. We mention that we have done the same thing. "How will I ever explain this experience to my family and my friends?" he laments. "It's so fantastic, really. Too crazy to believe. If this were not me, I wouldn't even believe it myself." We laugh and tell him we know the feeling and were just wondering some of those same things. Then we tell him about the interview, my dreams and visions and about the brain tumor and Sai's materializations."

"My God, how lucky you people are to be picked from a crowd of two thousand. At some seasons of the year there are more than a hundred thousand here. In Bombay the crowds approach a million. And to think that some people have been waiting daily for months for an interview and you get one in the last hour of your week's visit. Unbelievable. You must have something very special waiting for you to do in your life since you have received such a gift."

Why do people keep saying that? As the cab pulls away from the ashram apartment, an American woman, young and red-headed, dashes over breathlessly and knocks on the car window.

"What country are you from?" she asks.

"The U.S.," I answer.

"Good! Then this is for you! Don, an American here, asked me to be sure to give this piece of paper to you." She thrust a rumpled, sweaty piece of folded paper into my palm, waved, shouted "Sai Ram!" and was gone.

When I opened the folded note it said, mysteriously, without greeting or signature, "This is the address and phone number of the Littleton, Colorado, Sai Baba Center." Jim and I laughed and shook our heads at Sai Baba's wondrous ways. Before we left Colorado to spend a year in Singapore, we had never heard of Sai Baba or of a local Sai Baba Center. When I first saw His photo on the hotel desk in Aurangabad in 1979, on our honeymoon, I had no idea that He was the One for whom I would spend a year searching throughout Asia. When, in 1981, I saw His photo on book covers at the Book Fair, I felt He couldn't be the One I sought because God would probably look like Jesus or Moses!

Now Baba has drawn us to Him in His own Divine timing and has showered us with His love, has healed me, has proven His Omnipresence and Omnipotence and has captivated us fully with His tenderness and compassion for all beings. Who could have guessed that our Beloved Lord would be so very fun, whimsical, loving, adorable, inscrutable and yet, wholly approachable?

We happily settle into the back seat for the long ride over the familiar bumpy roads, completely unaffected by the dust and the heat. New meaning comes to us now in the expression that heaven is in consciousness, not place or form. Now that I have been to India three times, it's not so bad. In fact, in several years I'd like to return, but not before I implement Baba's directives.

CHAPTER 18
SHED SHOCK

"There is nothing like silence to still the restlessness of the heart."
Sathya Sai Baba, TOSSSB P 128

Littleton, Colorado
April, 1982

Immediately upon our return home from Asia to our beloved Colorado, we noticed changes in ourselves. But before realizing that we had changed, we reveled in the peace and quiet of our suburban neighborhood. After living in Singapore, one of the most populous areas on earth, it was a relief to be back in the dry, clear air of our fair state. We never tire of the view of the Rocky Mountains in the distance as we walk out the front door, nor the fragrance of Austrian pines and Russian olive trees in the back yard. It was comforting to us to once again revel in the vast sky-scapes of puffy, scumbled cumulous clouds, the wide, unobstructed views of the plains, and the smell of ponderosa pine, spring lilac and forsythia blossoms and mountain wildflowers dappling sunny meadows. We gave thanks for the chilly lakes and rippling streams, the rushing waterfalls and the fertile farmland with its crops of alfalfa, corn, barley and sugar beets.

I have noticed that everywhere I look – whether at trees, shrubs, people or animals – that everything has a golden glow around it, like a soft halo that suffuses the landscape and overlays it with a soft yellow light. I feel so blissful that it is hard to get into gear in my work. I sit and stare for hours with a big smile on my face. The fact that Baba is now in our lives is a delicious secret that buoys us continuously. Very few people, we find, are interested in the fact that the Avatar is on the earth now. Baba says that it's not time yet for the world to know about Him. He will decide when to announce His Presence on the planet.

Baba has begun to appear beside my bed at 3:00 A.M. and has told me many things. He says that "He is going to make a healer, a teacher and a leader out of me. First, though, there will be lots of purification of the body and the mind. He is activating the light body and says I must stop eating chicken and eggs as in the U.S. they are filthy. Also, I must drink eight or more glasses of water a day."

Baba also gave Jim a "snoring healing" in response to my prayers, since Jim's snoring was so loud it threatened to bring down the rafters. Now we can both sleep peacefully. I intend to begin management consulting again soon.

Littleton, Colorado
October 31, 1982

We have just learned that Swami Mukthananda has left his body. Apparently his successor will be a very young woman in her twenties, who is Self-realized. Mukthananda didn't look well when we saw him in

Oakland, for our first and only darshan, about a year and a half ago. I have a feeling that his successor will prove to be very popular and helpful to people, though she is young. There may be some initial resistance to her until she "proves herself" as a worthy spiritual master. It's about time that we have Realized women being given the opportunity to serve and to lead. Oh, how the earth needs the nurturing, feminine/mother energy for its healing and restoration! I am thankful beyond words that Sathya Sai Baba is my Satguru, my Father-Mother, my Lord.

Littleton, Colorado
May, 1983

Baba has been giving me many dreams, has appeared many times in our house and He's given us vibhuti on photos. I've read nearly everything in English about Baba and am implementing His teachings in all aspects of life – otherwise, what's the use of reading His teachings?

Jim and I have become active in the local Sai Center and we're doing a variety of service projects. We had only been back in the States a short while, and had only attended the local Littleton Sai Center for a few months when a very odd and funny thing happened. Baba continued to appear beside my bed about 3:00 A.M. Mary, Jesus and Archangel Michael also began coming more frequently. Finally, one morning Baba tapped me on the shoulder and I awakened, startled. I thought Jim had tapped me but he was still sleeping.

Baba tapped me on the shoulder again. As I rolled over, I saw Him standing, smiling, beside the bed.

"Oh, hello Baba, what are You doing here?" I asked sleepily.

"I've come to ask you something," He replied sweetly.

"Of course, ask me anything, just anything," I answered. "What can I do for You?"

"I want you to assume the presidency of the Littleton Sai Center," He replied.

"What?! You want me to do what?! That's impossible, Baba. First of all, the members are practically all Indian. Secondly, the whole format is too foreign for me to know what to do or how to lead them. Those people are very strong-willed. Thirdly, they won't even let us sing any of the songs and make us sit in the back of the room, lip-syncing the songs! How will we ever learn that way? And fourthly, Vic Sharma, the doctor who is the president, as You well know, would never in a million years accept a non-Indian, AND a woman, AND a brand new devotee to preside over the Indians. He'd think I was on a power trip and would never believe that You are actually coming to me like this, especially since You're not appearing at 3:00 in the morning to any of them – or at least they haven't said so. There, I've given You all the reasons why it's impossible. Thank You for coming." I waved good night and turned over, hoping that would be the end of such a request.

The next night, at 3:00 A.M., Baba came again and tapped me on the shoulder, awakening me from a sound sleep.

"I've come to ask you the same question," He said sweetly.

"Now Baba, I've told You the four reasons that it simply wouldn't work. They'd never accept me as the Sai Center president. Besides, those Sanskrit words are very long and complicated and I know virtually nothing about Hindu culture. I've only been to India three times," I said, flustered, grasping at straws.

"Sai Centers are supposed to reflect the culture of the country where they are," Baba said patiently. "You don't need to know Sanskrit to be a good center president. I know who is the best person to serve. You would do a good job. Besides, I will tell the same thing to Vic that I'm telling you. Please say that you will do the job."

"But Baba, I wouldn't be very good at being a Sai president when I'm a brand new devotee," I pleaded.

"I'll be the judge of that. Your current life experience is but a small fraction of your overall skills, abilities and experience," Baba countered.

"Surely there must be other people who would be much better at the job," I whined.

"I've made my selection," Baba said, then disappeared.

Finally, on the third night, when Baba came again, I was ready for Him.

"You're just going to continue coming until I give in, aren't You, Baba?" I volleyed, before He could ask me the same question.

He laughed and smiled genially, waiting for my answer.

"Oh alright. I can see that saying 'yes' is the only way I'm going to get some sleep! But I'll only do it on one condition: You have to help me every step of the way. I'm quite certain that I don't know what I'm doing in that realm."

"Of course I'll help you. You couldn't do that or any job without my help, nor could anyone. Don't worry, I've told Vic what I would like three times, just as I have told you. Make your announcement next week at the Sai meeting."

After weekly bhajans, before I could make my announcement that Baba had asked me, three nights in a row, to accept the office of Sai Center president, Vic made a similar announcement, through tears. Baba had asked him, three times, to step down as president. Vic resisted, just as I had, and didn't want to relinquish his post. Then Vic said that Baba had told him to accept the leadership of a surprising person.

"It's her, it's Connie Shaw. Baba said she should step up and lead us and that we should all help her. Finally, I told Him that I would support her but that I didn't want to do so."

At Vic's announcement, I then shared what Baba had said to me. The group members were dumb-founded. After the shock had set in, they graciously agreed to support me and to educate me about the functioning of Sai Centers in general. This recent turn of events has to be one of life's great surprises for me. There's no doubt that I'll learn a lot.

Littleton, Colorado
June, 1984

Most of the people in the Sai Center were transferred out of town so we have moved the Sai Center to our house on Dover Street. Two new people who came to the Sai Center meeting at our house had healings of addictions by Baba. A man had been a drug addict (pot) for thirty years and had just completed ninety days of attending Twelve Step meetings – ninety meetings in ninety days. He sang and meditated with us – "us" being about nine people. As I opened my eyes after the silent meditation, I saw that there was something like talcum powder all over his hands. I bent over to get a closer look and nearly fell off my chair when I realized that it was Baba's fragrant vibhuti ash!

A woman who had been a chain smoker for thirty years came to one meeting. She spoke to Baba on the way home. She heard Him tell her to throw away all of her cigarettes and smoking paraphernalia, which she did. Her mouth filled up immediately with the taste and scent of vibhuti and she was healed of her tobacco addiction.

Jim and I have attended many Sai functions and now we're involved in many service projects. We're tutoring Chinese people in reading, writing, speaking and spelling English through the Laubach Literacy Program. Also, we volunteer at a nursing home where we sing, do manicures, write letters and play games with the residents.

When we first started the nursing home project, the residents wore pajamas, didn't know their names or what day it was. Now they are dressed in dresses and earrings and like to chat and to interact. Angie plays the piano and we sing old-fashioned songs that the residents enjoy.

One sad bit of news from David Hock, our American friend from Singapore, was that our beloved friend Tati Shariff, his girlfriend, died from the head injury she sustained on one of the boat trips in the South China Sea when she fell off and hit her head on a rock. She kept telling us she had headaches and she obviously had a closed head injury which went undetected by doctors.

A few months after the accident she was found dead in the shower with the water running. We were all grief-stricken; Tati was beautiful, smart, lively and humble. She was only in her late twenties. I wonder what she is doing on the Other Side and if she sees us and what we are doing.

Bangalore, India
October 28, 1985

Our first serendipitous trip to Prashanti Nilayam was the conclusion of a long search, and grew out of ardent longing mixed with keen curiosity. This second one, after three years away, is to obtain fresh inspiration and instruction for spiritual progress and a deepening in life of the Spirit. I told Baba in my prayers that I'd not return to India until I had implemented His teachings thoroughly and had taken seriously His advice to us in the first interview.

Just as Sai Baba predicted, there was no brain operation, nor were there any further headaches. I was completely healed. Since returning to the States, Jim and I have spent a brief amount of time in Israel, have changed our diet to a quasi-vegetarian one, have relinquished lots of weight and many old habits. Though we still travel extensively, our life-style is much quieter and we feel more aware than ever, but realize that we are just now embarking on a brand new journey into the invisible realm which has fewer signs and milestones than the exterior paths we've previously taken. *There's a great deal of both inner and outer work to be done. My heart thirsts for You, Lord. Purify me, sanctify me. Burn up my dross.*

From the Woodlands Hotel we arrange with Althaf, of Babu's cab company, to take us the three-hour ride to Puttaparthi. When we were here in March of 1982, it was 105 degrees at Puttaparthi but now in Bangalore it is surprisingly cool - about seventy degrees. Bangalore is pretty in its way with shaded streets and flowering shrubs, though it, like most of India, is fiercely crowded. That always comes as a shock to me, to re-experience the density of the throngs each time I come here. By now, my fourth trip to India, I relish Bharat (India) and find my heart beating faster as we drive toward Puttaparthi. Last night on the phone the hotel desk operator told us that Sai Baba is, indeed, at Prashanti Nilayam now. We are filled with relief that He is there, rather than in another city far away.

Out on the country road we see oxen pulling covered carts and wagons alongside vendors hawking coconuts, apples and sugarcane juice. Large billboards announce the upcoming concert appearances of the American musician, Maynard Ferguson. Graceful women glide along the roadside carrying jugs and baskets on their heads, oblivious of the several head-on collisions we pass where police have removed the injured and have left the crumpled trucks, buses and cars locked together until they can be pried apart and towed away.

Two immediate impressions have struck me so far about this part of India. One, we were not met with the usual extortionist airport officials nor asked for any bribes of liquor or cigarettes as on all past trips. Apparently Rajiv Gandhi, the vibrant new leader of India, is really having success at cleaning up the corruption in officialdom. The second impression is that the circumstances of the local people here in South India have vastly improved over three years ago. There is an active stone quarry which is supplying stone to replace the mud and grass huts that were the usual housing materials. There are new wells, schools, roads, shrines, temples and community halls to be seen as well.

The road to Puttaparthi, which has taken over fifteen years to build, is nearly complete. That means that the incredibly bumpy, dusty, arduous trip is now only mildly dusty and moderately jangly. Of course the driver,

Althaf, still drives, as is the custom, hell-bent for self-destruction in the middle of the road while leaning on the horn all the way, like a Kamikaze pilot on a sacrifice mission who is about to end his short life in some sort of ecstatic frontal smash-up to permanent Nirvana. My knuckles are yellow-white and I stare at the floor during a great part of the trip to preserve both my sanity and my lunch. Althaf is a sweet man, however, and is devoted to his Beloved, as well as being very conscientious about his work.

During a calm moment of neither blaring horn nor oncoming vehicles I peek up ahead and catch a glimpse of a gray monkey loping across the road with a fistful of grapes from a neighboring farmer's arbor. Our brief coffee stop at Chickballapur reveals further prosperity in the health, dress, and possessions of the people. There's even a new billboard advertising Trot shoes - "like walking on air." Further on, the landscape shimmers with a lushness that wasn't evident in the dry season of our first ashram visit. My feelings of "being home" startle me, especially in light of the fact that my initial reaction to India on the first trip was one of aversion - that passed within the first day, however.

Puttaparthi, India
October 28th

The most amazing changes have occurred at Prashanti Nilayam. The main street of town is being paved and there are pretty pastel cottages and apartments in the place of old thatched shacks and mud huts. Everyone is better dressed, both in town and at the ashram itself. Prashanti Nilayam is bustling with "sixtieth birthday preparations" for the upcoming November 23rd celebration and the World Council meetings the week before.

At the Accommodations Office we are told that not only has my letter not been opened along with thousands of others that have swamped the workers, but that there are no rooms whatsoever left.

"The only thing I can tell you, Madame, is that unless you want to turn around and return immediately to the U.S. you can walk up the hill to Hall 27 and ask the foreigners there if they can squeeze their sleeping mats closer together and make room for you and your husband. That's Hall 27. It accommodates 200 people and there are other Westerners there that you can speak with about this.

We knew before we came that this might be the case and still we have come. Since hope springs eternal in the human breast, I'm optimistic that there will be room and there is... in a manner of speaking. Very broadly speaking to be exact.

Fran Earley of Tasmania and her friend Sue of Australia offer to reduce their space so that we can make a three by five foot spot for our luggage and upper bodies while we sleep. Our knees and legs stick out into the narrow aisle. We're very appreciative of their generosity and feel chagrinned that all during the night people have to step over our legs to walk outside to the community showers and bathrooms. There are colorful sheets and bedspreads hanging everywhere from ropes and clotheslines tied to the ceiling's open steel rafters. It looks like a refugee camp in here and reminds me that millions of people all over the world live like this every day. It's a good experience and I'm glad we're staying here instead of in a room so that we can help the others and do whatever is needed. Can this be me saying this? I've really changed since the last visit when I was so horrified that the room was unfurnished! Now such a room would seem like the Hilton yet this should be lots more fun - more like camping with two hundred like-minded friends.

October 29th

We've been offered the "room" of a Swedish couple across the corridor here in Shed 27 when they leave tomorrow. What a welcome surprise! It's a heavenly room. The four-foot-high walls consist of white sheets that match and provide enough privacy to undress while crouching down. Instead of a space that's three feet by four feet, we'll have a spot that is about seven feet by seven feet. The current occupants are even donating their straw floor mats to us along with their cooking equipment, some bottled water, matches, fruit and clothespins. The precious items here are clothespins, air mattresses, safety pins, shampoo and cream rinse, cough drops, hats and scarves, cups, buckets, soap and toilet paper.

I brought extra hand cream and toiletries which I've given away to those who've been so kind to us. Before we leave I plan to give away absolutely everything I can to those who are staying on since it makes such a difference to them in this remote spot.

This morning an American woman named Rose strolled over and told us the secret of "making a house in the shed."

"You're lucky that you inherited a ready-made room," she said. "When I came I had to figure it out for myself. But it's easy. Here's what you do — just think of it as five easy steps.

How to Make a Private Room in a Shed

First, find four large flattish rocks outside about the size of a football. Take your rope or parachute cord and tie it around the first rock firmly.

Next, you swing it around and around your head, after first checking to ensure that no one is standing nearby. You wouldn't want to knock one of your devotee neighbors unconscious while swinging your rock! You aim for the horizontal metal beams overhead and just toss the rock over the beam and bring it down to the floor. It may take several tries until you develop your aim. Pretty soon you'll get the hang of it and you'll really enjoy the process.

You do this four times because each vertical rope becomes one of the four vital pillars of your new house or room.

Next, you tie horizontal ropes between the four vertical ones and then attach sheets or bedspreads to the horizontal ropes with clothespins or safety pins. Be sure to tie the horizontal ropes high enough so that tall people can't see you undressing and low enough so that the bedspreads reach the floor in order to keep stray dogs and curious kids from walking under your "walls" into your room.

Finally, you come to the fun part: decorating. You can make a small altar on top of a cardboard box, if you can find one, or on a little-used suitcase. You just add candles, Sai pictures, a grass mat, a few cots and bedding, and a darshan cushion. Voila – home sweet home.

"It's easy and fun and you'll find that you'll grow to love the sheds. Even though they refer to them in the administration office as "halls" or "dorms" they're still sheds. But, hey, when you're at God's house you can put up with anything, right? Besides, Baba says that He puts Westerners, especially, in sheds so that we can experience the way that the majority of people in the world live every day. We don't realize how soft we have it, in the States, especially. Just let me know if there's anything I can do for you while you're here. I've been coming for ten years now and I'm used to it. See you later."

With a smile and a wave Rose was off to cut vegetables in the canteen.

At the orientation session this morning we were told that the daily schedule will be very full and that it's best to be organized for the day upon arising so as not to waste time. Since the two hundred people in our shed will all be sharing the dozen cold-water showers and toilets each morning I plan to take the load off the lines by getting up at 5:00 A.M. to shower, dress, re-pack in our tiny cubicle and proceed to the canteen for breakfast. There are daily lectures and discourses, bhajan practice for foreigners who want or need to learn new songs, and darshan and bhajans twice each per day. The schedule, roughly is:

5:00 Arise and take cold shower from waist-high spigot by flashlight or candlelight.

5:30 Dress, unpack needed items from suitcases; re-pack nightclothes and laundry; move air mattresses; conserve space in the cubicle.

6:00 Walk down the hill to the canteen as soon as it is daylight.

6:10 Stand in line for Indian breakfast of rice, sauces, pancakes, coffee.

6:30 Take trays to canteen sinks; wash cups, plates, spoons.

6:45 Sit cross-legged in the darshan line with a few thousand women for about an hour and a half while meditating or writing in journal.

8:00 - 8:30 Sai Baba usually comes out for about 15 minutes to give darshan. He manifests vibhuti, heals, accepts letters, offers guidance, accepts interview requests.

9:00 Bhajans for half an hour.

10:00 Lectures by Al Drucker, Professor Kasturi, Dr. John Hislop or Rao.

11:30 Lunch (same as breakfast: stand in line, wash dishes one has used).

12:00 Wash clothing; shampoo; browse in bookstore; buy supplies.

1:00 Bhajan practice and review of previous day's songs and new Sanskrit words.

2:00 Rest or read in light clothes due to midday heat.

3:00 Change clothes again for darshan clothes (white) and re-pack and reorganize the cubicle to save space for sitting and walking (about a foot wide by five feet long - the "aisle" area).

4:00 Walk down the hill to darshan and sit in line for sixty to ninety minutes.

5:00 Baba comes out for afternoon darshan which can extend to 5:45 sunset.

6:00 Bhajans while the air cools sharply and the moon comes up. Sometimes Sai Baba comes out and gives a third darshan at this time.

7:00 Lecture.

8:00 Dinner line at the canteen.

9:00 Lights out.

9:15 Snoring starts in Hall 27.

9:30 All are exhausted and fall sound asleep.

Shed 27, Prashanti Nilayam
October 30th

This is hilarious - two hundred people from all over the world packed together in the most intimate of circumstances. And there are frogs in the toilets. Yes, frogs. They are about the size of plums, are wart-covered and greenish-brown in color. Like everyone else who discovers them, I was quietly sitting in one of the six or eight stalls when I suddenly felt something bump against me. Imagine the shock. I shrieked and jumped up, looking into the clear water of the toilet bowl to behold two green-brown frogs hopping about in fright. Again I shrieked at the unexpected sight. Then I ran out of the stall and ran back into the stall. By this time the two frogs were watching me from their new perch on the toilet seat, onto which they had jumped, so I shrieked again and ran into the next stall, checking on-the-run to insure that the next bowl in that compartment was frog-free.

Several times today we have all seen new arrivals quickly head for the bathroom before anyone could warn them. After a few moments we've heard shrieking and the sound of the bathroom door slamming. Since we've all been through this little initiation, it is no mystery. Those who are standing about in the large hall simply look at each other knowingly and chant in unison, "Frogs." We've petitioned the several young boys in the shed to try catching the frogs but they've reported that there are scores of frogs in the area and that once caught, others jump into the toilet bowls since water is scarce and the bathroom is a fairly dark and cool habitat for them.

There are also bats in the "belfry" or rafters of the open-beamed hall. They fly in at night and vie with birds for space to perch or to hang. Neighborhood dogs also attempt to run past the seva dals guarding the shed door to investigate the hall for unprotected snacks left on mattresses or beds inside.

Here in the sheds, as well as in the rest of the ashram, the water and the electricity keep going off a few times a week, at least. Naturally, this means we can't bathe, flush the toilets or shampoo our hair. Yesterday I heard someone in a nearby cubicle say, "God – it's hot. And my hair is so dirty that if it rains, I'm going to have a mudslide!"

We are all having to learn to not mind undressing while crouched down in our makeshift ceilingless bedspread-walled "rooms" while moving adroitly enough so as not to touch the cloth sides of the cubicle and risk knocking the whole delicate contraption down. This sort of accident would not only be a nuisance and a great social blunder to all of one's neighbors but would also immediately expose people napping on their sleeping mats, in the afternoon heat, in their underwear.

Since none of the improvised tents have tops on them you never know when company will come knocking at your tent flap to make an announcement, offer laundry service or to borrow something. Usually the women call ahead to ask if it's convenient to stop in but the men are so tall (Americans and Europeans, that is) that they just lean down and start a neighborly conversation. So far the tent has fallen down once while I had one arm through my shirt and one leg about to step into my slacks. A bedspread immediately became an improvised poncho until we could reassemble all the ropes and lines to the ceiling supports.

Today was the prize-winner. I was fresh from a cold-water shampoo in the shower, sitting in my undies on the air mattress, wrapped in a towel, combing my sopping wet hair. Suddenly the entire cubicle started to move sideways. Then, as some unseen hand jerked the far end of our interconnected bedspread-room contraption, all the connected cubicles in our row flew up in the air. A second later the fabric walls which had jerked four feet up in the air, moved sideways, flew over my head and came back down. What had been our neighbor's bedspread walls now partly surrounded our cot and luggage. Meanwhile, still wrapped in my towel with soaking wet hair, I was left sitting in what had become a new open aisle. Parisian Leonore and her small son Carlo came running to see what had happened.

"Oh, it is too funny!" she laughed. "Quick, Connie, you can hide in our room until we get this rearranged." Everyone else thought this episode was far funnier than I did at the time, since I was the object of the cosmic joke. Eventually we were able to tug on the ropes and to recover our own bedspread walls. However it's apparent that with so many people coming and going that we will need to warn and train the newcomers not to yank on our delicately-assembled spider-web of ropes. Also, we need some sort of leadership and a communication system.

Because of the fact that new people are arriving constantly we keep making the cubicles smaller each day to accommodate them. Despite the crowding though, there is tremendous cooperation and high spirits since we have all come from our various countries to have the darshan of our Beloved Lord.

October 31st

After three days here I've finally recovered from the worst of the jet lag, heat and crowding and feel happy and energetic whereas the first few days seemed rather dream-like, especially seeing Sai Baba again. My luck in the ground seating in the Mandir courtyard has been extraordinary in that nearly every darshan I've been in front of the Mandir door in the first, second or third rows. Today there were over 3,000 women packed in rows on the sand and in tight lines on the two new verandas at the edge of the yard. Women still sweep the sand to a virgin smoothness after each darshan and bhajan session. They place lovely fresh flower petal rangoli designs in front of doorways throughout the ashram.

So far Sai Baba has stopped right in front of me in the line and stood looking at me twice. Once He even turned around and stood and looked. Three times this week I have coincidentally been walking along one of the ashram roads when He has come right beside me in the car. What great luck this has been. It took all the restraint I had to keep from doing what I would normally do to acknowledge a welcome and surprise visit from a good friend: wave enthusiastically and greet the person with hearty voice. Thus, He's graced us with darshan and car darshan, or 'carshan,' as I call it.

Here, upon suddenly encountering Baba on the street, the people immediately stop, press hands together in the prayer-like Namaste fashion and gaze at Him with propriety in silence. We Westerners, even the most sensitive of us, need to work on propriety, as Americans have been repeatedly told in the newcomers' orientation lectures. We talk too much, waste too much energy dashing all over the ashram and we're not sensitive enough to the Indian culture and refinements of dress as far as what we rig up in the way of costuming.

Since Americans, especially, don't wear floor-length dresses or loose long shirts and baggy pants for everyday wear, we have had to either have more modest clothes made in town or purchase a close approximation. "Just because there's a lot of sand here doesn't mean this is the beach!" we've been told. Beach costumes won't do if they're skimpy little wraps or too short. (If the outfit is above the ankles it's too short. Period.) Jim and I were prepared by our last trip. Though some people feel the rules are strict, such regulations do help provide a serene atmosphere and keep order and maintain modesty among the burgeoning throngs.

Today there was a clash in Shed 27 between our appointed leader, a man named Adrian, and an Italian woman, Theresa or Resi for short. So many have lived in these conditions for six to eight weeks that they're wearing down, I think, from the cold showers, long food lines, snoring, crowding, Indian vegetarian diets and rigorous routine.

It was in the heat of naptime that tall Indian Adrian from Britain informed Resi that he had been elected by the committee to take responsibility for the needs of the Hall 27 occupants. It seems, Adrian told her sharply, that an Indian man, one of the loudest snorers, had had his leg yanked in the night by a weary, desperate person, apparently. Since Resi had repeatedly complained about the snorers the man accused her of having pulled and twisted his leg. She was outraged at being falsely accused. Adrian became defensive and told her she wasn't cooperating since she wasn't owning up to it.

She got furious and said she wasn't the sort of person who crawled along the floor in the dead of night to yank the leg of a stranger, even if he was noisy and disruptive of everyone's sleep. (The man, in fact, emitted amazing snorfling and snorting sounds combined with little strangulated inhalations that would have provided wonderful sound effects for a cartoon film of a snoring bear!) Adrian pointed out that snoring people simply can't help their affliction. We must have compassion for them and use earplugs if we have brought them.

The upshot of the argument was that Resi moved into the women's hall next door and both she and Adrian are upset with themselves that they behaved so badly toward each other. Adrian was so disheartened that I put a little note of encouragement and a new picture of Sai Baba inside his tent door as a means of letting him know we all appreciated his leadership. Strangely enough, Resi, who didn't know I had overheard the entire confrontation from my open-topped room, fell into step with me on the way to darshan and told me the whole story and how remorseful she was. I encouraged her to apologize to Adrian directly rather than carrying such a burden.

Later, amazingly enough, Adrian, who hadn't officially met me, told me the story again. I assured him that it was easy to see he was remorseful and that Resi would probably appreciate an apology. They're both fine people, it's obvious, and the strain has temporarily been too much. Yet such circumstances are the very material with which we have to work in life. What we make of these little annoyances is what we create of our lives. It's our opportunity to let the creative process work as it always does when we allow the action of Spirit.

Thirty-five times in a row I have been close enough to Baba to offer Him letters from Colorado devotees. Each time, He simply said, "Sit down." But I have summoned courage each darshan to try again. It seems I'm working on persistence, courage and humility. But He does give me the most magnificent deep, sweet and tender looks. How I do love the Lord.

These days I feel supremely contented. Recently Baba called a group of Mexicans for an interview. He told them that He had called them to India to save their lives from the recent devastating earthquake in Mexico City. He told them that Sai devotees were working without sleep, making meals for quake victims.

Last week I dreamed that Jim and I would make a short-term move of about three months to China. It would be thrilling to see the new changes in China since I was there in 1981 and to be able to travel to India from the People's Republic.

CHAPTER 19
THE PATH TO LIBERATION

"Liberation means that birth is finished with, that there is no more birth." Sathya Sai Baba, MBAI P 203

Puttaparthi, India
November 1, 1985

Sai Baba's Thought For The Day, written in chalk on the blackboard near the Admissions Office concerns "slights and affronts." We must not be the only hall that is having a little tension these days. Earlier today Resi and Adrian apologized to each other and each mentioned later how relieving it was to have humbled the self and dropped the burden of remorse and unforgiveness. But two more events have transpired as a result of their encounter and subsequent apologies. First, Adrian has announced that he is no longer willing to be the hall leader. From now on we will all have to be responsible for ourselves. Obviously that's how it must be every moment of our lives anyway.

The second event occurred today when Resi was at darshan, in the back of the line. "Baba did the most amazing thing, Connie. He didn't use the aisles today, but he walked right through the crowds directly to the woman beside me. He wasn't even looking at me, but His feet were uncovered and I thought to myself 'I've been to India five times now and I've never been this close to Him. It's now or never.' So I bent down and touched His feet. He patiently stood there until I was finished. I think He was giving me His grace since I had the courage to apologize to Adrian. How else can you explain such a thing?"

She is radiant and full of new resolve now. All day long I have heard the most extraordinary stories from Westerners about Sai Baba's recent healings, blessings and miracles. His love for us is sometimes so very overwhelming that I don't know whether to laugh, cry or sing. I feel such an upswelling of gratitude and emotional response at being alive on the planet at the same time that He is and to actually have the rare privilege of being here with Him. Daily I sense a deepening of faith and direction and Jim can hardly believe that I'm enjoying the hall so much, doing energy attunements and foot massages as service, and giving away little treats and surprises to our neighbors constantly. Just being in this rarified atmosphere is somehow changing me without my even having to try.

In fact, Jim confided today that when we were here the first time he secretly wanted to leave as fast as possible because he was in such physical torment from sitting for hours on the ground and concrete. He's still in pain and in darshan he actually times his various leg positions on his watch just as I did the first trip. He can endure having his knees up with feet flat for three minutes; legs beside him for two minutes and so on. Someone told me today that there are now sixty thousand people here in the ashram and I wouldn't have missed this for the world. How I would love to stay for the birthday but Jim has a very short vacation so we'll just be in India ten days and here for eight.

This evening we are attending a lecture by Al Drucker on "Sai Baba's Discourse on Bhakti Yoga, Discourse Number Nine," given during August and September of last year. It's a treat to actually be in this lecture hall with Al Drucker, who looks to be about forty-five or fifty but who, it is said, is some ten years older than he appears As people file in with their darshan cushions and seat themselves on the floor until the room is overflowing, I study Drucker's wiry build, smiling face, gray pompadour hairstyle and glasses. His lecture starts out at a gallop, filled with energy and enthusiasm, his expressive hands always dancing, like Kasturi's in their gestures. His hands swoop, flit and flutter about like lively birds as he talks and his ardent devotion and great vivacity are contagious. This man is alive in Spirit with a heart that is on fire! His fund of knowledge is immense, yet he's quite humble, like all the outstanding teachers here whom we've met so far. Professor Kasturi, near ninety, is bright and sharp and looks like a lively gnome with his balding head and impish smile. Both he and Drucker have sparkling eyes and the most marvelous sense of humor, always slipping in a joke or pun or witty remark into their teachings. This is the nearest I've ever been to the "heaven without." As for the "heaven within," the longest I've been able to sustain that state so far is about a year. In other words, to be constantly centered in Spirit. Then I allowed the seeming pressures and responsibilities of the world to intrude and had to start all over again through retreat attendance, spiritual classes, meditation and service. What we are after is to so consistently carry the Heavenly Garden within us that we extend it to our worlds by pouring out a blessing to others by letting Spirit express in our lives. It must really be something to be able to sustain that state indefinitely. But even that isn't total Self-realization.

Al Drucker has a very practical way of teaching, which is perhaps a result of his engineering and aviation background. He hits the high spots and leaves meaningful silences between the key elements for those of us who hastily scribble notes. The main points are:

- Still the thoughts to control desires. Still desire to conquer anger. To do this still the mind.
- Thoughts are charged with life and can be even stronger than the strongest matter.
- Thoughts result from the type of food we eat. From thoughts come actions and words.
- Bad or impure food leads to impure thoughts and actions. Don't kill any animals for food. (Uh-oh... we're still eating a little chicken and fish. This is an area of spiritual growth for us.)
- A strong and pure body is essential for the path.

Sri Sathya Sai Baba

Sathya Sai Superspeciality Hospital in Puttaparthi

Mandir darshan area in Puttaparthi, decorated for a festival

Halagappa's shrine at the Sathya Sai orphanage near Mysore – photo by Dr. Betty Broadhurst

Bas relief sculpture of Shirdi Sai's feet seeping amrit at Halagappa's orphanage – photo by Dr. Betty Broadhurst

Vibhuti constantly covers Sai Baba photos at the orphanage shrine room – photo by Dr. Betty Broadhurst

Vibhuti OM appeared on Sai photo in Rimal home, Salt Lake City, Utah

Bharosa Adhikari and Ramesh Nepali, priest and wife at Bharosa's home in
Kathmandu, Nepal. Lord Krishna dances in the flames.

Sai's vibhuti handprints appeared on chair in Adhikari home.

Manifested miniature silver sandals which dance in cum-cum powder on the Adhikari altar.

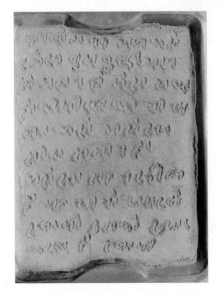

Message in tumeric powder from Baba, manifested in the Rimal home, Salt Lake City, Utah

Krishna ring Baba
manifested for
Ramesh Nepali

A watch-ring which Baba
created for the author
on November 8, 1999

Bananas which
manifested OM
symbols in Salt Lake
City, Utah

Krishna statue in Bharosa Adhikari's home, which manifested butter that fed hundreds of people.

Statue and rudraksha beads that manifested on the altar of Ramesh and Bharosa's home

The smiling Avatar

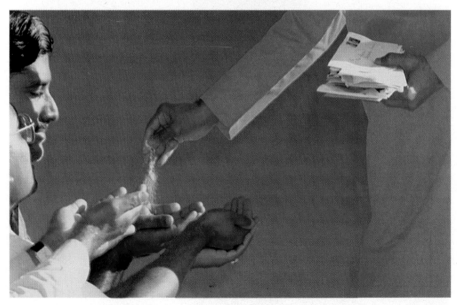

The Lord creates vibhuti ash for a devotee

⋄ Character is the only wealth; all else disappears. Wisdom remains as a companion, even after death.

⋄ We are all the worlds within us. (The universe is consciousness.) A devotee who wishes the Lord's grace must relinquish desire.

⋄ The first stage, dasohum, means being the servant, the messenger of God. But this must give way to the second stage: I AM He.

"Next," Al continues "The pure "I" principle emerges, then That Is All that remains. "I AM as I AM." When you know that all is the Lord, that is the final awareness - advaita. The idea of being a sinner is wrong for devotees. We are all saints. Let the past go. Don't identify with what is behind - it is not even part of us. Think "I AM pure bliss." Be without hatred towards any being." A fly buzzes loudly around Al's head and he makes a joke before continuing. "Now we'll consider some ways of controlling anger:

1. Drink cold water.

2. Take a cold shower.

3. Take a long walk." (This one's my favorite but I haven't had to use it in a long time.)

4. Examine the anger."

Regrettably our time is up so Al reflects a moment and concludes by saying "A weak person can never gain Self-realization." We all stand and flow from the lecture room infused with inspiration, fed on the Word of Spirit. In subdued but excited tones, the Westerners trail off to their rooms conversing in French, Swedish, German, Italian, and seven or eight varieties of English.

Saturday, November 2nd

Every day requires an earlier start for showers and meal lines because of the ever-increasing influx of people from throughout the world. It's nearly 8:00 A.M. and I've already been writing in my journal for a long time since Sai Baba is late today. He's been coming out four times a day lately in addition to His many car trips to survey the bustling construction activity around the ashram. Every day there's either a new building going up, a wall being painted or some sort of freshening up for the birthday. Yesterday I sat on the ground cross-legged for a grand total of five and a half hours; the body is screaming its complaints but it's being ignored. I shouldn't have been so proud yesterday about doing so well at enduring the physical privation.

Sai Baba looks the same as always, His erect form more like forty than sixty. He is so loving that His inspiration is a constant teacher to us in how to treat others. The question of His divinity has finally been settled in my mind. Here He is! The crowd inhales expectantly and sits up at attention. His graceful walk never fails to strike me as the quintessence of poise and dignity, combined with acute awareness and magnanimity.

He talks to one of the high school teachers, accepts letters from students and some nuts from a tray. He smiles, says a few words to students and accepts written petitions, then manifests vibhuti.

The second day we were here He gave about eighty of His orange robes to women in the darshan lines during bhajans. He has received a few bridal parties for interviews as well as groups of Australians, Americans, Italians and Mexicans. In ten minutes He goes to the men's side of the Mandir courtyard then, a few minutes after that goes to the Mandir veranda where He materializes vibhuti for one of the college boys. It comes to me more and more that I have a lot of spiritual work to do. After twenty years of active work on the path I now feel that I'm just now on the threshold of the classroom. But each new phase is like that; it's a type of dying of the old self until the more aware self gets established in consciousness.

Kasturi gives an inspiring morning lecture; the topic is "The Hand of Swami" and touches on the deep spiritual path toward illumination, prayer, silence and Sai Baba's omniscience. There is a brief clairsentient happening after the lecture by way of my experiencing a sandalwood fragrance from out of thin air right in front of my nose. During my first visit it happened several times.

This is the day of Akhanda Bhajans which is a twenty-four hour singing marathon that takes place all over the world to raise earthly vibrations and to purify the planet. We will sing spiritual songs from six o'clock tonight until six tomorrow night. The air is charged with an electric expectancy given off by the crowd.

So much has taken place these past three years in our lives that I wonder what will yet eventuate. After returning from Singapore I resumed my business, which has now taken a spiritual emphasis. Jim went to Israel for five months; I had an ovarian cyst removed and we have grown quite a lot from our associations with the local spiritual group. All three boys have become teen-agers with jobs, driver's licenses and social lives to manage along with family and school responsibilities. Travel has taken me to the Middle East; Paris, France; Puerto Rico; Virginia; Florida; California and elsewhere.

But inner travel has had the greatest impact, a liberating influence. As Al Drucker said in a recent discourse "We're all free - the jail door is unlocked. But we must know it."

November 3rd

How will we ever be able to summon the resolve to leave this gorgeous place tomorrow? I need to remember that the reason Sai Baba is with us on the planet is so that we can individually experience Self-realization. Therefore no matter how appealing He is because of His boundless love, it's not a good idea to become addicted to being with Him. Rather, we must resolve to be more like Him as our Exemplar and Way-shower.

So much has happened here in such a short time that I find myself reviewing all of the fascinating conversations and meetings with the people we've met. For example, there was the Australian woman whom Baba had cured of deafness and her six-year-old daughter who had been healed of muteness, deafness and Down's Syndrome. Fran Earley told us of the two momentous interviews which their Australian group were granted. In the first interview He asked an Australian woman who was a healer to hand Him her diamond ring, remarking that the stone wasn't a very good diamond, being quite small. He passed it around for all in the group to see. Then He blew on the diamond and instantly turned it into a clear, larger beautiful diamond and setting which He instructed her to wear on her healing hand. He was quite playful with the thirty-six people from New Zealand, Tasmania and Australia and commented that He likes the number nine, a spiritual number, which is the combination of 36. I noticed that His auto license plate is zero zero nine.

In the second Australian interview Sai Baba spoke to one of the women who was wearing a ring with a large crystal stone. Later a star formation appeared in the same ring. Other people who took part in the interview mentioned that Sai Baba also materialized "lollies" or lollipops for the participants as well as a crystal japamala of 108 beads.

A few days before we arrived there was a mass wedding at the ashram. Fran Earley estimated that in the group of tribal people that were married there were approximately six hundred couples and their families and guests for a total of over five thousand wedding revelers encamped for three days. In His boundless compassion He had learned that these poor villagers couldn't afford to marry or even to pay for bus fare to their own nuptials. He invited them all to come on the same day with many of them having to walk fifteen miles. It was arranged that He would marry them together in the huge Poornachandra building, would provide the wedding saris and chollies with matching petticoats, and would feed the families and guests for three days. When He was asked why all the saris were aqua with orange chollies and petticoats he replied "Ladies compare - so I'll give them all the same color." What a practical approach, as always.

There was gay paper bunting and streamers and He materialized prasad that did not run out the entire day. "I looked in the cooking pots and the food never went down more than a few inches from the rims," Fran told me in thrilled tones.

Her amazed excitement is easy to understand since I had felt that way myself last night at the conclusion of the twenty-four hour Akhanda Bhajans. After singing a total of six and a half consecutive voluntary hours while cross-legged on the sand I was feeling both quite high and on the verge of collapse at the finale. "What I'd really love right about now," I was thinking to myself at 5:30 P.M., "would be for Sai Baba to just materialize enough food for all of us so that all we'd have to do is to open our mouths, eat it, and go crawl into bed to sleep for about twelve hours. I'm just too exhausted to even stand in the canteen line for dinner." About five minutes later a stream of white-garbed volunteers in royal blue neckerchiefs walked single file through the Mandir archway, each carrying an aluminum cooking pot with lid. The boys lined fifty pots on the Mandir porch. Immediately I turned to my journal notes that I had scribbled earlier indicating that I had multiplied the number of people in the darshan lines (50) times the number of lines and had surmised that over seven thousand people were packed into and immediately around the Mandir courtyard, including villagers. If the food on the porch was really for all of us, and not only for the singers inside the Mandir, there couldn't possibly be enough unless Sai Baba were to multiply the food and feed the multitudes. After having read about this ability of His for years I was actually to experience it... and after wishing for such a fantastic boon in a wild moment of weariness. The mind boggles at such coincidences.

Next, Sai Baba walked out on the porch and blessed the vessels, touched each with His hand and announced that everyone was to sit facing the person in front of him, leaving an aisle between them. By this time bhajans finished and my heart was beating so fast I could hardly bear it. To occupy my racing mind, I decided to time this whole impending event on my watch. At precisely 6:00 P.M. the serving women swiftly passed out two braided coconut leaf cups to each person and immediately filled the cups with a mixture of spiced yellow rice in the left hand and served in our right- hand cups a sweet orange-colored dish like yams or pumpkin. Both were delicious and filling. The entire feeding of the crowd and the crowd's dispersal took twenty minutes flat. Then Sai Baba asked from the porch if everyone had had enough to eat. He's beyond understanding - and yet always so gracious, thoughtful and helpful in the most practical ways. The combination of His godliness and humanness is one of His most striking aspects to me.

On the way out of the courtyard I went over to the food vessels and peeked in, as Fran had done days before and, sure enough, there was food left over. If, in the future, when we have all become Self-realized and are doing "the greater works" mentioned in the Bible, it's going to be quite a spectacle with all of us materializing clothes, food and needed objects. Can't you just see it now - people who accidentally cut off a finger, just grow it right back. There'd be no need for Kleenex, drugs, hospitals, get well cards. It sure seems that we have a long way to go unless there would be some sort of pressurized upleveling in mass consciousness by specific stages until then. In any event, it's an exciting time to be alive as well as an unbelievable blessing to actually have Sai Baba's example of inexhaustible loving kindness. My heart overflows constantly now with love for Baba. There is a line by Rabindranath Tagore which I love: "In love I pay my endless debt to thee for what thou art." F P 55

Now the real work begins. People would bask in the glory of an Avatar as long as He would let them. What infant willingly gives up the warmth and nurturance of the breast of its mother? Yet we must all grow up and extend that which we have been given as best we can at our level of understanding, development and resources. I wonder what gifts Jim and I came to give. Does it just seem that we really don't know or will something new come forth?

Emerson said it best in his second series of essays, on New England Reformers and the life well lived:

> "That which befits us, embosomed in beauty and wonder as we are, is cheerfulness and courage, and the endeavor to realize our aspirations. The life of man is the true romance, which when it is valiantly conducted will yield the imagination a higher joy than any fiction.... Shall not the heart which has received so much, trust the Power by which it lives? May it not quit other leadings, and listen to the Soul that has guided it so gently and taught it so much."

We haven't received an interview yet. Since we leave soon I wonder if we'll see Him personally this trip for guidance and teaching. Of course on the plane of Reality He is with me every moment and talks to me in meditation and dreams continually so why am I so eager for an interview? The day before yesterday we, the crowd, waited for Him for four and a half hours in the rain. He says that these canteen lines, the heat, the crowds, ants, centipedes and other minor inconveniences build patience and character.

Now, at 10:00 A.M., we foreigners are all lining up outside the lecture hall half an hour early to hear Prof. Kasturi speak. Since he is so beloved, saintly and popular, not to mention hilarious, the hall fills up fast and soon every seat in the room is taken, both floor space and the row of folding chairs against the back wall.

Professor Kasturi, white-haired, bent and balding, shuffles to the empty chair that awaits him in the front of the room. He smiles as he sits and one gets the feeling that he loves being "on the lecture circuit" within these ashram walls. Love exudes from him as all eagerly lean forward to catch every syllable.

Kasturi bobbles his head and lifts his beautiful long-fingered hands in his characteristic fashion and, with a twinkle in his eye, we're off! Like a race horse shooting out of the gate he gallops along smoothly and we concentrate to catch his accent and the subtleties of his message, put forth in deceptively simple terms.

"I'm sharing the joy that bubbles in the heart with those who have come here. So... I dared to ask Swami if I could talk and He said "When your mind is fixed on Me it overcomes pain.""

We chant three Oms, then the Asathoma prayer before he starts the talk.

"This "Om," this Vedanta is the end of knowledge. It is in this one sound that you get Brahma. It is in this pursuit of knowledge that we are tempted to start on the path to Him. The road initially starts with the question "Who am I?" I don't think that many of us here have had this question put to us. We know more about our neighbor than about ourselves.

"Now when I was taught geography I was taught the subject by someone who knew and taught more about Texas than about India, where we were.

"Each new baby cries "Why have I come again?" This is not his first time here. So the word "Ohum" is the "start." After about five years one gets to the "Deho" stage where he thinks "I am the body, the senses, the mind. Or I am Dr. So-and-So! Therefore, many people do not bother to go on from this stage. At last you find out that that identification is not really you. Finally, as Swami says, "you get bumps and jumps." In other words, you get hurt, chastened, you suffer a million strokes (of pain, life). You get shaped. Each stroke shapes eventually a beautiful idol (i.e., statue). We also try to produce a statue or monument, a Ganesh of our lives and then we come to realize that the greatest achievements of man last only a short time.

"There is the Indian fable of the two brothers one ruled half of India and the other ruled the other half. One wanted to conquer and rule over all of India, from the Himalayas to the Cape. So he did. He wanted everyone to praise him with all of the positive adjectives in the dictionary and to inscribe these on all the peaks of the Himalayas. So he sent his subjects to seek suitable lofty spots for the inscriptions.

"His subjects eventually returned and said "Your Highness, there's no space. Every part of the Himalayas has already been taken by the names of those who have (in one way or another) conquered the country." He had thought that he was the first to have been a conqueror and was so surprised and humbled that he went and did penance and proceeded to seek that grander glory than mere human achievement. As he stood contemplating the glory of God, birds came and built nests in his hair. A statue now exists in Mysore representing this story of the pride of man in his little achievements. What are they before the grandeur and glory of God? If you pursue them, you have only become enslaved. Entombed. Swami has come to prick the bubble of the ego that has grown so big. This casket, ego. He smashes the ego to ash. "Scientists with big heads come and say "I have been to the moon," and so on, and He smashes that ego until it becomes ash, which He pours out of the box until the box is empty. Swami is a miracle. Whatever He does is a miracle." Suddenly Kasturi twinkles and perks up in his chair at the recollection of an amusing anecdote.

"Recently a man gave a speech saying he had smuggled a bottle of whiskey into Prashanti Nilayam and had opened it to find, in disappointment, that it had become water. 'Imagine my amazement! I of course hoped at the time that it would turn back into whiskey again after I left the ashram, but it didn't. So I have given up drinking. Swami can turn wine into water, as it were, therefore this Person must be my Master,' the speaker said.

"Now, speaking of Masters and Teachers, there was an American woman who alternated spending periods of her life between nunneries and slums and kept asking in her prayers that she be given a teacher as she felt she had gone as far as she could spiritually on her own. She kept asking and asking and finally shouted out soulfully one night 'I want a teacher! I ask it with all my heart. I want the best!' That very night Swami appeared in her dream and said 'You wanted the Best, here I am. You didn't know My Name so you called Me the Best.' "

"If the sage Valmiki were here he would write the story of Swami. Valmiki said 'Give me a person who will ask, 'What do you want and who will then give it.' " Leaning forward with merry brown eyes sparkling and long fingers spread wide on his thighs for dramatic effect, Kasturi chuckles and lowers his voice to a conspiratorial whisper. "Some people come here with long lists. Some say they want a new son-in-law, a new house, a way to keep the car, for example. But Valmiki asked for sixty items of good character, then Rama came."

"So mankind needs to have a great Person who knows the Reality of life and death. It is said, in one story, that there was reputed to be one such person near the Ganges but one day his successor, the heir apparent to the wise man, was questioned by a pilgrim as to the actual greatness of the supposedly holy man. The heir apparent thought a moment and responded 'Confidentially, if you find out, would you please inform?' " We all laugh but Kasturi turns serious a moment, just to keep us off balance and in the rhythm of his gallop.

"Swami says, 'Why search for others when I am in you?' Sometimes in a sudden flash of compassion, Swami reveals Himself in order to save us from devaluing the God that we have in Him. So it's done, this teaching, in Telugu, not English which is the language of shopkeepers to attract customers. You might say that He has, in fact, given us our troubles so that we might know that He is the Master and that we are the servant and that His will must prevail. He Who is the 'Only Is' must enter your soul."

Kasturi reads briefly from a book and asks "How do you change this "Is" to "Are"... to plural? You are all Sai. When you have seventy people sitting in a hall they are all Sai, there are seventy Sais.

"Da Sohum. The next stage. Many people come to the stage where there's no desire to go beyond when one has a Master. Swami says that the faithful servant may be trusted more than the son. The son always thinks of the Master's needs. He becomes an intimate and a confidante of the Master. You have to win the confidence of the Master."

At this point in the talk it hits me that this is precisely the stage where so much conflict has arisen within churches and even within the fast changing, tumultuous relationships within Sai centers throughout the world. So many devotees believe, at some level, that simply by coming to Baba they "have it made" and needn't really begin the work of being the faithful servant who carries out the work of subduing the ego and serving humanity. This has seemed to have caused a rift between those who want to go on and to carry out the vision of Sai Baba, and of Jesus, and those who seem to want to remain at a seeming plateau of ritualistic prayer and devotion.

A key point from *Sermon On The Mount* by Emmet Fox comes to mind. He says "Jesus came to carry the human race forward to the next great step, the most important step of all, which can indeed be the final step in the overcoming of all our limitations, if only we can understand clearly what that step implies, and take it. The heart of the whole Sermon on the Mount, which is itself the essence of the Christian message, is the insistence upon the need for this very step, the understanding that outer conformity, (to the law), absolutely essential as it is, is no longer sufficient in itself, but that now, if we are to "come of age" spiritually, we have not merely to conform outwardly to outer rules, but to change the inner man too."

Each time I come to the ashram I become aware of the amount of work that lies ahead of me, both personally, as well as in my leadership, if I am to really carry out Swami's message. At times it seems there's such a long way to go, yet I keep asking Baba to make me more willing to do His will and to be more loving and serving each day.

"Tourists note in their guidebooks," Kasturi intones, "I have seen such-and-such a town in India. Then when they come to Puttaparthi they say, and check off 'I have now seen Kasturi' with satisfaction. I have become just like a place to be checked off." He is, of course, referring to the treatment of the ashram and the people here as tourist objectives rather than to have the objective of imbibing the peaceful vibrations of Prashanti Nilayam into our being so that we can radiate that wherever we are. But since we all love Kasturi so, and have all wanted to "see him in person" we chuckle with him, wryly poking fun at himself. "But we are all a cell in the body of God. 'I am He.' Da Sohum. When you have surrendered so much and have become so intimate with the Master, then you become the Master. Then there is no difference.

"Oh, women get WILD if you say 'He', so in Sanskrit it is 'That' and not He or She," he laughs, obviously enjoying a dramatic memory of a "wild woman."

"Once a man came to Swami and asked for 'freedom.' Swami called him Freedom for six months. When the man returned to New York he and his friend called themselves This and That. He wrote me a letter which he signed "Freed Om." Freedom became freed. Therefore, when This goes, That goes. Then where is the 'This' that recognizes 'That'? If you take out So and Hum then your This and That goes and where is you?" (In other words, when we cease all separation and judgment between ourselves and others then we merge with them in consciousness and feel at one with all others. We cannot stay established in God-consciousness all the time unless we relinquish judgment.)

"When your mind goes haywire you say 'I MUST get a Master.' Swami answers. He hears a call. 'Is there no one who can help me?' you wail. Swami says 'If you won't open your heart to Me, I'll break it and enter!' Kasturi roars at this and we join him, enjoying his enjoyment of the quip, knowing he has indeed had brokenhearted moments in his long and lustrous life.

"So this girl I was telling you about, who was from the convent and in search of a teacher, cried out 'HELP me!' Swami suddenly appeared to her and said "Why do you shout so loud? You can even whisper and I am there. You needn't shout 'Swami! Swami!' Kasturi raises his shoulders and emits a falsetto voice, rolling his eyes like a helpless girl, which sets us all laughing so hard we can hardly stop. But he holds up his hand and continues

"So Swami helped this girl to a peaceful sleep and left. Such a Master He is. He is always with us. Let Him enter your mind, your intellect, your emotions. Then, in the last stage you find no difference between So and Hum and you become Om. The Gita says that if you repeat Om with your last breath the ladder of Heaven is sent down for you. To review, then: Ohum; Dasohum; Sohum; then Om. Om is the last stage."

Smiling sweetly Kasturi gets up and, after lavishing a loving look at all of us, he seems to retreat to an inward heaven as he leaves the hall. We sit rooted to the spot, too filled with happiness to move for a moment. Someone announces that Baba will give a discourse this afternoon and a quick flurry of excitement passes through the crowd at the news.

Many thoughts and memories whirl into my consciousness today as I realize I need to pack tonight and leave this heavenly place tomorrow. If I weren't married I would stay here indefinitely and that realization in itself is somewhat staggering to me. Just four years ago I was so attached to comfort that staying here a week was difficult and now I manage quite well with the food, climate, dust, and schedule. Baba will bless us with a Divine Discourse today.

It must be that one changes here without effort, just as a result of being here in Baba's Presence. One of the realizations that I've had is the enormous benefit of silence. This reminds me of the saying that "If you have something important to communicate, put your hand over your mouth and point." So much of our everyday conversation is a waste of energy and conveys very little. From the vantage point of the ashram it is easy to see how we waste our powers from so much talking, too much noise, the debilitating effects of pollution, too much unfocused activity and attentions directed to the outer world rather than to the inner Self, Source of all our energy and fulfillment.

Even my mind has slowed down, along with my rate of speech while here.

Jerry Jampolsky says, in *Goodbye to Guilt*, that "There's an old saying that a busy mind is a sick mind, a slow mind is a healthy mind, and a still mind is a divine mind." Yet even though my thoughts are more lucid and the mind is still a large part of the time, it seems that certain old issues can throw me off balance and start darting thoughts again - the cavortings of "monkey-mind" as the Asians call the restless consciousness.

Even though it seems that we've lost our chance for an interview, and we wanted one so much, despite our exterior nonchalance, I am thrilled to see the groups that troop in daily for interviews and who emerge calm and purified, even healed dramatically. In fact, Baba says "The sea may turn the rivers back but I will not neglect my devotees."

This experience, however, brings up the other side of the coin, which is that not everyone who comes here is magically freed or cured. Some experience this setting as a furnace which is burning all of the dross out of them; the more they resist the more emotionally painful the result. Each person's experience is unique to his faith, background, experience, and ability to let go, it seems.

There comes a time when everything becomes clear. We cannot expect the Avatar to make our path a flower-strewn one at every turn. That is not His job. His role is to reveal to us our own divinity within, which remains pure and unchanging, unaffected by the crashing waves on the sea of life. As Embodiments of Love, the love for which we have sought throughout eternity is already there inside us. The Avatar can and does employ any methods necessary which will take us inside ourselves. He can use disappointment, grief, divorce, illness, job loss, financial instability, disgrace, or trauma. He may build you up to test your resolve in the face of flattery and ephemeral triumph or crush your ego until you surrender to His Will. but His purpose is only to reveal to you your own reality and to give you true, dependable, eternal peace.

It's time to walk to the temple for the discourse. Eventually darshan line-up is completed and the rows of devotees enter the Mandir area. As I sit cross-legged on the sand of the Mandir courtyard the loud-speaker crackles as an indication that the discourse is about to begin. What good fortune piles upon me this month. In three years of knowing Baba, I've never had the chance to hear Him give a discourse. Hopefully I'll be able to understand His accent and the translator's interpretation. There's Baba's voice... we're starting. They're both speaking so fast, and sometimes simultaneously, that I'll merely be able to outline the key points of this talk.

Baba's voice, like His form, seems younger than His earthly years. It has a lilting, musical cadence that is quite charming. There are, in our audience, people of every ethnic background and every age, from babies through ancient great-grandparents. All are attentive, even the toddlers.

The seva dals finally take their seats and a hush falls over the crowd as the devotees lean forward to hear what the Avatar has to say. Some people begin to take notes. The birds stop chirping and singing. It is still.

Sai Baba's Discourse on the Topic of Music and Singing as a Selfless Community Service

Baba emphasizes the importance for people of singing and speaking of the qualities and glory of the Lord. He sings a melody then launches into an explanation that numbers have an equivalent melody so that in combination certain numbers would be musical. Next, He speaks of feeling in music and how important it is to convey feeling behind the song itself.

"Man and God are both essential for creation but those who may be atheistic have forgotten Who created fire. Fire is essential to life. We who are so many miles from the intense heat of the sun are delicately protected from its harm. The moon is cold and we're fairly close to it yet we are protected from it as well. The One Who is hotter than fire and cooler than the moon is God. Man simply cannot understand Divinity which is pure and extremely radiant.

"However, reciting the Name of the Lord helps us to reach God. It is even possible to convert poison to nectar through the process of repeating the Name. For example, Lord Krishna drank poison and it became nectar for Him. We must make the necessary effort to understand the efficacy of the Name. Whatever Name you think with your mind you have to also harmonize with your mind, thought, words and deeds while clapping with your hands. While chanting the Name to the glory of the Lord you must have purity of feeling so it can fructify. We can't have pure feeling without a pure mind. Whatever greatness one has achieved, there's no sweetness in his singing if his mind isn't purified. Thus, only with a pure mind can you have the sweetness of the experience of the singing.

"How can we strengthen our faith? Only by practicing what we believe. Life is extremely precious. It has to be lived. There is a goal in life, therefore. Without self-confidence, everything is dull and doubtful for a person. One without strong faith in himself and in God has no joy in life. Faith in self and in God - this is the secret of greatness.

"Sing of the sport of the Lord and of His play rather than of glorifying your crucible. (i.e., instead of modern songs of the body, sadness, and so forth) Sing the Name of the Lord. If you're a compassionate person you'll describe God as compassionate and there are many people who fit the description of compassionate ones. By merely describing the qualities of the Lord you can enjoy them but by saying the Name you can actually become one with Him. Group singing and praising of the Lord increases your Union with the Lord faster. In fact, Guru Nanak believed that it was possible to save all of humanity through group singing. All thus shine in a resplendent way. One who sings of God becomes one with God. The glory of Rama's face was reflected in Valmiki's face. Moses developed this glory also by repeating God's Name.

"When many people come together for ritual singing you have to consider all the people. If you select songs that can't be followed by all then the songs will be dull and unenthusiastic. Minds will wander. All must sing enthusiastically and then you can get Divine joy.

"Most people don't know what is to be done in group singing. One can only do what he can do. Take steps so that all can follow in community singing. Take steps so that the singing is useful. If it's singing for oneself it is not useful. If you want to transform the world, do community singing. This is applicable to all of society as whatever sound you produce, the sound waves go all around the world, the environment gets purified and your heart gets purified. Whatever feeling you are experiencing, gets into the song and its vibrations. So we must also inquire into our lives.

"Even after the death of a man his sound waves are still there. Today on earth there are bad feelings, bad words and bad deeds. The type of smoke you produce depends upon the type of fire you have. The type of crop that comes up depends on the type of rainfall. Your singing depends upon your thoughts and feelings. So develop sacred feelings, sacred thoughts. You can get into a state of bliss and forget yourself through singing. If you really want to enjoy Samadhi, spend time singing bhajans. But if the singing is slow and dull it will only lull people to sleep.

"Next, a combination of timing and feeling is important. If you mentally enjoy the feeling of it, if you can harmonize with it, you will enjoy supreme consciousness itself. But if we only care about ourselves and the tune it will be extremely selfish. We have to unify humanity. You'll be able to enjoy sanctity only with this type of unity.

"Where there's purity there's unity. Without unity there's no Divinity. So merge with Divinity and consider your attitudes and associations. But the Name will never change, therefore, establish the Name in your heart for Me. In singing the glory don't think about whether your voice will be in tune. If there's unity in your feeling then everything will be perfectly working. Don't divide your feelings - purify your feelings.

"When all the threads of a cotton cloth are put together how strong they can be! Picture the Lord in your heart - then you'll be able to enjoy the bliss when you love the Name (this way). This delight and joy can help you prove you can unify with God. Today, with Akhanda Bhajans, we will come to an end of the singing together but individually we can have endless singing of the Name. Singing this Name of Rama can remove all your desires and sins. With the help of the One Whose Name we sing we can get purified.

"From darkness to light. From death to immortality. We have to know what has to be known. We must learn the secret behind this singing of the Name."

Baba sings *Hare Ram* and we all join Him. Overhead the birds have ceased their chirping and the monkeys have stopped their rustlings in the tree branches. Bhajans begin with hearty tempo and attentive devotion. There are the soothing cadences of the old familiar songs and vibrant trills and tremolos of newer melodies. The Indian women sitting next to me are lost in the music, their cherubic vibratos voices telling of the longing of their hearts for the Lord.

CHAPTER 20
ZILLA

"Friendship is the expression of unshakable Love, Love that is noble, pure, free from desire or egoism." Sathya Sai Baba

Bangalore, India
October 15, 1986

The past year has flown and I'm back in India again. My dream last year was correct: Jim and I are moving to China for three months. I'm on my way to see Baba first, for a month, and will meet Jim in Guangzhou, China where he's building a new plant for his company, which will take until December or January to complete.

There were two exceptional happenings today and the second one puzzles me, though I don't know if I'll ever know the reason for it. The first event was the chance to drive out in the cab with Althaf, Babu's brother, to see Brindavan, Baba's ashram at Whitefield near Bangalore. Since I went there in the afternoon, it was deserted and I was quite surprised that the public area for darshan, under a corrugated metal roof beneath the crown of an old spreading tree, is so small. There's a pink-colored dorm and a faculty building as well as a small information center and some guest houses in the main courtyard.

Baba's house is within the ashram. Through an archway at the end of a walkway to the right of the dorm, in front of His home, there is a garden area which is made up of huge clean animal cages for ducks and other animals. The pens are maintained by the students who live there. It is quiet and peaceful on the campus and I was warmed to see photos of Walter and Elsie Cowan in the open-air entryway of the dorm quadrangle. They donated the building and, of course, Walter is one of the people Baba brought back from the dead. He led a stellar life of service as Elsie, herself quite elderly, still does in California.

Though I've known Baba for five years this was my first visit to Brindavan and I have a hunch that I'll have the chance to come back to Whitefield sometime during the month that I'm to stay in India this time. The visits in 1982 and 1985 were both to Puttaparthi and were but a week in length. This is my fifth trip to India.

Now for the other interesting item of the day: Julia and Albert Peters. The story about them actually began yesterday when our planeload of Bangalore-bound passengers had to endure the six and three-quarter hour layover in the plain, old-fashioned, uncomfortable Madras airport until the evening connection at six o'clock. While sitting there in the airport, telling Robert Gourley of Australia about Sai Baba, I met an elegant, wealthy-looking, dark complected couple named Julie and Francis Albert Peters who are actually Iraqis who've lived for thirty years in Surrey, England. (Later I learned that they are in the royal family of Iraq.) We met again, strangely enough, at breakfast in Bangalore's West End Hotel, though I had not planned to stay there at all. In fact, after arriving last night I went to the Rama Hotel, the Shilton, and the Windsor Manor, seeking a bathtub for a long soak of my aching bones. My exhausted body had withstood over thirty hours of continual sitting in cramped airplane or airport seats.

But there were no bathtubs in the simpler hotels and the Windsor Manor was booked. But Rama, the lobby manager of the Windsor Manor suggested the West End and even called ahead to ensure a room and to tell them I was on my way over. It turned out that the West End, also quite posh, was the very hotel where the film crew for the movie *A Passage To India* stayed for six months! The trees at the back of the hotel are breathtaking and are set amid winding walkways, colorful shrubs, rose gardens, and eye-catching plantings.

Today, precisely when I went downstairs to breakfast, whom should I meet but Julie and Albert Peters who asked me to join them for dinner tonight, at the Windsor Manor poolside restaurant under the stars. Actually, as it turned out, we were to meet the real host of the evening, a friend of theirs whose name is Madur Pi, a wealthy diamond merchant, member of parliament (I think) and all-around leader in Bangalore. Mr. Pi's driver came for us and we all joined this jovial raconteur's business associates at the Windsor Manor's garden for a scrumptious dinner. Among his friends were Sheshi of the Bangalore royal family and a fellow named Babu (somebody on his board of directors) and another chap. Actually, I've become a vegetarian now and can't abide the thought of fish, fowl or animals being killed for a few moments of pleasure to my palate. But vegetarian options were available, thankfully.

It turned out that Madur is a Sai devotee of thirty years, having met Baba when he was fourteen years old! All day I was singing the bhajan "Madura, Madura murali..." which simply wouldn't leave my mind. When Madur introduced himself and, on learning of my devotee status, told me of his also, the mysterious bhajan song became clear. It had been a musical premonition! Oddly enough, the Peterses didn't even want to hear a word about Baba, even though Albert has suffered severe sneezing attacks every ten days for ten days (ten on, ten off) for thirty years.

"We've spent a fortune on his doctors, medicines and handkerchiefs," Julie lamented. Madur seemed thrilled to have me join the group for dinner and a bit sad, too, that he seems to find very little time for Baba in his busy business life. So what was the evening about, I wonder.... It was perhaps a combination of things: pleasant company (and safe company) for me after a long trip before the rigors of the ashram. Baba's grace, definitely. Then, perhaps an introduction about Baba for Julie and Albert, which might be re-emphasized later by Madur. Then, perhaps a reminder for Madur that he must pay more attention to fleeting time and the spiritual life. But all of that is up to Baba.

Baba has arranged some of the most unusual interactions for me on my trips to India and, I must say, I usually end up talking at length about

Sathya Sai, at people's prompting, of course. Long ago I learned that the secret of happiness in speaking of your spiritual path is to "work with response." If there's no response, or interest beyond a superficial politeness, then avoid the topic altogether or there will be discomfort and/or unnecessary suffering. As the saying goes, "If there's no asking (sincerely about it), there's no listening!"

Also, I find that there are three types of people who are interested in Baba:

⋄ Those who have had a great shock, loss or emergency.

⋄ Those who are doing lots of service and are very ecumenical in outlook.

⋄ Those who are searching but are fed up with conventional religion.

Sometimes one person might embody all three aspects of a potentially interested person. Baba says He decides who has earned or deserved the grace to hear about Him and at what time and in what way.

Bangalore, India
October 16th

Babu and I left at 4:00 A.M. for the ashram, and arrived in time for morning darshan after halting for a camel crossing the road just past the boys' high school near the hospital. It is definitely a superior plan to leave before dawn when there is virtually no traffic and the evening stars give way gracefully to the pink and gray sky-wash of dawn.

Puttaparthi, India
October 16th

Baba emerged from the Mandir looking as regal and radiant, immaculate and poised as always, momentarily lifting the hem of His orange silk robe as He took the incline of the Mandir porch to step onto the peach-colored sand where the women are assembled. He walked toward the elderly and infirm, seated in metal folding chairs of blue or green, their faces expectant, their hands pointing heavenward in Namaste position of petition and greeting. Every head on the grounds was inclined toward Swami's every move, His slightest gesture, ears strained to catch a word directed to a lucky devotee.

As He rounded the curve of the first veranda and proceeded to walk gracefully along the perpendicular darshan line in front of the other women's veranda, all heads turned at the same moment, all eyes fastened on the divine form, all devotees as one body in united ecstatic connection with their Beloved. This rare, sincere, intense devotion must be seen to be believed; it outstrips the adulation so blatantly heaped on rock stars, movie moguls and other heroes by the ardent, though fickle public. This is real. Time stops. Nothing else matters in darshan. It all takes place in silence, which is a wonder in itself, especially considering the general hysteria and lack of discipline which can accompany gatherings of Indian villagers. Baba's darshan crowds, however, are quite a mix of urbane, sophisticated Indians, villagers and foreigners from throughout the globe.

How indescribably fine it feels to be back here near Baba's form, even though I have Him in my heart and carry on interior conversations with Him continually. Admittedly, I am foolish about God, but feel it is not at all foolish to love Him so, to yearn to be near Him.

Since I am here without Jim this time, as he is in China for three months, my darshan experience is totally focused. It is quite a luxury to have the entire month alone, with no family distractions or responsibilities.

October 17th

Yesterday, while dressed in my long white darshan dress and lacey shawl, I sat on the step of my assigned room in Prashanti for an hour and a half waiting for the occupant of the room to arrive. She supposedly had the room key. It turned out that there was no occupant and that the accommodations officer had made a mistake. I was given the key and let into the room, which had been vacant for a long time and was draped ceiling to floor in white cobwebs which had entrapped an enormous collection of spiders, flies, gnats and mosquitoes. After two hours of sweeping and scrubbing in the intense heat, I procured, from the village, an iron webwork cot and collapsed on it, drenched and exhausted.

The very moment I laid down, grimy, covered with cobwebs and ribboned with rivulets of dusty sweat, there came a knock at the door. I heaved myself over to the door to see who could be tapping and saw a sight even more appalling than that of my own wild-haired, red-faced, panting self. There in the sun-bright doorway of room R4A9 stood a thin, bent white-haired woman of seventy-eight years, covered elbow to wrist with large gauze bandages and sporting a purplish bruise on her forehead and a black eye. Poor, dear woman! She looked at me with a pleading, exhausted gaze from pale blue eyes. A pile of smart matching navy and beige luggage lay in a heap at her feet, having been dropped there by the shriveled porter who had grabbed her bags as she alighted from the taxi moments before.

"Well hello there.... I'm afraid I'm your new roommate. My name is Elizabeth Daniel, from Bangor, Maine. Zilla, for short – like Godzilla, the gorilla of movie fame."

I'm jubilant that I have a fellow countrywoman as a roommate, though I'd be just as happy with anyone, I'm sure. I engage the porter to come to the village with me to get another cot for Zilla so she can lie down and rest after the three-hour cab ride. As she unpacks and settles into the room before afternoon darshan, Zilla tells me that she used to be a labor organizer, retired from a position as a magazine proof-reader, lived at Findhorn, Scotland for two years, and is a healer and a dowser. What good fortune for me to have as a companion such an interesting person with whom I have so many common interests. She's such a tidy, quiet, considerate roommate. Thank you, Baba.

Zilla mentions that she's hearing impaired and that I'll have to shout, to look directly at her and enunciate clearly, if she's to hear me.

October 18th
We arise at five o'clock in the dark and take a cold shower. Though I'm tremendously grateful for a room in a round building (my first) instead of a shed, I'm a bit put off by the zigzagging traffic-columns of ants on the floor, the horrific smells in the gritty bathroom, the monkey bars on the windows, mosquitoes which evade our pitifully taped cheesecloth at the window openings. Will I be able to stand a month of this, in addition to the long food lines in the canteen, lines at the bank, post office, shops, bakery, and darshan? Though this is only my third day here, my mind is trying to insert a mood of depression at the idea of such austerity, relieved only by the brief sight of Baba during darshan and bhajans. I know this is a trick of the ego, yet feel myself succumbing to a mild blue funk, underscored by the oppressive heat.

On the way to breakfast, Zilla and I note Baba's Thought for the Day on the chalk board near the wall by the Public Relations Office:

"There are three groups of sadhakas (practices, service) which you have to take up – personal, social and universal. The individual's spiritual success, his beneficent nature and virtues when pooled with those of many others, become the wealth of society. Each one has to revere and to serve all. The divine in each is pooled into the concept of the Infinite Divine."

At eight o'clock Zilla and I negotiate with a trishaw driver to take us up to the hospital in order for Zilla to have her wounds inspected and dressed in clean bandages. On her way to India she was coming out of the women's restroom in the Changi Meridian Hotel in Singapore, when she tripped over the raised doorsill and went flying a short distance only to crash-land with great damage to her head, shoulder blade, collar bone, chest and arms. The fall took the skin off her forearms and battered the front of her upper body black and blue, so the woman doctor who attended her in Singapore gave instructions to have the wounds checked and re-wrapped on arrival in India. She's too weak to walk to the hospital so we squeeze into the trishaw and hold our breath. We fervently hope that the skinny little teenage bicyclist who strains to pull us in the rickshaw, will not collapse in a heap as a result of his zealousness in roping us into his conveyance. What an amusing sight we make as the creaky blue and silver cab of the rickshaw wobbles side to side on the dusty road.

The driver's slender frame is deceiving and conceals a Samson strength. Five minutes after arranging ourselves precariously on the narrow rickshaw seat, we arrive at the freshly painted hospital. Zilla and I leave our shoes on the front steps and pad shoeless into the cool silent lobby. It is ten minutes after eight and a short round woman emerges from a hallway to announce that a woman doctor will see Zilla directly after puja, or morning prayers and songs, which will now take place here in the lobby. We sit quietly, expectantly, comfortably, having just had breakfast and a lovely darshan.

A barefoot man with a bucket of fresh hibiscus blossoms walks up to the nine foot by four foot color photo of Baba and begins to arrange pink, yellow and red flowers on the nails at the top of the frame. It is continually thrilling to me to observe the devotion of Indian men and women to Baba.

To the left of the photo there is a statue of Krishna on a white table which holds a candle and incense. The only other furnishings in this simple lobby are three white-painted benches for patients, a telephone table and two olive green glass bookcases containing medical texts. Through the open front door of the hospital lobby streams a suffused morning lavender light onto the stone floor. Even at this early hour, a pressing humidity pervades everything.

Zilla tells me, while we await the doctor, a little prayer that is found in the back of the book *One Hundred and Eight Gems*.

"May the allotted span of my life
  Be as pure, fragrant and transparent
  as the camphor flame
  Spreading light and the warmth of love all around.
  May it be consumed in the fire
  And at the end of it all
  May there be nothing left to warrant another sojourn
  Between pleasure and pain."

From 1975 to 1977, Zilla went to Findhorn to live, then went back for a visit in 1979 and discovered there a book about Sai Baba, while she was staying at her friend's place. She decided to visit Baba and came last year with her friend Gordon for the first time. "In addition to Baba's extraordinary love," she said, "I was also very impressed with two of His sayings: The first was, 'There is only one religion, the religion of love.' The second was, 'Love all; serve all.' That reminds me of the old New England saying, 'Forget yourself for others and they'll not forget you,'" she said, smiling.

During the interview which Baba granted to Zilla and Gordon, He materialized a medal for her and let her hold His hand for several minutes. Baba told her then that she needed to get rid of all of her things, so after she and Gordon had stayed five weeks in the ashram she promptly went home to Maine and emptied her six room house.

"My friends thought I had become a fanatic, but a fanatic, as we say in Maine, is someone who is enthusiastic about interests that are different from your own." She chuckled at the memories.

She had just finished the monumental task of emptying her Maine house, when she embarked on the trip back here, alone this time and worn out. The accidental fall in Singapore was an unwelcome shock which had a dispiriting effect, as well as weakening her body considerably. I clown around with Zilla at every available moment, to try to cheer her up and keep her attention in the here and now until she can see a doctor.

In the corridor opposite our bench we see women and children lining up near a sign saying Out Patient Services. A large officious woman comes and takes Zilla away to the head of the line into a room marked Female OPD. Meanwhile many babies and toddlers simultaneously scream, squirm, cough, whimper, wriggle, and whine, setting up an unremitting din.

As I glance through the open hospital door, I can see a new building. Across the street from the hospital there's a hotel with shops - two stories, no less - describing itself as the Chai Thanya Shopping and Lodging Complex. It's rather a grand name yet the building is indeed the most pretentious one in the village and even has glass windows, making it quite a novelty for this area. Imagine - glass windows in Puttaparthi!

Suddenly a family rushes into the lobby with the staggering, corpulent mother, a heart patient, swooning as she steps across the threshold into the little hospital. A stretcher appears immediately and an orderly pops a nitroglycerine tablet under her tongue and a tape on her throat. She is unconscious now and is oblivious of being raced along the hallway to a room amid rows of curious onlookers, including babies who have stopped crying to observe the commotion. Expressions of pity and compassion mark the faces of the young mothers and toddlers.

Doctors and nurses arrive in the lobby for puja (morning prayers), light the candles and incense, sing *Ganesha Sharanam*, wave the camphor flame, take vibhuti to dot their foreheads, bow to Baba's photograph here in the lobby, and officially dedicate their work day to Him. In a matter of minutes, Zilla reappears with clean bandages, a big smile and compliments for the female doctor.

"I surreptitiously quizzed her on her medical background to ascertain whether or not she knows what she's doing and I decided she's not only competent but very sweet as well," Zilla announces.

"Don't worry, I was polite about my inquiry and I have total confidence in the staff here."

Since both of us are still jet-lagging back to normalcy, we return to the room to take a nap before lunch. To our dismay, however, our carefully duct-taped window netting has been mangled by monkeys. The white netting hangs limply in the breeze by a tangled strip of silver tape, admitting a horde of mosquitoes into our little room. Zilla confides that this isn't the first time monkeys have attempted to invite themselves into the room. She has shooed them away before, yet this is the first time they've done any damage. We have heard devotees in the canteen lines telling stories of monkeys having taken their passports away in their mouths, having eaten their lipstick and snatched their small makeup mirrors.

Zilla asks me to keep an eye on her so that she doesn't sleep excessively long in case she has an undetected concussion. I make more jokes after filling our water canteens from the sink, so that she won't realize that I'm actually quite worried about her.

Before the curtain of sleep sweeps over me, I wonder how it is that when I'm away from the Ashram I can hardly wait to get back and yet, when I have made the trip of about twelve thousand miles I'm always shocked again at the conditions. Have I made a mistake this time in planning to stay a month in the heat - amid the bugs, smells, dirt, and minor annoyances?

What will this trip bring in the way of new understanding, chastening, strengthening? Will we be granted an interview? Why am I here, other than to "report for duty to God" as I term it. After awakening from the nap, I print an inspirational sign for myself with a magic marker on a piece of white cardboard. It says, on the top line "The name of the Lord" and on the bottom line "Be joyful" as a reminder to stay fixed on the Tone all day, to speak as little as possible, and to remember that this is supposed to be, after all, a happy experience that I've chosen - being here with God!

On the way to the canteen for breakfast we jot down Baba's thought for the day. "Doubts will haunt a person until he cognizes the truth. When doubt enters through the front door, faith departs through the back door! Doubt comes upon people like a heart attack. It overwhelms a man all of a sudden. So enter upon your sadhana (spiritual practice) with full faith."

"Is that ever the truth!" I exclaim to Zilla, remembering my mood of discouragement that both arrived and departed last night.

"Oh look at this announcement about Al Drucker's talk this morning at 10:00," she says enthusiastically. We must get there early since the room fills up fast and we want to be able to hear what he says.

By 9:45 the simple lecture hall is packed with over seventy Westerners sitting quietly on the floor awaiting Al Drucker. He enters, tan and slender, wearing an immaculate white jacket and slacks, and opens the talk with a solo song in both Sanskrit and English called *Twameva Maata.* "Remember, musical ability doesn't count - it's the sweetness in the heart that matters."

After singing the Sanskrit, Al sings the English and teaches the prayer to us until he's sure we know the words:

You are my mother.
You are my father.
You are my nearest kin.
You are my dearest friend.

You are my wisdom.
You are my treasure.
You are my everything.
You are my Lord, my loving Lord.

We're all touched that he has taken the time to teach us such a lovely song and that we've mastered it so quickly at the outset of the lecture. Al flashes us a sparkling smile and rubs his hands together.

"Now, sing this to Swami in the interview room. He'll like that.... I've simplified my life greatly these two and a half years, teaching these Gita chapters that Swami has pointed out to us. In Sanskrit, particularly, the etymology of the words is very important. These are great discourses and they've not been published so they're still fresh. But we're not bound to that topic. This is a family meeting so if you have something you'd like to discuss, we can discuss your topic."

An older Australian woman immediately pipes up "Yes - what can you say about cremation?"

"Yes... what to do with these old worn out bodies. What do you do with an old milk bottle?" Al asks.

The group, unrehearsed, in unison: "Recycle it!"

We all laugh heartily at the perfectly timed, perfectly true and amusing response.

Smiling, Al nods and says "We recycle atoms in many ways. We think everything takes place in the waking state but everything you see is only the five elements - earth, air, water, fire, plasma; not the elements of chemistry in the West. The concept is much deeper than that. Out of the mention of the Lord came the Om sound. From that sound came space, ether, the akash. From that came touch. So... space, time, then air, then form, then fire, then taste manifesting itself as water. Then smell came, then earth, then seeds, then herbs, living beings and so on. First came the subtle, then the gross. We're all on the home-going path so we're moving from the gross to the subtle - back home. The most subjective feeling you can have is intense joy. If you're on the objective path it's not spiritual. We're moving away from objects to subject and even the Subject has to go eventually.

"A plant takes in carbon dioxide during the day. Breath is called prana - life. Even this chair is life in a more tamasic or torpid form. But none of this is real; not Self. All the countless variations of the five elements are changing. But divinity is always the same - unchanging - everywhere. That is Sath. The five elements that we mentioned are asath. Don't hold onto your bodies. Let go. Flowers dry up. Food spoils. The beautiful of today will become ugly tomorrow.

"No objects have any lasting value. Only the external senses hanker after the gross aspect of themselves so we must turn them around. Now, about sound: it is heard in the heart. Swami says the Bible is Veda, meaning given directly. It is also many other things.

"There are twenty-four principles having to do with Maya or illusion. They are the five yama indriyas - sound, sight, taste, smell, sensation. Then the five karma indriyas are eyes, ears, skin, tongue, nose. There are five koshas or sheaths or bodies. There are five pranas or vital energies such as breathing, elimination, circulation, upward flow of energy and digestion. Then there are the four parts of the mind - manas (attention); buddhi (intelligence or reason); ahamkara (ego); chitta (the total or collective sense of mind)."

The way in which Al delivers this news has us leaning forward, hanging on every syllable, all quite aware that just when we had thought we were about to receive a Ph.D. degree with honors we have in essence been informed that we have now qualified to enroll in first grade! There's vastly more to this Self-realization business than Western culture and education have led us to believe. Enjoying the dazed looks on all faces, Al smiles and waggles his head from side to side in Indian fashion, then chuckles. You can practically hear the wheels turning in the heads of this highly educated, earnest, well-traveled audience.

"The monkey mind always operates the senses. In primitive man the mind oversaw survival needs. That's manas. But the mind must now be used for other things. We have intuition. Buddhi or higher intellect knows why we are here. It's directly activated by Atma.

"We are still acting out a certain scene in this world from previous lives. So we must purify the chitta and have only pure tendencies. Ego is the mind; this is the aspect of God which has deluded itself into limitation. The spiritual path can be summarized as moving from limitation to unlimitedness.

"In other words, all of the twenty-four principles are under the sway of ignorance. All the joys imaginable ultimately bring us only sorrow. Only with control of the senses can you have peace of mind. Krishna taught a number of ways to control the sense organs. Neither joy nor peace of mind can be had without this. We all know how it is: we resolve to curb our appetites and then we stroll down the street, come to the bakery and lose all our will power!" The audience hoots in merriment since nearly everyone of us patronizes the cookies and mini-pizzas at the ashram bakery.

Al's eyes crinkle in a smile at our squirming and he announces that he's going to tell us a story that relates to his points. "Once there was a king who had five wives. He couldn't control them. He was a good king, though, who decided to hold a public meeting, inviting all the subjects in the kingdom to attend. Two large tents were set up on the grounds - one for those who had control of their wives and one for those who were controlled by their wives. As people arrived at the gathering the tent for those who were controlled by their wives filled to capacity. He went to the other tent and saw one lone man standing there and eagerly went over to ask him the secret of controlling his wife. The man, embarrassed, replied, 'No, it's not like that - my wife ordered me to come here!' The king then realized that no one is free from his wives. The king, of course, is the mind; the wives are the senses. Thus, everyone has five wives trying to control him.

"Our mind says it wants to travel, to hear fine music, and so on. The man who bases his life on his mind will become worse than an animal. His every moment is uncertain. Ramakrishna, who was also once Mohammed, was one day in great pain. In his last moments he struggled to speak and couldn't. Finally he said, 'I've been conquered by Maya but I struggle to say the name of God. Turn to God.'

"God takes care of everything - there's no worry. Live in this moment. The future takes care of itself. Until you reach total control of the senses you must subject yourself to some degree of trouble to start sadhana. You must control the out-going tendencies, the senses, ego. Then, what am I? Atma. You are Atma - the I AM that I AM. Of course, hearing it and Being It are two different things! We accomplish this by discrimination - by releasing ourselves from the changing. When we're in this new state the consciousness abides in Omni-consciousness.

"You know, Swami continually upsets our concepts. He constantly overturns our ideas of peace, war and imagination until we realize that we were never born, that we never truly die, and that this body is not us. He does this before we control the senses. Once we have this wisdom we can safely enter any field. Wisdom and renunciation permit us to fly home. They go hand in hand.

"Knowledge of the Atma alone is true knowledge. Then you experience that all is God. To know this, control your mind. The sense organs are very dangerous - like wild horses going in all directions. The body is a chariot. Therefore, to exercise a certain amount of self-control we must do sadhana, we must practice. It's just a few seconds before midnight for all of us. We must make rapid progress in constant remembrance of God. Understand that all things are impermanent.

"We should fill ourselves with Light. Then only can we speak, see and hear wisely. Select only good things to see, hear, think and say. Remember, all saints have a past and all sinners have a future, as Swami says.

"Control of the sense organs means that one can control the world - his world - otherwise one is a slave of the world. Swami urges us to learn the slokas in chapter twelve of the Gita. So start afresh for every moment is a new beginning. There's no trial period. Just start now. To gain the love of God just think of God and God thinks of you. We can do nothing on our own. He is the only Do-er."

With a flourishing hand to indicate that the lecture has ended, Al inclines his head and softly leads us in singing three times the prayer:

"Lokaa samasta sukino bhavantu." Let everyone in all the worlds be happy.

We are all electrified. There's a moment of silence as if we hang in space and time together, too contented to move a muscle. Then we shake off the spell that Al has cast over us and reluctantly rise to leave the hall. Zilla, wearing a grin, and more vivacious than I've ever seen her, confides enthusiastically that this one lecture by Al Drucker was definitely worth her long, arduous journey alone to India, including hauling her luggage, and even her fall and attendant injuries. We're unabashed fans and agree that this talk has been both inspiring and motivational in the highest sense.

It's obvious that my main task is to simplify my life and control desires. But how can one do this while living in Western society? It seems so easy here at the ashram where there is no media, nor ads or billboards or distractions. There is no social pressure to dress in the latest fashions or to maintain a certain lifestyle. There are no telephones, televisions, radios, magazines or junk mail.

Zilla and I agree that we must create an ashram of our homes, that is – a temple-like atmosphere – and relinquish our attraction to "sense objects" and comforts. As if the universe is conspiring against our resolve, a neighbor in our round building gives us a folding chair. It was left behind by a handicapped woman when she recently departed - for Europe, that is, not departed her body. Our own bodies are so stiff from sitting in darshan and bhajans six hours a day that we conveniently overlook our new austerity program and gratefully accept the chair. With our two cots of plastic woven strips, the straw floor mat, a photo of Baba and the chair, our room is lavishly decorated, all things being relative in these stark environs. However, if we had to live like this on a regular basis we would be considered (and would consider ourselves) abjectly poor. So how on earth are we going to winnow down our wants and possessions to any manageable situation permanently? That will take ingenuity and resolve.

October 21st

It seems that the chair wasn't a luxury after all. Zilla certainly needs it as she's so light and frail that sitting up in her cot is nearly impossible for her as she tips over quite easily. The chair is less tiring for her to read and write letters; she also uses it at 5:00 A.M. to meditate when we arise before dawn to prepare for the day. We meditate, bathe, make the "beds" and tidy up the room, then bundle the laundry for the dhobi who delivers yesterday's clothes at six. At six fifteen we leave the room, walk down the hill to copy the thought for the day, line up at the canteen for a breakfast of an idly pancake with spicy sauce and tea, then sit in the darshan line. We go inside the Mandir yard and wait in another line, experience Baba coming around to all of us in darshan, then do errands and come back for morning bhajans.

After bhajans we read until lunch then nap in the heat until it's time to put our clothes back on for afternoon darshan lineup, darshan, bhajans, then dinner. We usually go to bed at half past eight or nine at the very latest and are very tired for some reason, though we've done nothing very strenuous except wait in one line or another in the heat for five or six hours each day. While waiting in the lines we read or meditate so you'd think we'd be brimming over with pep but it isn't so. Why is this, I wonder? Is it jet lag, still, or the heat, or is it that our lower tendencies are being forced out of us in this rarified environment with the result that we feel as if we're working quite a bit internally all the time.

Yesterday I sat on the rain-soaked ground for six hours and today my hip joint was locked in place and aching fiercely. Since I could barely walk, my odd hopping limp caught the attention of Robin Adamson, a brand new devotee from Detroit who is a primal therapist. She does acupressure work and offered to come to the room to dig her elbow into the hip socket to release the pressure build-up. Her generously applied "digs" worked wonders, though excruciating to endure, and my appreciation knew no bounds. The limp is gone. Later we sat up for hours talking of Jane Roberts and Seth, various metaphysical books and authors, New Thought Philosophy and of Peter, her husband of thirty-eight years, who is very difficult.

Along with Zilla and me, Robin also came to India by herself, without mishap, and is thrilled to be here, as we are. On occasion, I wonder if Baba will see me in an interview before I go to China to join Jim for the next few months.

Now I understand why Baba blessed me with a roommate who is hearing impaired, or deaf to be more accurate. I've always been too talkative, both as a child and as an adult. My rationale for not curbing my excessive speech has always been that I am a naturally outgoing, energetic and vivacious person. Enthusiastic. I love life and people. But now I realize that an unbalanced diet of foods that have been too salty and too fatty (dairy products) have created a system imbalance wherein I'm too rajasic or too restless, hence overly-talkative. Baba says that too much talking creates lots of allergies. Living with Zilla, who is very strict and monastic, and who abhors any unnecessary talking, has forced me to go within and to listen to Baba inside my heart.

Baba may be going to Whitefield, near Bangalore, soon. In the back of my mind, I've been wanting to visit Halagappa's Sai Baba Orphanage in Sri Rangapathnam, near Mysore, sometime on this trip. I never go sightseeing these days, since seeing Baba in darshan is my sole reason for being in India. But I've had a persistent feeling that a trip to the orphanage would somehow benefit me in some way.

Since Zilla sits in the 'patient section,' for darshan, it's been delightful for me to be able to enjoy, in the darshan lines, the company of Robin Adamson, from Detroit. There are very few Americans here now and it was a tremendous joy to hear her New England accent in the darshan line one day, amid the Telugu and Tamil accents, and to have befriended her. Robin is, however, returning to the States in the next day or two. What will Baba have in store for me next, I wonder?

CHAPTER 21
MIRACLES IN MYSORE

"Baba will always provide." Robin Adamson

Bangalore, India, West End Hotel
October 25, 1986

All day long the words and melody of the song "Valderee, Valderah" kept running through my mind for no apparent reason. Then this afternoon when I received an unexpected phone call it became clear - it was another musical premonition. In the morning I had seen, in the veranda lobby of the West End Hotel, a tall, chubby red-haired woman whom I recognized had had a recent interview with Sai Baba at the ashram. Interested in making her acquaintance, I walked over to her and the woman she was speaking with and introduced myself, hoping to strike up a conversation.

Both of the women just stared at me, as if I had committed some sort of social faux pas, said they were very busy, and rushed away. I was a bit bewildered to say the least.

The phone call was from the red-head whose name is Valere Steen, it turns out, from South Africa. She called to apologize for "brushing me off this morning" even though we hadn't had a formal introduction, as she put it. At any rate, she offered to invite me to tea downstairs at the hotel and to relate the details of her interview.

During our get-together she mentioned that she had been hopelessly addicted to prescription drugs several years ago while she was recovering from a divorce. When she heard of Swami and eventually went to India, He cured her of the drug dependency in a matter of months. One of the things we have in common is writing. She's a writer who has published articles on Baba for a magazine in South Africa. Coincidentally enough, she is also considering writing a book of humorous accounts of Swami's leelas. When I told her that just as the phone rang I was contemplating abandoning *Wake Up Laughing* altogether, she discouraged me from becoming disheartened just because I haven't yet found the right publisher. I have been working on the book for four years and have nearly thrown it into the trash a number of times. It must be that there's a lot yet that needs to happen before it's ready for publication. What could that be?

Valere is extremely animated when she tells a story and elicits peals of laughter as she recounts how an acquaintance of hers in South Africa, an Agnes Logan, became seriously ill and in need of surgery. Ms. Logan, a Scottish psychic, was in her hospital room on the day of the operation when she felt a presence there, turned her head and saw, to her great surprise, Baba standing beside her bed in His orange silk robe topped with His Afro hairstyle - smiling at her.

She was frightened and unnerved since she didn't know Baba and immediately started shouting "And what are *you* doing in my room?! Go, go on out of here you wee funny little man!" Baba sweetly told her He was there to help her during the surgery and that all would be well. He then disappeared and she was wheeled to surgery; while she was out of the room a large, lovely vivid picture of Baba, like a stained glass window, appeared embedded in the window of her room. It immediately attracted the attention of nurses, doctors and staff who came in to look at it throughout the day as the patient peacefully slept off the surgical anesthesia and pain-killers.

When she awoke it faded and she was, indeed, recovered, as indicated by Baba in His gracious protective message to her.

Valere then tells me, with a sigh, that she was told in the recent interview by Baba, who addressed her as "Pakora" that she was too fat and that she must lose weight for her health. (A pakora is a stuffed fried flat-bread snack filled with onions, potatoes and green peas. It is rather like a stuffed dumpling in its implication here. Hence, the term would be like an American calling someone "Butterball" in a gently teasing manner.)

When Valere asked if she'd marry again, Swami assured her she would and that marriage would be good for her; He then said He would send the man to her.

"I just want to do the dharmic thing in all parts of my life," Valere said, folding her hands demurely in her lap.

"Absolutely," I responded. "You've heard of the Four W's, in regard to Baba?"

"No, what are they?" Valere asked.

"First, He woos you," I whispered impishly. "Then He wins you. Then He weans you – like a baby. Then, if you get too cocky, or too lost in the world, He wallops you (with karma)! Lovingly, of course." We both hooted, having been walloped a time or two.

Since we both have numerous Swami stories to share, I invite Valere to have dinner with me and our marathon conversation continues. I asked the dining room staff earlier today if they'd kindly pack a picnic lunch for Althaf and me for our trip to Mysore tomorrow. It's mystifying to me why I feel such a compulsion to go sightseeing in Mysore tomorrow, of all days, since Baba is at Whitefield and I'm here in Bangalore to see Him and not for any other reason.

These days I seldom go sightseeing randomly unless there is some larger purpose, such as to do research, to visit someone, or to take an actual rest. But oddly enough I actually feel as though Baba is guiding and directing me to go to Mysore for the day with the avowed purpose of sightseeing. I'm therefore trusting this instinct and preparing for the three-hour drive with a large picnic for the two of us. My feeling is that it needs to be ample since there may be no restaurants along the way.

As Valere and I swap tales of Sai Baba's grace and grandeur, Mr. Joy Paddayatty, the assistant dining room manager, comes over to the table three times to ascertain whether or not the picnic menu which he has selected will be sufficient. Each time I compliment him and tell him it will do quite nicely. Mr. Paddayatty is a dear fellow who is most anxious to please. The waiters welcome me back to the hotel by name and give outstanding service. Valere comments on the way everyone is bending over backwards to attend to our needs and I tell her that this must be Baba's work as it continually happens from place to place. We say farewell until the day after tomorrow and she briefly tells me the story of Halagappa, stressing the fact that I should visit his shrine to Sai Baba on the way to Mysore.

It seems that twenty years ago, roughly, a fellow named Halagappa, who was a pickpocket, regularly worked the darshan crowds at Puttaparthi. While all eyes were fastened on Baba and His help and benedictions to the adoring throngs, Halagappa was busily helping swell his own coffers with the wallets of unsuspecting devotees. One day when he dipped his hand into a pocket, out came a medal picturing Baba. As a surprised Halagappa-of-the-sticky-fingers stood there, the locket began to ooze, of its own accord, a clear, sweet fragrant liquid known as holy amrit. On the spot Halagappa became a convert to Baba's teachings, gave up the life of petty crime and decided to devote his life to opening and operating an orphanage for homeless children. He has a little school and shrine near the Cauvery River, outside of Mysore, that is well worth a visit, Valere assures me.

Bangalore, India
October 26th

At dawn, we're off to Mysore, Althaf and I, with water bottles, books, notepads, and the gigantic picnic box secured beside him in the front seat. The day has an aura of excitement about it and again, I wonder if I'm merely fooling myself that this trip is urged by Baba, rather than merely an ego desire of mine to escape the routine of sitting in the darshan line. Althaf, ever fashionable, is wearing a new shirt and is pleased to be able to show me the sights of Mysore.

It is a cool, cloudy day, this 26th of October and the drive to Mysore is exquisite. After we've been driving awhile a sign catches my attention at a highway rest area. It proclaims "Forest Picnic Spot" and announces "You and your vehicle need cooling for awhile. Nature invites you." A clean fenced area with picnic benches does indeed look inviting under shady trees in this lush, pastoral landscape. Around the bend we come upon stooped women scrubbing their laundry in shallow red streams against a background of coconut palms, pongoms and tamarind trees. Despite the bumpy, winding road I'm lulled into a reverie by scenes of the snowy egrets on emerald rice paddy fields. Black and white storks with slender red legs flap skyward over acres of sugar cane. Along the road, milky white oxen wear tinkling brass bells around their necks, heads bobbing and legs ambling along in a weary age-old rhythm.

Althaf starts to get restless as we near a little restaurant where he wants to stop for a leg-stretch and a tea break from the long drive. Over the Shimsa River bridge we rumble, past a pair of skinny brown legs carrying an enormous wobbling load of purple sugar cane, obscuring their owner. While Althaf drinks tea, I admire a stand of spectacular eucalyptus trees with swirled designs in the mottled trunks resembling a paint-by-number kit; there are pools of beige, purple, gray and brown color on the bark.

The closer we get to Mysore the more buses and trucks bear down on us then veer off at the last breath-catching moment. Every ten minutes I utter a hasty emergency prayer *"Oh, God! Baba - puleeze... get us to Mysore and back safely, and please prevent any children, donkeys, goats, dogs or chickens from running in front of our car."* Numerous tiny three-wheel cabs appear and zip around bikes and motorcycles that race beside a sign for this town. It seems we are in Mandya District and the sky is now releasing rain torrents on attractive little schoolgirls wearing red, black and white jumpers set off by red hair bows in their looped braids. They cover their heads with sweaters and dash about in all directions for cover. Our tires, racing through the sky-colored rain puddles go "shish-loosh...shish! loooosh." Suddenly I remember that Mandya District is the area where Prema Sai Baba, Sathya's next Incarnation, will be born.

"Two hours behind us - only one hour left," Althaf announces jubilantly as a spray of vivid water lilies catches my eye to our left. Purple and hot pink water lilies decorate a coffee-colored creek in a shaded ravine. But what is this odd, dramatic sign we see: 'Caution! Vertical curve ahead.' Is it a cliff, a wall, or an embankment toward which we speed? "Heh-heh! Vertical curve - they just mean a hill, and a little one at that," I shout to Althaf from the back seat over the road noise and dusty wind whooshing through the little cab.

Suddenly Althaf announces that we have come to Srirangapathnam. I find myself wondering what on earth we are doing on this supposed "sight-seeing" trip which I have felt so certain is being directed on the inner level by Baba.

"This is the first thing I will show you - the old ruined fort of the famous Tippu Sultan, an old warrior of South India," Althaf smiles. We drive through ochre-colored bunkers, ancient embattlements and moats, and, finally, a little village with a Vishnu Temple which I briefly inspect, efficiently tourist-like. Upon coming out of the temple to rejoin Althaf in the cab, I encounter some pundits chanting in Sanskrit "Lokaa samasta sukino bhavantu... May all the beings of all the worlds be happy." It startles and then delights them when I start chanting along with them and they all laugh and nod cheerily to me.

This brotherly mood is marred, however, by a pack of beggars which descends on me with the usual unnerving intensity, shrill cries, dogged determination and heavy desperation. They push each other aside, grab at my clothes, reach for my purse, scream and whine. Since I've been caught off guard and realize that I'm nearly out of change to distribute, I jog-trot to the car in frustration, shouting above the din "No, no - sorry. I have no money for you. Very sorry."

One persistent fellow about twenty runs shoulder-to-shoulder with me and says "Here, you buy my guidebook to Tippu Sultan's Summer Palace. I am no beggar like these; I am selling. Selling, not begging. Only four rupees. Good price."

"Okay, okay, here's four rupees for you and a pack of gum for all of you to share. Now that's all I can give you so good-bye and thank-you."

It was a mistake to give them the gum as they fly into a scrimmage that sets up an opaque cloud of yellow dust and gravel amid a fist-fight.

Seeing that I'm upset at the desperation of the begging and that I don't have any change to give them, Althaf tries to cheer me up as we drive along. He knows that I spend a lot of time thinking about the abominable state of the living conditions of millions of poor in India.

"Look, Madame - we are coming to the Sri Sathya Sai Baba Shrine. Just go inside this little shrine and you will like it. It will make you feel happy to see it. All people feel happy when they see this. I will wait here for you."

Remembering Valere's story of Halagappa, the pickpocket-turned-orphanage-teacher, I notice an old man surrounded by toddlers on the veranda of a small building set back from the road amid a tiny cluster of simple dwellings. This must be Halagappa and his orphans; since he's teaching the children the alphabet in English, with great concentration, I decide not to bother them but to simply walk through the open door to which he gestures behind him.

But the room is empty of furniture and is merely filled, floor-to-ceiling on every wall, with photographs of Sathya Sai Baba and Shirdi Sai Baba. The room is a bit dark and after a quick glance at the photos I decide that this can't be the famous shrine. There's nothing here - only pictures. And small children with an old man. Surely a famous shrine would be more impressive than this - or more different, somehow. This can't be the place.

"So. How did you like it?" Althaf asks, expectantly.

"This can't be the place, Althaf. There's nothing in there but some pictures."

"But yah, this is the shrine. Everybody likes this place but you. They always come out smiling and talking very excited. I don't understand."

"Neither do I, Althaf. I just didn't see anything special. And frankly, I wonder if we should have come for the day like this. Everyone says it's better to stay overnight since the drive is so long. But let's keep going. And it's not that I don't like these places, it's just that I'm not sure what I'm doing here when I came to India only to see Baba and not to go sight-seeing. But I feel like this is what I'm supposed to be doing - seeing the sights of Mysore for the day. Anyway, we can have lunch at the bird sanctuary pretty soon. That should be interesting, don't you think, with all those exotic birds flapping along the canals?"

"Yah. But first I want to show you Tippu Sultan's Summer Palace. Then we can go eat the picnic lunch and after that we can see the palace in Mysore and the famous Brindavan Gardens."

For some reason my heart starts beating faster as we drive up to the entrance of the summer palace and Althaf parks the cab under a shade tree for a nap, declining my offer to pay his admission. Still clutching the little guidebook which I bought to fob off the beggars, I walk up to the ticket window and see that the ticket booth is packed with half a dozen men who stare at me, then start talking all at once. One of the men comes rushing toward me after I've bought the ticket and pursues me down the path.

"Hello… I see you have my guidebook."

"Oh, you mean the guidebook that you sell here," I say a bit dryly, fearing that this is another beggar, spotting what he thinks is a soft touch, a "rich American."

"No. I mean that I am, in fact, the author of the book you are holding in your hand and that I was merely going to offer to take you on a guided tour of the summer palace. I'm a historian and my name is here on the title page of the book. See, Jayaramaiah, author. That's me. Since you're dressed all in white, I suppose you're a Sai devotee?"

As my face reddens in shame and embarrassment I see that this unassuming man is indeed not a beggar and is also wearing white. Baba's reminder about our personal interactions rings in my memory "We cannot always oblige everyone but we can always speak obligingly to everyone."

"I'm so sorry. Can you forgive me? I've just experienced so many pursuers, charlatans and beggars that I guess I'm a little shy of men approaching me and I over-reacted. You know, it's amazing, but just a few minutes ago I bought this little book from a boy at the fort and here you are - the author, right before me! I'd love to take your guided tour and I am indeed a Sai devotee here on a pilgrimage to Baba."

"And I am an old colleague of Kasturi's. I've taught history for years. Is Swami in Bangalore, now?" Jayaramaiah asks.

"Indeed He is. There were only about seven hundred people at darshan yesterday, which is a relief after the thousands at Puttaparthi." The peaceful vibrations of the lush grounds and many-pillared palace are compelling.

For some strange reason Robin Adamson pops into my mind and I wonder how she is doing, now that she is on her way back to Detroit and to her husband Peter and her Primal Scream clients. The hairs stand up on my arms and a persistent feeling that something is about to happen occurs to me.

"This is a mural of Tippu Sultan going into battle," Jayaramaiah says, warming up to his topic as we round a corner of the open-air palace.

"Robin!" I blink, thinking that I'm imagining Robin Adamson standing in front of me on the veranda of the palace out here in a remote rural area of South India.

"Connie! What on earth are you doing here?! Oh never mind - Baba has sent you to get me. How did you get here?"

"What are you talking about? How did you get here? I came by cab and Althaf and I would love to have you come sightseeing with us. We even have a huge picnic lunch that the hotel made for the trip," I exclaimed.

"Oh what a Godsend. Let me tell my tour guide. Oh! It has been awful. You wouldn't believe it. I decided to stay a day or two longer so I booked a bus trip to Mysore from Bangalore to see some of the sights since I haven't seen anything except the ashram since coming to India. The tour sounded so good in the brochure - you know how those brochures are - but as it turned out the bus is filled to capacity and the passengers immediately pulled the blinds down and turned the television on full blast. So after paying all that money for a tour to see the countryside I have a headache from the TV and wasn't able to even see out the window until the guide gave me his front seat. I prayed and prayed to Baba to improve the situation then I finally just said to myself jubilantly, 'Alright, Baba, if this is what you want, I accept it.' "

Robin jubilantly informs her guide that he may keep the tour fee and that she'll be going back to Bangalore with her American friend. Meanwhile my mind reels at the synchronicity of this situation and the time and space factors which had to be overcome in order for Robin and me to meet at this moment and for me to have come supplied with everything she needs now. In fact, merely by following a seemingly crazy inner prompting from Baba, the result is that I can perfectly serve Him and her at the same time. How much free will do we really have, I wonder.

Robin and I admire the enchanting architecture and grounds as we stroll beside our new guide. Professor Jayaramaiah rises to the occasion of having just inherited another client and launches with great enthusiasm into an abbreviated version of the interface between the history of South India in the 1770's and its interface with the history of pre-Revolutionary colonial America. As he waves his hands toward the murals, columns and ceilings of the airy arched wooden building, he verbally gallops along describing which faction opposed which other group, which in turn caused another revolt. Meanwhile, Robin and I are entranced at the romantic, open-air palace, lotus pools and spacious lawns.

Tippu Sultan certainly had an eye for highly ornamented teakwood design as every inch of this building is painted in elaborate paisleys and Moghul prints. Charming balconies overlook vast green lawns and ancient shaded groves. In fact, we are told that the term for this intricate style of architecture is Indosaracen. Nawab Tippu Sultan Bahadur named this gem of a summer palace the "Daria Dowlat" or "Wealth From The Sea." The more we see of the building and grounds the more enchanted we become; it is definitely a worthwhile destination and one to which I'd like to return many more times.

Professor Jayaramaiah's lively tour makes all the difference in our understanding and appreciating the palace museum artifacts as well as the accomplishments and values of people who lived two hundred years ago. It seems that Tippu Sultan was an extraordinary individual by anyone's standards. In addition to being a great statesman and warrior, he was a philanthropist, a patron of the arts, builder of factories, (which produced paper, sugar, glass, silk, watches and ammunition), and a champion of religious freedom for both Christians and Hindus, though he himself was a Muslim.

Gradually, through seeing the palace murals, glancing at the guide-book, and hearing the tour lecture, we're beginning to formulate a picture of the times at the end of the eighteenth century in pre-colonial India and of the intelligent, courageous Tippu Sultan. It helps to see the glass-encased artifacts in the museum since I've just come from Fort Srirangapathnam with its ochre-hued broken stones that form the bastions and secret passage-ways. There's mention of the famous water gate or secret escape route to the Cauvery River as well as the dungeons where British officers stayed until the tide turned and Tippu was eventually betrayed and killed by the British at the age of forty-nine in 1799. He was the first and only Indian ruler to take up arms against the British.

Three facts impress us in this colorful, unusual story of Tippu Sultan's important role in national liberation by way of his attempts to unify the many warring factions of South India before the inevitable British rule came about.

One is that this leader made many financial grants to Hindu mosques, Hindu temples and Christian churches and continually demonstrated charity for clergy and lay people of all religions.

Secondly, it interests me that Napoleon, through correspondence, vowed to help Tippu fight against the British but was, himself, ambushed by the British in Egypt and was banished to the island of Elba after his capture.

Third in interest is the information that Tippu's two sons, ages eight and ten, were sent as hostages to Lord Cornwallis for two years to pay off war debts to the British. The boys were met, however, with a twenty-one gun salute, were embraced by Cornwallis, and each was presented with a gold watch.

As we reach the small upstairs museum I feel as if I really comprehend the triumphant tragedy of Tippu and the main characters so skillfully drawn by our guide. We admire a fine portrait of Tippu, which has eyes that follow the viewer, like Mona Lisa's eyes. He had such clear, luminous eyes and an air of quiet dignity. There are costumes, coins, charcoal drawings of the sons and a letter of admiration from Lord Cornwallis.

We tip Professor Jayaramaiah for his stimulating stroll down history lane and join Althaf who is snoozing in the cab. Suddenly Robin has an idea. She suggests taking me to the Halagappa Shrine which we visited on the way to the palace and which I felt was highly over-rated. She just laughs and insists that we return to see "what is really there." "You just didn't know what to look for," Robin explains patiently. Althaf, overhearing this, is curious as to exactly what it is that Robin noticed in the shrine that I either overlooked or which didn't move me.

By the time we get back to the shrine, the children have disappeared and Halagappa comes up to greet us. The large sign at the roadside announces that this is indeed the Bhagawan Sri Sathya Sai Baba Krupa of Srirangapathnam, South Bridge, Mandya District, Karnataka. Once again I enter the dimly-lit room in expectation. Suddenly I see that many of the photographs are covered with vibhuti so that only the face of either Sai Baba of Shirdi or of Sathya Sai Baba peeks out of the ash. Ash has manifested from both the paper and the glass on some of the pictures, which show Sathya Sai in all ages and stages. These are rare old photos and the amount of vibhuti on them is astounding. Halagappa leaves to get a carpet for us, which he carefully spreads out on the floor.

"Can you bring us the buckets of amrit?" Robin asks.

"Buckets?!" I exclaim. "Buckets, actually?"

"Yes, the medals of Shirdi Sai and Sathya Sai have been oozing amrit for twenty years so Halagappa just keeps them in aluminum buckets and people keep coming and taking some away in little vials and tiny perfume bottles. See, I brought this little plastic tube to take a sample back to Detroit."

Halagappa brings in two shiny silver-colored buckets, each holding a photographic medal of Shirdi Sai or Sathya Sai. Without pomp or show he scoops out a medal from each bucket and places Shirdi Sai in Robin's palm and Sathya Sai in my palm. Immediately both medals start to secrete the holy nectar, which is clear, not as viscous as honey, and smells like flowers. We are dumbfounded and stare with sagging jaws.

"Robin," I whisper, "This is a miracle... do you realize that?!"

"Of course, that's why we came here, to see miracles. It's just like I always say, 'Baba provides'. He takes care of us and also does things like this so that other people can believe the truth, too. Isn't He absolutely wonderful?"

"Yes, that's an understatement...." My mind is numbed into silence.

"Let's each give Halagappa here a big bill to contribute to the orphans," Robin suggests.

We sit looking around the room in awe after making a donation and then, Halagappa, who senses our deep devotion to Baba, jumps up and says, with enormous pleasure and anticipation," Come - I show you something."

As if we haven't already seen enough with the vibhuti and the amrit, we scamper along behind the old gentleman down a hill beside the orphanage past a Krishna statue to an enclosed outdoor shrine. The shrine is a bas-relief statue of Shirdi Sai Baba's feet, cast in black metal, perched on a cube of home-made white porcelain tiles. We're instructed to take out our hankies and place them on top of the dry statue. Within seconds the hankies are soaked with fragrant amrit. Another miracle

After thanking Halagappa profusely for his time and generosity we dash back to the cab and relate everything to Althaf, who smiles in satisfaction that this is, indeed, a special place after all.

"See? If you had not been kind to Mrs. Adamson then she would not have had the chance to bring you here to see all these things. Swami says that in life our money comes and goes but love comes and grows. So it is good you are helping people. We must all be helping," Althaf proclaims.

Althaf is definitely showing more interest in and awareness of Baba's teachings these days and his ears are like trumpets every time Robin and I exchange stories of personal experiences with Baba's jokes, grace, healings or miracles.

We all decide to have the picnic lunch at the Ranganathittu Bird Sanctuary which is known as a winter stop-over for exotic birds from around the world. How perfect it is that we have plenty of hard-boiled eggs, sandwiches, cookies, fruit, soft drinks, water - and roast chicken for Althaf. Since birds are an endless delight to me, I'm touched that we can enjoy this park together while Althaf takes another nap.

Robin announces that since she saw me last she received the distinct instruction from Baba, through a vision and a dream, that she is not to leave her husband Peter but that she is to return home and heal the relationship. She definitely feels that Swami is a new, loving, tender Mother to her. "And I've needed one so badly all of my life," she confides.

We joke about Baba's materializations and how He has said that if He were to materialize large college buildings instead of waiting for us humans to complete them that it would attract too much attention and the government of India would panic and surround Him with armed guards as if He were a precious artifact or a national treasure.

But our lovely day isn't over as we have yet to see the Palace of Mysore, and the well-known Brindavan Gardens and Cauvery Reservoir. Since all three of us enjoy flowers enormously we find the Brindavan Gardens the perfect topper of the day with teal blue waterfall cascades, fountains, a lake and roiling waterfalls, water sprays in shapes of arcs and domes. The long vista at the base of the breath-taking stairway to the lake is vivid with colorful flowers. There are oblong pools displaying several different qualities of water surfaces such as ripples, waves, rivulets, and turbulent aspects. At night there is a sound and light show where colored water jets dance to music.

We marvel at our good fortune as we make the long climb back up the hill from the lake to take a last look at the panoramic view of the pools, lake and gardens from the old white honeymooners' hotel.

"Just think, Robin, our smallest needs and delights have been attended to by Baba. This is exactly the sort of thing that you and I love but I wasn't inclined to arrange it for myself since I just wanted to see Him in darshan. Even the tour you arranged wasn't as fine as this has turned out to be. He really is guiding us. In fact, there's a saying that "a coincidence is a miracle that God doesn't want to take direct credit for."

We both agree that Liberation is our goal in this life, God willing, and that, of the nearly six billion people in the world now, we are incomparably blessed to be able to spend this precious time with God Himself. Robin leaves India tomorrow. In about ten days I'll be leaving too, to join Jim in China. How I love Baba and India.

CHAPTER 22
AKHANDA BHAJAN INTERVIEW

"The end of wisdom is freedom. The end of culture is perfection. The end of knowledge is love. The end of education is character."
Sathya Sai Baba

Puttaparthi, India
November 9, 1986

We have been granted an interview with Baba! It is Sunday, November 9, l986, at approximately 7:20 A.M. It is also Akhanda Bhajans, second day, morning darshan, so we had given up hope that Baba would see us.

As I search the crowd from my vantage point on the Mandir veranda, yesterday's Thought for the Day flashes through my mind, as it certainly seems to be epitomized by the circumstance of our imminent interview with Baba. A few of us intend to ask Baba for Realization.

The 'Thought' states: "Every man yearns for only two boons – escape from sorrow and attainment of joy. When both are achieved, man is truly free; he has gained liberation. Do we reach liberation along the path of activity or of inquiry or of devotion? The argument will only fog the issue. These paths only cleanse the mind or clarify the intellect, or purify the emotions. If the Atmic Core of all things and beings is recognized, bliss will be ever present and full. Sai Baba"

As the rest of the group approaches the veranda and awaits Baba, I read my journal notes and today's Thought: "The Divine Principle is the Reality, the Base, the Essence, the Ocean in which the waves rise, roar and fall. Discard the name and form which are ever changing and contemplate on Existence – Consciousness – Bliss, of which each cell and particle are constructed. Then you can immerse yourself in Eternal bliss, Anand, which is Omnipresent. One has only to know how to discover it and derive it from the Source Which is everywhere. Sai Baba"

The Interview Participants

The participants of the interview are: Aleks and Lubov Babarin; Phoebe Gasich; Jann De Hoog; Dean Lusted, M.D.; Malini Angunawela; Vimila and spouse Srinivas and young daughter; Winnie Phelps; Suzi Elbert; Mrs. V. (wishes to remain anonymous); Connie Shaw.

(Note: This interview write-up was sent to a national Sai magazine by another interviewee. Thus, since it has already been printed in the 1990's, the actual names of participants are included, rather than giving the interviewees pseudonyms for anonymity.)

After our "American group" had assembled on the Mandir veranda Sai Baba told one of the party to leave, then He instructed us to enter the outer interview room. We formed a "women's side" on the right and a "men's side" on the left and all sat down on the floor. Baba closed the door and walked to the front of our group, which also included one or two people whom we hadn't met; He manifested vibhuti for the women, which He dropped into our outstretched palms and said "Eat."

Baba, to the group: "What do you want?" He then looked at Aleks, a Russian American from New York.

Aleks: "I want Sai Yuja - only to merge with You. To be love."

Baba: "Love... Not physical love."

Aleks: "What Sadhana should I do?"

Baba: "Don't think 'What work shall I do?' Think that only: Baba is doing work through this vehicle. Do Seva with the hands..." (while materializing a silver color "ID" type bracelet on which was etched the "Om" symbol) "Do Sohum meditation. Like this - (He inhaled deeply) Soooo ... Hummmmm. Soooo... Hummmmm. You must do this 21,600 times a day. Always Sohum, Sohum. All of you here should do this every day."

Then, turning swiftly to Dean, Baba asked him "What is your name?"

Dean: "Dean."

Baba: "Last name?"

Dean: "Lusted."

Baba: "Have faith in yourself. Without faith in yourself, faith in God is impossible."

Baba, to Connie: "Where are you from?"

Connie: (Since He'd asked me this twice this week in the darshan line, I thought I'd try the answer which my roommate, Zilla, had suggested that very morning which she had read in a book about Baba. "If He asks you again where you are from say, 'I'm from the Atma, going to the Atma.'") "I'm from the Atma, going to the Atma... meanwhile living in the USA!"

Baba: "No. All is Atma. This is a wrong answer. Atma is in you, in all. All this coming and going, going and coming... is not Atma." (I felt He meant that mere travel for pleasure is a waste of time and that I should sit still more and contemplate God.)

Baba, to group: "What is the road to immortality?"

Jann: "Morality."

Baba: "This is not a full answer... not immorality. The way to immortality is to remove immorality. Peace, love, truth, righteousness, harmlessness."

Then, turning to Malini, He said softly, "What do you want?"

Malini: "You, Baba."

Baba: "Here, here, here I am. You have Me. You are still a child… "
Then, to the group: "Come."

Connie: "All of us?"

Baba: "Yes". (He gestured for us to step into the inner room, behind the curtain. He noticed Dean looking at Aleks and said dramatically "Jealousy!" Dean later told us that he wasn't jealous that Baba had materialized a bracelet for Aleks but was, in fact jealous of Aleks' faith since faith was an area of difficulty for him personally.)

Swami saw to it that we were all seated on the floor in the far room then He sat in His brown corduroy easy chair and began the "personal" part of the interview.

Baba: "What do you want? Problems? Your problems?" (He was being playful and light and we should have known what was coming - jokes at our expense!)

Winnie: "Baba, should I move (from Mesa, Arizona) to Arkansas to be with Virginia?" (i.e., to set up a Sai group there)

Baba: "Yes. Do it."

Vimila quickly asked a question, presumably about the future.

(At this point I saw that Baba was operating on at least four levels with us. He was using every opportunity to not only answer each question on the practical level as well as on a subtle or jocular level, but that He was also using every available chance to teach the group and to hold our attention with mini-discourses. The fourth level of spiritual expression was His healing Presence which affected us on the physical, mental, emotional and spiritual levels and kept working within us even after the interview itself was over.)

Baba, to Vimila and the group: "Live only in the present, not the past or the future. Joy is an interval between two points of pain. Pain is a point between two periods of joy."

Mrs. V., anxiously, in Telugu: "Baba, what can you tell me about my son?" (Her son, in his early twenties, had suddenly disappeared a year and a half before and was feared dead.)

Baba, in Telugu: "Yes, he is fine. And where is he?"

Mrs. V: "I don't know. He left home."

Baba: "You're wondering if he's even alive, aren't you?"

Mrs. V: "Yes. Is he all right?"

Baba: "Yes, he's fine and you will be hearing from him soon. He couldn't face his father since he didn't want to disappoint him (and presumably wasn't very keen about following in his professional footsteps) so he dropped out of school and went to Canada where he is working and living with a girl who is also working. They are happy and he will come back. He left his car in a shopping center and you thought he was dead. He called several times and hung up as he wanted to hear his mother's voice. He feels guilty. Don't be hard on him. He's a good boy. Welcome and bless them both. They love each other. But he doesn't want to be forced to be a doctor like his father."

Mrs. V. later cried with great joy and relief and was immensely appreciative for the interview and news of her son, who had always been a model child and student.

Jann: "Swami, what about (my opening) the Sai School in Stanton (Orange County, California)?"

Baba: "Yes, open it."

Jann: "Any advice on that, Swami?"

Baba: "Advice?! My life is My message."

Jann: "But what to teach?"

Baba: "Character. Stories and plays on qualities… honesty, morality, confidence, love, courage, truth, righteousness. And no drugs. All are taking drugs – even adults. You know and I know - it affects the mind. Not good. We must be Divine." (He pronounces it Deevine) Then glancing and smiling at Aleks says, "Deevine, not deep wine!" We all laugh.

Baba, to Dean: "What do you want?"

Dean: "Faith, Swami."

Baba: "Yes, faith in Self. Without faith in Self there is no self-confidence. Without self-confidence there is no self-satisfaction. There must be self-confidence, self-satisfaction, self-sacrifice, then Self-realization."

Baba, to Winnie: "What are you doing, Sir?" (Meaning in her work, which had been a constant preoccupation or concern to her of late.)

Winnie: "Trying to serve you, Swami."

Baba: "No trying. You must DO, not try."

Baba, to Connie, abruptly: "Where is your band?"

Connie, puzzled: "My band? My what, Swami? How's that?!"

Baba, merrily, but pretending impatience: "Your band. BAND. HUS-band." (We later learned that 'band' means faithful servant.)

Connie: "Oh, my husband. He's in China."

Baba: "In China?"

Connie: "Yes - China. But I haven't seen him in a month; I think he's still there." (There was a long distance telephone operators' strike in India at the time so we had had no communication whatsoever.)

Baba: "How many husbands?" (He was setting me up for a joke but I didn't see it coming and was very serious.)

Connie, perplexed: "Only one." I (naturally) have one husband....

Baba: "No, you have two."

Connie, catching on: "Oh yes, I see. Yes, he's my second one. But Swami, I only had one husband at a time!" (After having been married for five and a half years after university graduation I was single for eight years and am happily remarried. I intend for this second marriage to be my last. By this time I was getting slightly irritated and embarrassed, not understanding that he was yet to tease me more. Was He intimating that He is also my husband and always has been?)

Baba: "But you're trying for a third husband."

Connie, shocked and mystified: "No! No, Swami, never!" (Huffing and puffing now, with hands on hips, challenging Him. How could He possibly say such a thing when I am such a virtuous wife?!)

Baba: "Ah, ah. Bumps and jumps. Your mind is making bumps and jumps." Then, to the group, he makes a metaphor: "She is trying for a third husband. The first husband (which we should all "try" for) is the moral life. The second husband is the spiritual life. The third husband is the Divine life (Self-realization). That's the third. Divine life. She wants Self realization." (So that's it: Baba was teasing me to make a point about the fact that I'm earnestly working to attain Self-realization. Why must He always tease and embarrass me so in front of interview groups?!)

Baba to Connie: "I will bless you with a long life, a healthy life, a happy life and a Divine life (Self-realization)."

Baba, to Aleks: "Do you have children? Do you want children?"

Aleks: "No."

Baba: "It's good to have children. You should have two children, a girl and a boy. The son is wisdom and the daughter is peace. Baba, to Aleks: Your wife – sometimes crying, sometimes happy. She is doubting you." Jokingly, Baba said, "Women are like that. Sometimes she is doubting. She loves you. She is good. Very good woman. (To Luba:) He's a good man."

Aleks: "She is your daughter (peace)."

Baba, to Phoebe: "Where is your husband?"

Phoebe: "Gone, Swami."

Baba: "Yes, gone. It's very good if Mother is God, Father is God, sister is God, brother is God." Then Swami spontaneously chanted the Sanskrit words to a song that Al Drucker had taught us recently in a lecture. Baba turned to Suzi and nodded.

Suzi: "May I speak Japanese?" He ignored this, although He speaks all the languages in the world. The author has heard Him speak Telugu, English, Japanese, Spanish, Hindi, and many Indian dialects.

Baba: "Be alike to everyone. Treat all alike. Treat all the same."

Jann: "Baba, should I marry?"

Baba: "Yes. Why do you want to marry? For five minutes of happiness in the day, why do you want 23 hours and 55 minutes of trouble? Marriage is not for social security. Go, get a husband."

Jann: "Swami, you're my security. You choose my husband."

Baba, to Connie: "And now, you. You will have a long life, a happy life, a healthy life, a peaceful life and... a Divine life (Self-realization). Now, come." He beckoned us out to the outer interview room again.

Baba: "Very happy. Very happy (with you)."

As everyone scrambled into the other room, Connie asked what to do with her book manuscript, to which He replied, "Yes, yes." (Whatever that means.)

Baba, to the reassembled group: "The first step: develop confidence. Without confidence there is no God. Where there is confidence there is love. Where there is love, there is peace. Where there is peace, there is truth. Where there is truth, there is God."

"I will have a surprise for all after Akhanda Bhajans."

Baba, to Connie: "When are you leaving?"

Connie: "Today."

Baba: "Today *night*, is it?"

Connie: "Yes."

Baba nods and starts a mini-discourse:

"Consciousness is the omnipresent, unchanging. Conscience is in your heart. You are three people - the one you think you are (physical and mental); the one others think you are (the personality); and the One You really are (obviously we must all identify more consistently with the I AM Presence within.)"

Baba, to Malini: "How are you, Mad Girl? Complete hysteria."

Malini: "Can I merge in you, Baba, in this life?"

Baba: "It's not easy. Do your work. Do your duty to family."

Then, to Jann: "How long are you staying, Sir?" (Jann had hoped and prayed He wouldn't address her as "Sir.")

Jann: "Until after Christmas, Swami."

Baba: "Until after Christmas? Yes, yes."

He then got up and took His basket of packaged vibhuti and dropped little packets into our hands, then announced that the interview had come to an end.

We were all a bit light-headed and blissful as we walked across the Mandir courtyard in front of the singing crowd and out the gate. We decided to go to Malini's place to re-create the interview and make it available and to collect odds and ends of food for a celebration and thanksgiving together. Phoebe quickly made lemonade into which we put a pinch of vibhuti. Luba brought a cake and Phoebe brought cookies and Danish cheese. A vegetable roll and a cheese puff appeared and lo, a feast!

"Let's propose a toast."

"This is communion. Oh, how fortunate we are."

"To Divine life, Self-Realization, to Swami!"

"Thank you, Swami! Om Sai Ram!"

On the way back to my room after our group meeting I came around the corner of the building swiftly and barely avoided colliding with a huge and exquisite black and cobalt blue butterfly. There were large luminous blue circles, about the size of a button, in the center of his wings and two shades of blue ruffles on the outer edges of the wings. He swerved sharply to avoid me and crashed into the wall in front of me. He fell to the ground, dead. I gasped, and felt awful as I bent over him, telling him how very sorry I was to have caused his untimely death.

Then I remembered Lazarus and decided to try to resurrect him.

"Come back, Lazarus Butterfly! Come back now! Your work in the world isn't finished. Return to bless humanity. Arise, Lazarus Butterfly! You can return now. In the Name of Sathya Sai Baba awake and arise!"

To my utter astonishment, he jerked his head up, flapped his spectacularly-colored wings and flapped away.

It was such a surprise that Lazarus Butterfly had resurrected himself, through Baba's grace, that I remembered the words of Jesus that "Greater works than these that I do, ye shall do, and even greater works." Immediately I began to will myself to create vibhuti. I've been practicing hundreds of times without success. As I was twirling my hand the way Baba does, attempting to manifest vibhuti, Zilla came around the corner. Embarrassed, I turned the vibhuti-making motion into a fly-swatting motion.

She had seen our group go onto the veranda and had not felt inclined to join us since she had been sitting in the patient section of darshan each day, and hadn't attended our meetings and didn't know the other group members. She also had felt ill at ease about her deafness and felt that most people "chattered far more than was good for them."

"Oh, Darling! I'm so happy for you. What happened? What did Baba say? Did He manifest anything for anyone?" Zilla asked.

"Thank you, Zilla. Yes, He manifested an identification bracelet for a Russian American named Aleks from New York. He teased me and then He told me He'd give me a long life, a healthy life, a happy life and Self-realization." I had been whispering, as is customary in the Ashram. We were standing directly under a sign that said "Silence."

"That's exceptional," Zilla said, in normal tones. "He gave you the ultimate grace. That's all that anyone could want."

Suddenly we both stopped breathing and stared at each other. Zilla was practically stone deaf. Or at least she had been until yesterday. Yet she had heard my whispering perfectly.

"Zilla! Can you hear me when I whisper like this or are you reading my lips," I asked with my lips closed, like a ventriloquist.

"Darling, I can hear you," she answered.

"That means you've been healed, Zilla!" I shouted.

We embraced and began to dance around and around in a little circle, chortling, crying, giggling, praising Baba, beside ourselves with joy. Tears ran down our cheeks.

"Oh, Connie," Zilla said breathlessly, "That little Swami Honey has healed my hearin' and I'm going to be grateful to him forever and ever."

We opened the door to our little ashram room and I could hardly see properly to pack my luggage for my departure today, because tears of gratitude kept flowing.

Oh My Lord, how wonderful Thou art. You love each of us more than we can possibly understand. How I will miss Your Sweet Form when I go back to China the next few months.

Guangzhou, China
November 12th

After having spent a month in India I'd like to return to Baba for Christmas with Jim and Scott, who is now eighteen, and is in school in Seattle, Washington. Jim is willing to go to Puttaparthi for Christmas if we can get tickets at this late date. We would leave a month from now, and would arrive back in India in mid-December.

There are many things which I've learned the past twenty years on the path of conscious spirituality. One is that the reward for patience is more patience. Another is that the reward for service is more service. Baba loves each of us more than we could ever imagine and gives us continual opportunities to know ourselves and to serve Him by showing love and compassion to others. What an inordinately blessed life this is; how did we become so incredibly fortunate?

CHAPTER 23
HOLY CHRISTMAS

"Jesus announced himself as the Messenger of God. He spent many years in austerities so that he could shower compassion and love on all humanity. Later, he asked himself, 'Am I just a messenger, or am I more closely related to God, a part of God with the divine as my essence?' Jesus spent twelve long years wandering alone in deserts engaged in this inquiry. At the end of this period, he returned to the society of men and announced, 'I am the Son of God.' "
Sathya Sai Baba, AEVJC

Guangzhou, China
December 15, 1986
Four weeks ago I left India and came to China to join Jim. In the past few days, however, Baba telepathically impressed me to attempt to get air tickets to India for Jim, Scott and me. Scott is in school in Seattle and would like to celebrate Christmas as a family in India with Baba.

After much gnashing of teeth due to the fact that our travel agents haven't been able to get air tickets for the three of us, at this late date, I sat down and wrote out a "telegram" to Baba today. I didn't mail the telegram, but put it in the drawer of the hotel room desk. I knew He'd get it anyway, as He says, since He knows all of our thoughts. It said:

"Dear Swami, Please help us! We need three round trip seat openings to leave within 48 hours to come see you. Can you please get Scott booked from Seattle to India and back so that he doesn't miss more than a few days of school? Jim and I can meet him there. All my love, Connie."

Meanwhile, I didn't give up hoping and praying and asking Swami to guide and protect Scott if he were able to travel alone to Asia to meet us. Since he's eighteen and hasn't been to India before, much less alone, I felt I should ask Baba to light his way, as He did mine when I went alone to India eight weeks ago. Also, I asked Baba mentally to please help Jim in his work so that we wouldn't have to always be moving overseas for several months at a time. I don't mind traveling but feel that we can't very well operate my business and provide leadership for the Sai Study Group and service projects if we're not available on a consistent basis.

December 16th
Swami really acts fast: I only sent my unmailed telegram yesterday, by putting it in the desk drawer with fervent prayers. Last night Jim came home from work to say that we have three air tickets to go to India. Scott will go to Bangkok, change planes on a tight connection, then go to Delhi and wait for ten hours for a flight to Bangalore. I have attempted to send telexes to the Babu Taxi Service and the West End Hotel so that Scott can be met by both the driver and the hotel staff, and be given a

meal. After he rests, he can come with the driver to the Bangalore Airport to meet us later in the day.

Jim also said that his boss informed him that he will have a new job description upon arriving in the States in mid-January. Jim will supervise those who set up plants and will travel extensively still, but won't have to live overseas in the future, it seems. Hooray! Thank you, Baba, for both miracles - and so speedily, too.

December, 17th

Jim's secretary, Dear Soul, sent the plane ticket to Seattle in time for Scott to get it only twenty-four hours before he was to leave on the trip. We have all been tested regarding our faith these past three weeks as we were told repeatedly that all flights were booked and that it would be impossible for all three of us to get to India at the same time.

This morning I finalized all packing details and took a cab to the Wampoa Ferry to meet Jim and proceed to Hong Kong to stay overnight before leaving for India via Kuala Lumpur, Malaysia.

December 19th

In K.L., which is a lovely, clean, modern city, we stayed at the simple but adequate Federal Hotel then left early for a flight to Madras. In Madras we went into town to have the buffet lunch at the Sheraton Chola and then Jim took a cab to Malaysian Airlines but the cab broke down and he had to walk. Meanwhile, while awaiting him in the Sheraton lobby I bought a huge white calf-length shawl to cover my (nearly transparent) punjabi suit that I had made by Miss Mo in Guangzhou. My underwear was showing right through it.... When I bought the fabric I should have unrolled the bolt and held the material up to the light to ascertain that it would pass the "modesty test."

From the Sheraton phone I called Babu to see if he had received my telex. He was surprised to hear from me. He hadn't met Scott at the airport, so I asked him to call Scott at the West End and tell him, if he had indeed arrived, that we are on our way and will see him tonight. Now I am wondering how he got to the West End Hotel and if there was a room available since they probably didn't receive a telex from China either. We seem to be having so many opportunities to give our concerns to Baba and not to worry, even though we have no idea where Scott is or even if he safely left Bangkok and Delhi, if he had enough money with him, and so on. Baba keeps telling us He's our Mother and Father so we'll just have to keep praying, knowing that He knows the correct outworking of all events, processes and circumstances.

December 20th

What an immense relief it is to see a loved one after a period of not knowing the condition, safety or whereabouts of that person. At the West End Hotel desk we were informed that Scott had, indeed, checked in several hours before. They were not expecting him or us, and did not know we were even related, as no telex had arrived. When we finally found Scott, he opened the hotel room door looking like a red-haired cadaver, with sunken eyes from having flown over twelve thousand miles, without sleep for nearly thirty hours. But he was full of stories about his adventuresome trip and was obviously glad to see us, though extremely confident and satisfied with his successful solo trip without parental chaperoning.

I enthusiastically thanked Baba aloud for taking such excellent care of him, start to finish. Scott told us, with Indian accents, rolling eyes and little dramatic touches, about his encounter with a charlatan taxi driver. He mentioned how, as he got off the plane at the Delhi Airport, he was approached enthusiastically by a cabby. The eager driver asked if he were an American and if he wanted to go to the domestic airport. Scott, stunned at the possibility that there were two airports, and that he had yet another one to reach, agreed to go with the driver. It turned out that the "taxi" was a three-wheeler and that the man drove him to the outskirts of town and asked him how much money he had.

Scott, suspecting trouble, said "Ten American dollars. See? Why? How much is this cab ride to the other airport going to cost me?" It was late at night and he was beginning to get scared. He also began to wonder how, if he were robbed or worse, at night in Delhi, India, he'd ever be able to let us know what happened to him.

"Ten dollars?! Oh no... this ride cost forty dollars.... But don't worry. Since you have only ten dollars I do it for that." He was way overcharged but at least he learned a lesson about settling the price first. He now knows to find out ahead of time the distance from someone other than the driver, and to see the cab first before agreeing to take that specific conveyance. The ride shouldn't have cost more than a few dollars.

After hearing about Scott's little taxi detour, the three of us, famished, went downstairs for lunch and then started filming the grounds and fabled trees of this lovely hotel.

It is so good to see Althaf, who, luckily enough, is in town and can take us to Puttaparthi tomorrow at 3:30 in the morning. This afternoon Scott and I went down to Mahatma Ghandi Road to get some provisions for the trip to the ashram. We needed some white kurta shirts for Jim and Scott, a hanging mirror, some plastic water bottles and some immersible coils in case we're lucky enough to have a room or even an electrical outlet nearby so that we can make tea and soup. We brought a few snacks, nuts, tea and coffee with us in case the canteen lines are too long because of the large Christmas crowds.

The West End staff sent a basket of chocolate and fruit to our room and are very glad to see me again and to meet Jim and Scott. They are friendly and warm to both of them but Scott and Jim haven't yet attuned their ears to the Indian accent here and can't understand much of what they say. They and the staff are frustrated at being unable to communicate with each other when I'm not around to interpret, so they usually have a brief exchange of smiling and nodding with much embarrassment on all sides. The staff think Jim and Scott mumble, "like all Americans" and Scott and Jim believe that the Indians are speaking a local dialect, even when they're speaking perfect British English. It takes practice in close listening to catch the British-Indian English rhythm of their speech and to understand the unfamiliar terminology to which we're unaccustomed. For example, they use the term 'lift', for elevator, 'chemist' for drug store, 'tiffin' for snack or meal and 'lorry' for truck.

Our room, number 8, has an enormously high ceiling, a fan, three twin beds, a sofa and chairs, a desk and wardrobe, and a funny old-fashioned bathroom containing an antique tub with ball-and-claw feet. It's charming, really, and a real luxury to have a bathtub in India. Jim and Scott love the local color, the many kind attentions of the staff, the garden walkways and spreading trees. There's a newly-finished pool and veranda with dining tables and wicker chairs.

Tomorrow we arrive in Puttaparthi again and I'm wondering if any of "the old American interview group" will still be there. I've written to Zilla several times but don't know if my letters ever got out of China. Hopefully the interview participants will have received the typed copies of the interview that I sent from Guangzhou. Mom told me on the phone that she hasn't received a card or letter in two months, though I've written many cards and a few lengthy letters to her and Dad from both India and China. It's always a thrill to get through to the States on the phone since one in nine or ten calls might go through on the ancient phone lines in Asia. The electricity still goes out all the time in China and India but I'm used to it now and don't mind.

December 21st

Groggily, we piled ourselves and our luggage into Althaf's number 357 cab. Somehow everything fit and we launched off toward Prashanti Nilayam around 3:00 A.M. this morning. The unfinished road to 'Parthi is so bumpy that we kept hitting our heads on the cab ceiling about three times a minute. We made a family joke that by arrival time the three of us would have such flat skulls from having hit our heads about six hundred times on the roof, that we would surely qualify for honorary initiation into the North American Indian Flathead Tribe.

After three hours of rattle-rattle-bumpety-bump, we drove up to the Accommodations Office at dawn and there, walking along in her intense, bent-over way was Zilla. I rolled down the window and said, in a stage whisper, so as not to disturb the silence so early

"Zilla! It's Connie - we're here! We made it - all three of us." She stood there a moment as if seeing a ghost then hurried over and hugged me through the window.

"Oh, my child, how good to see you...." Then she collected herself and reached across me to shake Jim's hand, saying "I've always loved the name Jim. I'm so glad you could come with Connie. She's such a wonderful person. And Scott, you've come too. How wonderful. And

Althaf - how are you doing? Well, I'm glad you all got here safely; now I must go quickly and have some breakfast before darshan. Won't you meet me when you've settled in a bit, Connie? By the way, I got that interview write-up you sent and what a memory you have. I loved reading it so." Zilla's hearing was still perfect since Baba's healing of her deafness a month ago.

Right beside the cab is the little black chalk board with Baba's Thought For The Day: "Sunday - Man is eager to collect information about everything else but he never asks 'Who am I?' Though he uses the expression "I" and "my" freely almost always. Remember, you are the forever, the body is the field. Sow the seeds of goodness - you can get the harvest of happiness. Sow the seeds of evil - you reap the harvest of grief. You yourself are the cause of either of these."

Later, as I glance around from the women's side of the Mandir court-yard, during darshan, I wonder how Jim and Scott are doing. Then I see them from where I'm sitting. They're in the front row. Swami comes out and floats along the ground toward the women patients and takes letters, blesses photos and creates vibhuti. As He comes toward me He manifests vibhuti for four women just a few yards from me and I am swept with the feeling that this is where I belong - here with Baba. It is unspeakably good to be back here. What good fortune to be able to have come to India twice in one year. Hopefully it will be a beneficial time for the whole family.

After darshan, at the Accommodations Office, we are informed that we will be in Hall 17/18 and may go there immediately to find a space. On walking into the shed/hall we are relieved to find that there are still several spaces available. It's not as crowded yet as it was last year when we had to sleep with our upper bodies inside the makeshift room while our knees and feet stuck out into the aisle. Crossing our fingers that we'll be able to find three cots available to rent in town, we are elated that some people in our hall are leaving at this very moment, and agree to let us accompany their porter who will return their cots on this rickshaw. At the shop, we check the cots back in and out in one smooth operation, then walk back to the hall and empty our bags of all "architectural supplies" in order to assess how we might rig up a little cubicle for the three of us.

Although Scott is quite adaptable for an American teenager, I am interested in his reactions to the ashram and the shed. He gets over his shock at the simple accommodations fairly quickly. Scott cheerfully helps me throw the parachute cord around the beam rafters so that we can attach white sheeting material to it with clothespins, and have some privacy for changing clothes and sleeping. We meet with curious stares of the other hall occupants, many of whom are overseas Indians. The luggage fits under the cots and the sheeting of our tiny cubicle touches the sides of Jim's and Scott's beds; my cot is in the middle, directly against the other two.

Across the shed I can hear some Indian-American kids complaining to their parents that they had not been adequately warned about the rigors of the ashram. Throughout the shed there is sympathetic chuckling from other shed occupants inside the various cubicles.

We investigate the latrines and Scott is disgusted. It smells. There are rows of sinks and mirrors, then a row of showers and behind that a row of enclosed Western toilets with separate doors. There are signs on the shower doors: "Please do not urinate in the showers. Please keep the facilities clean. Flush the toilets. Turn off the water faucets. Sai Ram"

Our hall is open near the rafters so dust and birds fly in but at least we have a roof over our heads and so many in the world live nearly like this every day for a lifetime. They never have hot water or a refrigerator or nice furniture and carpets on their floors. And they have no space or privacy, as most of us in the West do, and take quite for granted.

December 22nd

It seems that we have, in our hall, many toddlers and small children who run and yell from the wee hours onwards. The noise reverberates off the concrete and the racket is dreadful. We all have jet lag and yet are thrilled to be here despite the hardship of having to wait in lines for everything - food, bathrooms, showers, sinks, darshan, post office, stores. I won't even mention the bakery because the lines are so long one can't tell where they start or end and it's futile to approach the mob there.

Choir practice for foreigners promises to be a treat as Liz, the American singing teacher is leading Christmas carols for the Christmas day program. We hear that Maynard Ferguson, the American jazz trumpet player is here and that he will be a part of the program with us.

There's an American group here that meets daily under the tree near the bookstore. I was delighted to see that Phoebe, Jann and Dean are still here. Phoebe was able to obtain another interview just five days after our group interview of November 9th. She told me, gasping at the recollection, that Baba materialized a crystal japamala in that one but that He didn't give as many teachings and mini-discourses to the seven of them. He chatted a bit with each person. "It was lovely! He is so serene, impish, adorable and majestic - all at the same time. He allowed padnamaskar for all the ladies. I have to keep reminding myself that He really has given me so much and that I'm not dreaming." Phoebe has decided to stay for nearly a year, if she can manage to get a visa extension. She, as well as all the others I met here seem so much calmer than even a month ago. Their faces look very different; they look relaxed and radiant. Even the talkative, nervous ones have calmed down and tell me how happy they feel.

As Jim, Scott and I walk to afternoon darshan after hearing Phoebe's account of the second interview we see Baba's daily message: "You must realize that this life is a stage in the long pilgrimage and that now we are in a hotel, a temporary resting place which has also a watchman. The mind is that watchman. So do not feel permanently attached to the mind or the body."

December 23rd

After a few good nights of rest we're all feeling more human, strong, healthy and cheerful. Scott and Jim keep getting in the first few rows in darshan, so Scott has had perfect spots from which to view Baba blessing the old and young with His words, smiles, looks, pats, vibhuti, counsel and interviews. There's no place else we'd rather be during this strenuous yet merry adventure in Puttaparthi this Christmas.

Our family has decided to give each other service and more consideration all year long instead of gifts this Christmas. Baba keeps encouraging all of us to have a "Holy Christmas" in keeping with what Jesus had in mind with His ministry. He didn't intend that we should make of His birth anniversary a marathon of gorging ourselves on food, drink, lavish presents and noisy parties of nonsensical interchange and meaningless interactions.

Christine Spring from Switzerland - the therapist - is still here. She leaves the day after Christmas and is looking bright as always with her curly brown hair, translucent complexion and wry smile. She is terribly sad to be going after these months, as all are, but knows she must face it and get back home to start a new chapter. She introduced me to a wonderful woman named Claudia Zimmermann who was on her way to China when, the day before she left, a friend in Germany called her and insisted that she "visit someone named Sai Baba in South India." Claudia is a former fabric buyer and, most recently, a personnel manager and communications specialist for a large German company. She tells me that she had to leave her work as she only wanted to talk of spiritual things and was beginning to not fit in with her subordinates in the conventional ways anymore, though they were hungry to hear about the spiritual life.

Claudia's parents are coming here the first week of January to see what their daughter has found in this Sai Baba. Since He repeatedly says that no one can come to Him without His willing it, then Claudia is fortunate that her parents are coming so soon after her own discovery.

A few weeks ago, before going to sleep, I asked Swami if He'd be so good as to tell me specifically, in a dream, which members of our family would, if any, be coming to Him in our lifetime. I mentioned curiosity about my sister Bev, brothers Rod, Mike and Rick, and also about stepsons Jonathan and Benjamin. Naturally I'm also wondering if Mom and Dad will ever have any curiosity about Him.

The same night that I asked, I had a dream that all three of our boys would come to Baba and that my sister and all three brothers would come. My, my, what a marvelous message - and so fast. I suppose Mom and Dad will continue within Catholicism which is just fine, of course. They haven't shown the slightest interest in Sai Baba or in anything mystical or metaphysical these past twenty years so I'd be shocked at this point if they changed. And I've let go of wanting them to be more open to my own spiritual pursuits. We simply don't talk about spirituality much. Last summer, however, Mike told me that Mom and Dad think I've really gone too far in being so enthusiastic about the life of Spirit. They think I'm slipping away from the dock! If they only knew that I've found safe harbor in the Lord!

Each morning our American group gathers for a head count and passing of the sign-up sheet. Jack Hawley of California leads us in chanting three Oms and a five-minute meditation followed by an Om and three "Shanti's" for peace. This makes a very tight schedule as we arise at 5:00 and shower then organize the laundry for the daily pick-up and delivery at 6:00. At a quarter past six we sprint over the hill to the canteen for a quick breakfast and then jog to the darshan lineup about 6:45 A.M. Darshan lines enter about 7:00 and Baba comes out at 7:15. We stay for bhajans at 9:00 then meet our fellow countrymen at 9:30 and proceed to choir practice at 10:00 in Hall 25 with Liz and 200 foreigners.

Liz has let us know we will be practicing night and day for hours on end until our Christmas choir sounds perfect. She's extremely exacting but very professional, warm, and even saintly as well as funny. Everyone loves her. More crowds are coming and the halls are filling up daily but since we're kept so busy with the Christmas program preparation we barely notice. Everyone who arrives is made to feel welcome and quickly joins in the activities.

Strands of Christmas lights in pink, green and white are looped all over the Mandir, causing it to resemble a fairy castle at night. A cross and a star sparkle brightly from the front of the building as the twinkling garlands of light wink off and on in alternating patterns. Holiday excitement is building with Baba as the focus of this hallowed occasion. There has been no mention of food, gifts, or any of the usual nonsense that so dominates consciousness at this time of year elsewhere. What a delightful change.

This afternoon when I bumped into Dean, he told me he has greatly changed and wants nothing more upon returning home to the States than to get a "nice little room near a safe park and a library." He's unsure what he'll do next with a background as a physician, or how to dispose of his properties in New England. He's brimful of joy and contentment and says he has self-confidence and deep love for Baba, as per Baba's counsel to him in our interview. What new insights will Christmas bring us, I wonder?

December 23rd Evening

This day seems to have gone on for a week. We have been singing since early morning with a ferocious intensity focused on putting the final polishing touches on the five songs we'll sing on Christmas day. Liz seems to garner more energy the closer we get to the Big Day and becomes livelier by the hour. She is infinitely patient and loving with us. Baba has the most outstanding leaders and organizers for His various enterprises, including those involved with the Christmas program.

One of the benefits we receive from learning music from her, aside from being in her presence and sharpening up musically, is that she has immense knowledge of the deeper meanings of the Sanskrit words of the songs. There's a breathtakingly beautiful song called *Buddham Sharanam* which we're practicing now and when Liz sees that we're just not singing with the right spirit, she quietly halts our rather clunky wobble-warbling and gives some background on the song. "Now let's really look at these words a minute:

> Buddham sharanam, Gach cha mi.
> Dharmam sharanam, Gach cha mi.
> Sangham sharanam, Gach cha mi.
> Saisha sharanam, Gach cha mi."

"In volume two of *Sathya Sai Speaks* there's a discourse on this. Roughly, it's intelligence, the power of discrimination - I take refuge in the power to discriminate (Buddham). I take refuge in morality, justice. I take refuge in the family of man. When there's a problem with another I see God in my fellow and I don't let go until we reach concord. That's what this means. Now... let's try that again." Every single devotional song that we sing as Sai devotees is filled with instruction and inspiration. Liz is supremely skilled at making the music and words spring to life for the choir.

After a vigorous afternoon practice we're told to quickly get dinner after darshan and bhajans and then to return at 7:45 P.M. with flashlights. We will practice walking around with them as we'll do when we sing on Christmas morning before dawn.

At darshan today Baba materialized a gold ring with a green stone for one of the men. At bhajans I sat next to a Danish woman for whom He had materialized a white lingham (egg-shaped stone) either today or yesterday. A few days ago He materialized a lingham for an elderly Italian woman in darshan. With this sort of thing being done by our loving Lord in such a casual way here in the ashram, no wonder the energy and excitement are mounting among the foreigners.

Westerners have been told to assemble for Christmas carol procession practice tonight. We'll be dressed in sparkling white on Christmas morning as we walk in procession six abreast. At 7:30 we gather with flashlights in front of Hall 25 and notice that several of the seva volunteers have "bullhorn" microphones for giving us directions in the dark. Claudia, Christine, Louise and I cheer each other in between our walking choral singing and new directions from Liz and Al Drucker.

We sing and march, six abreast, then stop and receive more instructions. The consciousness required to walk in step and rhythm with the others in my row, and the rows before and aft, make me truly appreciate all of the intricate drill team maneuvers one sees on TV for football half-time shows and in the opening ceremonies of the Olympic games. To be successful it takes practice, focus, persistence and group telepathy.

It seems we can't be heard very well, so Al suggests that some of the altos on the outside be given the horns to amplify our voices and to ensure that we'll all be singing the same thing at the same time. We try this but it distorts the voices a bit. More singing, marching, stopping, waiting, talking. We begin again, and again. Everyone is tired but still we persist. Liz is energized and endlessly patient with us. Some of the singers, still suffering from jet lag, slip away in the darkness to their rooms or halls.

By 10:30, which is an hour and a half past "lights out" someone says from the crowd of marching singers "Oh come on, for heaven's sake - we're all tired and we have to save some energy and voice for the Christmas program. Let's go to bed." Slight applause follows. The crowd disperses as Liz asks us to come early for practice tomorrow.

Christmas Eve Day, December 24th

After darshan, bhajans, and the American meeting, we meet in the courtyard of Round Building 2 to practice our final selections for the Christmas choir. The choir has swelled its ranks the past few days but yesterday Liz closed it. While we enjoy the full sound created by the atrium-like garden of "R2" Scott leans over the balcony filming our practice. The women and men seated on the ground make a splendid sight; our ages range from early twenties to early seventies. In white attire the men contrast sharply with the colored saris and long skirts of the foreign women.

Liz, in a pale green sari, seems bathed in a pale green light or aura. Even her silver hair looks misted in light aqua as she revs up for another full day of vigorous leadership. Her clear voice rings out, belying her six or so decades on the earth, and she gives a short preamble in her New England-accented English. We feel her will and resolve and no one dares to joke around or goof off today as her fuse is a bit short. She glances at the harmonium on her lectern and at a paper in front of her, adjusting her spectacles that are attached to a neck cord for security in her more enthusiastic moments of conducting.

Here we go. We sense her high standards as we lift off together, telepathically attuned, hearts intertwined, all two hundred of us, reluctant to disappoint our strict task-master. Liz leads us to new heights, thrusting with fisted arms, rocking her body from side to side as if she's sawing down a redwood tree single-handedly, frowning, lips pursed. Suddenly she breaks the spell.

"No, no, no. This must be light. LIGHT. Like this. Not dah, dah, dah. Not mechanical. She rises up on tiptoe, raises her eyebrows, gracefully moves her arms as if she's rocking a baby, then makes bedspread-smoothing gestures accompanied by a beatific smile. We get the idea and try again. It's better but not close enough. We all hover, psychologically on the brink of feeling that we're practically hopeless, but that she's still trying for a miracle before Christmas and has enough faith to carry on with us. We sing again the songs *Dear Lord, Sweet Lord,*

Alleluia, Sai, Sai, Sai and *Swami We Adore You.* Liz then lights up with smiles, posture erect, and blows us kisses - a rare enough occurrence so that when it happens we know we've really achieved something worthwhile.

We'll meet again at Hall 25 later then back in R2 tonight. After our second practice of the day I head for the canteen for a quick lunch and have a feeling of expectancy for some unknown reason. It must be merely that it's Christmas Eve Day. As I enter the door of the dark, cool women's canteen, an inaudible voice tells me to sit near the front door as soon as I've picked up my food and buttermilk. It's a strange command since I virtually never sit near the door, which is the scene of traffic congestion from all of the coming and going of the lunch crowd.

Nevertheless, I sit by the door, eat the rice, vegetables and bread, then take the dishes to be washed in the back room. Then I walk to the canteen door and the glaring daylight, to see a sight that makes me think I'm hallucinating. It looks like William Wong, from Singapore, peering into the darkness of the women's canteen like a lost soul. It is William and he is lost.

"William! What are *you* doing here?!"

"Is it Connie? What on earth are *you* doing here? How wonderful to see you. It's great to see someone I know. You'll never believe this - I just got here five minutes ago and since I've never been here before I've just been looking around trying to figure out where to go and what I'm supposed to do next."

I chuckle at the fact William has actually come to Baba after all these years of hearing about him. Then I notice that one eye is bulging a bit and looks rather dead and drooping and a surge of pity for him wells up in me. Hastily I tell him about having come with Jim and Scott and about my month's stay from mid-October to mid-November. He's amazed that I've come twice in one year and wants to catch up on all that's happened since June but choir practice awaits, as well as a meeting with Claudia and Christine. Regretfully, I tell William we'll have to catch up later as I'm running late and have to dash to practice. As I say this, Jim and Scott come up behind us for quick introductions and renewed amazement that William has come.

Zilla passes by and tells me she's feeling very weak and nearly fainted at bhajans last night, so I tell her I'll walk with her to bhajans tonight if I can find her in the crowd. Christine then runs up to say she's down to her last forty-eight hours here and wants me to write to her when she's back home in Switzerland. Her eyes fill with tears that she's going at last. Claudia asks me if I have anything she can wear for Christmas Day since we're all supposed to wear pure, sparkling white for the choir performances and she hasn't anything. I'm thrilled to offer her my new white brocade silk dress that was made in China, especially since she's been in the fabric business and was on her way to China when she came here. How "fitting" as it were! She's pleased and we wonder at the way things work out so well when we let them.

Hall 25 is a large empty building used for singing practice; Liz has added color and warmth with a wooden chair for Baba, decorated with light blue needlepoint cushion and footstool, backed by a rose-colored wall hanging and carpet in case Swami joins us during the singing as He did a few days ago. There's a picture of Him with garlands and a small altar with candles and incense. Pink light comes through the windows and makes oblong squares on the gray-blue cement floor. The faces of the singers are pouring out light, their expressions look sweet and transfixed by the songs.

Liz is even more energized than before.

"Now ladies, be sure to pin your dresses and saris securely so that you don't lose them while we're marching in procession at 4:30 in the morning in the dark," she exclaims. "Also, please securely anchor your hair by tying it or firmly pinning it down. You people with fluffy hair or long tresses... we don't want you to have your hair set ablaze by someone behind you, since we'll be carrying candles and we'll be packed together in tight rows both across as well as front-to-back."

A titter ripples through the choir at the prospect of ardent white-garbed singers marching in the dark with hair ablaze, oblivious to their danger, while concentrating on Liz's exacting instructions to "stand tall, keep rhythm, sing lightly from the heart, don't bump your neighbor, don't fiddle with your clothing."

As we start to sing, the voices swell the hall like the sound of angels singing and some of the men are so overcome with the intricate descant of the sopranos over the rest of the voices, that they begin to weep. Liz is unaware of this and, deep in a conducting frenzy, makes imploring gestures to us, then threatening, aggressive jabs, stabbing the air with pointing index fingers. Next, she puffs up like a football player to indicate that we need to give more fullness of sound. Cradle-rocking motions follow. Then, oblivious to William Wong's entry in the back, and Scott's filming in the front of the room, she launches into an especially wild series of movements, arms flailing, eyes shooting Shiva-looks, and head flung back in total abandonment. Her glasses fly off, caught by the neck-cord and she shakes her head from left to right wondering momentarily what has happened. Recovering quickly she says merely "Oh, excuse me," in a prim, business-like way and then sings a few lines for us, then sings with us.

Fascinated, we all hang on her every word, every move. We become as one body. Smiling broadly, supremely happy, Liz makes great punching gestures, as if she's walloping the daylights out of a gigantic punching bag and loving every minute of it. Her pure-hearted effort, energetic stalking around and her range of abilities in music, drama, comedy and spiritual teaching leave us marveling in utter amazement. As she bounds along at a gallop, her shawl suddenly flies off, she trips backwards a bit but recovers her step.

Someone arrives with emergency telegrams for foreigners but the recipients are not among us. We're hot and sweating; she pushes us onward until we think we can't sing anymore. Finally practice is over and we rush to get in line for darshan. Baba calls a group of Romans for an interview. We have another practice for choir members tonight at 7:30 after bhajans and dinner. The intense, demanding pace is starting to get to us, and we'll be secretly happy when this program is all over.

Our last practice is lovely in the starlight under the papaya trees of R2. We put in two more hours of focused, relentless singing and get it nearly perfected. This morning we had singing from Italian, Australian and Canadian groups, as a treat, and the children's choir sang in rehearsal. We're told to be gracious hosts of the Lord in our singing tomorrow, to bring flashlights in the morning, and once again to secure our hair and saris so that we don't have any mishaps.

"Bring a seat to leave in place and be ready for anything. We may sing, we may not. With Swami you never know. He has to invite us, you know. Maynard Ferguson will play his trumpet and the college band will play too. Then the children's choir will sing and Swami will give a discourse after some guest speakers talk. Come at 2:00 and be ready to sit for at least three and a half hours if not much longer."

Then Liz blows us a kiss and we trot off to crash onto our cots for a few hours of precious sleep before Christmas Day. Two thorns that pierced my foot during our marching practice have become infected. Shame on me! I haven't been wearing socks.

Yesterday's Thought for the Day was: "Love alone can reveal the divinity latent in all. Love is God. Live in love. Love lives by giving and forgiving. Self lives by getting and forgetting. Love is self-lessness. Selfishness is love-lessness. Do not waste your life pursuing the narrow interests of the Self. Love! Love! Become what you really are - the embodiment of Love."

Today's message is "Do not imitate others in your spiritual sadhana. You have your own feelings, your own ideas, your own opinions, your own will. Why then imitate? Follow your own sadhana. Let your own experience of God be your guide, master and guru. Do not go into the groove, weakly imitating others."

Christmas Morning, December 25th

We gather at 4:30 at the Ganesh gate and prepare to walk and sing in procession with lighted candles. The Mandir lights wink delightfully and the morning has a special feel to it. As we begin to sing and walk, the townsfolk line the walkway, bewitched by the sight of the foreigners dressed in white, joyful faces illuminated by candles. This event is eagerly awaited all year by the local people and I can understand why that is so, since I myself am nearly too moved by the sight to sing. Surely these people are seraphim merely masquerading as humans.

Fortunately, however, the bullhorns come on and we all concentrate on our parts - the altos, sopranos and, in the men's section, the tenors and basses.

As the serpentine line of 200 singers ends up singing directly under Baba's balcony, He comes out, smiles tenderly and blesses us, like a doting mother well pleased with her children. This is a moment I'll never forget, so clear and happy do I feel. *Thank you again, Swami, for your bounteous love that our family is here with you at Christmas.*

Sun-up comes quickly and we line up for Christmas Day darshan. On the Mandir veranda Baba lights a birthday cake candle for Jesus and the college band plays Christmas carols inside the Mandir. Then seva dal volunteers distribute sweets to the crowd from Baba.

As devotees wish each other "Holy Christmas, Happy Christmas," I again silently thank the Lord for the most exalted, serene Christmas of my life. All of the discomforts have faded from memory and have definitely been worth the outcome. Surely this is how a genuine spiritual celebration of the birthday of our Beloved Jesus can always be arranged, if we decide to allow Christmas to have a much truer, deeper meaning for us.

While sitting in our final choir practice today, Christmas, I realized that the two infected thorns in my foot have simply disappeared! In fact, they had been gone for several hours, healed by Baba, and I had marched all over the ashram with our singing choir at dawn before I even realized it. *Thank you, Baba, for such a painless resolution and for the umpteenth favor.*

We've been told to come to the Poornachandra auditorium at 2:30 to line up and be seated inside for at least an hour before the afternoon Christmas program begins. Our choir, dressed all in stark white, looks stunning and we are excited that we are to be on the program with Maynard Ferguson, the American jazz trumpet player.

After sitting for an hour and a half we all sit at attention as Baba comes out on the stage and beckons forward a little cluster of white-clad boys who chant the opening to the Christmas program. Next, Victor Canu, a well-known devotee from Africa, gives a keynote speech which is well-received by the crowd.

Baba and the translator begin the Christmas Day talk then Al Drucker mounts the stage and announces the program, to include the Children's' Choir, the Overseas Devotees' Adult Choir, and Maynard Ferguson and the Band of the Sri Sathya Sai Institute. Dressed in white outfits with little red bow ties, the children, mostly pre-school and elementary age, sing rousing renditions of *Ave, Ave* and *Sathya Sai, Sathya Sai* (to the tune of *Jingle Bells*) which bring shouts of appreciative laughter and warm applause from the overflowing audience.

After the Adult Choir sings, the audience responds in a burst of appreciation and we nudge each other in the choir. The *Alleluia, Buddham Sharanam* and *Sai On Earth* have come off wonderfully and Baba smiles like a proud Father at Liz, who has worked unstintingly on this for months.

At last we are treated to the part we've all been waiting for: Maynard Ferguson and his trumpet. Maynard, who is about sixty-five and white-haired, looks like a friendly, overgrown Saint Bernard puppy, oozing with rhythm. As he plays his horn while directing the brass band in *Hark The Herald Angels Sing* he bobbles, wriggles, bounces and generally jazzes it up to our great delight and fond amusement. At the outset of his perform-ance he announces that he is dedicating his concert, as he does all of his concerts, to the Lotus Feet of Swami. Then Maynard performs a solo of *White Christmas* with uncanny trumpet squeals that sound just like a whinnying horse. He ends with a rambunctious version of *Swami We Adore You* which brings the house down.

We finish by having audience participation in singing *The Saints Go Marching In* and I must say that it's quite an experience singing that song in the company of the Avatar and many actual saints at Puttaparthi with twenty thousand voices!

What a contrast between the usual celebrations of Christmas throughout the world with parties, useless presents and too much eating and drinking and this sublime experience of hearing the Lord speak on the true meaning of life. On the way to the auditorium we jotted down Baba's "Thought for the Day" for Christmas Day. "Do not allow your body and senses to dictate your moves. Develop the inner vision. The body is the cart, the spirit is the horse. Do not put the cart before the horse. Spiritual practice is the only means of acquiring mental peace. Cultivate not riches, not comforts, not luxuries, but Divine Vision. Then you become fit to receive God's grace."

At Baba's Divine Discourse we're reminded of the significance of Christmas and of the life of Christ.

Baba's Christmas Discourse

"Striving to lead godly lives is the only truly sacred behavior. Jesus lived for the Divine Glory of this sacred planet. His every action was for those around Him. Nothing was too precious for Him to give up for His people. He sacrificed His body's own blood for the good of humanity. Today is the anniversary of the day when Jesus came to Earth. Of what meaning is it to spend such a divine day feasting? Is it divine to spend the entire Birthday of Jesus, the master of sense control, by over-indulging our own senses? Make this day meaningful and beneficial for yourself and mankind. Practice at least a few of the ideals that Jesus preached and gave His life for.

"It is ridiculous to spend the birthday of any great person gorging on expensive dishes. Who does that bring honor to? Celebrate a true day of rebirth in your life. Practice any ideal set forth by a great person. Your divine actions honor God who manifested as the ideal human you are guided by.

"You are embodiments of living Divine Love. In memory of Jesus' Birthday, you must begin to change your way of living. You must honor the living memory of Jesus by beginning to act as He acted."

Baba gives a lengthy discourse which lasts over an hour and a half and by the time we leave the auditorium I notice that it is after seven o'clock and that we have been sitting on the auditorium floor for four and a half hours. We're too tired to stand in the enormous canteen line so Scott picks up the little pizzas we had booked days ago at the ashram bakery and we each have a soft drink and a tiny pizza as our Christmas feast and then we all fall exhausted to sleep on our cots in Hall 17. This has been the best Christmas of my life.

December 26th

Jim, who looked a little green yesterday, has food poisoning, it seems. He's too weak to get to the hospital and just lies on his cot moaning. This morning an American woman, who was crippled with polio or something similar, and had to be carried everywhere in her husband's arms, was carried into Baba's interview room and, after the interview, walked out on her own legs, fully healed! Today Baba materialized a lingham for an Italian woman in darshan and He has been materializing rings and linghams as well as vibhuti during the holidays in the lines.

How long, oh Lord, are we going to have to stay in this shed or hall? Jim has to walk through two adjacent halls to get to the bathroom and is in agony. Scott and I are helping to ease his discomfort all we can but it keeps us hopping when added to the already rigorous schedule.

Hopefully Jim's case won't become more serious since we have to travel back to China in a few days which means getting in and out of five different airports, customs, immigration, and so on.

December 27th

This morning in darshan Baba stopped in front of me, turned around and gave me a long, compassionate look. Now why would He do that, I wonder? Maybe it was because of Jim's being so sick. I just shook my head, not comprehending, and smiled back. Puzzling.

As Scott and I were starting out on our very first walk since being at the ashram we were stopped by Vernette Maya of Hollywood, California. "Say, Connie, wait a minute, I have good news! There's a room in the round building where I'm staying that just became available. If you run over to accommodations right this minute, you can probably get it if you explain the problem about Jim's food poisoning."

For a moment it seems too good to be true. Scott and I just stare at her in disbelief. ("What, and leave our wonderful shed with all the crying babies, visiting dogs and monkeys, the frogs in the bathroom, crickets in the luggage?" I think to myself.)

"Thanks a million, Maya! Come on, Scott, let's run over and try our luck."

We're jubilant at even the thought that we might be so lucky as to get a room here at Christmas time, but at the same time warn ourselves not to get our hopes up too high.

We wait in line at the Accommodations Office for about half an hour. As requested, we let the man know our hall number, number in our family and about Jim's illness, and the lack of a nearby bathroom for him. The fact that Jim needs to be fit to travel all the way to China seems to be the final point that helps our situation.

"We just heard from our friend that there's a room available in Round Building 1," I mention, hoping that we can move in immediately.

"Sorry Madame, I can't give you that room. It needs cleaning and that will take some time."

"But I don't mind cleaning it myself, really," I plead.

"No, I can't have you doing that. What I'm trying to tell you is that I'll put you in another vacant room that has been cleaned and is very nice."

I can hardly believe my ears. "You mean we can move now? Actually? Out of the shed into a room? Wonderful! Thank you - I mean God bless you. And thank you, Baba. Hooray. Let's go tell Jim. He'll never believe this."

We're handed the key to our new abode when suddenly Scott and I both jerk to a halt at the same time with the same thought.

"Hey Mom... don't you think that first we'd better...."

"I know. We'd better take a look at the new place first before we rave about it to Jim, get his hopes up, and go to all the trouble of moving, in case it's not much of an improvement."

We dash over to the new room, unlock the door and immediately start to exclaim over the fact that there's a screen door, screened windows, shelves, hooks, and a fan. The final touch is the gorgeous view of the Administration Building, the green hillside and a few bullocks outside the window. What a boon.

Laughing as we run back to the shed, we hatch a plot as a way of kidding Jim since he's always pulling jokes on us. We sneak up on him then enter our tiny cubicle and announce that we're checking out of the ashram. "We've had it, Jim. Would you like to come with us or not?"

"What?! How can you say that, especially you, Connie, after having spent a month here. I don't believe it. Come on, you don't really want to leave. What's really happening?"

Scott and I, bursting with the good news, can hardly contain ourselves. "We just said that as a joke because the great news is that we now have a new room with the finest amenities - including screens - and here's the key. Just lie back down on your cot and we'll supervise the entire move. We've arranged the porters and they'll arrive in an hour. Isn't that exciting?"

Jim perks up considerably but is still way too sick to help pack and organize the move. Scott and I dismantle the elaborate webwork of rope and fabric that has comprised our ashram home the past week and we stack the luggage, cots, laundry bags, straw mats, and sheets for the porters. It is so sweltering that we are soaked after this rather mild exertion, and sit on the floor panting and discussing our remaining days - four of them - here at the ashram.

After moving into our clean new room, which seems palatial to us, we unpack and reorganize before going to afternoon darshan. Now maybe Jim can speed his recovery and we can have a few days of rest, which is what we came for, but which we haven't experienced yet, due to the hectic Christmas program practice.

A few hours later, as I'm reclining on my cot thinking with satisfaction how enjoyable the next few days are going to be, now that we can have a bit of comfort, it becomes clear to me why Baba was giving me a long look of compassion. Rest and comfort weren't in the plan, it seems.

Scott falls in the door looking vacant and pale. He turns to show me his back, which is covered from ankle to hairline with wet gravel and sand. He was standing in line at the bakery and had just stepped up to the window when the next thing he knew, he had passed out cold. When he woke up he was being slapped gently on the face while a crowd of people looked down with concern into his face and sprinkled vibhuti all over him.

He was shocked, scared and embarrassed. Mostly embarrassed. He lies down on his cot while I bring him some water and he admits that he has become dehydrated, after all of my warnings about how dangerous that can be in this climate. We can lose fluid through perspiration and can, with the excitement of being near Baba, forget to eat and drink sufficiently. He is obviously exhausted and I'm wondering if the entire experience of meeting India so frontally, as he has, with little preparation, was a mistake. But Scott has seemed to enjoy being here and has had the good fortune of nearly always getting to sit in the first few front rows for darshan. The privations of the ashram have been too much, however.

It's a good thing we have this room since it would really be over-whelming to be caring for two sick family members in the noise, dust and lack of privacy of the hall. We received this room in perfect timing for this latest challenge. Thanks again, dear Baba.

In a matter of days our priceless Christmas with God will come to an end and Scott will return to school while Jim and I return to China briefly for the conclusion of Jim's project. In spite of the fact that I'm thrilled to have the chance to live in China for a few months, that old feeling of danger or caution has returned each time I contemplate our return to Guangzhou.

CHAPTER 24
KIDNAPPING IN CHINA AND LEELAS

"There are three types of teachers: those who inspire, those who explain, and those who complain." Sathya Sai Baba

Guangzhou, China
January 2, 1987

Since my first trip to China in 1981, I have been back four more times. The changes are astounding in every area of life here. People wear Western clothing, debris from the Revolution has been cleaned up and building construction has accelerated enormously. With each trip to China I have again understood how naïve I was during my initial trips to Asia. I now see how the mind creates our entire reality and that overcoming cultural and gender conditioning, among other shackles, is essential for liberation. The mind is the cause of grief or happiness. Our happiness or misery is not dependent upon our circumstances, but upon what we think of our circumstances and our desires to have things be different.

Jim and I have only weeks remaining in China, from our three-month stay, before we return home to Colorado. Jim's commute is an hour and a half to work each way which means that he sits in the van for three hours a day and is ready to rest upon return to the hotel where we live. We meditate together after work each evening and share the day's insights and experiences.

Yesterday I booked a cab to take me to see some of Guangzhou, including temples and museums. After I explained where I wanted to go to the driver, and satisfied myself that he understood, I settled into the back seat with a new Sai Baba book that I had bought in Puttaparthi a few weeks ago.

After having been engrossed in the book for about half an hour, I suddenly looked up. We had driven away from town, not downtown as I had requested. We were nowhere near the city and a chill came over me. It abruptly dawned on me that the driver was intent on kidnapping me, that he intended to rob me and to abandon me at the remote and smelly landfill, or city dump, which loomed ahead.

He had been speaking in Mandarin to his supervisor over the taxi radio. I noticed the cabby's license that was clipped to his visor. It showed his photo, name (Tan Li) and the vehicle number.

"Where are you, Tan?" the supervisor barked over the radio.

"With the foreign lady customer, sightseeing," Tan had replied.

Nervously, Tan abruptly turned the cab into the dump, which was reeking with giant mounds of refuse from millions of Guangzhou residents. He began to speak softly to me, his quick brown eyes peering at me through the rear-view mirror. His voice quivered and perspiration trickled down his brow.

"Give me all your money. I am going to leave you here. No one will find you for days. You will not be able to get back. You must do as I say."

Sizing him up, it seemed that this was his first abduction and attempted robbery. He was shorter than I am, so I decided to have a show-down. No wimpy, audacious little cab driver was going to abduct and rob me and get away with it. Silently I prayed to Baba for guidance and help and apologized for the fact that I planned to scare the living daylights out of Tan Li, which is a tactic that I normally deplore. Tan Li, however, didn't seem like one who would easily take to calm, kind persuasion.

"I don't understand," I said. "Let's step outside so I can see your face and hear you better."

We both got out of the car and faced each other. I'm nearly five feet six and he was about five feet two inches tall. Although I'm non-violent by nature, I could easily take him on with a swift kick and a karate throw. But I hoped that intimidation would have an effect on him so that I wouldn't have to use violence. He trembled and looked apologetic.

"Give me all your money... purse... watch... jewelry."

"NO! Forget it! You should be ashamed of yourself, treating foreign guests this way," I shouted, indignantly. "Stand right there where you are and don't you dare move. I'm calling your supervisor on the cab phone. You'll be lucky to keep your job after he hears about this. Think of your family." Although I wasn't really angry, I scowled, hissed and growled in hopes that I looked threatening.

"Don't you even THINK of trying this sort of kidnapping and robbery again. You could go to prison for this. This is a crime. Do you want to spend your life in jail?!" I shrieked, for effect.

"Now, get over there by that pile of garbage and don't you move until I tell you to," I snarled.

Pressing the radio mic button as I had seen Tan Li do, I reported the taxi number and told the taxi dispatcher-manager that Tan Li had kidnapped me, tried to rob me, and had taken me to the city dump far outside of town with the intention of leaving me to the fate of marauding animals and other unscrupulous men.

There was a moment of silence on the other end. Then many voices all began talking at once. There was screaming and shouting. Finally, the dispatcher said, barely able to contain himself, "This is very, very bad. Tan Li is in very big trouble. What is he doing now?"

"He's standing about ten feet from the cab while I'm talking to you," I said. "Tan is going to take me back to my hotel now and then he will be reporting to your office after that. I have told you the entire story. My name is Connie Shaw. I'm living at the Garden Hotel. If you need to call me for further information, please feel free to do so. Tan will see you in about forty-five minutes to an hour. I'm very disappointed in your cab company's hospitality. This will hurt the reputation of China and the

Chinese people. You had better talk to your staff very firmly about these crazy robbery ideas. No good can come of it. It may look easy, but jail is the final result."

Mr. Mak, the supervisor, apologized profusely, assuring me that this was the first time such a thing had ever happened. He then asked to speak to Tan and, while I held the radio, gave Tan a fiery, screaming tongue-lashing. Tan and I both got into the cab and he slumped down in the driver's seat, shamed and humiliated, as we drove back to town. As I studied him in the mirror, I realized that Tan was probably only about twenty-two years old and no doubt lived with his parents, like most young men and women.

As we arrived at the hotel, I told Tan, who was still trembling, to consider this a warning from the gods.

"Think of the shame and disgrace you could bring on your parents. You could be a model son and citizen if you begin now, with remorse. Envy is poison. Count your blessings instead of plotting theft. If you do a good job of serving the customers you can get big tips and make more than you could from robbery."

Hopefully I have learned my lesson to never, never get lost in a book while riding in a vehicle with a strange person. I should have been paying attention as we drove out of town. Jim thinks I should ask someone to accompany me on my sightseeing tours. But who could I ask? Maybe I should stick to day tours while we finish our stay here. But I've never been a coward and don't intend to start now.

January 3rd

We must be in an astrological period of vulnerability to theft and privacy invasion. As amazing as it sounds, there was another incident today with inappropriate behavior from Chinese citizens. This time it was the hotel staff.

Because I still have a bit of jet lag from India, I decided to take a nap about 10:00 A.M., instead of leaving the hotel for the day. As I turtled deep under the covers, with quilt over my head, as usual, I heard voices in my room. It was the hotel manager, a man in his mid-twenties, and his young female assistant.

They were opening the closet, commenting on my clothes and luggage, and then began opening dresser drawers and taking out my underwear. Suddenly, the heat of indignation arose. This was the second time in twenty-four hours that my privacy was being violated. The nerve! *Who do these two think they are?*

Quickly, I decided once again on the strategy of surprise and intimidation. In one smooth maneuver, I yelled "Geronimo!" at the top of my lungs, simultaneously waving my arms up and down like a windmill, for added fright effect.

The petite manager and his assistant squeaked out a startled response as they stared at me, clad in blue floral flannel pajamas, hair standing out in all directions.

"How DARE you? Is there no end to the indignities brought upon foreign guests? You should be ashamed of yourselves. I know that you think most Americans are spies. That is no excuse for invading our room and my possessions. Neither I nor my husband are spies. We are simply trying to help China and the Chinese. But you make it very difficult. We are honest people and we don't like this treatment. Please don't ever, ever let this happen again or you will be very very sorry. Now good day."

I held the door open while simultaneously making a sweeping motion to indicate they should immediately leave the room. They fumbled. floundered, apologized and said they had made a mistake. I agreed.

Living in China has changed me. The mere necessity of constantly having to protect myself has made me both bolder and humbler. After having lived in Italy, Germany, China, India and Singapore, I feel I can handle anything. I have become less passive and now stand up for the underdog in any situation, if I feel it's indicated. Maybe Baba has given me these challenges so that I won't put up with being bullied.

He says, "Man should be courageous. Lack of courage leads to doubt, despair, dejection and depression. When obstacles come, meet them with courage. They harden you, make you tough." CTSSB P 97

There's a wonderful story told about Jesus by Baba. "Once a devotee went to Jesus and asked him, 'Oh Lord! What is the power by which one can protect oneself? Jesus replied, 'Son, when you love God, that power itself will protect you.' " CTSSB P 433

It must be my great love for Baba and His grace that acts as a dome of protection over me. But I'm not pushing my luck.

Littleton, Colorado
October, 1987

Jim and I spent two sublime weeks in India with Baba. There was no interview but the darshans were heavenly.

October, 1988

Time is flying. Three of us just returned from India. Baba was most loving; there was no interview but one can't expect that type of grace on every trip. I feel very blissful.

September, 1989

Baba blessed us with our seventh trip to see Him. It's funny how adamant I was about not wanting to return to India after the first and second trips. But God had other plans. I wonder how many trips to India I'll make in this lifetime. Imagine – some devotees have been there fifteen or twenty times. Every trip for us is different and we have both changed a lot. My focus is much more internal now, rather than in the world. My wardrobe colors have changed from reds to mostly blues and greens with a few whites and purples. Life without Baba would be unthinkable.

Next year Jim and I would like to travel to India via Hawaii. We both work all the time, seven days a week, like Swami, and need a rest. I'm organizing food for the homeless, leading Sai meetings, doing lectures and workshops, doing counseling, and attending many board meetings as seva.

Littleton, Colorado
October, 1989

Baba gave us a lovely string of leelas in the back yard this year. The first one concerned our crab apple tree, which stands next to the small Square-Foot-Garden of flowers and vegetables beside the house.

One day I was walking around the garden, speaking encouragement to all of the flowers, shrubs and trees, as I often do. After acknowledging the Austrian pines, the mugho pines, potentillas, aspen and honeysuckle, I came to the crab apple.

As I leaned against the tree, I began speaking mentally to Baba, telling Him that I had made a mistake in planting the crab apple since you can't give crab apples to the homeless, who get so little fresh fruit. In other words, if the tree were an apple tree, instead of a crab apple, we could feed people.

Our Sai Center takes peanut butter sandwiches to a women's shelter in Denver every Monday. Shortly after my blessing of the trees and little musing to Baba, a few weeks later, I couldn't believe my eyes when I went outside into the back yard. One half of the crab apple tree had produced little red crab apples, the size of marbles. The other half of the tree, against which I had leaned, when talking to Baba, had produced over a hundred green, granny apples!

I ran inside the house and told Jim, then called Geetha, a member of our center. We later put the granny apples in sandwich bags for the battered women at the shelter to eat.

Baba's generosity so inspired me that I began naming several dead trees in the neighborhood Lazarus, after Lazarus in the Bible. They are now Lazarus One through Seven. Each day as I walked to the neighborhood soccer field and back, as my two-mile exercise regime, I spoke to each dead tree. I held its withered branches in my hands and asked it to return to life to bless the neighborhood. For two or three weeks I did this. Baba restored six of the seven trees to life.

This year I have been teaching Therapeutic Touch to nurses and chiropractors with Judie. Recently Phil Michaels asked me to come over and heal his Afghan Ridgeback, Cahill, who was dying with hip dysplasia, incontinence and other problems. Cahill told me telepathically, upon arrival to the garage, that he was tired and depressed at being ignored, at being kept in a dark garage for weeks on end with no exercise or fresh air. He wanted to die. Phil and Diane were amazed that Cahill had given me such a graphic account of the truth. They vowed to take better care of him and to take him to the park daily, as they had until new projects claimed their time. I asked Cahill to consider living and to realize that he could bless Phil and Diane and the neighborhood if he would stay in his body. He recovered, was able to live without diapers and began to bound about healthily again.

Littleton, Colorado
December, 1989

Many odd things are happening. Sandy, a waitress at the Harvest Restaurant, asked me to heal her kitten, long distance, via holding its photo. The kitten had swallowed a needle and thread and was having surgery, as we spoke. It was not expected to live. As I placed my hands around the photo I asked Baba to heal the kitty, if it were His will.

The vet told Sandy the next day that the kitty had come out of anesthesia bouncing with energy and was having a record recovery. Sandy next asked me to do an energy session with her, which I did, explaining that God is the healer, not me.

To my astonishment, Sandy told me the next day, at lunch at the restaurant, that not only had her upset stomach been cleared, but that her Caesarian keloid scars had nearly disappeared.

"How did you do that?" she asked, gasping as she relayed the news.

"It wasn't me – it really was God," I said hastily, and rushed out of the restaurant.

Littleton, Colorado
April, 1990

Baba is calling me to India – alone this time. I seem to deepen more when I'm alone in India than when I'm with Jim or with a group and the inevitable responsibilities and distractions. It has been four years since Baba has blessed me with an interview but I am solid in my practices and in service. Ramana Maharshi and advaita still captivate me. What does our sweet Lord have in store this time, I wonder.

CHAPTER 25
TRIPLE INTERVIEW BLESSING

"Man has two varieties of troubles; the physical due to the imbalance between the three humors, Vatha, Pittha and Kapha, and the spiritual, due to the imbalance of the three gunas, Sathwa, Rajas and Thamas." Sathya Sai Baba, CTSSB P 38

Kadugodi Village, near Bangalore, India
May 11, 1990

Baba has allowed us to come to India once each year in 1987, 1988 and 1989. It has been four years since I have had an interview with Him and don't know if I'll ever have that great joy again in this lifetime.

After spending a week's vacation with Jim last week in Hawaii, I proceeded on to Bangalore, India, alone. Jim went to Toronto, Canada on business. My plan is to spend two weeks experiencing Baba's darshans, even though we were blessed with a trip to Puttaparthi only seven and a half months ago, in September. This is my tenth trip to India and I have no idea what I am to learn or to experience. It is seldom that I come to Baba with a request; I come because I love Him and want to be with His form every chance I get. He, of course, calls us to Himself for His own reasons, most of which we'll never know.

Recently, as I've been reviewing old journals, I've been horrified at the patterns I have seen in myself, such as conceit, arrogance, self-righteousness, selfishness and a tendency to control. How I wince and cringe to re-read my old letters and diary entries. Self-awareness inevitably humbles us; there's no way around that fact.

May 13th

Baba is at the Brindavan Ashram in Kadugodi Village, near Whitefield. He began giving darshan twice a day, instead of once, on the day I arrived. Sometimes His darshans have been quite brief and He merely came out of the gate, waved or took a few letters and entered His car to inspect the extensive ashram construction work and refurbishing that is taking place.

To my utter delight, the crowds during the week days have often numbered only three to four hundred people, with ample seating space and the possibility of everyone present being seated in the first, second or third row without difficulty. Thus, everyone has a good view of Baba and can clearly see Him manifesting vibhuti, taking letters, blessing photos and speaking briefly with devotees. My love for Baba is boundless now.

May 16th

Today a group of about ten Europeans were called in for an interview but as they approached the inner gate to proceed to the interview, Baba suddenly turned and quickly scrutinized their dress. After spending several weeks or months in the heat, crowds and confusion of India, away from one's routines, comforts, grooming equipment and culture, one can let standards of grooming and dress slip a bit. As a consequence, overseas devotees sometimes acquire a slightly worn-out, disheveled or even a "seedy" appearance. Many foreign ashram visitors would be unrecognizable to friends and families back home while dressed in simple "darshan whites," sans their familiar hair mousse, acrylic fingernails, high heels, and other modern primping aids. In India, while under the beneficent mind-altering influence of a Realized Master, one's attention moves naturally inward, away from the outer world, including one's appearance, which gradually assumes less importance. However, sloppiness is not tolerated. Further, Baba says, about clothes, "Remember also that dress is primarily for protection against heat and cold, not for vain display even at the cost of health." SSS VOL II P 78

Baba told three of the ten devotees to go in for an interview and told the others that they were not dressed in tidy enough fashion to receive an interview.

"Is this how you dress for the Avatar?!" He asked them.

A ripple of concern moved through the crowd. Next, we were informed by the head seva dal (volunteer service worker) for women that Baba had announced that only those who were clean and tidy in appearance would receive interviews henceforth. She elaborated by saying that hair must be clean and combed and men must be clean-shaven or have trim, tidy beards. Shawls must be neat, pants and skirts must be modest, reaching the ankle, saris must be fresh and crisp, and that if people were wearing white, the whites must match exactly and look clean and pressed. In other words, one was not to wear ivory-colored whites with pure whites as the effect was jarring or unsettling for those who had to endure seeing people who might dress thoughtlessly.

"You must not be careless in dressing for darshan. You have come to see God; this is a rare chance which will not last indefinitely since Baba is rapidly becoming well-known. He will not tolerate a casual attitude that takes Him or His precious darshans for granted," she said sharply. Her demeanor and hand-wringing gave us an indication that she felt a bit guilty, like the mother of a large family who felt that she had somehow failed in her duties to educate her children as to propriety, protocol, manners and consideration of others.

It was a tense moment. Some people hung their heads. Others whispered to their friends that they should immediately go to Bangalore for shaves, haircuts and new clothes. After the head seva dal had made her announcement and had sufficiently chastised us there was a second or two of contemplative silence.

Then, as the news sank into our psyches, there was a whoop and a whoosh from the crowd of foreigners who ran outside the ashram gates to commandeer the nearest taxis. It was unanimous – everyone felt moved to rush into town to buy fresh saris and punjabis in order to look neat for darshan the next day. The seva dal workers wore fresh saris the next few days as well and the crowd had a new sense of pride as evidenced by haircuts, beard trims and sparkling clean clothing. Baba indicated His approval of the crowd's re-adoption of high standards of grooming and cleanliness.

Next Baba evicted about twenty-five landlords and hotel owners from darshan for two weeks because they had hiked the room rates up considerably for the foreign devotees. Foreigners had been asked to leave the ashram in order to make room for the incoming Summer Course students that were arriving from three of Baba's colleges.

"Is this how you treat your foreign brothers and sisters who come to see God? Instead of receiving them with love as the Avatar asks, you try to take economic advantage of them because you are jealous of them! For most of these foreign devotees it is a hardship, it is sadhana (spiritual work) to come to India. They leave their jobs, homes and families and endure a strange climate and culture. They have true devotion. We must extend hospitality to them, not cheating. We will see how you yourselves like it not to go to darshan for two weeks. Maybe then you will learn compassion for overseas devotees."

But Baba wasn't finished. Babu, who owns the Sai Ram Taxi Service, told me that Baba had similarly chastened several cab drivers who were taking chances with their passengers. Even though the drivers are Muslims and not devotees (though many Muslims are devotees), Baba laid down regulations for drivers who ferry devotees:

1. Start early, go slowly, arrive (early and) safely.

2. Resist the temptation to overtake or pass other vehicles out of habit or for a sense of machismo or satisfaction (i.e., no competitive driving).

3. Do not take any unnecessary chances when approaching an oncoming truck, bus or train.

"Remember, drivers," Baba had said, "You have mothers, wives and children who are depending upon you and your work for their livelihood. If you die from carelessness they will be thrust into the street or they will become a responsibility of your brothers. Everyone – the families of devotees who are killed, and your own families - would be very sad if you died. Keep Allah in mind and deliver your precious cargo safely. I bless you."

The drivers agreed that they had been developing reckless driving habits, often because they were trying to impress their passengers with their skill and deftness. After Baba's announcement to cab drivers, many of them applied window decals to their vehicles that said: "Start early. Go slowly. Reach safely. Sai Baba"

Baba Heals My Foot

Within 3 days of arriving in India and walking around the Brindavan compound barefoot, I noticed that a tiny cut between the small toes of the right foot had become badly infected. The entire top of the foot was filled with yellow infectious matter and outlined in red lines. It was obvious that the foot needed to be treated at the hospital: lanced, drained and dressed. Minor foot surgery was in order.

But the uppermost errand in my mind was to deliver some letters from the States to Baba. The previous night I had become quite sick due to a temporary lapse of common sense by drinking local tap water and sugar cane juice from a street vendor. Though I had been coming to India for ten years, I had always avoided the tap water and food from street vendors but forgot this time as I was traveling alone.

Further, the night before delivering the letters to Baba, I was bitten on the face by an unseen insect, which I suspected was a centipede, in the cottage room of the Ananda Bhavan Hotel. Thus, in the middle of the night, after the bite, I awoke and switched on the light, started vomiting, saw my swollen face in the mirror, glanced down to see that my foot was dangerously infected, and let my ego get the better of me through self-pity. Somehow it seemed overwhelming to me that I was having to simultaneously endure a poisonous bite, vomiting and a badly infected foot without any aid or comfort from another human being.

At that moment a little leela began with Baba that was to last for two months.

Like a petulant, spoiled brat I started mumbling aloud to Baba, as if it were His fault that I had been careless. (Poor Baba, only God could endure the endless whining of six billion people.) Nevertheless, I was totally sunk in a delusional fog of victimhood.

"Alright, Swami, I've had it with India. This finishes it. Here I am, all alone in India - sick as can be with no one to comfort me. Now some creepy insect has bitten my face and I look like a monster. The foot probably has to be cut open at the hospital tomorrow after darshan. I feel awful. I'm not coming to India anymore for a long time. Probably a year and a half. So there!"

Swami's Inner Voice then spoke.

"Really? (chuckle, chuckle) Not coming to India for a long time? Really?!" The way He said it, I knew that He had a little surprise in store. Little did I know that it would come within 24 hours.

The next morning I went to darshan with letters in hand and sat down in the second row. Very shortly after that Baba walked swiftly over to where I was sitting and took the letters as one of His first acts in darshan. He did not speak to me nor touch me. The letters contained no petition for physical help nor did I ask Him to heal me as the only thing on my mind was to fulfill my duty in delivering letters to Him.

After He took the letters a light feeling came over me and I instinctively knew that something had happened to me, but it was a mystery as to what it was. After darshan, as I was walking to get my shoes from the shoe pile near the gate, I heard my Inner Voice say *"When you get into the cab (to return to Bangalore to the hotel) take off your sock and look at your foot."*

The removal of the white sock revealed that the sock was dry, the foot had not been punctured or lanced in any way, and the foot was healed! Though the oversized square Band-Aid was still in place and the yellow and red infection was gone, I began to doubt my senses. So I took off the other sock, thinking that somehow I had mistaken the right injured foot for the left one. Both feet matched - they looked equally healthy and normal.

As I sat back in the cab in astonishment I profusely thanked Baba and apologized for having been so peevish and full of self-pity the night before in the hotel room.

"Swami, please forgive me for being so mean. **Of course** *I'll come back to India again. Generally I do love it here...except for a few little things...Really, Baba, you are too kind to me, to all of us, all the time. You knew how I shrink from being cut upon and from taking antibiotics and going to hospitals. You not only saved me the anguish, you saved me the time and the money. Thank You, Lord, for Your constant grace. I really appreciate it and feel so ashamed that I was such a self-centered brat."*

The Four-Part Dream

May 17th

That night Baba seized His moment in a vivid dream which led to a series of events that resulted in my bringing a group of nine people right back to India just seven weeks after my return to Colorado.

The May 17th dream:

I am riding in a Western car with Swami wherein I am an honored guest in the back seat. The country seems to be India - green, tropical and a bit hilly. It's summer and very sunny with lush monstera (philodendron) plants, coleus and philodendron growing amid the verdant landscape beside the car.

In the front, in the left-hand driver's seat, is my Hungarian friend, Maria Ujfalushi, who is acting as Baba's chauffeur. She wears a navy blue and white sari with hair in upswept coiffeur - very efficient-looking. Swami, wearing an orange robe and His hair short and business-like, turns around from the front seat and begins to speak to me as I sit in the back seat.

In the back seat I think to myself: "Wow! Can you believe it? Here I am sitting in the car with Swami, just as if I were an important diplomat or something - just like Dr. Hislop. How did this happen that I'm getting such VIP treatment? This must be a dream."

Baba, in the dream, then said three things:

First, "When you get back home you must come back right away and bring the others (or the group). Second, "Tell everyone Baba is going to be in Bangalore all summer-then they will come." And finally, "Now, why should I give someone like you an interview?!"

At that moment I was puzzled, thinking, *"But I didn't ask You for an interview. Besides, being right here with You (in the car) is like an on-going interview anyway."* Then I awoke and realized that Baba was referring to my having fussed at Him the night before when I had a little temper tantrum after having been bitten on the face by the strange creature while in the cottage hotel room. I also realized that: Since Baba had instructed me to return to India virtually right away, I would have to do it. He would have to send the money if I were to come back. I should never again tell Him I will not do something in particular as that's the very thing He makes me do! (i.e., "I'm not coming back to India soon.")

Thus I'll be returning almost immediately. *Very funny joke, Swami.)* I wondered who would be coming with me and if they would be willing to come "merely" on the strength of His invitation in a dream.

May 24th

Now I'm returning to the States after two blessed weeks in India. I'm consciously resting in the deep peace that is my Self. What more is there? Is there any joy greater than this? I think not.

Littleton, Colorado
July, 1990

My solo trip to India in May thus ended happily, with a healed foot and with instructions to return very soon with a group.

Baba later gave me the names of those to ask, day by day. Twenty-two names were given to me, one at a time, and nine accepted.

Puttaparthi, India
July, 1990

We're back in India, six weeks after returning and have a group of eleven people, two of whom we didn't know, who joined us in India. Baba has told us that He'll see us more than once. It is only our second day here and He has called us inside to see Him.

Those who have formed our American group are dressed in darshan whites. We have, as our group insignia, a long, Olympic-style red-white-and blue ribbon around our necks.

Our group is comprised of a variety of people, mostly women, who are inexperienced travelers and who seem intimidated by India and the culture. We are:

Connie Shaw, group leader, outgoing Center president, administrator.
Jim Wright, Connie's spouse, and assistant leader, businessman.
Amy Ford, incoming Center president and seasoned businesswoman in her sixties.
Sally Dotson, incoming Center secretary, business woman in her forties.
Vera Karn, homemaker and senior citizen from a small Iowa town.
Justin Lang, a single man in his forties, chef from New Mexico.
Carol Cummings, retired truck driver, dog trainer, seamstress.
Andria Spring, clerical worker and hair-dresser in her forties.

Daisy Jones, healer, receptionist, who also has a small business.

Except for Jim, Connie and Justin, all of whom have been to India numerous times, the others are first-timers in India and had only heard of Sathya Sai Baba within the past several months.

In fact, Adrian, Carol, Daisy and Vera had only had knowledge of Him within about 100 days before they started planning to take the trip.

We held very detailed planning meetings for the group to instruct them as to what to take; Indian protocol; food; customs; how to dress for darshan, the hotels and sightseeing; history; Baba's mission and teachings.

During the six and a half weeks before we left Denver, there were various suspenseful delays with nearly each person, having to do with getting the time off work, the money for the trip, or the cooperation and support of friends and relatives to make the trip to Asia.

Amy's passport came the day before we left and we had to implore the Indian Attaché in Singapore to grant an emergency visa lest she be sent back to the US. He asked to hear some of our Sai Baba experiences, then asked Amy if she believed that Baba is genuine, even though she hadn't yet seen Him. She assented very enthusiastically. The attaché, a Muslim, then surprised us by saying, "Normally it would take two weeks for the granting of this visa. I understand that your transit flight is leaving Singapore in a matter of hours. Just consider this a miracle from your Sai Baba through me." He granted the visa that day, though others who had been waiting in line with us were told to return the following day with no guarantees of success in their visa-requests.

Baba graced the trip in many ways through sending help in airports, metro stations, restaurants and hotels when we needed it. Finally we arrived in Madras and were able to have a totally unplanned morning of sight-seeing on the Trident Hotel Coach to a Gandhi shrine, a snake and reptile zoo, Baba's Mandir and the world-famous Theosophical Society at Adyar, featuring the outstanding bookstore, lovely grounds, two ancient banyan trees and quarters for visiting scholars and students.

Along the Madras beach road there were women construction workers breaking rock into gravel with small hammers while traffic whizzed by on all sides. The chaotic oncoming cars seemed to converge in the middle of the road, as if bound for head-on collision - only to veer off at the last moment. The concept of remaining in one's own lane on the opposite side of the road from oncoming traffic was apparently a novel, untried idea as of yet in India.

Tea vendors and hawkers sold their wares from little blue carts at roadside and old men slept in the shade of dusty trees, oblivious to traffic.

From Madras Airport, an unusually large and clean plane from Indian Airways took us to Bangalore where we checked into the Holiday Inn and learned to our dismay that, though Baba had indeed been in Bangalore during April, May and part of June.

He had had to go to Puttaparthi and had not returned, nor was He expected by devotees to do so soon.

After absorbing the shocking news we decided to rest for a day and a half, to see the sights of Bangalore and then to proceed to Puttaparthi by three cabs. In Bangalore we took the group to see the Parliament Buildings, the parks, the Lal Bagh Botanical Gardens with deer park and glass conservatory, the exterior of the Science and Technology Museum (which was having a power failure!); the Bull Temple; the Sri Ramakrishna Ashram and rose garden with temple; and Tippu Sultan's Palace which was graced with large trees that bore sausage-like fruit or seed casings.

During sight-seeing in Bangalore, as we crossed the bumpy street, Daisy, who was wearing socks with slippery high-heeled wedgies, fell off her shoe and twisted her ankle.

Meanwhile, a steamy Indian romance film was being made in the lobby of the five-star Holiday Inn (now called Le Meridian) which featured doe-eyed satin-clad beauties dancing and shimmying up and down the wide marble stair-cases to the accompaniment of raucous music of strange stringed instruments. Kumar, the manager who met us on our arrival, mentioned that the film was "one of those musical romances" indicating that it was big on froth but small on plot.

At 2:30 A.M. our cab caravan departed from the luxurious accommodations of the Holiday Inn, saying farewell to sumptuous buffet tables, the lush swimming pool garden, shops, glass elevators, bellmen, marble lobbies, carpeted halls, bathtubs and hot water, electrical outlets, reading lamps, furniture, sheets and blankets, comfortable beds, refrigeration, air conditioning and other familiar Western amenities.

The trip was, thankfully, uneventful. As we pulled up the deserted road to Barren Hill before descending to the dry rocky valley containing Puttaparthi and other tiny villages, a spectacular rosy dawn tinted the landscape. There were white bullocks pulling painted carts; thatched huts with rough door-openings spilled out beige dogs, nude babies, grand-parents and sleepy-eyed men with towels slung over their shoulders who ambled down to the nearest well or stream for morning ablutions.

It was 6:00 A.M. as we arrived in the village of Puttaparthi; we needed to dash to the nearest stall outside the ashram car-gate to get darshan mats in hopes of arriving early enough to see Baba. Everyone began talking at once.

"What would He be like?"

"I wonder if I'll feel anything unusual when I see Him in person" our group members were murmuring.

"Do I look alright? Am I modest-looking enough?"

"Has He come out yet?"

"Where's the line?"

"What shall I say if He comes over and talks to me?!"

"This is the most exciting moment of my life!"

Swami came out for darshan, looking radiant and, as usual, floating along silently, first to the women's side, then to the men's side.

The Mandir compound was unexpectedly crowded the next several days with approximately 4,000 to 4,500 people inside, including visiting students and teachers from Baba's elementary and secondary schools. The college students, elementary and high school students and the male devotees, service workers, teachers and administrators wore white, as Baba has asked devotees to do. Our group wore white along with an Indonesian group, an Iranian group, an Australian group, a German group, some Canadians, and a sprinkling of other foreigners.

The first day at the ashram we were joined by Ed Davis, who is an administrator for a massage therapy school in Florida, and his friend Sara Kent, who is a social worker and who does TV and video work for her spiritual teacher, P. I. Khan.

After the first big shock of the trip - that Baba was in Puttaparthi, and not Bangalore as He had said He would be in the dream - the next shock awaited.

Shed Shock. By now, I have become accustomed to the sheds and even find them rather fun, but the others were not amused at the news. The Accommodations Office informed the group that the only space left in the ashram was in the "halls" or "dorms" as they euphemistically refer to them. A shed is a shed is a shed. The women blanched, went to town and got cots, mosquito nets, pails, and the usual supplies for shed camping and settled in, some in a deep funk upon seeing the stark condition of the sheds.

Meanwhile, as the women in our group adjusted to the reality of the situation, the funk deepened in Shed 15/16. Meanwhile, I, who had been assigned to the Family Shed 17/18 with Jim, was fervently praying that Swami would help me have the strength to endure the sharp disappointment and mounting wrath of the women in the group. Their seething was nearly palpable through the walls of their shed next door.

The morning of the second day of darshan Baba glanced at our women and walked over to Justin Lang, who was in the front row of darshan on the men's side. The women, who had drawn row 14 B were straining to see what was happening. I had just said "Now if anyone in our group gets called we all get to go in for an interview, so keep your eyes on our men so that we don't miss their going up on the veranda in case they get called in."

Swami talked to Justin and said "Are you ready to go in?" Justin, Jim and Ed arose silently as the ashram photographer took their picture, then ours as we women arose, hearts pounding. We knew that we had to make it to the veranda without being turned back. Then we needed to reach the interview room on the first floor of the Mandir temple without being sent out. We made the hurdles and sat down as fast as we could on the stone-tiled floor of the small green room which held Baba's red chair and foot stool, three gift clocks, some pictures and a table with the silver tray that holds letters to Baba.

As we all sat pressed closely together, crowded like honeycomb cells, more people came into the room until it seemed we couldn't hold another person. Six Indians joined the eleven of us: Connie, Jim, Justin, Ed, Amy, Sally, Sara Kent, Vera Karn, Carol, Andria and Daisy. Thus the room seemed full with eighteen people eagerly awaiting Baba's comments and inevitable surprises. What would He say and do? Would He acknowledge any of us directly? Would He tease us? If so, would we be able to take it well? My heart is bursting with love for the Lord. It's also clear to me that the only way to avoid reincarnation is to still the mind.

It seemed that the Indian family was from The Hague, Holland. Baba sat down with great finality in His chair and asked in a loud voice "Why have you come?"

"Because we love You, Swami," I replied with a laugh.

Baba then leaned down close to her ear and made as if to mumble "Baa Baa Black Sheep, Have You Any Wool...? This immediately set the group to thinking - at least those who could hear Baba over the fan and who could understand His accent. Several people later said that they wondered if He meant that He knew that they had always felt like the "black sheep of the family" due to their unconventional spiritual pursuits.

At the time, I was reading a book of short stories about India by Kipling. The first story was entitled "Baa Baa Black Sheep" so I wondered if Baba was indicating that Kipling, though a facile writer, was unsuitable reading due to his superior Colonial attitude toward the Indians of his day in the 1800's. Was this a message to be more universal? Or were some in the group prejudiced toward blacks; was this Baba's way to let them know He knew? In any event, Baba knows our every thought and everything we read, hear, see and say.

Demonstrating His omniscience, Baba next said "Yes, love." (You're here because You love Me.) You don't worship a picture. (One or two people from fundamentalist Christian backgrounds in the group initially felt that "pagan worship" was taking place at the ashram.) They had little travel experience and were put off by Hindu culture. We educated them about the symbolism of Hinduism and the fact that Hindus believe in one God with many aspects.

Baba indicated that we are all in God and God is in all people and things. He then moved His hand in large round circles, swiftly, whereupon a small, round, embossed silver vibhuti container appeared in His hand. Baba took the top off of the dainty silver case and showed us that it was filled to the brim with vibhuti ash which has curative properties. A gasp of delight went up in the room. Next, Baba rubbed vibhuti on the chest of the older man for whom He had manifested the silver box. He lovingly patted the man, who had some ailments. In deep gratitude the man attempted to stoop down to touch Baba's feet in the customary manner of Indian devotees when Baba restrained him out of concern for the gentleman's health.

Baba then manifested vibhuti for the women and, in some cases, put it into their hands with a firm touch (called sparshan) for an extra healing or blessing.

As the women were consuming their sacred ash (given to assist in detaching from desires) Baba ushered the elderly man and his wife into the rear interview room for a private interview that seemed to last for about fifteen minutes. After they emerged He gave each of them a large handful of vibhuti packets enclosed in small plastic "zip-lock"-type packets.

Another couple were called into the back room with their thirteen-year-old son for a private session. The woman later told us that she had prayed the previous night that Baba would bless their wedding rings, as they had gotten married in a court-house rather than a temple. In the rear room Baba blessed their rings and marriage and put the rings on their hands.

When Baba came out into our front interview room He sat in His chair and gave a mini-discourse with fast-flying commentary to the group and to individuals, with many subtle meanings for us.

Baba: "Where are you from?" as if He didn't know. He asks this so that others in the room might have the benefit of knowing the country of residency of those present. Obviously we are all from God.

Justin: "From the USA. Denver. We're Americans."

Baba: USA? There's a USA in India also. Near Bombay. U S Association. This was a joke that we failed to grasp. Baba obviously likes it and wants us to catch the meaning as He told this joke in each interview and it still went over our heads though the Indians laughed.

Baba: "Where is God?"

Connie: "God is everywhere - in all people and in all things."

Baba: "How do you know that?"

Connie: "Experience."

Baba: "What is the way to God?"

Connie: "Through service to others."

Baba: "Good answer." (Connie was greatly relieved to finally hit upon a correct answer in an interview as He had teased her in prior interviews and then said "No. That's not the correct answer.")

Next Baba held up His hankie that had been resting on the arm of His chair. "What is this?"

Group: "A hanky."

Baba: "First it is cotton. Then it is threads, then cloth - all the same. The cotton is in My hand. Now I cover it. Now I pull it out. It is still cotton. Still hanky. Still cotton all at the same time. Now: you are God. God is in you. But God is not so small as to be only in you. God is in all. All is in God. Always look up, not down. Remember - expansion, not contraction. Love is expansion."

Then Baba said, "Unity is strength," and mentioned the "Four F's":

Follow the Master - **F**ace the Devil - **F**ight to the end - **F**inish the game.

Justin leaned forward and began to put forth a question he had been pondering for several months. It had to do with the reaction of fundamentalist Christians to Baba in the future. Justin approached the question very obliquely at first.

Justin: "Sir, there are so many divergent religions... what are we to do...?

Baba: "You are separating. Dividing. All is one. One people. The sky is one with many stars. This is a dual mind (you have). You are thinking of the differences in people. No. All are one."

Next Baba got up from His chair, held aside the simple brown curtain from the doorway to the rear interview room and said "Americans - go in." There were some simple arm chairs along the wall of the interview room as well as a few photos and Baba's brown corduroy armchair. Daisy sat in an armchair next to Baba while Connie and Justin sat at Swami's feet on the bare floor in front of Him. Vera sat in a chair along a back wall and the rest of the group sat on the floor within a yard or two of Baba.

Justin held Baba's hand, then Connie held it briefly, then Daisy held His hand quite a long time. Daisy beamed throughout the interview and light seemed to pour from her face. Baba smiled tenderly to the group and exuded the pure love of the Divine Mother.

Of Justin, **Baba** asked, "How are you?"

Smiling, then floundering, flustered, Justin replied "Fine. I'm fine."

Baba: "Eh?"

Justin: "I'm uh... I'm a mess!" He laughed and we all laughed loudly at such a genuine reply when Baba held up His hand and shushed us. We abruptly ceased all laughter as we didn't want Justin to suddenly shut down in his first interview.

Justin:: "I'm so happy." (Indeed, Justin looked as if he were going to levitate up to the ceiling in the ecstasy of being with Baba.)

Baba: "Where is your wife?"

Justin: "Wife?" (He is 45, single. Baba started a game with him at this point, asking periodically "Where is your first wife?")

Baba: "Don't have one?" Sometimes you want a wife. Sometimes you don't. It is not good to change partners like musical chairs." (Seven of the eleven Americans were single.) "What are you doing? (meaning for work these days)"

Justin: "I'm going back to work."

Baba: "Lazy!" He affectionately tapped Justin as He said this.

Baba: "Where is your wife?" (to Jim)

Jim: "She's my wife," pointing to Connie.

Baba: "She's a good woman. He's a good man (meaning Jim.) Sometimes you fight."

Connie: "Yes, Swami, sometimes we fight, but not so much anymore." She laughed as she said this.

Baba: "No, not so much now. How many children (have you)?"

Connie: "Three boys."

Baba: "But you wanted a girl" (when you were of child-bearing age you had hoped to have a girl, also, someday.)

Connie, silently: "How on earth did He know about that - that I had always wanted a daughter, as well as a son?! I never told anyone - not my mother, sister, nor husband."

Baba: "All children are the same; girls and boys." (This statement meant a lot to Sara, who has two sons. Her second son, she says, didn't even have a name for four days because she was so certain she'd have a girl. Others also responded to this comment of Baba's.)

Baba to Jim: "How is your work? He works hard. Always working at this, that. (Baba made little fixing motions with His hands as Jim is always fixing things in the house, cars, and yard when he is not at the office or composing music or working at the computer.) Sometimes you have many disappointments... and some depression. (Baba then turned to Connie and spoke.) And he keeps secrets, things in his heart. (Connie and Jim often discuss their tendency to overwork as well as Jim's inclination to keep his thoughts and feelings to himself, to Connie's consternation.) Next Baba rubbed His thumb and fingers together and looked at Jim and said "Money... " as if to say that Jim worries about money, which is true.

Baba turned to Ed, who had been sitting quietly and attentively and asked "And what do you want?"

Ed: "A pure heart."

Baba: "What is your work?"

Ed: "I'm a school administrator, Baba. Sometimes I have bad thoughts." (i.e., that I need Your help with.)

Baba: "Even more than bad. I know. I will help." (Ed was perplexed that he had unaccountably experienced hostile thoughts toward Baba.)

Turning to Daisy, who was tearfully holding Baba's hand, face aglow, Baba spoke.

Baba: "You are 'Mommy'. Your name?

Daisy: "Daisy."

Baba: "You are devotion. Your middle name?"

Daisy: "Maria. That's what I want. (devotion)"

Baba: "Any sons?"

Daisy: "No."

Baba: "You have many sons. (Sons-in-law and young men that she mothers. Also, Baba says all men are our sons, all women are our daughters.) She is a good woman. She has cried for me for two years. (Though Daisy had only heard of Baba in February, her husband had died two years before and she had prayed to God fervently since then.) She has much pain in the left leg - and in the stomach, too. Ulcer. I will heal that. How is the finger?"

Daisy: "You knew about that, too?! It was a hangnail. It's fine, Swami."

Connie: "You know all of our little secrets, Baba!"

Baba to Daisy: "I will take care of you from now on." (i.e., She is a widow and her husband took care of her. Now Baba is her husband, as He is the husband of everyone, even men.)

Baba to Adrian: "How are you, Mommy?" "She is a good woman." (to the group, referring to Adrian)

Next, He turned to Sara and asked what she did as a line of work.

Sara: "Social work."

Baba: "Not much social work. TV, videos. All this TV and videos is not so good. Time waste is life waste. Don't waste time." (This seemed somewhat unsettling to Sara.)

To Vera, our senior homemaker from Iowa, Baba asked, "How are you, Madame?" In a trembling voice and with quavering lips, Vera replied, "If I have to answer, I'll cry."

Baba: "Your children are now with you."

Vera: "Not with me?"

Baba: "NOW with you." (meaning they would support her India trip and Sai experience when she got home, instead of fighting or rejecting the whole thing.)

After finishing with Vera for the moment, Baba turned to Sally and asked "How are you, Sir?" (Since she's a woman, and a pretty feminine one at that, this caused us all to giggle silently... until He began to address nearly all of our women as "Sir" as the days went on. Some of us thought that this meant that we are asSERtive women, whereas others felt that He said it because we believe we are equal to men, Indian men in particular, who seemed to overlook our women in various lines and service counters. Local people have told us that it means that a woman addressed as 'Sir' has the capacity for Realization in this lifetime.) After Sally said she was fine, Baba asked what she did for work.

Sally: "I manage real estate."

Baba: "Do you want children?" (She's single and would consider marriage to a spiritual man.)

Sally: "No."

Throughout the interview Baba made three more points:

1. Less luggage makes life's journey more pleasurable."

2. You are all like light bulbs connected to the same energy. Just increase your wattage!"

3. "Let your conscience be your guide. It is inside you. Use it."

Then, as Baba concluded the interview, which had lasted for an hour and twelve minutes, He said, "I'll see you again on Sunday - no - Saturday." (the next day)

Connie, eager to pin Him down asked "Now Swami, (smiling and teasingly) do You mean that You will actually see us again on this trip, in these bodies, in Your form and not just in our hearts or dreams?!"

Baba, laughing and imitating Connie: "Yes, I will see you again on this trip, in these bodies, in This form. Some people are thinking Sai Baba does not keep His Word when He happens to be in Puttaparthi. But you see... the crowds are very big now so when I came here (from Bangalore in June) I had to stay to see people. So I am seeing you here (instead of Whitefield, as per Connie's dream.) But Baba keeps His Word. I will see you. Now, come."

He ushered us to the door and we glided out to the darshan area contemplating our great fortune at having had the group interview, an interview in the rear room, and the promise of yet another interview. This was only our second day in Puttaparthi. Baba had asked us briefly how the sheds were. Silence. He asked how the food was. We responded "Fine" in a halfhearted manner. He thus let us know that He was aware that we were disappointed to be in the sheds in Puttaparthi instead of in

Bangalore hotels and that He was making up for it by seeing us more than once and giving generous attention to all in the interview.

We contemplated our extraordinary good fortune and the tremendous grace which the Lord had conferred upon us. How could He possibly outdo Himself and make us any happier?

CHAPTER 26
RING ON SHANKARA'S BIRTHDAY

"You are the embodiment of God. fill your thoughts with your almightiness, your majesty and your glory." Sathya Sai Baba, CTSSB P 335

Puttaparthi, India
Saturday, July 21, 1990

Interview No. 2

At 7:00 A.M. Baba called the group via the men's side and also called in four Italians, fifteen Indonesians, and some Indians from Pakistan, making a merry mob of thirty-eight people pressed intimately together in the outer interview room.

As someone sat on someone else's hand there was a startled "Oh! Excuse me." Then a reply, "Don't mention it - I'm used to this. I was a sardine in my last life!"

Baba asked each group where they came from, for the benefit of the others there. He asked where the rest of the large Indonesian group had gone. They were a lovely group dressed in white with a long red shawl as an insignia. They replied that most of the men had left the previous day to get back to work but that this contingent had re-booked until today in hopes of an interview. (Connie had told them the previous day that she felt they would be getting an interview soon, not dreaming that both groups would be seen together. On the strength of that comment they had changed their air tickets and, lo! - both groups sat happily side by side in the outer room.)

"Where is the group leader?" Baba asked the Indonesian women. A short-haired brunette raised her hand. Baba then made swift rotations with His hand and said "This is for the Mandir, for puja." He materialized a lovely gold statuette of Shirdi Sai which had a red robe.

Next, He made a jade-green lingham for a woman from Pakistan who said she wanted concentration. He told her that the lingham would help with concentration. The group from Pakistan asked about money and some financial help. Baba said He would help them.

"The situation in Pakistan is not good. All is contraction, contraction, contraction," He said. "No expansion."

It (the war there) all comes from bad politics. Politics without morality, science without humanity, education without character, colors without variety (in people) are all useless and dangerous!" Then Baba got up and manifested vibhuti ash for the closest women in the crowd.

He then turned to a tall thin student and said to him "Your consciousness is dead."

He turned to Justin and asked him "Where is your first wife?" Justin replied "I don't know." (Later this became a joke and Justin would come up to our group at the bakery or elsewhere in the ashram and say, spontaneously, "Hello, I'm fine and I don't know where my first wife is!") Later we learned that when Baba refers to the first or second wife, He means that one is at the first level of the path: the moral life. The second spouse, which one is seeking, is the spiritual life. The third spouse, which all will eventually have, is the divine life, or Realization. The two children which everyone needs, are a daughter – peace-and a son, which signifies wisdom. Thus, the Holy Family is within.

Baba stood by the door to the inner room and said "Indonesia, come now." Indonesia went in for a few minutes, then came out. Swami suddenly looked at the tall Italian woman in the blue silk outfit and said "She (the daughter) is fighting with you - she wants to marry." Then He asked the people from Pakistan what their names were. They had Muslim names. They went into the rear room for a few minutes and next the Italian couple who had a boy and girl went in. Baba had a box of rings which He blew upon, then closed the box. There were two rings, one of which was a diamond that was loosely sitting in the setting.

The Italian woman indicated that He had made the ring or the stone for her as she came back to her place in the outer room. Some students went into the back room briefly as the fan whirred gently overhead in the quiet outer room. In our tightly packed situation we were all afraid to breathe lest we would press too heavily on the persons on all sides of us.

Baba made the same joke about the USA in India, which we still did not appreciate or understand. Then He said "USA, go in." He took Ed by the arm and said "Come, Sir," and sat him down between Justin and Jim. He commented on the fact that we had mostly assumed our same places as in the previous day's interview, but He noted the exceptions. "See, I know," He said with a twinkle in His lustrous brown eyes.

Then He bent down and looked under Daisy's seat and said "Bag... is there a bag here?" rather enigmatically. (As it turned out, Sara had left her bag back in the darshan line when we were called for the third interview. Further, monkeys returned to Puttaparthi and we had to zip up our bags so that cats and monkeys wouldn't carry off items from our bags in the sheds. Additionally, we were forever counting and recounting our hand luggage and carry-on luggage at the numerous airports we transited on the trip to and from India.)

Baba's opening remarks to Justin were: "What do you want?"

Justin: "Strength, clarity, good vision, faithful and steady. Love of Sai."

Baba: "What? What? Sai is here. Sai is everywhere."

Baba then addressed Daisy, who held His hand: "How is your head?"

Daisy: "It's better."

Baba: "I am everywhere."

Next He asked Sara how she was and when she responded that she was fine, He said she was depressed. We had taken a tour to see Baba's elephant, Sai Gita, via rickshaw the day before, as well as to see the famous Wish-fulfilling Tree, the river (which was devoid of even a puddle of water) and the schools, Ganesh Gate, Meditation Tree and ashram grounds. Further, the men needed to get white darshan pajamas tailored and Sara needed to be fitted for a punjabi. We also had had to set up housekeeping, to get bottles of cold Bisleri water and to do errands to settle into the sheds.

Baba addressed all of our bustling about the village and spoke to us like a firm mother.

Baba: "Don't go outside the ashram because there are many beggars out there. Do not encourage them. They come from everywhere." (i.e., from other villages to prey on foreigners. Baba has offered to feed, house, clothe and educate all the village people but most are not interested.)

Baba to Justin: "You are giving money to beggars and they are taking alcohol, crack, stick, all those things."

Justin: "Oh… You caught that, huh? (donations to beggars) But Swami, there are good people out there."

Baba: "How do you know they are good?!" He said this with great sternness. "Don't form attachments when you come here. People will pretend to be nice and will say 'How are you, Sir,' so sweetly, when they are not sincere. Just tell people when they try to form attachments with you: 'I have come for Sai Baba, not you.' If you want to give them something, give them food. Liquor is no good. Your body is a temple."

"So… how is the food (in the ashram)?"

Group: A half-hearted "Fine."

Swami to Justin: "One heart. Two eyes, two ears, only one heart. Have only one wife, not like musical chairs."

Turning to Jim, **Baba** said: "You're a good man."

Then He started teasing Connie, who sometimes likes to make mischievous jokes and who sometimes feels great remorse at being too strict or self-righteous.

Baba: "You, are sometimes not good. Not bad, but not good." Connie worried about this for several days, as Swami intended she should. She concluded that she still has a strong smart-aleck streak and jokes around far too much.

He said to all, "Have one path, one teacher, one way."

At this point Connie asked, "Swami, is this a good time to ask about where our center should move? We're getting a bit crowded meeting at our house (where the Sai center for the Denver area has been located for the past three and a half years).Shall we go to Glendale Community Center? Or to a church. Would a church be better?"

Baba seemed to dodge the question by asking for someone to pass Him a silver box that lay on the window sill. As He opened the embossed box that was oval-shaped, about four inches by three inches, Connie, who sat holding Baba's foot, saw that the box contained three types of seeds or nuts. He removed one small brown seed and put it in His mouth. "I will see you all individually. When are you leaving?"

Connie: "In a week. Friday. Is it good for us to leave Friday, Swami?"

Baba: "Yes, then I can see you again. In the form!" We all laughed that He had anticipated Connie's wanting to pin Him down again about yet a third interview. "The crowd is large and I said I'd see the Indonesians so I can't see you individually today. But this week. Be good, Rowdy," He said to Justin.

Finally the Italian couple went in again, then the tall student. Baba rebuked a student and cuffed him. "When is your class?"

Student: "Ten."

Baba: "Sit down."

In conclusion, Baba got the red velvet vibhuti basket and passed out packets of vibhuti to the Indonesians. He told us we would not get any as this was not our last day to see Him. The comment created a happy expectancy that He would, in fact, really see us again, for a third interview. Such grace is virtually unknown as many people who have known Baba for ten or fifteen years or more have never had the chance to talk with Him, to touch His feet or to have an interview, not to mention the chance to have an interview in the rear room or to see materializations or to be given vibhuti, all of which our group was given.

As a result of being with Him at close range this time, it is clear to me now that most talking is a waste of time and a great seepage of precious energy. If the mind is kept still and drawn in, toward the spiritual Heart, there is constant contact with Baba and a renewal of energy. Also, I clearly realize now that when my own life is in order that I have no need to control others. Finally, being with Baba's form is giving me the insights and resolve to retrieve my own reality, feelings and motivations, instead of rescuing others in the name of service. Little by little, I am taking back the power which I unwittingly abdicated to men, to priests, ministers, doctors, managers and other authority figures in order to absolve myself of full responsibility for my life.

Interview No. 3

Wednesday, July 25, 1990

It was Wednesday morning and our next-to-last darshan. After having read *I Am That*, which appealed to me greatly two years ago, I've since discovered the teachings of dear Ramana Maharshi on advaita, or non-duality. This is my path. What a relief to know that there's an entire body of sacred literature on advaita. The two main ideas are: All is Consciousness. And, I am not this body, therefore, to whom do these thoughts arise and through whom is this life lived? I sat quietly in the darshan line reading Ramana. Eventually the chits were drawn by the head of each line.

Finally the women drew a low enough line number to get in the second and third rows. As Baba came past in darshan, I asked "Baba, will You see our group today?"

Baba noted the question without comment and proceeded to the men's side. asking "Americans? Americans?" Jim arose and asked Baba to see our eleven.

After we seated ourselves on the veranda, Baba called numerous Indians to the interview as well. There were a family of five, two couples, and some boys. As the Indians sat down Baba scolded a boy who was a young doctor.

Baba: "I told your Grandfather to come, then you and the family came instead. Selfish. Modern boys... You are a doctor. Doctors need the most patience!" Baba chuckled at His pun and we joined in, good-naturedly.

Then Baba turned to a beautiful Indian woman wearing a yellow punjabi and asked her what she wanted. She replied that she wanted peace of mind. Baba then waved His hand and manifested a stunning pair of diamond earrings for her. He told her that the design, which was a cluster of three large, simple diamonds, symbolized the three gunas, or qualities underlying all life: tamas (lethargy), rajas (restlessness or activity) and sathwas (spiritual balance).

Baba to Connie: "What do you want, Sir?" (Oh no - not "Sir!")

Connie: "Self-realization."

Baba then launched into a mini-discourse, most of which we didn't catch as the fan was whirring and He spoke very fast.

Baba: (In essence, He said -) "Self-realization is not religion. Religion is not Self-realization. Love - love is Self-realization."

He then made large circles with His hand and materialized a splendid silver ring which was in the shape of a drop, with a point at one end. He said "This is a Navaratna Shivalingham. It has nine gem-stones on the dome on top. It has the nine stones to ameliorate the planetary influences. It will protect you." The nine stones in a circle are the ruby, emerald, pearl, diamond, coral, topaz, sapphire, opal, and another stone. Twenty-one diamonds outline the tear-drop shape of the ring base. On either side of the ring there is an Om symbol. (Connie is the president of Om Productions which produces inspirational and educational materials about Baba and His work and mission.)

Baba: "Here, wear it on this finger (index finger, right hand). It's a bit big."

Connie, gasping: "No, it's fine, Baba. Oh, thank You, Swami, it's beautiful!"

Baba: "If you don't like it I'll make you a different one...."

Connie: (Stunned to have received a ring -) "Oh no, Swami, I like it very much!"

Baba: "Today is Shankara's birthday. I have waited eons to give you this. Today is a very auspicious day. That's why I gave it today."

Baba, to Justin: "How are you, Coconut tree?" Justin is six feet, four inches tall. "Where is God?"

Justin: "In my heart."

Baba:: "God is everywhere. The hanky is in My hand. All is IN God."

Baba then materialized a small gold statuette of Shirdi Sai Baba wearing a red robe for the same woman in the yellow punjabi for whom He had made the diamond earrings. "This is for your puja (prayer room altar). It will bring you peace of mind.

Next He materialized a spectacular gold watch for an older Indian woman in front of Him. "It says five after seven.... See? Even the time is right!" The woman took off her old watch and held it toward Baba.

Baba: "No, no. Keep it. Baba only gives, He doesn't take. Only one-way traffic with Baba. All giving, no taking!"

We all laughed at His loving ways and sweet little quips. Baba made a jade green lingham for an Indian woman.

"Jealousy," He remarked to the Indians.

Baba then turned to Jim and asked: "What is your name?"

Jim: "Jim"

Baba: "Jim, not gem. James, not games. There are games between husband and wife." (We had had a power struggle, like many couples, for a number of years.) Then, as soon as Jim and Connie followed Him into the rear interview room, alone, Baba gestured for them to sit down.

Baba said to Jim, about Connie: "She's a good girl, she's a good girl."

Then, to Jim, "Sometimes you are depressed." Jim then asked about our three sons.

Baba to Connie: "Such good boys, such good boys. Your son is a good boy."

Jim: "Baba, when shall we bring the boys to India to see you?"

Baba: "They can come next year. I will give you many blessings, don't worry. I called you in today because this is the birthday of Ishwara and of Shankara. This is a very auspicious day, very auspicious. That's why I waited until today to see your group. Today is the most important day of the year. It starts the most auspicious month of the year, also. From now on you will all hear only good news." (In the previous two years Connie had "lost" through death, about sixteen friends, acquaintances and relatives, so she had had lots of shocking news. She had further been a bit sad that she hadn't had an interview in three and a half years, during which time she had experienced many trials, lessons, and challenges.)

Next, Baba said the unthinkable. It had to do with His upcoming 65th birthday, the Golden Jubilee of His fifty years of world uplift. When our group had heard that Baba had seen Phyllis Krystal the previous week and that He had told her three times to come to Birthday, we immediately started making jokes about a person being out of his mind to come to Birthday as it would be thronged with two million people. We joked about most Americans having crowd phobia and so forth.

Baba looked at Jim and Connie and said "Come back in November. I will give you the money."

Picking up a prior on-going theme with Connie, Baba said, "I know you want Self-realization and I will give it to you, but not now. Now the children are still young, in school, and you have so many responsibilities that it would be better to wait a bit. So be patient and I will grant it in a few years. I WILL give it to you so just be patient until you have fulfilled duties and responsibilities to husband, children, family, work (Om Productions, new projects, counseling, healing work, Sai Center, service work, Colorado Sai Center advisory work for the state of Colorado, speaking engagements throughout Colorado and the U.S.)

"Birthday?! He wants us to come to Birthday?" Connie and Jim were asking silently, simultaneously. Jim looked shocked. Connie stiffened. Their jaws sagged. Seeing this response, Baba then said to Jim very sweetly "Of course if you think it will not be comfortable at Birthday you need not come. But I will send the money, then you can decide if you want to come. But it would be good to come. I will bless you. From now on you will have health, happy life, blessings for your family, for the group."

Connie, with tear-filled eyes: "Oh Baba, You are such a sweet, loving Mother to us! Thank You for everything." Baba smiled and patted her hand.

"Shall we move into a church?"

Baba, with vigor: "I will find you a church. I will give you a church. And I will help your sons. Today I will give you a robe."

Connie, not comprehending: "A robe, Swami?"

"Yes, a robe. For your Center. My robe. This afternoon I will give it."

"This very afternoon, Swami?!" Connie was breathless at yet another boon, unaware that Baba was leading her on another merry chase. He had had great fun previously in imitating Connie imitating Him and in correcting her American English to British pronunciation, telling her she speaks too "fahst" (quickly). Now the robe would prove to be a source of much anticipation and many jokes.

After having taken Jim and Connie for a private interview first, Baba next took Daisy, Sara, Ed and Sally into the rear room. He asked Ed how he was doing with his thoughts.

Ed replied that he was doing much better and said that Swami's medicine is powerful medicine.

Ed: "But how do I know that I'm hearing Your voice? What's Your voice and what is some other voice?"

Baba: "It is all My voice."

Ed:: (Ed had had a vigorous haircut in town yesterday. The man had hit him very severely on the head as part of the "massage treatment" that went with the haircut.) "Well, Baba, You really beat me on the head yesterday!"

Baba: "Yes."

Ed: "What about all these fears I have?"

Baba: "You have much confusion. I will bless you." Baba then tapped Ed on the head and pressed him on the head.

Baba to Sally: "What do you want?"

Sally: "I want Your grace and blessings."

Baba: "Do you have children?"

Sally: "No, Swami."

Baba: "Do you have a husband?"

Sally: "No, Swami."

Baba: "Do you want a husband?"

Sally: "Yes."

Baba: "You have much confusion. Sometimes you want, sometimes you don't want (a husband). I will find you a husband. And you come back after you are married with your husband, soon, and I will give you wedding rings and bless you. I will always be with you and will always bless you."

Baba then asked Sara how she was doing. She answered, "Fine."

Baba: "Your mind is up and down. You are thinking about leaving. It's okay. You'll be back. Keep a steady mind. You help him (Ed). You help him. I am always with you."

He took Daisy's hand and asked "How's the leg?"

Daisy: "Fine, but the right ankle hurts."

Baba: "That's because we don't walk as much as we should. What do you want?"

Daisy: "I want nothing, Swami. I have everything."

Baba: "You want love and devotion. You are Mommy. Not many are given that (love and devotion). There is a little confusion. Never fear as Sai is here. I bless you."

The next group to go in for a private interview were Justin, Vera, Adrian, Amy and Carol.

Baba to Vera: "How are you?"

Vera: "The aging process is working on me."

Baba: "You have grandchildren."

Vera: "Yes."

Baba: "Your son is too attached to Mama."

Vera: "He's a singer."

Baba: "Yes. Sometimes he's good, sometimes he's bad."

Vera: "Well he quit drinking and smoking."

Baba: "But he has many friends - many women and men friends who smoke and drink. Your husband... a habit (drinking) You are affectionate but your son is not." (Vera thought that he must mean her husband, who acts as if he is a son and not a husband.)

Baba to Justin: "Find a wife. You have many women and a monkey mind."

Justin: "What about my mother?" (who isn't well)

Baba: "Baba is your mother."

Justin: "My EARTH mother."

Baba: "Do your duty. Don't worry."

Next Baba held Adrian's hand and asked how she was.

Adrian: "Fine. What about my eyes?"

Baba: "You will not have to have the operation. Take vitamins A and D for one month. Your eyes are fine. No cataracts, no disease. Vitamin A. Your eyes are healthy."

Adrian: "I'm moving out of the state and will start a Sai Baba Center."

Baba: "I will bless. I will bless. I will bless."

Swami then bounced Amy's and Carol's heads.

He asked about Amy's health.

Amy: "It's fine, Swami." He had called her "Pakora" which is a tender term that means, essentially, "My little dumpling."

Then Swami said that they would all have a long life, a healthy life, a happy life. **Baba:** "And I will bless your families."

Baba to Carol: "How are you?"

Carol: "I'm great."

Baba: "You are not great. You stay too much in the intellect. What do you want?"

Carol: "The doors to my Inner Knowing opened."

Baba: "Your sons-in-law... one is acting mean to your daughter. She's a good girl. Her next husband will be good."

Carol: "One daughter has trouble with money."

Baba: "Next month one daughter will have money. You think about your children all the time."

After everyone entered the main interview room, Baba made a very attractive and unusual gold ring with diamond "lotus feet" on its flat surface for the Defense Minister from New Delhi.

The man was thrilled but the ring was too small. Baba took the man and the ring into the next room for a moment and blew on the ring to enlarge it.

He made a few doctor jokes and then created a lovely cloisonné picture frame with glass and a tiny photo of Baba for the young doctor whom He had first chastised. Then Baba said "Oh, here's the stand." He then blew on the back of the little frame and a gold stand flew out of the back of it, to our great astonishment and delight.

Our third interview concluded with distribution of vibhuti and Baba's blessings amid our hearty thanks and sense of wonder at our tremendous good fortune in being the recipients of incomparable grace. The interviews lasted from about an hour and ten minutes to an hour and twenty minutes each.

* * * * *

As per our custom, we met after the interview under the tree in front of sheds 15/16 and 17/18 where we had been meeting each morning at

5:45 to say "Om's," meditate, sing and to start the day with a strong, unified group focus. We had also met there at 2:00 P.M. in order to do spiritual reading and discussion together as well as to sing and to process the upheaved reactions of individual group members to the sheds, to Baba, to India, to village life, poverty, bats and insects and the usual reactions to "camping out" in the ashram.

Then at 2:35 we would again meditate and sing before group line-up for darshan and the wait for Baba to appear about 4:40 or 4:50 P.M. Thus, we sat on the ground for about six to eight hours a day. The theme for us was "staying unified and meeting each other in the present moment through taking responsibility for thoughts and perceptions."

We reviewed each interview under "our tree" with the intention of typing and copying the notes of our extraordinary experiences on the group pilgrimage to the Avatar. In our last interview Baba said "Today is a new life for all of your group."

As we prepared to pack, several of our members announced with great awe and utter astonishment: "I'm even going to miss my little corner in the shed.

I said I'd never come back to India as it was such a shock to my belief system and habits, but I will probably be back here. I already miss Baba. Of course He's where we are, as He says."

Naturally, our incomparable trip to Swami held many more treats in the way of exposure to Indian arts, architecture, history and artifacts, but they were anticlimactic after being with the Lord. We took a jaunt to Mysore, which was a thirteen-hour excursion delayed by traffic, detours and the illness of a group member who had been processing the results of three close encounters with the Divine Incarnation.

Highlights of the junket included views of rice paddies dotted with cranes, ibis, storks, herons and kingfishers. We stopped in at Halagappa's orphanage to see the yellow lingham, the large crystal lingham, the silver Avatar sandals, vibhuti on Baba's picture, the bas-relief statue of Shirdi Sai's feet, the holy Cauvery River (one of the five most important rivers in India) and to receive some amrit and vibhuti to take home in tiny hotel shampoo bottles.

As we strolled through the stunning architecture of the Srirangapath-nam area, I mentioned that Tippu Sultan, the great unifier of South India, had been defeated by the Army of Cornwallis. In our last hours in India we rambled around the famous Srirangapathnam island to visit Tippu Sultan's Fort and moats; his grave; the summer palace with its gardens and museum; his mausoleum; the mosque tower; and the twelve-hundred-year-old Vishnu temple with ancient banyan trees and temple stalls. A very interesting feature of the visit to the temple near the fort was the huge ancient carved teakwood chariot known as the juggernaut. Baba has changed me a great deal since I was last in Mysore with Robin Adamson. India definitely has a hold on me.

Our tour of the Sultan's Royal Palace of Mysore was like a time-travel journey to an ancient era of fairytale princesses and Arabian nights. We marveled at the vast mirrored ballroom, the embossed silver thrones, unparalleled paintings of gods and goddesses, the stained glass, stately pillars and carved doors. How grand it must have been for the royal family to have walked among fine sculpture, glasswork and ivory-inlaid furniture on the way to the palace rose gardens and courtyards as they passed under graceful arcades and scalloped arches. We were entranced with the unusual Muslim architectural influences mixed with breathtaking Hindu religious art.

Luncheon at the Lalith Mahal Palace Hotel began with our (ducking our heads) entrance through the crossed swords of richly costumed guards dressed in emerald green with burgundy silk helmets, white gloves, black boots and trim.

The sumptuous palace featured:

⬧ The making of a film in the marbled staircase and grand entryway.

⬧ A dining room of Wedgwood blue and white with about 20 large round tables set with fine white cloth, silver and glassware.

⬧ Sitting rooms off the main hallway were decorated in red velvet with mahogany tables and trim under extremely high ceilings. Huge waxy green plants accented alcoves, hallways, corners and libraries. The hotel interior was butter yellow and white with various accents; this theme is typical of Sultan's palaces the world over. We admired the immaculate paint, trim, decor, grounds and entryway of this unique palace hotel that has been preserved as a gem of India's past and culture.

As we left the palace – skipping down the wide marble entry steps - a snake charmer stood waiting for us at the base of the stairs. He entreated us to watch the entrancing of his venomless hooded cobra which undulated from a wooden box to the tune of a reed pipe. We stood in a cluster, safely admiring them both at a distance!

We also passed the Zoo, the Race Course, the view of Chamundi Hill which houses a temple and hotel with spectacular view. The drive home to Bangalore showed us a welcome rain, homey sights of little Indian villages, school children in varied and charming uniforms and donkeys and oxen ploughing fields and hauling fodder. As twilight stole over the landscape, lights began coming on in shops and monkeys scrabbled in tree branches. In the dusk we noted a vendor proudly displaying an attractive assortment of huge glass chandeliers on the dirt at his impromptu curbside "selling spot" under graceful old trees.

We had been incredibly graced and purified by the Lord. All of us were changed, even the veteran travelers. India - funny old, crazy old, wonderful India left its indelible thumbprint on our minds and hearts and we left some of our invisible baggage behind and came away lighter, brighter and more energized for the next chapter in our Soul's homeward saga.

Puttaparthi, India
July 26th

It has been fifteen years since I began meditating. The mind has become a clear lake, most of the time, during the past two years. Baba often says, "Nothing can be done with an untrained mind." Unless the mind is still and receptive, one cannot be utilized as an effective instrument of God.

Ramana says, "Desires are the cause of an insatiable activity orientation." How true.

After Baba had told me that He would give us one of His robes, I asked Him, from line one, row one in the next darshan, when He was going to give it to me.

He had set me up for another of His leelas. Just when I felt that I didn't want anything from Him, He hooked me into wanting the robe that He had promised. As I looked up at Him from the ground as He walked by the first row, He gazed all around me in an elaborate avoidance of direct connection with me.

"Swami!" (I was practically shouting since He'd soon walk by and I'd miss my chance before going back to the States. Devotees are supposed to remain silent in darshan and certainly are not to shout.)

"What?" Swami asked, barely concealing a smile. "What? I can't hear you!" He said, teasing me royally.

"You know, Swami... what You said this morning. The robe," I replied.

"The WHAT?" He asked, laughing.

"The ROBE. R-O-B-E. YOUR robe. You said you'd give it to us." By this time everyone was staring and I felt acutely embarrassed; my face was red.

"WHAT robe?" He asked, innocently, laughing even more.

When I asked the head Seva Dal, or usher, where I was supposed to procure the robe Baba had promised, she just laughed.

"Darling," she said, "You must learn to love Baba's uncertainty. He could give it to you tomorrow, next year, in ten years. That's the way He is. Now you have had so much grace and so many interviews, my advice to you is just be happy you have been so fortunate. When Swami wants to get something to You He knows all of the options. I have even known Him to send things back to other countries, using devotees as couriers. But my dear, Swami is God, as you know, and you can't always take Him literally."

Our group ran back to the sheds after darshan, thinking He had apported it to one of our cots. But, there was no robe. Next, in the Bangalore hotel, we all searched the cupboards and closets for the promised robe. No robe was to be found. Thus, my serene mind was disturbed by the Lord in the fruitless search for His robe.

Littleton, Colorado
August, 1990

The capstone on the robe leela came a few weeks later on the occasion of my presentation of a talk to scientists, inventors and healers at the Annual Global Sciences Congress in Denver, Colorado. My topic was "Miraculous Sai Baba – Planetary Avatar." There were about thirty speakers for the five-day event and it was considered quite an honor to have been invited to speak. The thirty speakers were selected from about seven hundred people who desired to speak at such a venue.

One of the speakers who was to make his presentation before my own, was a young math wizard who was a Baha'i. He opened his talk by greeting the audience, and then by looking directly at me, sitting in the front row of the large hall of several hundred attendees. I had never seen the young brunette man before.

"Welcome, Ladies and Gentlemen. Thank you for coming," he began. "I am a member of the Baha'i faith and I am a God-loving man. Before I begin my talk on New Approaches to Mathematics, I shall read from the words of the great prophet, Baha ullah." He opened a huge holy book, which rested on the lectern, then, while looking directly at me, began to read in a penetrating voice that was saturated with reverence.

"And the Lord said, 'I shall make of you My Robe, and It shall never become outworn.'"

Suddenly, a tingling vibration shot through me and I realized that Baba had meant something far more important than a mere promise of gifting me with perishable fabric. He was referring to the fact that each of us is Atma, immortal Spirit, temporarily clothed in a body. He is eventually going to erase my misidentification with body, mind, emotions, gender and culture. Overcoming cultural and personality conditioning is essential if we are to attain, and to become established in, Realization.

As I understood the joke about the robe, I chuckled inwardly. "Oh, Lord – how delightfully funny and wonderful You are! Such a good Joker and Supreme Tease! Thank You, My Darling Bhagavan, for the great reminder: I AM Thee and Thou Art me. Joy is my birthright."

CHAPTER 27
THE ANCIENT MANUSCRIPT: A COSMIC BLUEPRINT

"Do all karma as actors in a play, keeping your identity separate and not attaching yourself too much to your role. Remember that the whole thing is just a play and the Lord has assigned to you a part; act well your part; there your duty ends. He has designed the play and He enjoys it." Sathya Sai Baba, SS October 1995 P 273

BANGALORE, INDIA
July, 1990

Milestones In The Dream

Because of the loud, incessant Bangalore traffic noises outside the office window, I leaned closer to Mr. Ramakrishna Shastry, sitting across the desk from me, to better hear what he was about to tell me regarding the "Cosmic Blueprint" of my life. The well-known and popular interpreter of the ancient manuscripts, called the Shuka Nadi leaves, was instantly likeable. His plump radiant face and expressive gestures made him a compelling and picturesque figure in his long, immaculate white silk kurta and matching floor-length dhoti.

Mr. Shastry opened the stack of brown leaves and selected the top one from the pile. The leaves were actually palm leaf strips scribed in ancient vegetable dyes and sealed with a vegetable shellac. Each one was about fourteen inches long and about two inches wide. They looked like a stack of old brown wooden rulers and were tied together with frayed twine and kept in squares of silk in antique wooden boxes. The language was Sanskrit and the script was small and exact.

Thousands of years ago, as incredible as it seems, Sage Shuka devoted his entire life to the akashic record notations of about three thousand "remarkable lives" of people who would live in the twentieth and twenty-first centuries. The common thread between the people featured in the manuscripts is that they would have a connection to Sathya Sai Baba, planetary Avatar. Many, if not most, would have incarnated with Him in some of His other lifetimes. Together with Sai Baba, they would dedicate their lives to the uplift of the consciousness of the world and usher in a Golden Age of Peace and Plenty.

Since many of the characters in the manuscripts would have extremely difficult karma and challenges, the manuscripts served numerous helpful functions. They helped people to cognize the pattern of their current embodiment and to accept their lot in life. The manuscripts gave an overview of the key spiritual passages in each lifestream and mentioned when the person would leave the body. They told of one's spiritual status; of karmic debts to parents, siblings and spouses; of financial or economic circumstances; of achievements and distinctions; of major challenges and obstacles; and of grace and blessings, including whether one would experience interviews from the Avatar.

After Mr. Shastry intoned a Sanskrit prayer and blessing, he explained that he was going to give me a brief overview of this embodiment as far as two major themes: major spiritual tests and invisible guides who would be helping me throughout this lifetime. I nodded my approval. Like his father before him and their ancestors for thousands of years, the men of the Shastry lineage had carefully safeguarded the precious manuscripts from fires, flood, epidemics, wars, invasion, foreign occupation, and all of the uncertainties and upheavals which befall a family and a nation, throughout the course of history. He explained that after giving me the two dominant themes, he would detail certain events of this lifetime and mention a number of events yet to come. He said that the ancient manuscript foretold that I would return quite a few times for readings and that each time a certain topic would be revealed. One is only allowed to receive particular information at each visit. If we were to know the details of the entire life in advance we would not learn the lessons of that incarnation.

Behind him, on the wall, there was a picture of Sage Shuka wearing a topknot and white beard, a loincloth and some brown rudraksha beads around his neck. He sat on a deerskin under a large banyan tree and held a writing stylus and a scroll in his lap. The sage received his information while in a light, receptive trance and wrote it down faithfully for posterity. Sage Brighu, elsewhere in India, did the same thing and many people had received readings from both lineages, which, of course, coincided. Occasionally minor details would vary.

Beside the picture of Sage Shuka was a photograph of Mr. Shastry's deceased father who had read the Shuka Nadi Manuscript on Sai Baba many years ago. There was a paper wall calendar depicting goddess Laxmi and a picture of Lord Rama. The large brown desk and three brown wooden armchairs were the only furniture in the room.

After Mr. Shastry chanted "Om Shukaaya Namaha" and gave me his blessing, he introduced the Life Reading with a shocking and tantalizing commentary. As he cleared his throat to deliver the cargo-load of initial points, he chuckled, rolled his eyes in shyness and amazement, then saluted in Namaste prayer-fashion and came right to the point.

"Sage Shuka welcomes you and says that you are a Mahapurusha Yogi (Great Being) who has come many, many times with Sathya Sai Baba for helping with world uplift. You accompanied Him when He was Lord Rama, Lord Krishna, Shankara, and Shirdi Sai Baba, to name but a few of your incarnations. The key hallmarks in this lifetime are that it is a lifetime of worldwide spiritual teaching and healing which will evolve into Self-realization in this embodiment.

"But you will have many tests of courage and fortitude. It will be an extremely eventful life marked by many hair-raising experiences." At this point he laughed heartily, then cleared his throat in embarrassment and continued. "It's incredible the number of hair-raising experiences you will have in this life. It is, however, a very happy life in spite of it all because of your positive attitude and your ability to see the lighter side. Most people couldn't take even a fraction of what you'll go through.

Unseen Assistance From Great Masters

"In this lifetime, because it is so pivotal for you, and because you are facing so many challenges, you will have continual unseen assistance from Sathya Sai Baba, Mother Mary, Jesus, Archangel Michael, Kuan Yin, Lord Buddha and Teresa. It is a blessed life. Have Jesus and Mary and the other Holy Ones come to you yet?" Mr. Shastry smiled in anticipation of my response. He was obviously enjoying the reading as much as I was.

"Yes, they began coming in 1980. Baba has appeared in our home dozens of times and Mary and Jesus have as well."

Tests of Courage

As Mr. Shastry silently translated the Sanskrit for the next body of information I recalled, as if watching a movie unfold before my eyes, about two dozen different experiences which had indeed been a test of courage. Some of those which have already taken place follow. I had always thought of myself as extremely healthy and very bold and fearless. The totality of the challenges which I had surmounted, when recounted together, was staggering. They were:

Being knocked unconscious, at age twelve, through a spinal injury suffered when a childhood friend fell head-first from the top of a thirty-foot cherry tree on top of me. I blocked her fall and saved her life but had back problems thereafter as a result.

A near-death experience during the childbirth of my only son. We both hovered near death for a month.

A hi-jacking in Egypt by Arab terrorists while on a trip to see the pyramids. I talked my way out of it and eventually the entire group were freed, unharmed, in forty-eight hours.

Being stoned and "egged" by a riotous anti-American Communist mob in Naples, Italy, while shopping with a friend.

Several broken bones. I was a very adventuresome tomboy.

Five surgeries.

Received a blow to the head after landing a small rented plane I was using for flying lessons.

Escape from the seventeenth floor during a hotel fire in Singapore.

A brain tumor was healed instantaneously by Sai Baba at our first interview.

After meeting Baba, I was in a light state of ecstasy for a year.

Self-healing of ankylosing spondylitis in six weeks through massive doses of vitamin C.

A profound Samadhi Breakthrough took place, lasting a day.

A hold-up and kidnapping in China. I escaped injury and turned the man in to authorities.

A great "letting go" experience occurred, lasting two weeks.

Threats to my life during lectures.

Slander because of my affiliation with Sai Baba

Hassles during solo travel to many countries with inhospitable political environments to Americans.

Braving vast floods of India, horizon to horizon, as well as many cholera and malaria epidemics.

A swift, spectacular Samadhi Activation came, lasting three weeks.

Dangerous encounters with large seven-foot rattlesnakes in Colorado and Arizona, with a seven-foot cobra in a Puttaparthi hotel lobby, a centipede bite on the face, and an attack by a rhino mother and baby while riding on elephant back in Nepal

Yet to come, from 1996 to 1998 would be recovery from pneumonia, Epstein-Barr Syndrome and malaria, contracted in India.

Long-term endurance of numerous overwhelming kundalini activations

Endurance of debilitating and painful patterns of nausea, dizziness and joint pain from being extremely sensitive to storm fronts, inner earth movements and from being an earthquake empath. This physical vehicle, which is being used for healing, teaching and other aspects of Baba's work, is highly attuned to other realms.

My head was whirring. Suddenly, it struck me that I was rather like the cat with nine lives, only in this case it was at least twenty-five. No wonder there were so many angels and Ascended Masters guiding and protecting me. I needed a whole team, apparently, to keep from either getting bumped off or from being overwhelmed with discouragement at the tasks I'd agreed to before incarnating in this embodiment.

The amazing thing is that I have always looked upon my life as a very happy and fortunate one, because I had never looked back or dwelled on the past. I was feeling slightly overwhelmed as he spoke and observed my mind preparing to go into denial mode.

"Mr. Shastry, are you sure you have the correct palm leaf manuscript, I mean, that it belongs to me and to my life?" I asked, somewhat aghast. (Really, now, how many people's lives would fit such a description? I was grasping at straws to keep from integrating the awareness that, by most people's standards, my life had been extremely traumatic. But I simply would not, could not view it that way. It had been eventful and challenging, yes, but also filled to overflowing with grace and enormous opportunity. Each so-called catastrophe was, in my view, merely something which I had to encounter, as God's Will, and I endured it with as much cheer and good grace as I could muster. I refused to see it any other way.)

"Do you agree that you have had these many, many tests of courage and that many great saints and beings from the other side have already been in contact with you?" he counter-questioned. "Surely this must be the correct manuscript. There's your age, birth order in the family, your one son, your first and second marriages, your work, your association with Sai Baba and the interviews you have had."

"Yes, that's definitely my life, but the manuscript makes it sound very grand. That is, the part about the role I'm to play, with world-wide teaching and Realization in this life. I'm such an ordinary person that I can't imagine that I have such a big role to play in Sai's lifetime. Are you absolutely sure there's no mistake here? Though I have to admit, that if all of my difficulties were ordained thousands of years ago, then it must mean that we don't control our lives as we believe in the West."

"Every life is like a novel," he said. "Only most people aren't very conscious as they live their lives. The Shuka Nadi Manuscripts help us to be more aware of the role we are playing. The Life Reading also helps us to take the role more seriously in a way so that we can do it justice. Some lives are like a great spiritual epic, like those of Lord Buddha and Lord Rama. All the roles are assigned by God. You can't take credit for the role you have been given, nor should a person feel guilty about his life, since all the roles are needed for the play. Just play the role to the best of your ability."

"Now, then, we will begin. You were destined to get this reading today. You are the eldest child of your family. You had a normal schooling and college education. At age twenty-one to twenty-two you became independent and moved, after graduation. You found your first marriage partner then and after knowing him for eight years, the marriage developed some problems and ended.

"By this time, from age thirty to thirty-eight you were already very creative and were on a spiritual search. Your communications ability and personal energy built up. During the years from thirty-eight to thirty-nine you had a change of profession. You became a communications specialist and an organizer. From 1981 to 1982 you underwent many changes – a move overseas, a lot of travel, a health crisis. From 1982 to the present has been a period of rapid spiritual development. The key turning point was in 1985 to 1986. Your partner's key turning point was from 1982 to 1986.

"You knew him as an acquaintance in 1976 and married him, your second and present husband, in 1979. He joined you on the same spiritual path (Sai Baba). He is also a good healer and can be a good organizer of a healing center in the future. He is your soul partner. Your mutual goal now in this marriage is working for soul purposes. You are the one who has given him his support for his spiritual development in this lifetime.

"Your personality thrust now is that you are a good organizer and a good communicator. These two things are the purpose of this lifetime. You are destined to have a good sixth sense intuition and to heal and to have a positive personality. Before 1986 you were impatient but now you are very patient. After 1986 you started your own business and your negativity went down and positivity went up and your concentration increased. You then gave up personal ambition and decided to change the focus of your work from an economic/business focus to a spiritual focus working for the good of society.

"Money will come easily to hand and not be a problem for you. You and your husband will move to a larger tract of land which will be beautiful and quiet and where you will find great peace." (Two years later we moved to Harmony Farm, north of Denver, Colorado, where we have indeed experienced great peace.)

Major Incarnations

"You were born in India in many lifetimes. You taught many spiritual subjects such as yoga and meditation and your communications capability in this life comes from those Indian incarnations. Your step-sons in this lifetime were your natural sons in seven other lifetimes. That is why you take such a keen interest in them and their well-being in this incarnation.

"You were in Egypt in the royal family near the Nile and you liked to work as an artist in making gold jewelry. In this lifetime, however, you have already used and will use your extra money to help others.

"In Israel you were a man, a Christian priest. Now you have this priest quality and can be a medium of the spiritual masters for helping others with your sixth sense.

"You were a philosopher in Greece and traveled the world teaching the non-dualistic philosophy of Shankara. You were also one of the four disciples of Sage Shankara of the 700's and took his philosophy far and wide. You have also taught Christianity in various lifetimes and have taught Shirdi Sai Baba's teachings in your last lifetime as a member of British royalty who, as a woman, moved to India to be near Shirdi Sai.

"You will get a lot of help in this lifetime from Ganesha, Jesus, Baba, Durga, Teresa and a Buddhist monk. You will be a medium for the Ascended Masters for their work, healing, teaching and their beneficial influence on the planet."

"Mr. Shastry – that Teresa – is it St. Teresa, the Little Flower, or Mother Teresa, or which Teresa?"

"I'm sorry it doesn't say in the manuscript," he replied, shaking his head. "But it does say here that you'll be a good spiritual teacher, a good writer, a healer, a counselor, a mind-healer or psychologist and a very good communicator of philosophy. In fact, you will write a book on philosophy and will also write one on psychology. You'll write eleven books. You were in China and Tibet as a native healer in the past.

"In this life you will get pleasure from organizing but you will earn income from communication. Don't get confused by mixing these two.

"You will have good health. Any physical difficulties can be cured by meditation and asanas. You were destined to have only one natural child, a son, and you will be happy with him. He is a good boy and will be a good architect or he can even do architectural programming. He will be very successful. He will be a good consultant to others on the material as well as the spiritual plane eventually. When he is in his thirties he will become a Sai devotee. He will be a father by 1999. His wife will also love God. Your son, step-sons and their wives and your future grandchildren, when they come, will all be Sai devotees. You are very blessed.

"The reason for your first marriage was karma and to provide a vehicle for your son's birth. It was all in divine order. Your current or second husband is the spiritual one. You have known both of the men many, many times in other lifetimes. Your current husband was a teacher to you before and this marriage will be successful and happy. The last part of your life, from ages fifty-eight to eighty-eight will be the best part of your life as you will be Realized during that period.

"This is your last lifetime or you can return as a Bodhisattva to help uplift mankind during Prema Sai's incarnation. If you come back then to help Sai, you will be a male teaching yoga in His ashram.

"If you chant 'Om Dum Durgaya Namaha' you can have material or career success and eventual Realization. It will dissolve any problems.

"You will write and derive income from your future books and will have good contact and many interviews with Sai Baba in this life. You will live a life of service to others. By the way, did Baba give you a ring a few days ago? It was ordained thousands of years ago that He would. It was a gift of thanks for your help to Him as Shankara's disciple. Soon you will have some extraordinary kundalini experiences. Also, it says here that Baba will give you several gifts this lifetime from His hand. It is all because of your discipline and from making correct choices day to day, life to life.

"This is all that I am authorized to tell you at this time. You will come back many times, it says in the manuscript, and each time something new will be revealed. Every visit is ordained by God. Thank you so much for coming."

After recovering from my stupefaction and thanking, then paying Mr. Shastry, I wobbled out of the room and collected my shoes before entering the cab for the ride to the hotel. The reading had provided more than food for thought – it had provided a banquet for contemplation.

I mused about reincarnation and Baba's comments on rebirth.

"This son of yours has come as your son as a result of something which you or he may have done during his or your past birth. It is only to redeem some debt between you both, that he has come as your son in this life...." BTOS P 125

"If you are asked, what happens to man after death, you can point to yourselves and declare, "This is what happens; they are born again." BTOS P 143

Lord, am I really going to attain Realization in this lifetime, as You keep indicating to me?

As the cab made its way through the crowded streets of Bangalore, I opened the book I was reading, which was *The Yoga Sutras of Patanjali*. Since this is my fifth reading of the ancient classic, there were new items of interest, which I hadn't noticed before. Patanjali, in his great work, listed the primary obstacles to awakening. It seemed odd that I hadn't noticed them in my prior readings of the book.

The Nine Distractions Creating Obstacles In The Path

1. Disease
2. Languor or chronic fatigue
3. Doubt
4. Carelessness
5. Laziness
6. Worldly-mindedness
7. Delusion
8. Non-achievement of a state (i.e., lack of seeming progress)
9. Instability (i.e., character defects or attachment to persons, objects or ideas). TSOY P 78-82

Littleton, Colorado
August 1, 1990

On the return airplane trip to Colorado I had an alarming vision. It was that the U.S. will be involved in a war in the Persian Gulf very soon. I saw burning oil fields, planes being shot down and bombs dropping. (This vision of the Gulf War did indeed become fulfilled.)

August 3rd

Baba has manifested amrit nectar on some Sai photos in our house. Recently I was about to lead the song "Lord of the Universe" at our Sai meeting. As I glanced down at the page I noticed that fragrant vibhuti ash was forming next to the song title. This was a double leela. First, He showed me again that He knows my every thought, even that I had decided, but not yet announced to the group, that I was going to sing a particular song. And second, He is, indeed, the Lord of the Universe, the Resident in every heart.

Now I realize that *A Course in Miracles* is Christian Vedanta, and corresponds perfectly to Ramana Maharshi's advaita. We are not required, I understand, to change the world but to change our perception through seeing and stopping our projection. In any endeavor, as instruments of God, we do our best and let God do the rest. He is the only Doer.

Recently I have come across some of Baba's sayings about destiny. For example, "Remember that with every step, you are nearing God, and God, too, when you take one step towards Him, takes ten towards you. There is no stopping place in this pilgrimage; it is one continuous journey, through day and night, through valley and desert, through fears and smiles, through death and birth, through tomb and womb. When the road ends, and the goal is gained, the pilgrim finds that he has traveled only from himself to himself, that the way was long and lonesome, but, the God that led him unto, was all the while in him, around him, with him and beside him!" MBAI P 81

Further, "You are bound to go when the time comes, leaving behind everything. It is the Grace of God which alone is permanent." DD 1987 P 11

One is going to play the role which God has allotted to him in life. God is far, far more than the compelling Figure Whom we know as our Beloved Sathya Sai Baba. God, He says, suffuses everything in creation, both animate and inanimate objects alike. It is vast, this creation, and it is said, in Vedanta, that it is all resident within us, rather than the way which we perceive it, which is as outside of ourselves. *Thank You, Dear Lord, for being with us at this time and for allowing us to serve you, to see You, to know You and to love You increasingly.*

PART THREE

WHO
PRACTICES?

CHAPTER 28
KUNDALINI

"The awakening of man begins when he discovers his own identity
and at the same time, he begins to recognize the identity of all
around him, for all are one, all are Divine, all are part of the whole
and I am that whole." Sathya Sai Baba, FFWG P 269

Littleton, Colorado
August, 1990

In August of 1990, immediately after returning from our "Triple
Interview Trip" to India, I began to experience profound kundalini
activations which lasted for weeks. They were completely absorbing and
rendered me incapable of work or social life. It was as if I had, like a St.
Bernard pup, suddenly been picked up by the scruff of the neck by my
canine mother, and shaken, vigorously and helplessly, while seeing lights
and experiencing bliss all the while. At times I also felt as if I were falling
into a vortex of energy that was like a black void, drawing me ever
inward. Hopefully the following list of hallmarks of the experience which
took place during August will be helpful. Everyone experiences kundalini
or samadhi activations differently, according to their karma, culture,
physical and mental fitness and the grace of God.

List of Aspects of Three Samadhi Activations
Note: This "Awakening" is still incomplete and ongoing, though now
with more subtlety. I still move from duality to non-duality while carrying
on normal daily functions, work and interactions.

Author Gopi Krishna's well-known account of his joy and surprise at
his own kundalini activation are, in fact, similar to my own. He describes
his emotional reactions in his book, *Kundalini: The Evolutionary Energy in
Man*. "I went to bed that night in an excited and happy frame of mind.
After years of acute suffering I had at last been given a glimpse into the
supersensible and at the same time made the fortunate recipient of divine
grace, which all fitted admirably with the traditional concepts of
Kundalini. I could not believe my good luck; I felt it was too astounding
to be true. But when I looked within myself to find out what I had done
to deserve it, I felt extremely humbled. I had to my credit no
achievement remarkable enough to entitle me to the honor bestowed
upon me. I had lived an ordinary life, never done anything exceptionally
meritorious." KTEEIM P 209

Quite often, kundalini activations are accompanied by great pain or
discomfort. In my own case, there was virtually no suffering that
occurred prior to or during the kundalini activations, for which I am
extremely thankful. There occurred, at various times:

1. The spontaneous perception of auras.

2. The unsought, spontaneous ability to read the thoughts of others.

3. Exceptionally elevated body energies which interfered with electrical apparatus and caused malfunctions of a TV set, a friend's computer (as I stood beside it), and caused the automatic door locks on my car to lock by themselves three times.

4. A zigzag or "classic serpentine pattern" of kundalini movement as described by ancient yogis.

5. A "fire-fountain" in the spine that was non-painful.

6. A virtually pain-free experience throughout the activations, with a few very brief exceptions. This is highly unusual and extremely fortunate, obviously.

7. Waves of bliss lasting for days or weeks.

8. Great resolve to release any unforgiveness toward everyone and to release my many character "flaws."

9. Feelings of great compassion for those who had previously maligned and slandered me.

10. Great thirst and consumption of gallons of water in a day's time.

11. Waves of heat flicking the body in fiery sheets.

12. Sensations of deep compassion for humanity.

13. Strong sensations of imminent, uncontrollable levitation that caused me to walk about the room clutching the furniture for fear that I would suddenly fly up to the ceiling like Saint Padre Pio (who often shot up in the air when outside, having to call for help from an embarrassed entanglement in tree branches!). Actual levitations have not happened to me, but the phenomenon is, in fact, occurring to many in the U.S.

14. Pressure at the base of the spine at the root chakra.

15. Unaware, uncontrolled, undirected bi-location, or being seen simultaneously in two places at once in daylight hours. (e.g., I was seen by friends in three other states while I was with my husband, usually at home on the weekend. Seven other friends also called to say that they, too, had been seen elsewhere, though they were not having a kundalini activation. I tried to explain that I don't practice yogic siddhis, nor want them but the friends insisted that I not only "appeared to them" or "spoke in their ear" but that I gave explicit aid and advice on spiritual and practical matters, even on such subjects as quantum physics, about which I know virtually nothing, having read only a handful of books on the subject.)

16. This is unsought experience and sounds just as strange to me as it surely might to the reader. I am becoming more silent and reserved all the time.

17. "Mock" pains in the heart as if the body is being reconstructed.

18. Strange sensations in the cells as if every atom is being rearranged.

19. Staring into space for hours at a time.

20. Inability to concentrate on work for weeks at a time.

21. Tingling, puckering sensations at the brow chakra.

22. Precognition of coming events.

23. A feeling of falling through space for 6-12 hours.

24. Sensing oneself to be a part of All That Is.

25. Seeing a luminous golden glow emanating from people, plants, trees and rocks.

26. Telepathic connection with animals, people and plants.

27. Experiencing rapid, unsought manifestations of slight, mundane, unspoken desires.

28. Weeping very briefly upon fresh perception of the profound beauty and perfection of life.

29. Apparitions of saints who sometimes speak and sometimes remain silent.

30. Visions or visits by angels and Archangels.

31. Sensations of extreme heat and cold in the body.

32. Spontaneous execution of yogic mudras (symbolic gestures, hand motions).

33. Spontaneous writing of articles, songs, book chapters with great ease and speed.

34. Spontaneously providing insights for others while in an exalted state in a forceful, confident way that could be described as the spiritual gifts of wisdom and exhortation (not readily and continually available in the customary waking state where I usually experience myself).

35. Very brief sensations of sharp, stabbing, needle-like pains in the body - the eye, the head, the limbs - lasting but a few seconds.

36. Hearing the Music of the Spheres and angels singing.

37. Ability to attune to seeing the future (as a daily process) if it is desired by Mother Mary and Sai Baba.

38. Rolling back and forth on the floor (like saints Paramahansa Yogananda, Ramakrishna, Sri Anandamayi Ma) to "rebalance the electromagnetic currents of the physical body."

39. Reviewing childhood scenes from a new perspective - often seeing how difficult it was for my parents to have had to deal with such a willful and unusual child. This helped me to better understand and appreciate their extreme strictness and enforced discipline, and to appreciate their parental challenges.

40. Temporary loss of attachment to family members, followed by increased service to them.

41. Observance of silence for many days at a time.

42. Extreme sensitivity to odors of all kinds, including perfumes and food.

43. Extreme sensitivity to noise.

44. Aversion to the vibrations of aggressive or contentious people (who would yell at or insult me).

45. Desire to be alone.

46. Occasional grumpiness (no wonder!).

47. Temporary inability to carry on simple social conversation.

48. Periodic confusion.

49. Occasional dizziness.

50. Increased psychic awareness.

51. Painless piercing of the chakras.

52. "Buzzing" of the meridians.

53. Profound uncontrollable absorption, for two to four weeks at a time, in the scores of changes: spiritual, physical, etheric, mental, emotional and social.

54. Extremes in sleeping patterns: insomnia to oversleeping.

55. Weeks of unaccountably accessing high states of wisdom and knowledge.

56. Spontaneous execution of yoga postures.

57. Observing the self in "witness-consciousness."

58. Awareness of "having created the world I see from the Ground of Being in Consciousness."

59. Realization that we are all Love Itself and that Love and continued Revelation is all there is, for eternity. (i.e., This world of form is illusory, not real.)

60. "Seeing" bright kundalini energy move up the spine, variously like a silver-white serpent, like a fountain, like wax-blobs in a lava-lamp.

61. Feeling as if the top of the head were transparent.

62. Seeing the Atma standing above the body.

63. Experiencing a blissful "blue rain" shower unexpectedly down from the Atma, as in ancient yogic texts of this classic experience.

64. Feeling powerful waves of bliss strike the heart chakra from a radius of about five feet on either side of the physical body.

65. With eyes closed, seeing a single symbolic royal blue eye staring back. ("Let thine eye be single and thy whole body will be filled with Light.")

66. Seeing a blue dot in the third eye.

67. Seeing a blue pearl.

68. Sensing the coolness of mentholatum on the forehead.

69. Feelings of faintness, though not being prone to fainting and never actually fainting.

70. Temporary x-ray vision.

71. Feeling as if encased in honey, like an insect caught in amber.

72. Periodic ability to read the character and motives of others.

73. Suddenly receiving unsought "blocks" or units of knowledge in various disciplines of study.

74. Being pervaded with an "ominous" feeling about 24 hours prior to the death of friends or relatives.

75. Geophysical empath symptoms in the physical body a day or two prior to a large earthquake.

76. (Much to the chagrin of my husband) guilelessly, periodically blurting out truthful statements like a child without a shred of the customary socially acceptable filters of subtlety or thoughtfulness. (i.e., Becoming like a little child in observation and speech. This definitely does not win friends.)

77. Brief glimpses into past lives with issues or themes relating to the present.

78. Realizing, in the midst of the tumultuousness, that great Grace is being conferred while simultaneously feeling gratitude.

79. Knowing that the fireworks/symptoms are being activated by God, on schedule, though they always come most suddenly and unexpectedly. They cannot be controlled and it would be unthinkable to force them. To attempt to do so would be as unsacred as trying to force your own puberty or childbirth.

80. Feelings of awe at observing and participating in the overwhelming, uncontrollable, relentless, intelligent and wondrous process.

81. Sweet fragrances emanating from the body. I wear no colognes or perfumes.

82. Seeing foot-wide, silver spirals of energy, through my third eye, moving from the tips of the toes and fingers up the arms and legs toward the trunk.

83. A sensing that luminous energy was bathing and irradiating every cell.

84. An appallingly voracious appetite to fuel the energies of cell rebuilding.

85. Many strangers and acquaintances reported my appearing to them in their dreams, giving spiritual advice. I, myself had no awareness, interest, or ability to execute such.

Finally, I emphasize that this Samadhi Activation process is still incomplete. I am not, at this writing, fully Self-realized. The most important aspect of it is that I experienced myself as NOT A PERSONALITY, and as nothing and everything simultaneously. The illusion of 'being someone' was seen through, and I awoke from the dream-illusion of life, laughing. My mis-identification with body, mind, emotions, gender and roles was seen for what it was: nothing at all, a mere artifact of the mind. The mind is merely a bundle of thoughts and beliefs.

I share this highly intimate process in the hope that others might be helped through the potentially bewildering forest of unusual symptoms and processes in this evolutionary energetic process of the human species.

Meanwhile, I sought help, in prayer from Baba and from others, in hopes of finding relief or even understanding of the scores of unspeakable aspects and processes that were inexplicably, without invitation, marching purposefully, with fireworks and effrontery, through body and psyche.

"The only difference between you and Me, is that I am God, and I know it. You are also God, but you don't know it." Sathya Sai Baba

Mother Mary has mentioned several times that millions will soon be awakening globally. Baba has also said He is here to create a global awakening and a thousand years of peace.

On the individual level, the intense, delicate, consuming process of spontaneous kundalini activation needs to be handled with the utmost care for the protection of the mental, emotional and physical vehicles.

How Does One's Kundalini Become Activated?

Every person has a unique programming or "schedule," designed by God, for the awakening of his kundalini energies. It is dangerous to attempt to force kundalini activation. A prematurely fired kundalini energy could, in the case of an undisciplined, unaware, unprepared person cause permanent mental aberrations, intense pain, tantrums, power plays and a host of other unpleasant embarrassments and experiences. This is called a "Kundalini Crack-up" and few mental health professionals have accurately diagnosed or treated this phenomenon as it is seldom recognized and little understood in conventional American culture.

The process of the undulating spinal energies moving upward from the base chakra through the other chakras has been known in Asia for thousands of years. There is precise terminology in ancient Vedic literature of India that identifies the Samadhi symptoms and the stages to final illumination. The Sanskrit language, in fact, contains an expansive vocabulary of great nuance and subtlety for a process that is virtually unknown in English.

In the West, despite the abundance of Christian mystics and saints that have experienced the Great Undoing of Ego, there has been little written about Samadhi Activation until recent decades. Some of the most intelligent, remarkably talented people of every era and culture have described the experience. For example, St.Paul, St.John, St.Teresa, St.Catherine of Genoa, St.Catherine of Siena and Teilhard de Chardin are but a few Christians whose descriptions mimic those of Eastern yogis and adepts. Quakers and Shakers also describe these energies.

The process can last for days, weeks, months or years. Since many are already awakening with dozens of bewildering attendant symptoms, it seems prudent to alert holistic health workers, therapists and Lightworkers to possible symptomology.

The variety of phenomena, which are not to be sought or forced, depend on many aspects of one's life. They are influenced by diet (vegetarianism), sexuality (abstinence), discipline (meditation, prayer, yoga, service), lifestyle and other factors.

Possible Aspects/Phenomena of Samadhi Activation

Some, none or all of the following might occur in the spiritual aspirant. Obviously, however, the presence of any of the following aspects does not necessarily mean that one is having a Samadhi Activation.

⋄ Light-headedness, dizziness
⋄ Confusion
⋄ Levitation feelings or tendencies
⋄ Telepathy, clairvoyance, clairaudience
⋄ Trembling, shaking, shuddering
⋄ Spinal tingling, "buzzing," sheets of heat, or even pain
⋄ Panting, grunting, groaning
⋄ Swooning, fainting
⋄ Extreme, consuming thirst
⋄ Craving for carbohydrates
⋄ Absentmindedness
⋄ Becoming temporarily lost or disoriented in familiar surroundings
⋄ Inability to sleep
⋄ Oversleeping
⋄ Staring into space for hours or days
⋄ Copious weeping
⋄ Inappropriate laughing, loud talking or whispering
⋄ Hot flashes
⋄ Sensations of "letting go" and falling through space
⋄ X-ray vision

⋄ Accelerated personal magnetism
⋄ Speaking, moving, acting with either a new authority or new shyness and timidity in public
⋄ Temporary inability to grasp simple statements or simple jokes
⋄ Ability to see or feel auras as if they were a webwork of light
⋄ Ability to see, feel one's meridians, chakras
⋄ Ability to see chakras of others
⋄ Ability to "read" health, character, intentions of others
⋄ Ability to disappear and reappear
⋄ New humility or even a self-absorption
⋄ Ability to affect matter
⋄ Ability to heal one's body or that of others
⋄ Ability to raise the dead
⋄ Ability to manifest, materialize
⋄ Fragrances sometimes emanate from one's body or subtle sheaths
⋄ Spontaneous ability or inclination to write poetry/music or to sing devotional songs
⋄ The sensation of a fire-fountain in the spinal column
⋄ Losing bowel or bladder control without realizing it
⋄ Periodic depression
⋄ Inability to carry out simple daily tasks
⋄ Striking mudra poses with the hands or doing spontaneous sacred dancing
⋄ Fluttering, puckering, or pulling of the third eye
⋄ Feeling and demonstrating increased mental and spiritual clarity
⋄ Abidance in That (True Self) produces ecstasy.
⋄ Reality is easily differentiated as the Ground of Being from which all experience emanates.
⋄ Experiences come and go like passing clouds, without one's ego-self becoming caught in or identified with them.

This is by no means an exhaustive list but covers the more familiar aspects of the process. Literally hundreds of symptoms have been documented in the literature on the subject of kundalini awakening. One who has had one, two or even half a dozen kundalini or Samadhi Activations is not necessarily Self-realized as the complete process can continue over a decade or more. The phenomena are not the point, but the process itself attests to the divine plan for each human being in his own natural flowering of consciousness.

How To Assist One In Samadhi Activation

1. Do not administer pharmaceuticals, as a general rule.
2. Urge the person to stay quiet and to avoid all but closest friends and relatives.
3. Urge deep continual silence.
4. Normal breathing patterns are best.
5. Urge copious water intake.
6. Arrange for a companion, since the individual is unguarded and innocent as a child and can be easily led, influenced or taken advantage of.
7. Rest and relaxation help steady the person in the experience.
8. Don't react to the individual or treat him in either an exalted or a scornful fashion as he's extremely sensitive.
9. Pray, sing or meditate together as support when this is welcome.
10. Urge the person to abide deeper and deeper with the process.
11. Advise the person not to seek special powers or siddhis.
12. Firmly warn against showing off, displays or performances.
13. Ask, "Who is having this experience?" (Atma, "I AM" Presence)
14. Mention that outer life might or might not change as a result of the Awakening.
15. Stress love and selfless service as a general lifetime modus operandi.
16. Mention that, "They also serve who sit (in meditation)."
17. Encourage the aspirant in compassionate acts of thoughtfulness.
18. Shield the aspirant from gossip or from jealousy, criticism or slander of uninformed fundamentalists or other unaware, unsupportive persons.
19. Discourage the intake of all meat, alcohol, drugs, tobacco or caffeine.
20. Urge a diet of fruit, vegetables, grains and soups.
21. Firmly suggest the aspirant avoids crowds.
22. Suggest that the person avoid touching others as others could swoon, faint, become "slain in Spirit" or even succumb to a coma if the Kundalini shakti is especially powerful.
23. Place the feet on a large (baseball-size) chunk of amethyst to ground excited energies and/or to stop uncomfortable hot flashes. Both men and women get kundalini hot flashes.
24. Advise sitting in a cold bath several times a day to minimize sweating and excessive body heat.

Kundalini surges can come in waves that are days or years apart. Give thanks during the Samadhi Activation, whether yours or another's, and ask to be protected and to remain a pure vessel of love for God. Maintain a sacred atmosphere and use extreme caution not to become unnecessarily startled or unbalanced by loud noises, insufficient food or water, by odors or smoke, air pollution, raucous music or curiosity-seekers/unwelcome visitors.

A final caution: unwise or ignorant individuals may react in harsh, negative or aggressive ways toward the newly awakening person. They may polarize against the accelerating Light/Energy and, especially in the case of bewildered males encountering energized females, may attempt power struggles, attack or domination to the dismay of all involved. For this reason most ancient cultures have sequestered their awakening shamans, priests, healers, medicine men and women, goddesses, masters and spiritual Teachers until they have grounded, integrated and stabilized the attendant gifts and vibrations.

Samadhi Activation in its best, truest sense is merely experiencing oneself to be that which animates the body-mind-ego ("I AM," Atma), rather than being the body-mind-ego or false personality self. Eventually one is able to see Divine Love in all other beings.

Helen Keller is attributed to have said, "Life is either a daring adventure or nothing." May you let your willingness to more deeply experience your Inner Presence open for you a daring adventure. It's an ongoing ride you'll never forget, as well as a blessing for you and the planet.

As compelling as Samadhi Activation can be, however, it is not final by any means. Nor does Nirvikalpa Samadhi (incomplete awareness) mean anything, necessarily. Revelation continues throughout eternity; whatever experience comes and goes is, in the final analysis, not Real. It only arises from the substratum of Consciousness Itself.

Again, I emphasize that, at this writing, full and abiding Realization has not taken place. Meanwhile, our mail has, by this time, become voluminous, not to mention the phone calls, faxes, e-mails, videos and photos which people have been sending us about Sai apparitions, Marian sightings, prophecies and miracles throughout the planet. For years we have accepted invitations to speak on radio, TV and in person, in the hope that people might be benefited. But Baba has completely changed me. Now I experience myself as deep peace, as love, as others and as Him. He is continually showing me that there is no Doer other than God. Though the personality still remains, He has, indeed, led me to experience the One for Whom I sought as That, as Self within.

CHAPTER 29
VISION OF A TRIBAL ASSASSIN

"All are beggars at the gate of God. The hero is he who does not beg or cringe or flatter or fawn. He knows that the Lord knows best."
Sathya Sai Baba

Littleton, Colorado
January 26, 1991

The Spiritual Unity of the Tribes Gathering

My involvement with native people from various tribes and nations began in Colorado one night during a whistling, shrieking blizzard. Jim was away on business and I was sitting in the living room amid stacks of mail, bills, books and papers. The house was in disastrous condition because of debris-build-up during our recent respective business trips. We were behind on housework, correspondence, and personal upkeep. My hair was badly in need of a shampoo.

As I sat in the living room listening to the wailing and moaning wind of the snowstorm outside, I contemplated what task I should tackle first: shampooing my hair; paying some bills; sorting some clothes for the United Cerebral Palsy truck pick-up; writing overdue letters; placing some telephone calls for our Sai Service Project; or cleaning up the house. I was humming a bhajan and chuckling at the saying that "what every woman needs is a wife – but who can afford one?!" Just as I had decided to shampoo my hair, I stood up and was about to go upstairs to the shower when the phone rang.

"Hello, Connie, this is Jim Walton. I'm an Athabaskan Elder visiting some Baha'i friends in Longmont, about an hour from your house. I'm calling to tell you that I'm coming to your house in an hour with a carload of Indians – and a few Anglos. I've been directed by Great Spirit to come to the Lower Forty-eight States to visit two people – Rolling Thunder and you"

"I'm afraid you have the wrong number," I said. "I don't know any people from Alaska or any Native Americans either," I responded tentatively to the confident-sounding voice on the other end of the line.

"No," Jim chuckled softly, "I don't have the wrong number. We have a mutual friend named Jeff. You and he follow Sai Baba. You come highly recommended by him for a special mission that we Indians are planning. I'm coming to your house in an hour and we're going to smudge and purify you and then do a sacred pipe ceremony in your living room. This will be a test as well as a blessing for you. You need this pipe ceremony blessing. After we perform the ceremony I will tell you something and then I will ask you something."

"But, but... there's a snowstorm outside. It's dangerous to drive tonight," I stammered, grasping at straws. I looked a wreck, the house was a trash pit, we were in the midst of a blizzard and now a carload of Indians I'd never met wanted to do a pipe ceremony in the living room!

"*Swami – what shall I do, for heaven's sake?*" I prayed.

"*Be hospitable,*" He answered inside my heart.

"We've already driven thousands of miles with a broken car heater. A blizzard won't stop us. Nothing will stop us," Jim laughed good-naturedly. "So put on the tea kettle. We'll see you in about an hour and we'll be ready for a hot cup of tea. By the way, put a throw rug down for us and have a big pot or bowl ready for making a small fire."

An hour later Jim and his four friends, nearly frozen from the highway journey without an auto heater, banged on the front door and swooped into the front foyer covered with a white blanket of snow. As they shook the wetness from their jackets I could see that the two Anglo women were tall and thin, single and in their thirties. They had sweet vibrations and the simple, pretty, virtuous faces of Baha'is I had known. The native men were short, thin, rugged and were grinning shyly at my bewilderment. All of them were simply dressed in jeans and light jackets, snow boots and wool hats. They hung up their coats and hats and carefully unwrapped their sacred medicine pouches and deerskins on the throw rug I had laid in front of the coffee table. As I served them tea, Jim began to explain how a pipe ceremony was conducted. He instructed me to sit without speaking for the next three hours, preferably with my eyes closed. When the group shouted "Ho!" I could join them. When he prayed to Wakantonka, Great Spirit, I was to remain in a respectful state and pray to God silently. I was not to touch any of the sacred objects such as the eagle's wing, the medicine pouches, the beaded objects, the tobacco or the pipe. If the pipe was offered to me to smoke I was to take a puff and pass it on.

"I'm sorry," I said primly, "I don't smoke."

"This isn't that type of smoking for pleasure," Jim sighed at my ignorance. "Well, just sit there and be quiet for the next three hours. We won't require anything of you. If you see little sparkling lights in the room near the ceiling it's just the spirits of the ancestors who are helping and blessing us this evening. They're good beings and won't hurt you. If you notice them or see any ancestors, just be quiet and be reverent. We'll handle everything."

Jim, Jay, Susan and Barbara made a smudge pot from an abalone shell and began to wave sage smoke around my head and body to purify me and each other. They prayed to Grandfather Sky, Mother Earth, the four directions and to the Grandmothers and the ancestors to guard, guide and bless the proceedings and to give them their answer at the conclusion of the pipe ceremony. We all sat in a half-moon configuration, cross-legged on the floor with the sacred articles spread out in front of us. The mood was deeply devotional. Young Jay very deliberately donned his yellow buckskins, made for him by his beloved grandmother, and nodded that he was ready to begin the ceremony.

Jim began to pray in a haunting, crying style in his language, and the hair stood up on the back of my neck and on my arms. I felt like weeping and dancing simultaneously as I heard the seemingly-familiar sounds. But I sat obediently with my eyes mostly closed, surreptitiously peeking out from under my eyelashes at the proceedings for most of the next three hours. It was obvious that Jim and his friends were sincere in their prayers and that I was indeed being honored in a most unusual way. The reason for this soon became apparent.

"Okay, you'll do," Jim announced at the conclusion of the pipe ceremony.

"I'll do? I'll do what?" I asked, totally confused.

"It's like this," Jim began. "Spirit told me to come to meet you and to check you out by smudging you with sage to purify you. If you could be humble enough to sit quietly for three hours without speaking and without asking a lot of questions you would pass the first part of the test. You passed that. Then, we called in the ancestors to help us to know if you have a pure enough heart to offer some service to the Spiritual Unity of the Tribes Gathering several months from now in Nambe Pueblo, near Santa Fe. You passed that part of the test. Now I will ask you straight out – would you be willing to speak at this holy gathering on behalf of Mother Mary and Sai Baba to a collection of five hundred people from all over the world?"

"Jim! I have no idea why you have honored me with such a tremendous blessing but I doubt that Native Americans would be interested in hearing about Mary and Sai Baba from a blond-haired Anglo when they've suffered so much grief from fundamentalist Christians over the past two centuries," I answered.

"Forget about your blond hair. My wife is a blond Anglo and my kids look Anglo. Lots of Indians you'll be meeting have red hair and green eyes. There are very, very few pure-blooded Indians left these days. It's not about race. It's about spiritual unity, that's why we call it the Spiritual Unity of the Tribes. The tribes aspect also includes Anglos, Europeans, Icelanders, Australians and tribal people from the jungles of Mexico. You'll really enjoy the event. We'd also like to invite you to accept the great honor of serving on the Gathering Planning Committee. That means you'll need to get to New Mexico once a month at your own expense, find lodging, bring your food, stay the weekend, participate in the planning and stick with the process until the Gathering is completed. Will you do it? It's a great honor and will bless you more than you can ever guess."

It would have been an understatement to say that this turn of events surprised me so much that "you could have blown me over with Jim's eagle feather." But my heart began racing and I knew deep inside that Baba was arranging for yet another series of lessons in humility. What I didn't know was that the lessons would emphasize humiliation even more than humility.

"Jim I'd be pleased and honored to accept your offer," I told him. The others nodded and smiled. "You know, Sai Baba says "There's only one religion, the religion of love. There is only one God and He is omnipresent." "He also says "Love alone can integrate the human race into a brotherhood of man under the fatherhood of God."

Jim nodded. "That's what we Baha'is believe." "If you serve on the Planning Committee for the Gathering you won't be sorry," Jim replied as he finished his tea and nodded to the others that it was late and was time to depart.

"Oh, by the way," Jim mentioned to me after the others had taken their leave, hunching low into the frosty screaming blizzard on their dash to the car. "I think of myself as a person in the wrecking and salvage business. Only I'm not dealing in metals, I'm dealing in human flotsam and jetsam. Our people are a wreck... through substance abuse, abandonment, neglect, fetal alcohol syndrome in the babies, mistreatment by government agencies, high unemployment, hassling by local ranchers and small town police forces. You name it - any type of trouble or tragedy - they've experienced it. Just remember, wrecking and salvage, with emphasis on salvaging." With that cheery note Jim disappeared into the night in a swirl of snow.

Nambe Pueblo near Santa Fe, New Mexico

As I drove across the red desert terrain and arrived in Santa Fe, a bumper sticker caught my eye. It said, "If you must cry over spilt milk, condense it." Ten minutes later, I passed a sign outside a church that said, "Sunday service at 10:00. Come in and have your faith lifted."

My volunteer time with the Planning Committee for the Spiritual Unity of the Tribes Gathering was to have its moments of comedy and suspense. Many months and thousands of (my savings) dollars later, I had just barely survived the explosive Planning Committee meetings at Nambe Pueblo. Of the thirty-five or so members who had committed to the monthly meetings and hundreds of hours of coordinating work, less than half that number remained by the time the Gathering was a few weeks away. At the very first meeting I had attended, the local pueblo people informed me that they referred to themselves as 'Indians' ; the term 'Native Americans' had been concocted by the government for census purposes. It was clear that they had mixed feelings toward government employees since they depended on them for grants but resented the dependence.

As a newcomer to the committee, which had been meeting for a few months, I had a lot to learn. Nearly all of the Anglos who had been invited to offer their experience, expertise and resources had been alienated by the tribal in-fighting between tribal traditionals and progressives, by insults and slurs about "untrustworthy whites," and numerous other unsavory developments.

Baba has often spoken about anger and has this to say about anger and the classifications of people.

The Four Types

"There are four types of people. The anger of a person who is of a satwic nature will be very short-lived; it recedes immediately. The Gita has declared such a one as a great soul. The second type will have his anger for a number of minutes, but it will soon fade away. The third category of person will have his anger continuously, all day long. The one in the lowest category will have his anger for life." DBG P 86

"What on earth is going on here?!" several of the committee members asked in alarm. "We're supposed to be planning a Spiritual Unity of the Tribes Gathering and we're constantly sniping at each other."

"Don't worry," I'd tell them. "This is just the surfacing of suppressed ethnic rage. I've been through this sort of thing many, many times in my work with the Black Movement, the Hispanic Movement and the Women's Movement. After people develop the courage to feel their pain they realize that they have a lot of hurt and anger that needs to be healed. After healing there comes reconciliation and cooperation. So first anger, then healing, reconciliation and cooperation. Then the sacred hoops of relationship, family and community are healed.

Sometimes, however, it takes years or decades to get to the healing after they encounter buried rage. Anger and rage are a bottomless pit. I was in therapy for awhile because of repressed rage but nothing helped until I simply accepted that certain things happen in life that we don't understand and that to wallow in self-pity just continues the sorrow and pain. It's the old 'letting go and letting God' process that keeps working for me," I confided over and over to the few Anglo people who remained on the committee. "These days, if anger arises, I let it subside by not giving it any attention."

"Well I don't know about you but I am sick and tired of being insulted," one of my colleagues said. "We've all put in a few thousand dollars of our own annual vacation funds and have come to help these people but they seem to get their jollies out of petty attacks. If they aren't careful, pretty soon there won't be anybody left on the Planning Committee but them and then they can just fight it out among themselves until the whole thing collapses."

"I know, it's not a lot of fun being insulted but it does seem to be a necessary part of the process," I told him. "It's like parenting. In some respects it's a bit of a thankless job if you have a rebellious child but there are lots of wonderful rewards that far outweigh all of the heartache that comes with the territory."

"Besides," I continued, "I promised my spiritual Teacher, Sai Baba, that I'd stick to this process no matter how hard it gets. And we're learning a lot about humility, about community and about the sacredness of life, the sacredness of children and of the Grandmothers and other elders. We'll just have to take it a day at a time – or maybe five minutes at a time."

To further complicate interactions on the Planning Committee, there was mistrust of my role because I had been appointed to the committee by Jim Walton who lived in Alaska, who was guiding the Gathering long-distance, and whom many of the planners had never met.

Mid-way through the planning process a number of middle-aged pueblo residents on the committee began to have flash-backs about the humiliations, punishments and deprivations which they had suffered at Indian School as children. They recounted how they had been taken from their families at the ages of five or six, had been sent to boarding school, had been forbidden to speak their language, to preserve their sacred ways, or to communicate with their parents except infrequently. They were taught that they were "ignorant, stupid, dirty, unworthy, inadequate and that they would never amount to anything." They were taught to disrespect their parents and elders and to regard the culture and mores of the dominant culture as superior.

As I listened to their childhood experiences over the months, their 'frozen feelings' thawed out and the native people broke through their long-repressed denial of child abuse. A torrent of volatile, suppressed emotions spewed forth like water gushing through a broken water main; unaccountably they began to verbally attack me as a 'representative white.' It is well known that alcoholics treat their loved ones and family members the most wretchedly among their support circles since they are least likely to flee. Similarly, they trusted that I was a bit like family and wouldn't flee in the face of their wrath.

On my way back to Colorado each month, as I drove through the stark desert landscape of New Mexico I wept for them, having listened impassively to horrendous tales of long-held resentment month after month. I wept not only for their personal sorrows but for the so-called perpetrators of their torment. I wept for my inability to help them to heal in a deeper way. And I wept for the continual cruelty we earthlings continue, in our ignorance, to heap on each other. Increasingly, with more and more of the Native American committee members the lid flew off the simmering pot of repression and denial. They were in full awareness of all they had suffered and they were furious. It was a popularly-held belief that it was all the fault of Anglos that they had been taunted, harassed, punished, abused and deprived. In their minds they were blame-free. But every conflict has two sides and learning to love one's enemies is always the spiritual goal in any relationship, no matter how brutal or dysfunctional.

As for my own dawning awareness during the meetings and weekends we spent together, I began to realize that, as a city person, I had the typical unconscious arrogance of urban people, was too rushed in my rhythms, intimidated country people without realizing it and needed to simplify my vocabulary. I needed to open my heart, needed to listen more and to talk less and needed to dress more simply and to drop my unconscious façade. I realized I was thin-skinned, was controlling (like most of the human race), had an Anglo thought process that was very different from that of Indians and that I needed more humility.

While I was deeply appreciative of the insights the new awareness brought, I was keenly cognizant that I was clueless as to how to quickly change my undesirable characteristics. Finally I came to the conclusion that the overcoming of my cultural conditioning would take three things: abundant grace from Baba, constant awareness of my thoughts, and a more accepting attitude of daily life and events. I prayed for patience and humility constantly.

Each time that I found myself upset or disappointed I realized that I had been attached to some sort of outcome or result in a situation. Baba's sayings about ego came to me over and over as I examined my own.

"Considering oneself as different from others is called ego." CTSSB P 168

"Criticizing others and finding fault with them comes out of egoism." CTSSB P 168

He further says, "Like the tadpole's tail, the ego will fall away when one grows wisdom. It must fall away; if it is cut, the poor tadpole will die. So don't worry about the ego; develop wisdom, discriminate, know the ephemeral nature of all objective things – then the tail will no longer be evident."

Every time I experienced a new rebuff, and asked Baba in prayer how much more humility I needed, the answer was always, "More, much more."

Having lived on the unusually affluent pueblo or reservation most of their lives, the Nambe Pueblo Indians were unaware that they were financially better off than nearly all of the Anglos who would be coming to the Gathering and than the average Caucasian in the States. They were considerably more fortunate than most Native Americans. They lived on five acre plots of land in attractive ranch-style houses complete with dishwashers, televisions, modern bathrooms, three or four bedrooms, attractive gardens, patios with spectacular mountain and desert views, two cars, often a boat and boat trailer, a lovely community hall, tribal lakes, waterfalls, streams and camp grounds which garnered rent from tourist fishing and camping, and continual bounteous government grants. Generally they were in good health and lived a life of high quality in clean air, comfort, security, basic education and productivity. While all of us on the committee agree that Western culture had become spiritually sick the past few hundred years, the tribal people for the most part were heavily influenced, through the media and through U.S. culture, by the same culture about which we all felt so frustrated.

A source of misunderstanding and discontent existed because many of them compared their lifestyles to the luxurious homes and stage sets of imaginary characters of television dramas and mistakenly believed that mainstream Americans lived in such affluence.

Many, if not most of the tribal people, however, bore deep grudges, suspicions and resentments of strangers and of city people, which is often typical of small-towners everywhere. In addition to tribal squabbling and distrust of non-Indians, many of the pueblo people, like most American tribal people, had long ago succumbed to substance addiction as well as to television addiction – the 'plug-in drug' of the dominant culture.

During the Planning Committee meetings there had been many long, heated arguments about whether or not to record the proceedings on audiotape or videotape. There were many rumors that certain tribes were going to boycott the Gathering altogether, though the reasons weren't clear. It was decided by committee members to ban alcohol, guns, drugs and cameras from the Gathering so that a sacred tone could be maintained – although our own tone was anything but sacred. I continually prayed that I would be used as an instrument of the Holy Spirit for any healing that might be Baba's grace to grant.

By the time the Gathering arrived, most of the committee planners were burnt out, were nursing grievances against each other and were all praying for healings and miracles for everyone attending the event.

The day before the event our Littleton Sai Center members, who had been invited to attend, were given the task of serving as greeters and of selling mugs and tee-shirts as a fund-raiser to pay Event bills and expenses. By clumps and clusters, various groups arrived from throughout North America, Central America, Australia, Iceland, Finland, Europe, Africa and the Middle East. There were endless stories about how people had been sent by Spirit to the Gathering, having received no written information or invitation whatsoever.

Interestingly enough to me, a Marian visionary, I heard many stories of Beloved Mother Mary having appeared to many Indians, Inuit Eskimos, Israelis and others in recent years to alert them to coming earth changes. People reported that she had said that:

1. Difficult times lie ahead and calamities are about to befall the U.S.
2. There would be enormous floods in nearly every state.
3. Forest fires would proliferate.
4. There would be weather calamities of all sorts and the U.S., of all the world, would be especially hard hit.
5. Americans would begin recovery as Europe, Asia, Africa and South America would begin their own trials.
6. Prayer and need for personal change were always central to the messages.

The arrival of five hundred people from distant states and countries brought all of us on the Planning Committee sharply back to the reality of the big picture of our overall goals and objectives — to provide uplift, harmony and healing for the attendees. Further, the noble bearing, purity, integrity and accomplishments of the new arrivals were as refreshing as a splash of cold water against the face on a sweltering day.

As groups and families arrived and began setting up camp we noticed that there were, among us, sacred costumes and ceremonial dress of every conceivable type from every race and most tribes. Drummers and flutists arrived. Sacred hoop dancers came in a cloud of colored hoops and feathered armbands. Inuit grandmothers from Alaska gathered to tell of the wisdom of using herbal healing remedies. Shamans showed up with songs and campfire stories.

A teenage Sioux, named Arthur, chopped wood for the campfire. The back of his tee-shirt showed a picture of two pine trees, a tall one and a short one. It said, "You have to do your own growing, no matter how tall your grandfather was."

"Good work, Arthur," shouted Grandfather Edward. "He who rolls up his sleeves will never lose his shirt."

From the spot where I stood near the stream I noticed a red-haired, freckle-faced Scottish girl wearing her family tartan plaids and matching knee-socks skipping across the tree-encircled campground to greet a friend.

Evidently they were both Baha'is. He, a radiant black man wearing an African dashiki and matching fabric hat, was from Chicago. He was jubilant to see his Baha'i sister.

"Hey, Sister," he chuckled, "How's it going?" Then, indicating the colorfully costumed people setting up camp on all sides, he asked, as if he didn't know, "And who be all these splendid dudes and dudettes?!"

Next, my eyes fell on a tall, picturesque Santa Fe Anglo couple who deal in expensive native rugs and pottery. They had attended one of the planning meetings to assess the size of the expected crowd and to ascertain if any native people would be bringing art objects for sale. She was a raven-haired stunner dressed in a black polo shirt and A-line skirt which set off a spectacular turquoise and silver squash blossom necklace and a matching concho belt, accented by turquoise suede boots.

Her husband, who was equally fortunate in his movie-star good looks, wore a fringed buckskin jacket and trousers which were enhanced by his blond hair and tan, chiseled features. He nodded as they walked past me, suffused in a cloud of perfume and after-shave lotion.

Most of the Gathering attendees, however, were simple people, simply dressed, who used simple language, simple thought patterns and simple gestures. They were open, unpretentious and heartful. From the corner of my eye I could see a Navajo family named Begay greeting members of the Planning Committee and asking when they might be able to speak about tribal unity. Meanwhile, a marvelous old shaman dressed in an old cowboy hat and faded jeans shuffled from the stream to the arbor area where rocks were stacked for a campfire ring. His aura was sparkling white and the lines in his weathered face were wrinkled with the kindnesses of many years. Beside me, seated at a wooden picnic table, a woman named Two Moons carefully lettered a small sign announcing an upcoming sweat lodge ceremony. In a nearby grove there were half a dozen Huichol people from the jungles of Mexico playing flutes and offering prayers for the success of the Gathering.

Suddenly, as I gazed at the bustling new arrivals who were setting up camp, I was filled with deep gratitude for all the stiff challenges I had overcome during the months of planning for the Spiritual Unity of the Tribes Gathering. But even more than that, my appreciation for my six billion planetary brothers and sisters swelled my chest to nearly bursting. Oh! This vast, gorgeous humanity – you radiant offshoots of our Beloved Creator – how I love you!

Among the trees white canvas teepee lodges were erected and a large open flat-roofed sacred arbor for the speakers and singers was built in the center of the campground beside the clear rushing stream.

The prospective program filled the Gathering participants with excitement and anticipation. There would be sweat lodges, stories by the Grandmothers, singing, community circle dancing around the evening campfire, drumming, talking circles, sacred pipe ceremonies, and hikes to a high waterfall on the pueblo-owned campground property.

The Warning Vision

That night, I was preparing for bed in the small clean hotel room of a Santa Fe Motel 6 with my roommate of the night, Annie Rose, a concert pianist/housewife and fellow Sai devotee from the Denver area. As I sat on my twin bed contemplating the successful Gathering set-up preparations we had made during the day, I suddenly gasped.

About two feet in front of me, on the white hotel room wall next to my bed I began to see a vision, like a movie being played. First I saw a malevolent, angry-looking Native American dressed all in black from head to foot. I had never seen him before and his name had not appeared on any of our Planning Committee mailing lists, if the name which came to me were correct. The name Jasper Black Fox occurred to me, though I had never before heard his name In the next scene Jasper Black Fox was standing under the lovely arbor we had all erected. It seemed that he had been secretly invited to speak by some of the more militant members of the Planning Committee without clearing the invitation with the organizing group in advance.

The Gathering participants were sitting in the audience on the ground before him as he shook his fist repeatedly in an attempt to incite the crowd to polarize against all non-native people in attendance. He was advocating violence. Some Indians were nodding in agreement. Others were horrified. People from other countries looked worried and it seemed that the Gathering might be spoiled by violence or, at the least, by ugly outbursts and clashes.

In the next scene the Gathering speakers for the afternoon agenda had finished their talks and there was a free-time break before dinner and the evening's events. The crowd was disbursing and I realized that I was the speaker who had just spoken and was walking away from the arbor, alone, toward a shade tree. Just as I neared the tree, which I intended to lean against, I felt someone approaching me from behind. As I turned my head to see who it was, I saw a young, thin, five-foot-seven inch Indian bearing down on me with murder in his eyes. He was wearing a red baseball cap, had a long pony tail, was wearing faded jeans, a red-white-and-black plaid shirt with rolled-up sleeves, and white tennis shoes.

Angrily he stalked toward me. Although I had never met this man in real life, in the vision he grimaced in hatred toward me and the veins stood out on his neck as he reached out toward my neck with the intention of choking me.

The vision then abruptly ended. I was stunned. If this were a warning about the next day's events and potential danger, it certainly was graphic and I felt sufficiently warned.

After telling Annie about the vision, I wished her sweet Sai dreams and slept peacefully.

The next morning I accepted the kind invitation of the pueblo's Lt. Governor to stay at her home during the Gathering and moved onto the reservation. The vibrations which emanated from the Gathering campsite were harmonious as I parked my car and walked over to the registration booth. The sweet fragrance of pine smoke curled up through the trees as breakfast campfires enhanced the aroma of cooked bread, oatmeal and coffee throughout the peaceful, colorful camp. There were RV's, blue pup tents, army surplus tents, teepees, station wagons, old hippie buses, Volkswagen vans, pop-up tents and every conceivable type of family and group camp housing strewn about the lovely grounds.

Ben Rhodd, of the Pottawatamy tribe, and several other spokespeople opened the ceremonies requesting that all those who had any grievances put them aside so that all the sacred hoops might be mended. "This is essential if we are to have peace in the larger society and in the world," Ben pleaded. "We must respect the authority of God, of our ancestors, of our elders, of the grandmothers, and of our Inner Spirit."

Sai Baba's words came to mind: "Having an open heart, do not relish the narrow path of restricted love; love all, do not develop prejudices against men in power and position. They too are our kith and kin; we all sail together." SSS VOL VII P 478

"We must set the example for our children and leave them a legacy of knowing how to solve problems and to get along with all types of people," another Native American had exhorted after Ben's talk. It reminded me of Baba's statement that "Culture must be directed toward the reform of character."

More people spoke extemporaneously about the need to end conflict and competition.

"We are all on a spiritual journey, whether we know it or not," said a woman named Fleet Deer.

Then Ben's uncle Chauncey, known as Yellow Horse, spoke about treasuring each moment of this uncertain life. "Mend the hoops of your family and tribe while you still have time," he urged the crowd. There was general nodding of agreement throughout the audience.

Then a shy native woman named Red Feather stood up and said, "Today's world is throwing all of us into an initiation of gigantic proportions. We need to hold each other's hands in this inescapable experience."

Many people shed tears throughout the morning and several of the most contentious Native Americans stood up and offered apologies for previous outbursts or unkindnesses toward various members of the Gathering Planning Committee. Three people who had heaped continual insults on me over the past three months apologized with sincerity and remorse. I had prayed incessantly to Baba to help me to stay with the Planning Committee when I was tempted to leave on half a dozen occasions.

I fully realized that some of the most wounded Indians were projecting past injuries upon me as a symbolic Anglo, rather than as a personal affront, and that their animosity was actually a call for love. But it was difficult for me to remain compassionate toward people who seemed insensitive to me, told frequent lies to me and to each other, and who seemed determined to humiliate me whenever possible. Thus my main lesson the past few months has been to remain aware and compassionate while not taking any hostilities personally. Consequently I have had to continually trust myself, trust Baba and trust them in the face of many disillusionments.

"In all effort, if you trust in a Higher Power which is ready to come to your aid, your work is made easy. This comes from true devotion and reliance upon God, the source of all Power." TOSSSB P 141

A palpable spiritual mood swept through the Gathering as prayers were intoned and songs were offered to Great Spirit, requesting unity, cooperation, harmony and peace throughout the proceedings.

At one point, while I was sitting on a rock by the river during a break, a very beautiful Indian woman named Ricky Bowers came and sat beside me. As she sat down on the stream bank, she threw back her long, glossy hair, smoothed her red cotton blouse and covered her knees modestly with her floral calico-printed skirt. She told me how she and her mother were still recovering from the grief of having been banished from the tribe for something they had done. They had come to ask forgiveness of the tribe and were hoping to be reinstated after the Gathering.

Several members of our Sai group and I had decided to offer reflexology and energy attunements to anyone who would like them as a free service during the Gathering. My first offers of energy work were extended to the people who had been so hostile to me and they wept after the sessions and apologized to me. *"Healing is happening, Baba, and for that we are deeply grateful, Lord,"* I prayed.

There were a number of program openers which were extremely moving. Ted Liew, a Chinese American did a magnificent "Whistling T'ai Chi" wherein he actually whistled melodies as he performed the dance-like movements in the open space beside the arbor. Johnson Blue Horse spoke of having been sent to Viet Nam against his will and of having become an alcoholic upon his return because of the shock of war upon his psyche. He joined Twelve Step work, was healed and has become a medicine man. After he spoke, Alvin Bitsilly, a Navajo Baha'i, made numerous light, friendly contributions. Someone announced that there would be an Alcoholics Anonymous meeting in one of the lodges at 10:30 P.M.

Finally the time arrived for the scheduled speakers and one after another, they dazzled us with their message. Ben Rhodd, the vigorous Baha'i and archeologist, touched me deeply with his competence and humility as a spokesman and leader. Maori people spoke of the need for unity between tribes and nations. They were brief, frank, friendly, humble and compelling as speakers. The Grandmothers, who had been too shy to come forth and speak, finally did so and were eloquent in their simple messages oriented to the need for women of all ages everywhere to keep the family on the spiritual path, regardless of obstacles.

Baba's words on this came to mind. "Motherhood is the most precious gift of God. Mothers are the makers of a nation's fortune or misfortune. They should teach two lessons, fear of sin and fondness for virtue. Both these are based on faith in God, being the inner motivator of all. If you want to know how advanced a nation is, study the mothers; are they free from fear and anxiety, are they full of Love towards all, are they trained in fortitude and virtue? If you like to imbibe the glory of a culture, watch the mothers, rocking the cradles, feeding, fostering, teaching and fondling the babies." SSS VOL VII, CH 6, P 22

As various women stepped up to speak, we continually heard the terms "walk in beauty," "hold each other in a sacred way," "honor the elders of all races," and "cherish your children and hold onto them, instilling character by example until they are fully grown."

After lunch, which was served cafeteria style under the open-air ramadas or shelters, we assembled again under the leafy arbor. It had rained in the night, and continued to rain each evening so the ground was damp. People settled into their lawn chairs and onto their cushions or ground blankets to hear the introduction to the next speaker. Suddenly, a lean, angry-looking man dressed entirely in black approached the microphone after being introduced as a "surprise speaker who is well-known to most Indians everywhere – Jasper Black Fox!"

The audience reaction was mixed. Half of the people cheered and yelled their approval.

"Go get 'em, Jasper. Tell it like it is," some shouted.

"Indian power!" Somebody yelled, holding a clenched fist aloft. A companion of Jasper held up a cardboard that read "Power to the people. American Indian Movement."

"Hey, none of that here, this is a spiritual gathering," one of the Baha'i Indians shot back as the jeering threatened to increase.

In the mayhem that ensued before the crowd could be subdued, I overheard a man sitting in front of me nudge his friend.

"Hey, I've got a joke for you. What does an Indian fortune cookie look like?"

"I give up – like what?" responded his friend.

"It's a piece of fry bread with a food stamp baked in it!"

His friend hooted, slapped his knee and said, "That's a good one. I'm going to tell it tonight at the campfire."

Finally the crowd became quiet and everyone rearranged themselves on their lawn chairs and ground cushions to hear what Black Fox had to say.

Jasper Black Fox did not mince words. His plea was for a hard-line, anti-white movement to form as a result of the Gathering. He was adamant.

"Whites have never done anything for you. Why should you have anything to do with them? Anybody who goes in for all this harmony bunk is a pansy sell-out to our people. Show these people that we won't be bullied anymore. Kick the government out. Tell the Bureau of Indian Affairs it's our way or the highway. Power to the people. Progressives to the forefront. Use the Money People the way they've used us. We're having a meeting tonight in one of the lodges for Indians only. We're having Indian-only sweat lodges at a location we'll announce later so it can be kept secret. These whites are just Indian wanabees. (want-to-be's) They've already taken everything from us, now they want our sacred religious practices for their own. We have to be militant if we're going to get anywhere as a people. We have to be progressive and savvy."

After Black Fox concluded his speech and left the microphone, with mixed audience reactions in his wake, it was announced that I would be the next speaker. A few announcements were made about pottery classes for children and about evening campfire talks. There was a request for non-native parents to prevent their children from urinating in the stream and from climbing on dangerous rock outcroppings near the waterfall.

Hastily I prayed to Baba, Jesus and Mary to guide my heart and words and walked slowly to the microphone at the far end of the arbor where speakers were instructed to stand. A weak sun filtered through gray clouds and I was acutely aware that all eyes were on me. *"Help me, please, Baba; let this be clear and meaningful to those gathered here,"* I asked again.

As I gathered my thoughts and discerned the vibrations and mood of the audience, I became aware of four uniformed Native American park police sitting on top of a picnic bench at the back of the crowd on the opposite end of the open-air arbor. I began the talk by telling about how I had met Baba, about His healing me instantaneously of a brain tumor and about His mission of inaugurating - with all of us - a thousand years of peace. I stressed this period in history as one wherein we must heal our marriages, the sacred hoops of our families, of our communities, the family of the entire planet and of Mother Earth.

Coming directly to the point of Baba's identity, I told them about Baba being God, the Father of Jesus, but that He loves all people everywhere and that it is not necessary for one to change his religion in order to benefit from Baba's love and help. I mentioned Baba's teachings, His resurrections and His multiplication of the food for multitudes numbering in the thousands.

During this part of the talk I noticed that the Native American uniformed park police sitting on the picnic bench at the back of the crowd were wiping their eyes with hankies. One man on the bench held his head in his hands and his shoulders shook.

Many times I stressed that everyone is loved, guarded, guided and protected. The emphasis was on our similarities and upon the fact that soon, according to many native prophecies, Native Americans will be healed of addictions. Further, they will rise up and will take their rightful places as teachers and healers in North America and elsewhere. But first we must all be purified by forgiveness, abstinence from substance abuse, violence and gambling and must make time each day for Great Spirit to speak with us in our hearts.

"As planetary consciousness rises," I said, "the things that were formerly held sacred and secret in all religions and paths will be shared for the benefit of all mankind. Every culture has a role to play in the great unfolding drama of our age."

At the request of the planners, I mentioned Mary's multi-cultural messages for humanity. The talk stressed brotherhood, forgiveness, harmony and love. I mentioned over and over that everyone is beloved of Great Spirit. No one has been abandoned, nor could it be possible that anyone could be bereft of God, no matter by what name He is called. There was a lot of self-revelation, many stories of healing and miracles and some humor. I ended with a few devotional songs and again urged everyone to enjoy the lovely assemblage of radiant brothers and sisters from across the planet and to stay centered in Spirit throughout the sacred Gathering in order to receive maximum spiritual benefit.

Suddenly, during the close of the presentation, a slight movement caught my attention in the front row of people who sat on the ground about four feet from me. To my surprise, as I spoke, Baba's gray vibhuti ash appeared on the calf area of the jeans of an Indian sitting cross-legged there. It appeared during the closing moments when I told stories of Baba spontaneously healing people of drug, alcohol and smoking addictions.

After the talk, the smiling white-haired Indian, named James, excitedly told me that he was a recovering alcoholic and that he believed Baba was helping and blessing him vis-à-vis the encouragement of the vibhuti appearance on his jeans. We both examined, smelled and tasted the fragrant vibhuti and then laughed simultaneously with glee.

"Oh, thank You, Baba, You really do show Your love for us in the most amazing ways!" I chortled to James. Then James, whose eyes were welling up with tears, awkwardly adjusted his red cowboy kerchief head-band to cover his embarrassment, and hastily thanked me and kissed me on the cheek before departing.

"Don't thank me, thank Baba," I called after him.

As the crowd disbursed and several people congratulated me on the talk, I left the arbor and moved in the direction of an attractive shade tree. By this time nearly everyone had left the area to return to their tents or to the snack truck.

Before I had taken four steps I felt someone approaching me from behind. Suddenly, as I wheeled around I simultaneously had the deja-vu recognition that I was in the scene which I had witnessed in the hotel room vision-on-the-wall. The same angry-looking young Indian in a red baseball cap, jeans, white tennis shoes and red and black plaid shirt was stalking toward me. There was murder in his eyes.

I backed up, instinctively. He bore down on me. I backed up again until I slammed into the tree, still facing the man.

"Stop right there, Sister," he yelled.

I stood still and gazed into his eyes. Then it occurred to me to send him love from all of my chakras and to relax in the knowledge that Baba would protect me.

"Above all, cherish faith in God. God is your sole protector." SS MAY 1996, P 122

He clamped one hand down hard on my shoulder with the thumb moving toward my throat. I gazed lovingly into his eyes

"Let's stop right here and talk," he began. "Sister, while you were first talking, I said to myself, 'Just who does that white woman think she is?! Why should I listen to her when I hate all white people for what they did to me and my people!' I tried to work up a ball of hatred in my gut as I listened to you but it just kept collapsing. The more I heard you talking the more sick I felt. Then when I heard you talking about how we're all brothers and sisters, I knew this to be true. So I decided I needed to tell you something... close up... but, but..." he faltered, then continued.

"The thing is, I'm just now realizing that while you were speaking about all that love and harmony stuff I was really just blaming you and other white people for my failures.... This isn't easy to talk about, Sister. This is the first time I've really even realized it – how much I've hurt myself and others by this lifelong hatred I've been dragging around inside of me."

His hand loosened from around my throat and I relaxed against the tree trunk. There were still about a dozen people on the sacred arbor grounds within shouting distance if I needed them but no one seemed to notice us. Meanwhile, my assailant's face was contorting with shame, guilt, awe and tears. Wet streaks coursed down his cheeks. He hid his face in his hands and wept against my shoulder, sobbing.

"Oh Sister, oh Sister," he moaned miserably, "I am so very sorry. I am so sorry about all this hatred I've kept in my heart toward whites. And now I want to be your brother."

At this point I, too, began to cry. We looked at each other. We embraced. And we wept. Then I told him that he was innocent and had done nothing wrong, that we all have unresolved issues of hatred and guilt.

"You will always be my brother," I said, "and I love you, whether or not you believe that. Great Spirit loves you. Now you can love and forgive yourself."

He held me tightly for a few more moments, like a little boy, then he thanked me profusely and, dazed and confused, he stumbled off in the direction of the teepees, wiping his tears on his shirtsleeve.

There's a line from *A Course In Miracles* which I've always loved that says, "There is no holier spot on earth than the place where an ancient hatred becomes a present love." For that matter wherever **you** are standing is holy ground, since each of us at any moment can ask to see another person or situation differently by asking our Divine Presence for assistance. *Baba, how richly You bless me, how mysterious are Your ways.*

The healings and changes of heart provided by the Gathering to the attendees were multifarious. Some took place in sweat lodges whereas others happened during the building of the giant medicine wheel or the offering of sacred cornmeal during the final closing circle on the last day. At last – I had passed my tests of many months! Before packing up my supplies and equipment I sat down on a rock near the stream and laughed at my previous glamorizing of Native Americans and at how thin-skinned I had been when I first started working on the Planning Committee. Once again all romantic ethnic ideas had vanished and in their place was a deep love and respect of an entirely new group of friends – toward whom I felt a genuine brotherhood born of compassion, struggle, misunderstanding and reconciliation.

Baba's famous words ran through my mind.

"I preach only one religion of love for all, which alone can integrate the human race into the brotherhood of man under the fatherhood of God. I know only one language of the heart beyond the mind or intellect which relates man to man and mankind to God, thereby creating mutual understanding, cooperation and community life in peace and harmony. On this basis, I want to build one humanity without any religious, caste or other barriers in a universal empire of love which could enable my devotees to feel the whole world as their own family." SATM P 258

For the last time I left Nambe Pueblo and headed home to Colorado. While I drove along, admiring the desert's beauty, I thanked Baba for His abundant grace. Then I rolled down the car windows and, as the soft pastels of the southwestern landscape swept by, I began to sing a bhajan. A scene from the Gathering flashed into my mind, causing me to laugh. Jovial Grandfather Edward had been telling anecdotes about Native Americans being recently robbed, threatened and beaten up.

"But we know our day is coming," he said. "We take our tips from the singing teakettle. Like the Indian, it's up to its neck in hot water, and still – it sings!"

For hours I sang praises to Baba. Enormously large, puffy white cumulous clouds sailed along the Wedgwood blue sky as I crossed the New Mexico state line into Colorado. The air smelled fresh and sweet, dry and clear. At that moment, there was no way that I could have guessed that Baba would have another adventure in store for me, in the Himalayas, halfway around the world, which would also entail a vision.

CHAPTER 30
VISION IN A SECRET CAVE

"Take the world as it is – never expect it to conform to your needs and standards." Sathya Sai Baba, TOSSSB P 126

Puttaparthi, India
January, 1995

Before the Cave

Two other Sai Baba devotees and I were discussing the Patal Bhuvaneshwar Cave over dinner at the Sai Renaissance Hotel Restaurant. I was in Puttaparthi as the group leader of a three-week pilgrimage to Baba; it was my nineteenth trip to India. My initial impressions of those who had been among the first Sai devotees to visit the Patal Bhuvaneshwar Cave were mixed. Having just returned from the Cave, the individuals themselves actually exhibited bright ten-foot-wide auras. Their faces wore the classic "lustre of the divine" which develops in people who have been in darshan with a Master or who have been on a retreat.

Still I was skeptical about going to the cave myself. As we discussed their exploits, I found myself in great emotional resistance, which surprised me, since I had traveled in over 50 countries and actually enjoyed a bit of danger now and then. Further, I'd been lost overnight in the Mexican jungle, had been hijacked and released by Arab terrorists and had traveled in Nepal by dug-out canoe and elephant back. I liked adventure; so why was this resistance making its appearance?

Long ago, however, I had determined that I did not need drama and trauma for life to be exciting since Sathya Sai keeps everyone's life more than compelling, once they consciously become devoted to Him. Further, Baba continually tells us to look within. He had brought Jim and me to India nearly twenty years ago and had, since our first trip, graced us to return to His Form nearly a score of times. He had appeared in apparitional form in our home over fifty times and had been blessing us with increasingly clear guidance. After the usual struggles with our own weaknesses and conflicts, we have reached the ever-present inner peace to which Baba points us.

Therefore, why would I want to go exploring a cave in the Himalayas when the Avatar is ever in the heart? The Form of the Avatar of the Age resides in Puttaparthi, where the intriguing conversation was taking place. Why would I want to leave Baba's Form and go far away just to satisfy my curiosity? I was practicing Baba's Ceiling on Desires Program (self-control) and no longer attempted to satisfy the whims of the mind, having found the results to be unsatisfactory. Further, through the disciplines of concentration, contemplation and meditation, one comes into contact with the deeper mysteries.

"THE CAVE" has been the topic of conversation on most people's lips at the Abode of Peace Ashram this January of 1995. In every apartment block, restaurant and street corner, little clumps of people chattered and laughed about the "Shiva Caves" - who had been there and what had happened. Typical conversations went like this:

"Are you going?"

"You've actually BEEN?! How was it? What happened?"

"Really? How fantastic! I must, must go!"

I observed the fuss and fanfare coolly from the sidelines.

Mounting Resistance

As more and more people invited me to go with them or inquired as to why I wasn't aflame with enthusiastic passion to propel to Patal, I made a mental list of good reasons for not going:

1. I had grown up near magnificent, beautifully-illuminated caves in the U.S. and had even done a bit of spelunking in my university days. This Patal Cave would have to be really spectacular to outshine those nationally-known caves.

2. This cave was difficult to reach and the route traversed treacherous cliff-hung roads replete with hundreds of hairpin turns. Why would I want to put myself through a round-trip drive of four days of dangerous, miserable travel just to scramble down a dark hole filled with rats and bats?

3. There were no accommodations to speak of and we'd no doubt end up sleeping outside to the serenading of jackals and leopards or packed tightly on the floor of a minuscule hut.

4. Only one floor of the seven-story cave was currently accessible. People who had been in its bowels reported that visitors would automatically become covered with soot and black mud from slithering down the steep incline of the "birth-canal-like" entrance.

5. Years before, when I had been doing lots of international travel, Baba had said to me "All this traveling here and there (of foreigners for vacation trips) is not Atma." Travel inside," had been the message. Was the Cave in this category? If Baba wanted me to go, He'd make it very clear.

The two most enthusiastic pilgrims to the Cave, were two Sai devotees, Dave and Craig. Their experience, to quote James Thurber, "had roused them to hosannahs of hysterical praise."

"Look," my friends said in exasperation, "If Baba wants you to experience the divine grace of visiting one of the holiest spots on earth, you'll go, whether or not you wish to do so!" Both they and I were puzzled at my lack of interest in the fact that visits to Patal Bhuvaneshwar were said to confer Self-realization upon a person. Further, a visit also "provided boons both backward and forward in time to their nearest relatives." Such a concept seemed vague at best, although intriguing if it were true.

Titillating Tales

It was reported that an ancient book, the *Skanda Purana*, mentioned that in about 1989 the cave would be rediscovered by a man connected with the army. It had, in fact, been rediscovered by General Kantilal Taylor, a Sai devotee, retired Army officer and overseer of pilgrimages to the cave. People reported that they were somehow transformed from a visit to the cave. Those not given to visions had seen saints and even angels and had heard choirs singing. The Patal Cave was reported to be the place where deities (saints and sages) paid obeisance to God twenty-four hours a day in another dimension superimposed on the cave. And the stories of people seeing visions and developing powers were remarkable.

Such experiences were already part of my life experience and I was unmoved. Tales of increased powers or siddhis left me unconvinced and unresponsive, especially since most devotees know that yogic siddhis are the worst nightmare of the spiritual aspirant. I myself could attest to the truth of that statement since many unsought "gifts" had been suddenly thrust upon me since childhood, making my life extremely difficult at times, to say nothing of continually trying to hide them to appear as "normal" as possible among my peers. No, I didn't need any more troublesome accoutrements, thank you.

Soon I left Puttaparthi to return to the U.S. En route, in Bombay, I was to stop for an appointment with a Nadi reader (ancient manuscript interpreter), a man whom I had never met, and who knew nothing about me. His main role in life is reading from the ancient Book of Brighu, which is similar to the Shuka Nadi readings, except that Lord Brighu was the channel and scribe many centuries ago.

The Prediction

As soon as I took a seat in Kantilal Pandya's office, the Bombay Brighu reader, he reviewed the manuscript and chuckled. Then he announced that I'd be coming back to India twice more in 1995 and that I'd go to the Himalayas - and would in fact lead a group to a most auspicious pilgrimage spot there (which I did). He said that Baba would bless us with an interview (which He did). Still, I laughed and tossed it off.

Meanwhile after I had returned home to the U.S. in January, letters, calls and little booklets on Patal Bhuvaneshwar began to arrive. James Redmond, whom I greatly respected and admired, reported that he had actually been to the cave three times. Dr. Dave Johns and Craig Lewis had been there. Finally, after Baba had sent about ten people to impress upon me that it was indeed my dharma to undertake the "cave adventure," I caved in and surrendered all resistance to Baba. In meditation, He showed me vivid pictures of those who were supposed to accompany me, as usual, and we made plans to launch in June.

Littleton, Colorado
June, 1995

Mr. Pandya was correct. I will be leading a group of five people to the Patal Caves. There will be, in the group, Monty, a NASA engineer who is completely new to Baba; Robin, a retired seventy-year-old Primal (Scream) therapist who wears a pacemaker; Bert, another retired psychologist; Bobbie, a nurse; and myself, an author-publisher. It was a congenial group which had, with one exception, been in India a number of times. Little did we suspect that we would encounter innumerable obstacles, several close-calls, peculiar challenges, and enough story material for a book chapter apiece.

Delhi, India
June, 1995

Heatwave, A (Bund) Shoot-out and an Abduction

(Perhaps at some deep subconscious level in me there lurked a dim precognition of what was to befall us on the cave trip and my subsequent purifications as a result of the pilgrimage. But that comes later.)

Launch date for India has arrived. As we arrived in Delhi's sweltering heat wave, which has already claimed several hundred lives, we were, nevertheless, in high spirits. The heat didn't deter us, nor did the prospect of the long drive, raging cholera and malaria epidemics, the raucous fireworks in nearby streets or prospects of highway bandits en route to our destination. It was only later that we learned that the "fireworks" in the neighborhood had actually been a bund or shoot-out of opposing political factions wherein ten people had been killed.

At the hotel in Delhi we were to meet two more traveling companions, Bert and Bobbie. Bert arrived safely. When our pretty, delightful friend Bobbie, a nurse, never arrived to rendezvous with us at our Delhi hotel, we grew worried. We later learned, when we met her in Rishikesh, that she had been abducted by an amorous Delhi rickshaw driver who drove her to an alley and began molesting her, much to her shock and terror. She had escaped unharmed with her luggage and had been exploited again by another cab driver who overcharged her by about US$225 to drive her to Rishikesh. This was adding insult to injury!

Women travelling alone anywhere in the world need to be especially cautious for their personal safety.

Rishikesh, India
June, 1995

Eventually the cabs arrived in Rishikesh, which, surprisingly, has lots of air pollution. Bobbie is safe. Even though she is an experienced world traveler, Bobbie was pale and agitated when we met her. Later in the day she discharged the shock of the horrid abduction experience through repeated vomiting. We're so thankful that she wasn't killed and left in an alley in Delhi.

General Taylor, who gave us a most gracious welcome, assuaged some of her upset, though, by explaining that to actually reach the cave requires a sacrifice. Perhaps hers had been monetary.

Why were we being summoned to the cave? And why this particular group of five? Would we ever learn the answers to these questions?

En Route to the Caves
Shrine-room Miracles, Epidemics,
Landslides, Forest Fires, Auto Breakdowns

The trip to higher elevations from Rishikesh began most auspiciously with a generous invitation to visit the home of General Taylor's young assistant, Geetha Sharma. Geetha's prayer room is well-known among local people for its manifestations of vibhuti ash and vermilion powder on photos of Sathya Sai, Shirdi Sai and General Taylor, whom Geetha addresses as Guru-ji.

The simple, lime-sherbet-colored room is bare of carpet and furniture and features a low altar inset upon which rests four clear crystal linghams (ellipsoids), articles of worship and the photos. The tiled room is charged with the beneficent energy of prayer and devotional singing. Seeing the photos of Baba reminds me of His saying that "Only a great teacher can mold a great student." How fortunate we are to be blessed by the Greatest Teacher of all to visit the Cave which is destined to become a profoundly significant hermitage in future years. Surely this trip is the boon of a lifetime.

After singing bhajans at Geetha's home and readjusting the luggage on the overhead racks of the cream-colored cabs, the caravan of five cars set out for the cave. The journey is two thirteen-hour days of driving from Rishikesh. The scenery along the way is lovely and seems suffused in a golden light.

There were eucalyptus groves in purple shadow and narrow, shallow streams meandered through scrub oak meadows. Small villages composed of beige or white cinderblock homes were graced by simple gardens and groves of tall shade trees.

Our caravan of cab drivers needed to stop every two hours or so for a smoke, a tea break or a look at the engines. There were flat tires and car engines overheated. As we climbed higher into the foothills of the Himalayas, we could see forest fires that had deliberately been set on the hills by local farmers in a dispute. We were blissfully unaware of any personal danger, though, feeling secure in Baba's inner Presence. Climbing higher yet through the rocky terrain, we noticed scraps of blue-gray shale lying beside the road and smoke-plumes curling from small cliff-hung cottages.

In the vicinity of Rishikesh we encountered rock and mudslides but were unaffected by them. The same day, ahead of us on the route, a van had shot off the cliff road like toothpaste out of a tube and all the occupants had been killed. (We didn't learn this until days later, however.) We learned at a tea stop that there are cholera epidemics in the area.

More forest fires among the hills created a vaporous smoky haze on the landscape of biscuit-colored hills and the pastel hamlets that clung precariously to the cliffs. Still we remained in bliss, humming bhajans and telling Sai stories of miracles and deliverance. By now we energetically intoned the Gayatri Mantra together whenever an obstacle threatened to halt our procession. Within five to seven minutes the way cleared and we resumed our course, humming happily.

Eventually we ceased to inhale sharply as trucks or busses suddenly careened around curves on the narrow road, threatening to send us to heaven several decades before we were ready. At the various stops along the way to visit temples and shrines, we were mysteriously met nine or ten times by priests, usually one at a time, who blessed us, prayed over us, and daubed us with cum-cum powder and vibhuti ash. We noticed that other tourist pilgrims in the precincts of the temples usually did not receive the same blessings and that the priests simply disappeared after performing their pujas for us. Were they angels in disguise? We grew more silent as the import of the pilgrimage dawned upon us.

Meanwhile, I thought about the teachings of Ramana Maharshi, who urges us to observe the mind thinking, and to interrupt our negative trains of thought in order to sink into peace, ever-present peace. Chanting mantras has the same effect initially but Ramana's method is more efficacious as it erases the thought patterns.

Non-existent Hotel Reservations

After thirteen hours of rocking to and fro on hairpin curves and slick, precipitous roads, our exhausted group yearned to crash into a comfortable hotel bed at Almora. The hotel reservation clerk, however, had no record of our reservations. "You can't sleep outside because of the danger of jackals, leopards and thieves," he announced matter-of-factly. "And you certainly can't sleep in the lobby of this hotel. So you'll simply have to go elsewhere."

"But we're Sai Baba devotees on a pilgrimage to the Patal Bhuvaneshwar Cave," I explained. "Sai Baba never lets us down, so if you don't mind, we'll just sit here for about fifteen minutes and chant the Gayatri Mantra until Baba creates a miracle for us."

We did so and after fifteen minutes, four men vacated rooms (at 11:00 P.M.) and we were moved into them. The five of us women took turns showering - Bobbie, Robin, and I and the two Japanese women in the caravan, Emico and Su. We each sprayed off the grit and gravel which had accumulated through the cab windows in thirteen hours of uphill driving. There was so much debris in our hair and clothes, that there were sounds of clinking in the shower as small pebbles hit the floor. We were thankful for a good night's sleep and, in the morning, emerged from our five-person room refreshed and ready again for more arduous travel.

After another long day's drive, we finally reached the village nearest the cave, about an hour from Patal. Badly needing a rest stop and some liquid for our dehydrated bodies, we scrambled out of the cabs seeking water, soft drinks or even the ice cream advertised on local signs. "Sorry, Sir" the man said to me, "No water, no drinks, no ice cream. Wedding today. All out of everything. No toilets. Sorry." We were parched, but there was still an hour to go before reaching our destination.

Back into the cabs we piled, hoping for any liquid and a snack upon arrival at the new ashram at the cave site.

At The Cave

General Taylor and Geetha had arrived ahead of us and had prepared tea and biscuits (cookies) for our arrival. There were even western toilets! Whoops of joy rang out as we assembled under large old trees in the courtyard of the new ashram-under-construction. The entire village had come out in curiosity to line the roads upon our arrival; they seldom saw Westerners, especially blond ones and women traveling without husbands, sons, brothers or uncles. After we stashed our luggage in the rooms, we gathered under the old trees for instructions about the schedule.

Suddenly my name was called from several directions at once by Hugh George, Craig Lewis and others. It was a reunion of Sai devotees from the U.S., Australia, Japan, India and Europe. There were forty-six of us who would share the Cave Experience over the next few days.

After a delicious dinner of potato and onion soup with flat bread and tea, cooked by Geetha Sharma and staff, we set up camp in our brand new rooms. The rooms were so brand new, in fact, that the cement hadn't fully dried. There was no window frame or glass or door so it was necessary to hang a sheet at the window to discourage the local men and boys who unabashedly crowded at the window and door to attempt to watch us undress for the night.

"Shoo! Go! Please leave," we pleaded in escalating tones as we realized that we were the local entertainment for the evening.

General Taylor had promised to have some brand new beds constructed for us but they never materialized. (I'm not complaining, just explaining.) It was about this point in the weekend that we learned the wisdom of the line from the American bumper sticker: She who laughs, lasts!

We were extremely grateful for the sparse, but adequate bathroom arrangements. The showers and toilets were enclosed and were set over a cliff, from which could be seen magnificent terraced hills below. Forty-six people shared three Western toilets and showers whose doors were large rusty sheets of metal. A porcelain sink was cemented to the outside wall of one of the bathrooms and people did their open-air ablutions in the wee morning hours. Many devotees slept under the trees in the courtyard so we counted ourselves fortunate to have rooms, crowded as they were. The forceful realization came home to me that the majority of the world's population sleeps in conditions like these every night, without relief. Surely we could manage without complaint for a few nights as we so often had over the years while visiting various other countries and sacred sites.

After dinner we walked to the cave, several hundred yards through a forest of the most beautifully-skirted spruce and fir trees,. in fact the only trees we had seen in the region. There was a sacred silence amid the thick stand of dark green trees as we strolled the newly-installed cement sidewalk to the cave.

In all directions below, we could see paisley-shaped rice paddies stacked fifty tiers high in the distance. Farmers had denuded the hills of verdure and the Ganges was horribly polluted. These two eventualities, deforestation of the Himalayas and the poisoning of the Holy Ganges, fulfilled ancient Vedic prophecies that when this happened there would be many disasters around the world before the public announcement of the Kalki Avatar Who would redeem a confused, corrupt world and create a New Golden Age. The prophecies are being fulfilled.

A ripple of excitement raced through the crowd as we assembled to enter the cave. In addition to the able-bodied adults present, there were children, the elderly and the handicapped. One man from England, handicapped and on crutches from a motorcycle wreck in England, was here for the third or fourth time. His strategy was to toss his crutches down the tunnel and to drag his body up and down with his arms. If he could do this, many were musing, we could certainly manage to climb down and back safely as well.

Many people were wondering whether or not they would experience a vision or have any unusual sensations in the Cave. That question brought to mind Baba's words: "When you practice the attitude that God is everywhere as the witness of every act of yours, that God is in every being that you will serve, then you will certainly be rewarded by a vision of the Lord." Some chatted softly, others meditated or hummed bhajans as we waited for the first courageous souls to plunge down the tunnel and into the yawning black cavern beyond.

Into the Abyss

Handbags and cameras had to be left at the cave entry in the care of an overseer of possessions. The sight of the cameras reminded me of Baba's saying that "If you wish to see Me in your heart, first you have to focus the lens of the camera there." Shoes had to be removed and one had to enter the low three-foot high cave entrance in a squatting position. Before squatting down to crawl into the cave, I had tucked a pair of Singapore Airline slipper socks into my belt, under my sweatshirt, for wearing on the cold, clammy cave floor.

We crawled and scooted into the yawning cave opening single file, leaving about six feet of space between us, lest anyone suddenly feel claustrophobic. Almost immediately upon entering the pitch-black cavern it became obvious that intuition and faith would have to be our steady companions in the steep descent. The naked sixty-watt light bulb overhead merely threw a weak orange circle of light in its immediate vicinity.

Down below me I could hear the soft voices of people emerging into the large room from midway in the canal where I was spread-eagled with hands and feet pressed against the curved cave walls. It was at this inopportune moment (with a line of people below me and a line of eager explorers above me) that Baba chose to give me a Maha-Vision.

The Vision and the Divine Message
June, 1995

The first part of the vision was fleeting and personal. Faces of various people raced past me and the knowledge which accompanied this phenomenon was that I was unconsciously harboring grudges against them for injustices which I believed they had enacted against me. I surrendered any unforgiveness and asked Baba's pardon. Immediately I was given a vast panoramic vision of millions of needy people throughout the planet. There were Chinese beggars living under slimy culverts in Hong Kong. Toothless Indian lepers lay on crowded filthy city streets as naked children held up their arms in supplication for food and love.

There was a procession of millions of sick, lonely, crazed, forlorn, desperate people, reaching out for basic nourishment, beds, housing, companionship, safety and love.

"*Oh! Baba! Please let me do something to help alleviate the vast misery and suffering of humanity,*" I pleaded. "*Please, Lord,*" I begged, realizing that the decades of service which I had done in tutoring, serving meals, counseling and visiting the needy had been but a drop in the ocean of desperate privation and that I had indeed been privileged to have taken part in even such paltry service as I had been given.

"Hey, what's the problem down there?" someone above me asked.

"Is everything alright, Connie?" Monty shouted up from below.

"Yes, everything's fine!" I shouted back, wondering why Baba was picking such an odd time to give me such momentous information.

Meanwhile, Baba said in sonorous tones, "*I'm going to give you a very big job.*"

"*A very big job, Swami? How can you give me a very big job if I'm just one little person?*"

"*Just as in the past,*" He answered. "*I'm the Doer. I've always given you the resources and help you have needed when I've given you a job. This will be no different.*"

"Thank You, Swami," I murmured as perspiration dripped into my eyes and my sweaty hand-hold began to slip and my tentative toe-holds gave way. I scrambled down the tunnel as quickly as I could and laid down on my back and rolled over the final flat ledge that led into the dome-shaped chamber. There, half a dozen people were waiting barefoot on the clammy black mud in a silent semi-circle. They patiently waited for each intrepid climber to emerge from the "birth canal" into the womb-like dark room.

General Taylor began pointing out the Shesh Nag, or giant snake sculpture that wound its way through the cavern and told us of the many natural sculptures of gods and goddesses who could be seen in relief on the cave walls. There were small pools of water in the various adjoining rooms of the main floor. In the darkness we could hear the chittering of bats and the rustle of rats.

General Taylor asked us to sit down in a small prayer-room inside the large cavern. We were invited to sing bhajans and to thank Baba for our good fortune. Geetha and General Taylor set up a puja area and we began to sing. Our bhajans sounded haunting in the cave acoustics and nearly everyone in the group had visions during our long meditations there. The Japanese devotees were the most disciplined meditators. Some of us saw Ganesh, angels, saints or rishis. Later, we discussed the strange "lights" people had seen: blue flashes, golden sparkles, eerie yellow auras around people.

Throughout our stay, General Taylor and Geetha were extraordinarily hospitable in the preparation of food, explanations of the cave's lore and history and in arranging many special rituals and ceremonies called hovens (rhymes with ovens). During the total of five hours which we spent in the cave throughout the weekend, I experienced myself in an altered state much of the time. Still, however, a lingering sense of dread stayed with me. This odd underlying sensation later proved to have been a prescient awareness of my near-death a little over a year later.

Our stay at the cave entailed lovely meals, inspiring bhajans, good satsang and exceptional hospitality from Geetha and General Taylor. The time to leave came too quickly.

Meanwhile, as departure time arrived, I was feeling more jubilant by the hour, despite the hunch that the cave would purify me, ultimately, more than I would have wished. I whistled a little bhajan as I packed my bags and remembered Baba's injunction to "Be eager and earnest to know more and more about the art of joyful living." We certainly had laughed a lot thus far on the trip. The weekend had fled, brimful as it had been with cave-descents, singing, meals, walks, meditations, rituals and silent appreciation of the vast Himalayan ranges from our cliff-side rooms.

As we packed our cabs for the two-day trip back to Delhi, we felt a surge of energy move through us which felt, to me, rather like etheric ginger ale, bubbling and coursing through my entire being and all of its systems, glands and organs.

While I sat in the cab as we bounced down the mountain, Baba's voice boomed into my ears. *"I am very pleased with you and the group. The way you chanted the Gayatri Mantra to clear the way before every obstacle encountered is the way I would like for you (all) to conduct your lives from now on. You helped each other at each stage of the descent and ascent in the cave itself and on the trip. This is what I like (cooperation and team effort)."*

Two things occurred as we sped toward Delhi for our plane trip to Puttaparthi to receive Baba's darshan. First, the strange infusion of unusual energy began to make us giddy - drunk on the Divine. Although Bobbie, Robin and I are normally cheerful people, we became nearly hysterical, giggling like chickens the rest of the day.

Secondly, my friend Robin, our seventy-year-old wearing a pace-maker, began to itch all over. Her skin developed welts and her jubilant mood turned dark. By the time we reached New Delhi, Robin was in the throes of a Dark Night of the Soul. Her welts had become suppurating sores to which she had attached billowing white hankies for protection.

"You look like an American leper," someone joked, vainly trying to cheer her up. She was not amused. Robin, who had entertained us by recounting her cave-visions of a charming, dancing Ganesha, was in a black, black mood. The rest of the trip she had to be assisted in dressing, turning door knobs and in performing most functions since her hands, trunk and limbs became marked with running sores. (Baba later told her it was an allergic reaction she was experiencing. But to what?!)

Upon our return to the Delhi hotel, we met my friend Dr. Flo Covell and her husband John, from Middletown, New York who would be traveling with us the remainder of the trip.

Our friends, Mr. and Mrs. Ram Patel, from Delhi, insisted on feeding us several magnificent meals, arranging bhajan sessions, and eagerly listened to our accounts of the cave. Mr. Patel called us at the hotel numerous times to try to persuade us to go with him and his wife Uma to visit with a Himalayan yogi who was staying for a month at the home of a wealthy Sikh Sai devotee named Mr. Singh. We declined. He insisted. We declined.

Finally, in exasperation, Mrs. Patel explained, "Shiv Yogi, who himself has lived a life of austerity in a cave, has not even had the chances you Americans have had to go to the Patal Bhuvaneshwar Cave. Don't you think you could be so kind as to share even one hour with him to describe your experiences? Is that too much to ask for one who has served humanity by meditating so many years for all mankind?!"

How could we refuse? Of course we agreed to visit Shiv yogi for an hour. The record-breaking heat-wave was still taking lives in Delhi. The moment we stepped out of the cool air-con of the hotel lobby, the reflected heat of the hotel driveway slammed into our faces and sucked our breath away. We scrambled into the two waiting cars and hurried across town to Mr. Singh and Shiv Yogi.

After entering Mr. Singh's cool two-story home, we were ushered into the master bed-room where ancient, white-bearded Shiv Yogi, dressed in orange turban and orange robe, sat meditating in lotus position on the gold brocade bedspread atop the king-sized bed. As we entered, he gestured for us to be seated on the floor, men on one side, women on the other. Mr. Singh acted as translator and asked us, for Shiv Yogi, to please sing devotional songs to our teacher (Baba) in English. One by one, we each led a bhajan; since we were still in bliss from the Cave Experience, we sang with great ardor and tenderness.

At one point I happened to open my eyes and noticed that Mr. and Mrs. Patel were weeping and that Shiv Yogi had tears in his eyes. (They later told us that they hadn't met many Americans, and previously had the impression that most Americans were - as depicted on TV - wealthy movie stars, gangsters or generally aggressive and unsavory! Thus they were surprised at our deep devotion and simple lifestyles.)

Next, we were asked to tell our experiences in the cave with Mr. Singh translating for Shiv Yogi. We spoke of visions, lights, music, transformations, hovens, surrender and new humility. Shiv Yogi, with obvious appreciation and grave demeanor, told us that we had been given, by Sai Baba, a reward for many prior lifetimes of service. "Even I, a renunciate, have not had this great boon. You are all going to be doing much healing and great works in this, your last lifetime," he announced. "This trip is the fulfillment of previous desires in other lifetimes - to visit the primary holy places of India. Going to Patal Bhuvaneshwar is worth more than visiting all the holy places and temples of India combined. Your relatives will also benefit greatly." Again he repeated, "You will teach and heal. You have been richly blessed among humankind."

Reeling at the import of Shiv Yogi's message, we thanked our host and Shiv Yogi and ambled back into the heat wave. The temperature was 122 degrees Fahrenheit. Hundreds had expired in the past few days. Unfortunately I alarmed the group (since I was the group leader) by fainting as we left the cab to enter the hotel. After my compatriots had helped me off the sizzling pavement, I fainted again as I entered the cool interior of the building. It must have been the sharp 52 degree contrast between both Mr. Singh's house and the hotel (both 70 degrees F.), and the outdoor temperature of 122 degrees which overtaxed the body. I had never experienced temperatures of 122 degrees until then and the body simply collapsed.

Puttaparthi, India
June, 1995

After more hospitality from the Patels, we departed New Delhi and headed for Baba's darshan in Puttaparthi. We were so exhausted from the ordeals of the trip that we could barely summon the energy to walk to darshan and return to our rooms to flop thankfully on a real bed with an actual mattress. Just being in Puttaparthi was a balm for our spirits. Baba acknowledged our arrival in Puttaparthi in a variety of ways. He glided past the crowd of thousands in darshan, signing photos and making vibhuti. As He walked by our group, He teased us by tossing out a few questions and phrases each day. "Wait, wait, I will see you. How many in group? Where are you from? (As if He didn't know every freckle on our bodies and every secret in each heart!)

It was glorious to feast our eyes on the Avatar's form. We could see Him joking with the students, who sat in rows in front of the veranda. He would stroll among them, making occasional comments and provoking roars of laughter. Many of the boys had tear-filled eyes and a few handed Baba a red or a pink rose. We were deeply touched to see the devotion of boys from age six to twenty-three.

We were finally called for an interview. As Baba pointed to our American flag group-identity scarves, He chuckled and said, "America. Very happy, very happy."

We were still bone-tired and reeling from the Delhi Heat Wave. We learned about the fatal bund shoot-out and the cholera and malaria epidemics. We joked about Robin's sores, the rock-slides and mud-slides, Bobbie's abduction, the forest fires, the cab break-downs, the wet-cement ashram room three feet from a cliff and the energetic-upheaval of the Patal Cave itself. (Had we somehow worked off cargo-loads of karma or did we simply happen to arrive in North India during a very eventful period?) Those words "Very happy, very happy" were music to our ears., as we scurried to the veranda to await the Lord's directives.

During the interview He answered questions, blessed various personal articles and told us that everything that had taken place in the Cave had been ordained by Him. "I bless you to go back to the Cave many times," He said to me. "Oh no, I thought I was finished with the Cave."

"Do you know what your name means?" Baba asked me.

"My name? (Shaw). Yes, Shaw means 'the forest' or the one who dwells in the forest."

"No, it means change," Baba replied. "Change."

"You, too, change." He looked at Bobbie as He spoke.

After the Cave

It transpired that Mr. Pandya, the Brighu reader, was correct: I did (somehow) go to India three times in 1995. However, after the publication of my book, *Mary's Miracles and Prophecies - Intimate Revelations of a Visionary,* blessed by Baba in November of that year, I nearly died. Most of the time during the next six months was spent in bed recovering from a strange malady that seemed to be Epstein-Barr Virus.

A year and a half before the cave trip, my husband, Jim, had made two flying leaps off a twenty-foot ladder onto his back, the injuries of which created such constant pain that neither he nor I slept through the night for three years. We were severely sleep-deprived for a year and a half before the cave trip and a year and a half afterwards.

Then our circumstances turned around and I was healed but Jim was still in frequent pain. I began to travel again and to conduct lectures and book signings. The Cave Purification seemed to be waning and I was gaining new strength.

On June 9th, 1996, Baba blessed us to start a fledgling Sai Center in Northern Colorado - the fifth which we have begun for Sai in Colorado. He has graciously allowed us to begin Center service projects which now include Habitat for Humanity, blood donations, food donations, a prison library project, a public library project, Adopt-a-Family at Christmas, the Poudre River Cleanup and sending food and blankets to Native Americans on reservations.

On September 15th, 1996 we received momentous grace during Bonfire Bhajans at our country home. About 22 of our friends had gathered around our garden bonfire pit for outdoor devotional singing. A local psychic, who had never before attended our functions, saw Baba (in His Etheric or Energetic Body) walk around the circle and bless each one present, then perform psychic surgery on Jim's spine. Baba did so by lifting it out of the body and removing several blobs of energetic accretions. Baba then, according to our gifted clairvoyant friend, "unzipped Connie's back, similarly, did some healing maneuvers and zipped it back up. He blessed Jim and Connie with His hand on their heads for a long time, smiled and vanished." (This was unusual in that Baba allowed Himself to be seen only by a non-devotee as grace to that person and to inform us of what had transpired.)

For the next four days Jim was in excruciating pain, as if he had indeed endured physical surgery. On the fifth day he could sleep through the night for the first time in three years. We were deeply thankful to Baba for our purifications and for pain relief.

Baba's key message to me during the 1995 post-Cave interview was that my life would change. Many people began to write and to call us after the publication of our book. The media did dozens of interviews and life is changing very quickly - just as Baba had foretold. However, as to whether there is even an inkling of the "big job" on the horizon to which He referred in the Cave-Vision, I have no clue. It doesn't seem as if we're doing anything remotely resembling such a grandiose term. There are thousands of Sai Centers throughout the world and most of them are steeped in service projects, educational efforts and the same kinds of things which occupy our own group. Surely the results of the Cave Pilgrimage will continue for many years with outworkings both subtle and overt.

Now that it has been about five years since I first visited the Patal Bhuvaneshwar Cave, I believe that I have healed my resistance to it and have emerged obviously unscathed from the near-death experience. We have also recovered from three years without sleep, and have adjusted to being forced to lead a more public life (than I would have desired) in order to do Baba's work through writing, speaking, publishing and service. Since I have now had many Shuka Nadi readings from the ancient manuscript, I realize that Baba will grant me Realization in this lifetime, whenever He decides to confer it, and that the extreme number of traumas and losses which I have experienced in this lifetime, is as a result of compressing the karma from two lifetimes together in one. That is, any future lifetime with Prema Sai will be voluntary and the karma from that life is now being lived.

On final reflection, I would say that I now realize I was being healed of various aversions (which, of course, are the flip side of desires!). Further, it is a profound privilege to have gone to the Cave. Obviously, the experience is a purgative, one which may not confer immediate blessings of the sort to which we'd like to become accustomed. But every event has its blessing - of which the form is not the aspect of primary import. That we are willing to do His Will and to bear whatever happens in life is the lesson of the Cave, of encounters with Baba, and in our on-going abidance in the Indwelling Presence.

Surely Baba has great work in store for all devotees as He becomes more widely known as the Avatar. It will take countless millions of devotees to inform, educate and inspire the thirsty souls who seek refreshment from Baba. Much, much will be asked of those fabulously blessed devotees who have had the unspeakable good fortune to have known and loved Him for a long time and who have seen and spoken with His physical form. I believe the Cave Experience was a boon from Baba to me and my friends that we might more quickly cease our identification with body, mind and emotions. The more we continually rest in True Identification, the more easily His Light can shine through us without obstruction for the unique ways in which He'll utilize each of us for His planetary mission of world uplift. World uplift depends on each of us. Baba reminds us:

"The end of knowledge is wisdom.
The end of culture is perfection.
The end of wisdom is freedom.
The end of education is character."

Finally, our Beloved Lord exhorts us, "I have told you for long that My life is My message. Now I tell you, your life is My message.... Are you ready to love and to educate those I send to you as I have loved you all these years? Resolve to sacrifice everything you have for the sake of the pure-hearted who rely on you for guidance."

Most importantly, one becomes established in contemplation and meditation as he moves through each day. It is through contemplation of the blissful, peaceful aspect of the Atma, or Self within, that one becomes aware of the deep peace that pervades the manifest world of form. One realizes that, beneath the seeming violent disharmonies that exist in the world, there also exists an exquisite serenity. The waves on the ocean's surface are constant but the vast deeps are still, still, still.

Note: In recent years the sacred Patal Bhuvaneshwar Cave has been closed by Baba and the auspicious energy has been removed. Local land disputes, political tensions in North India and desecration of the cave by Asian tourists, were apparently only a few of Baba's reasons for its closure. When the time is right, He may announce the transfer of Patal Cave energy to another location in the Himalayas. Or not. Meanwhile, the Boon-Conferring Avatar is ever available in each heart.

CHAPTER 31
THE MIRACULOUS MANGRU SHRINE AT COLUSA

"Without first becoming a servant, you cannot become a leader."
Sathya Sai Baba

Johnstown, Colorado
July, 1997

Since I have written, published and distributed *Mary's Miracles and Prophecies*, Baba has healed scores of people who prayed to Him by putting the Sai Lingham Photo, in the book, on their bodies. The mail, faxes and phone calls we receive about this are quite astonishing. I keep wondering what more could possibly happen since Baba has now graced us with twenty trips to India, with a dozen interviews, with fifty-four apparitions in our house, and with innumerable healings at our Sai Baba meetings over the years. We have seen Him perform miracles and manifestations hundreds of times in person and feel steeped in His bliss and love. How can He possibly give us any more, show us any more, do anything more for us that could top all that He has so far done, been and given to us and to the world?

His love for each of us is beyond measure. Our gratitude, of necessity and in responding love, must be the implementing of His teachings in our daily lives.

Mother Mary recently told me that, even though I believe that the work for her and Baba is waning, and that I have done all they have asked, that it is truly just beginning. She said that I am at the threshold of the Greater Work. I wonder what that means. Just before she said this, I was reflecting on the hundreds of spiritual talks I have given, on the thirty-five audio tapes I've made, the workshops and retreats we've organized, the dozens of service projects undertaken, the articles I've written, the books we've written and the videos and radio shows in which we have been featured. Yes, Baba is the Doer, but we have to do our part.

We are continually contented. In fact, Baba often says that "For the contented, life is one long festival." That is how my life's journey has seemed, the past two decades, in spite of the usual collection of challenges, difficulties, illnesses, tragedies and traumas which everyone must endure in order to learn wisdom and compassion. There had, it is true, been many disappointments since we have become Sai devotees, but Baba tells us to see disappointments as our friends. "Welcome disappointments, for they toughen you and test your fortitude."

Baba has patiently and gently taught us that "Good and bad, happiness and sorrow, which appear to be different and opposite, are in reality two faces of the same coin." In other words, we have created our own lessons and obstacles.

As I was musing over the thrilling life we have had in Baba's care since we met Him nearly two decades ago, I received a visit from a friend that was to inaugurate the next round of extraordinary leelas (surprising events) and manifestations of God's love. After the entire Colusa Wedding Episode played itself out, we were invited to tell the story many times and, ultimately, to provide the seva (service) of featuring it in an article for its appreciation by an international audience. The following is the synopsis of the story as it appeared in the *Spiritual Impressions* magazine which is an international journal published in India.

The Miraculous Mangru Shrine at Colusa
Marvelous Rumors About Colusa

We had begun to hear of miracles at the home of the Mangru family in Colusa, California, about a year before we seriously considered going there. There were stories that the Indian family had been feeding huge crowds of 200 or more weekly for three years and that the food had often multiplied so that all had enough to eat. We had heard tales of vibhuti, amrit and cum-cum forming on photos of saints and of Baba. People had apparently been healed of incurable diseases there and recently Baba had told some Japanese devotees in an interview that they could find the Mangru household by searching the internet!

One of the members of our Northern Colorado Sai Center had recently confirmed the miracles and manifestations upon her return from Colusa. "It's genuine phenomena," she had assured our members as we sat listening to her experiences, bug-eyed.

"Water pours out of a picture of Lord Shiva and falls on the floor. This so impressed my own brother, who isn't a Sai devotee, that, as he saw this, he began to weep and then decided to go to India to see Baba," our friend exclaimed. Our Center was abuzz with the delights of Colusa. We wondered if any of us would ever be so lucky as to go there.

Who Is Ami Mangru?
"Who was this Mangru man?" many were wondering. What was the extent of his "special powers?" How long had he exhibited them? Were they genuine? What was the rest of the family like? What was the depth of the man's devotion or understanding?

Mr. Ami Mangru, who was born December 9, 1943 in Fiji, of Indian parents, was reputedly very generous, highly intelligent yet very humble, extremely telepathic, yet quietly charismatic in his magnetism. How did one explain the cataracts of grace that he and his family had been so privileged to receive? Were these phenomena created by Baba primarily to alert the world to the Avatar's Presence in form on the planet? Was Ami a fore-runner of the type of devotee who will be common in the rapidly-approaching Golden Age of Peace when mankind awakens to his True Nature as Divinity?

A Special Request

In May of 1997 our friend Beth Blade approached me with a request. She was beaming and sighing, while clasping and unclasping her hands - the way she does when about to ask someone a really big favor. Beth wanted Jim and me to fly to California to attend her marriage to Elmer Woods. Beth, an entrepreneur, and El, an author, poet and retired forester, are extremely creative and wanted to have a unique wedding. Nothing fancy, but definitely unique. Not only that, she wanted to be married in the home of Ami and Ram Mangru. Not only that, she wanted to be married in the shrine room where devotees gather weekly to sing devotional songs to Baba. Not only that, she wanted me to call Mr. Ami Mangru, whom I had never met, and who was unaware of me, and convince him that this would be a good idea. Not only that, she wanted Jim and me to pay our own way by air to California. Not only that, she wanted me to conduct the wedding!

I could tell by the determined look in Beth's eyes that this was not the time to remind Beth about Baba's Ceiling on Desires Program (curbing the ceaseless wants of the mind).

"Look, Beth," I began, hoping she would change her mind, "It's true that I do have a ministerial license and can perform weddings, christenings, vow renewals and sacred ceremonies. In fact, I've studied enough theology and comparative religion to have earned two Ph.D.'s.

But after I decided to turn down a full doctoral scholarship to study art history at an Eastern university, and a law school scholarship in Oregon, I couldn't find a graduate program in the U.S. which was as all-encompassing of Eastern and Western traditions as I required to better understand my lifetime of transcendent mystical experiences, miracles and healings. So I kept studying with advanced teachers all over the world and ceased all interest in obtaining graduate credits. Finally, so many people asked me to do funerals, christenings and healings that I decided to get a ministerial license from Universal Life Church in California. It's a mail order license. Perfectly legal. But I don't have a doctorate in theology or comparative religion. Since Baba has healed people that have come to me, I decided it would be a good umbrella of protection so that I couldn't be accused of practicing medicine without a license! By the way, in many states a minister or a justice of the peace is no longer necessary to perform weddings. People can marry themselves."

She showed no signs of relenting on implementing her inspired plan. Beth was about fifty years old and had never married. El was nearly eighty and had recently had a pace-maker installed, thus wasn't quite up to taking a wedding trip to India. They were sure that I could persuade Ami and Ram Mangru that their small suburban ranch house in the Colusa farming community would be the ideal place for two strangers and their four friends to conduct a wedding.

"El and I thought we'd like to have Jim (my husband) be the best man and our friend Lynn be the maid of honor. My friend Lorie would be attending, too."

A Green Light from Baba

"Faith in ourselves and faith in God. This is the secret of greatness," Baba says.

Eventually, after several conversations with Ami by phone, and with the help of another mutual friend and her daughter, the arrangements were made. Ami told me by telephone that Baba had directed him and Ram to allow the wedding in their shrine room. Ami and his family had decided that the best time to conduct the wedding would be in the afternoon, just before the family's weekly Saturday bhajans which are open to the public.

Meanwhile, El and Beth wrote their own ceremony, complete with music, chanting and poetry. The tiny wedding party rehearsed before arriving at the Mangru's white, one-story stucco house on a shaded corner lot in a quiet suburban neighborhood. Ami and Ram greeted the seven of us as we huddled apprehensively on the front step, wondering what Baba had in store for us. We also began to realize how audacious we had been to presume that people who had never met us would be willing to allow a wedding ceremony of strangers in their house.

When Ami and his family met the seven of us at the door, we were surprised that Ami was so short of stature - less than five feet five inches - and that he seemed self-effacing in the extreme.

Ami introduced us to Sangeetha and Moneeta, his two beautiful daughters, explaining that his son Nirlesh had just left to visit Baba in India, thus was not at home. Someone had paid for his ticket and Nirlesh was the first member of this family to actually see Baba in physical form. "Blessed are they that have not seen (Him) and still believe."

Ami wore an air of quiet expectancy; his wife Ram and daughters were dressed in their best festive clothes, lovely bright-colored silk saris.

The Shrine Room

As we stepped into the shrine room we gasped: there were dozens of photos, floor-to-ceiling, and dozens of statues on small tables beneath the pictures of Avatars and saints. There were lots of red and orange tones in the pictures and overhead there were tinsel garlands looped from the ceiling. The overall effect was startling and dramatic and the vibrations were indeed what you would expect to encounter in such a sanctified location where healings and miracles had taken place for three years.

Extraordinary Gurupurnima Wedding

The Mangru family stood at the back of the shrine room as we made our preparations to begin the ceremony. Ami had just pointed out the vibhuti on numerous pictures of Baba. There was a half-inch-thick flow of dried amrit and honey on pictures of Jesus and Baba; an empty bronze container sometimes would fill with water, we had been told. As the wedding began and the vows were exchanged, I happened to notice out of the corner of my eye that more vibhuti had formed on a large photo of Baba's head, nearly encircling it. Amrit flowed and glistened from His hand in two other photos. Honey flowed from the Jesus picture as it had in the past. A six-inch-wide band of golden amrit flowed from a photo of Baba's feet. Suddenly, water spontaneously began to appear in the bronze vessel that rested on a table about eighteen inches from my left knee. The day had just begun and already it had become quite eventful!

After the ceremony was "official, legal and complete," we embraced the bride and groom and extended our heartiest blessings and wishes for a happy wedded life. Ami placed his hand on the heads of the newly wedded couple. Vibhuti appeared on their hair. As this occurred, I stepped over to the altar area to get a better look at something that was sitting on a small table to my left. It was glistening white, in a mound of approximately two cups in volume, at the base of Baba's full-length photo which also rested there.

As I stood bent over the table inspecting the sparkling, faceted little rock-like objects, Ami came over immediately, asking, "Did you put that on the table?"

"No," I replied, bewildered, "None of us touched anything in this shrine area. I wonder what it is... jewels, salt, moth crystals...?"

The seven in the wedding party and the four Mangrus stood transfixed for a moment, stooping over the low table staring at the opaque, glistening, emerald-faceted crystal-like squares that lay heaped in a pile several inches high. Suddenly it occurred to me that it must be rock candy that had been materialized by Baba as the fortunate couple had exchanged their vows.

"Taste it, Ami, I bet it's rock candy!" I exclaimed.

Rock candy it was. Ami passed some around for each of us to sample.

"Oh! Of course! El's nickname is Crystal Elmer because he collects exceptionally fine rock and crystal specimens. How generous of Baba to bless this sweet union with crystal-faceted rock candy," I laughed.

The mood in the room became mirthful as devotees began to arrive for weekly bhajans and we arranged ourselves directly in front of the altar in order to get a good view of any immanent miracles.

Suddenly a white object seemed to fall from the ceiling onto the altar as we sang. Was it a flower? Was it more rock candy? More vibhuti appeared on the large photo of Baba's face, lightly encircling it.

After three hours of ardent devotional singing we were lovingly served a fruit dish and a full dinner by Ami's wife Ram. The Mangrus, in true hospitable Indian fashion, gave a set of dishes to the bride and groom as a wedding gift, even though they are on a tight budget from gratis weekly feedings of hundreds who come to their home for bhajan singing.

Gurupurnima Night

As devotees surged around us after dinner we shared Sai stories; the evening grew late. After the wedding party left, Jim and I stayed a few more hours until midnight. Someone exclaimed, "It's Gurupurnima Night and the moon is full. Let's go outside in the front yard and admire it!"

As we prepared to go outside with the others, I overheard someone mention something Baba had said about the Inner Guru in a discourse on Gurupurnima that was printed in the ashram magazine, *Sanathana Sarathi*, in the August issue of 1996. "You are a guru unto yourself. All potencies are within you. This is indicated by the Gayatri Mantra."

About twenty people dashed outside to stand in the small front yard inside the fence, gazing at the moon. Within a few minutes Ami indicated that vibhuti ash had appeared on his hands as soon as he had concentrated on the Lord Shiva aspect of Sai, his preceptor.

Friends of Ami who had experienced the phenomenon previously, began to "high five" Ami in order to wipe vibhuti from his hands. It reappeared until everyone had received some vibhuti from his hand. As we walked into the house Ami indicated he was ready to tell me more about his recent life. It also dawned on me, lest we begin to feel special, that even though vibhuti ash had appeared on Ami, on Wilma Bronkey, on Millie Epstein, on myself and on other Sai devotees I knew, that it was all Baba's Will. We were all merely playing delightful and fortunate roles which had nothing to do with That Which we really Are - the Divine Presence. These roles are no more important, in the ultimate sense, than roles of someone pumping gas at the corner station in Arizona or of another person doing highway construction on a remote stretch in Texas in the blazing summer sun. All beings are aspects of my Self. Nevertheless, we were thrilled with Baba's incomparable grace.

As we sat down again inside the house, Ami remarked that yet additional phenomena had taken place in his home.

"A clear crystal lingham suddenly appeared here. And water appears in an empty glass (the size of an empty votive candle holder) in our hall closet shrine. In fact, Jared Phillip, a former Sacramento Sai Center president, took nine gallons of holy water from it one night. When we turn off the hall light and blow out the candle, the holy water production stops (or else it would flood the floor). All of this happens spontaneously. I've never promoted myself or my home. At least fifteen thousand people have come from throughout the world to view these miracles. We are just Baba's instruments."

It was quite apparent that Ami deeply respects Baba and doesn't want any show. To emphasize this, Ami mentioned that several individuals had brought video cameras to his shrine room, in spite of his having requested that they not do so. When Ami discovered that videos had been taken he silently asked Baba to erase the film, which Baba did.

Next, Ami explained the sequence of events as they took place in his home. First vibhuti appeared on pictures, then cum-cum powder, then, January 28, 1994, holy water began flowing. Ami mentioned that although he had known Baba since 1958, he wasn't really a devotee. His faith has intensified since 1994.

Ami's wife Ram and his two daughters Sangeetha and Moneeta have frequent Sai Baba dreams. As any devotee knows, Sai dreams are specifically ordained and orchestrated by Sai Baba and are eagerly received when they occur.

Ami continued in his soft-spoken, no-nonsense way, "We (people) have attachments. So our family has satsangs here to try to teach people about God. You either believe what's happening here or you don't. Our minds are limited and we don't understand God but Baba knows all fourteen lokas or realms. I am confused as to why Baba is having all these things happen here. Besides, people think that all these materializations are miracles. I'll tell you about *real* miracles.

"On February 28, 1997, I received a call from Oklahoma City to leave immediately to visit a comatose man in Oklahoma City. Awhile later, after I had packed a bag, two people appeared at my door to drive me to the Sacramento Airport, gave me the ticket and disappeared. After I deplaned at the destination I was met by two others who drove me to the hospital and straight to Intensive Care where I was to meet the patient. I saw Baba sitting there watching the patient. I put my finger on the man's third eye area. He blinked, his toes moved and he woke up!

"Different people then took me to another airport where I met two more people in Oklahoma City. I didn't know them and they didn't speak in the car. They took me to another Intensive Care Unit to a forty-two-year-old man that was a motel owner. This patient had fallen in his motel and was brain-dead but his heart was beating. The doctor asked me to tell the family what I thought. They were only going to keep the body alive another seventy-two hours. I told them to pull the plug and donate his organs since I saw he'd be lying there inert his whole life. Then I left. I went to my hotel and freshened up. People took me to my plane. I returned to Sacramento.

"Each time I traveled on the plane the seat next to me was empty. I ate and drank nothing on the journeys as I was full with love for Baba.

"When I left the airport the last time there was no one there to meet me. I wondered how I was going to get home in the middle of the night. Just then a small five-year-old girl came up to me outside the airport and beckoned for me to come with her to her grandfather's awaiting car. I got in. No one spoke to me. There was a special bhajan going on at our house in my absence. The grandfather asked if he could attend the bhajan. I naturally told them they were welcome and as soon as we walked inside I had a plate of food prepared for them. I gave it to them and turned around a second, then turned back to them immediately and they had vanished!

"I don't know who paid the plane expenses or who the people were. Now *these* things I call miracles! We have no secrets here. We feed all who come and we always have just enough food for all who come. We've been feeding them since 1994.

"I was a building contractor and made a lot of money. But I was out of work for one full year, during which time I was heavily tested by Baba. He said to me, 'Teach your family discipline first, then teach others!' We had no money and even had to collect aluminum cans to get the $22.00 to buy the food ingredients to make dinner for the 200 people who came to eat at our house. The food multiplied.

"Then, with no income, we had no money for the mortgage payment on this house. It went into foreclosure but at the last day we got word from the county clerk's office that someone had mysteriously paid a check for the $68,000 balance on the house. We stayed. My work from 1970 to 1989 was general construction, contracting and building. I'm also a pilot; I flew helicopters for the sheriff's department and was also a deputy. Then I became unemployed and went to the bottom. My wife had to get a job and it's very humiliating for an Indian man to have his wife work to support the family. Every day I'd watch my wife and my neighbors go to work while I stayed behind.

"Finally, after a year, I gave Baba an ultimatum to give me work five days a week. I didn't care what type of job it was. I would take anything, however simple. A few days later I got a call to be an apartment manager. That was two and a half years ago. I got a job and kept my house. So, I went from a high income to no income. For one year my house was open all day long, while I wasn't working. Finally we had to put a limit on it and have people just come during bhajans. The food has continued to multiply; we even had over five hundred people at Shivarathri.

"So many other things have happened. Infertile couples have been blessed with babies. I have had many visions of Sai Baba, of Shiva and Parvati. There have been healings of cancer and of a brain tumor.

"Another time someone asked me what the difference was between Shirdi Sai and Sathya Sai. I replied that there was no difference. At that moment amrit flowed from the Shirdi Sai and the Sathya Sai pictures simultaneously.

"A certain man from the Sai Organization came here and wanted us to form an affiliated Sai Center since so many people are coming here all the time. We asked Baba inside and He said, "No Center." We were also told by Baba that where the hearts of Center officers and other leaders are contracted there will be no expansion. We are just His instruments. We want no show."

Lita Burgos, a long-time Sai devotee from the Philippines who lives in California, later told us that Ami had been the houseguest of her daughter and son-in-law, Alile and Phillip Brown in San Francisco, the weekend of July 5, 1997. On Saturday morning when Ami was praying to Mother Mary, vibhuti appeared on Her face in a picture there. It also appeared on the face of Jesus, on His eyebrows and beard.

"It was most plentiful on Baba's face and on Mary's face," she said. "A week later another small photo of Baba was discovered to have been producing vibhuti also. Furthermore, when Ami sits in bhajans, vibhuti appears on his body. He doesn't want to make a scene, so he quietly steps into the other room when this happens. When he touched me on the head, red cum-cum powder appeared on my forehead. Vibhuti appears on the head of all he touches. We know this is Baba's doing.

"I can tell you this: I know in my heart that Baba will be profusely giving His powers to the devotees who have been purified and who have fully surrendered their lives to Baba. Therefore I feel that Ami's powers will be increasing the power of Baba's Presence through healing because people can easily relate to other people. This helps people develop faith that God is truly present to all."

We were extremely appreciative to have been given the gift of meeting Ami Mangru and his family and to have experienced the many boons which Baba provided for us during our stay there. We were equally grateful to Lita and her family for the many favors they did for us and for the continual love they extended. How could we have known that Baba was soon to "amp up His leela action" in our own lives, however?

The following list outlines some of the primary blessings which Baba has provided for the Mangru family and for their guests over the years.

Miracles, Manifestations and Healings
The Mangru Family Shrine at Colusa, California

Since 1994 there has been an outpouring of spontaneous spiritual phenomena at the three bedroom ranch-style Colusa home of Ami and Ram Mangru and their three children. The following list is but an attempt to chronicle the continuing blessings of the planetary Avatar, Sri Sathya Sai Baba, as He makes His earthly Presence known in the home of the very fortunate Fijian-Indian family, who have been visited by thousands.

1. Sai Baba's curative vibhuti ash has spontaneously appeared on photos of both Eastern and Western saints and Avatars. Thousands have witnessed this.

2. A small round crystal lingham (sphere/ovoid) materialized and has since enlarged.

3. Water spontaneously appeared on the lingham.

4. Two cups of crystal-faceted rock candy unexpectedly appeared during the wedding ceremony of two Sai devotees, on July 19, 1997. This was witnessed by eleven people. The couple, the wedding party and the Mangru family also witnessed the appearance of vibhuti, amrit and honey during the ceremony.

5. Sandal paste appears on pictures in the home.

6. Amrit cascades from photos and is captured in plastic containers beneath them.

7. Honey flows from pictures of the Sacred Heart of Jesus and the feet of Sai Baba.

8. Water appears in a three-inch tall glass in a hall closet shrine and overflows into bowls and then overflows into other water collectors.

9. Red cum-cum powder (used in Hindu prayer rituals) sprinkles pictures by itself.

10. Holy water spontaneously appears in a small bronze container on the altar.

11. Holy water flows from the head of Lord Shiva in a picture above the altar.

12. Vibhuti appears on Ami's hands periodically.

13. Vibhuti ash as well as red powder appears on the heads of people that Ami touches.

14. It sometimes appears on objects that he touches.

15. Ami has been instrumental in the healing of cancer, brain tumors and other maladies.

16. At least one comatose patient (in a hospital Intensive Care Unit) has been brought out of a coma by God through the instrument of Ami Mangru.

17. A videotape which was taken of the shrine room expressly without permission turned out blank after Ami asked Baba to erase all images recorded.

18. A small brass sandal/footprint about two inches long spontaneously appeared in the water of the hall closet. This symbolizes the sacred foot of the Teacher (or Guru).

19. Food multiplies at the Mangru home (when they serve large crowds each week).

20. Infertile couples have been blessed with pregnancy after singing or praying in the shrine room.

Sai Baba is well-known for all of the above phenomena and announced that after 1985 He would send His Divine powers through His followers throughout the world. This is currently happening. (Unannounced visitors are not received because of heavy family work schedules.)

Johnstown, Colorado
September, 1997

Baba has directed me to take a small group of devotees to India. There will be seven of us going to see Baba.

Puttaparthi, India
October, 1997

Our pilgrimage to the Lord has been eventful in several ways. First, Baba provided the magnanimous grace of giving us two interviews, during the first of which He made a huge diamond ring in a gold setting for Alvin Cook, the husband of my friend Kay and one of the men in our group. In fact, it was at Alvin's first darshan of his life that we were called into the interview room wherein Baba manifested Alvin's ring.

Secondly, our group decided, at the request of Helen Locker, an American devotee with cancer, to undertake group seva for her. We took turns taking her out for short walks, taking her to darshan, and bringing her food and beverages. We also told her Sai stories, jokes and generally tried to cheer her as we packed her belongings for her return to the States to live with her aged mother.

Thirdly, I contracted malaria. There are many stagnant puddles and filthy ponds near the hotels around Puttaparthi which served as a breeding ground for mosquitoes. Although the hospital staff said my blood test showed no malaria parasites, I have been extremely ill in India. Malaria parasites hide in the liver between bouts of chills and fever, thus they are very hard to detect. When I return home, I'll see a doctor and start a vigorous recovery process if I don't recover here.

Johnstown, Colorado
January, 1998

A local physician in Colorado told me that I definitely have malaria. He said there are four main types. He was a malaria specialist in New Guinea for four years. Since my return from India, I have been sufficiently ill that I have been bedridden for months, periodically suffering the chills and fever associated with malaria. The doctor informed me that the parasites hide in the liver and rampage in cycles. Most people are too ill to travel to a doctor during the raging cycle but, instead, seek him out when they feel a bit better. By this time the parasites have resumed their refuge in the liver and do not necessarily show up in blood tests. The situation is as I had thought, unfortunately.

After nearly four months of unabated malarial anguish, I have learned of an unusually gifted Nepalese Sai devotee who is visiting her daughter and son-in-law in Salt Lake City, Utah. Her name is Bharosa Adhikari and she was raised from the dead by Baba on October 6, 1996. I have been very eager to meet her and, since she has spoken with other devotees around the U.S. by phone, she is also interested in meeting me. Thus it has been that our Lord has begun to amp up His healings and miracles and our next adventure begins.

CHAPTER 32
Meeting With a Resurrected Woman

"What is resurrection, really? It is the revelation of the divinity inherent in man. That is the result of contact with the God-head; that can come only after years of contrition, which serves to remove evil from the heart of man." Sathya Sai Baba, SSS VOL III Chap 42, P 216

Johnstown, Colorado
January 7, 1998

There has been a big flurry recently regarding Bharosa Adhikari, from Kathmandu, Nepal, who is visiting her daughter and son-in-law in Salt Lake City, Utah. She has been to Little Rock, Arkansas, to Phoenix, Arizona and elsewhere at the invitation of Sai devotees. Ever since Bharosa was resurrected by Baba a few years ago, when she died of a heart attack in Puttaparthi, amazing things have been happening around her. Numerous people of sound mind and good repute have attested to the wonders.

For one thing, every time she enters the home of a devotee, photos of Baba begin to manifest vibhuti. For another, countless people have been healed by Baba through Bharosa.

On January 12, 1998 I had a most interesting telephone conversation with Rhonda Krieg, an officer of the Phoenix Center. She told me that Bharosa and her husband Ramesh, together with their daughter Sujata, Sujata's husband Sarit, and their children all came to Phoenix while staying with a relative in Tucson, Arizona. Rhonda, who is a chemical engineer, told me that upon Bharosa's visit to Phoenix, vibhuti appeared on a Sai photo there and it continued to accumulate day after day.

Rhonda mentioned that Didi North, a well-known devotee from Montana, visited Bharosa's home in Kathmandu and saw amrit appear from tiny Ganesh pictures. Rhonda's photo of Baba also manifested Sai's ash and vibhuti even appeared on the photo at the photo counter in Price Club!

Bharosa was reputed to be very humble. Upon hearing of the many manifestations around her, I recalled Baba's words, "One's personality blossoms only when one has humility along with knowledge." SS December 1996 P 333

Further, it seems that on December 27th, 1997, phenomena began to occur at Rhonda's house the moment that Ramesh and Bharosa walked in the door. Om symbols appeared on bananas and upon her Sai Baba photo. The next day, after the meeting with Bharosa, Rhonda woke up sobbing and wept for eight hours as a result of the healing of an old experience of grief. A woman named Sherry Dell also wept for hours the next day.

Murali Thirumal of Georgia also told us many unusual and wondrous things about Bharosa's trip to the South. When Bharosa's family and I finally spoke on the phone, she invited me and several friends to visit her at her daughter's house in Salt Lake City. She and I were equally eager to meet each other. At the end of January, 1998, just a few weeks after hearing about the phenomena surrounding Bharosa, we hastily made arrangements to drive to Salt Lake City since we couldn't, at that late date, locate reasonable air fares which everyone in the group could afford.

As we planned our trip to Salt Lake City, I mused on Baba's well-known words about His miracles. "Besides being spontaneous tokens of my love, my so-called miracles are to plant the seed of faith in unbelievers and to foster veneration toward God."

* * * * *

En Route to Salt Lake City, Utah
January 19, 1998

Seven of us were driving to Salt Lake City, Utah from the Loveland, Colorado area in two vans (over icy mountain roads in the snowy month of January) merely on the strength of the reports which I had been hearing for over a month. Bharosa and Ramesh would be staying with Sarit and Sujata Rimal, their son-in-law and daughter, for a few months. As we drove along I told the group again that Bharosa had even figured in the healing of emotions as well as the erasures of addictions, in addition to physical healings. I mentioned that vibhuti appeared on Sai Baba photos which were brought to the Rimal home.

After several telephone conversations with the family I had received an invitation to visit them (and I asked if I might bring my friends) for satsang, singing and to have dinner on Tuesday, January 20th at their home. Thus, at 2:00 P.M. on January 19, 1998, our two white vans (occupied by two men and five women) pulled out of the driveway at Harmony Farm and headed for Salt Lake City, Utah. Our friend Marsh Richards, a new devotee, had generously rented one of the vans and had volunteered to do most of the driving for Rena Phipps, Bonnie Marr and me. My new friend Maria Santo, though not yet a devotee, was very intrigued with Sai phenomena and was a devotee of Mary. My friends John and Trish Free, from Pagosa Springs, had been to India with me a few times and were always ready for a good adventure. Maria would ride in John and Trish's van. Rena Phipps and Bonnie Marr were also new devotees and quite curious about what the trip would provide in the way of healings and miracles.

What were we getting into? What if this venture proved to be unsuccessful, either due to severe weather and closed highways or to exaggerated reports about the healing abilities of Bharosa and the Sai manifestations at her daughter's home and in the homes of others? We realized we were taking a chance with icy roads and a potentially disappointing outcome but decided to surrender our expectations and to consider the trip a mid-winter adventure.

Our ten-and-a-half hour journey was delayed a bit by a blizzard with white-out conditions and road closures but Baba helped us to arrive safely in Salt Lake City. On the way to the hotel we passed a church which had a signboard in the front lawn that said, "Contentment is the power to get out of any situation all there is in it." The next day we were in high spirits as we followed our written directions to the Rimal home.

Salt Lake City, Utah
January 19, 1998

Since we wanted to bring some flowers and fruit for Bharosa's altar, we drove to a florist and a grocery store before going to the Rimals. Next to the flower shop there was a pick-up truck which bore a bumper sticker which said: "The wildest colts make the best horses." I felt that the bumper sticker message had something to do with Bharosa's husband, Ramesh, whom we'd be meeting within the hour.

After purchasing some flowers for the family altar, we arrived about 2:30 and were warmly welcomed by Ramesh and Bharosa, their daughter, Sujata, and by Sarit, their ebullient travel agent son-in-law. We introduced ourselves in the living room, then we were ushered into the tiny six-by-nine foot prayer room, beside the kitchen, which consisted of a low cloth-covered altar and dozens of photos of Sai Baba.

There was a chair for Sai Baba which was covered with a growing pile of manifested vibhuti ash that was so profuse that it fell into a nine-inch-wide container at the foot of the chair. Red vermilion powder covered other pictures and turmeric powder also lay on the altar.

We immediately placed our giant bag of fruit (vivid green pears, mottled red apples, and clear yellow bananas) on a tray on the floor in front of the altar, then sat down and sang about seven or eight devotional songs together. The vibrations of the prayer room were electric and most of us in the group of seven felt as if our heart chakras were being significantly expanded.

About twenty-five minutes later, as we arose to leave the prayer room in order to join the family in the living room, I noticed something on the sleeveless multi-colored sweater worn by Maria Santo. There was a three-inch wide spot of vibhuti on the left shoulder, over the lung area.

"Look! Maria, there's vibhuti on the back of your sweater!" I exclaimed. "Oh, thank You, Swami!" We all gathered around and I suggested that we take photos of the vibhuti while it was still fresh and undisturbed. After doing so, we went to the living room and sat down to listen to Ramesh tell Sai miracle stories and to drink Indian chai prepared by Sujata. Bharosa (and I) smelled a sacred fragrance; Bharosa, who didn't speak English, indicated that we should go into the prayer room because something may have happened. Whenever she smells a sacred fragrance such as jasmine, sandalwood or vibhuti, it is an indication that something has materialized in the prayer room. As we hurried through the kitchen and approached the altar in the kitchen alcove prayer room, we saw that brown Om symbols had been incised into the pears and bananas about 3:00 P.M. The symbols were about an inch and a half high and looked as if someone had used a wood-burning tool to create the Om. In fact, the entire group of about 23, which by now included ten local devotees, were gathered in the living room when the manifestation occurred in the prayer room on the other side of the kitchen. Human hands had not touched the fruit.

The Story of Bharosa Adhikari and Ramesh Nepali

Ramesh showed us photos of the manifestations which had taken place in their home in Nepal and talked to us for two hours. Bharosa, who has been a long-time Sai devotee and who now does healing as a service for Baba, has had a remarkable life. As a child of nine she was playing outside at a place near her home which was coincidentally the birthplace of Lord Buddha. At the time the area was under authoritarian government rule, which made the following event especially interesting.

As nine-year-old Bharosa scampered about, a small whirlwind which we call a mini-cyclone or "dust devil," arose nearby. Instead of running away from it, she ran directly into the center of the vortex. Her arms were outstretched and into them plopped, to her astonishment, a lovely carved trimurthi or three-faced statuette of goddesses Durga, Lakshmi and Saraswathi! Excited, she ran home with the new statue, only to be rebuked soundly by her parents. Naturally they assumed that their playful child had appropriated it from one of the temples, so they were eager to return it to the proper authorities. The statue was gratefully received by the government and placed in a shrine at a nearby orphanage at the birthplace of Gautama Buddha.

Many years later when Ramesh first saw Bharosa at her parent's home, he fell in love and they later married. In the great drama which is called life, while Bharosa was under the spell of God, however, Ramesh was under the spell of alcohol for dozens of years. For this reason, he says, he was unable to take his wife's spiritual experiences and Sai Baba's manifestations seriously. He ignored the phenomena in his own home and was meanwhile busy and productive for twenty-seven years primarily as a pioneer for the installation of Nepal's telecommunications industry.

Ramesh reports that he was so hostile to Baba that once he even threw Baba's photo down and that he doubted that the phenomena was genuine. Bharosa suffered for twenty-six years with his drinking and his attitudes toward her and toward Sai. Then hard times arrived, concealing blessings as they always do. In 1992 Ramesh no longer had a job; he had been fired. He had no money and Bharosa wanted to travel to India to see Sai Baba. Funds for a journey were provided and Bharosa went to India with a group of Shiva devotees for whom the trip was quite eventful.

One day in darshan a woman next to Bharosa began to scratch and pick at Bharosa's clothing. As Bharosa glanced down in slight annoyance and surprise, she saw that vibhuti ash had appeared on her sari and that the woman was helping herself to some ash. The next day the group was blessed with an interview with Sai. During the interview Baba took Bharosa's hand and placed her beside Him. During this brief period, Sai showed a very playful side of His Divinity and teased and made pinching gestures, like a schoolboy. Baba will sometimes be extremely light and playful with people who have successfully endured long trials and grueling tribulations.

Sai instructed Bharosa to visit her daughter in America. "Your daughter is a good devotee," He remarked.

"But we have no money, Baba," Bharosa replied.

"It will be arranged," Sai replied. "What is your husband doing? He is drinking."

Ramesh, with eyes twinkling, said, "At that very moment I was at a family dinner having a drink with relatives." Shortly thereafter their son-in-law, Sarit, arrived in Nepal with money for two airline tickets for Ramesh and Bharosa to go to the U.S. to see their daughter. Thus, through Sarit, Baba provided the funds for them to carry out His directive to go to the U.S.

Sai not only provided for their needs monetarily, but finally brought Ramesh out of his addicted trance and into a conscious life of devotion. But it apparently wasn't easy, according to Ramesh, who told us that he had steadfastly refused to attend devotional singing either outside or inside his home. Once, when he was inebriated, an insistent person came to their home and insisted that devotional singing should take place. Ramesh replied that the home was not a sacred place as he drank there. But devotional singing took place nevertheless. Vibhuti appeared. Bharosa took (tipsy) Ramesh's hand and rubbed it in the vibhuti to make an impression on him. He merely replied, in his stupor, "Huh! That's not much!"

Later, the sacred ash appeared on many photos throughout the night. But Ramesh told us that he was still resistant. "Huh! It only happens on Sai Baba photos. Not good," he snorted derisively. "After that it appeared on Shirdi Sai Baba's photos (the previous incarnation of Sathya Sai Baba). I have three married daughters and a son. After all this, my youngest daughter wanted to have some vibhuti manifest. It came. Then more and more vibhuti appeared on my bed cover. Next amrit nectar came on our photo from Japan where gold dust had appeared. After that, a deep pile of vibhuti ash appeared on my floor!"

Ramesh related that as the manifestations began to proliferate he created his own worship ritual and began to read about Sai Baba. Daily he and Bharosa did pujas or spiritual rituals. And daily there were manifestations.

Eventually Ramesh and Bharosa discerned that there had been three main phases of phenomena and blessings:

The First Phase involved vibhuti ash appearing on photos and on surfaces in the house.

The Second Phase, which lasted for six months, entailed simultaneous manifestations of ash, amrit nectar, turmeric powder and vermilion cum-cum powder.

By the Third Phase Bharosa had begun to receive the gift of sacred fragrances when there was a manifestation of a spiritual phenomenon elsewhere in the house. This was a playful indication from Baba and was a sign to begin searching until it was found. Statuettes and other objects began manifesting in the last phase.

For example, on one Shivarathri day Ramesh received a manifested four-faced Shiva lingham (stone egg) about two inches long. After fifteen minutes a powerful fragrance or, as Ramesh calls it, a "deep smell," pervaded the room. They ran to the basement prayer room and there noticed a most strange sight. There, on the chair which they kept for Sai Baba, was seen a large ball; a yellow triangle was striking the ball. This lasted for twenty-five to thirty seconds. Finally, an eighteen-inch statue of Shiva appeared. This ardhanara shor, or statuette, was made of black iron. (Over about a two-year period, the black statue turned to gold, vibhuti ash appeared on it and human hair began to grow out of its head!) Later, another sacred fragrance alerted the couple to more developments whereupon they discovered that a rudraksha rosary had appeared around the Shiva statue.

In order that Ramesh and Bharosa might know how to proceed with the caretaking of the extraordinary statue, a Ms. Parveg Murghelia appeared on the scene from Bombay. She instructed them in the Hindu worship protocol: "Pour water on the Shiva statue while chanting the Sai Gayatri Mantra."

When Ramesh obeyed the instructions he was startled that white liquid streams flowed over his hands. At first he thought the statue was melting. But no, he realized that the water had turned to milk! Next, without his comprehending it quickly enough, the marble streams turned to flowing white marble, which he tried to drink. As he sank his teeth into the snowy "streams" he nearly broke them... in pain and perplexity. As he sprang back, the marble then returned to milk. "Quick," he shouted to Bharosa, "Bring a bowl or something to hold this statue and the milk."

After they cleaned up the area and installed the newly manifested statue in the prayer room, Ramesh went to his room and wept. But that was not the end of the water-into milk miracle. For sixty-two days the prayer ritual water turned into milk and Ramesh fed thousands from it. At the conclusion of the ritual, yogurt appeared for Ramesh to ingest. Meanwhile, the two-inch lingham "grew" to about seven inches in length.

A Message of Correction From Baba

One day Bharosa was given a message for Ramesh from Sai. "Baba told me the milk will stop," she reported to Ramesh. In response Ramesh pleaded with Baba, "I have been corrected. I have gone down the wrong path. Be kind to me." Ramesh said the 108 Names of God with 108 flowers as an offering during the lingham ritual. Then, to his utter astonishment, nectar began to appear. A rose and other flowers "jumped up on the lingham." The ceremonial flowers continued to "jump up" on the lingham for four years during the daily worship. The Shiva statue slowly turned from iron to gold.

On May 6th at 4:00, the day honoring the Holy Mother, a six-inch, cum-cum covered silver statue of Goddess Bhagavati appeared on the altar. Two tiny two-inch silver avatar sandals appeared, then abruptly began "walking" to and fro around the Bhagavati statue, leaving footprints in the red cum-cum powder that had covered the area.

Every day when Ramesh placed flowers on Baba's chair, vibhuti appeared. As flowers were placed in the prayer room, ash manifested on them.

As if all of this were not blessing enough, Baba's hand prints appeared on a purple cloth. Then His footprints came forth as well.

When Ramesh went to see Sai in India he was given a spectacular gold-domed ring with a picture of Krishna inside, during an interview, which is detailed in the next section.

Once, while cleaning his plate of vibhuti ash, a six-inch Om symbol appeared. The second day he received a cross imprinted in vibhuti, then later there appeared a moon and a sarva dharma symbol or the representation of the unity of all faiths.

Another time when Ramesh was corrected by Baba he was at home in his prayer room. He received a written message from Sai in turmeric powder on a prayer room tray. "Baba, ke pas ao." Translated, it said, "Come to Puttaparthi. Baba"

Much Is Given and Much Is Expected

Within a short time Bharosa and Ramesh were to learn that a new chapter was beginning for them and that what Baba was to ask of them would not always be easy. After they arrived in India, Ramesh began to beg for an interview, like the many others present in darshan. When the request was granted, Baba called the group into His interview room and manifested objects for those present in the other three groups who had also been called.

The fourth group, of which the Nepalis were members, were finally taken in to the adjoining room for a smaller group meeting whereupon Baba teased Ramesh, who was frustrated and eager to know if he was taking proper care of all the manifested objects that Baba had caused to appear in his home in Nepal.

Playfully, in reply to Ramesh's question, Baba asked, "Do you have gas?!"

By this time Ramesh was beside himself with impatience and frustration. He replied, "No. Please tell me. Am I taking proper care of these objects?!"

Baba took compassion on him and fondly patted his shoulder, whereupon Ramesh felt a cool breeze on the shoulder and in his body.

"Please guide me, Baba," he begged.

"Yes," replied Baba, "I will guide you. I am in you, around you. I will guide you all the time. Do you have any friends?"

Ramesh: "No."

"Alright," Baba said, "Make Me your friend. How much did you pay for that ring?"

Ramesh answered that he had paid about two rupees for a simple ring on his hand.

"I will make you a very beautiful ring of Krishna," Baba announced. He then effortlessly produced a domed gold locket ring that opens to reveal a charming picture of the face of young Krishna.

To Bharosa, Sai next gave the gift of healing those people whom He'd send to her. He told Bharosa three times that "healing is a public welfare job that you have to do." Since then countless people have sought all types of healing and balance - spiritual, mental, emotional and physical - from Bharosa. Baba indicated that Ramesh wasn't quite ready at the time for his eventual healing role.

During his long period of unemployment Ramesh occupied himself by selling small articles from a small storehouse of wares near his home. When it appeared that someone had set fire to his small storehouse, neighbors actually ridiculed and derided Ramesh as it burned. One of the unusual but heartening circumstances which took place at this time was the appearance of a message from Baba on the tray of "yellow vibhuti" or turmeric powder which rested on the altar of the prayer room. It came at just the right time and said, "Don't worry, Baba is with you."

One of the most unique of the dozens of phenomena surrounding the Nepali family is that of butter appearing at the mouth of a Krishna statue. As readers may recall from Hindu lore and literature, young Krishna vexed his mother by eating butter whenever she wasn't looking. He is remembered in countless songs as the "adorable little butter thief and stealer of hearts."

Ramesh fed over seven hundred people from the materialized butter which increased after it had appeared for three days. There are many possible interpretations of each of the materializations, most of which would probably be centered around trusting God to provide for one's well-being in all matters.

Baba's Midnight Talks

Baba often comes at midnight and speaks with Bharosa. He blesses all in the house and specifically blesses each room there.

Cooking Without Fuel

Once when Bharosa was cooking a meal she found that she was without kerosene. Baba still allowed the stove to function as if it had a ready supply of fuel. Sai graces the Nepali family with many favors.

Rings

For Bharosa's daughter Sujata, a square black onyx ring in a gold setting appeared with no explanation. Bharosa was given a gold ring depicting a watch whereon the hands say 10:10, the exact time that she left on a Singapore-Nepal flight.

Resurrection From the Dead

There is one grace, the most spectacular of all, in the minds of many. It is the fact that while the Nepalis were on a visit to Puttaparthi, South India, Bharosa fell ill and had to be taken to the Sathya Sai Baba Superspecialty Hospital there. While in the hospital she expired on October 3, 1995. Naturally Ramesh was overcome with grief. He and the physician filled out the death certificate. After she had been confirmed "deceased" for forty-five minutes, the corpse sat up... alive!

As Ramesh spoke, we sat on various sofas and chairs in his daughter's living room. We were enthralled. He spoke very fast, showing us photos from a small album to illustrate various incidents. Since this was the first "Sai miracle experience" for most of our group of seven, their mouths were nearly hanging open in astonishment.

After awhile, I remarked that I smelled another sacred fragrance so we hurried into the prayer room again and saw that vibhuti had appeared on the oranges and upon the altar cloth and on the eight by ten inch photo of Baba's feet and on three other photos I had brought. Ash also speckled photos that had been brought by others. We whooped in appreciation and returned to the living room to continue the stories by Ramesh.

The number and type of manifestations which have taken place in the Adhikari family home for thirty-one years is staggering. A partial list follows:

1. Baba has written scores of messages in yellow turmeric powder about a third of an inch thick which rests on a small tray. The family jokingly refers to this as Baba's divine fax.

2. Vibhuti manifests on photos.

3. People have been healed both emotionally and physically by Baba through Bharosa.

4. Statues have appeared.

5. A tiny pair of silver sandals (a few inches in length) appeared and walked around the silver statue unassisted.

6. Baba's hand prints have appeared on pieces of cloth.

7. Baba speaks locutionally to Bharosa.

8. Rupee notes appear on the street as Bharosa is walking outside.

9. Ramesh was healed of drinking.

10. Amrit nectar has appeared on photos.

11. Sacred fragrances appear.

12. Turmeric powder dusts photos.

13. Vermilion powder sprays statues and photos.

14. During a worship ceremony, water poured onto a statue turned into milk, then yogurt, then marble!

15. An iron statue turned to gold.

16. Flowers "jump" from the prayer table onto a small two-inch lingham (stone egg that represents the cosmic womb of creation).

17. Baba writes sacred symbols in vibhuti ash or other powders on the prayer table: an Om, a cross, a sarva dharma symbol (symbol of the unity and sanctity of all religions).

18. Once Baba helped Bharosa cook a meal when she was out of kerosene for the stove.

19. Rings and precious stones have appeared for the family members.

20. So many phenomena have taken place in the home that such events are now considered by the family to be regular occurrences.

21. Great quantities of butter, which fed seven hundred people, appeared on a Krishna statue, which was manifested by Baba.

22. Sai manifested one large diamond and two small ones, for Bharosa and her grand-daughter, respectively.

After our minds had been boggled by Ramesh's divulgences, I glanced down and noticed that a cluster of vibhuti ash had appeared on the right knee of my slacks. Trish Free had noticed a dusting of vibhuti on her Sai medallion and others in our group, John Free, Rena Phipps and Bonnie Marr, all experienced a dusting of the light gray holy ash on their chests in the vicinity of the heart chakra.

Maria and John were given a healing by Baba, via Bharosa, on the evening of January 20th. Maria wept several times during the evening. (The next day a Sikh from Salt Lake named Mr. Singh, received a healing of his poor night vision after he returned to Bharosa.) Toward the end of the evening, the two dozen people re-arranged themselves cross-legged on the floor for extremely soulful devotional singing after which a lovely Indian vegetarian meal was served to all present. I was deeply touched by the copious weeping of various devotees and remembered that Ovid had said, "It is some relief to weep; grief is satisfied and carried off by tears."

But I was also keenly aware, from having studied and practiced advaita, or witness-consciousness, that most humans are addicted to negative as well as positive emotions. If one is not observing his thoughts and feelings, then he will continually be reacting to life circumstances, from misidentification with the body, mind and emotions, and reeling from pain and grief at every turn. Recently, I have been observing my own heart pains and periodic malaria symptoms while remaining in the deepest peace. My happiness is not dependent upon my circumstances, this I know for certain.

As we left we were given fruit upon which Om symbols had appeared and our vibhuti-covered photos which we placed in plastic zip-lock bags or a magazine. Baba had once again overwhelmed us with His grace, a most memorable satsang and miraculous manifestations.

A Brief Chronicle of the Personal Experiences of Our Group at the Rimal Home:

Marsh Richards (new Sai devotee; cattle broker; healer; first "Sai miracles")

1. All three photos which he had brought manifested vibhuti.
2. Tears of gratitude trickled down his cheeks as he realized that Baba had blessed his photos with vibhuti. Marsh doesn't weep easily.
3. A sense of deep calm, openness and amazement came over him in the prayer room alcove and in the living room.
4. Marsh felt a sense of oneness with everyone in the house, though most of the people there were strangers to us and were from different cultures and religions (Hindus, Sikhs, Hari Krishnas, etc.)

Maria Santo (non-devotee - a bit skeptical; many ailments; though from Spain, lived in the Philippines during WW II and is settled in the U.S.; art collector; Mother Mary study group coordinator.)

1. Received sacred vibhuti ash on the back of her sweater (left shoulder, over the lung) very early in the afternoon.
2. Years ago, when she had been in a coma for six months, the oxygen she was given harmed her hearing and her lungs. Her hearing seems to have improved, according to John and Trish, and she didn't pant as much on Tuesday as she had during the previous day.
3. Maria was given a healing by Bharosa who told her that for three days she would have much pain, then the pain would be gone for good.
4. Her foot and back were hurting the three days after the trip.

John Free (retired Air Force Colonel; author of a book on dreams; college level psychology professor; had two brief trips to India)

1. Received a laying on of hands by Bharosa. He felt a vibration at the time that Bharosa's hands were placed on his shoulders, chest and abdomen.

2. Was visibly touched by the experience of being in the atmosphere of singing and vibhuti manifestations.

3. Received vibhuti ash on his black turtle neck sweater in the area of the heart.

4. Felt the earth shaking, as if a quake were taking place. (Kundalini energy?)

5. Experienced a tremendous sense of peace and well-being during the singing in the prayer room.

6. The next day he drove eleven hours straight from Salt Lake City without asking for driving relief. John is 71 years old.

7. Three small photos developed vibhuti.

8. An empty film case developed a sprinkling of vibhuti on the top.

9. Bharosa gave a small vibhuti packet to John and Trish and asked them to eat it.

10. Ash appeared on John's ring on his right hand ring finger.

11. One week later, at a routine blood pressure check-up with his physician, John learned that his blood pressure was much lower than usual and that his arrhythmia, or irregular heartbeat, was no longer present.

Trish Free (co-author of a dream book with her husband; healer; had taken two brief trips to India)

1. Vibhuti ash appeared on her photos.

2. Received vibhuti ash on her Sai Baba medallion inside her turtle neck sweater as her throat felt hot. She has a thyroid problem. Bharosa was gazing at Trish at this time.

3. Dreamed that night that her aged mother would be leaving the body soon.

4. Was deeply touched to see vibhuti ash on so many photos and on the fruit at the altar.

5. As Ramesh spoke to Maria, Trish began to weep with compassion for Maria, who had been aloof, detached and skeptical.

6. Trish felt very despondent after leaving the house and asked for a teaching dream, which she received about her mother.

7. Her third eye area turned red for awhile.

8. She was amazed that Oms began to appear on the bananas in our hands before we even sat down in the prayer room.

9. She smelled a sweet smell, like roses, at least five or six times.

Rena Phipps (healer; former cattle rancher; retired teacher; new Sai devotee; first "Sai manifestations")

1. Felt energy expand her heart chakra and move to third eye region of forehead.
2. She wept twice, as if she were experiencing a healing crisis.
3. Vibhuti ash appeared on her black pin-striped jacket in the region of the heart chakra.
4. Fruit which she had purchased and brought to the gathering developed Om symbols and vibhuti ash.
5. Sacred ash appeared on the well-known "Lingham Photo" of Sai Baba which she had placed in the prayer room.

Bonnie Marr (retired bookkeeper/secretary; healer; new Sai devotee)

1. Felt as if she had levitated while sitting on the floor of the prayer room in a cross-legged position. (She had not, however.)
2. Sacred ash appeared on the Lingham Photo which she had placed at the front of a tray on the alter.
3. A scattering of vibhuti ash appeared on her turquoise blouse in the area of the heart chakra.
4. She smelled the fragrance of vibhuti periodically while we were there from 2:30 P.M. until 7:00 P.M.
5. Although she was energized while we were visiting the Rimal family, she has experienced extreme fatigue and a headache since the trip. (She has had diabetes; perhaps this is a healing crisis.)
6. She has been feeling "weepy" since her return and feels she is processing at a deep level.
7. There is a tightness from her heart to her throat chakra.

Since the trip, Bonnie has seen Baba moving in His photos nearly every time she sees a picture of Baba. This started January 27th, a week after the trip. Next, on January 29th she saw a green aura around Baba's head in a large photo of Baba that is kept in our Sai Center meeting room.

Connie Shaw:

1. Sacred ash appeared on her right trouser leg at the knee-thigh area.
2. She smelled sacred fragrances throughout the day.
3. Oms appeared on the bananas as she traversed the kitchen on the way to the prayer room.
4. Fragrant ash sprinkled across the four photos she had placed on the altar.
5. She was given a packet of vibhuti by Bharosa to eat.

6. She felt, in the prayer room, as if she were levitating but was not, in fact.

7. She felt as if her heart chakra were expanding.

8. A deep feeling of peace and oneness pervaded her being all day, even before arrival at the house.

While the group was proceeding from a local restaurant to the Rimal home, she got out of the van to buy flowers for the altar. On the way to the florist she saw a handicapped man in a wheelchair at the traffic light of a busy city intersection. She heard Baba say, "I know you are running late, but please help that man. He is confused, his hands are freezing and deformed and he can't pull his gloves on." She went over to him, helped put on his gloves which were clipped to his wheelchair arms, and pushed the wheelchair to a shop near the florist which was his destination. As Connie looked into the man's eyes she felt, "This is my Self, manifesting as this handicapped brother."

Every member of the group was deeply appreciative to Baba and to Bharosa, Ramesh, Sarit and Sujata for their love, hospitality, lovely vegetarian meal, solace, informative sharing of experiences and enthusiastic devotional singing. Our time together was eventful and thrilling and we all felt changed in ways that are still difficult to describe in the limited language which is English. Our visit to the sacred precinct of their prayer room is a treasured memory and perhaps a turning point for many, if not all of our group.

After returning home the group members continued to experience deeper emotional and physical healings. On Sunday night following the trip to Salt Lake City three of us gave presentations to our Sai Center about the profuse healings and Sai phenomena which had taken place in the Rimal home. We were unprepared for the response of the audience: they decided, nearly to a man, to leave for Salt Lake City within the next several days! Thus it was that three of the seven members of the group returned almost immediately - plus seventeen others (including three from New Mexico, one from Nebraska and two from Texas). Considering that we had been graced beyond all belief on January 20th and had experienced a riveting reception to our talks on January 25th, what on earth might transpire on January 31st on our return trip with three times the crowd?

CHAPTER 33
MORE SALT LAKE SURPRISES

"The mind is the cause of both bondage and liberation. It is only by controlling the mind that man can achieve liberation."
Sathya Sai Baba, SS July 1994, P 169

Salt Lake City, Utah
January 19, 1998

Baba had more surprises in store for us after the first visit to Salt Lake City. Many of the twenty in the next group left for Salt Lake only five days after Rena, Bonnie and I gave short presentations about our adventures at our Sai Baba Center. Devotees and non-devotees alike came from Texas, Colorado, New Mexico and Nebraska to have healings with Bharosa and to sing devotional songs with Sarit, Sujata, Ramesh and Bharosa.

We were a jolly group, as usual, when going on any sort of pilgrimage, and shared Sai stories, Baba's maxims, humorous events of recent weeks and Sai's teachings. Just before we left I had received a lovely letter from my dear friend Deirdre West who is a British Sai devotee working with lepers in Baba's Whitefield Hospital. She sent me a quotation of Baba's that was concise and touching:

"Money can buy a bed, but not sleep.
Money can buy a book, but not brains.
Money can buy food, but not an appetite.
Money can buy clothes, but not beauty.
Money can buy a house, but not a home.
Money can buy medicines, but not health.
Money can buy luxuries, but not happiness.
Money can buy a crucifix, but not heaven.
Money can buy a temple, but not God."

For the second trip, there were eight from Colorado and one person from Nebraska who took the one hour and twenty minute Frontier Airlines flight together. Several other carloads arrived at the Rimal's yellow shingled house on Saturday night with high expectations. In addition to our twenty friends, there were Kristine and Glen Johnson from Bluffdale, south of Salt Lake City, Craig Lewis from Austin, Texas, and Bob Cunningham and Phil Roland from Salt Lake City. About thirty people were present as we sat on available sofas and floor cushions. People had physical, emotional and relationship needs. Most of those assembled were healers of one sort or another and were burnt out after years of helping, serving, healing without let-up. Now the healers needed healing. This sweet collection of humanity knew the meaning of Baba's many statements on service. For example, "When I say devotees should do selfless service to humanity as a way of serving God, it is only in your interest and for your spiritual uplift. SS January, 1999 P 20   God is the Doer and doesn't need our help. Through service we learn detachment, surrender and humility.

Baba's Message to Us

After everyone was seated that Saturday night shortly after 8:00 P.M., I thanked the Rimal and Nepali families for inviting us to come again and told the group that Sarit had shared some tremendous news the previous day on the phone. When he and the other family members went into the prayer room on Friday, they had two surprises awaiting them. An empty cut glass bowl was filled with about a pound of vivid yellow-orange turmeric powder. Furthermore, on the altar tray of turmeric powder there was a most intriguing message in Hindi from Baba:

"Give my love to all. Do a nice puja (on Sunday for Nepali Spring). Feed everyone and heal everyone. Love, Baba."

"This group you are bringing is very, very fortunate," Sarit had said. "We were all so excited when we saw the turmeric in the bowl and when we read Baba's message. So, we will see what happens on Saturday night during the healings and on Sunday during the singing and the puja (ceremony)."

Immediate Manifestations

After removing our shoes and coats in the front hallway, we brought gifts of candles, incense and fruit to celebrate Nepali Spring, February 1st. As we filed through the living room and passed through the kitchen into the prayer room, Oms began to form on the bananas held by Carol Meyerowitz. I placed eight wallet sized unframed Sai lingham photos in front of Baba's chair on a red velvet runner that lay on the floor. Within minutes vibhuti formed across the photos and on a small wooden box I had brought, and ash sprayed the framed photos brought by our group.

Vibhuti Inside Envelopes

When Bharosa placed the gifts I had brought to her at the altar, she also put my thank you note there as well. About five minutes later she indicated that she had a feeling that maybe something had appeared in the envelope. I looked inside and saw to my utter amazement that vibhuti had filled up the envelope and had adhered over the word "Thank" on the front of the note, obscuring it. Someone else placed a prayer request in an envelope at the altar and later found that it, too, was covered with ash, inside the envelope.

Baba says that "Vibhuti is the most precious object in a truly spiritual sense (as it represents the burning of desires that agitate the mind and cause confusion)."

As we sat in the living room, we made lists of healing requests of Baba on small scraps of paper. A short time later, Sarit announced that his mother-in-law, Bharosa, would begin the healings one at a time. They took me into the prayer room first and gestured to a dinette chair in which I was to sit. Then Bharosa asked me to lean back and keep my eyes open as she poured rice water into them. She then placed her hands on my chest, abdomen, back, arms and legs. The session lasted about five or six minutes. I felt deeply moved and appreciative.

Healing of a Long-Term Back Injury

The next morning at 6:30 A.M., I experienced two dramatic and unexpected healings as I lay in bed. All of my cells began to stir and to vibrate at once, as if they were being purified in an accelerated way. Next, energy moved up the spine and five fused vertebrae unclicked painlessly by themselves as if I were having an etheric chiropractic adjustment. There was no pain. This was especially interesting to me since I had forgotten to list the fused vertebrae in my prayer request the night before. The back injury had occurred when I was twelve years old and had, seemingly by a mere fluke of luck, saved a friend's life.

At the time I was living in Frankfurt, Germany with my parents and siblings. On the day in question there were about half a dozen kids playing under an old thirty-foot high cherry tree next door. I was picking up cherries on my hands and knees when Jackie, a few years younger, suddenly screamed from high up in the cherry tree, which we were all forbidden to climb. She torpedoed head-first, down through the branches and landed on my spine, knocking us both unconscious, and sending us both by ambulance to the hospital for a few days.

When we eventually woke up in the hospital, she had a headache and was sharply rebuked for having climbed the forbidden cherry tree. I was informed that, although my presence had saved Jackie's life, five of my vertebrae had been fused together, causing one leg to become temporarily slightly shorter than the other. In addition, I now had scoliosis of the spine, and would have to wear corrective shoes. Further, it would now be necessary for me to go to physical therapy to learn how to pick up marbles and pencils with my toes in order to correct damage done to my feet and legs. A year later I developed severe allergies and asthma due to poor circulation in the area of the back injury.

Many years later, as I now contemplated the sunrise in Salt Lake City, while lying in bed at my host's home, a spinal healing spontaneously occurred as a result of Bharosa's loving healing touch the night before.

An Eventful Saturday Night

On Saturday night after we had assembled in the living room, Bharosa took the women one-by-one into the prayer room for healings. Ramesh showed the group some photos of the manifestations which had occurred over the past few decades at the Nepali home in Kathmandu. People would emerge from their ten-minute healing with Bharosa and would alternately smile broadly or weep - or announce that a particular painful condition had vanished. The very air in the living room and the prayer room was charged with expectation, love, gratitude and joy.

Bharosa's Resurrection In Detail

Since we had learned, about two months prior to our Utah visits, that Bharosa had been resurrected by Baba, I had wanted to hear about the experience in greater detail. Ramesh was kind enough to supply details and to answer all of my questions as Bharosa was doing healings. On October 3, 1995, as was mentioned earlier, Bharosa had a heart attack at the Abode of Peace in the women's section of the open-air Mandir temple area during devotional singing.

On the men's side of the darshan hall, Baba stopped in His rounds to speak to a Dr. Ayer. Ramesh, who saw this exchange but was unaware of Bharosa's situation, was wishing that Baba would come and speak to him also. But Baba glanced at Ramesh and glided by without speaking.

When Bharosa later went to the hospital the same Dr. Ayer was there, weeping, saying, "Baba sent me to the hospital, asking, 'Where is daughter Bharosa?'" Sai had in fact sent Dr. Ayer to the General Hospital to attend to Bharosa, who took a turn for the worse there. Finally, Bharosa was rushed to the Super Specialty Hospital on the outskirts of Puttaparthi.

Heart Surgery and Death

By 11:00 A.M. Bharosa was undergoing heart surgery. Suddenly, her vital signs stopped. "She's no longer with us," the doctor announced sorrowfully." The heart pump was tried. No response. Finally they laid the body on the floor and chanted Om Sai Ram. The death certificate was signed by Ramesh and by the doctor who instructed Ramesh to remove the body as it couldn't be kept there.

Meanwhile, what was transpiring for Bharosa on "the Other Side?" "As soon as she went out of her body," Ramesh intoned seriously, "dark entities from the astral realm swooped upon her in a vicious attack in which they began, in another realm or loka, to beat her etheric body." Naturally she was terrified and began to doubt the value of having dedicated her entire life to Baba since she was now alone in defending herself at the moment of expiration.

Super-Baba to the Rescue

Just then she saw snow falling and noticed a small red dot in the center of the snowfall. It grew larger quickly and suddenly Baba was there in His red silk gown instructing Bharosa to open her mouth. He then sent a yellow flame arching from His Divine mouth to hers and took her swiftly by the hand to another loka for safety. There they came before a man who was flipping the pages of a large registration book. There were about ten or twelve people in the area as Baba signed a paper that released Bharosa to return with Baba to her body back on earth in Puttaparthi. Baba gave her etheric finger an injection which manifested as a hole in her physical finger upon her return to the body. Before returning Bharosa to her body, Baba told her that He was removing her karma and extending her life. But there would be three conditions which she would have to endure in order to receive the restoration and life-extension:

1. She would henceforth have diabetes.
2. She would have high blood pressure and would have to be careful not to overstress her heart.
3. She would become a world-famous healer.

After-Effects of Dying

The ordeal of the heart attack, the departure from the body and the attack by the dark forces before her rescue, had had such a devastating effect on Bharosa both physically and emotionally that she couldn't speak for 26 hours after being resurrected. Perhaps there was yet some karma to be erased, as well as an enormous service of healing on a massive scale yet to be enacted. Bharosa has high blood pressure and diabetes now and often becomes so exhausted from the healing sessions that she must rest in bed for a day or two, in order to recover enough afterwards to perform daily household functions. On average, about a hundred people come to her home in Nepal each morning and a hundred each evening, seven days a week. That's fourteen hundred people a week or fifty-six hundred a month!

Ramesh also related that an interesting thing had taken place one time when Bharosa had vowed not to eat meat. She slipped and ate it one day and immediately became sick. As she was returning from the bathroom, after having vomited, she looked down and saw that her body was covered with vibhuti. Ramesh mentioned that when Baba corrects either of them, He usually follows the correction with a loving treat to soften the chastisement.

Healings Galore

In the Rimal living room in Salt Lake City more and more people emerged from their healing sessions to report to the group what had transpired or to weep quietly into their hankies on the sofa. Since the healings and manifestations were so profuse and on-going, we'll list the ones of which we are currently aware:

1. Connie Shaw: Experienced the vanishing of "black dot floaters" in her eyes; healing of fused vertebrae; an emotional healing; a financial healing. Upon unpacking her luggage from the trip, Connie discovered that two pieces of fruit given to her by Bharosa's family, a pear and a banana, had developed Om symbols.
2. Donna Kuczek: Her lungs cleared and a chronic cough has lessened. Her wheeze is gone.
3. Sheryl Mack: She had sustained a broken jaw from being mugged and robbed. As a result, she couldn't move her head and had carpal tunnel syndrome in the right arm. Both conditions seem to have cleared immediately.

4. Barbara Verde: Her stiff neck and shoulder were relieved and she has received the confidence she prayed, to immediately begin a new practice of Healing Touch right away in Santa Fe, New Mexico. She did begin a healing practice shortly thereafter.

5. Bob Cunningham: He had placed small bottles of essential oils and Bach Flower Remedies on the alter; vibhuti appeared on them. Bob served the group by tirelessly offering acupressure throughout the weekend. His stamina was staggering.

6. Jo Whit: Her liver cancer surgery was postponed.

7. Bonnie Marr: Wondered if her diabetes had been healed. She experienced more energy.

8. Rena Phipps: Wept at an inexplicable emotional release. She had been widowed a few years prior to the trip and had recently remarried.

9. Nana Rios: Had a spiritual healing and experienced more confidence about spiritual values and her mission on earth.

10. Manny Rios: Asked for spiritual strength to do his life's mission of service and to be less attached to material things.

11. Mary Toro: Received a healing of pain in her fingers and palms. Vibhuti formed on her photo as she watched.

12. Forest Phipps: Experienced a health improvement.

13. Josie Regal: Stopped smoking.

14. Craig Lewis: Felt new energy surges.

15. Sam George: Felt very ebullient and energized.

16. Lanny Wills: Felt positive energy.

17. Sheila Jones: Received a release of life-long neck and shoulder tension from a traumatic birth which was said to be brought over from a past life. She felt supported as a healer to see Bharosa work with others so simply, confidently and humbly. Sheila was told, "Now you'll have a quick spiritual expansion."

18. Phil Roland: Released grief.

19. Kristine Johnson: No follow-up information.

20. Glen Johnson: Felt uplifted.

21. Larry Kuczek: Released some anger.

22. Kay Cook: Her neck and shoulder tension were released. Vibhuti appeared inside the envelope of her letter to Baba.

23. Alvin Cook: Felt more uplifted, ultimately, eventually obtained a new job and was restored to his sweet personality after a long-term depression.

As we prepared to sing a few devotional songs to Baba in thanksgiving, we noticed that vibhuti had been added to some Sai Baba photos in the front hallway to the kitchen. Next, we saw that a pile of ash had gathered on the flat wooden tambourine handle as I passed it to Ramesh. Finally we took our leave at 11:30 P.M. and the line of cars silently left the Rimal neighborhood to return for more adventures the next day.

That night some of the group received Sai Baba dreams or were so electrified they couldn't sleep much at all. Others continued to have pain relief and new awarenesses. The next day was the celebration of Nepali Spring via the Laksha Archana Ceremony, which roughly means "Achieving Your Target" through requesting a favor of God.

Vibhuti Appears Under Cellophane

Shortly after our arrival, several of us stood in the kitchen talking with Bharosa and some other devotees in the kitchen. Bharosa had just placed a large rice and raisin pudding in a huge aluminum pan and covered it with cellophane wrap. She turned away from the pan for a moment to speak with someone and then turned back toward the pan. There, to her astonishment, she saw that fresh vibhuti ash had sprinkled itself over the top of the white pudding, under the cellophane!

More and more people entered the small living room and arranged themselves in every cranny and corner of the house before bhajans began. There were people sitting in the hallway in front of the door, in the hallway to the bedrooms, behind the sofa, under a table, in the coat closet and in the kitchen. Somehow over sixty-five people were smashed together in a room that could comfortably seat about twenty.

Later, as we sang devotional songs in the living room, vibhuti sprinklings on three hanging photos grew as we sang. Next, Sarit gave instructions for chanting the mantra "Aum Bhagavan Sri Sathya Baba A Namaha" as we tossed grains of dried rice from our containers into a paper plate for over an hour. We sang joyful bhajans and were deeply moved at the devotion emanating from those who were present.

A lovely Nepali vegetarian feast was served after the Laksha Archana and the happy crowd reluctantly trickled out the door, well-fed and with auras and hearts greatly expanded.

Healings at Harmony Farm

Naturally we were deeply appreciative of having had two opportunities to visit Bharosa's lovely family in the same month. Surely we had seen enough healings to last for a lifetime of happy recollections. But Baba had other plans. The week after our return from Salt Lake City, the second time, we were astonished that a continual parade of visitors to Harmony Farm began to experience spontaneous healings. Baba had told Bharosa that those who would be healed by Him through her would, in turn, be instruments for the healing of others. We had no idea, however, that Baba was referring to a scale much greater than a mere handful of healings in our own case.

CHAPTER 34
ASTONISHED BY GRACE

"...purity, patience and perseverance. If you follow these three tenets you will not be affected by any disease." Sathya Sai Baba, SS March 1994 P 69

"Worry causes hurry, and both of them together bring about ill health. So worry, hurry and curry (fatty foods) are the root cause of cardiac ailments." Sathya Sai Baba, SSN Summer 1994 P 4

More of Sai Baba's Healings in the U.S.

For some reason, as soon as we returned from seeing Bharosa Adhikari in Salt Lake City, a flurry of spontaneous healings began to take place at our home and in the homes of friends, both Sai devotees and non-devotees alike. The telephone lines throughout the U.S. were humming with fantastic reports of telephone healings, sudden blessings of gifts of the Spirit and a host of other remarkable outworkings. Why was this torrent of grace occurring? Only God knows... and He wasn't saying!

"If the heart is turned toward God, some grace will be received." I had just given this statement of Baba's to a friend on the telephone. She, like so many of our friends and acquaintances, is not a Sai devotee. These days, when pressed by my friends for a news update, I find myself combining periodic home-work-Sai-group updates with a bit of background on Baba since He's the Doer in every aspect of our lives.

My friend Dee, a "borderline Catholic" ("more spiritual than religious," by her account) had just relayed that, one hour after she had nearly decided not to attend her monthly women's (boring) meditation group any longer, extraordinary things took place. " People just started having healings left and right!" she nearly shouted through the phone receiver. "I know what you mean," I blurted out. "It's been happening here, too. Dee, you wouldn't believe it, beyond our wildest imagination!"

Another friend, Henry, from Texas, also Catholic, like Dee, and not open to the idea of Sai Baba at all, called with his news. "People have been calling and have received healings over the phone. Not only that: lots of them have been slain in the Spirit over the phone, but they have fallen out of their chairs on the kitchen floor. They don't get hurt, though, as the Power of God falls upon them. They sometimes call back and ask if we can do it again! Now when they call, the first thing I ask them is "Are you sitting on a sofa or armchair in case something powerful and unusual happens?"

But the strain of so many calls was affecting Henry's health. "We may have to get an unlisted number," he chuckled. We laughed heartily at the sudden, very welcome spiritual revolution in healing which is now happening in the United States, to everyone's enormous surprise. But then, Sri Sathya Sai Baba is the ultimate Master of Surprise.

To say that 1998 was an eventful year for Colorado devotees and spiritual aspirants is a major understatement. Jim and I have been in the world-wide Sai Movement for nearly twenty years and yes, it's true that Baba has healed us several times and saved our lives on numerous occasions. It's also true that we have been richly blessed (who knows why?) with His directive to speak in numerous countries about Him, to receive amrit and vibhuti on household and Sai Center photos and to travel to India two dozen times and receive countless interviews. We feel deeply blessed and profoundly grateful for such bounteous grace.

These blessings and the changes of heart and temperament He has brought about, would surely be enough for any twenty people. So we were content and have been abiding in the Atma, or Indwelling Presence, doing our daily work and service and minding our own business. You may have heard the adage that "There are three kinds of business: yours, mine and God's." Over and over again we have been firmly taught by Baba that paying attention to other people's business is simply a waste of time - as well as being an unhealthy (co-dependent) focus of living.

The Master of Surprise Drops Hints

Now, you may know that Our Beloved Sathya Sai often drops a few Hansel-and-Gretel breadcrumbs on the spiritual path leading to the next stage of service and awareness. As we look back, we can see that He has been preparing us for the breathtaking events which have recently thrust themselves upon us and our Northern Colorado Sai Group.

Not that it's been a rose-strewn path of ease and bliss every moment, by any means. All of us have been tried and tested in the refiner's fire continually, like people everywhere. As Sai says, "My Grace is proportional to your effort. Try to win Grace by reforming your habits, reducing your desires and refining your higher nature. One step makes the next step easier; that is the excellence of the spiritual journey. With each step, your strength and confidence increase and you get bigger and bigger installments of Grace." Sathya Sai Baba, ACSSBS P 125

When we watched Baba heal, deliver divine discourses and multiply food for the multitudes, like Jesus, we were impressed. Seeing vibhuti pour from photos in countless homes throughout the world has also been touching and thought-provoking. Baba's transformation of our own hearts and minds has been profound and continual.

Wilma Bronkey and Enchanted Acres

Baba eventually arranged for us to visit the extraordinary elder devotee, Wilma Bronkey, twice and to speak at her retreat at Grants Pass, Oregon, where three devotees reported that Baba had healed them during the talk. On the same day, Wilma had a vision of Baba walking on the grounds and I saw Mother Mary standing next to Diane, a lead bhajan singer. We also noted the profusion of vibhuti ash and amrit at Wilma's home altar-alcove in the living room.

Harmony Farm

On February 8, 1998, a spate of healings began to take place at our home, which has stupefied us. They began with a small leela as I was unpacking from my second trip to Salt Lake City, Utah within two weeks. As soon as I opened my suitcase I noticed that a banana which Sarit had given me had developed an Om symbol inside the suitcase, during the flight! When I placed an apple on the kitchen counter to have a snack, I turned away a moment, then turned to pick it up and saw that vibhuti covered the top of the apple.

Several nights later, as we held our regular Sunday night Sai Baba meeting, a visitor from Greeley named Susan, whom we'd never met, was healed of forty years of blindness. A few days later someone else was healed of deafness, the first of about eight such cases. Then the momentum picked up and two years later we have been privileged to have witnessed at least 90 healings of people from several states - as well as a pet feline from Colorado named Henry.

The healings have been physical, emotional, mental and have included the healing of various addictions. When we lived in Littleton, Colorado, there were about a dozen healings of various types. We have been very clear about the fact that we have nothing to do with the miracles and healings. God is the Doer and it's His business whom He will heal and when - or even if healing is in order. Baba has often said in this regard, that one's karma plays a role and the extent of service one is doing has an effect.

There have been days when we have wondered whether the healings have just been hysterical psychological manifestations as a result of listening to the devotional singing in the serene atmosphere of candles, flowers and Sai photos. But upon further reflection, we realized that the bhajan singing of our fledgling devotees, though well-intended, hardly has the capacity at this undeveloped stage to inspire instantaneous healing! Further, if people were going to be healed just by sitting in a devotional setting, you'd think that every church in the land would be putting up flyers to the effect.

Each time that a doubt as to the veracity of a particular healing would creep into my mind, Baba would confirm that His work was genuine through someone else. He often appeared to devotees far away and told them to "Call Connie Shaw and tell her that I am going to perform many, many healings and miracles at Harmony Farm." The persons who received the visions or the dreams had no idea what the messages of Sai meant or why they had been selected to convey them. Since there has, unfortunately, been jealousy and controversy between various Sai Centers (both affiliated and unaffiliated with the Sai Organization), Baba often gives confirming signs to the families at the scene of the manifestations and healings lest they begin, in the face of certain intimidating pressures, to doubt their own experience or to lose heart in the face of nay-sayers.

"Faith in ourselves and faith in God. This," says Baba, "is the secret of greatness. For God is Love." Sathya Sai Baba, ACSSBS P 186

There have been about 90 cases of healing of which we are aware. Surely there are other healings which were deemed too personal or too embarrassing by visitors or members to mention to us, thus - they have gone unrecorded. There have been many cases of permanent relief from deafness, grief and depression, as well as healings from arthritis, addictions, insomnia, back pain and poor eyesight, to name but a few of the healings. In the majority of cases, Baba sent strangers to our meetings and they often called later to report having experienced a healing.

A Growthful Process

Naturally, having experienced hundreds of Sai miracles and manifestations, both in the U.S. as well as in India and other countries, we have made many changes. We now have increased faith in the unseen and in the gracious Lord's Plan for World Uplift - one human being at a time. We have also had to stretch our capacities and inclinations toward service, hospitality, setting up and running Sai meetings for nearly two decades, and learning to lead disparate groups of people who are often troubled, confused and cantankerous, if not ill, undisciplined and undependable. That is, Baba says He often sends the most needy, difficult people to Sai Centers since they would not, in their various states of unease, be welcome in their local churches and temples.

The various constituencies with whom we have worked over the years have also had to be patient with us as we have worked through various snits, projections and ego-attacks, recovered from hurt feelings, and moved through the various levels of leadership/followership maturity. For example, we moved from rigidity and control-freak managerial expressions to a less autocratic, more group-centered leadership approach to meetings and service activities.

Our various Sai Center members have learned, through service and trips to India, how unspeakably fortunate we are, presently, in America, in every material respect, yet how unconsciously we treat our children, the elderly, infirm, shut-ins, handicapped, homeless and incarcerated citizens. They have been individually humbled, over the years, as Sai devotees, through experiencing Baba's Tough Love Curriculum. It has entailed death of loved ones, illness, divorce, bankruptcy, job loss, incapacitation, unhappy marriages, car wrecks, house fires, burglary, financial loss, and a jolly good assortment of travails seemingly designed by the Surprise-Meister to get one's complete and undivided attention. And to keep it. But Baba says it is not He who deals out bad luck like a nasty punishment. It is we ourselves who bring forth our own lessons in order to really comprehend that "our happiness is not dependent upon our outer circumstances," contrary to the message of cultural myths and worldly advertisements.

The Lord's Promise to Us

It does no good to rail and flail at Baba, accusing our dear Lord of abandoning us for our self-created messes. No, it is better to ask to see the lesson and to abide in the heart, serenely above the fray, even though our troubles may threaten to last a lifetime. Regarding His promise and support for our future, Baba says, "It is God's word that if you have devotion to God, He will look after your future. He will look after all the welfare that is due to you." Sathya Sai Baba, ACSSBS P 332

Not everyone who has come seeking a healing has received one, though all have been blessed in other ways. Some people have asked us why we believe they have been so fortunate as to have been healed when others have not. We tell them that Baba says, "Your progress is reflected back as Grace." Sathya Sai Baba, ACSSBS P 186

As we have struggled to gather some understanding from the bonanza of blessings and boatload of challenges Sai has laid before us of late, we have seen some patterns in the healings. First, and most importantly, the visitors were not physically touched by us and may not have realized that they had been healed until they were driving home.

Furthermore, the healings were not necessarily physical or emotional. Some involved the restoration of faith in God. Many visitors, at least ten with whom we have spoken, have seen Baba, Mother Mary, Jesus, Yogananda, Sri Yukteshwar (Yogananda's teacher), other masters and/or angels in our meeting room.

Perhaps Baba has graced the various homes of aspirants throughout the world to hearten the residents during times of especially harsh treatment by others, or in the face of great trials and keen losses. Maybe they earned the opportunity through serving Him in other lifetimes. Actually, it is futile to speculate on why some have the responsibility of such seemingly unasked-for, high-profile service or sadhana. The fact is, this life is a vast play with six billion characters, directed by Sri Sathya Sai, Poorna Avatar, Divinity in Form. Everyone has a part in the play and each life is a story in itself - of gain, loss, adversity and triumph. Somebody has to play the part of Halagappa, Wilma Bronkey, Indulal Shah, Ami Mangru, Bharosa Adhikari and others.

Those roles are quite temporary - just the blink of an eyelash in eternity. That the roles are played with good humor, compassion, heartfulness, focus and awareness of the Self is the key.

Baba assures us that His Will and His mission indeed will be accomplished. Referring to Himself, He tells us, "There can be no limit or obstacle to His Will, nor bounds to the manifestation of His Power and His Glory. He fructifies all that He wills. He can manifest in whatever form He wills. He is unique, incomparable, equal to Himself alone. He is our own measure, witness, authority. God alone knows the ways of God!" Sathya Sai Baba, ACSSBS P 328

Although the witnessing of healings is indeed thrilling, we hope we have finally learned, through nearly having died several times the past few decades, that healing is no substitute for wholeness. That is, it is better by far to cling to the Atma, or Indwelling Presence, rather than to worry over health as health comes and goes. When we stay established in God-consciousness our state of health is not only more bearable, it is quite beside the point.

A Joyful Prescription

This resting in God can be done by simple attunement to your Inner Tone, through hearing devotional music, by repeating God's Name or reflecting on Baba or the Atmic Presence. All of these promote joy. "The more joy, the more disease will go. Joy is the medicine." Sathya Sai Baba, ACSSBS P 154

Further, Baba says, "Purity of mind is the pathway to progress. Purity of mind means mighty power; a pure mind is like a precious pearl in the sea." He also says, "Chitta is the internal mental consciousness. The general nature of the chitta is to waver and hesitate and flutter in search for happiness and peace. When the chitta gives up the attachment to external objects, when it is saturated with repentance for past foolishness, when it is filled with remorse, renunciation and understanding, when it directly fosters the development of head and heart, then truly it becomes fit to join the ideal. Whatever ideas and pictures it may form, instruct it to find only God in those creations of mind-stuff. It has to be watched and trained. It must be made to flow, single-pointed and steady." Sathya Sai Baba, ACSSBS P 154

Finally, through continual study of Sai's teachings and through keeping our minds fixed on the True Self, we learn that the true healing is the overcoming of our cultural conditioning and the relinquishment of our misidentification with the body, mind and emotions. Happiness is not dependent upon our circumstances. Whether one is rich or poor, married or single, employed or unemployed, sick or well, every life event and circumstance points to the fact that true and lasting happiness cannot be found in the material world. However, it is possible and necessary to discover happiness within, regardless of outer circumstances.

Repeatedly, in His divine discourses, Our Beloved Baba tells us, "You are the embodiment of God. Fill yourselves with the thought of your almightiness, your majesty and your glory." Sathya Sai Baba, DACSSBS P 186. He announced at His 70th Birthday that the Golden Age of Peace and Plenty has dawned. The more we allow the veils of consciousness to be lifted, the more easily He can utilize each of us as instruments of His Love to restore to the planet the Sanathana Dharma. The soon return of the Sanathana Dharma means the Eternal Values that sustain the nobility of life on earth.

Author's Note: The first part of this chapter was reprinted with permission from *Spiritual Impressions* Magazine where it first appeared as an article.

*   *   *   *   *

Although individual devotees have experienced countless miracles and continual grace, Sathya Sai has remarkably transformed His native India in the past sixty years. During the past two decades in which my husband and I have been coming to India, we have seen enormous improvements in the infrastructure of the country by way of roads, housing, schools, hospitals and clinics, village water supplies, factories and vocational training institutes. Such advancements tremendously impact the well-being and lifestyles of our Indian brothers and sisters.

When we first traveled to the sub-continent, the night-time streets and sidewalks were packed with millions of sleeping homeless. Most Indians had to either walk or take a crowded public bus to their workplace or the market. Very few enjoyed hot water, a small refrigerator, a wristwatch, a radio or a good pair of shoes. Now every community has a television set, many people own a moped for family transport and South Indian women no longer need to spend the day walking many miles over rocks and thorns in bare feet to carry water for family use. The majority of Indians are well-dressed by Asian standards and the number of children per family has declined from ten or twelve to four or five. More children than ever are being educated at trade or vocational schools and the exploitation of children for 'sweat labor' is diminishing.

Many improvements in cleanliness and standard of living have been due to the vast contributions of millions of Sai Baba devotees who volunteer their time once or twice a week to clean slums, teach hygiene, dispense medicines and to otherwise lovingly assist the poor and the discouraged. They instruct the disadvantaged throughout India to tidy up their living areas, to raise their skill and aspiration levels and to trust that God will help them in the most mundane matters, which He indeed does.

Thus, the Avatar has undertaken three gargantuan tasks: the clean-up of India, the prevention of all-out nuclear destruction of the planet and the restoration of dharma through the purification of humanity. The Perennial Philosophy, or Sanathana Dharma, which sustains high conscious awareness of life purpose is implied in the ancient and famous Yamas and Niyamas, or the "Do's and Don'ts for Awakening." The secret of sacred living is found in implementing the Yamas and Niyamas of the sincere spiritual aspirant. The yamas represent the 'great vows' of personal restraint: honesty and truthfulness, non-violence, continence and freedom from greed and desires.

The Niyamas emphasize renunciation of wrong and include study of scriptures, purity, internal and external contentment, discipline of body, speech and mind and surrender to God (Your Will, not my will, oh Lord).

Our Beloved Baba has provided countless spiritual paths and religions for humankind, all of which lead to God. One need not become a Sai devotee since becoming a more devout Muslim, Buddhist, Hindu or

Christian can have a powerful impact on oneself and one's loved ones. However, Sathya Sai has created Sai Centers in 150 countries for the education, inspiration and uplift of people in those countries who wish to avail themselves of the centers.

Because of His stupendous accomplishments on physical as well as subtle levels, the Avatar is enormously sought-after. The poor and desperate as well as the powerful and celebrated flock to His daily darshans. It is becoming more rare and difficult to obtain an interview with Him. For this reason I was overcome with joy and surprise when He suddenly called me.

CHAPTER 35
THE ADVAITA INTERVIEW

"When people follow the path of truth and righteousness, love will sprout naturally in their hearts." Sathya Sai Baba, SS February 1995, P 35

Brindavan Ashram, Kadugodi Village near Bangalore, India
November 3, 1999

This morning I was reading *Insights* on Ramana's teachings when I came across a line from Ramana that I had written inside the cover of the book that has been part of my experience for about six years. It is that "The delusion of a personal self is the first set of shackles which must be broken." Several years ago I had two forceful experiences of not being a personality, but merely condensed Light, through which God's energy, thoughts and actions continually flow. The accompanying knowledge was that thus, one cannot legitimately feel guilt or self-congratulations for anything which one does as one is definitely not the Doer.

It is so very clear to me now that unillumined human life generally revolves around one's getting what he wants. When we 'accept what is' (surrender), there is peace and joy. Unmasking the ego, moment to moment, is in my opinion the most enjoyable game on the planet. We are all movie critics of our own unacknowledged, critical projections on others. Now, when people try to tell me their victim story, I simply show them how to reverse the grievance and to see that they are displeased with themselves unknowingly. The result of catching themselves in a fit of anger, jealousy or fear is that they immediately feel compassion for the object of their projection and finally, for themselves.

"Relax. Be easy with yourself," I tell them. "We've all merely been confused. Wake up and smell the vibhuti!"

Now I want to relate a funny story. We heard of an amusing incident which happened here in Kadugodi Village sometime in the past year, it seems. The Prince Carriers Café, a simple outdoor coffee shop across from the ashram, was the site for the incident. A local snake charmer, squatting at the roadside a few yards from the café, tried to coax a lethargic cobra from his round raffia basket. The cobra was apparently not in the mood to entertain the arriving streams of devotees who were coming from morning darshan.

Finally, the snake charmer gave up his wheedling and walked away for a few moments to get a cigarette from a friend lounging against a post. The cagey cobra seized upon his opportunity to escape and slithered from beneath the loose basket lid and undulated his way under the half-dozen outdoor café tables. Meanwhile, about twenty starry-eyed devotees laughed, told Sai stories and sipped coffee in the drowsy morning sunshine.

Suddenly, someone yelled "Snake! Cobra!" In a flash, the twenty lounging, laughing devotees speedily jumped onto their chairs and tabletops, shrieking and tap-dancing. Eventually the cobra was retrieved and returned to the shady confines of his round raffia basket at the side of the dusty road. The incident was followed by a steady procession of people mounting the stairs to the computer shop over the café. Devotees formed lines behind the four computers to await their turn to fax or e-mail the folks at home about the cobra scare and the events of morning darshan.

As I walked back to the room after darshan this morning, I noted some lepers sitting under a tree at the roadside. It reminded me that two years ago Baba healed me of my aversion to lepers. As I passed four men who were sitting on a blanket under a tree begging, I noted that each was missing at least an arm or a leg. I felt deep compassion for them and nodded to them. Suddenly, a flood of light came from the entire group and I could see Baba's essence in them. Since then, I have helped Deirdre West in the wound-dressing room at the Sathya Sai Hospital in Whitefield when lepers have come to her for colloidal silver ointment and fresh dressings. Deirdre is getting healing results with lepers in six months instead of the usual fifteen or twenty years that such healings from leprosy normally take with conventional treatments. Baba leaves soon for Puttaparthi. We'll be here until His Birthday.

Puttaparthi, India
November 8th

We came to Puttaparthi a few days ago from Brindavan. As we sat in the darshan line today awaiting Baba's emergence into the hall, I was flooded with deep love and appreciation for the inordinate grace Baba has showered on our family in the past eighteen years. By now He has appeared in our home fifty-five times – to teach, to bless, to heal and to warn. In 1988, when my parents were both suddenly sent to different hospitals on the East Coast of the U.S., without my knowledge, He appeared in my prayer room to inform me. He was thirty feet tall, and His waist, at ceiling level, went through the roof in the apparition He provided. "Trust Me; I am caring for your parents. They will have the best care in the best facilities available. Do not worry. I am their Mother and Father."

Later, when my sister had called with the dire news, I said, "I know what you're going to say. It's that Mom and Dad have both been taken to the hospital – different facilities – and they're getting the best care available."

"How could you possibly know that?" she had asked, astounded.

"Sai Baba just appeared to me in a vision and told me," I replied. "He said not to worry as He is their Mother and Father. " My sister and I both wept at Baba's thoughtfulness and at His having shown Himself to me as a giant, symbolizing a tower of strength in all times, and especially in family emergencies.

Among Baba's manifestations to us have been vibhuti, amrit, a ring, vibhuti fragrance in my mouth and in front of my nose, sandalwood and jasmine fragrance, and gold leaf flecks on His photo. He has showered me with vibhuti a dozen times and has manifested fragrances, amrit, apparitions, honey, cum-cum and candy at my talks. He has healed audience members at workshops. Several times He has saved my life: from car wrecks, from a brain tumor, a high-jacking in Egypt, a kidnapping in China, a near-highjacking in India, ptomaine poisoning in China, malaria, congestive heart failure, pneumonia from India, an assailant in Texas and an assailant in New Mexico.

Thank You for all the adventures, Lord, but I think I've had enough for the rest of this lifetime, if You don't mind. But if it's part of Your Plan, naturally I want to be as surrendered as possible to what may come.

It was Monday, November 8, 1999 at 6:40 A.M. in the Sai Kulwant Hall at Sathya Sai Baba's Abode of Peace Ashram in Puttaparthi, South India. Since Sai Baba's seventy-fourth birthday was only two and a half weeks away and incoming crowds would be enormous by November 23rd, our small American group of three women did not have high expectations that we would be fortunate enough to be blessed with an interview, or audience, with Our Beloved Lord.

The only inkling that Baba might even consider seeing us came in January of 1999 when He graced me with a dream wherein I was sitting directly in front of Him, slightly to His left, in an interview. During the dream interview He suddenly said to me "You're on back pay!"

"Back pay, Swami?" I had asked, puzzled.

"Yes, back pay," He had responded, twinkling but enigmatic. The dream then suddenly ended.

In February of 1999 He had called me to India for five weeks and then again for three weeks in June and July. But while there had been enormous grace, many talks and workshops presented by my dear friend Kay and me wherein He had silently healed many attendees, there had been no interview. But long ago we learned to attune to His Inner View and guidance and to come to His lotus feet and radiant form without expectations. The October-November trip was my third journey to India in 1999 and I had become extremely quiet throughout the year, savoring inner stillness. At last I had been able to tolerate sitting on the ground for up to ten hours a day and was no longer bothered by India's minor inconveniences.

Unexpectedly, on the morning of November 8th, 1999, during my twenty-sixth trip to India, our pre-darshan line-up row drew a token for line one. Amazingly enough, there was no pre-seating of VIP's or dignitaries that morning and we were seated in the front row of the darshan hall. Soon thereafter the darshan music began playing over the loudspeakers announcing the Avatar's arrival. Baba came floating out of His doorway in the Poornachandra Hall where He has a small room for His quarters.

As He approached the arched gate to the women's side of the hall, the teary-eyed ladies on both sides of the red-carpeted aisle leaned out, smiling and holding out articles to be blessed and letters to be accepted. Hastily, I fumbled for a pen and for the book manuscript I had brought to be blessed by the Lord. He stopped briefly here and there on both sides of the aisle giving a word here, an upraised hand of blessing there. Then, as my heart pounded in a threat to jump its ribcage, He walked straight toward me. Could it be? Was He going to suddenly turn away as He so often does, to tease the devotee and to force one's attention back inside to the vast interior of the Self? He kept coming. Finally He stood before me and began speaking.

"When are you going (back home)?" He asked, as if He didn't know, since He always gives me, in meditation, the precise dates to leave and return for each trip.

"November 24th, the day after Birthday," I replied.

"I will see you," He said, slightly turning His head as if to walk on by. This might be my last chance in this entire lifetime for an interview, especially since He had fobbed me off countless times before with "I will see you," or "Wait, wait (until later)."

"But will You just please sign my book, Lord," I pleaded, kneeling and beseeching Him with pen and manuscript held toward Him. He smiled slightly at my antics.

"How many (in your group)?" He asked, as if He hadn't told me whom to invite, as usual.

"Only three, Baba" I answered, genuinely startled, since the words that every devotee longs to hear from Him are "How many?" and "Go!"

"Only three?" He answered, imitating me, as He so often does, to my chagrin and delight.

With a sideways Indian-style head-jiggle which means "yes," He said "Go!" and swept His index finger away from His body emphatically.

My friend Kay, a social worker from Houston, Texas, and I were then joined on the veranda by our new friend, Marilyn Wilkinson, a rancher from Ellensburg, Washington, who had been sitting in the patients' section. She had come to the Mandir temple veranda on crutches because of severely painful and swollen legs. Double knee-replacement surgery had necessitated the insertion of plastic knee-caps and metal rods in her shins. It was Marilyn's first trip to India; she had only learned of Baba's authenticity as God in May of 1999 and was overwhelmed with a series of miracles which lead up to her departure for India in October.

One by one we were joined on the veranda by misty-eyed devotees from other states, most of whom we didn't know. There were two women, Jo-Anne Powell and J.P. Riggs, from New England. From Sedona, Arizona, there were John and Ann Marks, Elvin Johnson, a woman named Jan and a woman named Star. An Indian family composed of a husband, wife and a son who was in Baba's school were also called, along with Dr. Sam Sandweiss, author and professor, and Dr. Mike Goldstein, cardiologist, both from California. Some ladies from the U.K. came to the veranda but Baba said, "Not now, go." They left and He then turned to the men on the veranda.

Baba signaled for Sam Sandweiss and Mike Goldstein to go into the interview room, then He indicated that the women should follow them. In the basket beside Baba's chair I placed the letters that had been entrusted to me from Colorado and California devotees who could not make the trip. Then I sat in the exact spot where I had been sitting in the Sai interview dream ten months before! Marilyn was behind me, Kay was to my left, directly in front of Baba, and the other ladies sat behind us. The ladies sat down first, to make room for those still trickling through the doorway.

The Large Group Interview

Several people were dabbing at their eyes, still overcome with the surprise of having been suddenly called for a private audience with God Incarnate, after months, years or decades of longing for such an eventuality. Fully aware of this, Baba engaged in preliminary gestures and comments to make each person feel welcome, at ease and grounded enough to enjoy the long-awaited interview. The love which filled the room, both towards and from Baba, was nearly palpable. Every gaze was riveted, adoringly, on the Avatar.

Baba to the men: "Sit down, Gentlemen."

Men: "Thank You, Swami."

Baba, standing, accepted a small family photo album from Dr. Goldstein. He looked through it and asked: "Is this your boy?" (Baba performed a marriage ceremony for Dr. Goldstein's second son on November 22, 1999 in the interview room, but that event was still more than two weeks away.)

Mike Goldstein: "Grandson."

Baba: "He is his mother's son, not his father's son." (Presumably closer or more like his mother, more affinity with mother.) Then, teasingly, Baba asked, "Do you want a (another) son?"

Mike Goldstein: "Oh no!" Everyone laughed good-naturedly.

Baba asked about various family members and said that He would bless them as He patted the small photo album. Then Baba sat down in His red velvet chair facing the group.

Baba to the student, to let him know that he was in august company with Dr. Goldstein and Dr. Sandweiss: "He is a doctor. He is a professor."

Baba to Jo-Anne Powell: "Do you know Goldstein?"

Jo-Anne Powell: "Yes, Baba, he pushes my wheelchair."

Baba: "Yes, Goldstein helps." (A few weeks later Baba gave an extraordinary ten-minute eulogy to Mike after Mike's very inspirational speech at the University Convocation. Baba said that Dr. Goldstein, the guest of honor, exemplifies duty, discipline and devotion, has worked very hard for the Sai Organization and is very successful. Long-time devotees know how exceedingly rare such a tribute to an individual has been over the years.)

Next, Baba manifested some grainy, chalky white medicinal vibhuti for Kay, Connie, Marilyn and the Indian lady. As the four women sat there holding it, **Baba** said, "Take, eat, now." It had no fragrance and was thick and grainy but not unpleasant. Connie had a very severe cough and chest phlegm; Marilyn's seventy-three-year-old legs with implants were hurting, and Kay was "a bit weak" according to Baba.

Then **Baba** addressed Connie and asked, "Do you know this Sandweiss?"

Connie: "Yes, Swami, we know this Sandweiss."

Baba: "How?"

Connie: "We have spoken with him on the phone over the years and we have seen him here over the years at the ashram and at conferences."

Baba: "But how do you know him?"

Connie: "Because he's famous, Swami. Everybody knows Sandweiss."

Baba: "(His) titles?"

Connie: "Yes, his titles… He has written *The Holy Man and the Psychiatrist* and *Spirit and the Mind.*"

Baba: "Yes. You know him because he is famous."

Baba addressed Connie and asked, pointing to Marilyn Wilkinson, "Who is SHE?" (as if He didn't know)

Connie, for the benefit of the others: "She is Marilyn Wilkinson, from Washington state."

Baba: "Who?"

Connie: "She is Atma (Spirit), known as Marilyn in this form."

Baba, nodding: "She is Atma!"

Connie: "Yes, Atma."

Baba, pointing to the ring He had manifested for me nine years before: "What is this?"

Connie: "It's a Navaratna Shivalingham ring that You made for me in 1990."

Baba: "When?" (For the benefit of the group so that they might know the history of the ring before it disappeared.)

Connie: "On Shankara's Birthday, July 25, 1990." (Shankara, known as Jagadguru Adi Shankaracharya was one of Baba's great Incarnations as the famous poet, mystic, philosopher, logician and architect of the Shankara system of philosophy which is expounded today by Sri Sathya Sai. Shankara is said to have lived in the 700's. When Baba had materialized the ring in 1990 He said, slowly and deliberately, "I have waited eons to give you this ring. Today is Shankara's Birthday. Wear the ring on the right index finger."

Two days later Mr. Ramakrishna Shastry, now deceased, in reading an ancient Shuka Nadi manuscript said, "It says here that Baba should have given you a Navaratna Shivalingham ring two days ago to commemorate your relationship with Him as one of His four disciples when He was the great sage Shankara." The implications of that reading and its many astounding statements hit me with great force. If it had been foretold thousands of years ago that I would bring a group to India in 1990 and that we would be blessed with three interviews and a lingham ring on Shankara's Birthday, then where did the concept of free will enter into any life?

My burgeoning interest in advaita, or non-duality was kicked into high gear as I realized that within my Causal Body must reside full knowledge of Baba/Shankara's teachings since, as His disciple, I had also been an instrument for taking His teachings on non-duality far and wide, just as in this lifetime.

The implications of simultaneous realities were not lost on me, nor were the implications that our "future" lifetimes; just as our "past" lifetimes are all known to the Lord and, in fact, designed by Him, as roles in His endless fascinating drama. The mind, which is but a bundle of thoughts and beliefs, is staggered at the implications of Sai's revelations, surprises, teachings, lines of questioning, benedictions, grace, healings, miracles and manifestations.)

Baba, holding Connie's finger, pretending that the loosely-fitting ring was a tight fit, made as if it took great effort to pull it off: "Yes, yes, ten years back (I made it). I know, I know. Do you want this ring or do you want a change?"

Connie: "It's up to You, Swami."

Baba, mimicking Connie: "It's up to You, Swami. BUT... Do you want this or some other?"

Connie: "Whatever You'd like to do, Swami, is fine with me. ANYTHING is fine."

Baba: "Sure?"

Connie: "Yes."

Baba quickly tossed the lingham ring to Mike Goldstein who accidentally dropped it on the floor where it then bounced. He must have felt very bad. Then Baba asked Mike Goldstein to pass it around to the men. The men didn't understand that they were to examine it and pass it around.

Baba to an Arizona man: "Take it."

Elvin: "What?"

Connie: "Baba means take it and have a look at it."

Elvin: "Oh." He examined the ring a moment.

Baba: "She (Jo-Anne Powell) wants a ring. No, she still wants the wheelchair."

Baba: "What is it?"

He indicated that the boy student should answer. No one seemed to know what the lingham ring was or what it signified (the Cosmic Egg of Creation; the Beginninglessness and eternality of Atma, of ourselves; all of Creation is enfolded within each of us in the vastness and Omnipresence of Atma within). Baba paused and there was silence for awhile. Finally Connie spoke.

Connie: "It's a lingham."

Elvin: "It's beautiful."

Baba: "Beautiful or beauty-fool?" (Meaning that Baba was making a private joke with Elvin that one/humans should not be a fool for worldly beauty.)

Elvin: "Will You make me one like it?"

Baba ignored this as the men passed the ring around among them. Baba then held out His hand to retrieve the silver-colored lingham ring which had a dome of nine gemstones encircled by twenty-one diamonds. There were Om symbols on the sides of the tear-drop face, along the band. (When Baba had given the ring to Connie He had said, "This ring will protect you." Since then, while she gave inspirational talks at large gatherings there had subsequently been two attempts on her life – one a thwarted verbal attack in Houston and one an attempted choking by a Native American in New Mexico.)

Baba blew on the lingham ring three times. Between the second and third puffs the silver-colored pancha-loha metal ring (five-metal amalgam) turned into gold. He opened His hand and Connie gasped. The new ring was a ring-watch with a gold expandable band, gold minute and second hands on a black face surrounded by twenty-six diamonds, and a tiny gold dial. He looked at her meaningfully and placed the watch-ring on her ring finger of the right hand. She had been telling Baba internally for about two months, "Baba, you have given me a wonderful earthly husband in Jim. He is loving and serving and is so very good to me. But You, Lord, are my spiritual husband. I surrender all my concerns to you and totally trust You to care for me in every way. All people are married to You as the Beloved and so am I, Lord."

Connie, feeling extremely undeserving of such generosity: "Oh! Swami, THANK You!"

Baba: "Why do you say 'Thank you?' "

Connie: "Because I've been well brought-up, Lord. My Mother taught me to always say 'Thank you.' "

Baba: "Don't thank Me. I am Your Mother."

Baba: "What is this?"

Connie: "Lord, it's a watch-ring."

Baba: "What is the meaning of a watch?"

Connie: "W-A-T-C-H. W is for watch your words. A is for watch your actions. T means watch your thoughts. C means watch your character. H is for watch your heart. And watch your time!" She laughed at the pop quiz, not realizing that it was just beginning and would last about half an hour. Baba, how can we ever thank You for such love and grace (as You dispense to all) except by loving everybody?!

Baba, to Connie: "What is love?"

Connie: "Love is to see everyone as my Self (Atma) – all species, all people."

Baba: "Why do you come here (to the Abode of Peace)?"

Connie: "Because You call me for Your reasons."

Baba: "Why do you come here?"

Connie: "You draw each of us here for reasons that only You know."

Baba: "But why do YOU come here?!"

Connie: "Because I LOVE You, Baba!"

Baba: "I love YOU. What is surrender?"

Connie: "To accept what is."

Baba: "No – what is surrender?"

Connie: "Letting go. Accepting what comes to us."

Baba: "What is surrender?"

Connie: "Doing Your Will, accepting Your Will… God's Will. Your Will is my will."

Baba: "Yes, this is not free will. Free will is not doing your will – this is not freedom. The only freedom is in doing God's Will. Surrender is being One, not two. All is One. God is One." (Baba has often said that man has about as much free will as a donkey tethered to a post.)

Connie: "You and I are One."

Baba: "No, not you and I are One. We and We are One."

Connie: "Yes, even We two is one too many. Only One. Only One. Everyone is my very Self."

Baba: "What is this myself, myself?"

Connie: "Self, Baba. My Self. Advaita…"(YOU know, Lord, why are You teasing me like this?! she was thinking.)

Baba: "All are One.

I AM One with all." (i.e., Each of us is That. We must experience this continually.)

I AM the embodiment of peace. (i.e., Each of us is That)

I AM the embodiment of love.

I AM the embodiment of truth."

He pointed to the group at large (humanity) – Here (in the world of form, while mis-identified with our personality, mind, body and emotions) there is no peace, no love, no truth.

Connie: "God is everywhere, in all people, in all things, all species, all places."

Baba: "Here (in this room, i.e., Baba, and when we are with devotees) … or there?" (Outside the room, back in our countries – do we take God, Atma with us, remember God?)

Baba to Connie: "Where is God?"

Connie: "Everywhere! And He is in my heart (everyone's spiritual heart-center). YOU are in my heart."

Baba: "Yes, this is the spiritual heart. What is the heart? Where is the heart?"

Connie: "The Heart is everywhere all at once, in all times and places and dimensions. There is no death. I just want to ABIDE in the heart (to abide in peace moment-to-moment in the heart-center)."

Baba: "Yes, no death. Spiritual heart. Pointing to Connie's heart – This is PHYSICAL heart."

Connie: "Well, Baba, this physical heart has a mitral valve problem." (Connie nearly died of congestive heart failure on April 7, 1998. She had been shown on the hospital heart monitor that her mitral valve wasn't closing properly as she had been born with a heart murmur and had recently developed severe chest pains, swollen ankles and feet and shortness of breath. The doctors told her she had nearly died and that she would be a cardiac patient the rest of her life. She politely refused their medications and turned solely to the Divine Physician, having taken no medication or treatment since paying several thousand dollars for one night in the hospital.)

Baba: "No. there is no problem with the physical heart."

Connie, feeling perplexed and amazed: "No problem with the physical heart, Swami? Has it been healed?!"

Baba: "Yes, yes, no problem. What do you want?"

Connie: "I only want to do Your Will perfectly, with love, energy, enthusiasm AND... IF it IS Your Will, to set hearts on fire for the love of God. But, if this is not Your Will for me, that is fine."

Baba: "Yes, yes."

Then, turning to the student, He said, about Connie, "She is a lady who has been coming here for many years (nearly twenty, in fact.) These Americans have good answers!" Everyone laughed. Then He spoke a few words to the student in Telugu. Then He smiled warmly at Connie and said, "She is a good talker!"

Connie, teasing Him right back and not missing a chance to clarify His meaning: "Swami! I HOPE you see that it (the talking) matches the way I live."

Baba: "Yes, yes. You're a good girl. You're a good girl." Then, turning to Mike Goldstein, "She's a good girl!"

Next Baba made a gold watch for the boy student and seemed to fumble with the catch. "Does anyone have a pin?" Kay offered Him her ballpoint pen.

Baba: "No PIN, not pen."

Marilyn: "Here – I've got a safety-pin He can use. It's on my (ace) bandage." (She had wrapped an ace bandage, which Kay had purchased at the Puttaparthi Pharmacy at Marilyn's request, on her swollen knees.) The project of opening the latch on the band of the newly-materialized gold wristwatch gave the men something to do as each of them tried a hand at flipping the catch with the safety-pin. At one point Marilyn said under her breath "I've got to remember to get that safety-pin back. It's been touched by God!"

Connie, whispering: "Yes, maybe you could even frame it!" (So others could enjoy it)

Marilyn, whispering: "No, I'll keep it on me forever!"

Connie: "Of course!"

Baba: "You (three) Americans. Go inside (to the private interview room behind the curtain)."

While the men discussed how to flip the catch on the wristwatch, Connie, Kay and Marilyn scurried into the other room. Baba left the door behind the curtain ajar and as she sat down to Baba's left, Connie could see the little cluster of women in the main room closing their eyes to meditate.

Connie: (For nearly two decades she had wanted to pat Baba's hair, out of a deep love for Him as Sai-Ma, Mother Sai or Divine Mother). "May I touch Your hair, Swami?"

Baba: "Yes, yes. He leaned forward for her to touch it as He reached out to sign a photo of Himself and her new book manuscript about His many miracles, lessons, teachings and healings in her life."

Kay, to His right: "May I touch Your feet?"

Baba: "Yes, yes." She placed her right hand on His foot.

Marilyn, in the middle: "May I touch Your feet?"

Baba: "Yes, yes."

Connie, lost in time and space, touched His hair gently with her right hand, then decided to make the most of a tremendous opportunity and touched more hair with her left hand, so that both hands were experiencing the very light, fine silky texture of the Lord's hair. She was thinking to herself, "Since His hair is so very light and finely textured, I wonder how He gets it to stand out so nicely and puffily like that. You'd think it wouldn't have enough body and would collapse."

At that moment, Connie gasped quietly as she began to see, in Swami's aura and hair, a series of fast-moving images, like a video playing. About ten years ago she had been told in a dream that one day she would see images in people's auras that would seem to her as if she were seeing movies around their heads. This was the first time this had happened and she was astonished at what she saw.

She saw the following scenes: Baba was calling devotees to Himself in India to instruct them in His trip abroad. Next, He was stressing the need for harmony and unity. Then, in another scene, He was walking around in the U.S. It seemed to be summer or about May, June or July and devotees were giving talks about Him and introducing Him to crowds. Meanwhile, in the interview room, Baba was busy signing photos.

Connie wondered whether she was inadvertently seeing His thought-forms at close-range or whether Baba had purposely shown her a preview of coming attractions starring the Planetary Avatar as a "back-pay bonus" about which He had hinted in her January, 1999 Sai dream.

Connie, startled and delighted at what she was seeing: "Swami! Are you coming to the U.S. in May-June (or) – July, next year?"

Baba, gasping, and imitating Connie, as He often does: "Yes! I am coming to the U.S. in May-June-(or) July!" Baba was mentioned in the May 1, 2000 issue of Newsweek in the U.S. Good joke.

Connie: "WOW!" Then, collecting herself, Connie remembered she had a question. "Swami, may we start a school and ashram for You in Colorado?" He had already taken a letter to this effect in October, 1997, when He granted Connie's group two interviews, directly after which Connie came down with malaria for five months.

Baba: "Not this year. In 2000. About the other (trip to U.S.) – ask Goldstein."

Later, in the large room Connie asked Mike Goldstein if Baba had said He were coming abroad to the U.S. but Mike drew a blank and seemed not to understand the question. Baba had recently said in two discourses "Why should I leave India?" The Avatar keeps us guessing. One of His favorite lines is "Learn to love My uncertainty."

Baba addressed Kay: "How are you?"

Kay: "I'm happy."

Baba: "Your health is weak. Sometimes you get depressed and confused."

Kay: "Yes, will You help me?"

Baba nodded and asked Kay about her husband.

Kay: "He's fine. He has questions...."

Baba, interrupting her: "He is NOT fine. He is not happy. You are not compatible."

Kay: "What, Baba?"

Baba: "Thoughts, thoughts, not compatible." He put His two index fingers together and separated them, meaning the two partners have different ideas about things.

Kay looked completely blank.

Connie: "He said 'not compatible.' "

Baba nodded.

Baba to Marilyn: "You have a problem with your knees." No response.

Baba: "Your knees. Your knees. I will help. I will see you separately."

Marilyn: "What?"

Connie: "Separately. Baba, do You mean that You'll see her again, alone, by herself?"

Baba: "Yes. I will make medicine for you. It is rheumatic. You (Connie) have rheumatism too!"

Connie: "It's not arthritis?!"

Baba: "No, rheumatism. I will take care (of it, i.e., heal it)."

Connie: "But what about this little left-hand finger (that is stiff)?"

Baba, laughing: "Oh alright, I will take this (stiffness away) too!"

Next He stood and walked into the other room. Meanwhile, Connie and Kay helped Marilyn up since she had left her new crutches on the veranda outside the interview rooms.

Since the three women were taking about twenty seconds to get Marilyn on her feet and the others were eager to go in privately with Baba He mockingly snapped His fingers and said, "Come on!"

Baba to the New England and Arizona devotees: "You other Americans, go."

As Jo-Anne and J.P. determined where to sit in the back interview room, Jo-Anne Powell indicated that J.P. should take a chair. J.P. demurred as she felt it would be impolite and against spiritual protocol to be seated on the same "chair elevation" as God. Finally, though, she was convinced to sit in a chair because of her bad knees. Later, J.P. from New England, explained that "I have had bad knees from doing the twist in a disco in 1960 which caused a bone to chip. I've had two knee surgeries on my left knee which is arthritic."

Baba to J.P. in the back room: "How's your leg? Knee? Left knee?"

J.P.: "So-so."

Baba grabbed her hand and shook it (sending healing energy into her). "How long are you staying?"

J.P.: "November 28th."

Baba: "So happy. Another interview. A long one, on the 16th. Everyone assumed this meant the 16th of November."

Others: "Oh no, Swami, the 11th. We're leaving on the 11th." (Elvin, John, Star, Jan, Ann).

J.P.: "Swami, they're leaving on the 11th" (as if He didn't know).

Baba then asked the Sedona people to leave and Jo-Anne and J.P. to stay a moment. He brought Elvin back in. J.P. and Jo-Anne then sat on the floor.

Baba to Elvin: "What do you want?" Elvin responded.

Baba to Jo-Anne: "How's your health? You love God but you worry. You worry about the future, your family. Don't worry. You have a monkey mind. Don't worry. I'll take care. I'll help you."

Baba to Elvin: "What do you want?"

Elvin responded the same way. Baba repeated Elvin's response.

Jo-Anne said later that she felt energetic healing surge through her body as well as feeling emotional healing take place. During the interview in the main room Baba gave Jo-Anne lots of eye contact and both Jo-Anne and J.P. were blessed with padnamaskar at the conclusion of the interview.

Meanwhile, after the New England and Sedona people had finished their private interview, Baba brought in the student for a few brief moments, after which He brought the boy's parents into the back interview room.

Then Baba invited Dr. Sam Sandweiss and Dr. Michael Goldstein into the rear interview room. They stayed about five to seven minutes.

Marilyn then asked the student for the return of the safety-pin-touched-by-God so she could put it back on the bandage.

Connie: "She would like to have her safety pin back to secure her knee-bandage, please."

He took it from his pocket and returned it as Baba emerged into the large room again and Baba asked to have His vibhuti basket handed to Him for distribution. As the Lord bent over to pass out vibhuti packets, Connie leaned up and whispered, "Oh, thank You so much, Baba for everything today!"

Baba: "Yes, (I'm) very happy, very happy (with you)." He smiled and distributed packets to all.

Both Jo-Anne and J.P. took padnamaskar or the touching of His feet.

Baba then indicated to the group that the interview was at an end. The time was 7:40 A.M.. Thus the Lord manifested medicinal vibhuti, a gold and diamond watch-ring and a gold watch; healed at least five people – three of whom had leg and/or knee problems and two of whom had rheumatism. One heart valve was healed without surgery and a depressed person was healed. He gave advice, blessed individuals, relationships and families, gave homilies and enacted a pop quiz in Vedanta. He made jokes, calmed fears and nervousness, clarified issues and problems and, as ever, acted as the Divine Mother and the Consummate Host. *How great Thou art, oh Lord, how great Thou art.*

Postscript:
There are many reasons for the fact that devotees often respond to Baba's questions with a blank stare or "I beg your pardon?" Some of them are that: many do not understand His accent. His voice is soft.

Some devotees are too emotionally overcome to hear properly. Others are stunned that He knows everything about each of us. Some are buying time until they can give a suitable answer in public that doesn't incriminate themselves. Since the author has had many interviews and has lived abroad in Europe and in Asia, she understands the many varieties of English accents, American accents and Indian accents, hence feels free to assist people in interviews who may not understand what is taking place or what Baba is asking of them.

Baba did not see Jo-Anne Powell on the 16th of November; perhaps on another 16th He'll see her unless He "saw" her in her sleep. Nor did He see Marilyn Wilkinson separately. He did not say specifically that He would see her on this trip. He did, however, heal her dear friend Esther, in Florida, of cancer while we were still at Puttaparthi. She had been given three weeks to live by her doctors and was disbursing her belongings to her children when, after using the Golden Lingham Photo of Baba which Connie had given Marilyn, she was completely healed.

We learned of this great blessing by fax. Another friend of Marilyn's had placed the Lingham Photo on her face and was blessed with a shower of vibhuti on her forehead. Finally, a counselor friend of Marilyn's was healed of a disabled hand from Parkinson's Disease in September when Connie, while visiting Washington, touched her third eye with vibhuti at her request.

Baba is the only Doer. Of ourselves we are nothing while operating in personality consciousness. Although we are, as He says, Divine, too, we do not experience ourselves Thus because of obscuring veils of ignorance covering our ever-present Atmic Reality. His interviews, healings, benedictions and decrees erase the veils to our True Nature. He, in all of us, is Everything, our Atma, Our Lord.

Puttaparthi, India
November 24, 1999

The month of November has been over-flowing with festivals and special events. There has been Women's Day, wherein Goldie Hawn, the American actress, offered, with five other women, a bouquet to Baba. There was a University Convocation, processions, bands, World Youth Day, the Youth Conference and the release of a Commemorative Stamp for the Sri Sathya Sai Water Project which has brought water to nearly a thousand villages in India.

Baba's seventy-fourth Birthday celebration was lovely, in Sai Kulwant Hall, and He looked like a young man in His twenties as He sat in His chair before the crowd. He wore a white silk robe and looked quite diminutive in the royal blue velvet chair with its silver trim, charming silver umbrella overhead, and footstool for the Lotus Feet.

This month, Baba exhorted us, in His five discourses, to have bhakti, shakti and rhakti. Devotion (bhakti) creates energy (shakti), which then spreads (rhakti) to those nearby.

He constantly urges us to implement His teachings each day so that we might exhibit the twenty-six characteristics of the true devotee. I have made a list called the Daily Reminder Program from the booklet *Who Is A Devotee of the Lord?* by M.V.N. Murthy. It encompasses the twenty-six qualities in a condensed checklist.

The 26 Qualities – A Daily Reminder Program

1. He has no hatred (in thought, word or deed)
2. He is friendly, kind, compassionate
3. He is unselfish
4. Bears sorrow and joy equally
5. Has contentment
6. Shows self-control
7. Has conviction
8. His mind is in God
9. He doesn't harass the world
10. He is not harassed
11. He has no desires or expectations
12. He displays purity
13. He has competence
14. He shows detachment
15. He resides in Spirit
16. He has no spurts of joy or sorrow
17. He does not judge
18. He has equanimity
19. He has calmness in heat and cold
20. There is stability in both praise or blame
21. He observes silence
22. He has contentment, acceptance of life
23. He is "at home" wherever he is
24. The mind is unwavering
25. There is fortitude
26. He has faith.

Striving for the twenty-six characteristics is still the long, slow road, compared to advaita. When the Lord sees our efforts, He can, at any time, whether we are bhaktis, karma yogis or advaitists, dispense such Grace that our veils are lifted and we see automatically that those qualities have always been ours as embodiments of love, as Atma.

Recently, someone gave me one of Baba's quotations, which I have kept in my journal. I don't know when He said the following words, but I enjoy reading them.

"No matter where you go, always do your duty as you see it, and know that I will be there inside you, guiding you every step of the way. In the years to come, you will experience Me in many different manifestations of My form. I will protect you as the eyelid protects the eyes. I will never leave you and you can never leave Me. From this point on, do not hanker after anything. Do your duty with unwavering Love, seeing all as God. Be patient. In time, everything will be given to you. Be happy. There is no need to worry about anything. Whatever is experienced, whatever happens, know that this Avatar willed it so. There is no force on earth which can delay for an instant the mission for which this Avatar has come. You are all sacred souls and you will have your parts to play in the unfolding drama of the new Golden Age, which is coming."

Baba is interested in bringing each of us back to the very Source of manifestation – to our mergence in Him, while in these bodies. Our mistaken identity as an independent individual is the source of all of our suffering.

Over and over, He has told me: "This is NOT YOUR LIFE. This is My life, lived through you as a vehicle." Even your thinking is not yours. Don't take it personally. You are not doing it. It flows through you.

Acceptance of the ego and of the idea that 'This too, shall pass,' both joy and sorrow, leaves in its wake, an expanded awareness. Finally, when Realization comes that one is not separate from God, and never could be, one wakes up laughing, laughing, laughing.

GLOSSARY

Advaita	Non-duality; the body of teachings/non-teachings that emphasize witness-consciousness and abidance in the Self. The main idea is that "consciousness is all there is." The objective is freedom from cultural conditioning and from mis-identification of body, mind and emotions.
Ahimsa	Non-violence
Amah	Mother; polite address to an Indian girl or woman; Asian house-keeper
Ananda	Bliss
Arati, arathi	The honorific circular waving of a flame on a tray in front of a deity statue, photo or a Master; the ritual presentation of the flame, which signifies the Inner Presence in all, before or after devotional singing or prayers or a special function
Ashram	Monastery; hermitage; place of spiritual retreat
Atma	The True Self; Indwelling Presence; Spirit within
Avatar	A Divine manifestation of God. Sathya Sai Baba is the Poorna Avatar, the fullest Incarnation of God ever to take human embodiment. He is all knowing, all powerful, all present in all beings and is everywhere all at once. He has control over ego, fire, earth, air, water, and He created the entire cosmos. He speaks every language in the world and knows everything. It is an incomparable blessing to be alive on earth while He is in human form. To be able to catch sight of Him in one's lifetime is an unspeakable grace. He is also continually available to each person inside the heart and responds to each prayer individually on inner levels.
Baju kurung	Traditional Malay women's cotton dress of elbow-length sleeves, close-fitting, scooped-neck over-blouse, long floor-length skirt
Bhajan	Leader-response devotional singing
Bhakatavatsala	One Who showers profuse grace on His devotees or spiritual aspirants
Bhakta	Devotee

Bhakti	Devotion, love, honor; the heart's attitude of yielded love and devotion to God
Bodhisattva	Someone who has finished karma and no longer needs to return to earth unless as a volunteer to help to uplift humanity
Bomoh	Islamic spiritual leader; natural healer and/or psychic
Brahma	The Creator, God
Brahman	The Absolute; the Supreme Being; the Reality at the source of all being
Brahmin	The priestly class charged with learning, teaching and performing sacred rites and sacrifices, chants, pujas, ceremonies of Hindu culture
Chakra	Center of spiritual energy; place of energy entry or exit within the body
Chapatti	Griddle-fried whole-wheat flat bread
Charpoy	Rope bed
Cheong sam	Loose Chinese street-wear pajamas
Darshan	To see a Holy Person; the place where the faithful gather to see Baba or a saint; when a saint blesses the crowd or shares His Presence with devotees
Deva	Angel, spirit, ethereal being
Devi	Goddess; can refer to any of thousands of local goddesses, each of which has a function
Devotee	Spiritual aspirant; one who is devoted, in thought, word and deed to God
Dhal	Pureed lentils
The Dhammapada	The religious masterpiece which preserves the Buddha's teachings on "the way of perfection"
Dharma	Duty; righteousness; role in life; proscribed way of spiritual living; right livelihood
Dhoti	Indian sarong skirt for men
Dim sum	Cantonese for Chinese sweet and savory buns, snacks and dumplings served at breakfast and lunch in steamed wicker baskets
Rajiv Ghandi	The late Prime Minister of India who was assassinated
Ghee	clarified butter

Gompa	Shrine; monastery
Guru	Spiritual teacher
Japamala	Rosary beads; prayer beads
Kampong	Village; village on stilts over water
Karma	Law of cause and effect
Kirtan	Singing of devotional songs; a ballad
Krishna	Lord Krishna was one of the great Avatars of all time. He was one of Sai Baba's previous Incarnations, was the hero of India and the advisor of Arjuna in the Mahabharata war and the Bhagavad Gita.
Kundalini	Spiritual energy within the spine which lies coiled at the base of the spine when dormant
Kum-kum	Also, cum-cum. A red powder made from lead which is used for cosmetic purposes as well as to anoint the forehead after saying morning prayers
Kurta	A loose, collar-less shirt that reaches the knees
Lamasery	Buddhist monastery; abode of lamas or monks
Leela, lila	Play of God; joke; prank; surprise; lesson
Lingham	An egg-shaped stone symbolizing the womb of creation; the focus of Shiva worship
Locution	Inner ear messages or guidance from God, saints or Ascended Masters
Loka	Realm, region in other dimensions
Longhi	Indian skirt for men, tied around the waist
Mahatma	Great Soul
Maha Purusha	Great being or personality
Mala	Rosary; garland
Mandir	Temple
Mantra	Word or phrase of power and devotion
Maya	Illusion
Padnamaskar	To touch the feet of a Master, either with the hands or with the forehead. This is considered to be one of life's great blessings as it removes karma and confers grace.
Pakora	Indian vegetable fritter; when used as a nickname – "Butterball"

Peraq headpiece	Festive Tibetan woman's traditional hat-veil covering the back of the head; red, turquiose and black felt hat worn with Tibetan national dress-up costume for special occasions
Prakriti	Root, primal or universal matter or substance
Prana	Life force
Prasad	Blessed food
Prasanthi Nilayam	Abode of Highest Peace, Sai's ashram at Puttaparthi; also Prashanti Nilayam
Puja	Devotional service; daily prayers of Hindus
Raja	King; ruler
Rambutan	Sweet, white, round, golf-ball size Asian fruit in a red leathery casing; it resembles a huge leechee.
Sadhakas	Holy men and women; renunciates
Sadhu	Holy man or renunciate; mendicant; wandering monk
Samadhi	Merging into Universal Consciousness; Superconsciousness; an exalted state
Sambhashan	Conversation with a Master; being acknowledged by the spoken word, greeting, advice or interaction with a Guru
Samosa	Indian vegetable-filled pastry snack or appetizer; pastry triangle filled with potatoes and peas
Samsara	Cycles of birth and death caused by delusion and attachment to form
Samskara	The tendencies, patterns, habits which lead to rebirth
Sannyasi	Wandering monk
Sarawak	A state in East Malaysia
Sari	South Asian woman's dress consisting of several yards of fabric which is wrapped so that the bottom forms a skirt and the top covers the upper body as a shawl. It is worn with a floor-length petticoat and a short-sleeved blouse
Satsang	Sharing truth; spiritual sharing; being in the presence of a spiritual teacher
Shakti	Spiritual power
Shastra	Teaching, body of teachings
Shastry	One who reads, conveys, translates, gives a body of teachings. A contemporary meaning refers to a per-

son who translates ancient manuscripts containing prophetic information for a particular recipient.

Shikara	Long North Indian paddle boat, which often has a cloth sun canopy for the passengers
Shirdi Sai Baba	Sai Baba of Shirdi, North India, Who was the Previous Incarnation of Sathya Sai Baba
Shiva, Lord	The Aspect of the Hindu trinity Who rules dissolution, destruction, finality
Siddhi	Spiritual power
Sparshan	The touch of a Master (e.g., a pat on the head, tweak on the cheek, tap on the shoulder); such a touch is considered very auspicious
Swami	Spiritual Teacher
Swami	Sai Baba
Tandoori	Indian clay-oven cooking of marinated meat, usually chicken
Tankas	Silk Buddhist instructive hangings depicting gods and angels; they are collector's pieces
Tapas	Penance; austerity; sacrifice or discomfort with a spiritual emphasis or purpose
Tsampa meal	Simple cooked grain eaten by Himalayan monks
Vasana	Latent tendency
Vedas	Holy texts of Hinduism

CHARACTERS IN *WAKE UP LAUGHING*

Robin Adamson – Connie's friend who is a therapist and a great sevak

Bharosa Adhikari – Nepalese devotee who was resurrected by Baba, is a great healer and a great sevak.

Malini Angunawela – Sai devotee who was in an interview with the author

Wahid Awi – Connie and Jim's driver and friend in Singapore

Sri Sathya Sai Baba – Creator of the universe; the Avatar; God; the hero of the story

Aleks and Luba Babarin – Russian-American devotees whom Connie met in India

Babu – Founder and owner of S. Babu Sai Ram Taxi Service

Heather Bayliss – A Canadian tourist from Montreal who was visiting India with Brendan Tours

Bert Barns – A retired therapist friend of Connie and Jim's

Wilma Bronkey – A well-known, beloved American devotee from Oregon

Regine Burgoin – French woman who was Connie's roommate on the trip to Little Tibet and North India

Lita Burgos – A long-time Philippine-American devotee from California who started a Sai school and who does much service for others

Alvin Cook – Devotee and spouse of Kay Cook

Kay Cook – Devotee, nurse, spiritual teacher, good friend of Connie's

Carol Cummings – Friend of Connie's who is a healer, dog trainer, horse-woman

Zilla Daniel – American devotee, healer, dowser, writer who was healed of deafness by Baba

Ed Davis – Healer, acupuncturist, health educator

Maria de Castillo – Latin American devotee

Jann de Hoog – Lovely American devotee, yogini, spiritual teacher

Maria de Servent – Latin American devotee

Sherry Dell – An Arizona devotee

Indra Devi – Also known as Mataji (Dearest Mother), Russian-American yoga teacher, author, devotee

Sally Dotson – American businesswoman, friend of Connie's

Al Drucker – American author, teacher, scientist, healer who taught at Baba's school

Suzi Elbert – A devotee who was in a Sai interview with the author in the 1980's

Jane English – American photographer and physicist married to Gia-fu Feng, the author

Faiz – Tibetan tour guide of Little Tibet and Nepal

Gia-fu Feng – One of Connie's first spiritual mentors; Chinese translator of the *Tao te Ching*; spiritual teacher and leader of Stillpoint

Norma Jean Ferguson – American tour organizer in Singapore

Brian Flemming – Tour guide on Connie and Jim's wedding trip to India

Amy Ford – American businesswoman devotee who is Connie's friend

John Free – A retired Air Force colonel, a college professor, author and media personality

Trish Free – An author, healer, radio and TV personality and friend of Connie's

Teddy and Olga Frett – American tourists from Manhattan

Phoebe Gasich – American devotee who resides at the ashram

Elizabeth George – American nurse and acupuncturist from Borneo

Rajiv Gandhi – Former Prime Minister of India

Althaf Sayed Ghoush – Babu's brother, Muslim cab driver and shop owner

Michael Goldstein, M.D. – A well-known, long-time American devotee who is a cardiologist, a leader in the Sai organization and an inspiring speaker

Robert Gourley – An Australian tourist

Halagappa – former pickpocket-turned-orphanage-founder near Mysore

Sally Hillis – Connie's American yoga teacher in Singapore

Bobbie Johnson – Connie's friend who is a nurse and Sai devotee

Elvin Johnson – An American devotee that Connie met in an interview

Daisy Jones – American devotee who is a healer

Vera Karn – Retired home-maker from Iowa

Professor N. Kasturi – Baba's biographer, great saint, professor, radio personality, editor of the *Sanathana Sarathi*, the ashram newsletter, author known for his soaring prose and wit.

Sara Kent – American friend of Ed Davis; social worker

Rhonda Krieg – A Sai devotee from Arizona

Justin Lang – A chef from New Mexico

Craig Lewis – friend of Connie's, retired veterinarian and great sevak

Gracia Lewis – Distinguished Singaporean of British ancestry whose father developed Hong Kong on elephant-back. She was a prize-winning orchid-grower and the first red orchid of Singapore was created by her and bore her name. She was a world traveler, a yoga teacher and raconteur.

Beijing Mr. Lo – Ik Chin Travel Company's PRC contact for China tours

Danny and Yu Lan Loh – Singaporean tour companions on Connie's first China trip

Muey Low – Connie's Singaporean roommate on her first China trip

Dean Lusted, M.D. – An American physician who was in an interview with the author

Ami and Rama Mangru – Fijian Indian-American Sai devotees from Colusa, California through whom food multiplies continually and at whose household shrine room many Sai manifestations and healings occur

John and Ann Marks – American devotees Connie met in an interview

Bonnie Marr – A friend of Connie's who is a healer

Vernette Maya – American devotee from California

Swami Mukthananda – Well-known Indian guru and author

Ramesh Nepali – Husband of the Nepalese healer, Bharosa Adhikari

Jimmy Ng – Singaporean driver who helped Connie and others on her first trip to China

Julie and Albert Peters – Iraquis from Surrey, England

Winnie Phelps – An American who is a very loving and ardent long-time devotee and permanent ashram resident

Rena Phipps – A healer who is a friend of Connie's

Madur Pi – Long-time Indian devotee and businessman

Jo-Anne Powell – An American Sai devotee from New England

Jaya Rajamanikam – a very helpful devotee who lives in Singapore

Rasool – Muslim cook and sherpa on Connie's trip to Little Tibet

James Redmond – An American Sai devotee who is well-known for his kindness, sense of humor and his outstanding, prolific, professional videos of Sai Baba

Ben Rhodd – Well-known and beloved Baha'i Native American archeologist

(Ms) J. P. Riggs – An American Sai devotee from New England

Sarit Rimal – The ebullient son-in-law of Nepalese healer Bharosa Adhikari

Len Rodrigo – Singaporean attorney, author, devotee, great sevak

Monty San Carlo – aeronautical engineer from Houston area, healer, great sevak

Maria Santo – Connie's friend who is an art collector and Marian devotee

Shirdi Sai Baba – Sathya Sai's most recent Incarnation who left His body in 1918

Geetha Sharma – Great devotee, selfless server of many devotees, helped Gen. Taylor to Organize and lead trips to the Patal Caves

Andria Spring – American devotee who is a healer

Val Steen – South African devotee

Tippu Sultan – Great leader who unified South India, inventor, merchant, great Muslim, Philanthropist

General Taylor – Long-time devotee, retired Army general, former leader of groups to the Patal Caves, constructed a small ashram at the Patal Bhuvaneshwar Cave

Murali Thirumal – Sai devotee and Asst. Director of Lockerly Arboretum in Georgia

Sandy Tucker – American spiritual teacher, speaker

Maria Ujfalusi – Connie's Hungarian-South African friend, microbiologist, spiritual teacher, Artist, animal rights advocate

Jim Walton – Athabaskan elder and shaman who mentored the Spiritual Unity of the Tribes Gatherings

Mr. Wee – A Singaporean tour companion on Connie's first trip to China who became a hero

Deirdre West – Connie's English friend who is a former university professor of English in China, healer, sevak extraordinaire, composer, musician, writer, works with lepers at the Sri Sathya Sai Hospital in Whitefield, India

J. Marilyn Wilkinson – Educator, rancher, retired librarian, horsewoman, dog trainer, Sai devotee, friend.

William Wong – Sai devotee and Professor at Singapore University

B.P. Yap – Great sevak and devotee for whom Baba manifested a ring of Jesus. B.P. is a founder of the Swami Home nursing home in Singapore, which is a world prototype.

Bibliography

AA   *An Autobiography*, Frank Lloyd Wright, London, Longmans, Green and company, N.Y., 1938.

ACIM   *A Course in Miracles,* Foundation for Inner Peace, Tiburon, CA 94920, 1985.

ACTSSB   *A Compendium of the Teachings of Sathya Sai Baba,* compiled by Charlene Leslie-Chaden, Sai Towers Publishing, Prasanthi Nilyam, India 515134, 1997

AEVOFC   *An Eastern View of Jesus Christ, Divine Discourses of Sathya Sai Baba,* Sai Publications, London, 1982.

ANOJ   *A Net of Jewels*, Ramesh S. Balsekar, Edited by Gary Starbuck, Advaita Press, 1996.

BIH   *Baba is Here*, Graciela Busto, Leela Press, Inc., Faber, VA, 1998.

CWTI   *Collision With the Infinite*, Suzanne Segal, Blue dove Press, San Diego, CA, 1996

DACOSSSBS   *Digest, A Collection of Sri Sathya Sai Baba's Sayings,* Tumuluru Krishna Murthy, Italy, 1985.

F   *Fireflies*, Rabindranath Tagore, Collier Books, N.Y., 1955.

IFOTSM   *In Favor of the Sensitive Man and Other Essays*, Anais Nin, Harcourt Brace Jovanovich, N.Y., 1976.

IITRW   *Insights into the Ramana Way*, A.R. Natarajan, Ramana Maharshi Centre for Learning, Bangalore, India, 1996.

KTEEIM   *Kundalini, The Evolutionary Energy in Man*, Gopi Krishna, Shambhala, Boulder, CO, 1971.

M   *Markings*, Dag Hammerskjold, Alfred A. Knopf, N.Y., 1964.

MMAP   *Mary's Miracles and Prophecies*, Connie Shaw, Om Productions, Inc., Loveland, Colorado, 1995.

OTYRTIN   *Other Than Your Refuge There is None*, Smt. Vijayakumari, Sai Shriram Printers, Ekkattuthangal, Channai, India, 1999.

POTO   *Poetry of the Orient*, Alfred a. Knopf, N.Y., 1928.

SBIB   *Sai Baba in Brief,* Connie Shaw, Om Productions, Inc., Denver, Colorado, 1989.

SUBDOR   *Self Unfoldment by Disciplines of Realization*, Manly P. Hall, The Philosophical Research Society, Inc., Los Angeles, 1977.

TCEAOW   *The Complete Essays and Other Writings of Ralph Waldo Emerson*, Modern Library, N.Y., 1950

TD   *The Dhammapada, Translated by Eknath Easwaran, Nilgiri Press, Tomales, CA, 1985.*

TER   *The Essential Rumi,* Coleman Barks, Harper Collins, 1995.

TSOY   *The Science of Yoga,* I.K. Taimni, The Theosophical Publishing House, Adyar, India, 1993.

TUR   *The Unknown Reality*, Vol. 2, Jane Roberts, Prentice-Hall, Inc., Englewood, N.J., 1979

WIADOTL   *Who is a Devotee of the Lord?,* Dr. MVN Murthy, Edited by Connie Shaw, Om Productions, Inc., Denver, Colorado, 1991.

WWAW   *War Within and Without*, Anne Morrow Lindbergh, Harcourt Brace Jovanovich, N.Y., 1980

YSOP   *The Yoga Sutras of Patanjali,* B. K. S. Iyengar, Bombay, India

THE WORKS AND WONDERS OF SAI BABA

It is no exaggeration to state that any attempt to categorize and to catalogue the stupendous healings, miracles and works of Sai Baba is but a feeble attempt at a massive undertaking. Why is this so?

There are several reasons:

1. **Many are unknown.** The Avatar does many of His works in the privacy of homes and they are not divulged.
2. **He seeks no publicity.** He is modest and does not advertise His activities and miracles.
3. **They are vast in number and type.**
4. **He takes no credit.** Often the recipients do not realize that He is the author.
5. **They are new powers.** Many fall outside the realm of science or human experience, hence there are no names or terms for them.
6. **He is multi-dimensional** and is constantly performing them as loving expressions.

ADOPT-A-VILLAGE PROJECTS: The loving lifestyle transformation of citizens of nearly a thousand villages throughout India by providing the Five Essentials: clean, accessible pumped water within the village; a good road to the village; a school; a community hall; a mosque or temple for worship.

APPARITIONS: The appearance of Sathya Sai Baba, Shirdi Sai Baba, Krishna, Rama or other aspects of God as well as saints, to spiritual aspirants or to those in need in order to teach, to warn, to increase faith, to heal, to protect, to uplift or to inspire.

APPORTATIONS: To bring an object from one realm or place to another through invisible means.
Example: Baba brought to Australian author Howard Murphet a rare American five dollar gold piece which was a collector's item, minted in San Francisco in 1905, the year Murphet was born.

BI-LOCATIONS: The simultaneous appearance of an individual in two or more places, in the body. Sathya Sai Baba has been seen in Australia and India at the same time. He has been seen in two or more places in India simultaneously.

BI-LOCATION OF DEVOTEES: Sai Baba has bi-located a number of devotees to various destinations to speak, heal, teach or to rescue someone without the knowledge of that devotee. He bi-located the author on the following occasions:

- To Idaho to give a formula and a special motor for an invention to a physicist, 1994
- To Texas to counsel distraught people on several occasions, 1994, 1995, 1996, 1998, 1999
- To India to do service, 1996
- To the U.S. to visit a depressed Colorado man three times while the author was in India in 1999

CONTROL OF THE WEATHER: Sathya Sai stops rain within a small area for the comfort of devotees. He controls storms, has created a vertical rainbow for Joel Riordan and has stopped flood waters on command. He controls wind, outside temperatures and brings rain and breezes, when necessary, as grace.

DAILY DARSHAN: To bless, grace and walk among one's devotees so that they might see, talk with and touch Him. Sai Baba has accomplished the prodigious feat of offering twice-daily darshans to his crowds of admirers for over sixty years, seven days a week, weekends and holidays included. He does this barefoot, in all weathers, dressed in a simple robe.

DIVINE DISCOURSES: When the Avatar dispenses grace, wisdom and practical teaching to vast crowds for the sake of educating and informing them. In the past, Sai has given such talks as often as twice a month or more. Currently, He usually gives a discourse at such festivals as Gurupoornima, Rama's Birthday, Krishna's Birthday, Sai Baba's Birthday, Dasara, Onam, Christmas and Shivarathri. One remarkable feature of His talks is knowledge of unknown aspects of all previous Avatars and saints and their thoughts, comments and miracles, though they have been long gone from the stage of the earth.

DIVINE IMPRESSIONS: The creation of Baba's image or other aspects of Him upon material substance. For example, Baba creates images of His face or form in people's photographs of family members, friends, buildings or nature. He also impresses His footprints onto piles of vibhuti ash, footstools, carpets and other surfaces, long distance. He also takes bites out of food offerings on the altars of devotees – in locked rooms!

DIVINE PLACEMENT: The Lord puts rings and gems inside coconuts, locked boxes, taped-up containers, and various other objects.

DREAM APPEARANCES AND GUIDANCE: Sathya Sai appears in dreams in order to teach, warn or guide. He says that one cannot dream of Him of one's own volition.

FEEDING MIRACLES: Sai manifests food for tens of thousands that is hot, tasty and plentiful. He does this by tapping on the lids of a few large cooking pots to will that there be an abundance of food until all present at the particular function have been fed.

* He has multiplied food weekly for a number of years at the home of Ami and Ram Mangru in Colusa, California.
* He has multiplied food at American homeless shelters and feeding sites.
* He increased the available food at a Thanksgiving dinner for the homeless in Detroit.

FEEDING THE POOR: On a regular basis Sai Baba feeds the hungry of Puttaparthi in a ceremony or service known as Narayan Seva. He fed the poor as a child of four until He was an adult and transacted this feat on a massive scale. He often performs mass weddings for the poor and feeds thousands of people three meals a day for three days.

FIRE MASTER: Sathya Sai is the producer of fire and can extinguish fire, both close at hand and at a distance. He has extinguished home fires, clothing fires and office fires in numerous countries.

FRAGRANCES: Baba manifests sacred fragrances in front of people's faces, such as vibhuti, roses, jasmine and sandalwood. This indicates His love and His Presence.

FUNDS: He has provided billions of dollars for people and organizations throughout the world on a continual basis, a little at a time, as needed. He creates miracles to provide for college educations, home mortgages, transportation, trips to India, new jobs, promotions, loan payoffs, the meeting of hospital bills and so forth.

HOSPITALS: The Avatar has built many small hospitals, numerous eyebanks, countless clinics, and two super-specialty hospitals. All surgeries and medical treatments are free. Hospitals and clinics are staffed with competent, loving, self-sacrificing staff.

IMPERSONATION/BI-LOCATION: Baba has impersonated nurses, army officers, cowboys, athletes and countless other people to deliver babies, fix flat tires, fend off assailants, give information and save lives. He impersonated the author in Switzerland by giving a talk to devotees on Mother Mary's prophecies for Switzerland, using the author's name and particulars but assuming the charming form of an Indian woman in a white dress!

LANGUAGES: Sai Baba speaks every language in the world since He created them all. He speaks and understands the erudite versions as well as the common vernacular of those languages. The author has heard Him speak English, Tamil, Telugu, Spanish, Japanese and Malayalam.

MANIFESTATIONS OR MATERIALIZATIONS: To create an item from nothing.

Examples:

On-The-Spot Materializations -

* Vibhuti ash for healing
* Photos
* Jewelry such as rings, watches, medallions, bracelets, earrings, brooches
* Medical instruments for performing immediate surgery
* Fruit
* A live monkey
* Candy
* Gold statues
* Linghams from "thin air" as well as from His stomach through His mouth. Linghams are egg-shaped objects which have been made of alabaster, brass, silver, gold, crystal and other substances. One was ejected from His stomach complete with a three-legged stand!
* Amrit nectar
* A black onyx map of India studded with 18 diamonds, created for students in 1985
* Crystal japamala rosaries
* Buddha statues
* Gold statues of Shirdi Sai Baba
* A silver bowl or patra for a group of renunciate devotees who went to the Himalayas to the Gufa Ashram to meditate the rest of their lives.

Long-Distance Manifestations -

* Food was created in the silver patra bowl on demand by Baba for the devotees at the Gufa Ashram cave in the Himalayas each time one of them was hungry (e.g., yogurt, grapes, rice, vegetables, etc.).
* Cum-cum powder (vermilion)
* Tumeric powder on a tray with messages written in the powder
* Vibhuti ash in flavors of peppermint, peanut butter, flowers, talcum
* Vibhuti ash on the inside roof of a car; sprinkled on people's clothes; in their mouth; in the middle of their forehead, on their shoes; on their books; on kitchen counters; on computers; in wallets; in letters; on people's hands; on their hair; on chairs and furniture; on their pet dogs; on photos and statues; on manuscripts and dissertations; on His chair at Sai centers; on pictures of devotees, Jesus and Mary, Sathya Sai, Shirdi Sai.
* Pearls
* Amrit nectar
* Sandal paste
* Om's on pieces of fruit
* Om's on walls, photos, altars

* A photo of Shirdi Sai in a pail of milk
* Rings hidden in a pile of vibhuti on altars
* Unset diamonds in prayer rooms
* Rings suddenly appearing on one's hand
* A ring suddenly disappearing from one's finger
* Rice and sandalwood powder from the ceiling
* Amrit nectar from the hair-part on the head of a Nepalese woman daily for   over a year
* Amrit nectar from the ears of a Texas woman who is a talk show host

LEVITATION: Baba has defied gravity numerous times by floating or rushing from the base of a hill to the top in a matter of seconds, in full view of a crowd. He has levitated a car He was driving on at least two occasions. Once He drove it a foot off the ground, around Puttaparthi. Another time, while on a trip with Dr. John Hislop and other devotees, Baba casued the car to rise a few inches off the ground while it was in motion. The Avatar also levitates other objects at times when necessary or to prove a point.

LIMB SEPARATION: Like His previous Incarnation, Shirdi Sai Baba, Sathya Sai also has been observed to have separated his arms and legs from His torso and has subsequently drawn them back to their proper positioning without any injury to Himself!

MEDICAL MIRACLES: Baba heals the sick and incurables of every disease known on the planet. He performs surgeries; comforts and cures the mentally and emotionally ill; restores hearing, eyesight and speech to the afflicted and returns mobility to the lame. He repairs organs, glands, tissues, cells and systems while patients sleep. He stitches bodies without anesthesia, bleeding or pain. He improves eyesight, breathing, thinking, feeling sensations and memory. He heals snoring, coughing, sneezing, fears and phobias.

OMNIPOTENCE, OMNIPRESENCE, OMNISCIENCE: Sathya Sai is all powerful, all present and all knowing. He knows every thought, word and deed of every being on the planet as well as the past, present and future of all beings. He has perfect love for all people, regardless of their past or current actions.

PROTECTION: Strange and wonderful are the protections He affords: stopping bullets aimed at devotees; causing a bullet to bounce out of the mouth of a woman who was shot; saving devotees from head-on collisions by warping time at a distance.

PURITY: Baba is purity and has no lust, desire or addictions. He can heal the addictions of any who ask, provided that He feels He wants to remove that person's karma or lessons. He can change our habits and outlooks so that we, too, can become pure and selfless.

RESCUE: Sending help to devotees to fix flat tires, pass examinations, get free of muggers, escape fires, escape from large snakes, pay the rent, fix disabled autos on the highway, escape attack or abuse, get medical help, find lost children, pets and objects, remember speeches, perform in recitals and prevent drowning.

RESURRECTIONS: To return the Spirit to the body of a person who has been declared or observed to be dead. Baba has raised numerous people from the dead. For example, He resurrected Dr. Walter Cowan of California; Bharosa Adhikari of Kathmandu, Nepal; V. Radhakrishna of Kuppam, Andra Pradesh, India; Krishnaswamy of Kota, Rajasthan, India; Prem Dutt Verma of Vasant Kunj, New Delhi, India; Bhagwandas Daswani of Hong Kong; Charles Penn of Australia; Dr. S.K. Bose of India during a Divine Discourse in Prashanti Nilayam. Although these are some of the most well-known resurrections, no doubt there are countless others which are unknown to the author.

SIZE AND WEIGHT: Baba has made Himself so small as to dance both on the head of a pin and to dance on the hood ornament of a devotee's car. He has appeared to the author as a thirty-foot giant in her prayer room, with His waist touching the ceiling and His head standing above the roof. He can make Himself very heavy or very light.

TRANSFER OF ILLNESS: Sathya Sai has taken the illnesses and ailments of devotees upon His own body to alleviate the sufferings of others.

TRANSFER OF POWERS TO DEVOTEES: Healing, bi-location, pre-cognition, manifestation, food multiplication, resurrection, teaching, exhortation

TRANSFORMATIONS: To change the form, essence or consciousness of an object or being.
Baba has changed the minds and hearts of hundreds of millions of people. He has also changed objects from one substance or material to another.
Example:
* Turning glass into sugar candy
* Changing water into gasoline
* Changing gasoline into water
* Turning captured frogs into pigeons in order to free them
* Changing flowers into medallions
* Making Himself into Rama, Krishna or a small crowd of people
* Changing a tiny button rose into a diamond ring for author Howard Murphet
* Changing rings from one style or form to another
* Changing a spider into a gold and ruby spider brooch and back again

VISIONS: The Avatar shows a variety of unusual scenes to devotees in many novel ways.

Examples:

* To a student who denied having smoked, against school rules, Baba showed the boy smoking in a scene from the recent past enacted on Baba's palm.

* On His chest, He has manifested pictures of the Preceptors of ashram visitors.

* To devotees in interviews, He has shown visions which have appeared like slide transparencies on the wall of the interview room.

* He has manifested a small TV on the palm of his hand more than once to show future scenes and scenes from across the world to devotees.

* He has made Himself appear as a combination of Shiva and Shakthi to devotees.

VISITATIONS: Baba appears in person to warn, to teach, to guide, to inform, to educate, to invite, to chastise, to comfort, to surprise and to inspire.

ABOUT THE AUTHOR

Connie Shaw, a graduate of James Madison University, is an author, publisher, speaker, healer and spiritual teacher who has lectured and taught classes in spirituality, Advaita (non-duality) and the teachings of Sathya Sai Baba in the U.S., Canada, Mexico, China, India, Singapore and Nepal. Her travels to fifty countries, and temporary residence in Germany, Italy, China and Singapore have provided a broad understanding of humanity. She has worked with Israelis, Eskimos, Native Americans, Asians, East Indians, Chinese and Westerners from many countries.

After meeting Sathya Sai Baba in early 1981, Connie traveled to India nearly thirty times and has been blessed with many personal meetings, or 'interviews,' with the Avatar. Although Connie has been active in social service to the community all of her life, after her first encounter with Sai Baba, she began to devote much more time to such activities.

Connie has served as a board member on numerous boards of directors. She and her fellow Sai devotees have collected food for the feeding of the homeless and for women's shelters. They have entertained and befriended nursing home residents, homeless children and shut-ins. Connie has tutored Chinese-Americans in English literacy and has obtained Rotary grant funds for books for homeless children. Other service projects which have utilized her talents are Habitat for Humanity; Poudre River Clean-Up; food and clothing drives for Native Americans; spiritual counseling; distribution of flowering bulbs for shut-ins and students; and Meals on Wheels.

While Connie's career has centered on communications and psychology, the emphasis has been on management consulting; organization development and training; trans-personal psychology and personal growth; and spiritual healing. Her avocations have included research in radionics and alternative healing. Her hobbies have included gardening, languages, landscape design, art and travel.

Connie says that she has been blessed to start a number of Sai Baba Centers in Colorado and further served her state for several years as the State Advisor to the Southwestern Regional Council, of which she was a Member-at-Large.

Connie says, "When one finally wakes up to the reality that we have very little free will and that God is moving us about like puppets, we realize two things. One is that we needn't feel guilty and remorseful about our past mistakes. Secondly, we can't take credit for our current role in the perennial play of life. The entire drama is much more vast in its implications than we had imagined. God is the Doer. Further, That for which we have sought is within. Sathya Sai Baba, planetary Avatar is here to help us to experience That Essence and to usher in a new Golden Age of Peace and Plenty, revolutionizing society and world culture in the process."